# Augustine the Reader

# AUGUSTINE THE READER

*Meditation, Self-Knowledge,*
*and the Ethics of Interpretation*

Brian Stock

THE BELKNAP PRESS OF
HARVARD UNIVERSITY PRESS

*Cambridge, Massachusetts*
*London, England*
*1996*

*Library of Congress Cataloging-in-Publication Data*

Stock, Brian.
Augustine the reader : meditation, self-knowledge, and the ethics
of interpretation / Brian Stock.
p.   cm.
Includes bibliographical references and index.
ISBN 0-674-05276-5 (alk. paper)
1. Augustine, Saint, Bishop of Hippo. Confessiones.
2. Augustine, Saint, Bishop of Hippo—Books and reading.
3. Augustine, Saint, Bishop of Hippo—Knowledge and learning.
4. Augustine, Saint, Bishop of Hippo—Influence.   5. Books and
reading.   6. Spirituality—History.   I. Title.
BR65.A62S76 1996
270.2'092—dc20
95-34831

*For Maxime*

# ACKNOWLEDGMENTS

I wish to express my thanks to Goulven Madec, who graciously agreed to read this study, and to Peter Brown and Pierre Hadot, who kindly commented on the Introduction. I am grateful to have had the opportunity of discussing my ideas with Jerome Bruner, Maruja Jackman, Aviad M. Kleinberg, and Jeremy Worthen. Ann Hawthorne edited the manuscript with great care and made many suggestions for improvement.

A number of institutions have kindly invited me to speak on the themes of this book. I thank M. Robert Favreau, at the Centre d'Etudes Supérieures de Civilisation Médiévale, Poitiers; Jacques Le Goff and Jean-Claude Schmitt, at the Ecole des Hautes Etudes en Sciences Sociales, Paris; Georges Duby, at the Collège de France; and Giles Constable, at the Institute for Advanced Study, Princeton. I am indebted to Victoria College, University of Toronto, for the privilege of delivering the twenty-fifth Erasmus Lecture in 1989; and to Ralph Cohen for invitations to the Commonwealth Center for Literary and Cultural Change of the University of Virginia in 1990 and 1993. I also wish to express my gratitude to the staff of Baker Library, Dartmouth College, during my stay as William H. Morton Senior Fellow in the Humanities in 1990; and to the generous librarians of the Pontifical Institute of Mediaeval Studies, Toronto, and the Institut d'Etudes Augustiniennes, Paris.

This book has been written with the financial help of the Social Sciences and Humanities Research Council of Canada and the Connaught Foundation of the University of Toronto.

# CONTENTS

✶✷✺

Cum legerem, per me ipse cognoui. Itane est?

—*De Utilitate Credendi* 7.17

# INTRODUCTION

This is a study of Augustine's attempt to lay the theoretical foundation for a reading culture.

Augustine was convinced that words and images play a fundamental role in mediating perceptions of reality. From the spring of 386, when his interest in Christianity was renewed, he attempted to situate his inquiries into such transfers of meaning within a programme of scriptural studies. The subsequent union of philosophical, psychological, and literary insights gave birth to the West's first developed theory of reading.

This theory deals with, among other things, mental representations, memory, emotion, cognition, and the ethics of interpretation. These themes are unified by Augustine's concern with the self as a reader, that is, with the personal understanding that can be created through a mental "rereading" of the narratives of previous events lodged in memory. He contrasts the inner certainty of the self's existence[1] with the uncertainty of information acquired through such accounts. If our presentations of self are in this respect like such rereadings, we cannot hope for objective knowledge of ourselves any more than we can be certain that an interpretation of a given text is correct.

As a guide to self-analysis, therefore, reading occupies an ambivalent position in Augustine's thinking.[2] On the negative side, the knowledge acquired through reading is inseparable from sense perceptions, which are limited by time, place, and circumstances. Yet, in the presence of a sufficiently authoritative text (such as the Bible), the reader can approach a higher understanding, even if he or she rarely transcends the senses entirely.[3] An act of reading is then a critical step upwards in a mental ascent: it is both an awakening from sensory illusion[4] and a rite of initiation, in which the reader crosses the threshold from the outside to the inside world.

This upward and inward movement takes place when the appropriate text is transformed into an object of contemplation.[5] *Lectio* becomes *medi-*

*tatio.*[6] Words, created in silence, return to silence in the subject's mind:[7] the Many become the One as they are united in reflective thought.[8] The reading process concentrates the subject's attention, and the normal flow of time, which is measured by the passing sounds and letters, is replaced by an awareness of an extensive present—a "distending" of thought that creates the illusion of permanence. Needless to say, in order to achieve this desired end, the student of scripture has to leave behind all linguistic and literary conceptions of selfhood.

Augustine drew on many ancient authorities in the formation of these ideas, through which he was able to bring together his spiritual concerns and his metaphysical reflections. Yet it is his writings rather than those of his predecessors that provide Western reflection on reading, inwardness, and transcendence with their earliest synthetic statement. His design for reading is one of the distinguished intellectual achievements of his age.[9] He tells us more about the subject than does anyone else in antiquity.[10] Equally important, his theory is consistent with his authorial practice: he is one of the earliest masters of a type of prose whose "phenomenological"[11] qualities depend on the presence of a speaking and reading "I."[12] There is no autobiographical voice quite like his[13]—a fact that Edmund Husserl was quick to recognize in claiming the bishop of Hippo's patronage for his own *ego cogito.*[14] Philo, Origen, and Jerome rival his interpretive skill but lack his ability to combine meditative reading, exploration of the self, and first-person narrative.[15] Augustine also consolidates the role of reading and meditation in Western mystical thought: he differs from Plotinus and some Christian authors in not reducing but accentuating the distinction between subject and object[16] through patient, line-by-line exegesis.

Augustine is by far the most influential thinker in the field during the medieval and early modern periods. Inevitably, as well, his admirers subtly altered his views.[17] Medieval monastic authors frequently gave reading a higher priority in devotional activity than he did,[18] just as scholastic theologians used his critical vocabulary to engage in a philosophical type of hermeneutics that rarely appears in his writings. As interest in his ideas grew, one branch of his thinking on language passed to philosophers from Henry of Ghent to Duns Scotus,[19] while another proceeded from Ramón Lull to fourteenth-century French prose stylists.[20] Authors such as Petrarch, Montaigne, Pascal,[21] and Rousseau popularized the *Confessions* as a literary genre, whereas Augustine himself was more interested in exploring the value of the *Confessions* as a "spiritual exercise." Luther was indebted to his programme of Bible study,[22] as was his erudite critic Erasmus,[23] but neither replicated his ideas on Christian education. Seventeenth-century English poetry rediscovered and transformed his biblical meditations.[24] Iconographic tradition associated him with Jerome as a father of Western book culture.[25] Contemporary literary theorists have confirmed this view.[26]

While I recognize the historical relevance of these developments, my aim in this study is to analyse Augustine's own various statements about reading within the evolution of his ideas[27] and to describe his responses to specific occasions, audiences, and controversies.[28] I propose that the notion of the self-conscious reader plays an important part in his resolution of key issues in the philosophy of mind. Furthermore, I offer an interpretation of his formative years that emphasizes the consistency of his thinking, on the basis of his approach to reading, in contrast to the once fashionable tendency of scholars to distinguish sharply between the writings of the early and middle phases of his career.[29] The best narrative account of the role of reading in his education remains books 1–9 of the *Confessions,* despite their often noted weakness as a historical record, and that is where I begin. In the story of his early years he explains why he adopted reading as a means of acquiring edifying knowledge; in particular, why he replaced the type of verbal ratiocination that was common to both Manichaean dualism and pagan philosophy with an inward search for wisdom in which answers to existential questions devolved from a scriptural (if no less verbal) authority, the word of God. The life history tells us how he pursued the most elusive of antiquity's philosophical goals, truth and eternal life, only to discover at the story's dénouement that their timeless values are not a part of the reader's world.[30]

Throughout the study I adhere to Augustine's vocabulary for reading, speaking, and thinking. Also, I restrict myself to his explicit statements, since it is here rather than in his implicit views that he stands out most notably among ancient authors. My emphasis is on the structure of his ideas in an attempt to reveal what Goulven Madec calls "le mouvement propre de son discours et de sa pensée."[31] His normal unit of thought is the book: accordingly, I follow his arguments through his works or lengthy segments of them without trying to isolate problems that are best brought into focus by grouping texts written at different times and places.

❦

THE TOPIC can be approached in essentially three ways: through what Augustine read in the course of his education, through his comments on ancient methods of instruction in literate disciplines, and through some subjects to which he gives special attention, namely authority, reason, silence, and the theory of signs.

It is difficult to generalize about his use of his sources.[32] We are ill-informed about the occasions on which he read many of the books at his disposal.[33] Nor are we certain what he read. He knows some authors whom he does not quote; he quotes others (such as Virgil) selectively and interprets them as he wishes.[34] Plato is known through intermediaries—Cicero, Plotinus, and Porphyry.

Augustine reshapes everything that he reads: the critical factor in understanding his literary debts is the context of the references in his own writings. Where precise borrowings occur, "the quotations form an essential constituent of the argument," amounting to "a documentary exposition" of his text.[35] In his use of the Bible, it is frequently the arrangement of the texts rather than an interpretive gloss that offers guidance to his meaning:[36] the phrases from the Psalms that interlace the narrative of the *Confessions* provide its textual foundation as well as sources of doctrine.[37] In commenting on classical and Christian works, moreover, he alters, supplements, and occasionally disagrees with the ancient manuals of instruction that he is thought to have had at his disposal.[38] His knowledge of Greek—both in his early writings and after 410, when he acquired greater expertise—remains a subject of speculation, each student of the question, as Pierre Courcelle noted, proposing the degree of competence that "he finds convenient."[39] His handling of patristic authors likewise resists simplification:[40] it is at once "a christianizing of hellenism" and "a hellenizing of Christianity."[41] As a young man, he eagerly studied the classics, as he did after 413 when he wrote *De Ciuitate Dei* and *De Trinitate* 12–15. By contrast, in works composed between 391 and that date, his only extensively cited source is the Bible.

In order to provide an alternative to this unclear picture, we can turn to Augustine's method of reading, which is reasonably stable over time. His habits reflect a typically fourth-century Latin education, whose often emphasized weaknesses[42] include a rigid curriculum of set texts, an academic attitude toward speaking and writing correctly, and a commitment to the dated ideal of the learned orator. He paints a vivid picture of this type of schooling in a decadent phase, objecting to archaism, thoughtless mimicry, and the preference for style over moral values. In his recollection of *grammatica,* that is, instruction in grammar and literature,[43] he speaks of practices that had remained unchanged for generations: reading set texts in class,[44] teaching by dialogue with a master,[45] memorization and recitation of "classics,"[46] intensive study of pronunciation,[47] exercises in composition, scrutiny of commentaries,[48] and fabrication of stories based on exemplars.[49] Much of the literature was not read in the original but drawn from anthologies.[50] Recognizing the superficial nature of such studies, he came to detest all instructors in wordplay *(litteriones)*.[51] He later reproached himself for having allowed literary exercises of this type to lure him from the teachings of his pious mother, whose faith was sure, even if her spoken Latin was unpolished.[52]

In raising questions of sources and methods, it is necessary to remind ourselves that reading in the ancient world placed a considerably greater semantic burden on the voice than it does nowadays. Silent reading was not unknown,[53] as Augustine's examples will demonstrate. Yet books of a literary, philosophical, or theological nature were normally read aloud. The ancient reader's first acquaintance with style, genre, and subject matter occurred when he or she listened to the vocal modulations of the text as the words were pronounced.[54]

Oral reading was necessitated by the format of scrolls and codices, which were not punctuated.[55] In order to understand a lengthy passage of verse or prose, a student had to sound out the words, syllable by syllable.[56] Memory was an aid, since the texts that were read in class were frequently those that had been read before. After the literal—that is, the vocal—sense was clear,[57] the reader engaged in higher interpretive activities—philological commentary, textual criticism, analysis of style, and aesthetic judgement.[58] The rules were applied to written as well as to nonwritten texts;[59] the former were often transcribed so that they could be performed before live audiences.[60] Oral methods of reading and composition overlapped.[61] Augustine's attitude on these matters is typical of later ancient and early medieval authors.[62] Visual reading did not make serious progress until Latin was recognized to be a foreign language, word-separation became common in manuscripts,[63] and punctuation gave rise to what Malcolm Parkes calls "a grammar of legibility."[64]

Augustine's mature writings are rich in oral genres, primarily those of an exegetical and meditative type, such as the *sermo, enarratio, tractatus, expositio, commentum,* and *explanatio*.[65] A unique description of his oral and meditative reading is found at *Confessions* 9.4, where he recites psalms in Monica's company as they stroll in the villa garden at Cassiciacum.[66] Within the life history, this performance is a public symbol of the maturing of his private spiritual life; however, by the time it was written, he was accustomed to the oral, rhetorical reading of scripture in his daily sermons. Some 546 are extant,[67] eloquent witnesses to the growth in his ability to combine spoken and reflective theology.[68] During delivery[69] he occasionally had moments of meditative withdrawal, that is, short periods of time when he stopped talking and reflected on the biblical text's meaning,[70] and these intervals may have contributed to the formation of readable commentaries out of groups of sermons: an example is the *Enarrationes in Psalmos,* which were preached in Carthage before large audiences,[71] the lector[72] reading parts of the same psalm over several days. There was considerable variety in his methods: some sermons were "dictated" for use by his brethren and not "preached";[73] others were too long to be read aloud.[74] Another variant occurred in the 124 sermons of the *Tractatus in Iohannis Euangelium,* which were conceived as a commentary, even though their composition appears to have been frequently interrupted.[75] Normally he delivered his sermons from notes, or occasionally *ex tempore;* secretaries took down what was said.[76] The audience "read" what was "heard" and "known": the public reading was a "commemoration."[77]

We possess an inadequate vocabulary for describing the oral qualities of such readings. The generalizations of contemporary literary theorists are based on the age of mass produced books, which began in the eighteenth century,[78] rather than on the practices of the ancient world, in which an "edition" meant the production of a single, handwritten copy.[79] The reader is assumed to be an individual, and silent reading is taken as the norm.[80] Studies of orality and literacy, which have proliferated in recent decades, have inadvertently widened the gap between ancient readers and ourselves by placing the concept of reading within the orbit of writing, thereby restricting orality to spontaneous forms of speech.[81] Analytic and continental philosophy, in concert with linguistics, has confirmed the bias. Since Austin and Wittgenstein, Anglo-American philosophy has been concerned chiefly with meaning arising in spoken sentences,[82] whereas in ancient authors such as Augustine there was an equal interest in words that occurred in speech, texts, and thought.[83] European philosophy since Husserl, which shares a phenomenological focus with Augustine,[84] occasionally privileges speech.[85] Even when it does not,[86] there is little attempt to distinguish between the ancient speaker and oral reader.[87]

One area in which Augustine illustrates the difference is his thinking about reason and authority.[88] There are early statements in which the topic is taken up in the absence of textual considerations.[89] On other occasions readers are implicated, as at *De Ordine* 2.8–9, where he speaks of "the very law of God, transcribed, so to speak, onto the souls of the wise."[90] Authority is said to precede reason in time; yet reason has a certain precedence,[91] since it consists of "the motion of the mind capable of separating or connecting what is learned."[92] At the same time, it is authority, guided by reason, that orients studies, while a higher rationality remains a distant goal.[93] In *De Moribus Ecclesiae Catholicae* (388)[94] the two ideas appear as dimensions of biblical study: authority has priority, owing to the weakness of unsupported reason,[95] which is said to be frustrated in its search for wisdom unless scripture comes to its aid by means of marvels and books.[96] It is a short step from such a statement to the studious discipline[97] of moral reform in *De Doctrina Christiana* and to the view that authority derives from the Bible, while reason consists of the intellectual exercise of making sense of the text.

The themes of oral reading and literary authority are linked to another major issue in Augustine's thinking—meditative silence. In the *Confessions,* the connection occurs in the well-known scenes in which the Milanese professor of rhetoric observes the reading habits of Ambrose (6.3) and at the moment of conversion, when he is called by unseen voices to "take up" and "read" in Paul's Epistle to the Romans (8.12).[98] An analytic account of the phenomenon occurs in book 11, where the distinction between the oral and silent recreation of the first line of the Ambrosian hymn *Deus creator omnium,* is critical for the resolution of the problem of time (11.27).[99] Elsewhere Augustine compares silence to sound as the darkness was to light when God created the world.[100] He believes that the silences in biblical texts kindle our interest in topics on which they do not explicitly speak, such as the nature of the soul.[101] He contrasts the sensory appeal of music with the silence of truth, which steals into our hearts and invites us to seek the blessed life.[102] Aesthetics are involved: in a well-composed song, the intervals between the notes contribute to the impression of an orderly, pleasing whole; similarly, the shadows in paintings throw prominent features into relief.[103] As speech incorporates intervals of silence, silence involves an interior type of speech.[104] Silence is a hermeneutic space that is emptied of outer, physical sound so that it can be opened to inner, permanent knowledge.[105]

Augustine's way of approaching these and other questions concerning reading is through the theory of signs. He is the first to have proposed a relationship between the sender, the receiver, and the sign (normally a word),[106] which subsequently becomes a standard feature of medieval and modern theories of language.[107] In the application of his ideas on speaking to reading, the role of signification remains unchanged: the sender is replaced by the text and the receiver by the reader. Other triads involving sending, receiving, and appropriate intermediaries account for a variety of mental activities, including thinking about what has been heard or read.[108] Augustine believes that meaning is created out of the individual sounds or letters of a word in the same way that the soul gives rise to the body's vitality.[109] The theological model for mediation between the temporal and nontemporal elements is Christ, whose incarnation is the basis for the concept of a sacred sign.[110]

The essentials of Augustine's teaching on signs are straightforward.[111] He asserts that all instruction *(doctrina)* concerns things *(res)* or signs *(signa)*. The distinction depends on whether a word that refers to an object such as "wood" is understood as wood or signifies something else, as it might in a symbolic, figurative, or metaphorical expression. When we read at Exodus 15:25 that Moses "made the waters sweet" by casting into them a tree drawn to his attention by God,[112] an object, a piece of wood, becomes a sign. In his view, words alone can perform this transformative function.[113]

A sign in this respect is a thing[114] that is capable of standing for another thing. Wood, stones, and cattle are things; however, if I *see* a track and *think* of an animal or *see* smoke and *think* of fire, I use "tracks" and "smoke" to signify other objects—"animal" and "fire"—which differ from tracks and smoke. Augustine calls this generation of meaning signifying *(significare)* and the result signification *(significatio)*. When an entity is perceived as a sign, a connection is made in the mind of the sender and the receiver between the thing (tracks, smoke) and what it stands for (animal, fire). Moreover, it is through the recognition of such signs[115] by means of recollection rather than their immediate perception through the ears or eyes that we communicate our thoughts about objects to each other.[116]

Signs are natural *(naturalia)* or given *(data)*.[117] The meaning of a natural sign arises from an object or event and our thoughts about it,[118] such as tracks and an animal. By contrast, given signs are so named because people offer them to one another "for the purpose of demonstrating insofar as they are able the motions in their minds, on the basis of what is perceived or understood."[119] In addition to these general distinctions, Augustine speaks of a special class of signs that are found in written texts *(scripta)*, called either proper *(propria)* or figurative *(translata)*. I can say *bos* in Latin and mean "ox," or I can speak as Paul does when he quotes the law of Moses forbidding us to "muzzle an ox when it is treading out the grain" (1 Corinthians 9:9), where the ox is taken to signify a preacher.[120] In the one case, I am speaking "properly," in the other, "figuratively." This division is a way of handling the two main sorts of obscurity in scripture, "unknown" and "ambiguous" signs. It is also an indication of Augustine's dependence on writings during the biblical phase of his thinking, since, in order for Moses to signify Christ, the sense has to reveal the intentions of an author, a text, or a reader.[121] As a receiver of the message, he can grasp what is meant only if he understands the language in which the Bible is written.[122]

Signs thus express intentions,[123] which can be either divine or human.[124]

At the human level, Augustine is as convinced as John Searle that "people have mental states which are intrinsically intentional."[125] The purpose of speaking is to transmit these states from one mind to another with the aid of external signs.[126] Unfortunately, signs imperfectly reproduce the content of thought:[127] this is true of words, the commonest type of signs, as well as the sign systems of gesture, dance, music, and art. Even greater obscurities surround divine signs, since we are never certain that we are correctly interpreting God's intentions.[128] This impediment can be overcome only by some form of direct communication from above.[129]

Although Augustine often used abstract language in referring to these issues, he was reluctant to make a systematic statement on the subject of signs. He summarized his position in *De Doctrina Christiana* 2–3 in 396; yet even there his objective was not to present an independent theory of communication.[130] He initially employed signs to deal with questions involving spoken language, chiefly in *De Dialectica* and *De Magistro.* After his ordination in 391, his interest shifted to the study of signs in the written text of the Bible.[131] From 397, he utilized signs creatively in the verbal and visual images of the *Confessions,*[132] thereby illustrating his view that the beauty of the universe displays a divinely inspired eloquence in which signs and realities participate equally. Novel words, if employed with restraint, enhance human language, just as God's eloquence becomes more noteworthy through the power of extraordinary events.[133] In his handling of the most complex of signs, *sacramenta* (sacred signs), he does not attempt to fix firm conceptual boundaries.[134] The major role is played by "scripture, which is ceaselessly meditated upon,[135] and ever present in his thought,"[136] providing him with a way of integrating his theoretical postulates with occasions of reading.[137]

NONE OF Augustine's theoretical works is devoted specifically to problems of reading. The reader nonetheless plays an important role in relating theory to practice within his philosophy of life. The reading of scripture is the key element in the pursuit of wisdom, the *amor* or *studium sapientiae.*[138]

The usual approach to philosophizing among ancient thinkers,[139] Pierre Hadot reminds us,[140] involved a preference for oral over written interchange.[141] Although Augustine thought, wrote, and read through the medium of the spoken word, he was committed to a permanent communication of his ideas through writing. In pursuit of this goal, he incorporated many ancient notions about spoken discourse into a textual hermeneutics. He adapted the Platonic distinction between the sensible and the intelligible to the literal and nonliteral dimensions of interpretation,[142] and in a comparable way he may have reconceived the Stoic doctrine that related sensations to mental intentions.[143]

Above all, however, his exegetical programme was buttressed by a number of widely held neoplatonic doctrines.[144] Like Plotinus and Porphyry, he saw existence as a "ladder" of levels of being,[145] in which, at the highest point, the *summa essentia,* there was absolute repose *(requies)* and changelessness *(incommutabilitas),* while at lower levels there was a ceaseless desire for upward movement *(motus)* and change *(mutatio)* in an effort to reach the dynamic equilibrium of the One, where the reciprocal principles of constancy *(constantia)* and potency *(uirtus, uis, potentia)* were in balance. God, the highest substance *(substantia),* existed in and of himself, while other substances, including human souls, derived their existence from him, demanding his continual action to maintain their precarious states of being.[146] The human soul, which was the vital principle of life, was immaterial but subject to time: it occupied a midpoint between the divine and the corporeal and had the capacity to move upwards or downwards in accord with its desire *(appetitus);* however, its natural tendency was to ascend.[147] The movements of the soul revealed by the senses were the emotions of desire *(cupiditas),* joy *(laetitia),* fear *(metus),* and sorrow *(tristitia).*[148] The soul's upward movement was looked upon as a conversion *(conuersio)* or return *(reuersio),* in contrast to its descent, which was seen as a deterioration *(corruptio)* or even as perversion *(peruersio).*[149] Its ascent was an imitation of unity *(imitatio unitatis),* a harmony of diverse parts *(concordia partium).*[150] As a principle of motion in bodies, the soul was the source of its own movement, and the knowledge of its ability to displace itself was the motivation behind its will to bring motion about.[151]

Into this composite view of neoplatonic doctrines, which I have sketched very roughly, Augustine introduced a concern with the philosophy of language. An early example of his approach is found in *De Quantitate Animae* 32.[152] In a typically neoplatonic discussion of the soul, he illustrates the central point in his argument by pointing out that the difference between the aural and mental perception of a word's meaning depends on the human consciousness of time—a principle that is explored at greater length in *Confessions* 11 and underpins his theory of narrative. The meaning of the word "Lucifer" cannot depend on the length of time that it takes to pronounce the syllables, since the word's signification survives after the sounds have ceased.[153] Conversely, although the meaning is not physically extended over time like waves of sound, it encapsulates the temporal expression of the word's letters, their pauses and periods of duration, animating them, so to speak, and bringing them to completion.[154] Through this type of intellectual strategy, he reasons that the behaviour of the soul provides a foundation for his philosophy of language, and vice versa.

Augustine's argument works equally well for spoken and written words. However, in his mature theology, it is applied mainly to scripture, which mediates between ordinary language and God's word, just as the human soul exists between the realms of the divine and the corporeal.[155] Scripture is partly temporal, since it consists of words written on parchment, and partly eternal, since it represents divine speech.[156] Not surprisingly, the word in the text reappears in the mind of the faithful as a changeless Word, an immaterial vehicle of communication that is unlike the utterances with which we normally express ourselves.[157] Our ability to perceive this inner design begins with a material medium, the written biblical text, and our sensory ability to decode its meaning.[158] The Old Testament is "the autograph of God,"[159] in which "we read the law written by his hand,"[160] since Hebrew, its original tongue, was from the beginning a written language.[161] There is a rough parallel in the New Testament: when the gospel is read aloud, we "listen" to the words of Christ,[162] who dictated the texts of the evangelists and the apostles.[163] Students of the Bible have to distinguish between what Christ signified in his preaching and the vehicles of his message—the mechanics of the voice, the sounds of the words, and the graphic symbols recorded on parchment with ink.[164]

Augustine's sensitivity to textual concerns is well illustrated by his attitude toward his own writings.[165] In the preface to the *Retractions*—the "confessions" of his later years—he critically reassessed the entire corpus.[166] The chronology of his publications[167] offered him a retrospective view on his literary achievements and failures,[168] complementing the account of his intellectual progress in *Confessions* 1–9 and the "philosophical dialogues." The book is also a self-defence,[169] since, as early as 412,[170] he planned for a "collected edition"[171] of his doctrinal and polemical works in order to eliminate misconceptions among his readers.[172] During his career his mind became so thoroughly imbued with the reader's mentality that it is necessary to distinguish between the act of reading orally or silently *(legere)* and the accompanying "intention" or "attention" of the mind *(intentio* or *attentio animi).*[173] He read and reflected on *Confessions* 1–9 while composing book 10;[174] later, he was as deeply moved by rereading his account as when he wrote it.[175] During the siege of Hippo in 430, while he was dying, the seven "penitential psalms" were copied and hung beside his bed so that he could read, weep, and repent.[176]

Among the philosophical issues that affect his approach to reading, a special role is played by the will.[177] As an aspect of his theory of verbal intentions, Augustine speculates on the manner in which the will, which in principle expresses the mind's desire, is actually expressed in words that may lead to contrasting or adverse actions.[178] As the divine will is unknowable with certainty by humans,[179] we are unaware of God's impress on our thinking, even on the occasions when he inspires our decisions. As a consequence of these disjunctions, our thoughts can frequently affect our actions differently from the way in which we think they should.[180]

Our only access to the certainties of the divine order lies through an authoritative source outside ourselves—scripture. In Augustine's thinking, therefore, reading takes precedence over other ways of understanding the future course of events. The idea itself was not new.[181] In late antiquity, the rise of a reading culture among Christians gradually put limits on the range of validity of other forms of understanding the future, namely those that were based on omens, magic, weather, oracles, stars, or deities.[182] These were either rejected outright, as in the case of astrology, or brought within the range of what could be read into biblical texts. If the latter course was taken, they ceased to operate as independent explanations of change and were incorporated into a growing field of interpretation.[183] Into the vacuum created when other causal notions were abandoned, Augustine introduced the view, already popular among Platonists, that there was a single deity who wilfully disposed and arranged the natural forces of the universe; to this he added a novel ingredient, namely the notion that God's will for us is demonstrated through our innate desire to know him[184] by means of the transcript of his message. For this reason, it is the reader rather than the speaker who brings the issues into focus as they affect the future of the soul or self. Scripture offers the reader—either the private reader or the audience at a reading—a privileged medium, through which God's will, framed in narrative, can be internalized and directed outwards as ethically informed action.

Another philosophical topic that impinges on Augustine's theory of reading is memory. He criticized classical reminiscence,[185] restricting inquiry into memory to the mental life of the individual;[186] he also distinguished between sensory and mental origins for memories.[187] Through introspective experiments he implicitly modified rhetorical approaches to the subject, which he may have reviewed in Carthage or Milan, and discredited the rote memorization recommended by the *Rhetorica ad Herennium, De Oratore,* and Quintilian.[188] He had some awareness of the distinction between "episodic" and "semantic" memory,[189] which he characterized by their relationship to temporally organized information. He likewise preceded one of this century's distinguished psychologists of memory, Frederic Bartlett, in separating memory from remembering and in emphasizing the part played in recollection by sensory encoding and recoding. On this view, short-term traces *(uestigia)* are enabling vehicles for transforming thoughts into words, and they are stored somewhere in the mind; later, "a stimulus reexcites the trace, and, as the trace carries with it a temporal sign, the reexcitement is equivalent to recall."[190] There is also a modern ring to his notion that memory arises from a combination of mental attention and linguistic intentions. Hearing differs from listening, seeing from looking: only the latter pair provides the basis for the word recognition that underpins a theory of signs. Before I speak, he proposes, the understanding of what I want to say fills my thoughts; however, as soon as I speak, I am guided by a mental image of the original ideas, whose imprint lasts only as long as verbal communication takes place.[191]

In addition to grounding his theory of reading in thought-experiments involving memory, Augustine was the Western originator of the notion of autobiographical memory.[192] He was the earliest writer to give memory a critical role in sustaining the individual's personal continuity[193] and in creating self-knowledge[194]—a view in which he differed decisively from his intellectual mentor on problems of consciousness, Plotinus.[195] He also distinguished between the simple reliving of an episode in the past and fitting such an episode into a schema, that is, a pattern of information already shaped in discursive or narrative form in the mind. In *Confessions* 8 he utilized this device in the account of his conversion, thus incorporating events that were experienced into a "generic image" of conversion that included elements that were by-products of his subsequent reading.[196]

Finally, he viewed external memory as a type of societal archive. The thesis was extensively documented in *De Ciuitate Dei*, where he contrasted pagan and Christian views, and it made an earlier appearance in *De Quantitate Animae* 33, when he spoke about the seven dimensions of the soul's greatness. Here he argued that external memory, as contrasted with internally operating habits, has a privileged position in relation to the soul's ability to animate the body and to coordinate the work of the senses. Only humans construct such a reference library in order to organize their purposeful activities.[197] Looking forward to Vico, Augustine saw memory as the basis of culture: the subjects included in his inventory ranged from farming and building to different symbolic systems—letters, words, gestures, sounds, paintings, and statues. They incorporated the languages and institutions of peoples (both new and revived); books, records, offices, powers, and honours; reasoning, conceptualizing, public speaking, poetic composition, acting, and music; and the arts of surveying, enumerating, and prognostication.

In the *Confessions,* Augustine linked the experience of narrative and memory through ethics, stressing the role of personal obligation in attaining a way of life that is improvable, if never perfect.[198] A detailed outline of his ideas is found in book 10, chapters 17–35, which unite study, remembering, and self-examination in a plan for disciplining the body.[199] The aesthetic motives for reading that are criticized in the autobiographical books (1–9) are replaced by an ascetic programme. Moral precepts are read (or heard); they are then transformed from thought to practice as they are recalled. The specific recollections are the points of departure for a meditative ascent. As this proceeds, the study of scripture gradually becomes a form of life *(forma uiuendi)*.[200]

Augustine took inspiration from a lengthy tradition of writings that related reading and asceticism.[201] The procedure is hinted at in the Qumran fragments and clearly expressed by the desert fathers, whose ambivalence toward books fills the pages of Palladius' *Lausiac History*.[202] The Stoic variant is given a classic statement in Seneca's *Epistulae Morales*.[203] Comparable ideas found their way into the "spiritual exercises" of the neoplatonists[204] as well as Pharisaic[205] and gospel traditions.[206] By the time Augustine wrote, reading and writing had for some generations been united with oral habits in producing a "technology" of self-reform,[207] thereby opening a new chapter in a philosophy of the ascetic life that went back as far as Philo.[208] The bishop's *Rule* was not edited for publication but was intended to be an aid to memory based on verbatim teaching:[209] he thus ascended from *scientia* to *sapientia,* as Etienne Gilson noted, by transforming philosophic virtues into monastic rules.[210] He recreated the ascetic life as a literary ideal while maintaining that it had no meaning unless it was lived.[211] In this respect, he regarded memory as a source of both "being" and "becoming."[212]

To entertain this double vision, Augustine had to believe that reading and writing provided the individual with a means of intellectual ascent through memory, even though, by the time he wrote the *Confessions,* he was convinced that true happiness could be realized only in the next life through the resurrection of the body[213] (not, as he may have believed in youth, through mystical or ecstatic experiences in this world).[214] Moreover, he balanced the innerwordly demands of writing[215] with the view of reading as an otherworldly activity. Leisured reading isolated the self and permitted a detached recollection and examination of mental activities.

During these moments of "illumination," the text was not sensorially decoded but became an object on which the mind focused its attention as it began an inward journey propelled by itself. In sum, he argued that if the contemplative frame of mind is our only experience of the blessed life while we are alive, the person most likely to achieve temporary happiness is the reader (whence his admiration for the silent, leisured study periods of Ambrose). Reading and post-reading experiences thereby paralleled the manner in which a life of Christian discipline could be followed by an afterlife of blessedness.

The two ideas went hand in hand, forming a union of hermeneutic and mystical possibilities. Augustine would have agreed with the contemporary observation that reading is an invitation to live temporarily within the thoughts of someone else;[216] but in his view, both the invitation and the response are issued by ourselves. We cannot truly inhabit another person's mind.[217] We are separated from each other by a gulf that our external and internal senses cannot bridge.[218] We are like sojourners in a foreign land,[219] participants in a "pilgrimage of the life of the flesh," in which "hearts are closed off from each other."[220] Men and women, we are equally abandoned by God in "the world."[221] We are estranged from our "native land" by an "ocean": we are able to see the distant shore but unable to reach it.[222]

Yet through reading and meditation it is possible for us to people our hearts and minds temporarily with a community of thoughts,[223] which live within us as something other than our selves.[224] They are harbingers of things to come and reminders that we pass our lives in what Plato aptly termed "a zone of unlikeness,"[225] a locality in which we have only a transient awareness of the nontransience of higher things. We can over-come this sense of alienation in moments of inspiration, when we directly experience God's power.[226] Failing this, we fall back on memory, which permits us to maintain a semipermanent continuity of thought.[227] This is "reminiscence," but not of a Platonic type,[228] since souls, as frames for memory, have become like texts, as instruments of record. The external and internal types of memory are paralleled in Augustine's notions of formal and informal religious groups.[229] In both, a community is formed: in the one, it consists of people living under a "rule"; in the other, of people united by their intentions, that is, by their social expression of faith.

AUGUSTINE'S ideas on these issues arose out of a traditional Christian position. He believed that reading and writing were among the labours imposed on the first couple as a result of their disobedience in the garden of Eden.[230] They were the consequences of human curiosity and pride.[231] Before the fall, there was no need of such cumbersome instruments of communication. God spoke to Adam and Eve directly, as he did to the Hebrew prophets, or made his will known without the use of language.[232] Reading and writing arose in time and were to disappear at the end of time, when the soul would be restored to unity with God.[233] Meanwhile, humans adhered to temporal principles, although they served eternal ones;[234] among these were the linguistic and grammatical skills that enabled them to understand the Bible.[235]

By following a positive line of thinking within this uncompromising outlook, Augustine was led to unusual insights on the relationship between the self and narrative.[236] If language, from which reading and writing derive, is definable through a community of speakers, then selves, souls, or minds, which depend on language for their human expression, have to have their communities too. Their lives consist of what Charles Taylor calls a "web of interlocutions."[237] It is this intersubjective quality that makes Augustine's *Confessions* unique in the ancient literature of the soul rather than the doctrine that the inner self is veiled, mysterious, or inaccessible. His story hovers between thought and the world before it enters the world in words that are intended to be interpreted by others.[238] *Confessio* becomes *narratio,*[239] and it is retransformed into a mental confession by its readers.[240] Furthermore, he establishes the view that knowledge about the self is revealed when the moral habits and internal patterns of a life proceed from the private to the public realm;[241] when they pass wilfully through stages of thought, language, and expression and are, so to speak, published. He distinguishes between the events of his life that he personally recalls[242] and the discourse in which those events are presented, which is inevitably a literary genre.[243] He knows that the life is not a revision of events: it is a revision of his interpretation of them.

His major vehicle for conveying these ideas is *Confessions* 1–9, where he contrasts the opinions that he held at the time when the episodes took place with those that arose at the time of writing. He sees the person who writes in 397 engaging in a process of self-redefinition rather than setting down a definitive version of the life. Final publication, to extend the metaphor, is endlessly postponed, and this too is intentional. The variants appear as early as 386–87; they are still taking shape when he writes the *Retractions* in 426–27.[244] "Take up my books . . . of *Confessions,*" he tells his friend Darius at age seventy-three, just a year before his death. "Pay attention to the person I was there: see what I was, in myself and through myself."[245] These are the words of a literary artist who refuses to separate the representational value[246] of his life from his evaluation of the person he has become.

His primary objective was to describe the manner in which his life had changed, not to produce a text. In moving from life to text and back to life, his concern was ethical before it was literary, and it was literary only in combination with ethics.[247] The purpose of living "in the house of discipline" was to learn how to live well *(bene uiuere)*.[248] He saw a potential fit between the inner and outer "readings" of the self as an instrument for bringing about personal improvement.[249] Working toward this equilibrium required that he introduce into Christian theology the notion of the self-conscious reader, who realized, like Montaigne centuries later, that "by studying and questioning . . . authors in the light of his own opinions and experience he was studying himself."[250]

In pursuit of this goal, he reoriented thinking on Genesis 1:26, the much-commented-on statement that God created humans in his "image and likeness."[251] His "departure" from tradition, Robert Markus noted, "appears to have been prompted by purely logical, linguistic considerations, not by disagreement with the theology of sin, grace, and sanctification."[252] Its vehicle was the understanding of speech in an ancient theory of reading, through which he stamped his personal interpretation on Paul's statements concerning the transition from the "old" to the "new,"[253] delicately positioning the student of the Bible in the ontological space between the inner and outer person.[254] This contrast separated the domain of the body, signs, language, and the reader's skills from that of the spirit, the undivided intellect, and God.[255] The appropriate moment for the transition to take place was at the end of "grammatical" education.[256] Living "according to the inner man,"[257] as Paul recommended, was like an advanced literary exercise: it was a "reediting" of the self in which one narrative, a life to come, was traced over another, a life already lived.[258] As one passed from youth to maturity, the Christian ideal of self-reform and the meditative life of the reader grew closer together. Reading became indispensable for the acquisition of salvific knowledge and beneficial self-discipline.

There are three stages in this progression. At the most basic level, reading is an empirical activity, inasmuch as it involves the senses of hearing and sight. At the same time, it is cognitive and interpretive, since the reader engages in intentional thinking and utilizes the memory while forming an understanding of what is signified by verbal and written signs. Finally, reading is a stimulus to meditation: the reader, focusing on the sensations created by words, uncouples the mental images of those same sensations from his or her thoughts about them, and is "taught from within." The reader thus follows a purely intellectual trajectory which leaves the physical text far behind.[259] In this respect, reading is a prelude to mystical experience.

In this reconstruction, the reading process is conceived as an "odyssey,"[260] in which the evidence of the senses permits the individual to ascend through a metaphorical "infancy" and "adolescence" to a certain level of maturity.[261] Beyond that point, the soul is guided by means that lie beyond the faculties of interpretation and judgement. The point is driven home in the final episode of the narrative segment of the *Confessions,* the "vision at Ostia" (9.10), where words, bodies, and genders are all transcended at once.[262] With good reason,[263] it is a woman who is strong in faith but weak in booklearning who accompanies Augustine during his momentary experience of beatitude.[264] In a complementary discussion in *De Trinitate* 12–14, he argues that even the highest type of contemplation attainable in this life will not exist in the next, except through "traces of memory."[265]

These ascents are about the way in which the self achieves spiritual interdependencies. They are not about an independent self. One of the lessons of the *Confessions* is that a plausible narrative is a precondition to the building of a bounded and believable self. Yet the writing has no autonomous status of its own, either as an act of composition or as a literary product.[266] Augustine would not have agreed with the view of his achievement that took shape after Petrarch, when he was looked upon as the ancient spokesman on behalf of a "modern" notion[267] of the reader: the "individual," alone with a book, self-absorbed in a silent world of his own creation. He is interested in the subjective element in the response to texts, but he does not believe in the text's or the reader's self-sufficiency. He likewise resists the temptation of literary Pelagianism, namely the belief that the individual is improvable beyond the limits of a fallen condition through education. There is a hint of this view in his twelfth-century admirer Hugh of St. Victor, as there is later in Erasmus. It is not found in his own writings.[268] Well before he encountered the works of Pelagius in 410–11, he had studied examples of this type of thinking, among them Faustus of Mileu and the anonymous Milanese who procured Marius Victorinus' translation of Plotinus.[269] He rejected them.

As an alternative, he invented a number of new roles for the later ancient reader. His reference point for the many writings in which he explored his novel ideas was the *Confessions.* Controversy has surrounded the life history since Adolf von Harnack drew attention to the differences in the account of his intellectual development in *Confessions* 1–9, begun in 397, and the early dialogues, especially *De Beata Vita, Contra Academicos,* and *De Ordine,* written in the winter of 386–87.[270] Scholars have continued to have misgivings about the factual value of the autobiography, especially concerning the critical account of the final conversion, which is not reiterated elsewhere. Mistrust reached its high point between Prosper Alfaric (1918) and Pierre Courcelle (1950), both of whom were convinced, for philosophical and philological reasons respectively, that *Confessions* 8 was largely a literary creation.

Courcelle saw his task as setting the historical record straight. "The words of Augustine," he stated, "invite us to engage in a twofold inquiry: to attempt to reestablish chronology as precisely as possible, notably for the Milanese period . . . about which we are well supplied with information, and, beyond that, to seek in the works of Augustine or his contemporaries either a historical context or direct allusions . . . testimonials against which the narrative of the *Confessions* can be tested." Courcelle's studies marked a turning point in historical research on the *Confessions* by replacing "the subjective reconstitution" of Augustine's "intellectual or religious development" with "an inquiry . . . carried out in a methodical manner"[271] which made use of the entire corpus of his autobiographical writings. Subsequent figures in the debate,[272] whether they have questioned or confirmed his position, have worked mostly within a tradition of thinking that asks whether a "correct" version of Augustine's life and thought can be established using the tools of textual criticism, source typification, and philology.[273]

Despite the advantages of this approach from a philological standpoint, it leaves a central question unanswered. This concerns Augustine's philosophical arguments for adopting a literary strategy in the first place. His reasoning is partly revealed in *Confessions* 10–13, but a full account requires an examination of a series of books dealing with words, texts, and reading that were written from 386 onwards. My purpose in what follows is to study the relations among these writings, and in particular to reexamine the narrative about reading in *Confessions* 1–9, which is taken up in Part I, in the light of the various analytical statements on the subject, which are the subject of Part II. I divide Augustine's writings on the subject into "narrative" and "analytical" types of discussion: in the one, reading is a story that is told to a real or implied audience, while in the other it is conceived in a nonnarrative manner as part of an inquiry into emotion, cognition, and principles of interpretation. Needless to say, I view these as operating interdependently, as does Augustine in his revision of later ancient views on the functions of the literary imagination.[274]

# I

## CONFESSIONS 1–9

✹

The topic of Part I is Augustine's narrative of his progress as a reader in *Confessions* 1–9. The account begins in infancy and moves to his classroom at Thagaste in 361; it then leaps forward to 373, when he discovers Cicero's *Hortensius,* takes up the study of philosophy, and begins a nine-year period as a Manichaean auditor. In 384, his interest in Catholicism is reawakened by the sermons of Ambrose, who teaches him to distinguish between the literal and spiritual senses of edifying texts and provides a model of meditative silence by means of reading. From May to July 386 he engages in a comparative study of Christian and neoplatonist writings, assimilating some ideas and rejecting doctrines unacceptable to Catholicism. He subsequently reads Paul's epistles and becomes acquainted with the life of Anthony. His conversion to the religious life in the garden of his house in Milan takes place through an act of reading, although its cause is divine. He follows a programme of biblical studies under Ambrose's direction during the winter and early spring of 386–87; he then sojourns at Verecundus' villa at Cassiciacum, where he begins the "philosophical dialogues." The story concludes at Ostia in late autumn 387, where he and his pious mother have a vision in which earthly forms of communication are transcended by a momentary experience of the blessed life.

# 1

## LEARNING TO READ

❧

### Words

Augustine's story[1] of his experience as a reader begins with a prayer (1.1–6) and a reconstruction of how he learned to speak (1.6–8).[2]

The prayer introduces some of the *Confessions'* major themes—language, memory, time, sin, and spiritual ascent (compare 5.1, 10.1–6). Augustine also acquaints the reader with the "confession" as an act of praise directed toward God and as a work of literature[3] directed toward humans, including himself. As author, he is engaged as both a reader and a writer.[4] The theme of oral, meditative, and commemorative reading[5] is established through multiple evocations of the Psalms,[6] while the content of the quoted texts draws attention to God's omnipresence and ineffability.[7] Augustine begs compassion and opens "the ears of his heart" (1.5.6–9); his restless soul seeks repose,[8] and this unquietness, issuing in his first sounds, begins his narrative in infancy,[9] that is, a speechless state.[10] The origin of his ability to speak and the composition of the discourse that is his autobiography[11] thus make up a single theme,[12] beginning in the first of the traditional six ages of man.[13]

These issues are involved with another of the *Confessions'* major topics, memory. Augustine has no recollection of his earliest infancy;[14] yet he is convinced that infants attain self-consciousness from the time when they can remember past events.[15] He notes that he has to learn what he can of this period from the reports of his parents (1.6.6–8) and nurses (1.6.9–10; 1.7.22–23). By observing mothers with their children, he acquires information about pregnancy, breast-feeding, and infants' sleeping habits, none of which he recalls from experience.[16]

The narrative following 1.8.4 lies within the domain of recall. Augustine's ignorance about infancy is meant to illustrate a general feature of our beliefs about the past. When we have no knowledge of events that have taken place, we have to put our trust in authorities other than ourselves (1.6.49–52). We believe what we cannot know or recall (1.6.21–23; 1.7.37–41).[17] The absence of memory benefits the infant in one respect, inasmuch as it is guilty of original sin[18] but has no recollection of sinfulness; instead, it is motivated by the desire to satisfy its physical needs.[19] And, because it cannot speak, it is exempted from the ethical consequences of human communication.[20] As an infant, Augustine was uncorrectable through words, but he was unable to be corrupted by them either.[21] Once he learned to speak, he had the power to use words for good or evil.[22]

In these opening statements, Augustine is thus speaking symbolically of the first stages of interpretive activity[23] and of the ancient education of the soul, which implied the control of emotion by reason.[24] At *De Doctrina Christiana* 2.12, he notes that understanding is eternal but faith is nourished on temporal matters, just as children in their cradles are fed with milk.[25] Similar comparisons are found in the *Sermones ad Infantes,* where the term "infants" refers to catechumens who have completed a programme of basic instruction and are to be taken before their bishop for baptism,[26] normally at Easter.[27] This was "the week of the infants,"[28] since baptized neophytes received lessons on the meaning of the eucharist.[29] The sermons that Augustine delivered on these occasions refer to infancy as the metaphorical point of departure for a Christian life.[30] A similar viewpoint is expressed in *De Catechizandis Rudibus*[31] and echoed in numerous letters.[32]

The innovative feature of his account in comparison to other ancient writers lies in making the soul's education depend on the infant's acquisition of speech. In his view, this occurs in three overlapping phases: instinct (1.6.9–20), gesture (1.6.23–31), and communication through words (1.8).[33]

The preconscious stage is limited to crude emotional responses, namely pleasure or dissatisfaction.[34] As an infant, Augustine is fed by his nurse, but he depends on the nutritional "riches" implanted in nature by God. Reciprocity prevails over self-interest: he does not desire more than God is able to give, nor do his wet-nurses offer more than they receive from God. Both parties are aware that "the good" comes through them but not from them (1.6.6–17).[35] Verbal communication is unnecessary. The sense that is utilized most is sight, which expresses self-interest (even jealousy).[36]

In the gestural phase, Augustine introduces the idea of imaginary communication within the infant's mind through a prespeech language of thought. At first he merely moved his limbs and made incoherent noises;[37] later, he learned a few words of Latin[38] in pleasurable circumstances as his nurses[39] and elders chatted and laughed. He attempted to imitate their speech gestures, and, within his mind, they provided him with an audience for his mental verbalizations (1.14.8–15). (Elsewhere he argues that nurses and mothers wag their tongues and truncate words in an effort to speak in a way that they think infants understand.)[40] Gesture, thus connected to audience, is a first transitional stage of language learning (see 1.8.14–18; 1.14.8–11).[41] And just as we do not forget childhood when we are adults, so, in our acquisition of speech, we do not altogether transcend gesture when we learn how to communicate in words.[42]

In the third phase (1.8), which is also concerned with mimesis,[43] Augustine deals with external rules and innate capacities, with habits of thought and practice, and with levels of recall (1.8.4–5). He emphasizes that there was no formal method by which he learned to speak.[44] The critical element in the learning process was access to memory.[45] When a thing was named, and when, guided by sound, those around him moved towards it, he saw what was happening, and he realized that the name was intended to draw attention to the designated object.[46] The connection was evident from adults' facial, eye, and limb movements, as well as from their voices, which he (subsequently) recognized as the outer signs of inner mental dispositions.[47] He listened to words as they occurred in different sentences until his lips were trained to make audible statements.[48] The ability to say what he wished thus resulted from the connections that he made between seeing, hearing, recollection, and habit. He also learned to associate the creation of verbal meaning with social interaction (1.8.20–24).

This brief account of infant speech acquisition parallels his description of the intentional states of mind that are envisaged between the writers and readers of texts.[49] His analysis also directs the reader's attention to the problem of metacognition,[50] to which he returns in books 10 and 11, and to issues that link him with contemporary theorists—namely prespeech language,[51] the play element,[52] and linguistic competence.[53] He also discusses the psychological[54] and social[55] aspects of language learning, which require the participation of a real or imagined audience.[56]

Yet the core of the description is empirical. Augustine mentions aspects of language development which investigators place before the second year: the use of deixis or indexicals, that is, "words that pick up or point to things in relation to the participants in speech situations";[57] the division of attention between an object and the person with whom the object is associated,[58] as well as the substitution of one gesture for another in an effort to gain adults' attention;[59] the capacity to distinguish between social and nonsocial play;[60] and ritualizing gestures, that is, actions that an infant performs again and again.[61] Conflated with these ideas are changes that take place from the second through the fifth years: the use of "commonsense realism";[62] the making of some conceptual distinctions between doing, knowing, and understanding;[63] the isolation of the factual from the non-factual; and at a later stage the conscious distinction of nonfactual mental states such as thinking, believing, and remembering.[64] As a child, Augustine is able to separate the world from his mental configuration of the world,[65] even if he has no semantic awareness of how the model relates to the world.[66] As he passes from infancy to early childhood he also acquires the ability to describe the world that he knows, as well as other worlds that are the by-products of his thinking.

Intentionality is central to his explanation, and this is understood both as a general feature of thinking and as specific acts of will.[67] In 1.6, it is God's beneficent will that programs the satisfaction of his basic needs; later, when he is able to point to what he wants, two wills are involved, his and his nurse's (1.6.23–29). In these first dialogic expressions of will arise the beginnings of his "moral personality."[68] Again, when he learns to speak, he expresses what he wills via particular signs (1.8.18–20). More specifically still, he demonstrates an awareness of the difference between noncondi-tional and conditional intentions. God's intentions for him, whether minor or major, do not require his satisfying any prerequisites, whereas the intentions that arise within himself presuppose the particular contexts in which his desires take place, such as feeding, grasping, and trying to speak. As an infant, he knows that intending an action, such as speaking, is not the same as intending a consequence, such as getting food by gesturing for it. Even as a young child, he appears to be aware of the recursive nature of some intentions; that is, he knows what others intend for him. In the next phase of his education, this includes learning to read and to write.

## Reading and Writing

The second phase of Augustine's education consists in the acquisition of these literate skills,[69] which he takes up in the remainder of book 1.[70] The scene is set in his native Thagaste and, from age eleven to sixteen, in the university town of Madaura.[71]

As he looks back on these years, he sees some four transitions taking place. He distinguishes between the activity of reading and the content of the texts that he is taught to read. He connects the memorization of the basic skills of reading and writing with the reform of his habitual behaviour. At the same time, he differentiates between reading for pleasure and reading for self-improvement: the one is an "aesthetic" impulse, the other, "ascetic." Finally, he asks his first questions about the value of spoken words versus

written texts as models for understanding how God's law is imprinted on
the human heart.

In his description of his studies he stresses his inadequacies. Talented[72]
and endowed with an outstanding memory,[73] he nonetheless "had no great
love of reading books" and "learned nothing from them unless . . . forced
to do so."[74] His work habits were disciplined by periodic flogging.[75] The
subsidizing[76] of his education was viewed as an investment (1.12.6–9):
spiritual benefits were not discussed (1.10.4–5). Understandably so; with
the exception of Romanianus, his patrons were people of modest means.[77]
Nonetheless, he blamed himself for his neglect of "reading, writing, and
book-learning" (1.9.29–30). His punishment was a disordered mind
(1.12.14–15). He had no incentives to improve his work habits and obeyed
no recognized precepts for disciplining his behaviour (1.10.1–4). He devoted much of his time to sports,[78] to fictions, and to spectacles—pastimes
that "tantalized" his senses and "whetted" his idle curiosity.[79] It was a short
step from these fleeting pleasures to the "carnal corruption of his soul" a
few years later through sex, carousing, and petty theft—topics that are
discussed at length in book 2.[80]

He undoubtedly exaggerated his waywardness. Independent evidence,
though not abundant, suggests that he was a studious, well-organized pupil,
whose literary interests surfaced at an early age.[81] In works written before
the *Confessions,* he refers in positive terms to the benefits of grammatical
and literary training.[82] The *Confessions* presents the critical view of liberal
education that is typical of the period after his ordination. As early as 398,
when the autobiography was in progress, he put a group of bishops on
guard against worldly uses of education among laymen and clerics, contrasting the potential for materialistic values[83] with an ethic of "living
well."[84] The play element[85] must also be seen in the context of three
important episodes later in the story.[86] In book 6, Alypius, his "alter ego,"[87]
fails to resist the attractions of the public games; as a result, he is unable to
direct his energies toward moral improvement (6.8). In book 8, when
Ponticianus tells the story of Anthony, he finds the letters of Paul on
Augustine's gaming table and recognizes that he is a Catholic.[88] And
when Augustine takes up and reads Romans 13:13–14 later in the same
book, he asks himself whether he has ever before heard *tolle, lege* chanted
by children as they played.[89] As Augustine passes from youth to early
manhood, therefore, it can be argued that the playing of games is superseded by the interplay of his interpretive efforts. At 1.6–8 his desire to excel
at sports contrasts with his inability to win a victory within himself; later
the playing field becomes the classroom, and the metaphors focus on

theatre, legal debate, and Manichaean preaching. In books 7 and 8, the false dramas of his student years are replaced by the internal drama of his salvation.[90]

The cumulative effect of these episodes is to draw attention to the bishop Augustine's ambivalence toward the role of formal education in the individual's spiritual progress. Augustine was an unbaptized child when he first learned of the incarnation and salvation (1.1.1–2, 23–35). This and other preschool lessons in theology were delivered at home by his mother (2.3.52–71). And when he was gravely ill, he was saved, he believed, by Monica's appeal to the deity (1.11.5–14). Not long afterward he had personal thoughts about God's interventive power while observing men at prayer: he envisaged the deity as "a great force" which was capable of perceiving him while remaining unperceived (1.9.10–13). He and his friends demanded an end to daily flogging. When the request went unanswered, he asked himself whether God worked from the outside, as they wished, or from within. In a revealing phrase, he speaks of invoking God at the very moment when his maker "undid" and "forced open" the "knot of his tongue" (1.9.13–15). He was aware that through prayer he "sensed" God's presence without the intervention of his external senses. He thus arrived at his earliest critique of the truth-value of sensory knowledge. This was another lesson that did not require that he know how to read or write.[91] Its catalyst was Monica, who generally operates outside the later ancient institutions of literate education.

This theme of transcendence reaches its finest statement in the "vision at Ostia" in book 9. In the other chapters of book 1 (1.13–20), Augustine focuses on the moral implications of his early education.[92] Within his general distaste for reading, writing, and arithmetic,[93] he distinguishes between struggling to learn Greek and the pleasure of Latin, once he moved beyond grammar to literature.[94] The bishop Augustine knows that the *grammatici* commercialize literate education:[95] the curtains before the doorways of their teaching stalls, far from inspiring respect, all too often conceal moral and intellectual backwardness (1.13.31–33). Yet his words do not imply a criticism of "grammar":[96] he is aware that a knowledge of reading and writing is more valuable than the transient pleasures that he derived from his recitations of set texts.[97] He notes that his best lesson was the earliest.[98] Although he was charmed by Virgil,[99] he cherished most the instruments through which he acquired and retained the ability to read what he came upon in written form and to write down whatever he wished for his personal use.[100]

In this statement, he extends the idea, prevalent among the ancients,[101] that infants learn to speak by remembering what they have observed when adults are conversing. Their capacities vary greatly: some youngsters cannot even memorize the alphabet,[102] while others find this type of rote learning so uninspiring that, like the precocious Augustine, they develop a strong antipathy toward it.[103] Augustine was more amused by the tale of Troy than by committing sums and syntax to memory (1.13.48–51). And when he mastered a literary text for his amusement—for instance, a few lines of Terence (1.16.34–36)—he mostly sought his masters' praise and feared their displeasure (1.17.8–11; compare 4.2.2–5).[104] He was able to recall Aeneas' misfortunes but unable to attend to his own; he wept over luckless Dido but shed no tears over the state of his own soul (1.13.11–19).[105] Worst of all, he failed to recognize the role of memory in building a foundation for the moral life, notwithstanding the model of the "true church" offered by his mother's simple faith (1.11.8–9). He only later realized that what he had learned from her by word of mouth[106] was firmly impressed on his mind (1.11.16–19); and she, noting his feeble resistance to temptation, sought to reshape this interior matter out of which his true being was made rather than troubling herself with the transient form in which it then appeared (1.11.32–35). She thus taught him a lesson that he would teach himself in book 7.

As the story proceeds, memorization proves to be an important force in Augustine's programme of reform. Its potential arises from the close relations that he perceives between memory and habit.[107] In his youthful recitations of pagan texts, habitual memory works against moral improvement (1.16); however, in book 10, where the texts are biblical, improvements in his customary behaviour take place through a combination of reading and recall. By retaining selected passages of scripture in memory and by organizing his thoughts around them, he creates a "plan for living," that is, a personalized rule that is capable of "ordering" theory into practice and offering resistance to the misleading attractions of the senses. Working from the inside, this procedure implements Paul's idea of reform; however, it does so by means of an Augustinian method: the later developments are envisaged at 1.15, where he asks that the basic disciplines that he learned in school—namely, speaking, writing, reading, and counting—be devoted to God's service, since it is the deity who first imposed a morally beneficial discipline on him.[108]

His emphasis on the value of this training is a clue to another issue raised in book 1, namely the distinction between the "aesthetic" and "ascetic" aspects of reading. The aesthetic can be defined as a type of reader's response in which the pleasure of the text is an end in itself,[109] while the ascetic assumes that the text is a means for attaining a higher, more pleasurable end. In an extreme form, the aesthetic response sees nothing beyond the text; the ascetic sees nothing of lasting value in the text. In the one, ethical considerations are subordinated to enjoyment; in the other, enjoyment is postponed until ethical imperatives are met. For the ascetic reader, this moment does not have to coincide with the time of reading; it may occur during thinking, meditation, or recollection at some remove from the aural or visual experience of the text; it may even lie beyond the physical life of the reader, namely in the afterlife. Augustine's suggestions build on comparable statements made in *De Utilitate Credendi* in 391 and in *De Doctrina Christiana*. In both cases, he envisages a hermeneutics of "using" and "enjoying" in which he distinguishes between the texts that we read, which are a means of communication, and the higher truths toward which they are directed.[110]

Within the autobiography, the aesthetic pleasure of the text is incorporated into a well-defined ascetic plan. The search for beauty is transformed into the satisfaction that results from the quest for a world-denying way of life through the study of the Bible. Reading ceases to be a "wandering" from one literary delight to another and becomes a "pilgrimage," in which all textual experiences are directed toward a single goal. We perceive the formation of this idea as Augustine isolates the experience from the content of his reading. He realizes that if his studies are to have a lasting value, he has to search for something beyond performances that engages his inner self morally and intellectually with an edifying text. This consciousness of himself as a reader develops during the course of his reading but is not detached from his progress through the text.

Detachment and self-awareness in turn help him to separate the false and true narratives of desire. In book 1, he associates the topos of youthful inexperience with the aesthetics of reading. The literary diversions pander to his vanity: he sees himself as "flesh" or "perambulating spirit," which is unable to "turn away" from temptation.[111] His only concern is for the expression and satisfaction of his emotions. Had he been told not to read about Dido,[112] he notes, he would have been saddened by not being able to be made sad (1.13.24–25). Seduced by the language of the set texts, he is likewise unable to recognize the immorality of pagan mythology: he overlooks Homer's ascription of divine impulses to many pernicious acts, through which the sexual lust of the pagan deities is simply disguised (1.16.10–13). Also, he fails to see that the repetition of similar scenes in different works suggests that one unreal situation is taking another for its reality. He offers the example of Homer's account of how Danaë was

seduced by Jupiter in a shower of gold when she was shut up for safe-keeping in a small chamber. In Terence's *Eunuch,* a youth of ill repute, looking
at a mural of the Homeric scene in a brothel, states that he too can make
love "in thunder."[113] Augustine memorized and recited Terence's lines,
creating still another level of encouragement for his own lust (1.16.19–
36).[114] With equally superficial ends in view, he was set the task of
inventing speeches in the *Aeneid* that were never made, and of transforming
its poetry into prose. The literary competitions caused him deep anxiety—
though not enough to make him withdraw from them—since praise was
given for finding appropriate words to express imaginary anger and sorrow
in already imaginary characters. Only later, as a professor of rhetoric, did
he come to see that in performances of this type the spoken word is
detached from any moral context and is supported only by the position
that the speaker is advocating at a particular time and place (1.17.2–11).

In sum, it is through his reading of the *Aeneid* (and other classical texts)
that Augustine's ambivalence as a reader first surfaces.[115] He wishes to
appropriate the text because it gives him pleasure; at the same time, he
wishes to isolate himself from it because he understands that the pleasure
is illusory. Through this experience he eventually learns that his inner life,
in which his being presumably resides, is at once dependent and autonomous: dependent because he needs the illusions of reading to believe in
the continuity of its existence; autonomous because he knows that the
reality existing in himself cannot be a part of such illusions.[116]

There is one other element that is introduced into this picture of the
emergent reader in book 1. This is the notion of rule, method, or law,
which results from Augustine's combined reflections on readership and
memory. The ease with which he learns Latin in contrast to Greek[117]
teaches him that "free curiosity" is a better teacher than "fearful coercion."
Yet the bishop and moralist observes that human curiosity knows no limits;
it can be restrained only by divine "laws."[118] He connects the notions of
reading and law in a simple example at the end of his discussion of the
*Aeneid.* Ask a group of students whether Aeneas really came to Carthage,
he proposes, and each will reply according to his level of instruction. But
this cannot be the basis of a general literary understanding, since the
responses will vary with the individuals' information. True knowledge, like
the thoughts that stand behind signs, must arise from a source common to
all. This can be illustrated by asking the students to spell Aeneas' name.
They have no choice but to reply in agreement with the conventions by
which letters create comprehensible words.[119]

By 397 Augustine had worked out a general way of describing such relations. It sufficed to think of divine laws, the rules governing conscience, and the commands of scripture as variants of the same principle.[120] Just as graphic signs were equated with fixed laws, so the acquisition of literate skills opened the door to the deeper, unchanging meaning that lay behind the sensory flow of words. The line between the spoken and the written was finely drawn: the oral vocabulary was seen to penetrate the literary expressions, just as scripture underpinned the concern with the voice. There was nonetheless an attempt to implant into his early learning experiences a sense of the superiority of fixedness over disordered fluctuations. His train of thought reaches its conclusion at 1.16–19, where he reiterates his objections to useless imitation and performance but introduces the notion that what is in one's conscience—the inner, ethical self that controls and guides one's actions—is produced by the same type of rules that apply to reading and writing. His early recitals of texts and his later readings were symbols of this difference: the words, being mere sounds, vanished, while the texts, which were based on scripture, endured.

How could this be so? A complete answer is not found in the *Confessions:* I return to these issues in Part II of this study. Within book 1, Augustine reasons by analogy from two learning situations, custom versus law and the transition from gestures to words. He cries out against the "river of routine" into which the sons of Eve have fallen, a torrent symbolized mainly by the incessant flow of words in human communication. Meanings are learned, eloquence acquired, business advanced,[121] and thoughts expressed, but, lacking divine guidance, to what end? In this situation man is like an actor who imitates a story that is shown to him by means of a series of wall paintings (1.16.1–26). To have meaning, Augustine argues, the pictures would have to be annotated in order to give specific significance to the events portrayed.[122] In communication through gestures (which he believes unscribed pictures resemble), this is never the case. What is presented is like a series of words in which there is no agreed meaning for the whole; therefore, what we can imitate and draw lessons from is only another person's representation of himself. This, ultimately, is an example of worldliness and vanity: for, if words are realities, then style is the man.

Working with such analogies, Augustine reaches a general statement of his position at 1.18.18–29,[123] where he proposes that there are two sorts of arrangements by which the conventional expressions of language give rise to meaning among humans. These are the relations between letters and syllables, the *pacta litterarum et syllabarum,* and the eternal bonds of salvation, the *aeterna pacta . . . salutis.*[124] Humans utilize words: God is "withdrawn, dwelling on high in silence" (Isaiah 33:5),[125] beyond language. The problems in communication do not arise from words, which are technical instruments for transmitting meaning, but from the manner in which individuals are taught to use them, particularly in the schools. There, young minds are enebriated with "the wine of error";[126] the rules of pronunciation suggest that it is more important to say the word "man" correctly than to know what a man is. As Augustine speaks of the *disciplina grammatica* in 1.16–18, the meaning is broadened from grammar in a technical sense to any imitative performance involving language in which attention is focused on outer rather than inner relations. Among the inward ideas that benefit man, moreover, none is more germane to the understanding and regulation of the self than what he calls, echoing Paul, the *scripta conscientia,* the human conscience (or consciousness) that is informed by God's law.[127] He thus introduces into the *Confessions* a crucial idea—the notion of conscience as a superior type of rule or judgement, which is enjoined on all Christian readers from within.[128]

On this note he brings book 1 to a close. As far as the topic of reading is concerned, the major theme of the *Confessions* is introduced; in books 10 and 11, its development will resolve the problem that arises between the words he speaks *(lingua mea)* and the text written on his heart by God *(scripturae tuae,* 1.17.14–15). The "confession" praises God for allowing the narrative of words to unfold into the narrative of informed sacred writings. In that sense, the story waiting to be told is like a book that he has opened but has not yet read. He does not yet know how to read it. Youth is a time of untutored innocence,[129] when he plays with words and views life through the eyes of the stage-player (1.19.1–10).

## Self-Improvement

In the next period of his education, Augustine is taught how his emotional responses are shaped as a member of an audience; he is also "converted" to the study of philosophy upon reading Cicero's *Hortensius.*

In books 1–3, these changes are marked by his awareness that his biological and cognitive evolution are not taking place at the same rate.[130] He grows up physically but remains morally and intellectually immature. The gap between what he is and what he should be widens down to the moment of his conversion in book 8 (compare 6.11.12–14; 8.7.20–21). Yet the challenge that he laid down in *De Vera Religione*—to move upwards from "historical examples" through "spiritual states"—[131]begins to be met.

## Audiences

The story begins in book 2 as Augustine harshly reviews his emotional development during his school years and continues the debate on his earlier educational values begun in book 1.[132] He disdains the pursuit of social mobility through the study of letters (2.2.42–44; 2.3.60–66), conveniently overlooking the modest financial position of his parents.[133] His father, Patrick, was concerned with his social advancement rather than the state of his moral life.[134] Monica hoped that he would remain celibate, at least until taking a wife,[135] but she appears to have been reluctant to criticize other aspects of his personal life (2.3.58–59). His study habits were unable to provide the requisite discipline. He found himself tossed about on a sea of conflicting desires (2.4.17–21), and he relates unsavory events in book 2 as an illustration of the depths from which it is sometimes necessary for sinners to cry out to God for help (2.3.6–10; 2.4.14–15).

He thus introduces the theme of self-mastery into the *Confessions* as a prelude to his discovery of philosophy. Its enemy is peer group pressure. His internal tensions with his friends are always in the background of his account.[136] He tells them what they want to hear, boasting falsely of sexual exploits (2.3.43–51): their presence contributes to the much-commented-on theft of pears,[137] in which he anticipates his passage from "perversion" to "conversion,"[138] as well as his ascetic method for achieving self-control in book 10. His motive for this mischief could have been nothing more or less than evil itself[139]—a philosophical problem that in 397 he thought as troublesome for Christians as for Manichaeans.[140] In favour of this interpretation, he notes that the theft did not replace one good by another; nor was there a hidden incentive.[141] He did not disobey his parents' wishes; God too was silent;[142] and he had little or no understanding of general laws of morality.[143]

As an addendum to these observations, he invites his readers to think of "discipline" as the patterning of conduct into a sequence of events that we should wish to live. The choice of the script that we follow initially appears to be ours; and, once we make a generic decision, our behaviour is organized as a recognizable narrative, whose plot is revealed through memory, since we revise our lives on the basis of the type of conduct that we have previously experienced and are able to recall. He is in fact describing his own method:[144] his mental record of the events in book 2 is a guide to the narrative he has chosen not to follow, thanks in large part to the choice that God has made for him (2.7.1–2, 5–6).

He concludes his discussion with the abstract example of a person who commits an act out of pride, cruelty, sensory gratification, curiosity, idleness, luxury, or avarice (or alternately, out of anger, fear, or regret).[145] Whatever the cause, he is able to conceive a sentiment that is the opposite of his motivation. He may be impelled to act through pride, but one is able to entertain the idea of humility while acting proudly; and although pride alone is affecting the result of the act, both thoughts have an equal reality in his mind. Furthermore, these thoughts occur to him in a moral hierarchy that does not depend on the evaluation of specific actions but on knowledge that is provably not human in origin and must therefore be divine (2.6.18–43).

Augustine's basic idea here is that men and women are ceaselessly engaged in mimetic interplay with the persons that they want to be. People make the lives and the worlds that they wish to live in, using as their means of construction the only tools at their disposal, words and images. They thereby attempt to introduce into their insubstantial narratives something that has both the form and substance that is capable of raising them upwards; and they take as their model what they know to be superior to their own minds, something which, as a consequence, they can never fully know. The different levels of self-knowledge implied in this neoplatonic process of imitation also provide a reason why two audiences are envisaged in Augustine's life history: one is God, who teaches him but learns nothing from him; the other consists of human readers, who presumably learn from his errors.[146] Among the latter he counts himself.

The discussion of mimesis comes to a head in 3.1–3, where he reflects on the appeal of pagan theatricals during his student days in Carthage. He is between sixteen and nineteen, still "in love with love" (3.1.2; also 2.1.7–8), but a good deal less devoted than before to sexual love. Testing himself, he plots a seduction during a mass, but he is too embarrassed to carry it off. He also notes that he has made little progress in other aspects of his life. His studies give him no solace: he is eager to acquire information about anything, but convinced that his curiosity puts his dwindling faith further at risk (3.3.2–8). He associates with seniors who specialize in destroying freshmen's illusions, but their artificial self-assurance contrasts with his very real insecurity, and he becomes a studious recluse.[147] Add to this his isolation, as a provincial attempting to make his way in the established society of Carthage. It is natural that he fluctuates between seeing no value in relationships, since he is not sure that he has any authentic ones, and looking for a permanence in them, which, given his status, they are unable to offer (3.1.12–13; 3.3.21–25).

His remarks on drama, which are among the most extensive in antiquity after Aristotle,[148] reflect another aspect of his dissatisfaction during this period—his sense of himself as the passive member of an audience.[149] As in his adolescent recitations of Virgil, the issue is whether lasting values can arise from transient fictions.[150] However, in contrast to his earlier reflections, he speaks as a confident "performer"[151] whether in pleading cases (3.3.13–15), in composing laudatory verse (3.7.48–53), or (on the horizon) in Manichaean preaching (3.6).

He sees two issues in drama: the actors express emotions which they do not actually feel, and these are based on events that never took place; and the playgoers replicate these expressions of emotion in a personal manner.

Two levels of duplicity are also at work. In the first case, the actors respond, not to signs, but to signs of words, namely the text of the drama. In the second case, the audience is one stage further removed; their reaction is to signs of words as they are internalized, interpreted, and reperformed onstage. In passing from the first case to the second, therefore, one fiction gives rise to another.[152]

This is evidently a rhetorical as well as philosophical approach to the audience,[153] which asks at both levels, for instance, why we enjoy suffering in a play when the pain would undoubtedly grieve us if it had to be endured.[154] The appeal of tragedy arises from the authenticity of our emotions, even though we are virtually certain that their inspiration is inauthentic. While the play proceeds, we feel a passion; and that passion, rather than the events taking place, becomes the object of our desire. We may be uplifted by the spectacle of someone else's misfortunes; but no true compassion is involved, since it never occurs to us to render aid. We accept the unreality of the situation as the foundation for the reality of our response. The better the acting, the more we suffer; the more we suffer, the greater is our enjoyment (3.2.40–43). It does not matter whether the play is about events that took place; it only has to give rise to emotional events that are actually experienced. If it does, we pay close attention; if not, we go home disappointed (3.2.4–14). Moreover, our response takes place in the real world as well as in a world of make-believe. In that frame of mind we participate in the story as members of a temporary community, one that includes the actors themselves (3.2.15–39).

This argument rejects the living of fictions; yet here, more openly than in his discussion of Virgil, Augustine validates a role for the emotional spectrum that literary representations can create. His position in 3.1–3 is that the emotions we feel in the theatre are not at fault, any more than language can be "accused" of wrongdoing when we speak (1.16.31). A play, like a painting or a sculpture, while unable to be "true," is not "false" either.

His statement complements a point made at *Soliloquia* 2.10, where he underlines the difference between the wish to create a falsehood and the inability to create a truth. Comedies, tragedies, paintings, sculpture, and other representations, he concludes, establish truth in one way by establishing falsehood in another.[155] Furthermore, the recitation of a passage of Virgil is an isolated literary event, while a play replicates entire segments of human experience, often embodying numerous conflicts within a single narrative.

## The *Hortensius*

Augustine's comments on drama expressed his need for a vehicle through which his values could be shaped from within, one however that was independent of his personal emotional fluctuations. This was provided by philosophy, to which he "converted" at age nineteen on encountering Cicero's *Hortensius,* in 372–73.[156]

The idea of abandoning the world may have been inspired partly by the excesses of Carthaginian society.[157] Yet in Augustine's brief description of the event, it is not the social or intellectual environment that we hear about: it is a new type of reading experience, which leads him to adopt philosophy as a way of life in a manner that combines ascetic and contemplative values.[158]

He tells us that he was then engaged in mastering the handbooks of rhetoric.[159] He was critical of his worldly ambitions but nonetheless determined to excel in public speaking. In the course of his reading he came upon a volume by Cicero, a writer, he later realized, admired more for his elegance of expression than for the depth of his thought. Yet the book in question, the *Hortensius,* appeared to be an "exhortation" to the serious study of philosophy.[160] It quite altered the way he felt: his desire for success seemed vain, even pointless, in the face of its timeless wisdom. The transformation was brought about by a book that he did not read to sharpen his tongue or to improve his style but because of the personal relevance of its message.[161]

His discovery of Cicero was thus a moral, emotional, and cognitive awakening.[162] The timing was right. He found himself between two periods of dissatisfaction with his life, 369–70 and 372–73: the one covers his boyish exploits in book 2, while the other is concerned with the birth of his son Adeodatus and the beginnings of a lengthy debate within himself on the merits of the celibate life (6.12–13). The *Hortensius* is the first in a series of readings that takes place between Carthage and Milan, to be described in subsequent chapters, which have the cumulative effect of orienting his thoughts about the philosophical life toward a community of "innerworldly" contemplatives.[163]

Yet his brief account in 3.4 raises some questions that, scholars agree, it does not clearly answer. These concern the nature of the conversion, the actual role of reading, and the possible changes in Augustine's attitude toward Cicero between the time that he read the *Hortensius* and the period in which he wrote the *Confessions*.

The conversion is the easiest to deal with, since it fits into a well-known pattern. Personal conversions to philosophy, which were reasonably common in antiquity, consisted in a "turning from luxury and self-indulgence and superstition . . . to a life of discipline and sometimes to a life of contemplation."[164] Augustine's change nonetheless differed from others in its timing and its mechanism. Among pagans as well as Christians it was unusual to undergo a crisis of identity in youth.[165] More important, among the records of the ancients, "there is one famous instance of conversion by a book."[166] This is Augustine's.

Yet the role of a book is clearer than the function of reading. A distinction has to be made between the initial acquaintance with the text, which was instantly transformative, and a more gradual study of its doctrines, which took place during the period between age nineteen and the writing of the *Confessions,* when Augustine acquired a working knowledge of *multa philosophorum*.[167] The "enthusiastic narrative," Goulven Madec notes, "has been the subject of substantial commentaries: less attention has been paid to the doctrinal influence of the work, which continued throughout Augustine's life."[168] Augustine committed his favorite passages to memory and quoted them repeatedly.[169] At Cassiciacum in 386–87 he read the work to his student friends Licentius and Trygetius, and it appeared "in large part to have united them in the pursuit of philosophy."[170] He returned to this text in subsequent writings when he spoke of the central themes of his moral outlook, wisdom and happiness, for instance in the structure and argument of *De Trinitate* 13–15.[171]

One type of reading, then, consists in the normal study of a set text. The other, for which it is a backdrop, is not reading in the accepted sense, although it occurs during a reading and at first seems to be a part of the exercise.[172] As Augustine speaks of this moment, it is one of illumination; the verb *legere* does not appear in the text. What he describes is a change in "the heart." The operative terms are concerned with the inner life, such as *pectus* (referring to Cicero's attitude of mind) and *vota, desideria,* and *aestus cordis* (referring to his own). The critical sentence announcing the transformation is *Ille liber mutauit affectum meum* (This book changed my disposition, 3.4.6–7; see also 6.11.1–4).[173] In this statement he looks back to his emotional reactions to poetry and play-acting and forward to the conversion of the bureaucrats in Trier in book 6, as well as to his own conversion to the religious life in book 8.

In sum, we have a conversion by means of a book in which there is a designated reader but no reading in the accepted sense. It is as if Augustine were not "reading" but was struck in a manner that activated his mind and heart from within. He repeats *liber,* which resounds through the chapter like a tolling bell (3.4.4, 5, 6, and 14), drawing our attention to the effect as well as to its suddenness and permanence.[174] This is indeed a "turning" toward philosophy, but it is one in which the idea of an authoritative text is implanted into the reader's experience while it is disguised from his understanding of his actions.[175] As we read the brief account, we are transported from the writings, *illae litterae,* to the love of wisdom, *amor sapientiae,* without any intervening steps. Reading is not a *cause* of conversion; it is a new *symbol* of conversion.

Does this interpretation imply a change in his attitude toward Cicero? We can answer the question in one way through the information provided by 3.4. There is no summary of the argument of the *Hortensius;* nor does Augustine echo the reminiscences of this lost text that are found in *De Libero Arbitrio,* which was written during his second stay in Rome, in 387–88.[176] It is tempting to think that just as it was not a literal reading that converted him, it was not the content of the text either.[177]

Yet there is a plausible explanation for the omission. The *Hortensius* expresses the views of Crassus in *De Oratore,* who advocates the study of the liberal arts in the education of the *doctus orator.*[178] In writing after 397, there was little need for Augustine to offer another summary of this theme, which is so often echoed in the "philosophical dialogues."[179] It was more important to speak of a conversion from within based on a renunciation of wealth and worldly ambition. The compression of ideas is what one might expect some twelve years after the event.[180] The themes are found in other protreptic treatises, Cicero's *De Finibus* among them;[181] and world-renouncing theses appear elsewhere in the *Confessions,* where Cicero is not the only possible inspiration.[182] Augustine's style of quotation here as elsewhere supports the view that the *Hortensius* was the reference point for ideas drawn from different sources. He limits himself to "short and pregnant sayings which could easily be memorized."[183] They offer a précis, not a precise résumé, of the text.[184]

As an alternative to this view, some scholars have argued that there is not one Cicero in the text but two. The first is the author of the *Hortensius* who actually fostered Augustine's rethinking of his life's aims in 373. The other, a composite figure created in his imagination over time, was in his mind when he wrote the *Confessions*. The function of the Cicero in the later configuration was to provide a backdrop for the retelling of the story and to emphasize what he found instructive. The two Ciceros would parallel the two Augustines in books 1–9; their roles are literary as well as philosophical.[185] The reassessment of the *Hortensius* begins in the Cassiciacum dialogues of 386–87, where, as Harald Hagendahl noted, "the great majority" of actual quotations occur. It is continued in 421 in *Contra Julianum*[186] and in *De Trinitate* 13–14 between 416 and the 420s, where the lengthiest citations are found.

However, if this is Augustine's intention, it is a part of a larger project whose ultimate aim is worked out in advance. This view is reinforced by *Sermon* 51, written in 417, where the mature Augustine notes that he did not envisage the conversion to philosophy as an isolated event, but within the contrast between his facility for reading pagan philosophy and his ineptitude at reading the Bible.[187] As such, it was a symbolic moment in his lengthy transition in books 1–6 from pride to humility,[188] culminating in his transition from Plotinus (or Porphyry) to John and Paul in book 7. If this evidence is admitted, then we have to distinguish between the conversion, in which reading is a symbol of awakened interiority, and the actual reading, which is a step on his way to his appreciation of the Bible, a text whose transformative qualities he ignored in 372; he tried to read scripture around this time but was put off by what he regarded as its inferior style.[189]

This interpretation assumes that his initial evaluation of Cicero was positive, in terms of both ideas and style; later, and especially after becoming bishop, he criticized his youthful naïveté by rewriting the narrative of his discovery of philosophy, in which Cicero emerged as a point of transition. The positively evaluated pagan philosopher was still in his mind when he wrote his autobiography, but it is his less enthusiastic image that gives the discovery of the *Hortensius* its framework and, ultimately, its meaning. This is the Cicero who is described formally, even perhaps pejoratively, as *cuiusdam Ciceronis, cuius linguam fere omnes mirantur*:[190] the orator whom bishop Augustine, mindful of his youthful errors, wished to keep at a respectful distance. His problem was how to incorporate this conception into a story that saw Cicero as the initial guide in a series of critically important philosophical and religious experiences. Writing in maturity, he may also have distinguished between the fictional Hortensius of Cicero's dialogue, an advocate of philosophical wisdom, and the real Hortensius of Roman public oratory, who, after his consulship, decided to enjoy the pleasures of life and "renounced the high ideals of study that had burned in his youth."[191]

In my view, there can be no final resolution of these issues.[192] However, as a contribution to the discussion, it is worth considering the evidence about reading presented at 3.5. In 372, Augustine presumably read the *Hortensius* aloud; he does not mention silent reading before *Confessions* 6.3. We assume that it was the oral experience of the text that led to his inner conversion to philosophy. This "therapy of the word"[193] is the beginning of his adoption of Christ as his "healer": it is also an announcement of the Pauline theme of *foris/intus,* which will dominate book 7. Yet, while this image is before us, another Cicero emerges from 3.5: it is the portrait of a philosopher who was read, thought about, and meditated upon, just as Augustine later mulled over scripture. If that had not been the bishop's original goal, he later remarked, why would he or anyone else have troubled to work through "so many dialogues"?[194] And what better image could Augustine have found in his attempt to historicize the birth of his Christian philosophy? There is also a narrative reason why his initial attempt to read scripture had to fail: we are thus prepared for his subsequent understanding of the literal and spiritual senses, for the study programme leading to his baptism, and, indirectly, for his conversion. By introducing the contrast between these two experiences of reading, the pagan and the Christian, he effectively completes the account of his nascent interest in scripture, which was unrecognized by himself.[195]

Some of this (though far from all) is clarified in the brief exposition of 3.5. Augustine first describes the state of mind of the subject before reading is begun, summing matters up in the phrase *animum intendere,* which means to focus one's thoughts or to give them some direction (3.5.1). He then presents a series of images that combine the notion of reading and conversion. In accordance with the ancient norms, the moment of insight is one of seeing (*uidere,* 3.5.2).[196] But the inner vision also has a hermeneutic quality, since the "unveiling" reveals to Augustine the inner sense of a text that is read. In the end, it is not the words that enlighten this reader, still less an official interpretation that is passed from one person to another. He "enlightens" himself as he participates in a mind that is implanted in the literary work that is before him. Here, it is the mind of a human author; later, as he becomes acquainted with the Bible, it will be the mind of God.

In 3.4–5, then, Augustine used the *Hortensius* to illustrate his ambivalence about his first conversion through reading. What the student did not know but the bishop appreciated is that the fundamental change did not come about through this means at all: it was a gift of God. True, the student Augustine discovered philosophy, and this was a necessary step in the evolution of a Christian philosophical outlook. Yet he failed to link the humility which this philosophy taught with the humble style in which the Bible was written.[197] Scripture "resists the proud,"[198] but, seduced by rational thought,[199] he was unable to resist his own intellectual arrogance. Pride was still a major force in his life when he studied neoplatonism a decade later.[200] The illusion of intellectual progress through reason was not to be shattered until the moment of his final conversion. Until then scripture's true message remained "impenetrable," since it refused to be "paraded nude" before his untutored mind (3.5.8 and 3). At age nineteen, he portrayed himself as thinking that the interpreting mind was the developing mind. The new idea that he subtly introduced into later ancient thought was that interpretation in itself leads the ethically oriented reader nowhere.

# 2

# INTELLECTUAL

# HORIZONS

❧

## Manichaeism

In 372–73, the period in which he was won over to philosophy by the *Hortensius,* Augustine also became seriously interested in Manichaeism.[1] He was perhaps acquainted with the movement in Thagaste, but he did not become an adherent until the final year of his studies in Carthage. He remained an "auditor" from eighteen to twenty-eight, until 382–83,[2] when his interest waned after a series of debates with the African dualist bishop, Faustus of Mileu.

Disillusioned, he nonetheless remained in contact with his Manichaean friends in Rome, where he journeyed in the summer of 383. Their support was instrumental in securing him the chair of rhetoric in Milan in the autumn of 384. Only after coming under the influence of Ambrose did he make a decisive break with dualism. In the years after his conversion and baptism, he wrote no less than thirty-three treatises against the Manichaeans by the count of Possidius, beginning with *De Moribus Ecclesiae Catholicae* in the autumn of 388.[3] Yet he found it difficult to free himself from the lingering suspicion that he retained informal links with the movement. He was accused of doing so by Petilianus in 401 and by Julian of Eclanum as late as 420.[4]

Cicero and Mani represented different sorts of influence on Augustine, but they had one meeting-point—an orientation in the direction of the ascetic life. In this respect, Manichaeism had a slight edge. His imperfect Greek was not a liability, as it would have been if he had wished to explore Hellenistic wisdom beyond what he could glean from Latin translations.[5] Within Manichaeism, the Christian borrowings, which owed a debt to Paul,[6] had a familiar ring,[7] and Augustine was intrigued by the dualists' claim to have discovered a "rational" New Testament faith that was un-contaminated by Judaic ideas.[8] His Manichaean friends eased him out of his isolation in Carthage and provided him with congenial gatherings for discussing ethico-religious issues. As he knew nothing of Christian monasticism,[9] theirs were the only religious writings whose consequences for group conduct he took seriously during his student years.[10] They offered him, initially at least, a reliable means of creating self-discipline through a set of rules, taboos, and ceremonies. And they appeared initially to offer a model of institutional continuity over time.

Philosophy and dualism made different demands on him as a reader. He read the *Hortensius* for himself, possibly silently but more likely aloud. There was no classroom audience as there was when he commented on classical texts or performed rhetorical exercises. When he took part in Manichaean prayer, liturgy, or interpretation, he read as a member of a group of potential or convinced believers. Whereas in philosophy the domains of theory and practice were distinguishable, within the dualist movement they were not: as a rule, practice absorbed theory, which, for the auditors at least, lost its autonomy.[11] And whereas he read the *Hortensius* for its message, we hear little concerning the content of Manichaean writings until he set out to refute them, point by point. By then (after 388), he was a serious reader; but he was no longer a follow of Mani. Moreover, in contrast to his philosophical experience, there was no sudden intellectual transformation when he entered the sect. He appears to have undergone a gradual initiation and training; he left the movement only when he was fully convinced of its errors.

In short, in taking up Cicero and becoming a Manichaean at about the same time, Augustine passed imperceptibly from one stage of reading to another. In his discovery of Cicero, he completed his youthful search for a type of reason that could establish faith. On joining the Manichaeans, he began the process of conversion to a type of faith that sought to establish rational grounds for belief.[12] Within that transition, three topics are relevant to his growth as a reader: the spoken word, the internal organization of sectarian communities, and the uses of books.

## The Spoken Word

It is within the Manichaeans' abuse of language[13] that Augustine lodges his typical complaints concerning their preference for the false over the true, the carnal over the spiritual, and custom over law (3.6.6–3.7.6).[14] Their tongues wag,[15] he claims, but their hearts are empty.[16] They are "loquacious mutes."[17] Their leaders are unscrupulously eloquent (5.3.4).

This picture, which was accepted by commentators in the Middle Ages and during the Reformation, is obviously rhetorical. There is ample evidence that Manichaeism was a religion of the book; its adherents were profoundly influenced by the Bible.[18] Mani criticized the founders of other religions for not lodging their teachings in a transmittable form.[19] The sect's scriptural foundations have been confirmed by discoveries at Turfan in Central Asia and at Fayum in Egypt.[20] Mani's religious education was also scriptural: a Greek life from Oxyrhynchus informs us that from age four to twenty-four he was "a member of the Jewish Christian sect of the Elchesaites in southern Babylonia."[21]

Writings played a large role in disseminating the sect's ideas. In the East, instruction was accompanied by pictures[22] (possibly in imitation of Jewish missionary practices). Persian legend spoke of an illustrated version of the gospels that had been given to Mani, who was himself a noted artist.[23] Augustine cites numerous writings, including Mani's *Thesaurus*[24] and the *Epistula Fundamenti,* which survives mainly through his quotations.[25] Texts were copied for specific audiences: an example is a dualist codex in Cologne which was written in a miniature hand to minimize the risk of its detection by the authorities after imperial decrees in 381 and 382 forbidding the circulation of Manichaean ideas.[26] Even as an auditor, Augustine bears witness to the splendour of the ornamentation, recalling *tam multi et tam grandes et tam pretiosi codices.*[27] He may have participated in liturgical exercises, for which lectionaries are extant, such as the highly literary Psalm-book that was brought to Egypt in the third century by missionaries from Syria.[28] The liturgical and scriptural aspects of the sect's practices enter his discussions from many angles.[29] For example, in 404 he claims that the bishop Felix is *ineruditus liberalibus litteris;*[30] yet he subsequently asks for a point-by-point written denial of dualist doctrines.[31] He has a vivid recollection of Manichaean *libri* as late as 428–29.[32] In sum, he appears to have been well aware that Manichaeism had its "foundations in a corpus of scripture" through which the movement "was able to foresee a universal and definitive success to its efforts at verbal communication."[33]

Why did he engage in an extensive programme of disinformation?[34] The standard answer is that he wished to leave no doubt in his readers' minds about his reversion of allegiance to Catholicism.[35] He may also have realized that he was for a time taken in by the very force that he so vehemently condemned—the use of words. He suggests as much in his account of the attractions of dualism in *De Utilitate Credendi,* written in 391 to his former friend Honoratus, whom he converted to the sect. Reiterating the Manichaeans' claim to have propounded a reasonable set of doctrines,[36] as well as their dismissal of the Catholic faith as nothing but

superstition[37] propped up by parental authority,[38] he notes that their arguments would have carried less weight had they not found a willing listener
who was eager to employ his rhetorical skills: "Whatever I picked up by
my own wits or by reading, I attributed willingly and solely to their
instruction; and so, from their preaching, I grew in my desire for such
contests, and from success in such contests, my love for these people in
turn grew daily."[39]

By late 397, when the *Confessions* was begun, the verbal magic had long
since worn off.[40] A serious methodological weakness was concealed by the
Manichaeans' evangelical fervour, which was aimed at discrediting rival
religions rather than establishing firm underpinnings for dualism. Worse,
the canonical texts were known only to the higher ranks of the hierarchy—the *princeps, magistri, episcopi, presbyteri,* and *electi.* They were not
divulged in public (as he noted after witnessing a debate between
Manichaean preachers and the Catholic Elpidius) but were communicated
among themselves—"secretius" (5.11.4–9). Even within the intimacy of the
group, the *auditores* had little or no direct access to the canonical books, as
Secundinus reminded him in a letter expressing his disappointment at his
withdrawal from the movement.[41] For the nine years of his apprenticeship,
while his interpretive abilities grew in leaps and bounds, Augustine was not
given free access to the sacred texts of his chosen faith, nor was he
encouraged to read them critically. His participation consisted mainly in
prayer, hymns, recitations, and preaching.[42]

As time passed, he became disillusioned with the Manichaean practice
of transmitting doctrines by word of mouth among a knowledgeable few[43]
who were permitted to experience gnosis. The *Epistula Fundamenti,* the
most reliable among the unsure sources of information in this respect, was
evidently read aloud.[44] Comments[45] and interpretive discussions[46] do not
appear to have been the norm.[47] The problem is complicated by the fact
that we do not know whether, as an auditor, Augustine had the relevant
texts at hand or whether he read them sometime later, as bishop of Hippo.[48]
However, if the illuminatory experience took place in a group, it may have
consisted of little more than "salvific words."[49] Significantly, after Augustine
had left the movement, he opposed Faustus' notion of enlightenment[50]
with specific biblical quotations[51]—added evidence of his reluctance to play
a passive role in the reading process.[52] The religious beliefs of neoplatonism,
which he subsequently adopted, obviously played a part in this transformation, since they differed from Manichaeism in holding out the possibility
of an ascent toward wisdom and virtue through explicit stages of spirituality.[53]

Even when the Manichaeans are recognized to be readers, Augustine stresses their lack of sophistication with higher principles of interpretation.[54] He grants a certain expertise to his former literary friends Honoratus and Secundinus; the latter distinguishes between the commentator, who understands a text as a unit, and the listener, who follows word by word.[55] But in other cases polemics take over. He claims that Faustus speaks of fulfilment *(adimpletio)* but fails to separate the moral and ceremonial aspects of the Old Testament.[56] In his debate with Felix,[57] the *scripturae Manichaei* (1.1.6) are confiscated (1.12.14–15) and eventually returned—their suppression evidently distressed Augustine (2.1.22–23).[58] Yet when Felix has his copy of the *Epistula,* he is said to make little use of it in his arguments.

## A Sense of Community

If Manichaeism appealed to the young Augustine's naturally inquisitive mind through its claim to be "rational," it also attracted him through its commitment to world-renouncing asceticism.

Rethinking the issues after 397, he stressed the intellectual reasons for his joining and leaving the movement. Initially, he was fascinated by the possibility of logical and textual criticism; some nine years later, when he departed, he stated that it was the inadequacy of the Manichaean solution to the problem of good and evil that was chiefly on his mind. Yet this account leaves questions unanswered. We do not learn when his dissatisfaction with Manichaeism reached a turning-point. More important, we are given no explanation why a gifted and independent thinker did not reject an obviously flawed world-picture sooner than he did.

Clearly, another factor played its part, one that was less intellectual than affective.[59] This was the sect's "spirituality,"[60] which, in Augustine's eyes, was inseparable from his relationships with his Manichaean friends. He relied on their companionship, hospitality, and contacts; they constituted his only real "society."[61] Even as late as the summer of his departure for Rome in 383, when his enthusiasm for their doctrines had considerably waned, his personal commitment remained high (5.10.29–33).

This was a new role for classical *amicitia.*[62] When Augustine was in Carthage, dualism enabled him to win acceptance in an established circle and to distance himself from the "wasters" into whose company he had temporarily fallen (3.5.15–25). Returning to teach in Thagaste in the autumn of 374, he lost no time in winning over his former companions, among them Honoratus, Nebridius, and the wealthy Romanianus, in whose villa they frequently met.[63] In Carthage in 375 he rejoined former friends. The mood of this period is captured in *De Duabus Animabus*, a work written some five years before the *Confessions,* where he echoes the words he had addressed to Honoratus in *De Utilitate Credendi* a few months before and recalls the qualities that made Manichaeism difficult to resist: their sense of intimacy *(familiaritas),* which was like a "gentle cord around his neck," and their encouragement of his participation in public debate. No mention is made of his reading projects outside their sphere,[64] which were presumably undertaken about the same time.

Our conclusions about his experience as an auditor are speculative, since he left us no description of what actually took place within the community.[65] What is known from numerous sources is confirmed by an account in *Epistle* 236, which was written to Deuterius, a bishop of Mauretania, concerning a certain Victorinus, a subdeacon in the village of Mallia who attempted to conceal his dualist sympathies.[66] The lower ranks were active in proselytizing, and Victorinus was exposed as he tried to influence his students.[67] The auditors and the elect shared beliefs that included praying to the sun and moon, denying the miraculous in the life of Christ, rejecting the Old Testament, and adhering to a dualist mythology. However, the auditors were less ascetic than the elect: they were allowed to eat meat, to work farms, and to have wives. They nonetheless had to be deferential toward their superiors, kneeling in some ceremonies.[68] In addition to their general obligations[69]—confession, fasting, alms-giving, and obedience to the Manichaean commandments—they had to provide the elect with food, Augustine bitterly recalls (4.1.10–11), and, if their means permitted, with lodgings. The elect devoted themselves to spiritual pursuits, and thereby assured the auditors of salvation.

Augustine's friendships may have offered him an alternative to this hierarchical rigidity. This possibility is suggested by a story at *Confessions* 4.4–9 about a young Manichaean in Thagaste.[70] It consists of two episodes which reintroduce the topics of reading and false communities touched upon in books 1 and 2, in the accounts of pagan verse and delinquent friends. The person in question was an adolescent friend and a lapsed Catholic, to whom Augustine introduced the Manichaean *fabellae* (4.4.1– 12). As a result, they became inseparable,[71] but his companion fell seriously ill, and while he was delirious was baptised. When he regained consciousness, Augustine expressed doubts about the efficacy of a sacrament administered while he was in this state. The friend was angered, and before his teacher could find a more opportune moment to raise the subject again, he died.

In his comments, the bishop Augustine reproaches himself for leading a person into heresy and failing to reclaim him for the faith before he died.

However, we are also aware of the sentiments of the saddened professor of rhetoric who reflects on the frailty of human relationships, their transience and vulnerability.[72] Late in 376 Augustine returned to Carthage, where the passage of time and the presence of other friends eventually healed the wound, notably by the same means by which he had misled his friend. He tells us that they took his mind off his cares by reading with him, either for pleasure or for edification.[73] He vividly recalls the playful teaching—another echo of books 1 and 2.[74] He subsequently dismissed their "consolation" as a huge Manichaean "lie." However, the experience confirmed his mature view that the chief means at our disposal for reorienting our ethical lives has something to do with the recreation of subjective literary experience.

*Confessions* 4.4–9 presents Augustine's Manichaean associations in their most favorable light. He is rarely so generous. The point is illustrated by a pair of anecdotes concerning the Manichaeans' failure to live up to their ascetic ideals.[75]

The earlier example is recorded in *De Moribus* 20; the events took place during his stay in Rome at the end of the summer of 383. A wealthy auditor, known for his asceticism, educational values, and support of gnostic associations, was offended by the behaviour of certain *electi*. As a corrective, he provided lodgings in his house where they could live in accordance with Manichaean precepts *(uiuendi regula)*. He cleared the idea with the local bishop, asking him to join the community. To his dismay, only a few accepted, mainly out of deference to their superior, and those who turned up quickly tired of their mundane tasks. Bickering ensued, followed by revolt. All the would-be monks eventually departed, including the rustic bishop, last seen, Augustine notes, carrying off the supplies that had been smuggled into his host's house at his request.

The later example of a failed community is recorded in *Confessions* 6.14 and dates from 385, by which time Augustine's contact with the Manichaean movement was limited to a dispersed group of old cronies. Established in Milan through their support, he had been discussing with some ten of them, mostly men of wealth and leisure, how they might withdraw from the turmoil of daily affairs and direct their efforts toward the cultivated life *(otiose uiuere)*. Already sincere friends,[76] they grouped around Romanianus, who was then at court; they agreed that their property should be held in common and that two administrators, appointed yearly, should look after their needs. However, some of the potential members feared that their wives would not take kindly to a community of bachelors, among them the once libertine Augustine, who was contemplating a good match, or at least another concubine (6.14.15–16). He had

misgivings of his own, which arose from a potential conflict between the
otherworldly aims of the group and the worldly connections of their patron
(6.14.12–13). The idea was eventually abandoned.

These half-hearted efforts at monastic discipline taught him valuable
lessons. Just a year after the failed attempt to establish a communal society
in Rome, he retreated with a group of friends to Cassiciacum with a
different model in mind, and the house that he set up in Hippo on his
return from Italy in 388 appears to have drawn some inspiration, although
one is not sure how much, from Manichaean hostels and seminaries that
he may have known. Also, it is against the background of his nine-year
stint as a dualist that he introduced the ideal of a Catholic monastic
community into *De Moribus Ecclesiae Catholicae*.[77]

Indirect confirmation of these ideas is found in the dream of Monica in
*Confessions* 3.11–12,[78] which predicted that he would eventually live according to "the rule of faith." This event took place after his first stay in
Carthage, in the autumn of 374, when he was twenty. Converted to
Manichaeism, he horrified his devout mother, who was not sure she any
longer wanted him in the house. In her distress, she had a dream in which
she saw him standing on a "wooden rule." She was approached by a
cheerful young man who asked her why she was upset, not, as he put it,
"so that he could learn, but so that he might teach."[79] When she told him
why she was unhappy, he advised her to be patient. Presently, he said, she
would perceive that where she was so too was her son (3.11.10–17).
Monica related the dream to Augustine, who deliberately misinterpreted it
to mean that someday she would be where he was, that is, in Manichaeism
(3.11.21–25). She asked for a second explanation from the erudite bishop
of Thagaste, and she let slip her anxieties, asking that the bishop "unteach
her son his evil ways and instruct him in righteous ones." He wisely replied
that Augustine was "unteachable": his mind was stuffed with heretical
verbiage; worse, he was forcing his questions on those least able to answer
them. "Let him be," he added; "only remember him in your prayers. At
length he will discover the source of his waywardness and impiety through
reading" (3.12.5–13).[80] The bishop's prediction was right. It was through
his reading that Augustine grew disillusioned with Manichaean solutions
to moral problems and eventually returned to Catholicism.[81]


The Uses of Books

Another aspect of Augustine's attitude toward books in the light of his
Manichaean experience is illustrated by a pair of anecdotes in the *Confessions* concerned with astrology. The earlier is related in two parts.[82] In 4.3,

Augustine is counseled against relying on nativity tables by a knowledgeable physician, Vindicianus.[83] The story is taken up again and concluded
in 7.6, after an episode involving Firminus, a Milanese nobleman, in which
Augustine comes to his own conclusions regarding astrological determinism.[84]

By this time, the spring of 386, a second episode touching on the theme
has unfolded. This is related in 5.3–7 and consists of Augustine's recollections of the conversations that he had with Faustus of Mileu in 382–83.
The ostensible topic is the place of stellar movements in Manichaean
cosmology, and in particular their unscientific approach to astrological
calculation, which is an important factor in his disenchantment with Faustus' position;[85] however, his broader aim is to contrast Manichaean *fabella*
and Christian scriptural narrative, and thus to prepare the way for books 7
and 8. In other words, the later reworking of the discussion is largely
literary in inspiration,[86] and concludes the Manichaean chapter in his
narrative of his education as a reader.

Both stories share a single preoccupation, which was with Augustine in
372 as it was in 386 and beyond: whether our destinies are shaped by forces
outside ourselves or patterned by those within, and therefore subject to the
will.[87] He expressed himself forcefully on the subject during the Pelagian
debate, where, following Paul, he proposed that predestination is compat-
ible with free will: the rationale underlying the divine choice is just, but
the deliberations by which a decision concerning salvation is reached are
inaccessible to humans.[88] In the *Confessions,* the emphasis is on the inner
forces that prepare us for the possibility of grace and the role of narrative
in bringing that possibility into our conscious thoughts. One of the prem-
ises of Augustine's thinking is that we can be made one with God through
the assimilation of his unified Word. This cannot take place if God is dual.

Augustine's focus on the interior life may be one of the reasons lying
behind his shift in interests from the calculatory to the narrative aspects of
astrology. In any case, its predictive claims were rejected in *De Diuersis
Quaestionibus 83* between 388 and 395.[89] In the *Confessions,* he was concerned with its role in a christocentric myth involving the elemental
opposites of good and evil. For, beyond the personality cult associated with
Mani, who saw himself as a docetic answer to the historical Jesus,[90]
Manichaean views were centred on a narrative whose ethical implications
were inseparable from heavenly movements.[91] The method was unsophis-
ticated and unmathematical.[92]

Augustine's first account of these matters occurs at *Confessions* 4.3, which
records events from 370 through 372. The context is a discussion of sin:
whether, in particular, sinning and forgiving are parts of a personal rela-

tionship between man and God or, as the astrologers propose, "the predetermined cause of sinning lies in heaven." Vindicianus,[93] who had awarded
him a literary prize, dissuaded Augustine from consulting nativity tables,
arguing that he had a regular job and did not have to earn his living as a
charlatan. Despite the good advice, Augustine did not give up his dependence on astrology until many years later. The turning-point came in 386,
during the period when Nebridius, always a sceptic concerning such
matters (4.3.47–49), was engaged in a decisive debate with himself over
dualism (7.2), and Augustine was mulling over the issues of free will,
worldly evil, and determinism (7.3–7).[94] With the help of his companion
and the sharp-witted Vindicianus, he carefully analysed an account told to
him by the abovementioned Firminus. Two babies, born at the same
moment, should have had the same destinies, but their life histories differed,
a fact having more to do with their social origins than with stellar motions
(7.6.58–62). He concluded that astrology was at best an art posing as a
science.[95]

The reasoning that lies behind this observation is found in his first
discussion with Vindicianus in book 4. Augustine had asked the physician
how astrological predictions often managed to be right. After a standard
account of probabilities, Vindicianus offered Augustine a literary analogy
which is reworked by the bishop of Hippo in the dramatic conversion
scene at 8.12. His example was the reading of a book of poetry (another
echo of the grammar lessons of book 1). The author's interests may differ
from our own, and we may be engaged in reciting verses that have little
or nothing to do with what has previously been on our minds. Yet,
remarkably, we often find a line that confirms our antecedent thinking, as
if the soul has unwittingly acted in accordance with a higher authority. In
other words, the desire to interpret what we read may be implanted in us
for higher purposes which we do not always understand. As in astrological
prediction, we speak of the coincidence as operating by chance: that is just
a way of expressing our ignorance concerning the causal force involved.[96]

These thoughts may have been in Augustine's mind when he reconstructed his exchange of views with Faustus, which took place during the
first half of 383.[97] The dualist prelate had just returned from one of his
numerous visits to Rome. Augustine had previously witnessed his oratorical skill as a member of a large audience. He had not been able to arrange
a private interview. After nearly a decade of unsatisfactory replies to his
questions, he was eager for the encounter (5.6.1–7).

His attitude as a reader had changed over the years. At nineteen, studying
Cicero, he had been unable to extract a method from the *Hortensius* apart

from its contents (which, he ruefully acknowledged, nowhere mentioned the ethical narrative that was to have the most value for him, the story of Christ).[98] No such compromise was possible with Manichaeism, which linked canonical texts to sectarian practices. His readiness for debate likewise bore witness to his increased self-confidence in handling intellectual issues. By 383, he had read and memorized the doctrines of many different thinkers (5.3.10–11). His personal ability to cope with philosophical texts had grown, as testify his disparaging remarks about the note-takers in a class on Aristotle's *Categories* (4.16). He was not a child who could be offered sweet words *(suauiloquentia)* or tall tales *(longae fabellae,* 5.3.4, 12).[99] Looking back on his conversations after 397, the bishop of Hippo could state as a confirmed ascetic that he had no interest in worldly knowledge.[100] Yet that is the setting in which he recreated the exchange of views. Faustus, reputed to be "well-trained . . . and, above all, a master of erudition in the liberal arts" (5.3.8–10), turned out to know only bits of Seneca, some speeches of Cicero, excerpts from the Latin Manichaean writings, and a smattering of poetry (5.6.39–43). He was a delightful conversationalist and a charming individual, whose bearing, inventiveness, and self-control Augustine admired (5.6.7–8, 21–23, 28–31); but he had no authentic knowledge of any discipline (5.5.7–9; 5.6.7–10).

The portrait contrasts with that in *Contra Faustum,* where Faustus is presented as a serious thinker who rejects the church's authority and Old Testament prophesies in favour of a rational and relativistic approach to biblical texts.[101] And of course the caricature in the *Confessions* is deliberate: its purpose is to configure the young Augustine as the victor in an epic battle of books. He is pictured as knowing more about both the humane and the predictive sciences than his prospective mentor. After talking to Faustus, he despairs of making sense of the Manichaeans' "interminable fables about the sun, the moon, the constellations, and the heavens" (5.7.5–6). He realizes that he is in the presence of a teacher whose authority devolves from charisma rather than from facts (5.5.26–30).

## Ambrose

Sometime between 382–83, when his interest in Manichaeism waned, and the summer of 386, when he decided to enter the religious life, Augustine became what may be called "a Christian reader." He had begun to link his spiritual progress to his ability to read and interpret biblical texts. Well before he was converted through an unusual reading experience, he appears to have become a convert to reading itself.

This phase of his intellectual development took place in Milan, where he became professor of rhetoric in the autumn of 384.[102] The two principal causes were the preaching of Ambrose and his reading of neoplatonist philosophical texts. His instruction by Ambrose, which took place sometime during the autumn of 384 and the first six months of 385, is related in episodes in books 5 and 6. In book 7 we learn of the doctrines that he subsequently absorbed from the *libri Platonicorum*, which were translated by Marius Victorinus.[103]

Like his literary studies, his discovery of philosophy, and his adherence to Manichaeism, the Ambrosian chapter in Augustine's story is a distinctive period in his education as a reader. Cicero's protreptic had convinced him that his ideas and his way of life should somehow work in harmony.[104] Yet the goal remained elusive in the years that followed. His rhetorical studies in Carthage were arid and formalistic.[105] The Academics, to whom he was attracted on arriving in Rome,[106] questioned his assumptions but offered no positive direction.[107] It was during his lengthy period as a Manichaean auditor that he began to appreciate the role that individual reading might play in resolving his difficulties. By the time Faustus of Mileu arrived in Carthage, he had "read many things among the philosophers, committed them to memory, and had them ready" for comparison with dualist "fables" (5.3.10–15).

Ambrose reshaped the content of his ideas as well as his methods.[108] He was a major source of neoplatonic doctrines, even if it seems unlikely, as Courcelle proposed, that these derived from specific commentaries on scripture, the *Hexameron, De Isaac,* and *De Bono Mortis.*[109] The sermons freed Augustine from his dependence on materialism, possibly a hangover from Manichaeism: for the first time, he found himself capable of dealing with the spiritual sense of biblical texts while retaining his belief in their literal or historical truth.[110] These momentous changes took place in a relatively short space of time, between the end of 385 and May or June 386.

He left an incomplete record of the forces that shaped his thinking before and during this period.[111] The main biblical influence was Paul, to whose epistles he turned on putting down the "Platonic books" in the summer of 386 (7.21.1–2). Encouraged by the allegories of Ambrose, he came to understand that the reader could distinguish between what Paul called the "spirit" and the "letter" as a parallel to the "inner" and "outer" self. Texts and selves interpenetrated: it became possible to look upon the building of a new self as an exegetical and interpretive process. A piece of writing, when it was read and understood, mediated the reality that it described, as did our thoughts about the same reality when they were transformed into words. Augustine thus confirmed a Platonic style of thinking, placing realities above representations, while he linked self-improvement to the creation of mentally represented worlds. He envisaged his programme as the living out of a story whose meaning he inwardly understood before it was translated into action, and he did so by evolving a theory that did not depend on the imitation of specific pagan texts. He thus deepened the distinction between the observer and the observed that his earlier readings implied.[112]

It may help us to understand these changes if we review matters as Augustine does in an "interior monologue"[113] at 6.11. He notes that some ten years have passed since his quest for wisdom began at age nineteen.[114] He is as unable as ever to resist the temporary satisfaction of a good job and a convenient woman. But the picture is not entirely gloomy. He has a three-stage plan for self-improvement, which consists in abandoning former philosophies, returning to the Christian fold, and resolving his problems "in the church's books" through personal study and meditation.[115] The interpretive programme is the search for a message that is thought beforehand to be hidden in biblical texts. What troubles him is how to put it into operation.[116] Where can he look for the relevant books? Are they to be bought or borrowed? Can he find time for study? Periods must be set aside and hours fixed "if his soul is to regain its health." When is this to be? Lectures take time; so do appearances at the imperial court. He has to devote a portion of each working day to students, friends, and preferments. He mentally juggles his schedule. If he sees students in the morning, can other time be freed up? If not, how is his mind to be released from its cares (6.11.9–25)?

In sum, what he advocates is a union of reading and conduct as a replacement for the ethical relativism of the pagan classroom. Time is found for leisured reading and meditation within the normal activities of a busy day, and a plan of living is evolved from that reading which redirects behaviour in the long term. If memory is added and some footnotes on time, we have the complete foundation of the ascetic programme in the later books of the *Confessions*.

This is not a novel development in his thinking. His evolution toward self-styled reading is noticeable as far back as age twenty. Recall that it was the combination of reading and memory, first at school and later at university, that enabled him to become a successful autodidact. We learn this from the brief description of a class that he attended on Aristotle's *Categories* in Latin translation in 374.[117] Only a year after his conversion to philosophy, he speaks of himself as an autonomous interpreter of such complex texts,[118] thereby incorporating the interchange of the Platonic dialogue into the dialogic interchange between reader and text;[119] this is also a transfer of his own notion of the *soliloquium* from the mind to the page. He boasts that he "read and understood" all the treatises on the liberal arts in which he then took so benighted an interest.[120] Although the content was later devalued, the notion of progressing through systematic study was retained. Reading became his major means of acquiring power over knowledge: "Whatever I read on the art of speaking or debating, as well as on geometry, music, or arithmetic, I managed to understand easily without anyone's having to act as an intermediary."[121]

To reading, as an intellectual tool, we can add the activity of writing. We learn this from his account of a lost treatise, *De Pulchro et Apto,* which was composed in 380–81 and dedicated to the otherwise unknown Roman orator Hierius.[122] The work is introduced in book 4 as part of a discussion of fleeting experiences of beauty which touches on diverse types of transience—writings, friendships, and studies.[123] Augustine knew that publication was premature, but he was nonetheless devastated at the book's poor reception. His study of the aesthetics of pleasure appeared to please no one but himself. Hierius took no notice at all (4.14.42–47).

Looking back on his disappointment, he draws some conclusions concerning readers and audiences that extend the analysis undertaken at 3.2.[124] In discussing plays, he pictures himself as a member of the audience, whereas, in *De Pulchro et Apto,* he sees himself as an author writing for an audience. This is a new adaptation of the Ciceronian model of rhetorical imitation.[125] Those who offer praise in speech or writing are characterized by an absence of person-to-person communication: the "love" that he demonstrates in his preface is not transferred from his "mouth" to Hierius' "heart"; representations intervene. The expression of emotion by one party, as a sender of signs, arouses an imitative response on the other's part (or is intended to do so). This is another occasion on which trust is placed in beliefs, and for practical purposes in the words in which they are expressed.

The reasoning depends on an implicit distinction between art *(ars)* and imitation *(imitatio),* a point that Augustine makes forcefully in *De Musica* 1, written before 389.[126] There he lays the groundwork for the notion that instructive mimesis is based on a rational plan. Adapting the idea, he envisages at one end of a scale the unthinking devotion of a "fan" at the games; this is an "irrational" reaction which merely "imitates" sounds or gestures.[127] The spectator and the gladiator have no interests in common (the one's pleasure results from the other's pain),[128] whereas, at the other end of the scale, he and the renowned orator share a rationale—the pursuit of worldly success.[129]

Augustine tells us little about the content of *De Pulchro et Apto*. The thesis is summed up in a sentence,[130] which simply contrasts the "beautiful" and the "fitting." The beautiful is something that gives us pleasure because it is complete; the fitting, because it is "accommodated" to something else, in the way that a shoe fits a foot (4.13.5–9; 4.15.1–5). This is an adaptation of the distinction between the aesthetics and ascetics of reading, which is retrospectively attached to his early classroom experiences; it is also a premature summary of the distinction between things as means and as ends which lies behind his ethical position on the usefulness of signs in *De Doctrina Christiana*.[131] In 380–81 he remains far from that synthetic objective; his attempts at interpretation are confined to physical analogies for nonphysical entities.[132] After reading Aristotle, he tries to find a "category" in which God fits (4.16.18–29). For, as he then believed, either the mind is made of matter or it is nothing at all.[133]

When in the autumn of 384 the bishop of Milan introduced him to new thinking, he did so by directing him along a path that he had already chosen. This is essentially what the *Confessions* tells us in two important episodes, at 5.13–14 and 6.3–5.

These narratives occur at different times: 5.13–14 refers to some weeks near the end of 384, when Augustine first met the bishop and heard him preach; 6.3–5 refers to a period sometime after Monica's arrival in Milan in the spring of 385, and before April or May 386. The second account consolidates Augustine's solution to the problem of the spirit and the letter sometime before he read the *libri Platonicorum*. It also takes up the problem of silence in reading.

What we learn from these accounts is complicated by Augustine's literary portrait of his relationship with the bishop. One has the sense of a "retrospective schematization."[134] Both descriptions position him somewhat at a distance from his subject—in 5.13–14 as the member of a listening audience, and in 6.3–5 as a simple onlooker. The rhetorical effects are deliberate. The portrait of Ambrose is intended to contrast with that of Faustus at 5.3–7, just as, in describing Faustus, Augustine may already have had Ambrose in mind; and 6.3–5 follows the pattern, taking up the differences between the two men at the level of their respective styles of reading. The Manichaean is verbose and superficial (5.6.39–44), while Ambrose is confidently directed from within: oral recitation thus yields to silent contemplation, which is the evolution taking place in Augustine's own reading habits. Finally, both descriptions have literal and figurative dimensions—an application, so to speak, of the lesson in interpretation that is taking place. The symbolic note is sounded at 5.13, where Augustine introduces the typically neoplatonic metaphors of nearness and estrangement. His *peregrinatio* is not just a personal visit to an avuncular bishop: it is the beginning of his soul's upward journey, through which he achieves a better understanding of scripture and himself. God leads him to Ambrose without his knowing why, and he is then led back to God.[135]

The weight of the evidence suggests that the influence of Ambrose on Augustine was more intellectual than personal.[136] In a statement made nearer to the events than books 5–6, Augustine speaks mainly of the effect of his sermons[137]—a view confirmed by a later recollection.[138] Neither of his two meetings with Ambrose—the one late in 384, the other after Monica's arrival in June 385—touched on personal matters.[139] When the two finally got together, they appear to have chatted about nothing more serious than curing Monica of *refrigerium,* the custom of taking cakes and wine to a martyr's shrine.[140] The discussion of theological issues may have been postponed until 386, when he was a catechumen; then they were possibly taken up in correspondence.[141] It is unlikely that the bishop would have welcomed a professor of rhetoric recommended by Manichaeans in Rome and appointed by the prefect Symmachus, an outspoken defender of paganism, whose efforts to restore the altar of Victory to the Senate house he had frustrated that summer.[142] Add to this the inconvenient fact that Augustine's expertise lay in verbal argumentation, a field that he had openly criticized.[143]

Monica was thrilled to meet an idol; Augustine says a good deal about her piety and the bishop's expression of satisfaction (6.2). But we are left to surmise his own state of mind. It cannot have been settled. He was still reflecting on his disillusionment with Faustus. He had been attending church when he could find the time, but chiefly, it would appear, to calm his thoughts rather than for theological edification (8.6.4–6). He had deceived his mother about his departure for Rome (5.8). His punishment (so he thought) was a debilitating fever at sea (5.9). His Manichaean friends in the capital, who nursed him back to health, no longer inspired his confidence (5.10.3–6). Nor did the Academics, whose only certainty was that philosophy could not be certain of anything.[144] His career offered little solace. He left Carthage hoping for higher pay and better-behaved students; his accent gave him away, and he was frequently cheated out of his fees (5.8.8–10; 5.12). Milan offered him material security, but his self-esteem remained low. Even the possibility of advancement after "reciting" a panegyric to the boy emperor Valentinian II[145] did not cheer him up. He envied the simple happiness of a drunken beggar (6.6).

His description of the manner in which he was gradually attracted to the sermons of Ambrose can be compared to his acquaintance with Cicero's *Hortensius* (3.4) and the oratory of Faustus (5.3). In all three examples of verbal discourse, there is a contrast between inner meaning and outer words. In the case of Cicero, Augustine the bishop devalues the Cicero whom virtually everyone "admires" for his tongue *(lingua)* rather than for what is in his heart *(pectus,* 3.4.4–5), while Augustine the actor, on reading him, is "transformed" in "disposition" *(mutauit affectum,* 3.4.7). In the case of the bishop of Milan, the polarities are subtly reversed: it is the youthful Augustine rather than the elder bishop who has the genuine insight, which comes about through a recognition of the content rather than the style of Ambrose's words. Faustus, as the latter's foil, is positioned between the two accounts, offering Augustine a point of departure for his encounter with the bishop. When Augustine meets Faustus, he subsequently notes, he is unimpressed by what he says but impressed by his charm, his warmth, and his genuine desire for literary conversation. Similarly, when he goes to hear Ambrose, he speaks of the man rather than the potential teacher. One can even ask whether there is an implied parallel between his disillusionment in 382–83, when he found Manichaeism inadequate, and his temporary confusion in 386, when he was still not sure that he could find a way to truth through Catholicism.

If he initially gave the bishop his attention, it was because this distant figure appeared to be kindly disposed toward him,[146] and because he had a professional curiosity about his reputation for eloquence. Initially he focused on the preacher's language and phrasing, paying little attention to the content of his message; subsequently, he noticed that Ambrose offered his listeners sound instruction based on a close reading of scripture, especially on their salvation (5.13.13–23), whereas Faustus was the victim of his own verbal strategies. Augustine's recognition of the value of the experience is mirrored in the narrative device by which the bishop is presented. In contrast to the presentation of Cicero at 3.4, where one time-frame is deliberately superimposed on another, the youthful and mature Augustines in 5.13 are part of the same episode, as, suddenly growing up and virtually converting to a new point of view, he finds his attention shifted by means of forces he does not fully understand from the exterior words to the interior message of his future mentor.[147] Furthermore, Augustine's initial description of his experience as one of those listeners contains the germ of what will become the bishop's instruction on reading; this is one of the many occasions in the *Confessions* when he implants into his characters what will become the motivation for his own action. Augustine moves beyond the contrast between the surface effects[148] and inner meaning of Ambrose's

words[149] to the position that he had reached by 391,[150] according to which
the recognition of truth in reading commences from a perception of one's
personal moral failings in relation to an exemplary text. This is the thinking
that relates the distinction between *uerba* and *res* (5.13.17–18; 5.14.4) to his
undefined attraction to Ambrose's message (5.13.24–25),[151] the "permanent" understanding which he finds "wholly unable to dislodge."[152]

There are good reasons why the content of Ambrose's preaching would
have attracted a disenchanted Manichaean auditor already interested in
Catholicism. Under Origen's influence, the bishop radically opposed flesh
to spirit, while maintaining a neoplatonic trust in God's essential goodness.
His themes were taken mainly from the Hebrew Bible, which the
Manichaeans disdained. Through allegory, the Jewish narratives were
shown to contain a poetic account of the progress of the human soul.[153]
The elements of Plotinus that Ambrose silently incorporated into his
sermons further attracted Augustine by giving the Christian message a
patina of mystical philosophy.[154] The bishop thus provided him with the
starting point for his rather different theology of the image of God in
man.[155] Above all, Ambrose appeared to be thinking as he was reading and
to be reading as he was thinking: he combined exegesis with meditative
philosophy. He offered Augustine an alternative to the misdirected polemics of Manichaean evangelism.[156] The effect was dramatic. Within a few
weeks, one stage of his future student's reading experience was finished and
another begun.

Augustine's mistrust of the alleged textual criticism practised by
Manichaeans was not new. It surfaced initially in Carthage, where he
sought superior expertise, though from whom we do not learn. About the
same time he witnessed the Catholic Elpidius, who debated publicly with
the Manichaeans and stymied them with precise quotations from scripture
(5.11.1–9). Ambrose confirmed his growing doubts about the way in which
auditors handled critical issues in open debate. The bishop of Milan was
unafraid of a full discussion of his views.[157] He responded directly to the
dualists' major challenge, the revision of the canon, persuading Augustine
that the Old Testament law and prophets could withstand philological
criticism, provided that the texts were explained *spiritualiter* (5.14.12–16).[158]
Augustine was captivated by this notion, which he makes no attempt to
define in the early phase of the narrative: it is introduced mainly for its
transformative effects, through which the professional rhetorician, already
attuned to the surface treatment of words, turns his power of concentration[159] to the demolition of his own erroneous views. Augustine was not
sufficiently inspired to "convert" there and then; his position was still close

to Academic scepticism, which permitted arguments to be taken up without necessarily accepting their conclusions (5.14.29–30). Yet Ambrose
reawakened his interest in finding a "rational" solution to theological
problems (5.14.20–26), while proposing that this goal could best be reached
by recognizing the limits of reason.

Augustine does not offer us a detailed description of the content of
Ambrose's sermons (any more than he gives us an idea of the education of
Faustus). He talks chiefly about their emotional and intellectual effects. He
also underlines the difference between two sorts of behaviourally related
reading experiences: in the one, which is represented by the *Hortensius* and
by his final conversion, a sudden transformation takes place; in the other,
although it is represented by the opposites of Manichaeism and Christian
hermeneutics, the changes are gradual and largely self-conscious. Ambrose's
message is of the second type; it penetrated his "heart" in degrees (5.14.4–
7). There was no instant of illumination or mystical intuition. Inspiration
was tempered by progressive stages of learning; neoplatonic alienation was
gradually overcome.[160] The bishop proceeded deliberately from the literal
to the spiritual sense of the text: it was not the one or the other that
disarmed the wary Augustine, but their combination into an effective
unit.[161] The systematic nature of Ambrose's approach revealed the weaknesses in Manichaean arguments point by point (5.14.10–19, 27–29). Referring to an earlier image, Augustine says that Ambrose "undid the knots
of artifice" with which the truths of the Bible had been bound:[162] he
believed he had at last found a way "to cure his languishing soul" (6.4.34–
37). Toward the end of 384, he became a catechumen.[163]

In the spring of 385, Ambrose taught him another invaluable lesson. This
concerned the relationship between reading and contemplative silence.

Augustine had taken up the problem in *De Musica,* when he discussed
the function of rests in the reading aloud of quantitative verse.[164] This
argument reappears at a critical moment in the analysis of eternity and time
in book 11; however, it does so in combination with the issues raised in
6.3, where his concern is not with silence as a feature of recitation but as
a symbol for the interior life.[165] Augustine tells us that when Ambrose read
to himself, he did so without pronouncing the words aloud, in contrast to
the normal manner of reading in the ancient period.[166] His eyes proceeded
across the page, while he sought out the sense with his heart.[167] In order
to appreciate the context of this statement, one must keep in mind that
Augustine was desperate to escape from himself (5.14.2–3; 6.3.1–5). Viewing the bishop, even at a distance, he saw something that he had apparently not seen before—the silent decoding of written signs as a means of

withdrawing from the world and of focusing attention on one's inner life. Silent reading was the technique: the silent reader, into whose interior world the outsider could not penetrate, was the sign that the desired state had been attained. A psychological mechanism and a philosophical ideal became one.

This portrait of the silent reader is inseparable from the notion that someone, in this case Augustine, is observing silent reading taking place. It is the observation of another person's contemplativeness, rather than the technique of reading itself, that makes the moment unique in the ancient literature of interiority. In one sense, both the reader and the observer are isolated: each is alone with his thoughts. However, in another sense Augustine is aware that he is not isolated. He is a member of an audience of observers of a silent reader: their silence is the sole basis of his emotional bond with them. He and the others present, the well-wishers whom Ambrose did not have the heart to send away, are not waiting for words to be spoken to them, as they would be in church. They are all outsiders attempting to interpret thoughts within a mind whose operations offer no outward, audible sign of its inner activity.

The technique of silent reading is presented as a part of Ambrose's normal daily routine. "We saw him reading silently," Augustine notes, "and never otherwise."[168] Ambrose had practical reasons for withdrawing in this manner: to preserve his weak voice and to keep the curious at a distance, one of whom, of course, was the admiring Augustine, who wanted nothing more than to break the bishop's concentration and to ask a number of pressing questions (6.3.20–32). Yet his major reason for this unusual style of reading was personal: he sustained his mind with books, just as he nourished his body with food[169] (as Augustine himself advises in book 10). Silent reading was a means to an end. The scene contrasts Augustine's restlessness with Ambrose's tranquillity: it is also a reminder within the Pauline design of books 5–7 that one's proper business lies not in the world but with oneself.

Finally, silent reading in 6.3 is an *exemplum* of self-reliance within a scheme of reliance on God. Augustine's lack of opportunity for exchanging ideas with the bishop in depth fits into the narrative design. The picture of Ambrose that Augustine wished to present to posterity is that of a man who enjoyed his periods of leisure by himself. The lesson that Augustine is eventually taught, after his baptism and Monica's death, is how to acquire the power of self-recreation on his own. It is difficult to see Christ in a crowd, he wrote elsewhere: God can be perceived only in the solitude of intention.[170]

The psychological effect of silent reading on Augustine is reasonably easy to understand, as his memoir in 6.3 is self-contained. The episode is a step in the direction of controlled interiority after the initial encounter with Ambrose's preaching in 5.13–14. As noted, there is an implied contrast with Faustus, who virtually becomes Augustine's pupil (5.7.24–28). In the case of Ambrose, there can be no such reversal of roles: it is the bishop who teaches Augustine that apparent absurdities *in libris ecclesiasticis* can be explained through careful exegesis and theological allegory (6.11.10–11). Yet the long-term influence of silent reading on his methods of study is difficult to assess. He shows little interest in the technique for its own sake.[171] Nor is the notion of a silent review without reading unusual in his thinking.[172] Silent reading is best understood as a complex symbol that is adapted to different ends at *Confessions* 6.3, 8.12, and 11.27. The description of Ambrose reading silently prefaces the conversions of Augustine and Alypius, where the silence does not direct our attention to the isolation of one mind but to the separate illumination of two minds.[173] The episode at 6.3 tells a part of the story in a manner that prepares the reader for the climax of the narrative books but avoids a direct anticipation.

The other major issue taken up in Augustine's recollection of Ambrose in 6.4–5 concerns the letter, the spirit, and the authority of biblical texts. Listening to Ambrose preach each Sunday, Augustine realized that he had been living in error (6.3). Through a combination of literary and philosophical insights, he concluded that Christianity was based not on carnal fictions[174] but on realities not apparent to the senses. The example that most frequently came to mind was the bishop's definition of man as a "spiritual substance" made in the "image of God,"[175] in which two ideas were fused. The "image" of which Ambrose spoke was invisible, although man occupied space, just as the intended meaning of the biblical text was invisible to the literalist (that is, Manichaean) reader, although it penetrated his mind via the ears and the eyes. Once Augustine grasped this relationship, one theological paradox after another was resolved: God could be on high and yet very near; he could be wholly everywhere, and yet located in no specific place (6.3.46–48; 7.20.5–9). He could be in the world and inside man.

These problems all seemed to lie within the connotative field of the term "spiritual." What precisely did this notion mean?[176] A tentative answer is given in 6.4.[177] The spiritual element is something that combines an agreed interpretation with an affective response in the recipient's mind. In this respect, the scene of reading is not unlike that described at 6.3, except that two people are involved, a reader and a listener. Ambrose reads aloud and comments on what he reads, while Augustine rehearses what is read to him in his memory, adding his own gloss. It is a *silent* reading of the bishop's *audible* words. He is "first confounded, then converted" (6.4.11–12; Psalms 6:11). When he hears Ambrose commenting on 2 Corinthians 3:6, "The letter kills, but the spirit gives life," what chiefly occurs to him is that a text can be like a rule,[178] if literalism is abandoned and the spirit truly allowed to live in the hearer's mind (6.4.25).[179]

The reader's sensibility, then, as an interpretation of Paul, is the mediator between the spirit in Christ and the spirit in man. In order to elucidate the interior sense, one has to listen as if one were reading. Initially, Augustine is just a listener. Trained in auditory memory in the schools, he is unable to separate the meaning of the words from the effect of hearing them spoken. Later, presumably in 385, he performs interpretive exercises via the ear by remembering what Ambrose has said, thereby obviating the necessity of hearing him each time or of having a written text in front of him. He then imitates what he thinks the bishop is doing: he reads to himself, reflecting on the spiritual sense, that is, the sense applied to *his* spirit. We do not know whether this was oral or silent reading; presumably it was a little of both, since Ambrose addressed his audience vocally but asked each member to reread and interpret what he had said mentally. Just as Ambrose read for himself, Augustine now isolates himself with the mental text and performs interpretive operations on it.

His chief concern is not with the correctness of Catholic doctrines—his views did not change definitively until the writing of *De Moribus Ecclesiae Catholicae* in 388[180]—but with an implication of the spiritual sense, namely that everything in which one believes does not have to be demonstrated before one's eyes: *crederetur quod non demonstrabatur* (6.5.3). The literal, or demonstrable, is what the ear hears or the eye sees; the spiritual, or nondemonstrable to the senses, is what the mind makes of the internalized verbal or written text. It is a short step from this statement to a new version of Augustine's now familiar theory of narrative. In life many things are taken on faith, such as who our parents are. We also trust what our friends tell us and what we read in historical accounts. If we had to verify all the facts in a given situation, we would never have enough evidence to be sure of anything. We could not act on our beliefs. Scripture now appears to him to offer a canonical example of this type of reasoning, since the stories come down to us on a higher than human authority (6.5.7–20).[181] But they cannot simply be accepted as related. If Ambrose is right, they have to be interpreted[182] through their "spiritual" element. It follows that for belief to take place the text needs an audience of at least one person.

## Neoplatonism

The influence of Ambrose coincided with Augustine's extensive studies in neoplatonism. His chief sources were the third-century philosopher and mystic Plotinus (d. 270)[183] and his pupil Porphyry (d. 304–05). Despite wider reading later in life, his understanding of Platonic doctrines remained within the orbit of their teaching.[184] In 397, when he began the *Confessions,* it was this pair of writers and Cicero who supplied most of his themes.[185]

His adaptation of Platonic and neoplatonic commonplaces to his theory of reading has been noted. The One became the Word. The distinction between the sensible and the intelligible became a hermeneutic tool, while the separation of the thinking mind from the objects of thought[186] reappeared as the meaning in the reader and the text. It was within this interpretive scheme that he found a language for discussing otherwise intractable moral issues (such as the problem of evil).[187] In general, Platonic influences[188] permitted him to adopt an unplatonic position in favour of reading as a method, while he adhered to many of its strictures regarding sensory perception.

He also broke new ground in reinterpreting the concept of mediation, through which he responded to neoplatonic elitism, in particular to Plotinus' restriction of ascent to a chosen few.[189] Well before he wrote the *Confessions,* he abandoned such rarefied notions[190] as being unacceptable to Christianity.[191] In *De Vera Religione* (390), he denounced the ancient contradiction between the teaching of philosophy and the practice of religion.[192] The Donatist controversy reinforced his suspicion of sectarian views based on inherited intellectual privilege.[193] In *Confessions* 7, he took a step in a new direction: he effectively domesticated the neoplatonic ascent by uniting its goals to those of Christian reading and meditation.[194] The move permitted him to remain critical of philosophy while incorporating the key feature of meditative reflection into a programme accessible to all.[195] In his view, pagans did not err in adopting the notion of an intermediary but in failing to recognize its embodiment in Christ.[196]

Book 7 is an attempt to unite the themes of incarnation[197] and mediation.[198] The first topics are types of nonmediation, namely the inadequacy of his notions of God and of self-knowledge (7.1–2). In 7.3–6, the question of intermediaries is raised within God's creative activity.[199] The introduction of the *libri Platonicorum* then takes place within a restatement of the prologue to the gospel of John (7.9.1–19), a classic meeting point for the ideas of creation, divine intervention, and illumination. Utilizing this text,[200] the hymn from the Epistle to the Philippians, and the first chapter of the Epistle to the Romans, Augustine elaborates a set of contrasts

between pride and humility, presumption and confession.[201] The life of
Christ thus becomes his point of reference for evaluating Platonist doctrines.[202] For, in his view, the incarnation personalized truth as no abstract
philosophy could.

The search for mediation is linked to an even more original idea in book
7: this is a new configuration of the narrator, which evolves in two segments, chapters 3–6 and 9–21. The clue to the change of priorities lies in
the contrast between the treatment of written sources. In 7.3–6, there are
few quotations, none from pagan sources and only a handful from the
Bible. In 7.9–21, both scripture and philosophy are well represented. The
texts are presented as if they were read, not cited from memory.

There are other possible reasons why these contrasting approaches are
adopted. Augustine may simply have relied on memory on one occasion
and on texts on another. Yet, if his citational practices elsewhere are a
guide, this type of division seems unlikely. Of the two segments, 7.9–21 is
a narrative, while 7.3–6 consists of a series of discourses; and it is in previous
narrative episodes, rather than in his discussions of ideas, that he is dependent on what he can recall.[203] His strategy may also have been dictated by
the nature of the sources. Yet no answer is found here either, since the
background material is complicated throughout. In 7.3–6, the subjects of
free will (7.3) and the incorruptible (7.4) may be derived from sermons of
Ambrose, the latter echoing *Enneads* 6.8.[204] The topic of evil (7.5) and the
errors of astrology (7.6) sum up long-standing arguments against
Manichaeism.[205] Chapters 9–21 have a more unified theme, but the sources
are no less difficult to unravel.[206]

If these options are rejected, then the situating of the references in 7.3–6
and 7.9–21 can be viewed as a literary device. Since there are no external
events to be related in book 7, Augustine may have substituted the stages
by which he rejected neoplatonism and adopted Christianity. Indirect
support for this interpretation arises from book 8, where a comparable
technique of narration is found, as well as from the timing within the
*Confessions*. Six books have passed, and six are to come. Augustine the actor
replaces outer illusions with inner truths and adopts humility in place of
pride.[207] His turn toward reading and toward writing about what he reads
is the confessional symbol of this reorientation.

The lesson of book 7, then, is that the person who assimilates texts,
comparing their doctrines, has to be a transformer of texts, who creates
writings out of what he reads. This is an expression of Augustine's belief
that it is the mind of the reader that creates coherent philosophies for life.
There are anticipations of this moment when he compares the style of the

*Hortensius* to that of Isaiah (3.5) and when he speaks of the composition of *De Pulchro et Apto* (4.13–14); however, the formative influence behind the scenes is Ambrose. Chapters 9–21 mark a stage in the evolution of an interpretive method that comes into being while Augustine listens to the bishop preach and observes him silently reading and meditating (5.13–14; 6.3).

In books 5–6, the narrator is pictured as a pupil sitting at his master's feet; in book 7 we see the emergence of an independent thinker and writer. The books that Augustine studies are before him on his desk: he leafs through them as he writes, frequently telling us where he is in the text as he pens (or dictates) his thoughts (for example, 7.9.20–48; 7.21.1–32). He is not the member of a listening audience; he is alone in his library, where the voices that speak to him are from the codices that he has in hand: they enter his mind as he attempts to enter their thoughts. His awareness that he is reading plays a role in his conception of himself as an author and remains in his thoughts as he engages in the writing that comprises book 7, in which mimesis involves literary production rather than performative reproduction as it does in the literary exercises of books 1 and 2.[208]

These transitions are confirmed by two chapters, 7–8, which link the statements in 7.3–6 and 7.9–21 and provide a rare glimpse of his mental "fluctuations" (7.7.3) as he passes from instability to stability via what he reads. In the logic of the discussion, a set of problems is addressed and turned over in his mind; they are resolved when he can compare different positions point by point (7.9 and following). He will undertake a similar comparison without texts in 8.7–11. In both instances, the sequencing of emotional changes creates a narrative that prepares the reader for higher nonnarrative experiences. Within the space of a few paragraphs in 7.7–8, a boundary is created between his prereading confusion and his tranquil- lizing re-entry into himself via neoplatonism (7.10). The elevation of the soul in 7.10 then prefaces a lengthy period of comparative reading (7.12– 16). A second elevation follows in 7.17: this is the dénouement in the internal narrative, before the truth of scripture is reaffirmed through the writings of Paul (7.21.1–2).

Augustine's entry into himself in 7.10 and its relationship to Plotinus have attracted much scholarly comment.[209] Less attention has been paid to the account of his instability, which is his alternative to the narrative of silence at 6.3. As he contrasts his futile search for the origin of evil with the promise of eventual salvation (7.7.6, 8–10), he forms a mental picture of his sufferings in which "the groans of torment to which the heart gives birth" appear to remain unheard, even though God is listening, unknown to him.[210] The situation is the reverse of the voiceless reading of Ambrose: silence is not a symbol of inner tranquillity but of unobserved confusion. Mindful of his mentor, he speaks ironically of himself, envisaging "the speechless contrition of his mind" as "a loud voice," pleading for God's "mercy."[211] The role of the audience is likewise inverted. In 6.3, those attempting to understand Ambrose's tacit thoughts are left without answers, which is the bishop's wish. Augustine, too, is isolated, but in silence he cries out for an end to his separation from the deity. What arrests the flux of his thoughts is the idea that no force within himself can ensure his spiritual progress. Certainty can arise only from God, who acts, condescending towards him through his ability to reach upwards through interpretation. It is a praise of the Word, a humbling of the reader (7.9.1–19).

The references to speech and silence in 7.7 introduce the topic of the self's alienation and potential return. This is accomplished by a gentle shift in metaphors from hearing to visual perception.[212] The scriptural text on which the change is based is Psalms 37:9–11, which speaks of the groaning of the supplicant's heart and the desire to be with God, concluding with the statement, "The light of my eyes was not with me." Augustine interprets this to mean that his mind or soul was not in its proper place.[213] As a consequence, the immaterial "place" in which he might have found permanent repose continually eluded him through analogies with physical incorporation.[214] He pictures himself striving upwards but continually being held back; recognizing himself to be superior to material things, but unable to free himself from his fascination with their mental images.[215] He endured his torments until, through insight into himself, God was a certainty for him.[216]

In this context, he introduces the "Platonic books" into *Confessions* 7. God wished to show him how "to resist the proud and show grace to the humble" (1 Peter 5:5; compare 1.1.4–5) in order to demonstrate how his mercy could serve as "a pathway to humility" for mortals, since his word "was made flesh and dwelt among men" (John 1:14; 7.9.1–4). To that end, it was by means of "someone inflated with tremendous pride" that the deity procured for him the *libri Platonicorum* which had been translated from Greek into Latin.[217] The unknown person who brought him these works thus reactivated the topos of his pagan pride, which first surfaced when he read Cicero's *Hortensius*.[218] In his critical reading of the "Platonic books," he reverses his position and places the *sermo humilis* above the eloquence of philosophy (7.9.38–43).

He is imprecise on the number of books or authors that he read.[219] Also, the views expressed in 7.9–21 are "highly nuanced,"[220] reflecting the superimposition of several readings and, within them, periodic responses from scripture (7.20.25–26).[221] The frequent references are intended to create an impression of scholarly thoroughness.[222] Within 7.9–21, two types of experience are configured, comparative reading (7.9; 7.20–21) and spiritual elevation (7.10; 7.17; 7.20). Their presence is part of a pattern, now well established, by which Augustine's spiritual progress takes place in alternating moments of sudden illumination and gradual, disciplined exercises. In the carefully reconstructed experiences of 7.9–21, he attempts to combine the two. The result is a union of neoplatonic mysticism, hitherto uninfluenced by reading theory, with his ascetic programme of reform.[223]

There is independent support for this interpretation in the much-quoted statement in *De Beata Vita* 1.4, written at Cassiciacum in the winter of 386–87, in which he briefly recapitulates the stages of his philosophical education.[224] He recalls the suddenness of his "conversion" on reading the *Hortensius,* which "so inflamed a desire for philosophy" that he "considered giving himself over to it at once."[225] He rejected the "childish superstition" of believing everything he was told;[226] yet, in his search for reason, he fell in with teachers who were blinded by "the light of their own eyes." He reconceives his Manichaean period in such metaphors as a lengthy journey, when his way was obscured, his course unclear, and his gaze fixed on "sinking stars."[227] He awaited the revelation of their secrets, "covered by veils," but none was forthcoming.[228] His period with the Academics in Rome and his attendance at Ambrose's sermons are also viewed as regular periods of study, lacking sudden illumination.[229] So are the neoplatonic books: "Having read a small number of the books of Plotinus," he states, "and having compared them as well as I was able with the authority of those who have handed down divine mysteries, I should have broken anchor, had the good advice of a small group of men not steadied my course."[230]

In the narratives written in 386–87 and after 397, Augustine is less concerned with the precise sources of each type of experience than with setting up a succession of experiences, in which the nature of each is clearly delineated. The causal links between reading and mental ascent are deemphasized in order that stress can be placed on the sudden, unanticipated effects.[231] The result is a complex narrative scheme, which is directed toward our understanding of his spiritual evolution as well as toward our own spiritual life. At the end of book 7, he wants us to be students of scripture like himself, not neoplatonic mystics. If this design is to work as a convincing narrative, his "attempts at Plotinian ecstasy" have to be "in vain."[232] An intellectual vacuum is created, which is filled by the internalist phase of his story. This is what happens in 7.9–21.

It is here that the idea of the incarnation is invaluable.[233] As previously remarked, Augustine's chief (retrospective) opposition to the purely philosophical programme of reform in the *Hortensius* is that "the name of Christ was not there."[234] The theme of the incarnation is virtually absent in books 3–6: this lacuna has to be understood as a narrative rather than a theological strategy, as his christology was well articulated by 397. In book 8, he turns his attention from philosophical issues to the model lives of holy men. The framework for this discussion arises between 7.9, where the gospel of John is introduced, and 7.18.1–8, where he recapitulates a number of developmental concepts under the rubric of Christ as "mediator." These include seeking and finding *(quaerebam . . . inueniebam),* means and ends *(quod esset idoneum ad fruendum),* and the metaphor of humble food, suitable for "infants," as a symbol of the literal flesh, within the magisterium of the Bible *(quoniam uerbum caro factum est, ut infantiae nostrae lactesceret sapientia tua . . .).* In these reversals, he indicates that he read the *Enneads* as a Christian, just as his translator, Marius Victorinus, read the prologue of John as a neoplatonist.[235]

Augustine attributes the neoplatonists' inadequacy partly to polytheistic influences (7.9.49–66).[236] But its main source is their preference for abstract moral ideas over the physical reality of a model life. As a consequence, he is able to find parallels in neoplatonism for philosophical statements in the Bible (for example, John 1:1–12),[237] but not for the incarnation[238] and the literal story of Christ.[239] These reflections translate his concern with materiality (7.1) to the literary sphere, where it reemerges in a more positive light as the literal or historical sense of the biblical text. What is disparaged as a remnant of worldliness in the individual seeking God is reevalued as a condescending spirituality in the world. From this vantage point his commentary proceeds from the literal to the interior and spiritual dimensions. This is a movement from a real life represented by a text to an inner text that is intended to be lived.[240] Because the model is the historical Christ, the search for the nonliteral in himself has to begin with the physical in himself, that is, in his body's narrative in time. He thereby combines the ambivalence toward the body that is typical of patristic exegesis (notably Origen)[241] with the idea that anyone's body can in principle become the "text" on which the story of the incarnation is written. If that were not the case, there would be no point in locating the reader in the literary structure of the *Confessions.*

In 7.9, he shifts the reader's interest away from charismatic teachers such as Ambrose and toward the written page (or, more precisely, toward the inward experience for which the page is an "admonishment"). Our attention is drawn to the texts through the omission of the name of the individual who purveyed them. There is no mention of Plotinus or Porphyry, whence no authority transcends the text and enlightens the uninitiated reader; the emphasis is placed on Augustine's interpretive activities. He seeks a single meaning in the text despite different styles of expression (7.9.23–24). Traditions of interpretation are *scripta* (7.19.7–8). Learning results from intensive study (7.9.43–44), from trial and error (7.16). Writings are distinguished from speech, e.g., "the text" of Paul's "discourse" (*textus sermonis,* 7.21.4).[242] Throughout, his arguments *(rationes)* are based on comparative reading (for example, 7.9.6–8). He quotes scripture as if it were philosophy.

Convincing evidence of planning arises from the arrangement of the biblical texts, whose ordering principles have been analysed by Olivier du Roy.[243] There are four antitheses which are introduced by either "I read there" *(ibi legi)* or "I did not read there" *(ibi non legi).* In each case, what is found or not found in the Platonic books is framed by a pair of quotations from scripture[244] in a "frequently employed"[245] schema. The same "grouping" characterises the incarnation in *De Genesi contra Manichaeos* (388 or 389), *De Fide et Symbolo* (393), *Sermo* 292 (preached before 412),[246] and *Enarratio in Psalmos* 130[247] (probably preached before 408).[248] Thus 7.9–21 is a rereading of scripture and a remembering of the neoplatonic writings[249] in which the presence of a pattern of interpretation answers many of the relevant questions before they are asked.

Once this framework is in place, Augustine introduces the first of the mental ascents in 7.10. The initial step occurs at 7.9.1 in the statement *Et primo uolens ostendere mihi . . .* (First you wanted to show me . . .), which presents the *libri Platonicorum* as a foil to scripture. The next step is the search for the doctrine of the incarnation; it is revealed at 7.9.23 when he says *Indagaui . . . in illis litteris uarie dictum et multis modis* (I investigated . . . in those books what was said in varied and different ways). The mention of idol worship in 7.9.49–66 focuses the reader's attention on externalities before Augustine turns to the realm of interiority. This is accomplished in a single statement that begins 7.10, *Et inde admonitus redire ad memet ipsum intraui in intima mea duce te . . .* (And thence, admonished to return into myself, I entered my intimate depths, with you as my guide . . .). The key adverb, *inde,* refers to the *libri,* while *intraui* echoes *indagaui,* as he proceeds from inquiry to the inner life of the soul. Neither the impulsion nor the result of this experience is strictly speaking a reading experience. The book is a point of transition between outer and inner teaching.[250]

This is not an isolated "turning" inwards, but a "returning" *(redire); it is* a "reminding" and "admonishing," in which God acts as Augustine's "helper."[251] The clue to his meaning is the adjective *admonitus,* a technical term that he frequently employs when referring to a divinely inspired "external event that triggers an internal effect."[252] In *De Magistro,* the model event is a sign;[253] when Augustine is converted to philosophy by the *Hortensius,* it is God's "advice."[254] Before the conversion at 8.12, he notes that he "had heard concerning Anthony that he had taken a piece of advice from a reading of the gospel that came his way by chance, as if what was being read aloud was being said to him directly."[255] Alypius, let us add, failed to follow him in his exercises in scripture;[256] yet, at the moment of his conversion, he was "admonished" by Romans 14:1.[257]

The turning point in this series is the reading of the *libri Platonicorum,* whence Augustine was "admonished" to look for the immaterial component of God's creativity.[258] This is his indication that 7.10 is a preconversion ascent of the mind, guided by reading. In contrast to Plotinus, he affirms that the soul in the course of purification cannot move upwards guided only by itself.[259] It needs a helper *(adiutor).* This aid is configured in the text by metaphors of light,[260] which are to be understood as a Platonist commonplace (the inner light in the mind) and as a symbol of progressive enlightenment through the understanding of scripture. He speaks in Plotinian terms of an ascent from physical to spiritual vision: entering into himself,[261] he sees a light source with his soul's eye. Yet, while retaining the force of these metaphors, he speaks of the light as "truth, eternity, and love"—a replica of the Christian trinity. The light is created above; he is created below (7.10.8–11).[262] The strength of his desire for Christian ascent is indicated by his replacement of *meditabitur* with *suspiro* from the paraphrased text of Psalms 1:2.[263]

These references are presented to the reader as aspects of a psychological experience. In reality, they reflect the content of his reading: the entire episode is framed by his careful study of Paul,[264] while the language of mental ascent is culled from Plotinus,[265] Porphyry, and scripture. He describes the manner in which he awakens, is borne upwards, and has an inner glimpse of the "being" that he is not: he "trembles with quaking fear," aware that he is far from God in "a land of unlikeness."[266] Like the quotations from scripture that make up the statement of his inadequacies in 7.7, this ascent is a reconstruction whose potential effect on the reader is worked out in advance.[267]

After addressing the issues with which book 7 begins (including the nonexistence of evil, the weakness of the dualist views on the good, and his carnal habits, 7.12–15, 7.17.3–4), he reinterprets the meaning of mental ascent at 7.17. Whereas in 7.10 an attempt is made to recreate the voice and feelings of the young Augustine, 7.17 reflects the views of a mature figure, who distances himself from his earlier enthusiasm. The quotations from Plotinus do not emphasize transcendental radiance but the transience of his response.[268] He seeks an inward power in the soul, but fails to locate it amid externals.[269] His vision proves unsustainable (7.17.1–6). He has a momentary glimpse of God's "invisible nature," but he lacks the strength of mind to keep it before him (7.17.29–30). This is not the world of Plotinus, in which there is a "fusion of self-knowledge and a vision of the One": "there is no such continuity between the 'otherness' of God . . . and the mutability of human nature."[270] What we have in its place is a traditional "encounter between a sinful man and a holy God."[271]

Another indication that the issues have been rethought arises from the number of concerns fitted into the episode, such as "using" and "enjoying" *(uti/frui)* as it appears after 388,[272] and the relation between *phantasma* and reality.[273] The theme of memory anticipates book 10,[274] and the stage is set for the vision at Ostia, where genuine transcendence occurs. Most significantly, the ascent at 7.17 is incomplete. As Augustine describes the transition, he rises through the body, the soul that perceives through the body, and the inward power by which the body's senses report what is outside, arriving at length at the potential for rational thinking, which judges what the senses bring forward; and he discovers through the changeableness of his judgements that reason has to be reinforced by a purer understanding if his degrading habits are to be overcome. Images and fantasies are at length beaten back: reason is enveloped in its own light. A fearful Augustine has a momentary glimpse of "that which is," then returns to his normal state of mind, in which he is left with only memory and desire (7.17.16–32).

This is a reflection on a failed ecstatic experience and, even more emphatically, on the inability to transcend the limits of the mind. Augustine counters with a positive view of outside authority in the remainder of book 7 (7.18–21).[275] The argument takes shape under the rubrics of the life of Christ and the alternatives to scripture, which are connected in 7.18. Conscious of the infirmity that prevented more than a glimpse of God in the ascent, he seeks the strength "to enjoy" *(ad fruendum)* a more permanent satisfaction. He finds this as he discovers the meaning of the statement, "The Word was made flesh" (John 1:14), thereby returning to 7.7,[276] with a change in emphasis. He is no longer attempting to find correlates in neoplatonism for the philosophical principles in John. Instead, he interprets the text itself. In order to attain the humility that he needs to understand the humbling of Christ in the world, he has to learn the worldly lesson of his own intellectual frailty.[277]

The final three chapters of book 7 recapitulate the manner in which he passed through pagan, heretical, and neoplatonist interpretations of Christ's life[278] to the point at which Paul revealed the meaning of this "mystery" (*sacramentum*, 7.21.1–2; compare 7.19.5–6). He initially favoured Porphyry's view[279] that Christ was just a man (7.19.1–2, 21), an *exemplum* of authoritative teaching and human concern;[280] alternately, he considered the heresy of Apollinaris of Laodicia (d. ca. 390), to the effect that Christ was "a god clad in flesh" (7.19.23–28). The salvific possibilities of John thus remained unexplored (7.19.16–18; 7.20.1–3): his failures at mental ascent become a symbolic statement of his inability to attain a state of Christian contemplation,[281] since he refused to profit from the theological knowledge that he thereby acquired.[282] He was no less a victim of his pride than the unnamed scholar who brought the *libri Platonicorum*.[283] Yet, if predestination operates, it was God who directed him to these books before he had an opportunity to think seriously about scripture *(priusquam scripturas tuas considerarem)*[284] so that the manner in which he was affected by such treatises might be imprinted on his memory *(ut imprimeretur memoriae meae);* only later, when he was made gentle by his writings *(cum postea in libris tuis mansuefactus essem),* did he distinguish between presumption and confession *(quid interesset inter praesumptionem et confessionem),* that is, between arid knowledge and true wisdom: "If my thoughts had been shaped by your sacred texts beforehand . . . and I had afterwards discovered these volumes, I might perhaps have been ripped from the foundation of my piety. On the other hand, had I remained in the state of mind created by what was imbibed to heal my soul, I might have believed that such ideas could be born in the mind of someone instructed by the [neoplatonist] books alone."[285] Through scripture, he learned to "rejoice with trembling" (Ps. 11:7): this was his biblically inspired rejoinder to the notion of a purely philosophical ascent, in which he briefly glimpsed God's eternal light, "trembling with love and awe" (7.10.16–17). Paul thus replaced Plotinus;[286] progress through reading superseded the ascent of the mind on its own. Moving upwards depended less on a hierarchy of being than on a synthesis of doctrines.[287]

# 3

## READING AND
## CONVERSION

Augustine's spiritual development culminated in his conversion to the religious life in Milan in August 386. This event was the climax of his reading experience in *Confessions* 1–9. The moment of commitment was anticipated by his sudden awakening to philosophy, as well as by his slower methodical instruction in interpretation, which began in the schools of grammar and rhetoric, continued in association with Manichaeism, and was rethought during the Milanese period. The sermons of Ambrose, the *libri Platonicorum,* and the Pauline epistles completed his education.

He learned to think of the past, present, and future of his life as if he were interpreting a text. The "literal" dimension consisted of events experienced and recalled, while the "spiritual" was concerned with matters latent, potential, or about to take place. He was aware of the danger of living out fictions from his consideration of pagan poetry (1.13), ancient drama (3.2–3), and his dedication to Hierius (4.13–15). Through his reading of Paul, he hoped to find another way to repattern his life from within and to direct it outwards as he wished.

The philosophical and theological elements in the new approach make their appearance at 4.10–11 within a discussion of growth, decay, and temporal experience. The manner in which one phase of existence succeeds another is likened to the comprehension of a spoken sentence. Sounds cease[1] but meaning endures (4.10.9–14). A narrative is a complicated version of what we hear when sentences are pronounced, word after word. It is a whole made up of parts,[2] and it proceeds from one type of being to another and back again, offering one sort of pleasure as we hear it, and another when it is understood. From the listener's (or reader's) perspective, the words impinge on the senses, then on the mind. Moreover, the narrative becomes an object of thought while retaining its links with sense perception, since, in constructing its meaning, we have to recall the words that have passed before (4.11.20–22).

In Augustine's view, all narrative phenomena are alike in their sensory impermanence. However, within Christian history, the appearance of narrative also symbolizes the passage from an eternal to a temporal mode. Human narratives entered through the first couple's disobedience, as recounted in Genesis, and the temporal element yielded to the eternal again during the life of Christ, which reintroduced permanent being on earth. Like thought becoming words, the saviour was temporarily perceptible to the senses of man. In this respect he was a living narrative. Yet he withdrew from human sight, so that, with his terrestrial manifestation gone, we might rediscover him in our hearts, thereby bringing ourselves closer to reunion with God (4.12.25–27).[3] Even the events of a human life can have a purpose if they are conceived in this manner, since God designs such narratives so that their worlds are to the real world as the parts are to the whole.

Augustine extended this type of thinking to the *in principio* of Genesis 1:1 in *Confessions* 11 (discussed in Chapter 8). In his view, unformed matter is not anterior to the things that are formed: both creations take place together, but they are related separately in sequences of words.[4] The residual model of change therefore is speech. The voice is the "matter" of our words, and words are indications of the voice's "form." When a person speaks, he or she does not begin by uttering formless sounds, which are subsequently organized into words; similarly, God did not first create unformed matter, then determine the shape it was to have according to the nature of each created thing. Just as we speak words in their entirety, so he created matter already possessing its distinctive qualities.[5] It follows that the creative principle out of which things were formed preceded them, "not chronologically, but in some manner in its origin" *(non tempore, sed quadam origine)*.[6] Scripture, being a sequence of words, cannot recreate this simultaneity of creation: it has to divide into moments of narrative time what is taking place all at once.[7] Just as words arise out of silence, are spoken, and return to silence, so things proceed from essence to existence and return to being in God (4.10.1–24; 4.11.1–13).

Our personal narratives imitate the master narrative of scripture. However, we cannot understand their underlying logic through the evidence of our senses. We acquire knowledge of things created in time through narrative experience, that is, through our perception of sequentially ordered events in the external world. This knowledge tells us about the past but not about the future.[8] We know that it is the adolescent's "nature" to grow older by looking backwards from maturity, but we do not observe what was foreseen for the child in God's will, from which the developmental cycle originally issued. We assume that old age will follow; but this information is not accessible to us through our senses either. As a consequence we conclude that "a principle of agedness" is "hidden" in youth, just as adolescence is concealed in infancy. This knowledge is unavailable to sight but accessible to the mind; in a parallel manner, God's will operates in nature and determines grace.[9] Augustine's own story is told through the retrospective benefit of his experience.

Book 8 introduces a new feature into this pattern, which reflects a heightened tension between God's predestination and man's limited understanding of his fate. Augustine contrasts the unknown outcome of reading experiences in personal narratives with the interpretive certainty of his perusal of a single text, Paul's Epistle to the Romans, which acts as a unifying principle for the various episodes. Book 8 thus transforms the programme of study announced at 7.21.1–6.[10] At the same time, Augustine introduces a variant of typology into the *Confessions* in which foreshadowing and fulfilment take place not between historical events, figures, or stories in the Bible, but between secular figures, guided by providence, whose narratives are interlocked by means of a logic that is clarified to none of them before the events take place.

## Alypius

The analysis of these stories begins with Alypius, who was the appropriate person to have witnessed Augustine's conversion to celibacy. By the time the *Confessions* was begun, he was bishop in nearby Thagaste.[11] His reputation for asceticism[12] had spread to Italy, from where Paulinus of Nola and Therasia had written him in 394 asking for the story of his life.[13] A part of that uncompleted project, which Augustine subsequently agreed to undertake,[14] may have been incorporated into the *Confessions*,[15] together with the idea of an autobiography, not as an exemplary Life, like that of Anthony, but as *historia*,[16] a narrative of past events in which care was taken to distinguish between what could and could not be recalled. Paulinus asked Alypius for the sort of information that Augustine does not supply for his partial biography of his friend, but which he provides for the story of his own life: a record of his family, his place of origin, and his reasons for entering the priesthood, as well as an account of the role played by Ambrose.[17] The request was introduced with a Virgilian phrase in which Pallas, King Evander's son, asks Aeneas to reveal his identity after the adventurous voyage from Carthage to Italy[18]—words that would have struck a chord with Augustine, who configures the narrator of the *Confessions* somewhat as a Christian Aeneas.[19]

Alypius is a witness of a special sort: he follows Augustine's conversion from the outside. In the climactic chapters of book 8, he tells us what is seen and heard, but not what is taking place in his friend's "heart." He has to be told what has happened (8.12.39–40). Through his version of the story our attention is drawn to a central feature of Augustinian conversion—its interiority. He also establishes the historicity of the event by conveying the literal sense of a narrative that has a deeper symbolic meaning. We trust the account because it is related by a character whose historical reality is accepted beforehand.

Augustine's distant model for this type of story is the gospel narratives, which include the perspectives of ordinary men and women on the life of Christ. In 8.12, the conversion of Alypius strengthens the realism by making Augustine the outsider and narrator in turn. By presenting the internal and external stories of his conversion simultaneously, the bishop Augustine responds to the two major counterclaims against his views, the neoplatonic and the Manichaean. In having his conversion witnessed like that of Marius Victorinus, Augustine implicitly rejects the internal verification of religious experience typical of the neoplatonic elevation of the soul. In leading the reader from the literal to the figurative, he responds to what he considers to be the weaknesses of Manichaean imagism and *fabellae*.

The groundwork for Alypius' supporting role in book 8 is laid in 6.7–9. These chapters, which deal with Alypius' student years, may be parts of Augustine's unfinished life history of his friend. The events of 6.7 and 6.9 take place sometime after the autumn of 376, when Augustine begins to teach in Carthage; those of 6.8 take place before the summer of 383, when he sails for Rome.[20] They treat aspects of a single theme, the inability of Alypius to resist mundane diversions and to direct his life to otherworldly goals. Two of the stories anticipate the *tolle, lege* scene in giving reading an instrumental role in the narrative. In 6.7, the setting is the classroom, in which the plot turns on Augustine's commentary on a set text; in 6.9, it is the market-place in Carthage, where Alypius is accused of theft while rehearsing some memorized lines for another of his classes. In neither case do we learn the nature of the text in question. As narrator, Augustine's interest is focused on the act of reading as an agency of change, through which the student teaches his master[21] a lesson that he presumably already knows but must be laboriously retaught. To understand what this lesson is we must pause briefly over the accounts.

The first of the three[22] begins with Augustine's recollection of the

conversations that he had with his friends Nebridius and Alypius in Milan
in August 386, before his conversion, when he was still tempted by
honours, money, and the prospect of a good marriage (6.6.1). Alypius was
an "assessor" in the courts (6.10.7–8); Nebridius had left his comfortable
life in Carthage to be with them (6.10.29–35). The three met in private to
discuss their hopes and fears (6.11.26–45).

Alypius was a native of Thagaste, like Augustine, and had studied with
him there as well as in Carthage some two years later. The pair held each
other in high esteem: to Alypius, Augustine seemed to combine the
qualities of erudition and goodness; to Augustine, Alypius seemed to
possess a degree of virtue unusual in one so young.[23]

The events related in 6.7 alter these first impressions. The young
Augustine saw himself as a teacher who was concerned with a wide range
of ethical issues, but the bishop Augustine, who comments as he tells the
story, sees him engaging in the ethically questionable activity of teaching
rhetoric. Alypius' apparent virtue was also flawed: he was "fatally" attracted
by gladiatorial combat,[24] a senseless diversion that threatened his otherwise
promising career. Augustine recognized the problem but was unable to
intervene. A misunderstanding had arisen with Alypius' father, a prominent
citizen of Thagaste, resulting in the withdrawal of his favorite pupil from
regular attendance at school. For a time, he even thought that the son
shared the father's views.

This was evidently not so. Alypius continued to make an appearance in
class, despite his parent's interdict, greeting his former teacher and remaining for a part of the lesson. The idea of reproving him had slipped from
Augustine's mind.[25] But one day when he was surrounded by his students,
an unusual incident took place. Alypius entered, greeted his former master,
and directed his attention to a text that Augustine was then reading and
discussing. He had reached the point in the lesson where it was necessary
to provide an illustration of a point, and he chose the public games, thereby
introducing an indirect criticism of the leisure activity that "captivated"
many of his students. Although Alypius was not the specific target of his
remarks, he "seized upon" Augustine's words, "believing" that they were
intended for him alone. Augustine thought that he had somehow caused
offence, but he later learned that Alypius was only angry at himself, since
he had interpreted the commentary as an indication that he should mend
his ways. He subsequently gave up the games, at least for a time,[26] and
persuaded his father to let him study with Augustine again. Yet he was led
astray a second time. Augustine led him to the Manichaeans, and he was
entirely taken in by their "bogus display of continence."

This story is constructed around a well-known ancient *exemplum,* related by Diogenes Laertius and others, concerning Polemo, the son of Philostratus, who renounced his dissolute life and turned to philosophy after he chanced to hear a lecture by Xenocrates on the virtue of temperance.[27] Augustine knew the story;[28] Ambrose, who may be his direct source, refers to it in his lengthy diatribe against excesses of food and drink, *De Helia et Ieiunio.*[29] There are some similarities between the original and *Confessions* 6.7–8. In both, temperance is the motive for inward change (6.7.46; 6.8.32–34); and Polemo's drunken bravado may be in the back of Augustine's mind when, at 6.8.4–6 in the following story, Alypius is urged on by his companions, who are "returning from dinner."

In other respects Augustine's account is different. The original story has a happy ending: Polemo takes over the Academy and teaches others to follow the philosophical life. Alypius merely passes from one state of illusion to another. If 6.7 "arranges" an existing story, as Courcelle proposed,[30] it also makes Alypius a thinly disguised stand-in for Augustine. He too disobeys parental authority in order to pursue virtue, and his educational journey takes him from Thagaste to Carthage, where he is attracted by "spectacles." Alypius' *amici et condiscipuli* (6.8.4–5) differ little from the "time-wasters" who earlier misguided Augustine (3.3.18); his diversions are also described as *insania* (3.2.5; 6.7.9). Alypius is unlike Augustine in rejecting sexual contact (6.12.3–7); however, this detail is important in the narrative structure too: it makes him an ideal witness to his mentor's eventual conversion to the celibate life.

The stories at 6.7–9 effectively prepare the way for this event. They mark the beginning of a shift from distant models of virtue, in particular from Augustine's conversion to philosophy via the *Hortensius,* toward lives of holiness arising in the time-frame of human memory.[31] Augustine signals a move in this direction by constructing the narrative in 6.7 around habit, remembering, and forgetting—forces that operate within individuals' experience—and he contrasts these motives for conduct with the inscrutableness of God's ways, which operate beyond human time. Above all, he transforms Xenocrates' "lecture"[32] into a complex relationship between text, commentary, reader, and listener.

In this reconfiguration of the *exemplum,* the story is both about the influence of a teacher on a wayward pupil and about the master as well. Both Alypius and Augustine are pictured as slaves of habit, Alypius more obviously, as he follows "Carthaginian customs" (6.7.8), but Augustine no less, as he mindlessly teaches rhetoric (6.7.11). Thus busied, he conveniently "forgets" that he has planned "to intervene" with Alypius.[33] When he finally influences him, he does so unintentionally,[34] seated "as usual" before his class,[35] book in hand,[36] reading. He is only thinking of how he can make his text "more agreeable" and "to the point."[37] He speaks of himself as a "user" of discourse,[38] a term that recalls his disparaging remarks about *grammatici* in 1.13.31–33. Alypius is attracted to public spectacles just as Augustine was when he was a student in Carthage six years earlier, in 370.[39] Now Augustine is something of a "public" spectacle himself (6.7.11). He is still unable to resist the emotions aroused by rhetoric, but the seductive words are his own. He is as committed to verbalism as was Faustus (for example, 5.5.26–31), whom he presumably then admired.

The turning-point in the story is a two-sided reading experience which does not depend on the text read, of which we learn nothing, but rather on a verbal commentary whose relation to it, Augustine stresses, is as arbitrary as fate. Not knowing the work, our attention naturally shifts to where he wants it—away from the visible act of reading and toward the invisible action of God. The entire scene is predetermined. Early in the story, we are informed that Alypius is already destined to be "the minister of his sacrament": his "correction" is attributable to the deity, even though it "operates" through a human.[40] Reading becomes the enactment of a secular sacrament, that is, a performance in which a person and a text ritually implement God's intentions. There is a set of signs that Augustine and Alypius share; however, the text that Augustine reads and Alypius hears is not what brings about their mutual understanding. They realize this when they become aware that their initial interpretations of the connection between the text and the commentary differ. Their insight into the "truth" arises subsequently out of their respective awareness of their errors. They have no control over the referential system in which truth resides: what is expressed through their experience of reading is what God wills for them.

The relationship to the art of reading differs in each case. The effect of Alypius' interpretation of Augustine's verbal example of the games is to permit him to review a narrative that has nothing to do with the text that his teacher is explaining: it concerns a young man's attraction for gladiators and his teacher's plan to discourage him before his career is affected.[41] The fact that Augustine has let his plan for correcting his protégé slip from his mind can be viewed as a silent, critical commentary on the narrative in which he has already played a part. The professor of rhetoric does not understand what he is doing or what he has done: from his standpoint, Alypius is not "a wise man rebuked," since Augustine did not intend to rebuke *him*.[42] Rather it is God, "using everyone," knowing and ignorant, through the just "order" that God alone knows, who inflames his "heart" and "tongue" so that his pupil can be helped (6.7.39–42).

It is Alypius' will that sets events in motion (6.7.28–29; 6.7.46), not the words spoken by either party. The meaning that was intended by God for Augustine cannot be traced to what they say, nor can the understanding that God intended for Alypius. The Augustine in the narrative follows the meaning of the words, but it is Alypius who intuitively understands God's intentions through them. The scene of reading thus sets up a dual reminiscence, reactivating differing narratives that have been temporarily forgotten by their actors. In Augustine, memory operates through forgetting and remembering; in Alypius, it superimposes a recollected life narrative on what is said. In Alypius' case, the interpretation is a type of prereading, since the scenario is in his head when he enters the classroom and only needs Augustine's illustration to be complete. He believes that the *similitudo* applies to him alone[43] and, as a consequence, the mechanism of reading does not work "by chance," as it does for Augustine,[44] but by an internal design, which he implements. By contrast, in Augustine, the operative is not a text, but words—or, shall we say, extending God's "dominion,"[45] the Word, acting momentarily through his agent (6.7.26). What is unknown to him is that his words, which he is only "using" (6.7.10–11), are a means to an end, the curing[46] of Alypius, an action through which he is eventually set free to "enjoy" God. What Augustine has forgotten—namely "to have it out *[agere]* with him"—is implanted by God in Alypius' mind, as "he bent his thoughts to what was being discussed *[agebantur]*."[47] The content of the set text is inoperative; yet there is no doubt that Alypius is an auditor at a reading. And this is not the first time we have observed such a scene: it reiterates the intellectual development of Augustine in the presence of Ambrose in 5.13–14 and 6.3.[48] But here, ironically, Alypius is a stand-in for an inadequate Augustine, and his teacher of rhetoric is an inadequate replacement for the bishop of Milan.

To describe Alypius' experience, Augustine deliberately chooses the strong verb *rapere,* which means to seize, to ravish, to assault, or to plunder. The connotative field seems inappropriate to the figure of Alypius, for whom chastity is an ideal well before he enters the religious life. Some light is shed on the matter if we look closely at the type of interpretation that is taking place. The relationship between the set text and the example of the games which illustrates it is analogous to the understanding Augustine worked out under Ambrose for connections between the literal and the spiritual. It is a reworking of Pauline hermeneutics, in which emphasis is placed on the spirit in the text and in man. Alypius has in effect given a spiritual reading to Augustine's text or, more precisely, to what Augustine said. He interprets it silently, just as Ambrose read and meditated silently some four chapters before. Had he vocalized his response, Augustine would not have had any trouble interpreting it, as evidently he did, on the basis of Alypius' gestures alone (6.7.35–37).

Augustine's biblical source for this use of *rapere* may be Matthew 11:12, which is alluded to at 8.8.5, when he describes the inner struggle that preceded his conversion in Alypius' presence and compares their hitherto feeble spirituality with that of "the uneducated, who rise up and take heaven by storm." He has already spoken of "seizing souls" for God.[49] A Pauline text with a similar meaning is 2 Corinthians 12:2–4, where the adjective *raptus* is repeated twice as the apostle describes "a man . . . caught up into paradise, who heard secret sayings, which one is not permitted to divulge." Augustine devoted *De Genesi ad Litteram* 12 to an exposition of these verses; the work was envisaged by 401, the year he completed the *Confessions*. The term "source" must be used with caution here; it would be preferable to speak of an overlapping of references, as Augustine may be drawing on a number of texts simultaneously when he describes intellectual transport in books 7 and 8. His purpose in 6.7 is to look forward beyond the Plotinian "entry into the self" (7.10.1–2) to 7.21, to where his description of Alypius *(At ille in se rapuit)*[50] can be read as a preface to his reading of Paul *(Itaque auidissime arripui . . . apostolum Paulum)* and to his own conversion by Romans 13:13–14, where he tells us: *Arripui, aperui et legi in silentio.*[51]

One other feature of the reading experience in 6.7 is worth noting. The text that Augustine holds, whose title we do not know, is a symbol of our inability to know God's ways. Yet his ignorance is a stimulus to self-improvement, as becomes clear if we compare the reading experiences of books 1 and 6. In book 1, Augustine criticizes the rote learning of the later ancient schools, that is, the memorization and recitation of set texts which do not touch upon the interior lives of those who learn them. Enjoying this type of performance is reading for pleasure—that is, using the text, which should be a means to an end, as an end in itself. But was Augustine not doing this in his teaching in Carthage? The evidence is unclear. His concern with lives of virtue seems to be an afterthought; what motivates him to intervene with his young friend is the fear that Alypius will not realize his worldly ambitions. Also, he offers his students the example of the games because they are not paying sufficient attention to his lessons.[52] It is Alypius who carries the moral burden of the episode by making reading an effective instrument of self-reform. The set text, which is read in class, elicits a response that relates inwardly to him and, as a consequence, not outwardly to what is said. His reaction comes in a flash. It is similar to Augustine's conversion to philosophy except in one detail, namely that it pertains to two texts, one written and the other spoken. The second is the "law" influencing his heart of which Augustine spoke in book 1. The analogy that is in Augustine's mind concerns the way in which statements in the Old Testament are suddenly illuminated by those of the New, if, contrary to Manichaean expectations, the preacher's words are able to unite the two. Because this enlightenment takes place through reading, illumination implies the isolation of minds—otherwise a text would not be needed as an instrument of mutual understanding. It is this final lesson at 6.7 that foreshadows the conversion through reading in 8.12.

Similar themes are taken up in the stories in chapters 8–9. We move forward in time; Alypius passes from adolescence to youth; and, accordingly, the moral dimension of the narratives is deepened.

He preceded Augustine to Rome in order to pursue his legal studies. His career was still uppermost in his thoughts when he subsequently accompanied his former teacher to Milan (6.10.1–4). His attitude toward worldliness is the understated theme of chapter 8. Like the previous episode, the story centers upon a sudden redirection of his attention. The same phrase, *animum . . . intendere,* is used to describe this mental shift on both occasions.[53] But whereas in 6.7 Augustine describes Alypius as "seizing" his words "for himself" and "believing" they were intended for him, at 6.8.2–3 he refers to his "being seized" by something "unbelievable"—his passion for gladiatorial combat.[54] The repetition is deliberate: we must know the outcome of the episode in 6.7 in order to understand the plot of 6.8. For Alypius' knowledge of his successful resistance in 376 lies behind his reaction to his temptation in 383—and to his failure to understand it.

In general terms, the subject of 6.8 is the nature of sensory attractions and the illusions that we entertain about our ability to resist them on our own. The topic is not taken up in depth in 6.7. Chapter 8 also differs from its predecessor in other ways. In 6.7, Alypius is a part of Augustine's audience in class; in 6.8, he is himself playing to an audience comprised partly of "friends and fellow students." In 6.7, the rest of the audience is just a backdrop; in 6.8, it has an active role in shaping his response. In the second episode, therefore, Alypius takes the place in the narrative that is occupied by Augustine in 6.7. The "crowd"[55] is likewise the norm by which we, as Augustine the author's audience, measure Alypius' failure to live up to the standard that he sets for himself; and it is we, as well as

Augustine's friend, who come to appreciate the inferiority of friendship to the love of God. Our loyalty to such human relationships is placed on the same level as our responses to claims for our attention made via our senses. Both are worldly involvements.

As in 6.7, the central character interprets what takes place as happening "by chance."[56] Yet like Augustine before him, Alypius is unwittingly following a divine plan (6.8.23–24). The events took place at the time of the games,[57] when Alypius met some companions proceeding from dinner to watch the matches. He was invited to join them but flatly refused. However, his "strenuous resistance" was no match for their "friendly violence," and he found himself borne physically toward the amphitheatre. "Bring my body there if you will, and keep it there," he said, "but do not think you can direct my mind and my eyes to the spectacles. I will be present as if I were absent: I will defeat them as well as you." His friends paid no attention, and when they arrived, the emotions of the onlookers were running high. Alypius shut his eyes and hardened his resolve, but when a combattant was wounded and the crowd raised a great cry, he was overcome with curiosity. Thinking he would not lose control of himself, he opened his eyes. He was mesmerized by the sight of blood (6.8.24–27). "What more is there to say? He watched, he screamed, and he was carried away by the heat of his emotions. When he left, the madness went with him . . . He went back again and again, not only with those who had initially taken him there but with others whom he took with him in turn" (6.8.29–32).

The moral of the story is that Alypius tries to rely on himself, when he should have placed his trust in God (6.8.24). His flaw is his self-assurance; he learns his limitations only later in life (6.8.32–34). Augustine criticizes his own youthful arrogance through his friend. Alypius also retraces his mentor's steps in a more subtle way. To the bishop of Hippo, writing sometime after 397, putting one's trust in God means finding certainty in the Bible: as a consequence, this anecdote, which is not about the presence of reading, is nonetheless about its absence. This message is encoded in Alypius' statement to his friends. He thinks that by closing his eyes he can be present and absent at the same time; but Augustine the bishop knows, as we do, that only God can accomplish this, since he is everywhere and nowhere at once.[58] Alypius' wager is lost the moment it is made: his friends are the witnesses to the triumph of God's will over him. As he inevitably yields to temptation, Augustine does not discuss the outcome—this is decided. He spells out the sensory and mental changes that take place. When his friends drag Alypius off to the amphitheatre, they shut their ears to his protests; at the same time, he leaves his ears open to the spectacle's temptation. It is through his ears that his attention is diverted from within to without: they are a gateway by which the enemy enters the citadel of his eyes and his mind, whence he is taken prisoner.[59] He is separated from the inner self that he singlehandedly tried to construct. "He was no longer the person who had come there; he entered into the crowd as it had entered into him: he was an authentic member of the gang that had transported him there" (6.8.27–29).

Erich Auerbach saw in this account a stylistic representation of the overthrow of "enlightened classical culture," with its dependence on "individualistic, aristocratic, moderate, and rational self-discipline" by the forces of "lust," "magical power," and "the dominance of the mob"[60] arising in the later ancient world. But it is not "individualism" or "rationality" that is Augustine's major concern in 6.8: it is self-delusion. Alypius does not fail because he lacks self-discipline but because he puts too much faith in it; he is weak not because he is unaware of his inner life, but because he refuses to seek firm support for it. Like Augustine, he builds a type of self-reliance that can end only in "a region of dissemblance," in a self outside his true self. It is for this reason that the themes of 6.8 are so carefully chosen from the events of books 1–4: they include parental authority, peer pressure, the attraction of spectacles, and the deceptions of friendship; and, they foretell, in Alypius' failure, Augustine's eventual victory over himself. The clue lies in the hierarchy of the senses, which proceeds from hearing to sight before exerting an influence on the mind— an anticipation of the way in which the senses work in the conversion scene in 8.12. A confirmation of this pattern occurs in 10.33[61] when Augustine confesses his weakness for temptations of the ears: he resists the attraction by means of an inner discipline that depends on scripture in books 11–13.

Alypius "retained the memory" of these events "as a medicinal for his future" (6.9.1–2). He also recalled the incident recounted in 6.9, which took place while he was Augustine's pupil in Carthage (6.9.2–3); this constitutes the third episode in his unconstructed life. In this episode,[62] he was in the forum at noon, alone, mulling over some lines to be recited in class.[63] This was a habitual learning exercise, as was Augustine's method of instruction in 6.7.[64] As he paced back and forth before the law courts with his tablet and stylus, another student suddenly appeared in the forum; he carried a concealed hatchet, with which he began to hack at the lead grates above the silversmiths' workshops. The artisans below, hearing the noise, sent a party in pursuit. The student thief heard them, panicked, and fled, leaving the hatchet behind.

All the while, Alypius was lost in thought. He did not see the felon enter the forum, but he noted his hasty departure and, curious to learn the reason, approached the place where he had seen signs of activity, at length coming upon the abandoned hatchet. As he wondered what had happened, the pursuers suddenly arrived and mistook him for the criminal. He was arrested, put on display, and led away for judgement, imprisonment, and possibly torture. However, en route to the jail the crowd met the architect responsible for Carthage's public monuments. They were delighted: by producing a genuine thief they thought that they could dispel the suspicion that some of them had been stealing objects from the forum. But he was unconvinced by their tale. He had seen Alypius at a prominent senator's house, and in private he asked what had really happened. Ignoring jeers and threats, he then ordered the others to follow him to the true culprit's door, where a slave child recognized his master's hatchet.

This story resembles chapters 7 and 8 in details but differs in purpose. Reading again plays a role in setting up the plot, and Alypius falls victim to a potentially violent mob. God's omniscience is vindicated, although its agency is a child who speaks proverbial words of truth. Yet unlike 6.7 and 6.8, the story relates to Alypius' ecclesiastical future;[65] also, it subtly incorporates one use for memory within another. It is the story and its moral lesson that Alypius remembers; but that lesson implies a criticism of the sort of memory that he exercises in the town square, which involves only the performance of remembered lines. He is falsely accused while he is lost in thought:[66] an implied link is thereby created between that rote memorization, which is a learning "habit" (6.9.4), and the identity of a self which is not his. In this respect, the situation is similar to that of chapter 8: if he is the person whom the crowd thinks he is, then he is not his true self. This non-self, whose "exercise" is represented by mnemonics, is formally symbolized by the "true" thief,[67] who is, like himself, a student. By encoding this symbolism in a daylight theft, Augustine indicates that this is another story about the making public of the inner self. The point is emphasized by the two types of theft, the one by Alypius' fellow student, the other, reported subsequently, in which objects within "the care of public buildings"[68] are found missing.[69]

At the literal level, the accusation against Alypius is dropped when the true felon is discovered. At the symbolic level, the public denunciation of the student who committed the crime permits the truth of his self to be publicly witnessed. It would appear that there is some doubt about the reason for his release: he is recognized to be innocent simply because of his family background. But this detail has to be understood as having a historical and a figurative dimension. The superior social level of Alypius' family is the first thing we learn about him in 6.7; this fact precedes Augustine's description of his precocious virtue. In 6.8, his social status is once again the code by which Augustine indicates his spiritual status. The architect has parallel functions. He represents the classical *deus ex machina;* for, just as we are not told what Augustine said to him, so we are not informed precisely how it is that he knows where to lead the angry crowd in order to find the genuine criminal: the statement "they came to the house of the adolescent who had committed the deed" (6.9.35–36) again echoes the gospel narratives, in which the uninformed many frequently oppose God's design only to become a part of it.

The contrast between the child who reveals the crime and the adolescent who commits it reiterates another familiar topos, the passage from guiltless innocence to irresponsible youth—the situation of Augustine in the pear-tree episode. The symbolic child here may be himself, commenting on his former guilt. The crowd, which witnesses Alypius' rite of transition, is like a chorus that helps him to relive and to remake his past. In the story, Alypius represents the good person who he was inwardly and was to become, while the other student stands for the thief in whose immature identity he temporarily hid. The gloating of the crowd can only stand for his false pride. The tenants likewise bear witness to the fact that one's interior nature is unknowable; they do this by not knowing who Alypius truly is.

The stage for the testing of Alypius is appropriately set as he wanders about the forum—a place that confuses the values of commerce and justice. Alypius stands for the ambiguity of the locale: he engages in purposeless self-absorption, standing apart from the world, lost in thought; but because of his neglect of self, he is abused by the world. In the end he is rescued. But by this time the narrative has reiterated the logic of 6.7–8; for his pursuers, who think he is a felon, are aroused by what they sense, first by the noise of the real thief hacking away at the grate protecting the silver-smiths' street,[70] then by the sight of a hapless student, who protests his innocence while holding the hatchet. As in Augustine's classroom in 6.7, only Alypius knows his inner thoughts; only he knows with certainty that he has not committed a crime. The deceitful images of the previous two chapters are recreated in the vulgar crowd that comes after him—a crowd that is no less the prisoner of its senses than Alypius himself, as, transfixed, he watched the lethal swordplay of the games.

In the friendship between himself and Alypius, Augustine found a convenient way of contrasting outer and inner behaviour. The stories in 6.7–9 center upon the one's ignorance of the other's thoughts, with the reading process acting as a means of passage from the outside to the inside of the mind. There is one further variation in this method in 6.12–13, not in a story but in the discussion of a topic—marriage versus celibacy. The two sides in the debate, Augustine and Alypius, are presented in different types of narrative: the virtuous life read or heard about, and the recon-structed personal history. Both are relived[71] through experience[72] as they are commented upon and put to the test in thought-experiments poten-tially applicable to life. Reflecting later on their exchange of views, Augustine takes himself to task for tempting the already chaste Alypius with tales of how marriage and the pursuit of wisdom can be reconciled. The effect on the reader of the *Confessions* is the opposite: it becomes clear that fictions are a less important influence on his friend than the events that he transforms into an internal narrative. Augustine's examples compel Alypius to reenact some unpleasant sexual encounters in the past. By doing so, he restates his experience as a counterargument to Augustine's position (6.12.3–7, 27–33). This is a technique of self-report that Augustine sub-sequently uses with impressive effect on himself.

## Simplicianus

The "life of Alypius" is a dress rehearsal for the resolution of problems of illusion and reality in the narratives of book 8. God works out his friend's destiny through dramas involving reading, remembering, and public en-actment; he arranges his conversion in Alypius' presence through the "taking up and reading" of a passage of Paul. In book 8, the narrator sees the events through Alypius' eyes. Augustine in turn witnesses his friend's conversion, thereby placing the already related episodes of his life in a larger context. Augustine's narrative brings that of Alypius to a close, but it is necessary that Alypius' stories anticipate Augustine's type of closure: two souls, freed from the world, then interpenetrate each other as the neopla-tonist Augustine wishes; yet they do so in narratives modelled typologically on a divine life, as God predestines. Augustine, a being in time, discovers the spiritual element in his own story, while God, a being out of time, reveals this meaning in his historical design.

The opening prayer (8.1.1–14), whose significance becomes clearer as the conversion nears, reestablishes the dual role of "confession,"[73] directing Augustine's devotions toward God and a memoir toward the reader.[74] Reiterating and transforming the prayer at 1.1.7–17,[75] Augustine asks that "the hand of his tongue" (Proverbs 18:21) find words to express "the sacrifice" of his "confessions" (5.1.1–2), while he promises the final chapter in the story of how God "broke" his "chains" (8.1.3–4; Psalms 155:16). The verb that links the statements, *dirumpere,* is close enough in sound and sense[76] to the formerly employed *rapere* and *arripere* to provide a metaphorical background for his definitive break with the past. The quotations from the Psalms in the opening lines[77] are complemented with phrases taken from Isaiah, John, and Paul (8.1.6–14). These offer the reader a symbolic point of contact with earlier events and prepare the way for the reintroduction of the narrative.

This segment consists of three interrelated stories of conversion, each of which is told by a different person.[78] Simplicianus, the successor of Ambrose as bishop in Milan in 397, tells Augustine of the conversion of Marius Victorinus, which took place in 355. Ponticianus, a Christian official of the imperial court, tells Augustine and Alypius of the conversion of two state agents, which occurred sometime after 381.[79] Finally, Augustine describes his and Alypius' conversions in the garden of their house in Milan in August 386.

An audience is present in each of these episodes. Augustine begins the story with Simplicianus as an addendum to the opening prayer, still addressing God in the second person (8.1.14–16); however, within the narrative, he is the only listener whose presence is felt by the implicit audience of his readers. In the second tale, the audience consists of himself and Alypius, while the deity reappears in his afterthoughts. In the third, Alypius is the observer of events but has to be informed of their meaning by Augustine.[80] In his explanation, Augustine addresses God, Alypius, and the reader at once. However, since God already knows what has happened, Augustine effectively speaks to the latter two, indeed, only to the reader through Alypius: for besides Augustine, only the reader has the three stories in mind, and without this knowledge a good deal of their cumulative effect is lost.[81]

As we proceed from the first to the third episode, therefore, we witness a change from the listening audience within the scenes to an abstract readership outside.[82] At the same time, the action moves from external to internal events, reiterating the pattern of book 7. These are significant methodological changes, which complete Augustine's transformation of

later ancient narrative by shifting interest from levels of style to questions
of audience.

The first story (8.1.14–8.5.54)[83] begins with a brief description of Simplicianus, who in contrast to Augustine, acquired "much learning through
study" and was devoted to God "from youth" (8.2.16–18). He is the
narrator of an edifying tale rather than the representative of a philosophical
position, just as Victorinus' story which he tells stresses the manner in
which "study" can inform a "a way of life."[84] Augustine visited him to sort
out the conflicts in his thinking in the hope that he could "direct his feet
along God's pathway" (8.1.20–22). He refers to his "erroneous wanderings"
(8.2.3): the weakly heroic phrase recalls his early literary education (8.2.3;
1.13.11–12), which contrasted his facility in Latin with the difficulty that
he experienced in learning Greek. Translation is the entry point for the
story of Victorinus, which is about the rejection of ancient rhetoric and
Greek philosophy in favour of Christianity. Although it is Simplicianus
who tells the story, he is in fact Augustine's auditor as the visitor[85] recounts,
not the events of Victorinus' life, but the milestones of his own studies, in
particular his recent sifting of neoplatonic philosophy and Catholic doctrine. When he recalls that he has been "reading certain books of the
Platonists translated into Latin by Victorinus," who was at one time a rhetor
in Rome and who died a Christian, Simplicianus expresses approval that
he has not taken up "the writings of other philosophers, which are filled
with errors and deceptions concerning fundamental issues," but these alone,
in which "God and his Word are everywhere implied."[86] Finally, in
reiterating his reasons for rejecting neoplatonism, Manichaeism,[87] and literary success[88] Augustine concludes on the theme of celibacy (compare
6.12–13): the detail does not preface Simplicianus' story but prepares the
way for the third episode of book 8, in which Alypius is present partly as
a symbol of chastity in order to witness his conversion. Augustine plays on
the language of ascent, stating that he has "risen above" the neoplatonists;
he has likewise been rescued from "that other breed of the impious," who
refuse to glorify God or to render him thanks (8.1.38–43; Rom. 1:21). His
remaining link with the world is through "woman" (8.1.28–29). He is
mindful that Paul did not forbid marriage but hoped for "something
better."[89]

Simplicianus places these events in the context of his encounter with
Ambrose, whose "fathering" of his studies at 5.13 his phrases recall.[90] This
is a symbolic way of describing an episcopal succession that looks back to
the baptism of Ambrose in 374, at which Simplicianus officiated, and
forward to Augustine's baptism by Ambrose at Easter 387. Paternity of

another sort is also at work. It was from Simplicianus that Ambrose learned much of his neoplatonism, which he in turn learned from Victorinus, the preeminent Latin Platonist of the time. On the basis of Simplicianus' teaching, Ambrose rejected neoplatonist magic, ritual, and spiritualism in favour of the Catholic doctrine of continence,[91] thereby influencing Augustine at a critical moment[92] and providing the *Confessions* with another theme that links books 8 and 10. With great narrative economy Augustine traces these changes in outlook to a brief critical period in the spring of 386. In patronizing *both* pagan and Christian traditions, moreover, Simplicianus legitimizes the fusion of ideas that Augustine tentatively proposes at the end of book 7. In this transition, the reader passes from the story of Augustine's troubles, which is referred to but not recapitulated, to the hitherto ummentioned person of Victorinus, whose conversion to Christianity follows.

This is not precisely the Victorinus of book 7. There, we are told that Augustine read the *libri Platonicorum* in Latin, but we are not given the translator's name. The source is added in 8.2 because this is the place at which the celebrated rhetorician enters the story: in parallel with the presentation of Simplicianus, it is not his philosophy but his narrative role that interests Augustine. Accordingly, he speaks of his acquaintance with neoplatonism as if the reading constituted a normal phase of his studies: he "came upon" the books (*incidissem,* 8.2.7), read them as a set of texts (*legisse, scripta,* 8.2.3, 7), and "found his way" through them (*insinuari,* 8.2.9). There is no talk of mystical elevation.

Augustine prepares the way for the interlocking of the three stories in book 8 through a comparable recourse to literary memory. The story of Victorinus' conversion is recounted by Simplicianus because of his recollection of what he has been reading (*commemoraui,* 8.2.3). Simplicianus then tells Augustine what he remembers concerning Victorinus.[93] Although this is a story within a story, the framing story has to be inferred: Augustine mentions his "circuit of errors" but does not provide any details, since we, the readers, already have them. In contrast to the statement in which he announces but does not tell of these events,[94] he says that he will "not remain silent concerning the story told" to him.[95] Simplicianus then "recalled Victorinus himself, whom he had known well when he was in Rome"[96] in order "to exhort" Augustine "toward the humility of Christ," a humility, he adds, "that is hidden from the wise and revealed to babes" (Matthew 11:25). Augustine thus establishes the opposites of telling and remaining silent *(narro, sileo)* within the interpretive distinction between hiding and revealing *(abscondo, reuelo).*

In the verb *exhortari,* he may even be thinking of his conversion to philosophy on reading the *Hortensius*[97] and his failure to understand the humble style of scripture (3.5.2–3). Accordingly, the story is an *exemplum* of the triumph of humility (8.2.25–27), through which "an elderly man" becomes a "child,"[98] as the pride of pagan learning "bends its head" and "submits to the yoke" of Christ.[99] Victorinus fulfils the expectation of the opening prayer[100] and counterbalances the arrogance of the unnamed person who purveyed neoplatonic texts to Augustine (7.9.4–5). He is portrayed as "a learned elder, highly skilled in interpreting the liberal arts, who had read and passed judgement on numerous philosophers." On becoming a Christian, "he was in the habit of reading the Bible and of carrying out serious research into Christian literature, which he scrutinized with great care."[101] And, while his thunderous rhetoric worked on others from the outside, scripture worked on him from within.[102] He asked Simplicianus one day, "not openly, but in a rather secretive and personal manner," whether he knew that he was already converted. His friend replied that he could not be counted "among the Christians" until he was seen "in the church of Christ." Victorinus, resisting public display, asked whether it was walls that made Christians.[103] Simplicianus then drew attention to his friend's preference for abstract doctrine over the integration of doctrine into public liturgy and worship.[104]

Victorinus may have refused a public profession of faith to avoid offending highly placed pagan patrons. He may also have had a lingering fear of the deities' wrath, despite his interest in Christianity. He was won over by the Psalms and the gospels, especially Luke, interpreting the incarnation as the *logos* foreseen by God to relieve humans of their sensory illusions.[105] His hesitations vanished before the frightening possibility that he would be denied by Christ (Luke 12:9). He realized that it was hypocritical to participate in the cults while refusing a public acknowledgement of God. Eventually he underwent catechism,[106] and the news of his imminent baptism spread. When the day of his profession of faith arrived, he was offered a private ceremony but insisted on reciting the creed before the congregation.[107] The response was appropriate: as he mounted the steps to the altar, a murmur rose up from the crowd, "Victorinus, Victorinus!"

Quite apart from its drama, this account provides a missing link in Augustine's own description of his comparative reading of philosophy and the Bible in book 7. Victorinus' reading of scripture is even described in terms that echo his language of neoplatonic ascent.[108] The accounts are in equilibrium: Victorinus struggles to make a public profession of faith, just as Augustine will struggle to make a private one; the latter's conversion will take place behind another type of wall—the individual mind. Also, the story provides a tentative transition from literary memory back to the presentness of oral memory.[109] It is apparently by word of mouth that Victorinus heard of Simplicianus' holiness;[110] the tale that Augustine is told is likewise a spoken account (8.2.11). After catechism,[111] Victorinus makes his profession of faith in the Roman fashion, reciting the creed along with "certain words, conceived and retained in memory."[112]

The move from private to public devotion is represented by the change of audience. In the first part of the story, Simplicianus is Victorinus' only listener; in the latter part, the auditors consist of the "faithful *populus* of Rome" (8.2.57). In contrast to Augustine's colloquies with Simplicianus, in which stress is laid on the ear, Victorinus appears in their "sight" (8.2.57, 61). The shift from the ear to the eye precedes the translation of Victorinus' faith from the "secret"[113] to the "public" realm.[114] The narrative technique recalls 6.8 and 6.9, where Alypius is effectively the prisoner of public emotion and opinion. The positive evaluation again sums up Augustine's thinking about the audience's reaction to the recitation of a sacred text rather than an oral performance. For, what Victorinus says is not just words: he realizes that there is "no salvation in the rhetoric that he taught" (8.2.61–62). The emotional bond that is created between him and the congregation results from their anticipation that they are about to hear something that they already know; it is as if Victorinus were recalling the details on their behalf. Three times in two sentences Augustine uses a verb of violent separation *(rapere)* to illustrate the dramatic changes: "Praise rose quickly to their lips when they saw him, and just as quickly they were silent, so that they could hear what he had to say. He pronounced the true words of the faith with magnificent assurance; and they wanted to take him up *[rapere]* at once into their heart: and they did take him up *[rapiebant]* in their love and joy—these were, so to speak, the hands taking him up *[rapientium]*."[115]

Augustine's commentary in 8.3.1–8.4.27 clarifies the memorial aspect of Victorinus' profession of faith through well-known passages from Luke 15:4–6 and 15:8–9, in which something lost is subsequently found. One of these is the parable of the hundred sheep: there is more rejoicing in heaven over one sinner who repents than over ninety-nine righteous persons who need no repentance (8.3.3–5; Luke 15:7). Another is the parallel story of the woman who had ten silver coins. When she lost one of them, she searched for it everywhere in her house; and when she found it, she called her friends together to rejoice in her happiness (8.3.7–9).[116] A line is also quoted from the story of the prodigal son (8.3.10–11; Luke 15:11–32).[117] These passages reinforce the notion of a special kind of reminiscence.

Augustine asks why the soul takes greater pleasure in things that it loves if they are rediscovered than if they are always in its possession.[118] The answer, already hinted at,[119] is that we frequently compare an experienced pleasure to its opposite, which we recognize through memory. The triumph of a victory is enhanced by the uncertainties of battle; food and drink please us through the recollection of hunger and thirst; and so on (8.3.18–23, 29–34). In order to be satisfying on this scale, it does not matter whether lost and found pleasures are licit or forbidden; their essential feature is a mentally recreated opposite to what is sensed (8.4.26–29). Moreover, while God, the highest pleasure, enjoys himself, beneath him and subject to his design there is a continual regress and progress as opposed forces are engaged and reconciled.[120] In these reflections, the Roman rhetorican's conversion invites comparison with Hierius, to whom Augustine dedicated *De Pulchro et Apto*. In place of an aesthetic theory of "the beautiful" and "the fitting," he now speaks of a "fitting mode"[121] of ascetic behaviour, which is illustrated by the paired opposites *defectus/profectus, offensiones/ conciliationes, summus/imus, initium/finis, excelsus/profundus,* and so on. These teach that God never completely deserts humans as they search for ethical values, even though humans have difficulty in returning to God.[122] It is in this context that a figure like Victorinus can act as an authoritative role model.[123]

When the story was finished, Augustine "was on fire to imitate him."[124] He was imprisoned by his continual failures of will, in which his desires arose, were satisfied, and became confirmed habits. A "new will" could not emerge: "old" and "new" persons coexisted in irresolvable tension (8.5.9–19). Yet a new chapter had been opened in his attempt to apply Pauline hermeneutics to life: he recognized that the literal and spiritual were present in his thinking before an ethically useful story like that of Victorinus was told. He "understood through his own experience what he had read," namely, "how the flesh works its desires against the spirit, and the spirit against the flesh."[125] In this frame of mind he could no longer complain that his perception of God's truth was "uncertain." Nor could he think of "the law of sin" as anything but "a type of violence that habitual behaviour commits against the inner self" (8.5.22–25, 27–30, 43–52).

## Ponticianus

The second of the three narratives in book 8 is contained in chapter 6, in which Ponticianus tells of the conversion of a pair of imperial agents in Trier. Augustine maintains stylistic continuity with the previous episode despite a change in actors and locale.[126] However, subtle changes involve the narrator, what the actors say, and the implied audience's knowledge.

In the first story, the events are related by Victorinus to Simplicianus, the principal narrator, who tells them to Augustine. This strategy makes Simplicianus the key figure in interpreting the internal changes that bring about the outward signs of a changed faith. In the second story, the roles of relating and interpreting are divided between the narrator and the audience. Ponticianus, like Simplicianus, discloses the events, but it is Augustine and, through him, the implied listeners to his *Confessions* who interpret what is taking place.

In continuity with book 7, this narrative technique works internally. As Ponticianus speaks, he tells one story that is heard by Augustine, while Augustine tells himself another that is heard through memory. The reason Augustine the bishop adopts this twofold manner of conveying the events is that Augustine the actor wishes to remake his life history into something resembling the composite, reformist story he is telling himself. While Ponticianus informs him (and us) what took place in Trier, we assume that Augustine is using his account silently as a basis for comparison with his own earlier life.[127] The shift to this type of narration introduces the Pauline dichotomy of the interior and exterior man into Augustine's lived experience, which is what he understands Paul to have intended his hearers to do; and, it moves the question of realism from the localizable outer world to the nonlocalized inner world, where, following Ambrosian neoplatonism, he now thinks that it belongs.[128]

As story two[129] begins, Augustine is pictured taking time from his teaching whenever he can in order to calm his nerves in church. By contrast, Alypius was compelled to be at leisure, having completed his final term as a public assessor (8.6.7). Whether employed or not, both ware traffickers in words: Alypius sold legal advice, while he peddled methods of persuasion.[130] Nebridius' situation was different. Like Alypius, he had come to Milan out of a desire to be with Augustine's circle of friends; but he had no need to earn his living.[131] He became a voluntary instructor for Verecundus, a pagan teacher of literature, who had requested that Augustine provide him with an assistant from among their acquaintances. Within this part of the story he is transformed into a symbol of scholarly detachment. In performing his duties, he avoided being singled out by his superiors lest worldly interests interfere with the pursuit of wisdom (8.6.20–21).

Through Nebridius, Augustine introduces a topic that has up to now remained in the story's background. This is the long-range programme of studious reading which was begun in Milan and continued at Cassiciacum in the winter and spring of 386–87. The link between the two periods of study is the figure of Verecundus, the owner of the villa where the dialogues take place, who withdraws from his secular duties as a teacher of literature. Later we learn of his desire to convert and of his premature death in Rome (9.3), through which (framed within the conversions of books 8–9) one life is finished and another begun. This is the way in which the narratives about reading in *Confessions* 1–9 will conclude at Ostia.

With these themes in place, Ponticianus[132] is then introduced, and a well-organized account begins.[133] Following the pattern of previous episodes, the reader's awareness of a divinely inspired design is created by the actor Augustine's perception that the events come about by chance. In this case, the effect is heightened by Augustine the bishop's inability to recall the date of or reason for the visit.[134] What stands out in his mind is the unusual nature of the visitor, a high official and a perfect stranger who arrives on his doorstep without warning. Yet he is an African and, "to that degree," one of them;[135] as a result, his visit lies within the range of the credible.[136] The readers share Augustine's lack of information, and they are thereby discouraged from thinking that he could be responsible for what follows.

The pair sat down, and a conversation began. Then Ponticianus noticed a book lying on a gaming table nearby; he took it up, opened it, and discovered, astonished but approving, that it was a text of Paul, whereas he had expected to find a professional manual.[137] This is the second apparently chance event in the story, and it directly foreshadows elements of Augustine's conversion. Now, as later, a codex is present, in presumed contrast to the *liber* from which rhetoric is taught. The action has three stages, as it will when "he took up, opened, and came upon the apostle Paul" (*tulit, aperuit, inuenit apostolum Paulum* 8.6.27) becomes "I took up, opened, and read the chapter" (*arripui, aperui, et legi . . . capitulum;* 8.12.32).[138] The instant (*statim*, 8.12.36) is anticipated by Ponticianus' immediate (*repente*, 8.6.30) awareness that he is in the presence of Christians. Silence is at work in both texts: at 8.12.32, Augustine is described as reading *in silentio*; at 8.6.27–28, Ponticianus is said to come upon (*inuenit*) the book and to have thought (*putauerat*) it something different without any mention of his pronouncing the words of the text.[139] Most important, the scene anticipates the problem of other minds in 8.12. The two Christians recognize each other through the offices of a third party—a book. Only Augustine is engaged in reading the Pauline epistles. Ponticianus knows what is being read, but the book is a symbol that alters his understanding of the inner life of someone else. And, by informing us that he has been studying Paul (8.6.31–34), Augustine makes it credible that his conversion could take place through a single verse of Romans later on.

Augustine notes that Ponticianus smiled and gave him a searching look (8.6.29). His visitor was taken aback to discover that he had "these texts, and these alone, before his eyes."[140] Ponticianus, he then tells us, was a Christian who frequently demonstrated his faith in God in church by prostrating himself in lengthy prayers: this detail completes the story of Victorinus, who was last seen converting publicly but not confirming his faith through repeated devotions. Augustine's mention of his studies in Paul is a reminder that he was engaged in comparative reading throughout the Milanese period[141]—another parallel (8.2.30–31). Moreover, as soon as Augustine informs Ponticianus about these studies, the story reiterates another theme. The mutual recognition of the two Christians—Alypius having conveniently dropped out of sight—gives way to the central concern of the Simplicianus episode, namely conversion.

The next phase involves a change of narrator, from Augustine to Ponticianus, as well as a move from the Pauline epistles to the living histories of Anthony and the monastic brethren who dwell outside the walls of Milan (8.6.34–48). Just as Augustine "reveals"[142] to Ponticianus that he has been studying Paul, so his visitor discloses a number of stories "which remained concealed down to that hour"[143] from Augustine and his friends. Moreover, in the first part of the story Augustine proceeds from the visual recognition of a text to the reader's implied state of mind, whereas in the second his interest lies in the internal "conversation"[144] that ensues: this is a commentary that involves two persons and two subjects and is thus a more complicated version of Augustine's interpretation of Ambrose's preaching, its obvious model. In this configuration, Paul represents the letter, that is, the basis for a common recognition of objective truth in two strangers—while the story of Anthony is the spirit, that is, what Augustine transforms subjectively and intentionally into a guide for his life. After he tells Ponticianus that he has been "deliberating" over "the sacred texts" of Paul, Ponticianus "tells the story of Anthony," thereby giving a new direction to their "discussion."[145] Paul's letters link the two phases of the narrative rather than the *Vita Antonii*, which Augustine gives no evidence of having read.[146]

In the telling of Anthony's story, what is said to Augustine and Alypius, as Ponticianus' audience, is not said to us, as their audience. We do not in fact learn the events of Anthony's life. Our knowledge will be completed only by Augustine's conversion, when we are informed of the central events through his paraphrase. What we are told about is the effect that "the ignorance" of Augustine and Alypius had on Ponticianus (8.6.37–39). When Ponticianus found out that they were uninstructed concerning this exemplary life, Augustine notes, "he lingered over it, elaborating what he had said . . . concerning so remarkable a man, marvelling all the while at our lack of knowledge." For their part, they "were stupefied, hearing of such wondrous events . . . witnessed so recently, virtually in their own time" (8.6.36–40).[147] They knew nothing of contemporary Egyptian or even Milanese monasticism.[148] The latter was personally patronized by the bishop of Milan, who reappears as a historical figure and as an influence on the interpretive methods taking shape.

Thus the middle segment of the Ponticianus episode ends (8.6.34–47). Writing some two years later, Augustine reveals that he was curious enough about the local brethren to seek them out for himself.[149] Yet it is not institutional arrangements that we hear about in *Confessions* 8, neither those of anchorites nor those of the wandering ascetics, whose imperfect imitation of the desert fathers he roundly criticized in 401,[150] the year the autobiography was completed. Instead, he juxtaposes the ascetic models of Paul and Anthony. Paul is a distant icon, whose words remind him that he can constrain his sensuality only through an effort of will; Anthony is nearer in time and holds out the possibility of a holy life that he can attempt to imitate. The same combination of a book and a living narrative appears in the final conversion scene, 8.12. The allusions to the monastic life also look beyond this event to the theme of transcendence in book 9. The suggestion arises from his use of images of a utopian community based on Psalms 77:52, in which he speaks of the "flocks of monasteries," the "customs so sweet" to God, and the "fertile deserts of the wilderness."[151]

The final episode of the story (8.6.47–86) returns to the topic of individual conversion. However, it differs from what has come before in having established a context of group participation and joint progress toward salvation, as if Augustine's earlier reference to kindred spirits "inflaming" each other (8.4.7–8) were becoming a reality. Through the interrelated stories of conversion which culminate in this *exemplum,* he likewise brings the secular and religious lifestyles together within a single narrative. The story of Anthony is a by-product of the mutual recognition of Paul; the stories of contemporary monasticism are illustrations; and the anecdote of two imperial officials in Trier provides an additional commentary[152] that brings the issues within the reach of men like Augustine and Alypius. Finally, this segment of Ponticianus' story presents the final variant in the uses of reading before the garden scene. The verbally related life of

Anthony is reconfigured as a book, and in this form it works its transfor-
mational magic as it is read. In the logic of the narrative, therefore, we
have an interlude of verbal discussion between two scenes built around a
single device, Augustine's reading of Paul and the anonymous officials'
reading of the life of Anthony. In the final conversion, the only novelty is
to collapse the different actors into the person of Augustine himself.

In this segment of the Ponticianus narrative, which we and Augustine
hear about simultaneously, there is an appropriate change in the location
of silence. In the preceding part, Augustine hears the story of Anthony,
but the reader remains in silence. Now it is Augustine and Alypius who
are silent, as they listen attentively to what Ponticianus says.[153] We know
that this story involves God's design, because its narrator offers us the
symbolic clue of not recalling when it happened.[154] Another indication is
the verbal echo of "circus spectacle," the most powerful image from the
fragmentary life history of Alypius, whose own story the two listeners know
but which Ponticianus presumably does not know.[155] While the emperor,
who is then in Trier, remains at the games (a symbol of false majesty and
of make-believe chance), Ponticianus and three companions go for a walk
in the gardens near the town walls. The detail reiterates and reinforces two
already present narrative motifs. Augustine will shortly employ the image
of the garden in the utopian setting of his own conversion; and he has
already mentioned the monastic communities living outside the walls of
Milan. The two references, separated by only one sentence, can be thought
of as parts of a single train of thought; and it is this, as well as the life of
Anthony, for which they furnish a typological *exemplum*.

The strollers divided into pairs, one remaining with Ponticianus, the
others wandering off on their own.[156] But their destination was worked
out in advance. They "made their way into a certain house," possibly
through the right of inspection. To their surprise, they found evidence that
it was inhabited by Christians,[157] humble brethren like those about whom
Ponticianus had been speaking. These were persons in God's service, the
meek in spirit living in "the kingdom of heaven."[158] Moreover, a codex
was found in the cottage in which the life of Anthony was written.[159] The
two officials were converted by reading it, one after the other, and decided
to leave the imperial service.

We have, then, a stage set within a woodland pleasaunce, and the absent
dwellers of this rustic but spiritually pure locale placed before us. The Life
that they found in the brethren's house was probably the Latin translation
of Evagrius of Antioch, completed around 371. Again we remain in
ignorance about what they actually saw, but we can guess: *Vita Antonii 2*,
in which the saint "entered church, at which time it happened that the

gospel was being read."[160] In place of the text, Augustine focuses on the response of one of the *agentes in rebus*. The description in 8.6.58–75 moves considerably beyond his earlier accounts of the psychology of conversion,[161] as becomes clear from the list of actions in the opening sentence (8.6.56–58):

| | |
|---|---|
| Quam [uitam] | One of them began |
| legere coepit unus eorum | to read [the Life], |
| et mirari | and he marvelled |
| et accendi | and was set ablaze, |
| et inter legendum | and, while he read, |
| meditari | he thought |
| arripere talem uitam | of seizing such a life |
| et relicta militia saeculari | and abandoning his |
| seruire tibi. | secular position in the military |
| | to serve you [God]. |

Around the major divisions of the sentence, *legere* and *meditari,* are grouped the developments found in earlier descriptions of conversion: wonder, the firing of the mind, and, while one reads, a transport of thought, with the result that one way of life is abandoned and another taken up. The novel element is the phrase *inter legendum meditari,* which indicates the role of literary memory, since the text in question is retained in the mind as the official reflects upon it. Another novel feature is the linking of the sudden decision to change *(arripere)* and the imposition of discipline *(seruire)*. We proceed from one Life, which is a text to be read *(legendum),* to another, which is a life to be lived: the text informs the life, as discipline informs conduct.

The official was filled with "sacred love" and "sobering shame."[162] He and his companion were members of an imperial service that was frequently engaged in gathering intelligence—worldly information that was useless for the soul's progress. The simple piety of the absent brethren laid bare the shallowness of these instrusive activities. They were humbled—not by what they knew of the cottage's inhabitants, since they were absent, but by the knowledge that was present, which was based on the codex. Moreover, from their reading of Anthony's life, they imaginatively reconstructed the lives of the cottagers—which is what Augustine was learning to do for himself. Augustine ties their lives to his by a literary and philosophical idea that has already appeared in one variant and is repeated in the final conversion scene—other minds. The official who read the life of Anthony is described as "turning his eyes toward his friend."[163] He does so because his friend cannot know what is in his thoughts; he has to be told. Only then does his companion ask what they hoped to achieve through their mundane activities. Could they attain anything higher than the perilous position of "friends of the Emperor"?[164] They conclude that in the secular world, the higher one mounts, the greater the risks, whereas in becoming the "friend of God" nothing is left to chance and everything is brought about at once (8.6.60–66).

These words are a sign that the official is "pregnant" with "new life" (compare Romans 6:4). The term *turgidus* (swollen) gives a positive meaning to a metaphor that is used negatively in the *Confessions'* opening prayer, in the conversion to philosophy by the *Hortensius,* and in the pride with which the unknown purveyor of his translation introduced him to neoplatonism (1.1.4–5; 3.5.7; 7.9.5). The ensuing experience also recalls the Ciceronian and neoplatonic conversions in describing how the official "turned his eyes back toward the pages; and within, where God has a privileged view, he was transformed, and his mind was cleansed of worldliness."[165] While the anonymous *agens in rebus* read, his heart was in turbulence; he then uttered a cry, and his decision was made;[166] he told his friend that he had broken with his former ambitions and had decided to serve God. To complete the metaphorical cycle, Augustine's term for this breaking off is *abrumpere,* a variant of the verbs formerly used to describe the abrupt change of heart brought about by the reading of scripture.

The convert asked his friend "to imitate" his example or, if he did not wish to do so, at least not to oppose his decision.[167] This is the first occurrence in chapter 6 of the verb *imitari;* yet mimesis is in Augustine's thoughts all along. Ponticianus then reappeared on the scene after having taken a different route through the park; this is a final detail in the episode's garden symbolism. The converts informed him of their desire to remain in the cottage. Ponticianus and the fourth companion wept and offered their congratulations, asking their friends to pray on their behalf. The unconverted pair returned, "dragging their hearts along the ground," while the others stayed on, "affixing their hearts to heaven." And their wives followed them into the monastic life (8.6.80–86).

## Augustine

The third episode of book 8 is the account of Augustine's conversion (8.7–12).[168] This is the subtlest of the stories in organization.[169] Augustine addresses the reader straightforwardly, recounting one event after the other in a paratactic style.[170] Syntactic subordination is less apparent than in other parts of the *Confessions,* but it reappears in the narrative structure.

This technique heightens the role of the reader's memory in relating the parts to the whole. The stories that have come before have to be kept in mind, as well as critical events and discussions in the previous seven books. At the same time, the preceding episode consolidates Augustine's thinking about past and future narratives. His understanding of the two threads of the story—the tale of the bureaucrats in Trier and the account of his failed attempts at reform—is comparable to the way in which he separates the "literal" and "spiritual" senses in book 7. The literal corresponds to what Ponticianus says; the spiritual grows out of his thinking about himself, which stands in relation to the enunciated narrative as a commentary does to a text.[171]

His narrative memories also form the basis of an internal dialogue in which the positions for and against a change of lifestyle are dramatized by three allegorized interlocuters, Conscience, Custom, and Continence (8.7.34–37). The conversation begins before Ponticianus stops speaking,[172] when Augustine asks Alypius, "Why are we passive? . . . Why do we just listen? The uninstructed rise up and seize the heavens, while we—educated but spineless—wallow in flesh and blood [Matt. 16:17]. They have gone before us. Why do we fear to follow?" (8.8.4–7).

A key expression in this animated statement is *caelum rapiunt* (8.8.5), which reiterates an already announced theme drawn from Matthew 5:3 and especially from Matthew 11:12, where it is written that "the kingdom of heaven has suffered violence, and men of violence take it by force."[173] At the moment of conversion, of course, the kingdom to be taken is Augustine's soul.[174] The statement that he makes to Alypius is a step between the long-range goal of achieving a contemplative utopia (Matt. 5:3) and the immediate desire for a violent break with the past (Matt. 11:12). Augustine the bishop observes: "I said this, not knowing quite what I was saying, and the commotion of my mind violently tore me from him [*abripuit*], while Alypius, astonished, remained silent, fixing his gaze on me" (8.8.7–9).[175]

In the space of a few lines, we witness changes in relations of gesture and speech, custom and innovation, and sound and silence. Alypius is cut off from Augustine's inner commotion and can observe what is taking place only through his friend's gestures. Augustine tries to escape from the "mortal burden of custom" (8.7.42) and speaks in a language that violates the customs of speech. While he attempts to resolve these tensions, the meaningful silence of his mute fear *(muta trepidatio)* is reflected in Alypius' speechlessness (*cum taceret*, 8.8.8). Alypius expresses the meaning of his silence: this is a step toward a dual conversion in which each participant witnesses the other's change of heart from the outside.

The friends proceed to the "little garden" of their rented house which is theirs to use while the landlord is absent. In speaking of use (*utor*), Augustine implies the complement, enjoyment (*frui*),[176] just as, in the literal garden, the *signum,* he has in mind the *res,* the symbolic reality for which it stands. This is an actual garden, a few steps from the house (8.8.24–25); it is also one of four gardens that have a symbolic significance in books 8 and 9. The conversion scene of the previous story takes place in a garden (8.6.51, 76); the villa of Cassiciacum provides the "philosophical dialogues" with a comparable setting (9.2.15–18); and the "vision at Ostia" occurs while Augustine and his mother stand before a window overlooking the yard of the house in which they are temporarily lodged (9.10.4–5).

The *agentes in rebus* in Trier had no idea what awaited them in the humble cottage into which they intruded; similarly, Augustine does not know what God has in store for him[177] when he takes "the tumult that is in his breast" outdoors (8.8.11–14).[178] Alypius follows "step by step," as did the companion of the bureaucrat who chanced upon the Life of Anthony.[179] Whereas this tale is unrelated to other events in *Confessions* 1–9, the behaviour of Alypius appears to complement that in the story told about him in book 6: at the Roman games Alypius maintained that he was able to be there in person but to direct his attention elsewhere; here he is present but absent from his friend's thoughts.[180] The isolation foreshadows the meditative state in which Augustine will convert after his attention has been diverted from the outer to the inner world by the *tolle, lege* chant. Finally, in narrating the initial phases of his conversion in this way, Augustine reverses still another established pattern in the previous books. Having repeatedly opposed religious esotericism, he forewarns the reader that his is to be a private conversion, a change of heart known only to him. Yet it is witnessed publicly by Alypius, and thereby responds to Augustine's criticism of gnostic and neoplatonic systems of ascent (the latter implied in the story of Victorinus) in which there are no exterior criteria of validation.

On entering the garden, Augustine finds himself able to resolve a number of hitherto intractable questions concerning the will. He realizes that when he performs actions over which he apparently has no control—for example, expressing strong emotions before Alypius—his will continues to operate, even though the signals between his mind and body are interrupted. Why is the mind obeyed instantly when it gives orders to the body and yet resisted when it gives orders to itself? In his view, the lack of coordination between thought and action is a legacy of the garden of Eden in which each person bears the responsibility for original sin but deals with that commitment in a distinctive way (8.9.1–5, 11–16; 8.10.18–20): "When I deliberated over the possibility of serving God as my lord, as I had long ago decided I should, it was 'I' who was willing and 'I' who was unwilling: it was just 'I.' I was not fully willing and I was not fully unwilling. I was thus in conflict with myself, even dissociated from myself ... Moreover, this state of affairs did not come about through the operation of someone else's mind: it was a pain endured by my own mind. Nor was it brought about by someone who was not yet me; for sin already dwelt in me [Romans 7:17, 20]. It was the punishment of someone freer than I was, since I was the son of Adam" (8.10.13–20). How then can the belief in the will's singularity be reconciled with conflicting worldly desires?[181] In contrast to the Manichaean argument for the existence of good and evil in everyone,[182] Augustine concludes that two wills can coexist in the same individual as long as the alternatives are considered simultaneously. Furthermore, although a pair of actions can be thought about at once, they cannot be spoken or carried out at once (that is, sequentialized by means of words or deeds).[183] The competing alternatives result in a single choice, which moves the soul upwards or downwards on an ethical scale (8.10.38–64).

The point about "following" the Trier bureaucrats is thereby clarified. The deity expresses his will for us in a form that we understand as a narrative, and, if we interpret this correctly, we have a basis for limited self-improvement. This type of imitation is an answer to dualism, in which man's soul can have no higher ethical basis for decision-making than the materiality of the self. Basing itself on a real life, mimetic self-reform is also a corrective to an overly Platonic interpretation of the literal and figurative, in which historical factors can be explained away.[184] If we return momentarily to the story of Victorinus at 8.5, we can see this thinking mirrored in two senses of *narrare* that are framed within the gerundive *ad imitandum* (8.5.1–2). The one refers to the earthly intentions of Simplicianus in telling the story, the other to God, who prearranges for it to be told. Out of these emerges the *uoluntas noua* (8.5.14–15).

Chapter 11 takes the reader back to the internal, first-person dialogue of 8.7.30–35, in which Conscience asks Augustine why his decision has taken so long. His break (*abrumpere*, 8.11.3, 6)[185] remains a distant goal. He repeats to himself, "Let it be now, let it be now," a refrain that is matched, at 8.12.20, with the audible words, "Take it up and read, take it up and read." Just as the command to read is the point at which his final conversion begins, the words that he utters internally move him toward a positive decision in his reflections.[186] He speaks of himself as an indecisive lover,[187] but this more accurately describes the state of mind that he was attempting to leave behind *(inolitum)* than the unaccustomed one *(insolitum)* that was emerging in his thoughts.

Moving inwards, he finds his tongue at last (compare 8.7.30–31). However, he answers a question that Conscience did not originally ask[188] concerning his sexual involvements and his entry into the religious life— the theme of 8.1 and the final instalment of his "life" of Alypius. The last hurdle[189] is his resistance to his libertine past, whose memories "tug at the garment of flesh," whispering, so to speak, behind his back as he departs, hurling barbs at him in the hope that he will succumb to his memories. But these voices have lost their persuasive power.[190] In the direction in which he has turned but toward which he fears to advance, "the chaste dignity of Continence"[191] suddenly appears, serene and joyous, enticing him honorably and calming his doubts (8.11.31–36). Her good "examples" are exemplary lives; he calls them *greges,* the term that he uses at 8.6.43 when recalling Ponticianus' description of the "flocks of monasteries" of contemporary religious life.

This utopia has been transformed from a living community to an ideal congregation[192] consisting of boys and girls, youths, widows, virgins, and Continence herself, who is portrayed as a fertile matron, wedded to the Lord, whose sons are her joys. Distantly echoing the *Hortensius,* which long ago "exhorted" Augustine to convert to philosophy, Continence delivers an "exhortation" in soft tones that mimic the immediately preceding appeal of Custom.[193] She mocks the self-reliance of his youthful philosophical rationalism, which he had himself used as an *exemplum* in the second story of Alypius. He blushes, since the voice of Custom is still within earshot.[194] Continence tells him to plug his ears against the call of his earthly members (8.11.40–47). Hearing nothing outside and seeing only inwardly, he avoids the error of Alypius at the games, when he closed his eyes but left his ears open to temptation (6.8.20–24).

Where did Augustine find the inspiration for this unusual vision?[195] One possibility is the allegory of the virtues in the Manichaean *Thesaurus,* which he quotes at length in *De Natura Boni* in 399.[196] In this fable, an all-powerful God reconfigures himself as a group of chaste men and women who battle the hostile, insatiable race that inhabit the heavens.[197] The light-giving youths implement God's will by appearing before their enemies disguised as their mates; in the ensuing sexual unions, entrapped particles of light are released from imprisonment, and the souls of the fallen return to their "native abode" on high. Augustine may have modeled his pair of allegories in 8.11 as a response to such fables, thereby satirizing their dualistic structure through his alternatives.

From "the hidden depths" of these ideas and his personal reflections on his life, his previous misfortunes are brought forward and displayed before "the gaze of his heart."[198] He weeps,[199] while Alypius looks on "in silence" at his "unaccustomed agitation."[200] The reappearance of his friend is a sign that the perspective of the narrator, the observer, and the reader are uniting in a single understanding of the events to come. In parallel with Simplicianus' story, Alypius takes the part of the congregation in the church in which Victorinus made his profession of faith; he also bears witness to its arcane, unknowable, and yet predestined nature. Augustine calls his process of self-examination *consideratio* (8.12.1); it is envisaged as a prelude to the conversion, in which his "struggle is changed into happiness" (8.12.55; Ps. 29:12) and he attains *contemplatio* (9.2.1–5). As Alypius stands by, he observes the two key steps in this transformation, the breaking with custom and the awareness of silence; these features are incorporated into the narrative of 8.12.

He withdraws to a more remote part of the garden, so that his friend's presence will not be a distraction.[201] *Negotium* implicitly contrasts with his goal of *otium* (as Alypius, who is present, contasts with Nebridius, who is absent). The "remoter" corner[202] is the place where his struggle is resolved, memorialized habits are overcome, and a vision of monastic utopia reappears. In this transformed *locus amoenus*[203] he finds himself beneath a real and symbolic fig tree.[204] Alypius configures the change of locale and draws attention to its inward, spiritual significance. "This was my state," Augustine observes, "and he sensed it: for I think I may have said something in which the sound of my voice already indicated that it was heavy with tears. And so I got up, while he remained where we had been seated, totally astonished" (8.12.7–9).

The phrases in which Augustine recaptures the words that he spoke[205] at that moment are those of Psalms 78:5.[206] To his question, "How long, how long," a voice, responding, mocks him with the words "Tomorrow, tomorrow." Yet his own voice reiterates, "Why not now?" (8.12.16–17). The poetic sing-song within his mind (*Quandiu, quandiu, cras, cras,* 8.12.16) then gives way to one that arises outside, as he hears from the neighbouring house the chanting of a boy or girl—again, he is not sure—repeating "Pick it up, read it, pick it up, read it . . ."[207] Emphasizing the inwardness, he reveals his state of mind as previously in external gestures.[208]

The words that are used to describe his thoughts have by now acquired definite associations within the narrative. The verb *mutare* is employed in the context of his reading of Cicero and in the conversion of the bureaucrats in Trier.[209] The fact that *tolle, lege* is not a habitual, or "customary," refrain of children in Milan is a reminder that he is about to break once and for all with his habitual past (for example, *solito*, 8.11.2; cf. 8.8.9). The *pueri an puellae* of 8.12.20 reinstates the motif of the *pueri et puellae* of 8.11.36. However, in 8.11, Augustine is entirely within his own thoughts, cut off from the world; in 8.12, his thinking[210] begins in a world that lies somewhere between the inner and the outer, the literal and the symbolic.[211] It is tempting to adopt the interpretation of the transcriber of the *Confessions* who replaced *uicina domo* with *diuina domo* (8.12.19), since it is not the neighbour's house but the house of God that is in his thoughts.[212]

The play element in 8.12.21–22 may recall a series of events that proceed from Augustine's childhood (1.10.9–13) to the moment of Ponticianus' chance discovery of the Pauline epistles in his possession (8.6.26)—events that underline the rudimentary level of his early interpretive skills and his former illusions concerning the power of reason.[213] However, at 8.12, the children's sing-song prefaces a more serious game of conversion concerning a book. This takes place both through predetermination, which is represented by a text established in advance, and chance (or freedom of will), which is symbolized by a random choice of verse to be read. When *tolle, lege* sounds, his tears cease—a sign that his attention to the sensory world is being replaced by a meditative state of mind. He interprets the chant as "a divine command to open the book and read the first chapter" that he comes upon.[214] When he sees the text of Romans 13:13–14, a second recollection comes into play: this is the mental record of his many sins, which are suddenly swept away as "the light of certainty infuses" his "heart."

The changes in these lines are from voices to silence and from words to texts. In his vision and in the refrain, Augustine is a listener; now he reads *in silentio* (8.12.32). The emphasis in the final scene is on writings.[215] In contrast to his conversion to philosophy, his turning toward the religious life involves hearing rather than sight.[216] The text in question is a codex, as was the discovered Pauline epistles.[217] Reading permits him to reintroduce the theme of a story within a story in an internalized manner, which lets a memorized text act as a guide for behaviour.[218] In the final act of the drama, he "takes up, opens, and reads" the text of Paul's Epistle to the Romans because he knows that Anthony was converted through a similar reading experience. The reading is the *result* of a behavioural pattern established in advance *before* it is a reading experience that can itself influence subsequent behaviour. We learn of Anthony's motive from Augustine's recollection of the text (compare 8.6.34–36). The mental record is in his thoughts as he hears the refrain *tolle, lege* (8.12.24).

His experience nonetheless differs from Anthony's on important points. True, both figures renounce the world in similar literary contexts. Anthony hears Matthew 19:21: "Go, sell all that you have, give to the poor, and you will have a treasure in heaven; and come, follow me"; the expressions *in caelis* and *ueni, sequere me* also recapture central themes in the stories of Simplicianus and Ponticianus, among them the search for the kingdom of heaven and the desire to find the right way to salvation through imitative narrative. But Anthony hears these words as he walks by an open church door: the gospel is read publicly by the celebrant of the mass, who presumably does not know of his presence. The text is thus a direct, unprecedented, and decisive intervention in his life.[219] Augustine reads Romans 13:13–14 privately. The message is a confirmation of what he already knows, since Paul is in his thoughts. The intervention is decisive, therefore, and direct, but not unprecedented. Rather it is an authoritative reminder, an example of reconceived "reminiscence."

The advice given to Anthony places his life within an already function-ing model narrative, the story of Christ. He does not create a new life history from reading, reflection, and interpretation. Augustine takes advice derived from an epistle in which Paul himself is engaged in an interpretive conversation with an implied audience: he advises Christians how to live within God's will in anticipation of the imminent return of Christ. Al-though Augustine's text asks him to renounce "the flesh and its lusts,"[220] its Pauline context also teaches his potential readers how to reorient their conduct within the overlapping narrative texts of the gospel, the *Vita Antonii,* and the *Confessions.* They "put on the garment"[221] of renewal through literature.

Augustine speaks of the life of Anthony as a story that he heard by word of mouth: "For I had heard, with respect to Anthony, that, from a reading of the gospel that he happened by chance to come upon, he was given a reminder, as if the words were addressed to him, when the text was read . . . and, by this divine pronouncement, he was instantly converted to you [Psalms 50:15]." However, we learn at 8.12.31 that Augustine leaves the text of Paul with Alypius when he withdraws into a more secluded part of the garden; and, on recalling the experience of Anthony, he hurries back to where Alypius is sitting.[222] It is only after interpreting the *tolle, lege* refrain as a "divine command" and recalling Anthony's conversion that he reiterates the threefold action that brings about his inner change: "I seized it, opened it, and read in silence the chapter on which my eyes fell."[223] He does not provide an account of how the reading affected his thinking, having already done so in the story of the first convert at Trier. He reiterates the conversion's immediacy and its irrevocable nature: "I did not wish to read further, nor was there any need. With the last of the sentence, all the clouds of doubt vanished, as if the light of certainty poured into my heart."[224]

Augustine marked his place and closed the book. With a mind now at peace he told Alypius what had taken place. He had no idea what his friend had been thinking. Alypius revealed his thoughts by repeating the sequence of events.[225] However, unlike the second convert at Trier, he was not merely persuaded by what Augustine experienced. He went through the ritual again, thereby confirming the readerly character of the conversion. He asked to see what Augustine had been reading; and, when Augustine reopened the book, his attention was drawn[226] to Romans 14:1: "Receive the person who is weak in faith." Augustine was ignorant of the text.[227] Therefore, Alypius could not simply follow his "narrative," as he had followed that of Ponticianus. Alypius took in what was written, presumably in silence; he then disclosed it to Augustine.[228] He accepted the words as divinely inspired; he decided to enter the religious life. They then went to Monica, who had evidently been in the house all the while,[229] and told the story of how it had come about—thus uniting their narratives. She rejoiced and thanked God that he had at last adopted "the rule of faith" (regula fidei, 8.12.54) as the wise bishop of Thagaste had predicted, "through his reading" (3.12.12–13).

A significant moment in Augustine's account occurs when he says that he does not know what was in Alypius' heart: it had to be revealed to him (8.12.41). This is a cumulative statement of his position on "other minds."[230] In his view, we can never really penetrate another person's thoughts. We know them only through language, that is, through the linguistic conventions by which what is private is made public. If we do not know ourselves (that is, if we cannot express what it is about ourselves that we know), then we cannot know others or express anything about them.[231] Moreover, to this revision of an ancient paradox, Augustine makes a unique contribution: his is the earliest analysis of the potential part played by reading in the creation of intersubjective thinking. Stated formally, the mediator between the private experience of two persons can be a single text. In the case of Ponticianus and Augustine, the recognition is based on a prereading. In the case of Augustine and Alypius, where different texts are involved, the common experience is reading itself.

Augustine thus returns to the problem with which his analysis of infancy begins the narrative segment of the *Confessions*. The manner in which we understand our mental activities is seen to be a function of our ability to frame our thoughts in speech. Moreover, as the story of his youth is related, the literary approach to consciousness takes shape as a direct result of his theory of narrative and self-knowledge. Our understanding of our lives is inseparable from the stories by which we represent our thoughts in words. Every understanding, therefore, is a reading of ourselves, every genuine insight, a rereading, until, progressing upwards by revisions, we have inwardly in view the essential source of knowledge, which is God. Reading, though not an end in itself, is a means of gaining higher understanding; the contents of the mind can in turn be conceptualized through the sensory relations of reading—listening and seeing. Augustine is the first to present a consistent analysis of the manner in which we organize the intentional structure of thought through this activity: he suggests that through reading a "language game" can become a "form of life."[232]

# 4

# FROM CASSICIACUM
# TO OSTIA

⁂

Two episodes in book 9 conclude Augustine's narrative about reading in the *Confessions*. The events took place at Cassiciacum and in Ostia between 22 August 386, when he resigned his chair of rhetoric, and autumn 388, when he departed for Africa.

During this period he began the "philosophical dialogues" (9.4.20–9.6),[1] whose relationship to his theory of reading is taken up in Part II. Here, as a conclusion to Part I, I am concerned with his description of oral reading at 9.2–9.4.19 and with his account of the manner in which human communication is transcended in a vision of the blessed life (9.10). These events are separated by his baptism in Milan at Easter 387 (9.6).[2]

Book 9 relates a number of stories of conversion and the afterlife. Verecundus, who lent Augustine his villa at Cassiciacum, was not yet a Christian in the autumn of 386; he became ill and converted on his deathbed (9.3.3, 9–11). Nebridius, then a Manichaean, was possibly converted in 390 and died in Africa after leading an ascetic life and bringing his aristocratic family to Christianity (9.3.24–26). Evodius, a member of the imperial police, also became a Catholic (9.8.1–4); it was he who read the psalter at Monica's funeral (9.12.25–26). Another death Augustine recalls is that of Adeodatus, who he believed "was destined to be educated in God's discipline" (9.6.20). In these episodes the second narrative of book 9 gradually takes shape, reaching its climax at Ostia.

Cassiciacum and Ostia are innerworldly and otherworldly vehicles[3] by which Augustine moves toward the concept of eternal happiness. The villa at Cassiciacum is presented in the rhetorical topos of the *locus amoenus:*[4] those staying there are suspended in time, "taking refuge from the commotion of the world in the pleasantness of God's eternally green paradise."[5] Augustine's final conversation with his mother at Ostia reflects the utopian theme in different terms: "Speaking to each other softly, and forgetting the past, we reached out to what lay before us in the future, seeking, as one, that truth already present in us, which is God, and, through it, what the future life of the saints was to be like, which no eye had seen, no ear heard, no man's heart fathomed."[6]

These alternate configurations of an ideal world stand on either side of a boundary represented by human discourse. At Cassiciacum, speaking, reading, and writing play the major roles; Augustine describes a Christianized version of classical *otium*. At Ostia, an unusual communion of minds anticipates the paradise of the elect, in which these instruments of communication have no function. Between these episodes—the one experienced temporally before baptism, the other atemporally afterwards—the logic of the *Confessions'* later books begins to be clarified.

## Cassiciacum

Augustine ascends to these visions by "steps" that are composed of psalms.[7]

Quotations from the Psalms are found throughout the *Confessions*. What is unique in book 9 is an extensive description of the reading of some verses of one psalm (Ps. 4). There is no parallel in his secular educational experience[8] for this type of reading, which reverses the negative associations of orality in grammatical instruction, Manichaean preaching, and training in rhetoric. We are not well informed on the stages by which Augustine reached this change in outlook: there was no radical break with his technique of reading before audiences at Cassiciacum (9.4.20–25) or in his method of composition through "soliloquy" or "conversation."[9] Yet the reading and writing of this period effectively transformed the later ancient "spiritual exercise" into a public literary experience while retaining its personal, private, and interior character.[10] "How I raised my voice to you, my God, in reading the Psalms of David," he recalls. "How I raised my voice in those psalms, and how I was inflamed in you because of them, how I burned to read them out, if I could have, to the whole world" (9.4.20–21, 25–27). His tears flowed[11] in a desire for emotional community.[12]

As James O'Donnell observes, there is "little in ancient literature" that "resembles" this description, which occurs near the *Confessions'* "midpoint."[13] However, there are precedents in the devotional and liturgical practices of Jews, Jewish-Christians, and the desert fathers, all of which utilized meditative reading of the Psalms. Up to now, Augustine has been concerned with learning to read (passively before book 7, actively afterwards): he now offers the first evidence of its "fruits" in his religious life. There are two audiences. Monica is literally present, since it is in her company that he will subsequently transcend the universe of signs. His readers are the designated audience of both the reading and the postreading episodes, since, with Monica gone, they are the only witnesses other than Augustine himself to the momentary experience of a higher reality which the pair enjoy.[14]

In describing his emotions, Augustine speaks in terms that recall the period just before his conversion in 8.12: "I trembled with fear and hope . . . and everything I felt came forth through my eyes and my voice."[15] He expresses inward thoughts before himself and God (*mecum et mihi coram te,* 9.4.40), thereby complementing the famous prayer at *Soliloquia* 2.1.1 *(Noverim me, noverim te)* through the mediation of the biblical text. However, in contrast to the garden scene in Milan, there is no dramatic change in outlook. Instead, he speaks of an Ambrosian programme of scriptural studies[16] interspersed with secular texts. The emphasis is much less on neoplatonic illumination than on sessions of deliberative reflection. Within that scheme, he wishes to reorient the ethical direction of his conduct rather than to collect information through a comparative scrutiny of texts. As he works toward this objective, words, phrases, and verses from the Psalms are reinterpreted within the narrative of the life that he intends to live.[17]

There is evidence that this type of thinking was relatively new to him in 386; it occurs in *Confessions* 10.33, where he recalls how difficult he once found resisting "the pleasures of the ears." Voice and song, he argues, affect our emotions in a secretive and yet familiar manner[18] that overpowers reason.[19] Shortly after the garden scene, he was moved to tears while listening to hymns sung in church; only later did his mind awaken to the content of the biblical statements.[20] He believed that liturgy should not be deprived of its beauty, but he was mindful of the advice given by Athanasius to his lector to "pronounce" rather than "make melodies" of the Psalms (10.33.18–25).

Reading aloud in the villa garden, he is led in a comparable fashion from aesthetics to ascetic exercises. He seeks the permanent message that lies beyond the auditory impressions; he thereby anticipates the transcending of those linguistic impressions at Ostia. Moreover, he makes an assumption that is not made in the case of secular texts, namely that the meaning of the whole can be retained in memory while the sensory effects are distributed among the parts. Reading, he listens, and listening, he recollects what he has read (9.4.88–98). He thus builds an internal tradition of his emotions.[21]

As in 11.27, memory is the key to this type of reading. In general, there are two types at work.

First, 9.4 vividly recreates the months spent in productive leisure at Cassiciacum (9.4.2–7, 99–101). The "commemoration of all God's benefits" (9.4.9–10) is "witnessed" by his books, by his letters to Nebridius,[22] and by prayer.[23] Reading and memory form an "inchoate meditation on his renewal."[24]

However, the purpose of this level of recall is to create a circumstantial backdrop for a more abstract, ethically oriented consideration of memory, in which two other levels can be distinguished. Memory sets up parallels between what he reads and the life he once led. A specific text thus acts as a touchstone for a narrative sequence and its negative moral values.[25] As he hears his voice, he trembles, recognizing the "falsehoods" that he has internalized as narratives, erroneously taking them for truths (9.4.58–59). Also, memory operates by means of allusion. The relationship between Psalm 4 and the "text" of his life is supported by words and phrases drawn from other psalms.[26] The vocabulary of his recent reading, so rearranged, is imposed on past experience, which is in turn reshaped.[27]

In the process, the theological context of the originals is altered. The references to the Psalms are framed within a Christocentric discussion that depends on quotations from Romans 2:5 (9.4.69), on 2 Corinthians 4:18 (9.4.72), and on Ephesians 5:8 (9.4.77) and 4:22 (9.4.82). These statements refer respectively to the obstinacy of man's heart, for which God has retribution in store; to God's power, which comes to our aid when we are confused and bewildered; to the good in man, which he rewards; and to the delusions of the carnal senses,[28] which is the persistent source of man's moral weakness.[29]

This approach is unlike that of Manichaean hermeneutics in uniting Old and New Testament themes (9.4.31–41; compare 9.4.65–69). But has Augustine put their methods entirely behind him? As he reads outside in eye and voice and inside in feeling and mind,[30] his experience of the Psalms contrasts with his failure to understand the first chapter of Isaiah, which Ambrose set him on his return from the country; and further back we are reminded of his indifference to the style of scripture after encountering the *Hortensius* (3.5). In view of his boast that he was able to comprehend difficult philosophical texts without the aid of tuition (4.16.6–7), what is the source of his emphatic *non intellegens* (9.5.10–11)? He may have retained a lingering distrust of the Hebrew prophetic books.[31] Or he may have paid attention only to what he wanted to hear in Psalm 4, which speaks in the first person *(inuocarem)*, asking God repeatedly to listen to the subject's prayer *(exaudiuit; exaudi orationem meam; exaudiet me dum clamauero)*, and makes mention of vanity and lies *(quid diligitis uanitatem et quaeretis men-dacium)*, in which statements he could see a gloss on his career ambitions; also the text dwells on the heart, hope, sacrifice, illumination, and peace—themes that were already in his thoughts.[32] Only later would he take up the general subject of sin in the Bible. Then he would write a very different book, *The City of God*.

## Ostia

In contrast to the utopian ideal at Cassiciacum, which is realized in the present, the vision at Ostia is a glimpse of the future blessed life.

The vision is shared by Monica, who plays no significant part in the discussions in the "philosophical dialogues." The episode is preceded by a lengthy portrait of her[33] at literal and figurative levels. The account of her adolescence and marriage is realistic (9.8–9), while, in deliberate contrast, the events at Ostia draw attention to her ideal qualities. Augustine knew her life history well enough to recall her youthful tipsiness (9.8.24–57; cf. 6.2.6–7). As her end neared, he was consoled that she thought him an obedient son who had never addressed her harshly (9.12.16–20). His devotion was unquestioning,[34] though marred by occasional deceptions. After the death of Patrick when he was about seventeen, she assumed the role of the Roman *paterfamilias*.[35] He repeatedly expresses his admiration for her uncluttered faith (for example, 9.12.67–69).

Beginning in infancy, she appears in episodes involving spiritual crisis and moral development. The stage is set in 1.11, where, as a child, Augustine is seriously ill with a fever. She prepares for his baptism at his request only to find that he has been mysteriously cured (1.11.1–16). During the turbulent period of his puberty, it is she alone who has some influence on his behaviour (2.3.27–32). She is the "Dido" who weeps for him at the shrine of St. Cyprian when he leaves Carthage secretively in 383. Her visions foretell his recovery from subsequent illness (5.8–9); her good cheer revives his low spirits in Milan (6.1.6–11). Her skill in divine matters is frequently noted.[36] These human details throw the extrahuman experience of book 9 into relief.[37]

Augustine advises her to "persist in her habits and ways of thinking,"[38] whereas he battles to overcome his own. He feels the need of documentary support for his statements on religious issues. She needs none, yet she speaks with authority.[39] At Ostia, as she stands before the window of their temporary lodgings, she communicates with him from within her heart: this capacity is subtly foreshadowed in the account of her education, which takes place entirely within.[40] She is not raised by her parents, merely entrusted to their care (9.9.1–2), in contrast to the young Augustine, who has to be disciplined by his teachers.[41] She is, by his standards at least, uneducated, and that is her advantage: she can teach him by example rather than by argument. She becomes his first model of saintliness.[42] She stands for inspired wisdom, while he represents those who learn in slow painful stages. She does not need to read;[43] he can learn only by reading. She has no need of interpretive theory.[44] Their meeting of minds is achieved despite a difference of methods.[45]

Only when details of Monica's life story have been related does Augustine lead the reader to the world of pure mind or spirit in 9.10.[46] The meaning of the scene is conveyed to the reader through the reiterated image of the garden. As Monica's departure from this life and Augustine's return to Africa near, he and his mother stand before a window overlooking the modest interior garden of their hostel at Ostia.[47] Like the garden in Milan, this is a place of internal action, and like the scene at Cassiciacum, it is presented in visual images[48] and perceived through the senses, in contrast to the Milanese garden, where the focus is not on scenic detail but on Augustine's confused thoughts. Moreover, the symbolic element arises out of an *act* of visual perception rather than from rhetorical topoi. Augustine and Monica are inside the house, and their view of the miniature landscape is literally framed by an open window, thereby representing a world that is close at hand but separated by a barrier, like the spiritual life that they ardently desire but have not yet attained. Even the window is a banal symbol of promise: it is their source of light.

The scene that anticipates this inward vision is Augustine's observation of Ambrose reading silently at 6.3. Like her son's mentor, Monica transcends her senses and finds the resources for spiritual ascent within herself.[49] Just as the bishop of Milan seeks leisure in self-imposed isolation, so Augustine and his mother look for peace and quiet amid the crowds milling about in the port.[50] However, in contrast to the earlier episode, neither Augustine nor Monica achieves inner calm through reading. Indeed, it is Augustine the bishop's design that they cannot. As they talk before the window, they ascend to higher levels of understanding while their conventional dependence on signs weakens to the point of vanishing.

In this respect, the setting at Ostia completes the symbolism of ideal states as the narrative of the *Confessions* nears its end. The three gardens, those of Milan, Cassiciacum, and Ostia, symbolize Augustine's views of the

blessed life before conversion, after it takes place, and as he looks forward
to the "eternal Jerusalem" (9.13.54–55). Also, as the pair of speakers interpenetrate each other's minds, they cease to be mother and son and become
spiritual kin.[51] The higher they rise toward union,[52] the more meaningless
their age and gender differences become. No longer a parent, Monica
becomes Augustine's companion and guide. If their dialogue echoes
Aeneas' meeting with his deceased father in the underworld in *Aeneid* 6, it
looks forward to the journey taken by Dante under the guidance of Virgil
and St. Bernard.

The moment of insight can be contrasted with Augustine's failed attempts at communication at school, with the Manichaeans, during the
tenure of his professorship, and, most movingly, in his conversations with
his fellow students in Carthage after the death of a close friend. At 9.10,
the occasion is fleeting, but a genuine meeting of minds takes place. This
is his final attempt to see his image of himself taking shape in dialogue with
another living person. From this moment, he envisages the self in isolation
from the world, as he reads, meditates, and "dialogues" with himself.

In invoking such themes, Ostia is not only a scene of remembering: it
is the other side of reminiscence.[53] Fixing their gaze on things to come,[54]
he and Monica leave behind them the past of their bodily lives while they
rediscover a state of mind that has been forgotten since Eden.[55] Conferring
"sweetly" with each other, they inquire into the perpetual life of the saints
(9.10.7–10). It is in this sense that they drink at the fountain of everlasting
life.[56]

The medium through which the pair's ascent takes place is human
language (*sermo*, 9.10.14; *dum loquimur*, 9.10.27). Their words to each other
are the steps of their mutual ascent beyond all corporeal things (including
the sun, the moon, and the stars; 9.10.14–19), just as Augustine's reading
of the Psalms is a *canticum graduum*. They move upwards and inwards,
"thinking, talking to each other, and marvelling at God's works": they enter
their minds mutually as they transcend those minds; they find themselves
at length in a region of unending abundance, where God nourishes "Israel"
on truth and where life consists of the wisdom in which all things are
created[57]—it is a place where the terms "past" and "future" have no
meaning.[58] Speaking gently to each other, they come within reach of their
goal in shared "heartbeats." Then, with a sigh, they abandon this realm of
pure mind: they hear each other speaking human words, physical sounds
that have a beginning and an end, in contrast to the ageless and ever-re-
newed Word of God.[59]

This celebrated episode, which defies paraphrase, has been much discussed, and one of the focal points of debate is the role of Plotinus, whose terminology for spiritual ascent appears to be echoed in Augustine's language, even if no single text of the *Enneads* is responsible for the conversation between mother and son.[60] As a consequence of the debts, it is legitimate to ask whether the ecstasy is genuinely Plotinian, or whether (as Augustine's point of departure in Paul suggests)[61] it is a mystical and contemplative transcending of the limits of human minds.[62] In other words, what sort of "heaven" does Augustine have in mind (9.10.19) in the context of a descriptive phrase evidently taken from Romans 8:23, namely "first things of the spirit" (*primitiae spiritus,* 9.10.29)?[63] Does the "firstness" refer to the beatitude of the saints in the next world, that is, to a primitivism recovered (as one might expect of his views in 397),[64] or to the soul in ascent in this world, as strict neoplatonism would require?[65]

The alternatives may be reconcilable. There is an intellectual component in the vision, as well as a mystical component in which the limitations of human knowledge are momentarily superseded. As in book 7, neoplatonic immanence and transcendence are absorbed into a Christian framework. The episode completes the purification by "light-giving"[66] that was begun by the comparative reading of the *libri Platonicorum* and Paul.[67] Augustine and his mother are led from their senses to beyond their mental capacities while they pass from a temporal to a temporarily eternal experience. This is what they will know of wisdom (*sapientia,* 9.10.23) and nothing more—a view that is reasserted in *De Trinitate* 12–15. The nontemporal otherness of the otherworld is emphasized: it is the "region," in which God dwells, where "life is the wisdom by which all things are made, both those that have been and those that are about to be."

In his earlier accounts of Plotinian ascent, Augustine stresses the manner in which a neoplatonic hierarchy of the senses proceeds from images of hearing toward those of outer and inner sight. At *Confessions* 9.10 the order is reversed. A visual framework—the sight of the garden outside the house—acts as a background for an ascent described largely in auditory terms. Although the experience is intense, it does not endure: Augustine hints at the fleeting nature of all such inspiration—a topic that he also touches upon in *De Doctrina Christiana* in another context.[68] He states that the pleasures of the senses are "hardly worthy of commemoration";[69] at the same time, the conversation is marked by sensorily perceived verbs of motion,[70] thereby creating the impression of a narrative sequence. Finally, the episode invites comparison with book 10, where he argues that the "places" of classical memory theory are not to be envisaged as physical locations in the brain but as functions of our ability to recall: at Ostia, the "pleasant place" is not a location but a point of departure for insight into mind or soul.[71]

This is also a region of silence. Beginning with speech (*dicebamus ergo*, 9.10.33; *dicebam*, 9.10.52), Monica prepares her departure from the world of time.[72] As we read of their conversation,[73] it becomes clear that Augustine is not referring solely to the unvoiced intervals between syllables: silence is a symbol for the ideal world. If certain "silences" prevailed, we would be able "to hear" God's word as it is, not through "the tongue of the flesh, the voice of an angel, the sound of thunder, or figurative comparison." For that to take place, everything that we know by means of our senses and our minds has to be "silent": "the tumult of the flesh, the mental images of earth, water, and air, the heavens and even the soul itself." The soul, in not thinking of itself, must somehow transcend itself: dreams, imaginary visions, all language, and every sort of sign must be silent— everything, in fact, that depends on the passage of time. For, at that moment, if we were to hear them, they would say in the psalmist's words, "We did not make ourselves but were made by him who dwells in eternity" (Ps. 99:3). The manner in which we would hear God's word without intermediaries is comparable to the way in which ordinary words are stretched out *(distentio)* and create an impression of permanence in "an instant of thought."[74]

Monica died at fifty-six, in the autumn of 387, when Augustine was thirty-three (9.11.37–38). The vision is completed by his account of her burial at Ostia. His first reaction was to give little outward sign of his grief, since inwardly, where his "words sought God," he was critical of his potential enslavement to his emotions. Even during the final prayers, when Monica's body was placed beside her tomb, he displayed no visible sign of suffering.

He bathed, slept, and awoke somewhat refreshed. As he lay on his bed, he "remembered the truths" found in his favorite Ambrosium hymn, *Deus creator omnium* (the hymn with which he will close the analytic discussion of time in book 11). The words reminded him that God arranges days and nights so that there is repose after labour, relief from cares, and an end to grief (9.12.50–66). He thereby reversed the direction of the vision at Ostia, proceeding from the eternal to the habitual, familiar, and temporal. Little by little, he was "led back" to his thoughts about Monica, when, in that brief moment of bliss, she appeared to be "the handmaid" of God. He likewise recalled the piety and holiness that she displayed throughout life. For the first time, his tears flowed freely. He knew that he was weeping not before his fellow men, who might misinterpret his expressions of grief, but before God, whose ears were now open to his cries.

Augustine's readers recall that this is the second death in the story; the first was that of his Manichaean friend in Carthage (4.7).[75] In the earlier event, he learns a lesson about transitoriness; in Monica's death, about eternal life. As book 9 nears its end, he briefly discusses another type of immortality, achieved through his writings. His literary activity after his mother's death offers him a way of validating his thoughts and emotions, since others can now see that his tears are genuine. In this respect the autobiography is a fitting memorial to his parents. At the same time, the confession is deliberately made to God "in writing."[76] Just as his memory of his dead mother has become an internal narrative, the *Confessions* is the external expression of his "heart, voice, and writings."[77] The final lesson of the narrative in that these writings have replaced Ambrose as the privileged mediator between his maker and himself.

# II

## THE ETHICS OF INTERPRETATION

# 5

# BEGINNINGS

It is now possible to ask what function is served by the episodes in *Confessions* 1–9 in which problems of reading are deliberately incorporated into the narrative.

The positive developments can be divided into three phases. These consist of Augustine's learning to speak, to read, and to write; his mastery of a variety of interpretive methods under such influences as the *grammatici,* the Manichaeans, Ambrose, and the *libri Platonicorum;* and, in books 7 and 8, the transformation of reading from an outside to an inside force in his life.

Given the anticipations, it is no surprise that reading plays a critical role in his decision to become a religious at 8.12. Yet here, as at 3.4, when he takes up philosophy, an act of reading is the vehicle rather than the cause of conversion. The text of the *Hortensius* is like a switch that permits a predestined event to occur; so does Romans 13:13–14. The final lesson of Augustine's education as a reader is that nothing is learned from reading itself.

If this is the case, we are entitled to ask whether any constructive role is played by the intervening mental representations. Are they indications of realities or appearances? Augustine argues that in one sense they are appearances inasmuch as they arise from the perception of words on a page, but that in another they are clues, reminders, or confirmations of inwardly understood realities. In other words, he proposes that they are false in one context and true in another, or, to put the matter more strongly, false because of the nonsensory nature of the truth in question.

Part II traces the development of Augustine's thoughts on this and related questions. This task entails shifting the discussion from his narrative about reading to certain topics connected to reading in his philosophy of mind. The first step is to discuss how he builds a theory of reading out of the analysis of language, and to ask what he hopes to gain from it in moral, ethical, or spiritual terms; these are the topics of Chapters 6 and 7. I then turn to a number of issues to which he gives special attention: memory, time, self-knowledge, and the pursuit of wisdom within the context of the reader's education; these are examined in Chapters 8 and 9.

My assumption throughout the inquiry is that for Augustine, as for Plato, Aristotle, and their later ancient successors, to talk about literature, profane or sacred, is to talk about ethical matters. Literary theory is intended to provide a means of understanding texts through the study of grammar and rhetoric, as well a guide to "discriminations of right and wrong, better or worse, higher or lower, which are not rendered valid by our own desires, inclinations, or choices, but rather stand independent of these and offer standards by which they can be judged."[1]

Augustine approaches these issues in one way through the narrative of *Confessions* 1–9. He tackles them in another in his analytical writings, where he argues that our moral outlook arises from instinctual or emotional reactions which are specific to each of us, and from acts of will by which we connect our selves to nonpersonal frameworks for ethical behaviour. He also maintains that our ethical choices are frequently made on the basis of habit, not through a rational weighing of potential benefits or liabilities. They are implicit rather than explicit options for courses of action, and, to the degree that we habitually live a life that we would not consciously choose to live, we dwell in what Plato terms "a zone of unlikeness." The problem is how to bring about change in the pattern of such a narrative, or, to put the matter in Pauline terms, to get from an outsider's to an insider's story. Needless to say, the more the self is guided by authentic narratives, the more easily it can be detached from inauthentic temporal concerns.

Part II begins with Augustine's deliberate break with his former way of life,[2] which took place when he resigned from the chair of rhetoric in Milan just before the "vintage vacation," that is, from 23 August to 15 October 386. In November he went to stay in a villa at Cassiciacum, near Como, which was loaned to him by his absent friend Verecundus, a Milanese grammarian.[3] He returned to Milan the following March and was baptized by Ambrose with Adeodatus and Alypius on Easter night, which fell on 24–25 April. He had been suffering from a lung ailment, which made lecturing onerous,[4] and he speaks of the necessity of replacing the voice with the pen.[5] Yet he left the classroom chiefly to pursue his philosophical interests. His anxiety over his course of action had all but disappeared.[6] His confidence was bolstered by the conversions of Verecundus and Nebridius, both educated men, whose faith, like his own, had its roots in self-analysis.[7] He retired happily to the country with a group of friends and relatives that included not only Monica, Alypius, and Adeodatus but also his favorite pupils, Trygetius and Licentius, and two cousins, Lartidianus and Rusticus.[8] There he tackled a wide range of philosophical topics, including scepticism, the pursuit of wisdom, the nature of universal order, and the organization of the liberal arts. Through these discussions[9] he laid the groundwork for his idea of Christian *otium*.[10]

He also embarked on his first serious programme of writing after the discouragement of *De Pulchro et Apto* in 380–81. As God had "unfettered his heart," he now "freed his tongue."[11] Treatises appeared in rapid succession—*Contra Academicos, De Beata Vita, De Ordine, Soliloquia,* and *De Immortalitate Animae*[12]—each bearing witness to conversations with others or with himself.[13] This was the beginning of the series of writings known as the "philosophical dialogues," which were modeled on Cicero's *Tusculan Disputations*.[14] They took shape in conversations at Cassiciacum and continued from 388 to 390 in *De Quantitate Animae* (388), *De Libero Arbitrio* (388, 391) *De Magistro* (389), and *De Vera Religione* (390). During the same period he undertook a group of studies in the liberal arts, of which *De Dialectica* (387) and *De Musica* (389) survive; and lengthy anti-Manichaean treatises, including *De Moribus Ecclesiae Catholicae et Manichaeorum* (from 388) and *De Genesi contra Manichaeos* (388 or 389). In these works there is little or no narrative of spiritual progress through reading.[15] Autobiography is subordinated to inquiries into philosophical and theological issues.[16]

## The Letters

A number of topics that are touched upon but not fully clarified in *Confessions* 1–9 are discussed in letters written between 386 and the time of composition of the life history, 397–401.

Among them is an important statement on Augustine's method of composition, which is found in the first letter to Nebridius (*Epistle* 3).[17] His young companion had put forward the view that mortals are denied complete wisdom; consequently, neither of them could hope for happiness in this life. Augustine writes[18] that he was thinking about the problem while he was reading the letter by lamplight after dinner, seated on his bed.[19] He was just about to say his prayers[20] when a dialogue arose in his thoughts that was similar to the internal conversation[21] in his recently completed *Soliloquia*.[22] Though described as if it were spoken *(loquelae)*, this dialogue began in one external text, Nebridius' letter, and finished in another, his reply. As the letter in turn arose from a verbal exchange of views to which

Augustine refers in his reply, so it was that the conversation reappeared orally in his thoughts when he wanted to bring it to a conclusion. The physical distance separating the two friends was transformed into a psychological distance that could then be bridged by inner speech. While this discourse was taking place, the speakers were not real and fictive, as if one were writing the letter and the other were configured. As in the case of Augustine in the *Confessions,* they were both historical *and* figurative.[23]

This letter was not an isolated case. In others, Augustine frequently expresses a desire for Nebridius' company, but he is just as eager for the literary pleasures that require his absence. Echoing Seneca, his companion speaks of his letters as a second pair of eyes,[24] and Augustine often uses visual metaphors to describe the philosophical insights that arise from their exchanges of views.[25] He admires his friend's "ability to sojourn happily within the confines of his mind,"[26] and he prefers correspondence to verbal discussion, since it allows him to build an archive of sifted ideas, some of which are destined for wider readership. He believes that the correspondence is educational,[27] despite Nebridius' occasional indiscretions,[28] and he makes a careful count of the letters that he sends, asking his pupil to do the same, since he sometimes forgets to make copies.[29] He limits discussions and avoids repetition; at one point he suggests that his protégé write nothing further until he is able to reach some conclusions on his own.[30] He expects his guidance to be followed. When Nebridius misunderstands his explanation of mental images in memory, he tells him bluntly to reread his letter and adds little by way of clarification.[31] Even on issues of common interest the student sends more letters than the teacher cares to acknowledge.[32] Augustine makes pointed references to his lack of time;[33] even paper seems to have been scarce.[34] But he never asks his student to be his editor.[35] Nor does he entertain the illusion that letters are a substitute for his companionship.[36] Nonetheless, meetings never take place at the prearranged times and places;[37] it is as if both parties had tacitly agreed on the literary preconditions for the *christianae uitae otium.*[38]

A different note is sounded in the exchange[39] between Augustine and Paulinus of Nola and his saintly wife, Therasia.[40] Alypius, as bishop of Thagaste, provided the couple with copies of some five of Augustine's treatises in 394—we do not know which ones; in return, they borrowed a manuscript of Eusebius' chronicle in Rome and had it sent to Carthage to be copied.[41] "How intimately I have come to know you," Paulinus writes to Augustine, "as I profit daily from the conversation I have with you through your books."[42] The parties do not meet, and, being far apart,[43] they resort to elaborate rhetorical strategies in order to recreate each other as a fictive audience.[44] Typical is *Epistle* 31, in which Augustine writes of two Italian clerics, Romanus and Agilis, who come briefly to Hippo and offer him a verbal portrait of their master.[45] Paulinus' letters are read aloud to the brethren at Hippo, and Augustine then writes to him to say that his image is "inscribed" on their hearts:[46] they are said to "carry away" his words for study even as they themselves "are carried away" by what they have heard.[47] The reading is a "sweet and sacred spectacle,"[48] which helps to sustain their community.[49]

Despite this literary play, the letters to Nebridius and Paulinus draw attention to Augustine's ambivalence toward friendship.[50] In *Epistle* 258, to Martianus, he speaks in Ciceronian phrases of a "harmony of the human and the divine in benevolence and love";[51] he believes that male friends (it is not clear that he had any female ones) are capable of inquiring together into the loftiest matters—the nature of the soul and the divine.[52] However, these sentiments contrast with his view that friendships can divert the seeker after truth from eternal to temporal values. By the time he went to Cassiciacum, he was aware that he could ascend the ladder of education through studies and discussion; yet, ironically, it was there, surrounded by pupils and relatives whom he liked, that he strenuously urged disengagement from worldly attractions and, by implication, from friendships.

In place of this companionship, or, frequently, in combination with it, he turned to reading (and, as time went on, to other literary pursuits, including writing, preaching, commentaries, and correspondence). He spiritualized reading despite its sensory origins, since it permitted the subject to approach truths that lay beyond verbal and written signs. He wrote to the convert Gaius in 390 that truth does not exist in books or authors but in the enlightened reader's mind.[53] He explained to his former mentor, Simplicianus, in 397 that his "literary labours" pleased him by appealing to the deity that dwelt within.[54] In 391 he reviewed his misspent youth for bishop Valerius, arguing that God intended him to "cure" his spiritual "illness" through the "close scrutiny" of his words, that is, through "reading" and "prayer."[55] Before ordination, he claimed, there was never enough time for study: now that ecclesiastical duties were thrust upon him, he asked for time off to become better acquainted with scripture.[56] In such statements, his ascetic attitude toward reading practices slowly took shape.[57]

Some instructive letters were written to pious women. In contrast to Monica, for whom booklearning was inessential, these females constituted an educated audience. The lengthiest letter *(De Videndo Deo)* is to Paulina, an aristocratic religious, in 413. Augustine's purpose is to emphasize the need for scriptural studies while not replacing her inner faith with outer oral or written instruction. He points out that the meek and humble "progress" through "reflection and prayer" rather than through "reading and listening."[58] In order for the inward person to be "renewed" through "the words of understanding" (compare 2 Corinthians 4:16), Paulina must free herself from the body, which burdens her among other things with gender and ethnicity,[59] and lodge her beliefs in the "authority" of scripture.

She can gain insight by studying the Bible or, if that is beyond her capacities, by adhering to truths that are revealed to her from within.[60] In either case, she must distinguish between external and internal sight (*uidere* versus *mentis obtutus* or *intuitus*)[61]. Augustine asks her to put his letter down and to think about the difference between the way in which she sees a physical event (for example, the sun moving in the sky) and the way in which she sees within her mind that she is alive, wishes to behold God, and seeks sacred knowledge;[62] furthermore, to consider the fact that although she has no doubt of the existence of her own mental activities,[63] she cannot through their exercise alone arrive at a clear understanding of God. She has to trust in what she can learn from outside sources,[64] which means placing confidence in "the signs of sounds, letters, or some other sort of documentation."[65]

By demonstrating the limits of what she can know on her own, therefore, Augustine argues in favor of a combination of scripture[66] and memory[67] in her efforts at self-improvement.[68] She reads that Christ rose from the dead (John 20:29); a visual or auditory image of the event is accordingly created in her mind which is based on the scriptural text,[69] and a combination of bodily and mental sight results.[70] "She sees in the mind whatever is understood to have been signified by the shapes of the letters or the sounds; she sees her own faith, to which her belief responds without hesitation; she sees the thought that her thinking has produced, and the benefit derived from it through belief; she sees the will, which attracts her to take up religion."[71] In a subsequent phase of reflection, she can proceed from internal images to the rule of understanding *(regula intellegentiae).*[72] Augustine thus briefly recapitulates the method that he acquired from Ambrose[73] and develops in *De Doctrina Christiana.*

## The Dialogues

Many of these ideas concerning readers and fictions are spelled out in detail in the Cassiciacum dialogues,[74] where, in contrast to the narrative plausibility of the *Confessions,* they create a sense of actuality through the scenery of their notation.[75]

Licentius loved the thrust and parry of the verbal arguments, but he was equally pleased that the words were written down so that they could be referred to at leisure.[76] The dialogues were read aloud to the assembled friends before they were published.[77] They were recorded with care; references to secretaries abound.[78] Inconsistencies are rare: on different occasions, Alypius and Licentius attempted to have ill-considered remarks removed from the record.[79] The timing, duration, and organization of the conversations was likewise determined by Augustine's insistence that they be recorded. Debates were broken off at nightfall and begun at daybreak so that scribes could continue their work;[80] they were stopped temporarily when the space on the wax tablets ran out.[81] Arguments that were taken down as notes, subsequently edited, and then made available to the group were described as "books."[82] Sessions were postponed for the task of correspondence.[83] The "ingenious invention" of the pen[84] trapped evanescent words[85] and prevented Augustine's students' labours from being "dispersed by the wind."[86] Memory was a faithless custodian;[87] texts made repetition unnecessary[88] and effectively ordered the audience's response.[89]

Doing philosophy did not entail reasoning from positions arrived at by the debaters but discussing texts by authors long dead.[90] The exchange of ideas required extensive reading of pagan writers, scripture, and, as the days passed, the transcriptions of the previous conversations.[91] In the upward progress of the soul inspired by the liberal arts, Socratic "reminiscence" was thus replaced by the memory of what had previously been said.[92] *De Beata Vita* can be described as a Platonic "banquet," but it is one that takes place in a library, or, as Augustine later described it, a museum of pre-Christian beliefs.[93] *Contra Academicos* and *De Ordine* had recesses for meals and for wearied speakers to return to the books that they were reading for their enjoyment.[94] Augustine's arrangements sometimes sound less like those of a philosopher than those of a seminar instructor.[95]

Yet this was true philosophy in the ancient sense of the pursuit of a way of life. The goal was the making of a better self. In a revealing aside, Augustine tells Alypius that, whereas he was his teacher of "words," his friend taught him through his actions.[96] In an epistolary poem[97] written some nine years later,[98] Licentius recalls a "golden age" of leisure and study,[99] in which the "master-teacher"[100] frequently revived his tepid interest in Virgil[101] through "the arduous labour of reading for the inner sense divulged in books and discovered through his ingenuity."[102] Yet Augustine is less interested in the content of the *Aeneid*, which is frequently cited,[103] than in creating a mental space for ethical discussion that is to be filled by instruction from within: he reproaches Licentius, whose literary talents he admired,[104] for mindlessly practicing the composition of hexameters.[105] At *Contra Academicos* 2.4, the debate was interrupted while he spent some seven days reading *Aeneid* 2 and 4 with Licentius and Trygetius before they were joined by Alypius, who caught up on the proceedings by reviewing their notes. However, this instruction was intended to alternate with periods of relaxation:[106] he asked his students not to talk during the evening about the books that they had read, since the soul had to have time "to be at home with itself."[107] What he had in mind is revealed in an anecdote at *De Beata Vita* 1.2, where he asked Trygetius whether the soul required nourishment like the body. When his student hesitated over his reply, Monica intervened,[108] reminding him that just a few moments before he was lost in thought while eating breakfast. Just as his body was nourished with food, his mind was evidently sustained with *theoriae et cogitationes*.[109]

The autonomous role that reading, internal writing, and meditative self-awareness plays in the letters and in the writings at Cassiciacum is occasionally foreshadowed but never fully paralleled in Augustine's predecessors in the dialogue genre. Nor can his literary approach be traced to his major sources of Platonic doctrines, Plotinus and Porphyry.[110] In his manner of conceiving relations between knowledge *(scientia)* and wisdom *(sapientia),*[111] frequent reiteration[112] produces no single definition[113] but instead a series of complementary roles[114] in which the mediators between man and the divine are chiefly reading and self-consciousness. The wise man has attained wisdom, while the reader–philosopher is desirous of doing so *(studioso);*[115] the goal is reached by few[116] through "continuous study."[117] Speaking in metaphors to Licentius in 395, he notes that Wisdom first fetters its devotees, then tames them through laborious exercises; later they are set free, and she gives herself over to enjoying them. The students who were bound by a temporary allegiance are thus united with her in an eternal embrace.[118]

It is in the context of man's desire for higher understanding and Augustine's criticism of the sceptical alternative that should be situated his well-known defence of the *cogito,*[119] through which he argues for the existence of knowledge on the basis of the certitude of consciousness. In *Soliloquia* 2.1, the argument follows his prayer for inner knowledge and precedes Reason's demonstration that he loves life for knowing rather than for living.[120] But his awareness that he is able to think is in fact brought about by a tool of thinking, that is, a discipline.[121] He considers two types of sensory information, one that arises outside and is coordinated by his inner sense before the data are taken up and sorted out by reason,[122] the other originating from sensory impressions in his mind, for example, the illusion that he is going somewhere. The fact that he can entertain such make-believe situations as if they were external events is proof that his mind cannot be the source of the truth that it inwardly knows with certainty, namely that it exists.

Augustine takes up the status of such fictional accounts in complementary discussions in *De Ordine* and *Soliloquia*. In *De Ordine* 2,[123] he introduces the topic by arguing that wisdom consists of both learning *(eruditio)* and a way of living *(uita):* it is configured in one way in the deity's changeless law and in another in wise souls.[124] The door to higher knowledge is opened by authority, which guides the uninstructed many. Once the threshold has been crossed, reason leads a select few to adopt an exemplary way of life.[125] The *rationale,* the faculty of reason in the soul, is distinguishable from the *rationabile,* what is done or spoken with reason.[126] In Augustine's view, one can be rational, even if one's thoughts and statements are not always reasonable.[127] Moreover, reasonable action deals with right living, while instruction and pleasure are reflected in disciplines of learning.[128] Reason itself does not create truths; it discovers them and, in doing so, renews individuals from within.[129] Those who use reason share a common rationality *(ratio communis),* by which they form a society. The "natural bond" that unites them is speech.[130]

Yet speech cannot perform its social functions without writing. To this end, meaningful sounds *(uocabula)* were originally affixed to things. As individuals heard one another enunciate these sounds, their ears acted as points of entry for their minds, where interpretation took place.[131] The system worked only for those who were present for exchanges of speech. Accordingly, Reason separated the various sounds and expressed them as letters, which could be transmitted soundlessly through writing.[132] Limits were also placed on the number of things that could be designated by spoken or written words.[133] Two professions, both based on assumptions of literacy *(litteratio),* thereby sprang into existence, the copyist and the calculator.[134] Later, Reason subdivided sounds and their written equivalents into vowels, semivowels, and mutes. Syllables were recognized, along with the eight parts of speech; short and long syllables were distinguished.[135] The "science of grammar," that is, "the discipline and the study of letters,"[136] was placed in a preeminent position among the other liberal arts, namely dialectic, rhetoric, metre, geometry, and astronomy. Other arts imitated these.[137]

When the programme was complete, Reason desired to be elevated to a contemplative state.[138] Yet she was impeded by the very senses on which she depended for essential information. Worse, each sense claimed to have a unique access to the truth—the ears, for example, proclaiming[139] that they had invented the words "grammar," "dialectic," and "rhetoric."[140] But Reason rejected this notion because she understood the difference between the sound *(sonum)* and the thing represented by the sign *(signum):*[141] the ears are restricted to registering sounds, whereas for meaning to arise sounds have to be ordered in time and modulated through pitch.[142] Out of her speculations arose the study of metre and accent[143] in poetry, as well as the recognition that the mathematical relationships involved in metre constitute an eternal "truth"[144] which is "the law of all art."[145] This "simple certainty"[146] is contrasted with the sensory aspects of the sciences of letters and numbers.[147] Therefore, someone who grasps "simple and intelligible numbers" (that is, the numerical relations illustrated by metre; 2.14.40) is in a good position to engage in intellectual ascent, assuming he has sufficient "talent, years, and leisure," as Augustine did, "from boyhood."

The allegorical journey concludes by reasserting the double value of reason, which is both the subject and object of the quest. The soul, looking into itself, is persuaded by its own erudition that the use of reason is an inseparable component of itself; yet it is also aware that it possesses an inner hidden motion, a force of reason itself, through which it is able to distinguish and interrelate everything that it has to learn.[148] The "well-taught soul"[149] thereby acquires the capacity to ascend through stages from the sensible to the intellectual and beyond, after "composing" and "ordering" itself within the principles of its own "harmonious beauty."[150] The "words" used in "everyday" expressions are left behind,[151] as they are by Augustine and Monica in the vision at Ostia. The person who catches sight of the "fountain" that is the source of "all truth"[152] is the one who "lives well, prays well, and studies well":[153] it is he or she whom God is most ready to hear.[154]

Similar issues are raised in *Soliloquia* 2, where Augustine adds an important conclusion to his theory of believable fictions. It is easy for the senses to mistake one object for another (assuming that deliberate deception is not involved). In a comparable way, the soul is one thing in reality and another as it is understood through sense perceptions: it is changelessly true, yet it varies with times, places, observations, and so on. Our self-understanding can thus be true and false at once.[155] Yet, if the senses deceive us on the true nature of ourselves, we nonetheless have to take into consideration the information that they provide; for, the only evidence that we have of the soul's existence arises from the sensory reflection of its vitality.[156] It is through the senses that its education begins.[157]

Truth or falseness in perception depends on the status that is accorded to the observer.[158] If nothing is true except what seems to be, if what seems to be is judged by the senses, if only the soul is able to make judgments through sense perception, and if an object in the world does not exist unless it is truly there, then it follows that a body cannot exist in sense perception unless the soul exists beforehand.[159] Truth is not a function of the perceiver's cognition of what seems to be:[160] it is "what exists," independently of observation.[161] Things are perceived to be "true" through a larger truth which is itself unperceived.[162] When we judge something that we see to be false, we have in mind an implicit "resemblance to the true."[163] Examples include pictures, mirror images, twins, and physical impressions.[164] In each case, the problem is to decide whether the copy is inferior to the original.[165]

On this view, there is nothing that can be truly called false except what is configured to be what it is not.[166] Furthermore, false things are distinguished by whether or not the intention is to deceive (*fallax* versus *mendax*).[167] In the case of actors, artists, and other creators of fiction, truth and falsehood go hand in hand: the representations are in some sense right because, in another sense, they are not.[168] It is not the representations that are "worthy of imitation,"[169] but the truth that is to be sought in their principles of organization. Reason and Augustine join forces in defence of this position,[170] using as their examples grammar and the laws of argumentation.[171] No one who learns and retains what is learned can be said to be without knowledge; in this sense, every discipline in itself is "true," and no one who acquires a discipline can be said to know things that are false.[172] Reason points out that the fictions that they have been discussing all relate to grammar,[173] through which we discover their qualities, not their truth or falseness.[174] Stories can instruct or give pleasure, but grammar, being ethically neutral, "is the discipline that acts as custodian and moderator of everything that is said: in this capacity, it has to gather together the whole of human language committed to memory or to writing, including the fictitious component." Language, then, can teach a kind of truth, even though the speaker seldom or never attains to truth.[175]

This argument is later reproduced at *Confessions* 1.13.22. It is not the pagan fables that Augustine learned as a schoolboy that profoundly influenced his educational development, but the techniques of "reading and writing," which gave him access to literature. Such a branch of learning can be "true" without imparting facts.[176] The purpose of a discipline is to establish "definitions, division, and principles of reasoning . . . to assign each element to its place without confusion, while overlooking nothing that pertains to the subject in question."[177] The pagans taught that we should believe in the content of myths, for example, that Daedalus actually flew toward the sun.[178] By contrast, Christians recognize the falseness of a story's content while focusing on the truth of the "grammatical" principles involved. The resulting combination of believing (credere) and knowing (nosse)[179] is close to the theory of narrative in the Confessions.

These disciplines are considered to be "true," and this truth resides in the soul. It is nonetheless necessary to explain the relationship between knowledge, disciplines, and the human mind. Reason accomplishes this by drawing attention to the fact that a thing can be said to be in another thing (aliquid in aliquo) in one of two ways. If I say, "The piece of wood is here" or "The sun is in the east," I can think of the wood and the sun at the same time as I think of their being somewhere else. It is also possible to speak of something as existing in the subject (aliquid in subjecto) in such a manner that this type of separation is impossible, for example, while I speak of "the form and appearance" of light in the sun, of heat in fire, or of a discipline in the mind (in animo disciplina).[180] Augustine concludes that if something resides inseparably in a subject, it cannot continue if the subject does not endure, and if what is separable ceases to exist, the subject can nonetheless continue over time indefinitely.[181] The colour of a wall can be changed, but the wall in which the colour inheres remains. A discipline exists in the mind in the manner in which something exists "in a subject." If learning is truth, and if truth endures, the mind or soul must be eternal.[182] It is a short step from this conclusion to Reason's affirmation of the reality of self-consciousness, from which devolves her proof of the soul's immortality.[183]

The central role played by the example of the study of literature (grammatica) in De Ordine and Soliloquia suggests that these works are Augustine's preface to the story of his education as a reader in Confessions 1–9. In De Ordine, the material is presented in an allegory of the birth of the liberal arts; in Soliloquia 2, the discussion moves forward by stages that are both logical and autobiographical. Forms of discourse and representation are fleeting and imitative; so were his youthful intellectual adventures. As a child, he was misled into believing that the images of things recorded by his senses were realities. As a student in Carthage, he was overwhelmed by dramatic performances.[184] Yet one lesson remained so firmly in his mind that he was later able to refer to it without any need "for deliberation":[185] this concerned the permanence of disciplines such as grammar and dialectic, which, paradoxically, retain their truth even though their applications may be false.

Reason reminds Augustine that the "byways" they have taken through "the forest of things" have not been in vain. The reader of the *Confessions* can agree too. For, at the end of the discussion of reading in *Soliloquia,* we find ourselves on the threshold of his discovery of the power of interpretation in Milan, in the spring of 386, under Ambrose's guidance. She points out that they should not "put aside" what they have undertaken and expect to find the answers in some book that might by chance fall into their hands—an oblique reference, perhaps, to the *Hortensius.* Many books have been written, she coyly adds, including some from their own time that they have not troubled to read, in which the ancient eloquence that they "mourned as dead was made to live again and was brought to perfection in a single figure,"—the bishop of Milan.[186] Augustine thus acknowledges that it was Ambrose who instructed him in an appropriate "mode of living." What he does not say is that his subsequent search for an explanation of how that was brought about involves a revision of ancient theories of discourse.

# 6

# SPEAKING AND

# READING

❧❧❧

## On Dialectic

As Augustine's autobiography begins with his learning to speak, the starting-point of his analytical account of reading is his discussion of the status of words. Two early statements of his position are *De Dialectica* and *De Magistro*. Neither work is complete. *De Dialectica* is missing crucial sections.[1] *De Magistro* is the revised version of a dialogue with Adeodatus which postpones "to another day" a full discussion of one of its key topics, "the utility of words."[2]

Despite its title, the subject of *De Dialectica* is not logic, narrowly defined, but the nature and function of words in a variety of logical and grammatical settings. If dialectic is "the science of disputing well," disputations nonetheless consist of words.[3] As planned, the treatise addressed this theme under four headings[4] of which only a part of one, *De Loquendo,* is extant; this is an abbreviated version of the section on simple and compound words (chapters 1–3), to which are appended chapters on dialectic (chapter 4), words, signs, and things (chapter 5), the origin and force of words (chapters 6–7), and obscurity, ambiguity, and equivocation (chapters 8–10).

It is clear from what remains that Augustine's programme is followed only until chapter 5, after which his ideas diverge from his major sources.[5] His initial concern is with the roles played by dialectic and rhetoric in oratorical debate;[6] his subsequent interest lies in the usefulness of these disciplines for solving problems dealing with words in written texts.[7] At the end of chapter 5, the "speaker" envisaged in *De Dialectica* is principally a reader.[8] In the other chapters (which probably originated as a dialogue)[9] the analysis of signs, which is his starting-point, is situated within a classroom where texts are discussed. The work's main task, therefore, is to reorient dialectic, and to a lesser degree grammar and rhetoric, toward the problems encountered by the reader in interpretation. The task of *De*

*Dialectica* is to inquire into the nature of these "representations"[10] and the role of the hearer in construing their meaning.

The topics covered in the handbooks of "grammar" dominate chapters 1–3;[11] Augustine then proceeds from styles of verbal expression to the problem of inference in propositions, in which ancient thinkers typically located sign theory.[12] By this route he arrives at the question of how words signify things, which is taken up in chapter 5.[13]

His statement is a novel synthesis in the field of later ancient semantics,[14] which makes the following points:

1. He proposes that a word *(uerbum)* can be the sign *(signum)* of any thing *(res)*;[15] it suffices that the word be uttered and understood (5.1–8). The thing is whatever is sensed, comprehended, or concealed[16] when utterance takes place; the sign is perceived sensorially in one way and understood intellectually in another (and it can be verbal or written).[17] He thus ties some traditional definitions of the elements of speech[18] to speakers and hearers[19] and to mental activities: by implication, speaking is an expression of the speaker's intentions.[20]

2. He then turns to the similarity between verbal and written signs (that is, the parallel between speaking and reading; 5.8–20).[21] In addition to grammarians,[22] two potential sources for his ideas are Aristotle's opening sentence in *De Interpretatione* and Stoic statements on the relationship between spoken and written expressions.[23] In both, however, sounds take priority rather than the written characters that represent them. At *De Interpretatione* 16a, it is "in sound" *(en tēi phōnēi)* that "the signs of the soul's passions" are reflected; what is written *(ta graphomena)* represents the sound.[24] Although it is hazardous to reduce Stoic views to a single position, most statements speak of a letter *(to gramma)* as a sound in speech *(to stoikeion)*, as the written symbol of that sound *(ho kharaktēr)*, or as the sound's name *(to onoma)*, that is, "alpha," the name of *a*.[25]

Echoing these ideas,[26] Augustine nonetheless suggests[27] that speaking and reading are parallel activities with respect to the mental recreation of signs.[28] Spoken words make sounds,[29] while written ones are "completely silent."[30] Does this mean that graphic representation makes a verbal sign into "the sign of a word"?[31] No: they are both signs; they merely enter the brain by different sensory channels. In speech, signs are heard; in reading, they are visually decoded.[32] The confusion arises from calling both "words." If the term "letter" (that is, *a, b, c,* and so on) referred only to "the minimal part of an articulated sound," there would be no problem. We unnecessarily complicate matters in speaking of groups of letters as "writings." A written word is really just "the sign of a signifying sound" (5.14–19).

3. He then turns to the grammarian's concern with the sound of words (5.20–26), proposing that the subject is not a normal part of dialectic until disputes arise over the meanings or contexts of words; otherwise, it is the *grammaticus* who deals with such matters as vowels, consonants, syllables, rhythm, and accent. Arriving at this distinction appears to be his principal objective in chapter 5.[33]

4. Accordingly, it is necessary to define four key semantic concepts: *uerbum, dicibile, dictio,* and *res* (5.27–45). The principal question is how words that exist in the mind as signs of signs can be said to signify objects. The reply (already given) is that when the disputation is the model for these relationships, the object to which the word refers is itself: the thing *(res)* that is the subject of the dispute is a word *(uerbum)*, which, proceding from the speaker's lips, is uttered on behalf of itself *(propter se)*.[34] As a consequence, we can speak of what the mind rather than the ear understands and retains through the *uerbum*:[35] this is labelled a *dicibile,* while the aural awareness of the *uerbum* is a *dictio,* that is, the word spoken not on its own behalf but in order to signify something else.[36] The *res* is what has not yet become either a spoken or a conceptualized word.[37] In other terms, the *uerbum* is both the word and what the word signifies. The *dicibile* is a word, but it signifies what there is in the word that is understood in the mind and "contained" by it.[38] The *dictio* combines the functions of the *uerbum* and the *dicibile:* it is both the spoken word and what occurs in the mind as a result of what the word signifies. *Res,* too, is a word once it enters speech; it is what remains to be signified.[39]

The *dicibile,* the most original of these concepts, may be a rendering of the problematical Stoic *lekton.* The other terms likewise echo Stoic usage in their emphasis on the verbal character of signification.[40] Yet in his argument in chapter 5, Augustine's chief interest does not appear to be signification for its own sake but the place of signifying in a philosophy of mind. In section 1, the signs that are spoken and heard are linked by understanding *(intellegere);* in 3, the sounds of words are disqualified from dialectic; and in 2 and 4, the topic is specifically the signs of signs, that is, their mental impressions: the *dictio* brings about meaning in the mind, and the *dicibile* understands and retains it.

5. The final topic is the dialectical and grammatical functions of words in a classroom example, *Aeneid* 1.1 (5.45–65).[41] Here Augustine is talking not about a verbal disputation but about the verbal debate over the meaning of a written text,[42] namely *Arma uirumque cano* . . . If a grammarian is questioning his class and asks what part of speech *arma* is, then "arms" is said for its own sake in the interchange between teacher and students.

The other words uttered by the teacher, that is, "What part of speech is . . .," are spoken because something is desired to be known about "arms" in context. "Arms," then, in such a discussion, is a *uerbum,* that is, the sign of a thing. Yet, as "arms" was originally uttered by Virgil in *Aeneid* 1.1, it was a *dictio:* it was said in order to signify the wars that Aeneas waged, the shield that he wore, or the arms that Vulcan made for him. These "wars" or "arms" actually existed, whether or not we have them in mind when we say *arma.* As such, they are things, *res.*[43]

This argument effectively substitutes *grammatica* (that is, the classroom study of pagan literature) for the Stoic division of deliberative, forensic, and panegyric rhetoric,[44] stopping at the threshold of hermeneutics.[45] The resulting model looks like this:

$$\text{speaker's mind}$$

$$\begin{array}{ccc} \textit{grammatica} & & \textit{dialectica} \\ \text{oral reading} & \text{solved by} & \text{oral argument} \\ \text{written signs} & & \text{verbal signs} \end{array}$$

$$\text{hearer's mind}$$

It is within this pattern that the subdivisions in signs are intended to work. For either written or verbal signs, the relationship is as follows:

$$\begin{array}{c} \rightarrow \textit{dicibile} \\ \textit{signum} \leftrightarrow \textit{res} \leftrightarrow \text{mind} \\ \rightarrow \textit{dictio} \end{array}$$

Confirmation of this view is found in section 3, where Augustine states that word sounds do not pertain to dialectic, while the "business of grammar" covers vowels, consonants, and syllables, which originate in speech, as well as "poetic rhythm and accent"—both of which are studied with the aid of texts. His explanation supplies a missing link in *Confessions* 1, where, writing some ten years later, he does not offer an adequate linguistic account of early reading experiences.[46] At a more abstract level, his critique of the reliance on verbal signs for information looks forward to the arguments of *De Magistro* and *De Doctrina Christiana,* as well as to his theological uses for *uerbum* after 389.[47]

From this point, *De Dialectica* adds only details to this interesting picture of signification. Three topics relevant to later discussions in this study are also taken up: the relation of meaning to sound (chapter 6), the force of words (chapter 7), and the roles of ambiguity and obscurity (chapters 8–9).

The use of the word in dialectic entails a knowledge of its origin, force, declension, and arrangement (6.4–6). Chapter 6 concerns itself with the question of "origin," that is, finding out why a word is called what it is.[48] There is no established method for this sort of inquiry.[49] Augustine considers[50] and rejects the Stoic account of relations between the sense impression and word meanings (6.35–119) which arise between words and things as well as between things and other things in cases of similarity, proximity, and contrareity.[51] The Stoics believed it possible to trace the "similitude" between "the sound and the thing"[52] in a word to its "cradle," that is, the point at which the sense perception of the thing to which the word refers harmonizes with the sense impression created by the sound; from this, they concluded that the licence for naming *(licentia nominandi)* proceeds from the similarity of a sound to the thing it names and to the similarity of one thing to another (6.49–52).[53]

Chapter 7[54] returns to the topic of speakers and hearers (7.1–37).[55] Modifying the position of section 5, Augustine argues that a word affects its hearer both because of itself and because of what it signifies, since the two normally act in concert (7.3–4). The concept of audience is thus broadened, and the concerns of dialectic and rhetoric are reintroduced (7.37–50).

There are three possible ways in which words reveal their capacities:

1. The word on account of itself *(secundum se,* 7.3–21) affects the hearer through sense *(sensus),* art *(ars),* or both of these together. The sense is affected by the word's nature *(natura)* or by custom *(consuetudo).*[56] Thus certain words, such as "Artaxerxes" and "Euryalus," intrinsically sound harsh and smooth, while others, such as "Motta" and "Cotta," acquire their acoustical qualities because the listener is habitually accustomed to hearing them that way (7.6–12). In the second case, the harshness or smoothness of the sounds is not relevant. The critical factor is whether the sounds are received as "friends" or "strangers" as they "sojourn briefly in the ear's inner chambers."[57]

As one hears the word spoken, one's attention is directed to its part of speech along with other matters that have been learned about "the disciplines of words" (7.15–17; cf. 5.20–25). The hearer is affected by both "nature" and "art" whenever reason notes what the ears measure and a name is put in place.[58] For example, if one says *optimus,* one long and two short syllables strike the ear, and the mind, having acquired the art of metre, recognizes[59] a dactylic foot (7.19–21).

2. A word's capacity also arises from what it signifies *(secundum id*

*quod significat*, 7.21–26).[60] If the word "Augustine" is pronounced, the hearer may think of the author of *De Dialectica* or someone else; in either case, the sign refers to a single thing, and each word affects the hearer only because of what it signifies.[61]

3. The word's meaning may depend on both of these together (*ex utroque communiter* (7.22–37), that is, on giving equal attention to the enunciation of the word *(ipsa enuntiatio)* and to what is enunciated by it *(id quod ab ea nuntiatur)*. When Sallust says, "He dissipated his inheritance through his hand, his stomach, and his penis,"[62] it is the appropriateness of the signifying word that effectively shields us from the off-putting reality that is signified (7.31–34). Similarly, if we speak of a whore who, when dressed respectably to appear in court, appears differently than she does in bed, again the hearer supplies the necessary context.[63]

These examples draw attention to an important difference between dialectical and rhetorical treatments of "words." Dialectic is concerned chiefly with giving an account of truth; rhetoric, with observing proprieties of expression.[64] An argument in dialectic need not be poorly expressed, nor is there a need for eloquence to misrepresent the truth. The situation reflects the difference between high and low culture: the well-educated few disapprove of what appeals only to the ear, while the poorly educated are drawn to a speaker through his verbal pyrotechnics, thinking that what is expressed ornately must necessarily be true. Public speakers must therefore pay attention to "the force of their words" (7.41–50) and their ethical implications.[65]

This conclusion is the unstated agenda in case 3 of chapter 7. It is also deducible in cases 1 and 2. In case 1, Augustine says that when a word is spoken on its own account, it affects the hearer through its "sense" or its "art." The sense represents the dialectical search for truth-values with which he concludes, while the art is concerned with the acquired disciplines of words, grammar, and rhetoric. The word's sense impression can be further broken down, revealing an inner parallel that reflects the outer pairs *sensus/dialectica* and *ars/rhetorica*: this is the distinction between *natura*, the essence or intrinsic meaning of the word based on its sound; and *consuetudo*, the conventional or habitual association between words (or things) of similar sounds. The nature of the word is independent of the speaker and hearer; it is an aspect of the word's truth-value. The customary associations of the word are completely dependent on speaker and hearer relations.

In chapters 8–9, Augustine turns to impediments to the hearer's understanding of the intended truths of words through obscurity, ambiguity, and equivocation. If a word is obscure, we have no guide to its meaning, whereas if it is ambiguous we are able to choose between possible meanings (8.4–7). An object can be obscure if it is known via the senses but not the mind (for example, the picture of an apple viewed by someone who has never seen the fruit). By contrast, I may not recognize a familiar object if viewing conditions are inadequate. There is also a type of obscurity that arises when someone who has never seen an apple is shown a picture of it in the dark (8.15–25).

These examples are visual, not auditory. The "pictures"[66] are implicitly signs of words: they thereby recreate the conditions of 5.8–20, the discussion which equates the signs of signs arising in speaking and reading; now, however, Augustine adds images as a third possibility.

Augustine asks us, in effect, to direct our minds "to the words for which such (pictures) as these are likenesses."[67] His example is a teacher of literature (grammaticus) who has convened his class. When the students are silent, he murmurs the single word, temetum (a rare Latin word for wine).[68] Those nearest him hear clearly, those farther away less clearly, and those still farther away not at all. These are the three levels of obscurity (compare the example of the pictured apple, 8.27–47) adapted to the literary context of temetum. Speaking of the students' ignorance, Augustine employs the phrase quid esset temetum (what "wine" is), without referring to the intermediary of a sign; in his logic, the reality has become the text. The relationship is that temetum in a text equals res, while temetum as spoken in class equals signum. The equations reproduce in a reading context the verbal situation of chapters 5–7, in which the hearer is affected by the word because of itself.[69]

By contrast, suppose the teacher says magnus (great), clearly and distinctly, so that everyone hears an easily recognizable word at once. The basic meaning is clear, but the students do not know what the adjective modifies. The teacher can be referring to a "name," a foot in verse, a great man such as Pompey or Virgil, or even, negatively, to his students, who may not be "greatly" industrious (8.48–57, 59–62). To the dialectician, therefore, every word is, in theory at least, "ambiguous" (9.1) and thus, like other verbal problems, subject to debate in words (9.11–19).

In parallel with his division of the signs of signs into those speaking and reading, Augustine also separates ambiguities into two broad classes, those that arise in speech (in his quae dicuntur) and those that exist in writing (in his . . . quae scribuntur, 9.20–21). Take the word acies, the term for "sharpness" that normally refers to a sword, a military unit, or keenness of sight.

Whether it is spoken or written, the sense is unclear if the sentence in which it occurs is not known. For instance, if one sees *leporem* (in a written context), one has to read the entire sentence of verse to know whether the penultimate syllable is long or short, and thus whether "wit" or "hare" is meant, whereas if it were read aloud the sense would be evident (9.22–29). Ambiguities in speech can themselves be subdivided into two kinds, "univocals" and "equivocals," that is, synonyms and homonyms.[70] In the case of homonyms arising from "art," the word affects the hearer on account of what it signifies; the thing signified is uncertain. However, in the case of those arising from "use," the word affects the hearer for its own sake: that is what is meant by words "in use."[71] For one can hear a word and have little interest in its part of speech, metre, or anything else concerned with "the discipline of words" (10.27–29; compare 5.20–25). One can hear the word "Tullius" and think of the person, his depiction in a painting or a statue, the codex containing his writings, or even what remains of him in his grave; the ambiguity arises from the different objects (10.30–33, 37–38).[72]

What are we to make of this fragmentary set of observations on dialectic, grammar, rhetoric, and "the force of words"? Basing his ideas on Stoic notions of relations between sounds and meanings, Augustine argues that words become signifiers of things (either of objects or of representations of them, that is, words, writings, or images) when they are recreated in the minds of those who hear the words spoken. For each situation in which meaning arises, both a sender and a receiver of a sign are assumed. The dialogue is the precondition for communication between two minds that are thinking of the same thing. Moreover, although words are the components on which the critical link depends, they are also the weak point in the system by which meaning is communicated, since there are many "impediments" to words' achieving their full capacity to signify the things to which they refer.

## The Teacher

*De Dialectica* makes the problem of words a central issue in Augustine's account of language. *De Magistro* considerably broadens the philosophical context of the discussion.

Some of the ideas in the earlier treatise are reiterated: the spoken word represents the sign,[73] meaning arises acoustically between the speaker and the hearer,[74] sound and sense are distinguished,[75] and, in general, speech is the model for human communication.[76] However, the treatment of signification differs. In *De Dialectica,* the topic is introduced in chapter 5 and plays a role in the analysis of factors adversely affecting spoken communication in chapters 6–10; the most important of these is the problematic connection between *uerbum* and *res,* through which words become obscure, ambiguous, or equivocable (chapters 8–10). To address this issue, Augustine must raise the question of mental representations.

Yet in *De Dialectica,* at least as we have it, he does not do this. The task is taken up in a number of subsequent works. A major exploration of the perceptual and cognitive issues is found in *De Trinitate* 8–15 (discussed in Chapter 9 of this book). The most informative statements on the role of verbal signs are found in *De Magistro*[77] and in *De Doctrina Christiana* 1–3 (discussed next, in Chapter 7). *De Magistro* is a sophisticated assessment of verbal signs; *De Doctrina* 1–3 takes up problems of written signs mainly as they are encountered by students of biblical theology. *De Doctrina* was possibly begun in 396 and revised in 426; *De Magistro* dates from 389 and results from a conversation between Augustine and Adeodatus before the latter's death at age sixteen.[78] The work may have been a memorial to his son, whose intellectual abilities he greatly admired.[79]

In *De Magistro* and *De Doctrina* there is an enduring influence from the Stoic logic that makes an appearance in *De Dialectica.*[80] Over time, however, Augustine's position evolves, and Stoic notions about utterances are increasingly embedded in a Christian-Platonic inquiry into words and things.[81] The shift begins in *De Dialectica.* Chapter 5 is indebted to Stoic ideas; yet the source is not mentioned until chapter 6, where Augustine echoes Cicero's derision at Stoic attempts to systematize relations between sound and sense through words.[82] He speaks of the movement in the past tense,[83] as if he were referring both to earlier history and to a previous phase of his thinking. From that point Stoicism ceases to be the major source of the argument; in chapters 8–10 reference is also made to Aristotle, Varro, and Cicero.[84] Augustine appears to be configuring the Stoics as purveyors of inadequate philosophical information and as *dramatis personae* in the story of his spiritual progress, which is related in parallel accounts in his dialogues, autobiography, letters, and theology. In *De Magistro,* as in the other "philosophical dialogues," Stoicism shares the stage with another abandoned perspective, scepticism. In *Contra Academicos,* Licentius maintains that people are happy as long as they are actively searching for truth, whether or not their objective is reached,[85] and this observation leads Nauigius to propose that the quest and the goal may well be identical.[86] In *De Beata Vita*[87] it is argued that the best that can be hoped for in this type of inquiry is "probability," not absolute truth.[88] In both works the problem of ethics is absorbed into the language of ethics—a strategy that is brilliantly deployed in *De Magistro*.[89] The result "is not a dialogue on the impossibility of dialoguing, still less on the impossibility of teaching, but on the conditions which render both possible."[90]

*De Magistro* is unique among Augustine's early dialogues in reproducing some features of an earlier work of philosophy, Plato's *Meno*.[91] Neither the father nor the son read the original;[92] but in *Epistle* 7, written in 389, Augustine speaks as if he is already acquainted with the Platonic doctrine of reminiscence and its critics,[93] among whom he later numbers himself.[94] His understanding is based on Cicero, whose vocabulary he echoes for the crucial relationship between teaching and learning *(docere, discere)* and remembering, reminiscing, or recognizing *(recordari, reminiscendo, recognoscere)*.[95] However, he disagrees with both Plato and Cicero on a critical element in the theory—the pre-existence of souls. He may have flirted with the pagan view as late as 389,[96] but no trace of it is found in the dialogue itself.

The similarity between the *Meno* and *De Magistro* is therefore formal, not substantive. The works occupy comparable positions in each author's thought. The *Meno* is reckoned to be among Plato's early dialogues, as *De Magistro* is among Augustine's. In the writings of this period, Plato is concerned with the nature of virtue and in particular with whether virtue can be taught. *De Magistro* is likewise concerned with teaching; its more restricted, linguistic context nevertheless includes ethical issues. Furthermore, the arguments of both Socrates and Augustine can be looked upon as parallel refutations of Meno's paradox: this is the sophistical view that, if we do not know what we are looking for, we will not recognize it when we find it; yet, if we know what we are seeking beforehand, our inquiry is pointless.

The idea is stated by Meno at the beginning of Socrates' account of reminiscence; in *De Magistro,* it occurs near the end, when Augustine sums up the reasons why we learn only from ourselves. Plato cites Meno's paradox as a point of departure, so that Socrates can find a way around it; Augustine refers to it in his conclusion because, obliquely, he affirms it, arguing that words inadequately convey our thoughts about things. Accordingly, each thinker has his evaluation of the place of verbal reasoning in determining what is taught or learned. Plato's view is positive: in the *Meno,* a slave-boy, untrained in geometry, solves a geometrical problem by following Socrates' questions alone. The necessary knowledge is acquired not through his sensory experience but through his understanding of logical relationships.[97] Socrates thus proves to his satisfaction that the truth of the solution is already "in" the boy's mind, and that it must have been there since birth: his questions are merely "reminders" of what the youngster has always known.

In *De Magistro,* the validity of interior knowledge is established through a negative version of the same type of thinking. Augustine tackles the issues through the manner in which a dialogue consisting of questions and answers proceeds, concluding that in all communication through signs, the relation of words to the things they signify does not arise from language itself.[98] We cannot learn anything from anyone without the use of signs (2.1–10.47), he points out, nor can we learn anything from anyone for certain by the use of signs alone (10.48–11.18).[99] The main goals of language, communication and recall (1.1–76), are thus facilitated and logically frustrated in verbal interchange. In Augustine's view, overcoming the difficulties requires a type of instruction that does not originate in external sounds but silently enlightens us from within. Ultimately, this enlightenment arises through a nonhuman source and requires an intermediary that is accessible to human senses and minds (10.43–14.45), such as speech, images, or texts.

## Speaking

The essentials of Augustine's approach to these issues are presented in chapter 1, where he proposes that speaking has a dual purpose, to "teach" something or "to call it to mind," either for others' benefit or for one's own.[100]

These notions require comment.[101] In *docere* (to teach) he does not refer primarily to teaching, but to informing in general, through showing, telling, or logical demonstration.[102] *Commemorare* (to recall) encompasses the ideas of reminding, remembering, and commemorating.[103] Neither concept requires the presence of texts; this has to be deduced later through an examination of a critical example taken from scripture, to which I turn presently. *De Magistro* also envisages different audiences as the dialogue moves from a positive to a negative position on the truth-value of verbal signs. When Augustine speaks of communication in words in the work's first segment (2.1–10.114), he thinks chiefly of what we can teach others or learn from them. When he turns to instruction from within in the second segment (10.115–14.45), the issues are taken up in relation to the individual mind.

The first task of the debate is to clarify the concepts of "teaching" and "recalling." This is done through the examples of song and prayer (chapter 1). The illustrations in *De Dialectica* 5 stand at either end of a scale consisting of physical sound and the mental recreation of meaning. In a melody to which no text is attached, Adeodatus points out, we utter connected sounds, but not words; and through them, although we derive pleasure, we teach and learn nothing; nor do we normally sing in order to recollect. Augustine is forced to acknowledge two "genres" of articulate sounds, melody and speech. Only speech, it would appear, has the dual role of "informing" *(docere)* and "calling to mind" *(commemorare,* 1.16–38).

The pair agree on this. Adeodatus then mentions a second exception, prayer. This too is a type of sound, since words are uttered (ancient prayer being oral). Yet God, to whom they are addressed, is neither taught nor reminded of anything (1.39–41).[104] Augustine's response draws attention to the contrast between hearing and insightful thinking, which looks forward to his argument for certain knowledge through inner illumination in 12.1–29. When I speak to someone, an outer sign, the uttered word, gives evidence of my intention. By contrast, when I pray, I also utter words; but these words arise from within, and the evidence of my intentions is the mental activity that brings them into being, not their sounds.

To put the issues in philosophical and Pauline terms respectively, prayer is a voluntary expression of signs through sounds that reveals what is in the rational soul, that is, the "interior man."[105] If we consider that the audience of prayer is God, the speech does not take place for his benefit, since he does not communicate in human language, but for the speaker's, as a type of *aide-mémoire*. There are numerous allusions to this sort of interiority in the New Testament, including, of course, Christ's instructions to his disciples about how and why they should pray (1.49–70). When I am deep in thought, I can think in words and utter them to myself without making a sound.[106] As in the case of prayer, this "speech" jogs the memory: I am reminded of the realities for which the words stand as vocal signs (1.74–76).

Augustine turns to these issues in the second section of *De Magistro;* in the remainder of the first section, he focuses on problems of words, taking up a question that arises from his two examples.[107] He asks whether significations arise *without* the use of such instruments. Activities that signify in themselves, such as walking or pointing to a wall, raise this possibility (3.1–84). One part of the ensuing discussion treats signs that relate to other signs (4.29–6.52). The other deals with actions that are not themselves signs: their natures are revealed by inquiries after the act or by signs that draw attention to the acts (4.29–40, 54–57; 8.25–10.48).[108] These are called significables *(significabilia)*.

In 2.1–10.47, he takes up the critical case of signs that signify by means of signs, thus transforming an argument from *De Dialectica*.[109] The discussion[110] results in distinctions between *nomen, uerbum, uocabulum,* and *onoma*.[111] A *nomen,* a noun or name, is the audible sign of other audible signs, such as "Romulus" or "river" (4.40–46); but each of these is also a word, a *uerbum*. A "word" is defined as the sign of "noun," in the way in which "animal" is the sign of "horse" (4.82–130). Among signs that signify things, therefore, "noun" and "word" signify themselves. For, just as *signum* is a sign, so *uerbum* is a word and *nomen* a noun or name. Also, "noun" and "word" are signs that signify each other, for *nomen* and *uerbum* are both words and nouns (4.131–5.26). Yet nouns and words differ as well: in etymology, which contrasts "naming" and "sounding" (5.54–57); in the capacity of nouns to be replaced by pronouns (5.60–91); and in a variety of functions in discourse, which specify the roles of parts of speech (5.58–219). Finally, while *nomen* can be distinguished from other word-names in Latin, such as *uocabulum,* which is not a part of speech,[112] it is identical to words serving the same grammatical function in other languages, such as *onoma* in Greek (6.1–53).

After Adeodatus lucidly summarizes the conversation to this point (7.3–86), Augustine turns to the problematic *significabilia*.[113] The Latin *ho/mo,* as spoken, consists physically of two syllables; yet what is signified by the sounds is a nonphysical reality, namely the mental notion of a "man" (8.32–46), since an audible sign invariably calls to mind the thing that it represents.[114] A fourfold scheme is then presented which gives logical precision to the distinctions implicit in *De Dialectica* 5 and 7:[115] this involves *nomen, res, cognitio nominis,* and *cognitio rei* (the name, the thing, the knowledge of the name, and the knowledge of the thing, 9.77–78). Augustine again argues that realities take priority over signs (even in dubious cases in which a sign is preferable to a less attractive reality, since the principle that creates order is judged to be superior to the order that is created by it, namely the sign).[116] He concludes that nothing can be taught by one person to another without the use of signs, except language itself and the notion of teaching (10.1–48).

The stated subject in this entire segment (2.1–10.47) is signs in spoken discourse; however, on close examination, this argument, like its predecessor in *De Dialectica,* is underpinned by illustrations that appear to imply the presence of written texts. Whereas in the earlier work these provide parallels for verbal relationships, Augustine now uses them to buttress his conclusion that, contrary to our intuitive understanding of language, we do not learn anything about reality from word-signs alone (10.49–11.44) but through a combination of verbal and mental activities. This is evident from his three types of examples in chapters 1–6, which involve grammar, unstated references, and what is potentially signified.

1. *Grammar.* In the analytical phase of the discussion of parts of speech, reference is made only to spoken words (5.66–91); yet the success of the argument depends on a harmonization of sounds and letters.[117] The introduction of a line of poetry, *Aeneid* 2.659, at *De Magistro* 3.6–7 during a crucial phase of the debate, transforms the verbal concerns previously outlined in *De Dialectica* 3 into the textual concerns of *De Dialectica* 5 and 7. A parallel effect is produced by the major illustrative quotation from scripture, 2 Corinthians 1:19: *Non erat in Christo est et non, sed est in illo erat* (There was not in Christ "is" and "is not," but "is" was in him). Augustine argues that what was "in Christ" was not the three letters, *est*, but what is signified in his name, that is, Christ (5.102–106). He confirms his position by stating that Paul's words are validated by the "authority" of correct usage as well as by their truth-value in the Bible (5.141–219). Looking ahead to *De Magistro* 12, his objective is to establish a link between knowledge gained from scripture through the senses (by hearing and seeing) and knowledge gained from within (by illumination).

2. *Unstated references.* This method involves both stated and unstated references. In the case of pagan works such as the *Aeneid* quoted in *De Dialectica,* Augustine does not presuppose that the text has been read in advance. Each line that is quoted is "grammatically" analysed. However, in his references to scripture, the meaning cannot be understood unless the speaker has already read the texts, compared them, and worked out an interpretive position (as in *Confessions* 7).

The best example of the second technique occurs in the passage (quoted above, in Chapter 1) on the relative value of song and prayer, in which an *analysis* of the semantics of melody is contrasted with a group of interlocked *quotations* from scripture. There are two quotations, each differing in the demands that they make on the implied hearer or reader. One, related indirectly, alludes to Christ's manner of teaching his disciples the Lord's Prayer.[118] The other works by drawing on unconnected passages of scripture that describe praying as an interior experience.[119] The critical link between the pair is effected by a text that is not cited; this is the statement upon which Augustine's metaphor of Christ as "the supreme teacher" rests. What Augustine says is that Christ taught his disciples not words, but things by means of words (1.63–68). What he does not say is that this application of his sign theory is derived from Matthew 6:7–8; there Christ tells the apostles not to be like the pagans, who think they can make themselves heard by using many words *(multiloquium);* instead, they should pray as he tells them, since their father knows their needs before they ask. His statement that in prayer God has no need of our spoken words[120] depends on a contrast between *loqui* and *orare* in the biblical text; and it is this juxtaposition, supported by similar statements elsewhere in scripture, which in turn underpins the notion of inner speech in the identifiable quotations of chapter 1. The notion of divine foreknowledge for man's words of prayer thus anticipates the view that in everything we understand we follow a truth that presides from within (11.44–46).

   3. *Significabilia*. A similar orientation appears in the discussion of "significables." The critical change is the introduction of the notion of writings as a kind of gesture and implying, as in *Confessions* 1.6–8, that such gestures give rise to acoustic patterns in the mind; graphic signs would then provide an example of linguistic gesturing between the sender and the receiver of a sign.[121] Within the class of gestures, however, writings are a special case. They differ from spoken words, since they are perceived visually rather than audibly; yet they are like spoken words insofar as the visual presence of the sign creates the mental equivalent of their being heard.[122] In this respect, *significabilia* parallel *uisibilia* and *audibilia*. They likewise recall the *dicibilia* of *De Dialectica* 5—that is, what the mind rather than the ear grasps by means of a word, but with the added notion of "inward seeing" (for example, 12.32).

## Of Bird-Snaring and Head-Gear

It can be argued that Augustine has this inwardness as his objective from the outset.[123] The first part of the dialogue (2.1–10.47) is a "playful" introduction to a serious subject:[124] this is nothing less than the understanding of truth (8.6–19), which is taken up in earnest in the third part (11.19–14.45). The second part, a mere two chapters (10.48–11.18), bridges these discussions. The brevity is understandable, if we assume that the thesis by which one gains information about reality through verbal signs alone has already been refuted. Augustine believes just the opposite. This is clear from the conceptual scheme laid down in chapters 3–4, where he demonstrates that signifying takes place in the absence of words; also, that there are privileged means for bringing this about, gestures and writings. The latter are adopted as models in chapters 10–11, where he shifts his inquiry from words to truth. In order to signify "wall," he argues, I can pronounce the Latin word *paries,* in which case the three syllables signify "a wall" in my mind; alternately, I can point to the wall, even though I cannot thus indicate its nonvisible qualities (such as how it feels, what it weighs, and its temperature). This limitation can be overcome if I switch from pointing to gesturing, as when deaf-mutes converse or when mimes enact dramas without words. Through such gestures, I can configure a wall as well as its nonvisible qualities.

These gestures *(gestus)* are signs that signify realities through the motion of a body *(motus corporis,* 3.1–52).[125] Accordingly, Augustine asks whether it is possible for me to distinguish between two states of the same activity, such as "walking" and "hurrying," by using gestures alone. His answer is negative. If I am asked what I am doing *while* I am walking or hurrying, I cannot indicate "the thing" through my bodily motions. The activity is already under way, and a gesture does not tell me where walking ends and hurrying begins. On the other hand, if I have not begun to walk or to hurry, and, if someone asks me to describe these activities, I can, after the question is put, clearly respond by means of gestures, distinguishing between two things, an unhurried and a hurried gait. This gesturing would provide a demonstration (in addition to those mentioned) that it is possible to signify something without actually using words (3.53–83; compare 10.1–17).[126] However, such signifiers would then consist of two sorts: those capable of being indicated by signs that we are not relating or performing when asked about them (for example, walking and hurrying), and those that are themselves signs while they are being related (for example, talking and making signs; 4.1–5).

In 4.29–40 Augustine divides these activities into gestures and writings. His purpose is unclear until the point at which Adeodatus' answer is criticized (10.62–90).[127] Augustine's refutation of his son's views is then documented by one example of each type of "gesture." These developments in turn depend on an important change in thinking that takes place at the beginning of chapter 10, when he asks Adeodatus to reconsider the nature of actions that signify on their own. His son recalls that there are two exceptions to the general rule, namely speaking and teaching; in both, the sign and the thing are the same. Yet, if this were the case, one could never teach except by speaking. Against this view, moreover, they have demonstrated that signs that are not words exist and things are made known through them (10.20–22). Therefore, "teaching" and "signifying" are evidently not the same. We give forth signs in order to teach, but we do not teach in order to give forth signs.[128]

One cannot even teach what teaching is without the use of signs. For, if teaching cannot be carried on without speaking, then it is not made evident by itself (10.38–47). Speaking, it would appear, is the only thing that is self-signifying. Yet even this conclusion, a pillar of Augustine's earlier interpretation of Stoic theory, seems to be of doubtful value, since the goal of the inquiry has shifted from the mechanics of verbal signification to an understanding of the reality that is signified (10.49–51). With these problems in mind, the pair take up two critical examples which conclude the discussion of the signs of words undertaken in *De Dialectica* and lay the foundation for Augustine's more general critique of verbal representations.

1. *Bird-snaring* (10.80–113). Two individuals meet on a country road. One of them carries equipment for snaring birds; the other is not familiar with this use for reeds and birdline and is curious to learn their purpose. If the hunter catches a bird, has he not shown the observer what he wants to know by the "art" of bird-snaring rather than by "signifying" (10.80–90)?[129]

Adeodatus recalls the case of walking (chapter 3). But Augustine has introduced a new element into the discussion; this is the assumption that an observer of a meaningful action is intelligent enough to grasp what is taking place after seeing *a part* of what is going on.[130] Certain things, though perhaps not all of any one of them, can thus be learned without signs.[131] Adeodatus agrees that an alert bystander understands what walking is when he sees someone take a few steps (10.98–100). As a consequence, it appears that their earlier view that nothing can be taught without signs is erroneous. Augustine adds that there are numerous examples of communication without verbal signs: they include actions as simple as a pantomime, in which a narrative is enacted silently; and, at a more complex level, objects which appear to be created in the world without the intermediary of signs, such as the sun, moon, stars, earth, and sea (10.108–113).

This argument compels him to restate his position. There is nothing taught by verbal signs in themselves. If I am presented with a sign, and I do not know the thing that it stands for, I can learn nothing. Conversely, if I know the thing it stands for before I become acquainted with the sign, I learn nothing from the sign.[132] As sources of knowledge, verbal signs are demoted from the primary role that they have had at the outset of the dialogue.

2. *Sarabarae.* (10.122–171). Augustine's second example is a biblical quotation: "And their *sarabarae* were not altered" (Daniel 3:94).[133] The context is the emergence, unharmed, of Shadrach, Meshach, and Abednego from the fire into which Nebuchadnezzar had them thrust after they refused to worship the golden statue he had erected in the plain of Dura. The *sarabarae* are the "head-gear" which they wore into the furnace. Thus protected, the three were unconsumed, bearing witness to God's limitless power.

The syllables of *sarabarae* do not inform the hearer that the reality in question is "head-coverings." This fact has to be learned beforehand as the sounds are repeated in the presence of the thing that they signify. The case of *sarabarae* is no different from that of a more familiar noun (such as *caput,* head). Anticipating his mimetic theory of child learning,[134] Augustine asserts that when the two syllables *ca/put* first reached his ears, he had no idea what they meant. However, as he heard them again and again, he "noted and observed" the thing for which the "vocal designation" stood— namely a "head." In sum, the sign was taken in by means of the thing as an object of thought *(res cognita)* rather than by means of a verbally given sign *(signum datum,* 10.130–133).

If I am ignorant of the thing signified, how can I acquire the knowledge that is evidently conveyed by the sign? Augustine's answer is by combining the aural and the visual. Suppose that I hear *caput* for the first time and I do not know whether the sound of the word signifies something or not. If, when I inquire, a head is pointed at, the sign—which until that moment I had heard but not understood—is learned by visual means. Echoing the language of *De Dialectica* 5, he concludes that every sign has two components, the sound and the signification *(sonus et significatio).* However, in place of the unique emphasis on sound in *De Dialectica,* he introduces a distinction between the ear and the eye. We perceive the sound when its waves strike the ear; but we perceive its signification by observing the thing signified.[135]

Sound and sight, it would appear, have different functions in signification. We cannot learn the reality of the sign through hearing or vision alone. If, for instance, I merely point to a head with my finger, I am unable to signify anything but what the finger indicates: that, obviously, is not the sign, but the thing. Nor do I truly "learn" of this reality, since, by pointing to it, I have demonstrated that I already know it. As Augustine stresses earlier, there is a difference between "pointing" and either "gesturing" or "writing": only the latter two can give rise to signification (3.24–83). The directing of a finger towards a thing is not the sign of a reality, since the intention is in the finger rather than in the sign (10.144–146). In this case, pointing has the same status with respect to things as saying "Look!" By the same reasoning, we do not learn the signification that is "hidden" in the sound by means of signifying; we learn of it after we recognize the reality that is in question.[136]

Let us not forget that Augustine is illustrating a single example, *sarabarae.* He argues that, as I learn about a "head," so I learn about *sarabarae.* They too can be indicated by gestures, by drawings, or by similar objects: in each case, I am taught what they are, but not by means of words alone. Alternately, someone might produce *sarabarae* and say to me, "Here they are." I would then learn of the reality by seeing it; and, after seeing it, I would know what it is and recognize it when I heard the word and saw it again. In learning what *sarabarae* are by these means, I would not be putting my trust in another person's words; and, if I did so temporarily, this would only be a directive to what I should seek out and observe myself.[137]

There is of course a problem with this empirical conclusion.[138] The difficulty arises from the fact that Augustine learned the meaning of *caput* and *sarabarae* in different ways. In the case of a "head," the sound and the sense of the word may have been united by visual means. Learning about a "head-covering" was another matter: the knowledge was not acquired after it was seen; nor was Augustine instructed by gestures, drawings, or objects that he recognized. His sole source of information, which he gained by reading, was a single, unrepeated line of scripture. Contrary to what he claims, he had to trust implicitly in someone else's words; these were originally God's words, but they were communicated through the transcriber of the story, and this communication involves another implicit assumption. Furthermore, the words are not directives to inquiry and observation; they are points of departure for his own mental operations. So, once again, we find ourselves in a dilemma similar to that of *De Dialectica*. The demonstration has been carried on as if nothing was involved but speech, complemented here by vision. But it appears that a good deal more is involved, including memory and narrative context.

Above all, it is not the word *sarabarae* that facilitates the understanding of the text of Daniel, as the logic of Augustine's argument seems to suggest, but the text of scripture that imposes a meaning on one type of head-gear—a relationship that can be clarified through a comparison with the quotations from scripture in chapters 1 and 5. There, meaning is constructed around words, phrases, and individual sentences *outside* their narrative contexts in the Bible. For example, in prayer, a number of separate quotations support a single idea, namely inner speech (1.49–56); in the statement taken from 2 Corinthians 1:19, a comparison is made between the phonetic and semantic dimensions of *est* (5.102–106).[139] These uses for scripture contrast with the comments on Daniel 1:94, where the illustrative passage is contextualized within a single biblical story. A similar idea is at work in the example of the bird-catcher, since it is assumed that one can grasp the significance of an activity by observing only a part of its performance. This "part" is within an account which the observer completes. In both cases, a meaning is created for events by putting them in a sequence, that is, in Augustine's terms, a narrative.

Like the observer of bird-snaring, then, the reader of Daniel 1:94 makes use of the "hermeneutic circle": he learns the part from the whole and the whole from the part.[140] Recognizing that this method is at work helps us to perceive the second type of contrast in the scriptural quotations. This is a variant on unstatedness. In the case of prayer, knowing Christ's words to his disciples strengthens the connections that Augustine makes between prayer and inner speech. Christ's words therefore stand in relation to what *De Magistro* tells us as an unstated text: *we,* as readers, complete the text. In the case of *sarabarae,* the meaning also arises out of the story in which the word occurs, although this story is not told by Augustine. In this case, *he* is the reader who completes the text. He thereby reiterates the principle of unstatedness, but in a personal narrative context (that is, by what the story means to him). When he turns to illumination, a similar method is at work; however, reading, as a human form of discourse, is no longer necessary. The role of the unstated text is taken by the knowledge that God implants in our minds or souls; the role of the stated knowledge is taken by words as they emerge from unconscious to conscious thinking and are heard as utterances. In this final phase, which is not clearly spelled out in *De Magistro,* we find a literary methodology coming to the aid of ontology.

## Beliefs, Knowledge, and Illumination

Augustine takes the analysis a decisive step further in chapter 11. Before doing so, he summarizes his fundamental disagreement with the position that he and Adeodatus forcefully put forward in 2.1–10.47. As he now sees matters, verbal signs are only "suggestions" for inquiries into a reality which they themselves cannot "show" us.[141] Lacking their referents, words signify nothing; they are only "sound and fury" (11.5–6). Moreover, speaking and teaching stand on opposite sides of a semantic boundary. Someone who teaches me about something, in contrast to someone who utters words, presents what I desire to know, either to my eyes, to my other senses, or to my mind (11.3–5).[142]

Augustine orients his argument to this position throughout. His initial contrast, song and prayer, is settled by the example of Christ, who did not teach mere words but taught realities by means of words (1.67–68). Later it is agreed by both parties that speaking is superior to words, since teaching has more value than speaking.[143] In a later stage of the discussion, the pair affirm that a knowledge of reality is preferable to a sign of reality, and that a knowledge of a signified reality is preferable in turn to a knowledge of its sign (9.69–80).

These statements are combined to arrive at a new point of departure in chapter 11, in which the argument of *De Magistro* is brought to its final phase (though left incomplete). Augustine's reasoning is based on what we do and do not know in the story of Shadrach, Meshach, and Abednego. Without his seeing *sarabarae,* he has made clear, the word is just uttered sound. Yet in reading Daniel, even if we do not know what "head-gear" is, we accept as a given the tale of how the three overcame the king and survived the flames through faith, sang the praises of God in gratitude, and were rewarded by their former enemy. We learned of these matters "by words alone": what they "signify" is acquired knowledge *(notitia)* at the time of relating,[144] that is, what is "boy," "furnace," "fire," and "king," and what is meant, or even implied, in the phrase "unharmed by fire." By contrast, there are other names that do not fall into the category of knowledge at hand: these include *sarabarae* as well as characters not mentioned—say, Ananias, Azarias, and Misael. In these cases, "nouns" or "names" do not provide a knowledge of realities. They remain mere vocal designations.

When we understand the story, the events are assumed to have taken place as they were written down. As Augustine frequently emphasizes, they are *believed* rather than *known*.[145] What I understand, I also believe; and everything I understand, I know. Yet I do not know all that I believe.[146] Indeed, most things that arise in narrative situations (including the narrative of the three youths in the furnace) cannot possibly be known, but believing them has a utilitarian value, since without such assumptions we cannot establish credibility for a narrative in which we ourselves have not taken part.[147]

This notion of truth is a hermeneutics of belief, inasmuch as truth is approached by interpretive stages involving the parts and the whole.[148] However, this truth is also concerned with narrative, because a continuity of beliefs is a by-product of stories that are told or read. In the search for truth, therefore, just as we unravel the spiritual sense of a text,[149] so we must turn from the externals of speech to the interiorities of mind,[150] that is, to the "rational soul" (11.46–51; compare 1.45–61). Moreover, the accuracy of our inner sight depends on the moral state of the will. Falling into error is like being unable to see an object when we are sure it is present and there is enough light for it to be perceived (11.51–55).[151]

As these thoughts are clarified, Augustine abandons the argument based on the signifiers and signifieds of verbal expression and adopts a Platonic approach. The visible and invisible are transferred to the biblical page as the overt and covert senses of the text. "Sensible" and "intelligible" are equated with "carnal" and "spiritual."[152] The carnal sense represents learning about signs from things physically present. For instance, in order to know what "new moon" signifies, I have to see the moon in the sky; otherwise, I lodge my beliefs about a new moon in the words alone. The parallel with the spiritual sense arises when I think of phenomena that are not physically present but known through memory, for example, last month's new moon. This type of image is put into words in the way in which a story is told *(narrare),* with the memory images acting like documentary proofs *(documenta)*[153] The type of proof to which Augustine refers is, of course, altogether personal. As a consequence, someone who hears the words "new moon" will not believe them solely on the basis of what I say. He or she must also have stored in memory the image of a new moon (12.14–29). Through the operation of memory, one narrative construction of reality thus supports another.

In these examples, exterior and interior perception differ. The stimulus of spoken words does not provoke a response; instead, it is through the faculties of "understanding" and "reason" that vocal expression is given to realities thrown into relief by "the interior light of truth" (12.30–33). If I speak of a "new moon" and my words are comprehended, the hearer recognizes their truth through his own internal reflections on them (12.33–35). I may speak a truth and he may see one: yet it is not I who inform him, but rather the reality which appears in his mind. The source of this principle of understanding cannot be physical, that is, lodged in words; it must be metaphysical, that is, arising directly or indirectly in God. The proof for the existence of a principle that is outside the boundaries of language is that the other party, if asked what a new moon is, can give an adequate reply, even though no moon is present. It is clear that a knowledge of the reality is in his mind before he is asked; and the accuracy of his response is not a measure of my power to communicate to him via words but of his capacity for self-instruction, which is based on his own concepts' becoming words. As an illustration of this point, Augustine analyses what sort of reality he and Adeodatus have been dealing with in their debate on the import of words (12.36–72). This is an ironic way of drawing attention to the propaedeutic purpose of section one (2.1–10.47), a debate in words that illustrates what words cannot do.

It is in this context that Augustine introduces his well-known doctrine of "illumination,"[154] namely the metaphorical approach to understanding, normally reserved for nonempirical information (for example, abstract notions, such as truth, justice, or faith), which assumes "that the act whereby the mind knows truth is comparable to the act whereby the eye sees a body."[155] His analogies are based on the notion that within the soul there is something called "understanding" or "mind," which is "enlightened" by a light that is superior to itself.[156] He alludes to the idea in *Contra Academicos*.[157] Typical expressions are also incorporated into *De Beata Vita* 4.35, where he speaks of "a type of recollection, or calling to mind, that acts within us, enabling us to remember and seek God, who acts like a hidden sun that brightens our eyes from within."[158] Similar ideas are explored in *Soliloquia*[159] and in *De Immortalitate Animae*.[160]

In *De Magistro,* neoplatonic metaphors of enlightenment are first coupled with explicit statements concerning interior instruction by means of Christ.[161] Augustine also makes clear that signs imply teaching from the outside. Most people are incapable of apprehending truth: they need the orderly methods of a discipline if they are to progress toward wisdom.[162] Illumination is a form of participation in God[163] that is brought about through scripture but is caused by him.[164] We speak of an enlightened man as "a luminary": yet it is only the light that truly enlightens.[165] Ignorance is its absence.[166] By contrast, words sound the same to someone who sees an object described as they do to someone who does not see it; and, when the image of that object is recalled from memory, it is only the sense impression that is brought out of storage and reexpressed in words[167] which answer no questions concerning realities in themselves (12.38–45).[168]

The direction of Augustine's thinking is well illustrated by a statement near the end of *Sermon* 54 on John, which is one of several reflections on the manner in which we are instructed through Christ's words. In order that humans might believe what they did not yet understand, the Lord's words were issued from human lips as audible sounds, making noises as they flew rapidly past and completed the term of their duration. However, the realities for which the sounds were the vocal signs were transferred into the memories of those who heard them, namely the apostles, and have come down to us by means of writings, which are visible signs. Yet these signs speak inwardly only to the minds of those who already understand; they address persons who are instructed without any sounds, whose hearts overflow with the light of understanding. God awakens in all of us a desire for this inner sweetness, but we acquire understanding only in stages of intellectual evolution, like children learning to walk.[169] In other words, it is through study that we are informed, but through inward teaching that we are illuminated.

This type of thinking lies behind the developmental scheme of *Confessions* 1 and some abstract discussion of language elsewhere in the "philosophical dialogues."[170] In *De Magistro,* Augustine satisfies himself with taking up negative cases. These arise when, through a variety of deceptions, words are not intended to stand for things (13.14–72). The treatise ends with a reaffirmation of the benefits of interiority. The person who sees with the inner eye is a "student of truth," who automatically becomes the judge of a "speaker," or at least of "what is spoken."[171] The teachers' thoughts are not adequately grasped and retained. What they pass on is just a "discipline."[172] Only later, in accord with their own capacities, do students judge what has been taught in the light of interior truth: then they really "learn" (14.5–12).[173] Similarly, in life, we cannot call another human our "teacher." For what is taught externally through signs is merely a "guideline" for what is taught when, turning inward towards God, one discovers "the blessed life"—a route that many seek but few find (14.18–27).[174]

As in *De Dialectica,* Augustine ends *De Magistro* by recalling the pragmatic world of teaching and learning in the liberal arts.[175] He reaffirms the distinctions between logic and truth put forward in *Soliloquia;*[176] at the same time, *De Magistro* is a turning point in his consideration of language and ethics through the introduction of the concept of illumination. He reasons that signification involves both the senses and the mind, since signs are one thing in sound and another in the understanding. The senses involved are chiefly hearing and sight, which are represented respectively by the activities of telling and showing. The mental parallel lies through memory and illumination: memory is "telling" through the remembering of relations between words and things; illumination is "showing," since realities are displayed directly. Writings have a special place in this scheme, since they combine visual and aural modes of communication. In reading, a sign, presented to the eyes, brings to mind a group of syllables as heard. Reading, therefore, and not speaking, is the new paradigm of signification, which can be configured as follows:

However, there is also a parallel between reading and remembering:

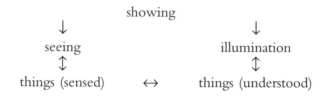

and between seeing and illumination:

Augustine is credited with introducing the notion of signification into theories of language. His approach can equally well be described as a defence of the power of mind at the expense of the belief that language can communicate unaided by anything else: his ideas represent the end of an age of innocence about the value of words and the beginning of one in which scepticism becomes the handmaiden of faith. What vanishes is the idea that there can be spontaneous meaning. In Augustine's view, linguistic instruction requires that we account for reality as something existing before the act of speaking, by which that same reality is given expression. He teaches us this lesson through *De Magistro*'s logic of the discussion and through its literary format. As the realities conveyed by words are questioned, so the functional role of debate is diminished. The turning point is chapter 10, after which Augustine speaks virtually alone. This development is appropriate, since the dominant theme has changed from "telling" to "showing." The ancient dialogue would appear to lose some of its force as its philosophical foundation crumbles.

## Defining the Reader

In the remainder of this chapter and in the next, I take up three works in which Augustine directly addresses the problems of readers and audiences raised in *De Dialectica* and *De Magistro: De Utilitate Credendi,* written in 391; *De Catechizandis Rudibus,* which the Maurists date from 399; and *De Doctrina Christiana.*

In *De Utilitate Credendi,*[177] Augustine responds to the Manichaean views of Honoratus, a friend from his school years,[178] in a first attempt at the delineation of the audience after his ordination. *De Catechizandis Rudibus* speaks chiefly of two types of auditors, the *rudes* and *eruditi* (the uninstructed and the instructed), both of whom are candidates for baptism but who represent different levels of instruction in grammar, rhetoric, and literary criticism. *De Doctrina* goes further still, distinguishing between novice and expert interpreters of texts; this work also separates the discussions of reading and preaching, and offers a general configuration for the educated Christian religious or layperson.

## Audience

In writing to Honoratus concerning the errors of Manichaeism, Augustine insists that his friend must not confuse a heretic *(haereticus)* with someone who believes heretics *(credens haereticis,* 1.1–2). The heretic is misled by his opinions *(opiniones);* the believer, by his mental recreation of them *(imaginatio,* 1.9–10). Neither the sender nor the receiver of signs apprehends a reality *(res,* 1.14); both depend on sense data (1.16–17). The speaker is an audience for himself as well as for others; the recipients are auditors through their reconstruction of what is said.

Beyond the rhetoric (for example, 1.7–9, 25–28) and the expected defensiveness of a sometime Manichaean auditor who had recently become an ordained priest (2.9–26), these remarks serve an important transitional purpose. The clue to *De Magistro*'s themes is in the phrase, *de inuenienda ac retinenda ueritate* (concerning a truth to be discovered and retained in memory) (1.12–13), where Augustine recalls the relationship between learning and memory (chapter 1) and the search for illuminative truth (chapters 13–14). In place of a comprehensive discussion of "the utility of words," which the earlier dialogue postpones, he turns to "the utility of believing." As the Manichaeans are recreated in his imagination, they personify the belief in spoken words against which the arguments of *De Magistro* are directed.[179]

In the dialogue with Adeodatus, Augustine opposes the transitoriness of verbal communication with certainties acquired through "illumination"; here he contrasts the words of heretics with an inwardness described in neoplatonic images of truth's unfathomable depths (1.20) and its remoteness from the spoken, the sensory, and the quotidian (1.14–15).[180] In contrast to *De Magistro,* moreover, he is overtly concerned with the readers and audiences of texts. He speaks of choosing not "to remain silent" (1.11–12), but he expresses himself through the silent pen rather than through the voice (compare 1.3–5); and he writes for Honoratus as well as for those "into whose hands his text *[litterae]* may fall" (1.22–25). He sees himself responding to the Manichaeans, who "tear asunder" the fabric of the Old Testament and "rip" its texts "to pieces," provoking an "infantile"[181] reaction among those unskilled in interpretation (*inperiti,* 4.2–3). He distinguishes between the masses *(ignari, turba credentium)* and an elite of careful readers (7.6–9), who can understand the Bible's "mysteries."[182] Catholicism, which the preaching of scripture opens to the many, nonetheless has to be expounded by the few, who avoid notoriety (unlike the dualists) and remain unknown except to those who persistently seek them out.[183]

As his interests shift from disputations to the interpretation of texts, he envisages two separate but similarly oriented states of mind held together by a common tradition. Conduct is reformed as individuals strive toward purity of mind using their agreed understanding of selected texts as an instrument of behavioural and intellectual change. From beginning to end, *De Utilitate Credendi* is concerned with the strength of habitual thinking *(mores),* its relation to innate desire *(libido),* and the consequent necessity for agreement between the learned *(doctissimi)* and the uneducated *(inperitum . . . uulgus)* in Christian hermeneutics (35.1–9). Honoratus is asked to take his friend's words as the reliable outer signs of his genuine inner thoughts, and to consider those thoughts as guides to morally informed actions, namely as a rationale for proving what is true *(ueri probandi causa).* The emotional force of his statement even suggests a "conversion," that is, a turning away from one way of life towards another,[184] since he recalls how difficult it is to enter and keep to the right path of wisdom *(iter rectum, uia sapientiae).*[185] He recommends that his friend direct his efforts toward a goal that he himself has not yet attained: his desire for understanding *between* himself and Honoratus thus becomes an expression of hope for enlightenment *within* himself. If that is the case, the audience to whom he directs his remarks is not Honoratus but God (compare 4.23–36).

Thus reading and the beliefs that result from a common interpretation of biblical texts emerge as a compromise: they represent unverifiable intentions in separate minds or souls. The one is envisaged as being in error and desiring the truth, while the other seeks the truth and desires not to fall back on past errors. These topics are developed in subsequent chapters. The theme of Augustine's personal conversion is reintroduced in chapter 20, and the distinction between the proponents and audiences for religious beliefs is the subject of chapters 23–32. Other chapters treat the four senses of scripture (chapters 5–9) and the potential errors of reading and writing (chapters 10–12). (The role of authority in the transmission of teachings—chapters 11–19—and the manner in which beliefs relate to such matters as faith, reason, study, and curiosity—chapters 20–22—are taken up in chapter 7.)

## The Senses of Scripture

The attack on Manichaeism begins with an analysis of *historia, aetiologia, analogia,* and *allegoria,*[186] terms which Augustine introduces hesitantly[187] and which, he initially claims, adhere rigidly to the Greek in order to avoid the pitfalls of attempted "translation" or "circumlocution."[188]

He interprets these notions in a way that makes other critical distinctions hinge on the meaning of *historia;* this notion is subdivided into two types in which the order of events and the order of the narrative are conceived interdependently (*gestum* and *scriptum*). Matters are said to be related historically when we are taught (1) what has been written or carried out or (2) what was not carried out, but is written up as if it had taken place.[189] Aetiology, analogy, and allegory complement this distinction through the different ways in which events are related in writings or related in a way in which writings figuratively stand for events. These are configured aetiologically "when a cause is made known why something has been done or spoken of."[190] The parallel *factum/dictum* is thus added to *gestum/scriptum* and forms the basis for *analogia,* which occurs "when it is demonstrated that the two Testaments, the Old and the New, are not opposed."[191] Allegory restates the initial interdependence between events and writings in a different way, teaching that "certain statements that are made in writing are not to be understood literally but figuratively."[192]

Augustine illustrates these terms with passages of scripture, at first suggesting that the choice of a method depends on the type of text[193] but subsequently revealing that his chief concern is with the audience's response. The contemporary reader (or listener) is instructed by the moral narratives of Christ and the apostles. In this scheme, the Old Testament foreshadows the New, and stories in the New Testament provide examples for educated religious or laypersons. The actors in the biblical narratives are configured as readers, thereby presenting a model of reading and interpretation for Augustine's readers and listeners to follow. In his view, Christ and the apostles are interpreters of the Old Testament even as they act; we interpret their readings and actions as we read and act, and so forth. It is through the model as well as the meaning of the stories that a community of readership overcomes the temporal distance that separates the two narratives in time.

He chooses to comment on passages in which interpretive situations

naturally arise. The cases of *historia* and *aetiologia* depend on Christ's interpretation of two principles of Israelite law and his claim to supersede its
authority. *Historia* is illustrated by Matthew 12:1–4, in which the disciples
accompanying Jesus through the fields consume some of the harvest,
thereby attracting the attention of a Pharisee, who points out that they are
contravening a sabbath law; their action is justified by 1 Samuel 21:4–7,[194]
in which David and his troops eat consecrated bread reserved for temple
priests.[195] *Aetiologia* is raised in the context of Moses' teachings on divorce
(Matt. 19:3–9). When he is questioned on the subject by the Pharisees,
Christ takes the position that the bond between man and woman can be
broken only if adultery has taken place (6.12–17).

These passages from Matthew recreate the conditions for disputation
described in *De Dialectica,* but within the context of a debate on Christian
doctrine. In each example there is a reference text which is known to both
parties, Jewish and Christian—a subtle countermove to the dualists' neglect
of the Old Testament. Jesus introduces the case of David by asking his
disciples whether they have "not read" about it (*non legistis,* Matt. 12:3). In
the instance of divorce, it is assumed that both parties know Deuteronomy
24:1–4; Augustine refers to the *libellum repudii* (bill of divorce), which is
mentioned in the Old Testament and the New (Deut. 24:1; Matt. 19:7).
He thus replaces the *causae* of rhetorical disputes with the reasons for
decisions given in the law.[196]

No quotation illustrates *analogia.* Instead, an attempt is made to refute
the Manichaean notion that there is no congruence between the two major
parts of the Bible. The dualists, Augustine argues, effectively grant the
authority of those who see the New Testament as supported by the Old,
inasmuch as in their rejection of the idea they are preoccupied with
showing how "the intermingling" of the two is due to "corrupters of the
truth." As the manuscript tradition of the gospel narratives does not go
back far enough to provide conclusive evidence one way or the other,[197]
it would be preferable if they asserted that the "transcribers" of the texts
did not "write down" the truth[198] (although it is not clear how evidence
for that position could have been brought forward either). He likewise
argues that the Manichaeans' claim of inconsistency in the New Testament
is itself inconsistent. In the interpretation of Acts 2:2–4, their grounds for
accepting some passages are no better than their grounds for rejecting
others as "falsified or interpolated." Their criticism is just an excuse for
altering the originals, and thereby for conceiving themselves (as did Faustus)
as "bearers of the holy spirit" (7.16–40).

Augustine's position is sounder than that of his opponents,[199] even if we bear in mind that we have only his version of their arguments;[200] this becomes evident as the discussion moves from *aetiologia* to *analogia* and *allegoria*. In his discussion of *analogia,* the focus shifts from *statements* in the New Testament, which refer back to the Old, to *interpretations* within two communities, Jewish and Christian, in which he alternately accepts and rejects the intratestamental references. In taking up *allegoria,* he combines a number of approaches into a complicated exegetical exercise in which the base text, Matthew 12:39–40, again involves questions and answers between Christ and a group of scribes and Pharisees. In addition to verbal debate, the Jews ask "to see a sign" (*signum uidere,* Matt. 12:38). Christ replies: "No sign will be given it but the sign of Jonas, the prophet. Just as Jonas was in the whale's stomach three days and nights [Jonas 2:1], so the son of man will be in the earth's heart three days and nights." Augustine does not quote the entire passage, which repeats *signum* four times (Matt. 12:38–40); nor does he explain the development within the Jewish-Christian dialogue. As he interprets Matthew, the scribes and Pharisees ask for a visible sign, and Christ replies that the only sign that they will receive is invisible. As a consequence, both he and Jonas have to be physically absent in order to become signifiers. Because they are unseen, their meaning in the text can only be understood. As a consequence, Christ's reply satisfies the criterion of communication through verbal signs and illustrates the principle of foreknowledge, since the verbal signs that are incorporated into the allegory have no meaning unless Jonah 2:1–2 is known beforehand (thus recalling the case of *sarabarae* in *De Magistro*). All in all, there is a threefold transformation. The visible sign becomes a verbal and a written sign as it is interpreted by Christ, and it becomes a written sign alone as Augustine reads the text in which the original debate is transcribed.

In his other examples of *allegoria,* the key text is 1 Corinthians 10:1–11.[201] This is taken up not as a prefigural narrative but as a strong interpretation of Exodus. In the order in which the original passages are rearranged in Paul, they speak of the crossing of the Red Sea (Exod. 14:15–31; 1 Cor. 10:1–2); the eating of the "manna" in the desert (Exod. 16:9–18; 1 Cor. 10:3); the water flowing from the rock at Horeb (Exod. 17:1–7; 1 Cor. 10:4); and the eating, drinking, and playing[202] that followed the making of the golden calf (Exod. 32:6; 1 Cor. 10:7, the only line quoted in part from the original).[203] These are seen to be illustrations of baptism (1 Cor. 10:2), the bread and wine of the Last Supper (1 Cor. 10:3–4), and God's relationship to his chosen people, who are "thrown down in the desert" (1 Cor. 10:5) because they refuse to recognize divinely inspired truth.

Augustine also perceives a more subtle development in Paul. This occurs at 1 Corinthians 10:5–7, in which he speaks of the events as "figures for us" (1 Cor. 10:6)—that is, his readers—in which the key episode concerns the idolatry, feasting, and gaming of the Israelites before the golden calf (Exod. 32:6). What Paul does not tell his readers but which many of them knew is that the contrast between the material and the spiritual on which his subsequent statement rests (1 Cor. 10:8–11) is contained in the narrative of Moses' descent from Mount Sinai and the story which in part he quotes. While the prophet is on the mountain and receives the Ten Commandments, the people of Israel, not knowing his whereabouts and fearful that he will not return, gather around Aaron and ask him "to fabricate gods." Aaron casts a golden calf from confiscated rings; the next day, the people make pious sacrifices, eat and drink, and amuse themselves (Exod. 31:18–32:6). In quoting this passage to illustrate *allegoria*,[204] Augustine takes the view that Paul refers to the historical account in Exodus *(historia)* in order to signify *(significare)* an allegory of the Christian people to come *(futurae christianae plebis allegoria,* 8.9–11). In Augustine, the terms "signify" and "allegory" relate to the words spoken and the significance of the text read, whereas Paul distinguishes between the events which took place "in figure" for the Israelites and those which "were written" for the "reprobation" of his readers, for whom the end of time is near (1 Cor. 10–11).

The notion of a spiritual union between past and present readers is developed in Augustine's comments on Galatians 4:22–26 (8.34–43), a text much discussed by Manichaean preachers (7.30–34), where Paul speaks of the birth of Abraham's sons, Ishmael and Isaac—the one by the slave-girl Hagar, the other by his free-born wife, Sarah. Ishmael is born "through the flesh"; Isaac, "through the promise" of God.[205] The respective statements in Genesis (16:15, 21:1–2) about their birth must have been made "in allegory" concerning the "two testaments." One of these, deriving from Mount Sinai, produces bondage. The other, coming from nearby Jerusalem, has two senses: it refers to the city that now exists, which is, so to speak, in bondage with its children, the Jews; and it refers to the Jerusalem above, "the mother of us all," which is free.[206]

In Paul's view, to inherit the "promise" it does not suffice to be among the biological progeny of Abraham. One also has to be a spiritual descendant.[207] Paul has in mind an eschatological view, while Augustine leans toward a hermeneutic one. Utilizing quotations from elsewhere in Galatians and from 2 Corinthians, he concludes that the "flesh" and the "promise" of Galatians 4:22–26 refer to two interpretive strategies, one relating biblical texts back to the historical events on which they are based, the other relating them forward in time to the lives of individual readers. The spiritual community of which he speaks is transferred from the next world to a status that is in this world while anticipating the next. Augustine identifies this community with a specific group of readers, to whom he thinks Paul referred in contrasting the text and its spiritual sense (2 Cor. 3:6).

In order to reach this conclusion, he assumes that the references to Mount Sinai in 1 Corinthians 10:1–11 and in Galatians 4:22–26 are parts of a single discussion which includes the notions of law-giving and bondage instead of dissociating scripture from the law in the Manichaean fashion (9.1–2). Galatians 5:4 is not a rejection of the Old Testament but an indication that the law is a stage in the historical and spiritual progress of mankind, referring to the mental state of the Jews who refuse to free themselves from the bondage of legalism, and more generally to literal and figurative interpretation. The bondage is a useful servitude (*utilis seruitus*, 9.7), because those who could not be brought to God through reason had to be obliged to obey through the law (9.6–11). By contrast, for believers, "the law" is a "pedagogue in Christ" (Gal. 3:24, 9:19–21). Augustine thus transforms the developmental metaphor into a way of talking about general spiritual progress, foreshadowing the narrative about reading in the *Confessions* as well as the transition from the earthly to the heavenly cities.[208]

## The Analysis of Error

Augustine's consideration of *analogia* and *allegoria* redirects his remarks in chapters 10–12 toward a fresh review of the audience's construction of a biblical text. He speaks of taking leave of "the heights of knowledge," accessible to "the learned," and engaging in a less formal type of discussion suitable to "friends" (10.1 3), but the analysis of complex Christian "mysteries" is taken up again at the beginning of chapter 14.

This statement outlines the potential errors of readers and writers. In chapter 10, the errors of reading are said to arise from the different understanding of a text in the mind of its author and its reader. The errors of writers arise from the differences between what they intend to say, what they say, and what they are understood to have said. Augustine thereby introduces a new idea into ancient interpretive theory—the notion that reading's ethical value can take place in a situation of perceived estrangement from truth.

The reader errs (1) when the false is taken for the true, despite the author's perception of the opposite, (2) when both parties make the same mistake, and (3) when the reader sees what is wrong but the writer does not.[209]

The third possibility intrigues Augustine because of its implications for the "use" and "enjoyment" of texts.[210] The understanding of a text is no guarantee that the reader has discovered the truth. A distinction has to be made between means and ends in the reading process. Along with parallel remarks in *De Diuersis Quaestionibus 83*,[211] written between the autumn of 388 and May 395, this view looks forward to the lengthier analysis of things to be "used" and "enjoyed" in *De Doctrina* (396) and *De Trinitate* (after 399).[212] The division of errors also echoes the three kinds of obscurity in *De Dialectica*,[213] within which *De Utilitate Credendi* argues, as does *De Magistro* 10–14, that the meaning of a text is rendered problematical by the isolation of individual thoughts; the failure of writers and readers to connect is a specific example of the weakness inherent in systems of signs, whether they are verbal, visual, or scribal. The logic of *De Magistro* is also radicalized. If the true meaning of the text is not derived from the writer, it can potentially arise in the reader; but Augustine argues that it cannot reside uniquely there either because the text from which the reader derives meaning is provably not his or her creation. Truth, to the degree that it is in texts, must involve a third party, who is neither the writer nor the reader; this is an implicit, unmentioned figure, present in all meaningful reading but not accessible to the senses as are the letters on the page. The ideal reader is thus identical with God.

Augustine is also concerned with an ethical implication of this view. His examples make clear that the three types of situation do not correspond to three reading errors: all are variants of one case, which is expanded and refined as the discussion proceeds.

Examples 1 and 2 are straightforward, involving conclusions drawn from quoted texts. In the first case, *Aeneid* 6.566–569, Rhadamanthus "hears and adjudicates the pleas of the dead." If someone "says or believes" this to be true, he does so because he has "read it" in Virgil's poem; that is, he believes something which should not be believed, and he thinks the author whom he is reading to have believed it as well.[214] Example 2 is Lucretius' thesis that the soul is made of atoms and dies with the individual.[215] In contrast to his treatment of Virgil, Augustine argues that the poet actually held this opinion. If the reader believes it as transcribed, he and the author are both in error (10.17–25).

Taken on their own, these examples assume that Christian views on death and the afterlife are "true" in advance of hearing pagan "opinions."

Honoratus can make an identical claim for Manichaean views; so can spokesmen for Virgil and Lucretius. Augustine is in a dilemma. If truths are determined before they are read, reading about them serves no purpose. If they are not, prior beliefs can be questioned, and the edifice of faith crumbles.

By way of solution, the third example takes up two cases, one dealing with the reading of a written text, the other with a parallel situation involving spoken discourse.

In the first case, a reader finds a passage in Epicurus in which continence[216] is praised as the highest good. He does not know that Epicurus believed that the highest good arises from bodily pleasures. Who is in error?

Augustine argues that it does not matter if the reader was in error with respect to the man or if Epicurus was in error himself. The reader has not indulged in bodily pleasures as a consequence of what he has read; moreover, the philosopher, as a result of this reading, enjoys a good reputation because he is thought to be free of vice. The example is more complicated than 1 and 2,[217] inasmuch as the truth that corresponds to the reader's presuppositions consists of a literary representation of another person's behaviour. Augustine does not prove that a reader can discover a truth in a text whose true meaning is not evident to its author; he does illustrate how appearances can play as significant a role as realities in leading a reader toward a previously agreed notion of what is good. What pleases him in Epicurus is his *thought* that the philosopher is free of vice; his intention is the critical element in his prior beliefs. In his view, "error" can arise even if one's intended conduct is virtuous.

In the second case of example 3, an admired friend, just before his death, swears in front of witnesses that his infancy and boyhood were the most agreeable periods of his life,[218] since he was free from the normal entanglements of mankind. Augustine, admiring the sentiment,[219] asks whether he can pass a positive judgement on the person's "goals and intentions" through his knowledge of what has been reported (10.24–52). He argues affirmatively, although the text is generated by a pattern of living (*uiuere*, 10.37), and it is the words that signify (*significare*, 10.39) what is intended. In the example of Epicurus, there is only one audience, namely the reader of the passage in question; here, there are three. The statement of the hypothetical friend is reported by unnamed individuals who communicate it to Augustine.[220] He listens to his thoughts as he weighs the alternative possibilities (10.50–52), and he envisages an external audience of those who may not agree with his interpretation.[221]

The intentions of the deceased friend are unknowable (10.46); as a consequence, we deal with those of the individuals who report his desires and those of Augustine, who interprets them. If we substitute the putative friend for the text of Epicurus (a model life transformed into a narrative report), then this life and its recipient stand in relation to the deceased as do the writer and reader of the Epicurean text. In the first case, there are only two possibilities: either Epicurus believed in continence or not. In the second, there are a host of other potential sources of misunderstanding (which Augustine suggests through the complicated language in which he relates the story). In effect, he is telling us that where the possibility of error increases, there is a greater moral weight on the reader/hearer to intend the good. Hence his conclusion that, in the absence of contrary evidence, he was well advised to think well *both* of the man and of what was said about him.

The ethical theme is further explored in chapters 11–12, where he takes up errors involving writing and directs the discussion back toward the Manichaeans' rejection of the Old Testament. The "conditions" and "distinctions" that pertain to "writings"[222] are not the mirror image of those of reading. They constitute a subclass of three logically different situations in which (1) something is written with useful ends in view, and these are not understood; or (2) a profitless situation arises for both writer and reader; or (3) the reader finds something useful in what is written even though the person whom he reads appears to have written the contrary.[223]

Augustine is not greatly concerned with the first or last types[224] but focuses on the converse of the second,[225] that is, the situation in which writer and reader have good ends in view.[226] He finds no fault with the writer who is misunderstood by his readers, nor is he concerned with one who does not perceive the truth, provided that he does nothing to harm them (11.6–9). Among writers who communicate truths to readers he envisages two problems in which there is a possibility of productive or beneficial error: the one is a variant of error 3 in chapter 10, in which both the writer and the reader understand the text in a profitable manner, but the one understanding is superior;[227] the other is a consequence of this, which shifts the issues from the intentions in the text to those of the author.[228]

In principle, error is impossible when the writer's and reader's conceptions of the good life are the same (11.15–18). But this situation rarely occurs; typically, there are a number of sources of misapprehension, which arise through the imprecision of the mediators between individuals' thoughts. The reading *(lectio)* may deal with matters that cannot be clearly known and must instead be believed.[229] Also, the writer's intentions can never be known in full. He may be absent or dead (as in the second case of example 3 of chapter 10); or, if present and questioned, he may conceal his true motives (11.20–24). There is a potential discrepancy between the intentions of the author and his text. We may know what sort of man the author is, but this knowledge may be of little help in assessing the value of what he has written.[230] The only relationship that Augustine thinks worthy of advocating is one that reflects what readers *believe* to have been the author's intentions, using as evidence the effect of his writings on a large portion of his readership. The author can be believed to be a good man who, by means of his writings, has a beneficial influence on those who follow his teachings (11.25–27). It follows that, if Aristotle cannot be understood by a disrespectful student[231] nor Archimedes be taught by Epicurus,[232] the Manichaeans cannot read the Old Testament in depth.[233] Augustine thus succeeds in establishing grounds for ethically valid readings while refuting the claims of his dualist opponents.

# 7

## TOWARD THEORY

❧❧

### Tradition and Beliefs

The second part of *De Utilitate Credendi* (chapters 14–36) provides an introduction to the issues raised in the two works in which Augustine's theory of reading is most clearly outlined, *De Catechizandis Rudibus* and *De Doctrina Christiana*. The original feature of this part of the work is Augustine's argument in favour of a hermeneutics of tradition as an answer to the problem of communication between readers and audiences.[1]

The relevant segment takes up the hypothetical case of a person who seeks a "true religion" based on the belief in the soul's immortality. He may or may not subscribe to this doctrine before the search begins,[2] but whether he does or not, he has to undertake a lengthy intellectual journey in search of a truth that he assumes can sooner or later be found (14.12–28). This, of course, is the story that Augustine tells about himself in the *Confessions* some six years later. *De Utilitate Credendi* complements the realistic account with an allegorical recreation of the soul's "wandering" in the potentially "erroneous" bypaths of texts. As early as chapter 10, Augustine plays on the idea in speaking of "the three kinds of error by which men lose their way when they read something."[3] Subsequently, the metaphor of errancy moves from the text to the soul: a narrative journey *in* the mind is transformed into a narrative journey *of* the mind. After chapter 14, the order is again reversed. The theme of the soul's truth-seeking (14.18, 20) reverts to a search for a "method" to guide this and future inquiries (20.1–5).

The hypothetical believer can be either Augustine or Honoratus.[4] Among conflicting spokesmen who claim to have the truth, they opt for (Manichaean and Catholic) teachers[5] of outstanding reputation. Augustine takes pains to recreate the atmosphere of contemporary oral teaching. The pair are described as listeners *(audisse);* the subject matter is taught by verbal instruction *(insinuator, professores);* the difference between teachers is verbal *(opinantes, opiniones);* and their celebrity is based on orally transmitted report *(fama).* Above all, the would-be professors gain credibility through the approval of their audiences *(occupatio populorum).* It is assumed that only a few of them have access to the religious truths in question.[6] Furthermore, Augustine reminds Honoratus that they have agreed to search out the would-be religion's teachers as if they were uninstructed *(quasi rudes,* 16.3). Their conclusions are based on what they derive as observers[7] from the relationship between the speakers and their listeners. If they do not know who these few are, they can infer nothing.[8]

This "truth," then, is an extension of the force of words, which is briefly outlined in *De Dialectica* 7. Augustine now asks how it is communicated from the few to the many. Are the latter united merely "by the name of reason"?[9] His answer is based on a parallel between the teaching of oratory and religion. He points out that few are genuinely eloquent (16.7–9, 14–15); yet the schools are filled with would-be orators, none of whom appears to resent being classified among the unlearned many *(inperitorum multitudo,* 16.9–10).[10] The majority of them, who lack education, attempt to master what the learned minority have judged worthy of handing down.[11] A "true religion" works in a similar way. As in the schools of rhetoric, there is a large group of people in the various churches who are unskilled in interpretive methods *(multitudo inperitorum,* 16.16–17). There is also a comparable form of revered authority. Just as some orators become famous, some churchgoers are "perfected" by religion's mysteries. In both fields there are many who desire knowledge but few who attain it (16.16–37).[12] And in both it is possible for the uninitiated to entertain illusions concerning their ability to progress without a competent teacher's help. When I read a text, Augustine asks, do I acquire knowledge on my own? It would appear not:[13] complex texts cannot be interpreted "without guidance."[14]

When Augustine was less sophisticated (as a dualist auditor), he frequently had his answers ready before the "scrolls" were "unrolled."[15] He took no account of the Bible's difficulty for plodding or inspired readers,[16] nor of its capacity for the concealment of the truth.[17] He recounts his change from pride to humility in chapter 20, where, in contrast to the narrative of *Confessions* 1–9, he speaks analytically[18] of his inquiry *(quaerere)* into "a true religion" both as the laying out of his argument *(causam exponere)* and the setting forth of his way *(edere . . . uiam,* 20.1–5). Parallel are also established between the external and internal events that took place between his departure from Carthage and his entering the catechumenate,[19] which can be listed as follows:

| | |
|---|---|
| crossing the sea | vacillations |
| encounter with Faustus | rejection of dualism |
| Academics | scepticism |
| authority | a way of seeking |
| a forest of ideas | confusion |
| divine providence | asking for help |
| Ambrose | Old Testament revealed |
| catechumenate | convincing himself |
| no obvious teacher | reflections on Catholic teachings |

The narrative line that emerges from these details stresses his development as a reader amid the false rationalities of Manichaeism[20] and scepticism.[21] He eventually retreats into himself and, discovering the potential of his mind, concludes that truth is concealed by the means of inquiry[22]—a notion that presupposes a superior authority[23] which is truth's true source.[24] Lost in the "impenetrable forest" of his own thinking, he is nonetheless unable to halt the progress of his thoughts toward a beneficial objective— proof that he is not ultimately their sponsor. Distancing himself from the dualists, he is guided by St. Ambrose (20.26–27), but he becomes a cate- chumen chiefly to find what he is looking for or to convince himself of the futility of the search. If he could have found the ideal teacher, he asserts, he would have been an eager student.[25]

The moral of this story is that a "true religion" cannot be located by an individual unless he first believes in its goals, which, supported by the influence of tradition, he will later understand.[26] The remaining chapters of *De Utilitate Credendi* attempt to convince Honoratus of the correctness of this position by constructing an imaginary dialogue with his friend (22.4–5),[27] dealing in turn with belief, reason, and authority.

Honoratus reiterates the Manichaean view that any belief that demands faith over reason is a type of credulity (22.17–19; compare 2.9–14). Augustine's response to this claim has so far been based on the fact that no one knows what is in another person's mind, and on the pragmatic logic of following the majority, guided by widely accepted teachings. He now introduces two parallel distinctions, one arising between credulity and legitimate doubt, the other between mere curiosity[28] and genuine study.[29] Honoratus notes that "credulity," that is, unreasonable belief, is something that is normally disdained. Whereas a suspicious person is at fault for distrusting the value of unproven facts, the credulous individual is subject to greater criticism, since he does not allow even for reasonable doubt. Augustine does not reply directly to this assertion but counters with another distinction. He states that we often speak ill of someone who is "curious," while we praise a person who is "studious" (22.6–14). Anticipating his friend's rejoinder, he adds that the curious person seeks to know of matters that have no relevance, whereas the studious person does just the opposite.[30] Honoratus offers the example of an individual living far away from his home, wife, and children,[31] but Augustine argues that he would qualify only if he did not wish to hear anything but news of his family and if, in his joy at such news, he wished to hear the same thing again and again,[32] not if he wanted to hear this message only once (22.30–36). He in turn presents the example of the person who has some interest in an after-dinner story, although he does not personally benefit from it (22.36–41). He thus distinguishes between an individual who is studious of a particular matter and one who is entirely devoted to study, in the same way that one can differentiate an interested and a curious person. If his distinction is valid, there is a comparable difference between belief and credulity.[33]

One way to clarify these academic distinctions is to point out that the audience situations in the two narratives are different. In the first hypothetical story, there are several speakers and one listener. The speakers all bring similar messages from home, and the listener's previous hopes concerning his family are successively confirmed. In the second, there are presumably one speaker and several listeners, one of whom is curious. All the listeners hear the same tale *(fabella),* which neither confirms nor denies their preexisting beliefs. There is also a rough similarity between the two situations, and it is on this that Augustine's subsequent argument hinges. Finally, both stories are told orally; in neither case is there any evidence beyond what the speaker says. Verification depends on internal criteria for belief. This is to argue that the difference between believing and credulity rests on belief itself.[34]

Augustine can hear Honoratus conceding that it is sometimes necessary to believe something without adequate proof, but asking him at the same time to explain why in religion it is not reprehensible to believe before one knows (23.10–12). His answer reshapes his arguments concerning the nature of error and audience and offers a solution to the problem of recreating tradition. He points out that the pair have been discussing not error but a type of fault[35] that is linked to the earlier discussion of the same topic (chapters 10–12) inasmuch as it involves logical misapprehension through language. As in chapters 21–22, Augustine takes up the question through a comparison of two mental states. He asks Honoratus which is a graver fault, to hand down a religion to someone unworthy of it, or to believe what is said concerning a religion by those who hand it down.[36] Clearly, the former: for the "unworthy" recipient approaches the issues "with a feigned heart."[37] He already believes something else—something which, by the criteria of the truth of the religion in question, is false.

He then asks his friend to consider the case of someone present who would like to pass on the doctrines of a given religion to him. Honoratus is in the hearer's situation. The proponent of the religion in question naturally wishes to know whether he is in a proper frame of mind, free of "deception or dissimulation" (23.20–23). Honoratus may make that claim with the words at his disposal,[38] but there is no way that the other party can tell whether he is sincere.[39] Knowing this, the speaker may respond by saying, "Indeed, I believe you: is it not fairer that you believe that there is truth in what I am saying, since I am about to bestow a benefit on you, and you are about to receive it?" If he is asked this, the only answer Honoratus can reasonably give is that he is obliged to believe[40] well before he knows.

Augustine is proposing that the possibility of belief arises between the words of a religion's proponents and the process by which principles are handed down (23.14, 15, 21). Beliefs are thereby related via spoken words to traditions of thought. It is this line of argument that he now pursues.

Instead of making assumptions about communication between the speaker and hearer of words, he might ask whether it would not be preferable to offer an argument; the listener would then follow the logic of the discussion wherever it leads, without the intervention of chance.[41] Augustine allows that Honoratus is clever enough to grasp what is involved and, as a consequence, capable of understanding the logical steps *(rationes)* by which one is led by a divine force to certain knowledge (24.6–13). But what about those who are less well endowed? Should they not be introduced to the innermost secrets gradually?[42]

In this solution, religious truths retain something of their esoteric nature while they become accessible, in theory at least, to everyone. No one who desires truth is "abandoned" or "rejected" (24.17–19). Instead, an assumption is made about all potential candidates as a consequence of their relative ignorance. There is no guarantee that all will reach the chosen objective. Yet they must all start out believing that success is possible, and in that frame of mind they must follow certain necessary directives *(praecepta)* in order to purify their way of life *(uitae actio)*. Otherwise, they forfeit any possibility they might have had of attaining truth. Even the knowledgeable few have to follow the programme, lest they mislead others "by their example" (24.19–29; 25.54–56). There is scarcely anyone who has an accurate idea of his own capabilities.[43] What makes true religion "providential" (that is, known to God but not fully knowable by humans) is that someone who underestimates his abilities is encouraged, while someone who overestimates them is restrained (24.34–36, 41–42).

It remains for Augustine to explain why those who promise to lead the uninitiated into religion by means of reason are not to be followed (25.1–2). He accomplishes this by shifting the question to those in search of religious truth who merit praise or censure, and by deriving from this a threefold schema relating understanding, belief, and opinion.[44]

Two sorts of persons who deserve praise as spokesmen on reason's behalf *(sponsores rationis, 25.4)* have been eliminated from consideration: those who have found what they are looking for and must be judged blessed; and those who are still looking for what they want to find, proceeding toward their goal in a studious and righteous fashion.[45] Three sorts of person merit censure among those who hold opinions: those who think they know but do not know, those who know they do not know and do not try to become knowledgeable, and those who neither think they know nor wish to seek to know.[46] Corresponding to this triad of censurable men, there is in the minds of men worthy of praise a triad consisting of understanding, belief, and opinion *(intellegere, credere, and opinari; 25.16–17)*.

The introduction of this threeway division invites comparison with those that have preceded and with Augustine's trinitarian schemes more generally. Earlier, the positive benefits of reading in *De Utilitate Credendi* grow out of a recognition of three potential errors in reading. Similarly, the virtues of a distinguished mind arise in the image of three types of "fault" among the seekers of truth.[47] In his final transformation of the triadic relationship, the problem between the author, the text, and the reader is internalized as a relationship between thinking, believing, and holding opinions. He argues that outwardly and inwardly one is never sure that one's expression truthfully represents thought, whence the value of beliefs arises from their "utility." Moreover, in his typology of praiseworthy individuals there is an extension of the third reading error and the second writing error, both of which are now viewed in a positive light. The person who has found true religion and the person who studiously seeks it are in the position, respectively, of the reader of a text who uncovers a truth not perceived by an author, and of the reader who purposefully reads a text as intended. In the one, the emphasis is on the mental activity of learning; in the other, on the means of communication by which learning takes place.

The parallel between the triads emerges in Augustine's discussion of understanding, belief, and opinion in relation to the human liability for error. In his view, understanding is faultless, belief is sometimes at fault, and opinion is always at fault.[48] There is only one type of belief that is wholly free of fault: believing while understanding that one does not "know."[49] What we understand, we owe to reason; what we believe, to authority; and what we hold in opinion, to error.[50] In matters of belief in which mediated knowledge is a factor, therefore, reason has to submit to authority. In such cases, if I understand, I imply that I believe, and if I hold an opinion, I likewise imply that I believe. However, if I believe, I do not necessarily understand; and if I hold an opinion, I do not understand. It follows that, in the cases of the two praiseworthy seekers of religious truth, those who are already blessed believe in truth itself, while those still seeking truth believe by means of authority. Of the three types of individual who deserve censure, the first is credulous; the second and third believe in nothing, for the one seeks truth with no hope of finding it, while the other does not seek truth at all (25.45–54).

Augustine gives special consideration to the priority of beliefs over knowledge in the active life (25.54–56). Even those who say that they follow the more probable of the alternatives of knowing or believing prefer to appear unable to know rather than unable to believe.[51] For, in general, people take the course of action of which they approve; otherwise, it would not seem probable to them that it would succeed. In a similar way, the two potential adversaries of truth—those who oppose knowledge but admit faith, and those who oppose both—are normally not found "in human affairs." These distinctions help us to understand how we free ourselves from thoughtless opinions by keeping faith in matters that we do not fully understand. Those who say they believe only what they know are protected against opinion; but it is also necesary to recognize a difference between thinking one knows and understanding that one does not know; in the case of the latter, belief invariably arises from authority (25.59–72).

Augustine terminates the discussion with three examples of relations between beliefs and authority in which such assumptions play a large role.[52] His solution to the problem of tradition appears to implicate the reader as well as to deny the reader a fundamental role. Like the dualists, whose notion of living "scripture" he passively absorbs, he believes that traditions exist as they are vitalized by readers and audiences. However, in contrast to the dualist position (as he understands it), he assumes that no amount of ratiocination (either in oral dialogue or in written argument) can solve the problem of why we should follow tradition in the first place. Here, he combines a sceptical argument concerning reason, which alternately fascinates and repels him throughout the "philosophical dialogues," with a rhetorical strategy that lodges the problem of tradition in the means by which traditional information creates communities of beliefs. The reader or auditor is a witness to the need for groups to authenticate them as well as to the fact that reading cannot constitute their authority on its own.

## The "Uninstructed"

Two mature treatments of the problem of reception raised in *De Utilitate Credendi* are *De Catechizandis Rudibus*[53] and *De Doctrina Christiana*. In the former, Augustine takes up a particular problem relating readers and audiences, namely the education of catechumens.[54] In the latter, he addresses more general questions of reading, exegesis, and preaching.[55] If these works are placed in a logical rather than a strictly chronological sequence, they inform us on how he dealt with a wide variety of readers, ranging from the neophyte to the well educated, at a critical time in the evolution of his thinking.

On returning to Africa, Augustine initially endeavoured to pursue the Christian life in seclusion.[56] From the spring of 391, the year of his ordination, he also appears to have had in mind a type of community in which reading and meditative study would play an important part.[57] Despite these plans, he led an increasingly active life. On 28–29 August 392, he vanquished the Manichaean Fortunatus in a debate in Hippo before a crowd of well-wishers of both parties. In December 393, at the Council of Africa, he spoke to the assembly of bishops on the subject of *De Fide et Symbolo*. In late spring of 394, he lectured to friends in Carthage on Paul's Epistle to the Romans. With the exception of *De Libero Arbitrio* 2–3, composed after 391, and *De Mendacio,* from 394–95, the works that followed have a pragmatic or polemical orientation. The defence of Catholic dogma is likewise at the centre of the half-dozen anti-Manichaean treatises written from 388 to 396.

One of his duties as a priest was to introduce candidates for baptism to Christian teachings.[58] *De Catechizandis Rudibus* is the earliest model treatise on catechism in the Latin West[59] and a summing-up of his personal experience.[60] The work also clarifies why the sender and receiver of an instructive text will interpret the information that it contains in different ways—a problem taken up but not solidly addressed in *De Utilitate Credendi*. Replying to the questions of an otherwise unknown deacon in Carthage, Deogratias,[61] Augustine analyses the nature of the conversation that takes place between catechist and catechumen. In doing so, he returns to two central themes of *De Magistro,* the strengths and weaknesses of signs[62] and the primacy of inner teaching as a source of belief.[63]

There are echoes of the vocabulary of illuminative ascent in the second stage of catechesis, in which the candidate for baptism, having advanced in slow, painful stages of learning, comes to knowledge via internalized ideas.[64] In the East, those ready for baptism were called "light-givers" after Paul, who spoke of the sacramental initiation as an "enlightening."[65] Baptismal imagery informs the notion of conversion in *De Magistro* 11–14,[66] as it describes the *rudes* who have completed their education in *De Catechizandis*.[67] The role of memory is likewise stressed: in ancient catechism, the creed was "handed down" to the *competentes* by word of mouth; they were given a week to memorize it, after which a recitation was demanded *(redditio symboli)*.[68]

Deogratias was concerned that he was not communicating with his catechumens. He never knew where to begin and end the Bible story *(narratio,* 1.8–10).[69] Worse, he was tired of reiterating the basics: he ran the risk of boring both his listeners and himself (1.12–18).

Behind his complaint looms a familiar group of issues. How do words, once uttered, affect the disposition of the speaker *and* the hearer? When one speaks, are thoughts accurately embodied in words? When words are heard, does the listener understand what one has in mind?

The treatise answers the deacon's questions and addresses these broader problems.[70] Catechistical narrative is the subject of chapters 3, 4, and 6; narrative commentary also takes up much of two specimen sermons[71] in chapters 16–25 and 26–27. Some six causes and cures of weariness in speaking are likewise examined in chapters 10–14. Speakers and hearers are dealt with in chapter 2. In chapters 5–6, the topic is uneducated catechumens; in 8, those trained in the liberal arts; in 9, students of literature and oratory; and in 15, how to adapt one's words to the needs of one's listeners.[72] Chapter 26 returns to baptism and the admission of catechumens to the church.

In answer to Deogratias' main question,[73] Augustine points out that speech inadequately configures thought. This is as true of one's own efforts at expression as well as for communication with others.[74] There are two schemas, and their assumptions are mutually supportive:

> *The individual:* thought → words
> *Speaker/hearer:* speaker → words → hearer
> ↓ ↓
> (thought) (thought)

Augustine derives the inadequacies of speech[75] from the incompatibility of two temporal modes. When he thinks about what he is going to say, understanding enters his mind in a flash of thought—a type of "illumination." Yet when he expresses the same understanding as spoken words, his ideas come forth slowly, one after the other. By the time he forms the word-ideas that give rise to his speech, their intellectual source has already withdrawn to a "secret recess" in the mind, leaving behind only a syllabic imprint in his memory, which endures as long as it is necessary for him to produce "signifying sounds."[76] The memory traces *(uestigia)* that remain temporarily in the mind during speech can be retained in thought or uttered as words (thereby paralleling the *dicibile* and *dictio* of *De Dialectica* 5). The understanding "shows" them to memory in the way in which a facial expression betrays a state of mind.[77] This showing has advantages over telling (as in *De Magistro*): the word "anger" differs in Latin, Greek, or Hebrew, but an angry look is understood in the same way, no matter what language one speaks.[78] Augustine thus distinguishes (as he does not elsewhere) between linguistic memory in the short and long term. Short-term traces are enabling vehicles for transforming thoughts into words; long-term storage is envisaged as an archive for what is understood and retained.[79]

In one respect, this is a simple scheme, in which communication takes place in a descending hierarchy through *intellectus, memoria, locutio, signa,* and *lingua* (understanding, memory, speech, signs, and the tongue). But understanding leads to two sorts of memory, long- and short-term; only the latter gives rise to words as they are speakable or spoken. Also, when short-term memory is involved, spoken signs are a type of telling, whereas in long-term memory the relationship to understanding is one of showing. Moreover, if we recall the scheme of *De Magistro,* Augustine retains the priority of showing over telling, since the information "secreted" into long-term memory is what gives rise to the possibility of conveying information through speech. Finally, it is possible to hypothesize that showing through understanding and memory is in parallel with the *dicibile* of *De Dialectica,* while telling corresponds to *dictio.*

Augustine next looks at the issues from the hearer's perspective. When a person speaks, he or she not only expresses a desire to communicate but

also responds to the listener's desire to hear what is to be said. The speaker
may be bored while the other party is instructed and amused (2.41–45,
59–61); as a consequence, Augustine advises Deogratias to make use of
humour, whether it suits his mood or not, in order to maintain the listener's
interest.[80] In any case, humans, constrained by their senses, never see things
as they are, but only "in an enigma and through a glass." Their love is
unable to "dispel darkness" and "penetrate the serene eternity," from which
transient things derive their "light" (for example, 1 Cor. 13:12).[81] Attempts
at instruction are not therefore futile. Just as day makes inroads on night,
so our words enlighten the uneducated in stages (2.51–59; compare 9.17–
18). The schema emerges in the form shown.[82]

$$
\begin{array}{ccc}
 & \text{knowledge} & \\
 & \text{(illumination)} & \\
\downarrow & \downarrow & \downarrow \\
\text{speaker} & & \text{hearer} \\
\textit{intellectus} & \text{(showing)} & \textit{intellectus} \\
\textit{memoria} & \downarrow & \textit{memoria} \\
\downarrow & & \downarrow \\
\textit{signa} & & \textit{signa} \\
 & \text{(telling)} & \\
 & \downarrow & \\
 & \textit{lingua} &
\end{array}
$$

In chapter 3 Augustine turns to the narratives that result, taking up the
types of story best suited to uneducated and educated catechumens. He
first deals with narratio plena. The term narratio is borrowed from rhetoric[83]
with a hint at broader literary issues;[84] however, he is concerned mainly
with the use of story for the teaching of Christian history.[85] By a "full
narrative" he means that the story omits no important phases (3.1–5) in the
first five ages of the church or the sixth, which begins with Christ and
continues to his time.[86] With the recipient's reaction in mind,[87] Deogratias
is advised not to recite the biblical story from memory, "unravelling" and
"expounding" each book.[88] Instead, he should present a summary, then
single out events that need further exposition. The goal is to "unveil" the
inner sense before the hearer's mind. Detail should not be raised for its
own sake but should appear in context.[89] Augustine thus calls for a type of
aural readership whose attention is focused on another person's understanding of what is essential in the text (compare 3.16–19).

Through his theory of narrative, he further proposes that Christian writings have given rise to two communities of response, one before and one after the coming of Christ (3.24–29). The earlier phase, paralleling the structure of the Pentateuch, is divided into five "epochs" (3.44–46); its writings are intended to instruct those of us who live in the later phase.[90] The statements in the first period are prophetic "figures"[91] and "announcements"; those of the second are "reminders" of Christ's love in divinely sanctioned "narratives."[92] All sacred writings—the law and the prophets, which were once "the only scripture," as well as the "divine literatures" that were written later—are memorials dedicated to our salvation (4.59–64). As a typological plan unfolds within the text, the historical communities provide guidelines for two types of contemporary readers, the carnal and the spiritual.[93] Carnal readers fear only physical chastisement; "spirituals" fear losing touch with the higher truths of Christ's "revealed" teachings.[94]

In the scheme of chapters 3–4, the literal and figurative senses are illustrated by paired metaphors: *in inuolucris/ostendere* (3.12), *scripta/figurae* (3.60), *occultatio/manifestatio* (4.65), and *carnales/spiritales* (4.67–68). The notion that links them is empathic love. It is not the purpose of love to generate interpretation, but vice versa. Yet the models of reading and loving operate in a similar way (12.4–6).[95] The reader intends his or her response: anticipation is love's strongest invitation; the unwillingness to anticipate is the mind's greatest discouragement. Like the reader and the hearer of the sacred text, the loving mind and the mind loved are fuelled by identical "fires" of expectation (4.10–38). One can read poetic trifles or a sacred story (6.19–25); similarly, there is a love that "consumes" and leads to "misery," as well as a love that is directed towards our fellow men and women as an act of "mercy" (4.40–41). The goal of reading is to create empathy between individuals; only in this way do words and texts supersede their limitations.

There is a parallel relationship, then, between the spiritual ascent of the catechumen through oral reading and the eschatological purpose of scripture, as reflected in its spiritual sense. The meaning in the text is to be matched by the subjective response of the reader or hearer. Augustine is also concerned with fitting the lived experience of the candidate into the intentional structure of the biblical narrative: ideally, the catechumen should then desire to be in reality what he had decided to be only in thought (5.12–15). In order to bring this about, he has to live a "representational" narrative; this is a story that is not externally untrue but that he realizes to be deliberately, self-consciously generated in himself.[96] The self becomes the subject and object of literary construction, as it did for Augustine, some three years before, when he embarked on his own "confessions."

No one can tell when the catechumen is in the right frame of mind to be "enlightened";[97] in this sense the audience of the catechist is unknowable. However, preliminary inquiries provide the teacher with essential information and help the candidate create the right preconditions (5.21–25). Within *De Catechizandis,* Augustine considers two classes of catechumen, the *rudes* (chapters 5–6) and the *eruditi* (chapters 8–9). The *rudes* are the uneducated and uninstructed, who have to be addressed in a humble, clear style *(sermo humilis).*[98] The *eruditi* are educated in the liberal arts and possibly the Bible.[99] In chapters 5–6, three types of potential ignorance among the *rudes* are taken up: the errors made by those who support Christianity, the errors made by those who oppose it, and the problems that arise from omens concerning the imminence of baptism. The needs of the uninstructed are also addressed in the two specimen sermons in chapters 16–27.

Augustine's analysis of these types of misinterpretation among the *rudes* is a transformation of the opening chapters of *De Utilitate Credendi* and can be summarized as follows:

1. The candidate may know Christianity but may wilfully misrepresent its aims; for instance, its spiritual goals may be interpreted as material advantages. What the catechumen states is therefore false. However, the catechist should not simply offer a refutation, since the candidate's "profession," as an act of will, is more valuable than its initial claims to truth. An effort should be made to build on the literary edifice already present in the hearer's mind and, if necessary, to reorient its purpose (5.25–32).

2. The candidate may hold views incompatible with Christian teaching. In this case, the potential convert is to be considered "ignorant" and "uninformed" and treated gently. No attempt should be made before the narrative is begun to impress doctrine on an unreceptive mind, lest, through a false simulation, a desire is "imposed" that has not yet been generated from within (5.33–40). The resulting internalization would not bring about moral reform.

3. The candidate may have had a "premonition" of God's interest in him through a dream, a vision, or a miracle.[100] Although fear is a condition of faith (5.5–7), such forewarnings should be only the point of de-

parture for spiritual development. "Intentions," if stimulated by the su-
pernatural, must be chanelled into "the surer oracle of scripture." The
individual has to understand that God would not have instructed him
by such "signs and revelations" had he not intended him to follow "the
pathway, already prepared, of sacred writings," in which he is to seek
not "visible" but "invisible meanings," and to look for them while he is
awake rather than when he is asleep (6.4–14).[101]

From these examples arises the view that a reformed life is a genre of
rewriting: its text is the self. *Narratio* is a means to an end. The life in a
hearer's mind takes on reality as it is actually lived. However, as story or
lived experience, it is also literature; and the catechist, no less than the
teacher of grammar or rhetoric, makes use of accepted methods of interpretation, differing from the pagan in the content of his texts and in his
long-range priorities. The *grammaticus,* if he does his job well, finds much
of value in "the fictive fables of the poets"; but his reflections, however
they may inform his auditor's minds, produce only sensual pleasure. The
Christian teacher discusses truths rather than trifles; and, in doing so, he
orients his narrative as well as his explanation to nonmaterial ends.[102] As
the shaping of a life is his aim, he must take care to tell his story without
digressing. The uncluttered truth will then be like a gold setting that
surrounds precious gems in a balanced design without drawing attention
to itself (6.26–31).

When the narrative is finished, objections answered, and the *rudis*
warned against nonbelievers, "the hope of resurrection" can be held out.
The "spiritual" reading in the *narratio* gives rise to the possibility of a
permanent life of the spirit, an anticipation of the "celestial city and its joy."
At the end of time the elect and the nonelect will be separated, but during
individuals' lifetimes the two "communities" coexist. In contrast to "the
perverse, who fill the churches with their many bodies" (7.1–19), there are
the "good Christians, the true citizens of the heavenly Jerusalem" (7.32–33),
who experience religion as a life of the spirit on earth.[103] These are the
catechumen's models. Yet it does not suffice to imitate their example. A
man cannot judge which man is just; his goal is to understand how we are
"justified" by God, who justifies us. Reform, therefore, depends on the
will to change, not on foreknowledge of the result. Scripture stands between the reader and hearer, preventing the catechumen from thinking
that changes in himself have come about through the mental activity of
either party alone (7.38–42).

Augustine then turns to the *eruditus,* the candidate for admission to the church who (like Victorinus) has some idea about the sacraments (8.1–6). He is familiar with methods of debate and interpretation and can be encouraged to think for himself. There is no need for the reiteration of well-known facts: brevity and discretion ought to be the rule (compare 26.24–30). When in doubt, the catechist should behave as if the candidate already knows the biblical material to which he is referring. Also, before instruction begins, he should familiarize himself with the intellectual background of the candidate. What books has he read? Are they doctrinally sound (8.7–50)? The catechumen should be looked upon not as someone who is uninitiated *(idiota)* but as a member of the Christian community *(societas populi christiani,* 8.51–52).

Augustine thus distinguishes catechumens as more and less educated, not as lettered and unlettered.[104] They are all assumed to be literates. *De Catechizandis Rudibus* is about a difference in teaching technique that is related to the levels of potential response in *rudes indoctique* (8.13) and the *eruditi* (8.14), that is, the *liberalibus doctrinis exculti* (8.2–3).[105] Whereas the uneducated person has to be told the Bible story, the educated candidate sees the events of Christian history as he or she reads of them.[106] Prereading is a condition for "participation,"[107] just as the methods of philosophical disputation are a prerequisite for understanding Christian doctrine (8.6–9, 56–60).

Augustine also distinguishes between "teaching" and "remembering" and between "believing" and "knowing": all are by-products of the ignorance that arises between the reader and the hearer—a transformation of the ideas of *De Magistro*. The *rudis* has to be "taught"; but the *eruditus* should be treated as if the catechist "believes" that he already "knows" the matter under discussion. The catechist should proceed as if the educated person has heard what he has to say: instead of being "taught" what "he does not know," he should pretend that the pair are "recollecting together" what the candidate already "has in mind" (8.11–16). For the educated candidate, already familiar with literary methods, the *narratio plena* is unnecessary (26.24–30). The "narrative" is already unfolding within himself.

The educated who enter the church are members of a new reading community.[108] The catechist must scrutinize what they have previously read (8.28–36),[109] as well as how they have read. If they have training in interpretation, they cannot be classified among the unlearned *(illiterati)* nor among the highly educated *(doctissimi)*. Possessing technical knowledge, but "illiterates" in humility, they must be taught that good conduct is preferable to well-chosen words, and a pure heart to a practised tongue (9.1–11).

Above all they must learn how "to hear the divine writings," that is, how to listen to the Bible as it is read aloud to them. As in the case of the *rudes,* but viewed from a different angle, the method is the *sermo humilis.*[110] As Augustine himself was instructed in Milan, they must be shown that "solid eloquence," because it is straightforward, is not demeaning: the "words" or "deeds" that are read about, though "sounded out in letters" and "covered" or "concealed" by "carnal overgarments," can yield understanding, if their meaning is "unravelled" and "disclosed."[111]

Augustine turns finally to some five impediments to effective communication between the catechist and the catechumen (chapters 10–14). He also rounds out his criticism of words. Even when speech is agreeable, we take greater pleasure in "hearing" something read aloud and in "reading" it for ourselves, since what is heard is already phrased for us and demands no effort of interpretation.[112] By contrast, when we pull together words of uncertain import for unknown minds, we leave to chance whether our utterances express what we mean and whether they are clearly understood by others (10.16–24). Oral reading, then, is a preferable pathway to truth as well as a corrective for oral memory. When we recall something that we have said, we invariably introduce inaccuracies into our original statements. Furthermore, the new version may be received differently from the old.[113]

How can we overcome the uncertainty of verbal communication, i.e., the unknowability of the "motivation of the auditors" (11.47–51)? The only way is to bypass ineffective understanding through an emotional union between speaker and hearer. Take the situation, familiar to catechists, in which statements suitable only for children have to be repeated (12.1–2). Neither the words spoken nor the text read can in themselves sustain the speaker's interest. He has "to call God into his heart" and to adopt an attitude of "a brother's, father's, and a mother's love": for, so great is the power of the mind's disposition that, just as it affects our listeners while we speak, so it affects us while they learn, with the result that we can, figuratively speaking, "dwell" in each other's thoughts.[114] Once again, Augustine argues that if minds cannot communicate with certainty through words, they have to do so by means of empathy.

The analogy between showing and telling is also instructive. If, as speaker, I show a potential auditor a pleasant vista that he has not seen, is my enjoyment not renewed and enhanced by his expression of pleasure? The deeper the friendship, the greater would appear to be our joy:[115] hence, in the bond between speaker and hearer, the greater the expression of love, the more old things can seem new. The progress that the teacher has made "in contemplating things" should be a stepping-stone for the learner, so that he too can ascend through study. His cheerfulness will in turn renew the speaker's interest in what he has to say (12.8–25).

Augustine's two specimen sermons[116] are prefaced by a final analysis of audiences in which he emphasizes the difference between oral discourse as it is delivered and a text that is prepared for future readers.[117] The speaker to audiences must distinguish between the single auditor and many auditors, the latter inevitably holding a variety of opinions.[118] It is important to note whether the speaker is seated before a small group, as in a discussion, or whether, standing above and apart from his hearers, he is observed silently from a distance (as Augustine observed Ambrose). The size and composition of the audience should likewise be reflected in the speaker's style: whether there are few or many listeners, whether they are learned, unlearned, or a mixture of the two, and whether they are countryfolk or townspeople. As the speaker affects them, they affect the speaker and one another. Speech expresses what is in the speaker's mind: the listeners are influenced by what they hear as well as by what is in their minds beforehand (15.19–24) The speaker must try to give verbal expression to his thoughts, and he must take account of different sorts of listeners—the clever and the dull-witted, the rich and the poor, the member of the community and the outsider. All deserve the same "charity," but they should not receive the same "medicine" (15.32–33).

## Christian Doctrine

Augustine did not explore the problem of audiences further in *De Catechizandis Rudibus,* possibly because some three years earlier he had written a draft of a treatise in which the topic was treated at greater length. This was *De Doctrina Christiana.* In this work the entire Christian community is envisaged, potentially at least, as a body of readers, either as clergy or as cultured laypersons.[119] The moral, intellectual, and spiritual improvement of the individual thus takes place within an aural or visual encounter with scripture.

Like *De Catechizandis Rudibus, De Doctrina* had its origin in a request. Shortly after Augustine's accession to the bishopric of Hippo, Aurelius, the primate of Carthage, asked him to draft a treatise on Christian education to serve as a manual of instruction for young clergymen.[120] Although the work that resulted is not a "fundamental charter of Christian culture" or a programme of "education for a Christian intellectual,"[121] as H.-I. Marrou proposed, it nonetheless makes space within a discussion of biblical hermeneutics for a "digression" on "the general principles of classical culture pertaining to the baptised."[122] In this endeavour, a large role is played by rhetoric,[123] and the version which may date from 426 shows significant influence from Tyconius' *Rules* of interpretation.[124]

In the treatise, the complexity of Augustine's approach to reading reflects the presence of three principles of organization. Books 1–3 deal with inquiries into doctrine, while book 4 is concerned with preaching. A second ordering principle is created by the concepts of signs *(signa)* and realities *(res)*. Signs are the specific subject of books 2 and 3 and an incidental subject in book 4; realities are the principal topic in book 1. Finally, throughout the treatise Augustine opposes the merely useful and the truly enjoyable. In doing so, he offers a parallel to the view with which he concludes *Confessions* 1–9, arguing that the purpose of reading is to permit one to ascend to a type of truth that lies beyond the reading process.

In the manner in which the treatise takes up the question of education, the work initially invites comparison with *De Magistro.* In both the point of departure is "learning" and "teaching." However, as in *De Catechizandis Rudibus,* the central issue in *De Doctrina* is how to derive meaning from biblical texts as well as commentaries and how to communicate what has been learned to others. The terms *modus inueniendi* (mode of discovery) and *modus proferendi* (mode of communicating) are introduced in parallel with *discere* and *docere:* what is to be discovered is "what is to be understood"; what is to be communicated is "what has been understood" (1.1.1– 3; compare 4.1). *Docere* does not mean "informing," as it does in *De Magistro,* but rather "instructing." *Disciplina* (from *discere*) refers to the discipline of education.[125]

The terminology is paralleled by a change of literary genre. In place of the dialogue[126] between father and son in the first half of *De Magistro,* we have a "treatise" *(tractatio)* which contains "some precepts for an ordered discussion of scripture."[127] A debate about words that takes place in words is superseded by a system of interpretation which utilizes reason to arrive at the meaning of specific biblical texts.[128] Accordingly, *De Doctrina* is presented not as the transcript of a verbal dialogue but as a book to be read, even to be studied slowly and laboriously section by section (4.31.3– 4). Books 1–2.9 deal with the first stage of the comprehension of scripture, that is, with doctrines related openly, while 2.10–3.37 takes up those related obscurely. Augustine is concerned throughout with readers' expectations (*exspectatio legentium,* 4.1.12).

## Prologue

The plan is outlined in the prologue,[129] where Augustine defines his terms of reference (sections 1 and 9) and answers potential objections to what he is setting out to do (sections 2–8). In a few paragraphs, he makes one of his clearest statements about the role of reading in intellectual and religious life. His thinking can be summed up as follows:

1. Whether one is reading for oneself or to an audience there are guidelines to be followed for revealing what is hidden in sacred writings.[130]

2. A person who reads aloud demonstrates that he is literate. If the skill is transmitted to others, they can read for themselves. In both cases received learning is passed on.[131] A person who interprets scripture for a listening audience thus performs a function that is comparable to that of the teacher of reading:[132] just as the one communicates literate skills, the other conveys the rules by which passages of scripture are to be understood.[133]

3. A person who knows how to read does not depend on what he hears in order to understand what is written. Likewise, those who know the rules of interpretation do not rely on others to think on their behalf; they interpret texts for themselves. Through the application of interpretive procedures, obscurities in biblical writings can be clarified and obvious errors avoided.[134]

These statements cover some of the same ground as *Confessions* 1–2, with which they may be contemporary. However, in place of the child's developmental cycle, Augustine speaks of individuals working within interpretive communities that succeed one another over time; he thereby makes the reading process an institution for the "transmission"[135] of knowledge. Also, in contrast to the early books of the autobiography, he is concerned with the psychology of the mature reader. The problem that is taken up is not how one learns to speak, then to read, but the manner in which, among literates, the eye, the ear, and the mind work together to communicate information.[136] The *intellector,* who is the reader, understands by remembering; the reading process is institutionalized through group memory. If memory fails, rules are of little use (2.9.16–18).

Augustine is aware that his approach may not suit everyone's taste. In sections 2–8 of the prologue he attempts to reply to potential objections. He considers those who cannot understand his precepts, those who cannot apply them, and those who think they can do without them (2.16–27; 3.28–38).[137]

The last group consists of inspired individuals who interpret scripture "through a divine gift";[138] an example is Anthony, who memorized passages of the gospels on hearing them and after due reflection interpreted them correctly "without a knowledge of letters."[139] Augustine does not deny such reports;[140] he points out that although the sources of inspiration differ, the interpreters all make use of the same conventions of language, which are learned from childhood.[141] "To hear and to learn the gospel, to read the Bible, or to hear someone reading or teaching" is to acknowledge this shared education. To deny it is to be tempted into error through wilfulness and pride (5.72–78; compare 3.1.10–13).

Inspiration, then, does not rule out the necessity of instruction;[142] for gifted individuals, it merely obviates a stage of the learning process. Augustine emphasizes the point through the functions of speech in Prologue 6 and 7. Paul was taught by God, but he was sent to another man to receive the sacraments (Acts 9:3–19). The centurion Cornelius was told by an angel that his prayers had been heard, but he was then handed over to Peter, who taught him what "to believe, hope for, and love" (Acts 10:1–4 ff., 19–48). Moses learned from his father-in-law how to govern (Exod. 18:14–27); Philip explained Isaiah's mysteries to a eunuch in words (Acts 8:27–35). The most persuasive example is charity, which would not bind men's minds were it not for what one soul taught another.[143]

In sum, the person who interprets scripture through inspiration glorifies God; the person who adheres to rules of interpretation desires to communicate his insights through speech. The inspired are advised to orient their minds and hearts toward heaven, so that their thoughts can inform others from within; however, their ways are judged unsuitable for teaching (8.115–127). In inspired understanding, there is no agreed methodology; the speaker transmits a personal interpretation of scripture. If there is a community, it consists initially of the reader and God. In guided reading, a method both encourages and constrains interpretation, and the community consists of the reader and the implied or intended audience. Finally, the inspired reader acts alone; only after the interpretation is completed does the audience come into the picture. The follower of precepts acts in concert. If he reads alone, he establishes his community with the previous interpreters of the text. If he reads to others, he brings it into being in accordance with commonly accepted norms. He also negotiates with his future readers, whose participation validates the rules by which interpreting is done.

## Book 1

Augustine returns to the hermeneutic concerns of the prologue in books 2 and 3. He does so having established another frame of reference for *De Doctrina;* this consists of rules for the guidance of the moral life.[144] The overall goal is the internal shaping of a lived narrative, as in *Confessions* 7–8. The personal reader is in his thoughts throughout books 1–3, where, Cornelius Mayer emphasizes, the incarnation is the "sacred sign" shown to man of the life to be lived.[145] In book 4, by contrast, the reader is identified with the preacher, the trained religious who has benefitted from the studies recommended in books 2–3, where the student of scripture appears to be at an earlier stage of training. As in the *Confessions,* both specific and general audiences are envisaged. In books 2 and 3, Augustine speaks to those entering the religious life; in book 1, his remarks are addressed to a broader implied readership, presumably including laypersons.

With the latter in mind, he begins book 1 by asking what realities are understood when scripture is read and interpreted.[146] In his reply, he summarizes his views on things and signs (1.2.1–2) and divides signifiable things into what is useful and what is enjoyable.[147] He also synthesizes his thinking about signs within his views on the ethics of interpretation.[148] The latter theme appears tentatively as early as *De Pulchro et Apto;*[149] it is touched upon in *De Dialectica* and *De Magistro* and formally incorporated into *De Utilitate Credendi.*[150] A statement is also made in *De Diuersis Quaestionibus 83,*[151] where it is linked to subjective and objective aspects of love rather than to the reading process.[152] *De Doctrina* combines these reflections into an effective unit.[153] Within sign theory, yet as a reader's version of that theory, the biblical text is considered to be the privileged means to an end: the enjoyment not of reading itself, but of its desired object, which is God's word. Reading is thus a way of overcoming "alienation,"[154] temporarily at least, and of conforming one's life to Christ's.[155]

But what is the status of the text read, that is, scripture? Is it an expression of thought or of words? In Augustine's view, it is both: just as there is inner and outer vision (1.12.1–3), so one can conceive an eternal and a mutable word, that is, a word as thought and a word as speech.[156] We express ourselves in a manner that permits what is in our minds to reach our listeners' minds (assuming that communication takes place). Our thought is not transformed into sound; it remains unaltered, merely assuming a vocal form, and reappears in the hearer's mind as it was in ours.[157] By analogy, the word of God represents the eternal expression of the divine mind; at the same time, this word was embodied in flesh and dwelt among us (John 1:14) in the way that physical sound incorporates a word's meaning.

All scripture, when read, has this two-sided quality, whose meeting-place is in the emotion of charitable love.[158] Through reading, we thus travel a road "not of places but of affections."[159] True, we learn many facts: these concern the ressurection (1.15), the church (1.16–17), life after death (1.19–21), and the dignity of man, who is created in God's image (1.22). But first and foremost, we have to understand the relationship between use, enjoyment, and love. Of many useful things, only four kinds are to be loved: those above us, in us, equal to us, and below us (1.23.6–9). Above us lie God and the angels, who enjoy what we desire (1.30.2); below us lies carnal and material lust (1.24). Within us is a natural love of self (1.35.4–5); this should be present not as an end but as a means, so that we can master the skill of loving ourselves profitably (1.25.1–2). Loving our equals means loving our fellow men (1.28.1–4); however, the most impor-tant type of desire, and the summation of Augustine's thinking in book 1, is the "love of a thing that can be fully enjoyed," namely God. This is the reason for "treating of" things in the context of divine law and scripture (1.35.1–5).

Someone who pretends to understand scripture, but whose interpreta-tion does not result in "a dual love of God and his neighbour," has taken the path of error.[160] Augustine again insists that a correct reading of the Bible can take place only when one is in the right frame of mind; minor inconsistencies can be overcome through faith (compare 3.10.5–8). The emphasis is placed on the mentality of the reader, not on the validity of the interpretation. Wilful falsification is prevented (1.36.4–7), as well as stage-acting, in which we associate "the highest good" with the most persuasive performance (1.29.8–22)—a doctrine that Augustine was taught as a student and taught others as a professor of rhetoric.[161] If we summarize these statements by means of a diagram (shown in the following figure), we can readily perceive the intellectual distance that he had travelled by 396.

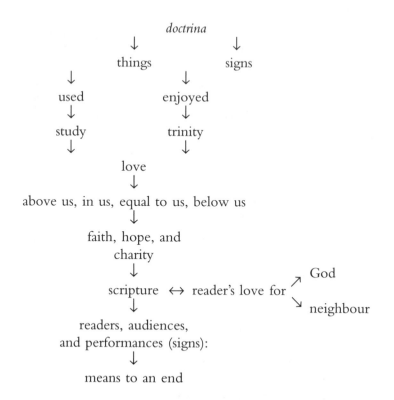

The reading process mediates between the doctrines about love in the texts and the comparable sentiment in our minds. In essentials, therefore, Augustine's proposal is this:

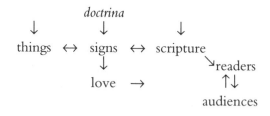

Love operates vertically, descending from the text to the reader, and horizontally, as readers relate to audiences. Christianity emerges as a textual community built around shared principles of interpretation.

## Books 2–3

Whereas book 1 deals with these "realities," books 2 and 3 constitute a unit in treating the means by which they are attained, namely signs (2.1.1–5):

in 2, the topic is unknown signs *(signa ignota);* in 3, ambiguous signs *(signa ambigua).* In the logic of *De Doctrina,* therefore, book 1 addresses the problem of love ontologically, but it does not discuss in detail how the knowledge of love gets into one's mind. This is the problem with which book 2 begins.[162]

Augustine's solution is that we acquire the knowledge from privileged writings.[163] Our only means of doing this is through reading.[164] The argument is found in 2.1–6 and grows out of a discussion of given or conventional signs (2.1.22–24); the latter are signs in which living creatures demonstrate to and for each other, to the degree they can, their mental reactions to what they sense or understand,[165] thereby intending to transfer "what the mind produces" from the giver to the receiver of the sign (2.2.1–6). His remarks on conventional signs in speech are applicable to scripture, which consists of verbal signs given by God and revealed to us in the transcriptions of men.[166]

Words, as they are spoken, have an obvious limitation as transmitters of thought: they consist of nothing but reverberations in the air. To endure, the signs that they transmit have to be expressed in written characters, which show them to the eyes—show them, that is, not as things, but as "sounding symbols."[167] The shift from an oral to a written medium indicates that reading has definitively replaced speaking as a way of giving and receiving signs. Augustine is aware that writing places a limitation on the spreading of God's word, for speech is common to all peoples,[168] while writing systems represent only specific languages (2.4.4–8). His solution is translation (2.5.1–4).

These views differ somewhat from what is proposed in *De Magistro,* his earlier systematic statement on signs. There, the poles of communication are signifiers and illumination. A middle ground exists, which is occupied by hermeneutic concerns, but, as the work is incomplete, the issues are left unresolved, and only some of the gaps are filled by the early chapters of *De Utilitate Credendi.* In *De Doctrina,* a fresh approach is undertaken (in parallel with *De Catechizandis Rudibus).* The limits of signs as sounds are outlined; also, while Augustine allows for the bypassing of reading through inspiration (2.6.7–15), he emphasizes the aesthetic appeal of literary expressions (2.6.15–42). With mere words discredited and pure enlightenment restricted to *sancti homines,* the text and the reader of scripture emerge as the chief parameters of communication. Reading is no longer one method among others; it lies at the root of our ability to acquire salvific knowledge.

Having discussed the nature of the text, Augustine turns to stages by which the individual believer attains wisdom.[169] This is taken up in 2.7–9.[170] In parallel with God's work of the seven days in the opening chapters of Genesis, he proposes seven steps in inner education. These begin with reading and proceed to meditation—a psychological state that is initiated with one's acquaintance with biblical texts but that is progressively detached from the sensory aspects of the reading process. The programme invites comparison with two earlier sevenfold schemes, those of *De Quantitate Animae* 33.70–76 and *De Vera Religione* 26.48–49, written respectively in 388 and 390.[171] In the former, depicting the third level of the soul's magnitude,[172] Augustine speaks of a number of ways in which mankind self-consciously creates a memory of its actions and thinking.[173] Reading and writing are on the list, but they are not singled out. Nor is the study of scripture. In *De Vera Religione,* there is a notable change in emphasis. Augustine is no longer discussing the potential greatness of any soul, but the possibility for regeneration in the soul of fallen man.[174] The mechanism is scripture, whose "medicine for the soul,"[175] working within "divine providence,"[176] replaces the tree in the garden of Eden (since it was not its knowledge that was evil but the human transgression of a divine precept).[177]

For the reintegration of the soul to begin, a cooperative effort is required between authority, which makes demands on one's faith and prepares the way for reasoning, and for reason itself, which, thus oriented, leads to understanding and knowledge.[178] The design of providence is thus worked out as a "temporal dispensation," which corresponds to the lifetime of a person. His bodily life begins when he enters the world, where the chief concerns are with the endowments of "nature" and their reshaping through "education." As in *Confessions* 1, the first stages of memory mark the boundary between infancy and childhood. In infancy the body is nourished, but no mental record is retained, while in childhood, the learning (presumably of language) is accompanied by recall.[179] Adolescence and early manhood follow, the one marked by puberty, the other by public and legal responsibilities;[180] then maturity, marked by relative tranquillity,[181] an age not mentioned in *Confessions* 1–9 but symbolized by the desired state of mind of *De Doctrina* 1; and finally, old age, the period of inevitable decline.[182]

This is the narrative of man's corporeal life; in Paul's terms, "the life of the old man, exterior and terrestrial" (compare Rom. 6:6),[183] a life not lacking in "happiness" if one has the benefit of a well-governed society.[184] Some individuals remain in this state from birth to death. However, others, granting its necessity, use it as a point of departure; they renew themselves within *(renascuntur interius),* eroding and burying their former selves, rising with spiritual strength through increments of wisdom, and binding their fates to heaven's laws, until the time of their visible death, when the soul is wholly restored *(totum instauretur)*.[185] Using a formula that will echo in *De Catechizandis Rudibus,* Augustine speaks of "a new man, directed within and toward heaven, who possesses stages in the life of his spirit, which are distinguished not by the passage of years, but by steps of progress."[186]

These seven *aetates* constitute a reading and postreading programme. The first is a kind of infancy, in which one is nourished by the useful examples of (biblical) history.[187] The second is like abandoning one's parents: it consists "in forgetting what is human, and in directing one's attention toward the divine," that is, leaving "the bosum of authority" and, "through steps of reason," striving after "the highest, eternal law."[188] The third is envisaged in the metaphors of a chaste marriage; it is a wedding between the appetite of the flesh and the force of reason, which produces an inward joy of conjugal sweetness when the soul mates with the mind and yet dons a veil of modesty, thus imposing on itself the constraint of living righteously, so that, when everything is permitted to it (in heaven), it will take no pleasure in sins of the flesh.[189] The fifth is the age of peace and tranquillity which passes amid the riches and untold abundance "of the realm of wisdom,"[190] while the sixth represents "a total transformation into the eternal life, in which the soul entirely forgets its temporal existence in the perfecting of its form, which is fashioned in the image and likeness of God."[191] The seventh is eternal repose, the state of complete happiness in which stages of life are no longer distinguished.[192]

In *De Quantitate Animae,* Augustine sees no reason why the soul, having attained the "tranquillity" of complete purification through the practice of virtue, should not advance from the "beginning" *(ingressio)* of momentary intuition of the divine to a secure "abiding" *(mansio)* of contemplative fruition, that is, to "a full and unshakable apprehension of the truth of God."[193] In *De Vera Religione,* a boundary is imposed between the realms of time and eternity, and the worldly steps are oriented to a programme of biblical study. *De Doctrina Christiana* furthers this transition, and the seven stages are once again reconfigured. In the first, the reader's initiation is through fear, a "turning" towards God's will as the arbiter of what is right and wrong. Fear engenders thoughts of mortality (2.7.1–4), thereby introducing an eschatological perspective. The second stage is the acquisition of meekness through piety, so that scripture is not opposed when it strikes against vice (2.7.7–10). This means believing that what is written is better and truer than what we can know on our own, even if much remains concealed from us.[194] The third stage, the acquisition of knowledge, is discussed separately in 2.7 and 2.8. In 2.8, which is logically prior to 2.7,

Augustine states that "the careful inquirer" is one who has read the whole
of the Bible (or at least the "canonical books") and retains that information,
even if he does not yet have a thorough understanding.[195] In 2.7, he
enumerates the psychological transformations that this education entails.
First, a "trinity" of love is realized (love of God, neighbour, and self). Next
comes an ascetic response: the reader learns that he has devoted himself to
temporal things; he now discovers the transcendental world of the spirit.
The fear of God's judgement completes the process; he deplores his own
situation and acquires courage, both of which "convert" him to the love
of the eternal triune God.[196] The remaining stages presumably take place
within his mind after he has thought about what he has read. They include
partial illumination, in which he sees the trinity "distantly radiating its light"
and the counsel of mercy, through which he exercises and perfects his love
of his neighbour. In the sixth stage, his inner vision is clarified, so that even
as a mortal he is able to fix his eyes directly on the threefold God. With
a purified mind and heart, the reader effectively becomes a contemplative,[197] ascending to the seventh stage, which is wisdom (2.7.36–61).

The case of the individual reader is taken up in 2.7 and 2.8, uniting the
neoplatonic notion of ascent with step-by-step progress through education;
2.9 offers the perspective of reading as an institution. Augustine reminds
the *studiosi* that their primary obligation is to become acquainted with the
Bible through frequent perusal and recall, even if at first their understanding
is limited.[198] But he adds a general rationale, which parallels the distinction
between basic and interpretive reading in the prologue. What is put to
readers openly in scripture is intended as precepts for living or rules for
believing (*praecepta uiuendi uel regulae credendi*, 2.9.6).[199]

On this note, he concludes his basic exposition. In 2.10 he begins
another phase of the discussion in which his topic is the potential misunderstanding of scripture through unknown or obscure signs (2.10.1–2). In
principle these can occur in oral or written forms, and they can be literal
or figurative. The literal relates a word to a thing, while the figurative
occurs when the thing designated by a literal sign is used to signify
something else (2.10.2–8). This is the distinction that is initially made
between things and signs (2.1–2); its reintroduction is an indication of a
shift in Augustine's interests from the world of which literature is a part to
literature itself.[200]

The meaning of the two stages of reading, that is, basic reading (1–2.9)
and interpretation (2.10–3.37), is also clarified as different relationships
between reading and behaviour. In 1–2.9, the assumption is that the model
reader knows little or nothing beyond how to read: the reading of scripture

is oral, and the lessons are directly applied. In 2.10–3.37, reading requires
that the student know a good deal (such as languages and laws of inference);[201] also, it is visual, reflective, and presumably silent in part, inasmuch
as it involves a simultaneous comparison of texts[202] or the consideration of
literal and figurative senses on the basis of alternative translations (2.12.4–
18). The relationship to conduct is likewise indirect. Before action can
result from understanding, reason has to coordinate diverse facts. The more
one knows in advance, the better one's chances would seem to be in
applying the lessons of the Bible to life.

Literal signs in scripture remain "unknown" mainly because of difficulties
in translation (2.11–15).[203] In taking them up, Augustine recognizes that
the reader needs information located both in language and in objects.[204]
The lengthy subsequent discussion (2.16–42) asks how pagan knowledge
can contribute to the understanding of scripture.[205] Excluding superstition
(2.19.3–7) and "pacts with demons" (2.24.20–24; 2.39.8–11), Augustine
singles out useful human institutions, "practices that have value . . . because
they are agreed upon and established" (2.25.4–6; compare 2.39.12–14),
including reading and writing (2.26.1–2). He also takes up sources of
knowledge not originating with men but with deities: these are brought
to light by inquiries, which he divides into those appealing to the senses
and those appealing to reason (2.27.1–5). In the former category he puts
history, scientific information, and an understanding of the technical arts
(2.28–30); in the latter, the sciences of disputation and of number, as well
as the rules of eloquence (2.31–38).

Initially bewildering, this classification breaks down into useless and
useful signs in pagan learning, and a discussion of how the latter can assist
the reader. His chief example of useless signs is "superstition," which
includes idolatry, that is, the worship of images or objects;[206] magic, that
is, pseudoscientific practices ranging from haruspicy and augury to amulets
and false remedies;[207] ritual "observances" (such as "kicking a stone to
destroy a friendship," 2.20.20–34); and astrology (2.21.1–3). His interpretation of these practices is reductive but original. He sees them all operating
through a misuse of signs. He hints at this approach as his list unfolds,
referring occasionally to the causal links as *significationes*.[208] A more general
statement is made in 2.24, near the end of his refutation of astrological
prediction. What makes magic work is previously established assumptions
about a language shared in common with malevolent spirits and binding
us to them (2.24.1–3; compare 2.20.3–5; 2.39.5–12). Demons desire to
ensnare us; but we too are trapped by our curiosity, anxiety, and enslavement to habit. Superstitions, like other sign systems, are conventional

arrangements *(pacta, conuenta)* between symbols and audiences; they achieve meaning and influence behaviour in accordance with a consensus *(consensio)* established beforehand in their respective societies. There is no agreement on symbolic languages, and so the signifiers of superstitious beliefs change with linguistic groups, rather like scripts. Yet, wherever they operate, one rule holds: they are not the subject of interest because they posssess an inherent validity; they are considered valid because attention has been drawn to their sign-generating activity (2.24.4–7, 18–24).

Useful signs, which are invented (2.25–26) or rediscovered (2.27.1–2),[209] are either made or not made by humans. The mimetic arts are man-made sign-givers (2.25.1–4), such as painting, sculpture, dress codes, weights, measures, coinage, and, above all, letters and languages (2.26.6–7), which seek "similitude through signifying" (2.25.15–16). Augustine's favorite example is pantomine dance,[210] which illustrates how the communicative arts differ from other man-made institutions in requiring us to know why, where, when, and by whose authority they are created. If that were not so, there would be no way of distinguishing genuine signifiers from "fictions and falsifications" (2.25.22–29).

By contrast, there are four means of understanding unknown figurative signs arising from knowledge not created by humans and known through their senses:[211] the narrative of facts about the past, that is, history;[212] the narrative of facts in the present, which is similar to a demonstration (2.29.1–2); the demonstration of knowledge of heavenly bodies, which is not a narrative (2.29.22–23); and other arts and skills, in which experience acts as a guide (2.30.7–8).[213] He rejects two types of predictive science, practical skills and codified disciplines, such as astrology and medicine; the latter can be judged only by the use that they provide.[214] As an alternative, he proposes "historical narrative," which treats the past and the future differently from natural occurrences.[215] Distantly anticipating Wilhelm Dilthey, he argues that whereas scientific laws predict the future of nature, a knowledge of the past informs the intentional world of the individual.[216] History has no greater value in predicting behaviour than astrology, since it tells us about human institutions but is not a human institution itself.[217] Historical narrative, however, makes different assumptions, and these provide a basis for guiding the individual in the future. As a consequence, astrology, in attempting to teach us what is to be done, fails, while history, in narrating what has been done faithfully and usefully (2.28.40–48), succeeds in influencing behaviour, not by imitating a predictive science, but through a method by which *writings* about the past are ethically related to the *reader's* present and future.[218] This conclusion, linking scripture, the source of *res*, with the reader, the perceiver of *signa*, through the medium of values, is the culmination of Augustine's theory of audiences and literary authority in *De Doctrina*.

In the second subdivision of non-man-made institutions, namely reason, he talks chiefly about disputation and number (2.31.1–3).[219] The "discipline of disputation" is discussed in detail (2.31–35), together with "the rules of eloquence" (2.36), a topic pursued at greater length in book 4. He argues that the logic of inferences has little to do with the truth of statements.[220] "Truth" means the facts as stated in scripture; "logic" refers to operations on those statements as words.[221] Truth comes before logic because things have priority over signs. A person who shows us animals, plants, and minerals, or who describes the motions of the stars, does not point out things created by himself: he draws attention to realities that already exist. Similarly, the narrator of a story is not the inventor of the order on which the sequence of events is based (2.32.4–11). As a sign indicates what a thing is, so, in exegesis, rules of logic draw attention to present, latent truths. And although inference can confirm truth, statements must be considered individually to establish whether they are true or false (2.34.6–9).[222] The following schema results:

$$\text{institutions of reason}$$

| truth of statements | truth of rules |
|:---:|:---:|
| ↓ | ↓ |
| meaning in text | meaning in reader |

Book 2 ends on a note of intellectual tolerance. The *studiosi,* who fear God and seek the blessed life, cannot achieve their goal through the study of pagan knowledge. But they cannot totally reject it either. Among man-made institutions, "they should not neglect teachings necessary for persons living together in society and necessary for its life" (2.39.1–6, 12–14). The maxim should be "Nothing in excess" (2.39.21; compare 2.40.23–27). Among non-man-made institutions, solutions vary. In the growing library of biblical knowledge, contemporary students can add to what is known. Yet this approach will not work for reasoning based on disputation, "since it binds the text of scripture like a network of nerves" (2.39.24–45). Pagan philosophy must also be viewed cumulatively. But Christians, when they convert, can take its "treasures" with them (2.40.13–

23), as did Augustine, provided they recall that "knowledge inflates, while charity edifies."[223]

Armed with languages, an understanding of similitudes, and correctly emended texts, the reader confidently proceeds to ambiguous signs (3.1.3–9).[224] Like unknown signs, these are either literal (3.2–4) or figurative (3.5–24). The literal can arise from errors in punctuation or in pronunciation, either in syllables, words, or expressions (3.2.1–3; 3.3.1–2).[225] In figurative signs there are two variables, the meaning in the reader and the meaning in the text. As in *Confessions* 1.19, Augustine's solution is to equate the improvable spirit in man with the spiritual sense derivable from scripture.[226] Change in the person is thereby brought about by an elimination of ambiguity in what one reads.[227] To understand a statement literally that is intended figuratively is to substitute flesh for spirit[228] and to eliminate signification from the doctrine of signs.[229] The result is a Pauline death or slavery for the soul,[230] whereas reading spiritually is a "liberation" (3.8.1–4).[231]

To understand the *historical* process relating God and man, man is therefore obliged to enter into a *psychological* relationship between the self and scripture. The point of entry is reading, and the key to becoming "a man spiritual and free"[232] is reading signs in scripture correctly. Whether one is "enslaved" or "freed" hinges on the state of one's knowledge, that is, whether one has "truly" understood what one has read: the slave worships a significant thing without knowing what it means; the free man does not venerate what he sees, but what is referred to, that is, the nontemporal meaning in the sign (3.9.1–6). Of course, figurative expressions can be mistaken for literal ones, and vice versa. But this possibility can be eliminated if one assumes that whatever in scripture does not literally refer to virtuous behaviour or to the truth of faith is intended figuratively (3.10.5–8; compare 3.24; 3.25.1–7). Augustine's train of thought thus returns by another route to charity.[233]

## Book 4

Book 4 turns from the "discovery" to the "making known" of scripture's hidden truth, the *modus proferendi* (4.1.1–11). Augustine thereby moves from the personal to the social dimension of communication.

Although this is a new theme, his method is in continuity with books 2 and 3; this is demonstrated in five introductory chapters on the acquisition of eloquence.[234] He reiterates his views that book-learning cannot replace youthful talent[235] and that students master linguistic skills mainly by habit *(consuetudo)*. The infant learns to speak by imitating speech; the child, knowing no grammar, nonetheless speaks grammatically. Similarly, one does not become eloquent by acquiring a theory of eloquence but by reading, hearing, and imitating eloquent people (4.3.40–50; compare 4.3.16–18; 4.5.33–40).

Augustine does not advocate secular rhetoric (4.1.12–17), in which persuasion is indifferent to moral values (4.2.1–6); yet he argues in favour of the construction of an internal narrative supported by a strong emotional appeal (4.4.7–15; 4.12; 4.17). If a capable individual reads the church's literature, he will become accustomed to its eloquence even if he is attracted more by the subject matter than by the style. If he practices writing, dictating, and speaking according to "the rule of piety and faith," the habit of eloquence will be confirmed.[236] The differing goals of eloquence and wisdom—the one seeking ornament, the other, truth—are thus resolved through the reading process (4.5.18–19). Augustine transforms Cicero's notion of the *doctus orator*[237] into a potent instrument of Christian education.[238]

Some read, but pay no attention; others read and remember what they have read, but fail to understand. The best reader—Augustine perhaps has himself in mind—is one who can recall the text when he wishes while fully understanding its meaning. The less gifted he is with words, the more he has to rely on recall, for it is his demonstrations that will delight the audience, not his expressions.[239] Some texts, too difficult for oral explication, should not be presented "to a popular audience": for a book, if understood, has a power that holds the reader's attention, and, if it remains unread, it cannot be misunderstood (4.19.1–7). With the basics established, Augustine divides book 4 into a treatment of two topics, the eloquence in scripture (4.6–7) and the eloquence of the Christian teacher (4.8–15). Here, his position is that Christian writings are eloquent, but not by classical criteria, and that Christians can speak wisely and well, but by reinterpreting the rules of oratorical style.

It is imprudent to speak of a "theory of reading" emerging from the reflections summarized here from *De Doctrina Christiana*. The prologue, perhaps as an afterthought, moves in the direction of hermeneutics; yet book 1 undermines its interpretive potential, and books 2–4 do not attempt to restore it completely. What is clear from the treatise's many themes is that it should not be studied in isolation from Augustine's other statements on the subject, in particular those in *De Utilitate Credendi* and *De Catechizandis Rudibus*. The common thread linking the three books is the recognition of the value of reading as a means, while denying its validity as an end. If reading is instrumental in gaining access to tradition, it is nonetheless a way of demonstrating the limits of interpretive reason. At the end of *De Doctrina,* Augustine arrives at a position comparable to that of *Confessions* 7–9. Through his analytical and autobiographical discussions, he concludes that it is illusory for men or women to believe that the narratives that they live are their own constructions, any more than they can be sure that a given interpretation of a text is completely correct. As predestination operates inscrutably in Augustine's life, scripture creates for him a readerly universe that is never fully knowable.

# 8

# MEMORY, SELF-REFORM,

# AND TIME

Two major topics envisaged in this study have now been taken up: the process by which Augustine "learns to read" in *Confessions* 1–9 and the presentation of his views on problems of interpretation in writings after 386. The remaining chapters examine some topics in his philosophy of mind in *Confessions* 10–13 and *De Trinitate* 8–15 that are related to the reading process: these deal with memory, reform, time, and the concept of the self.

In *Confessions* 10, with which the first and second parts of this chapter are concerned, I treat the links that Augustine perceives between memory, remembering, and self-reform. He argues that human conduct can obey ethical guidelines provided that the principles involved are continually present in individuals' thoughts. The guidelines he has in mind are drawn mainly from the Bible; as a consequence, his programme for personal reform links memory and the reader through the sacred text.

In *Confessions* 11, which is discussed in the third part of the chapter, he takes up a related matter, namely the experience of time that ensues from a meditative reading of a biblical text such as the opening chapters of Genesis; this topic gives rise to a lengthy exegetical discussion in books 12 and 13. In book 11, which is my chief focus of interest, he pursues a line of thinking that is introduced in book 10, arguing that just as we cannot know all the contents of memory, so we cannot fully understand the nature of time. We understand the passage of time in the way in which a reader or listener grasps the meaning of a text. As the sentences are read aloud, the ears decode the sounds in sequence, and the mind, aided by memory, makes sense out of the whole.

It is a short step from these reflections to the topic of self-knowledge, which I address in Chapter 9. In Augustine's view, we know that the self exists; however, we have no corresponding certainty about what the self is. We know ourselves through relationships that are derived from information provided by the senses or the mind. These sources offer temporary rather than permanent knowledge about the nature of the self. Furthermore, if wisdom is defined as complete self-knowledge, this goal is also beyond humans' grasp. We can pursue wisdom throughout our lives without ever being truly or fully wise.

In these discussions, Augustine frequently uses theory as a self-deflating device. He gives the discussions a theoretical preface whose function is partly to illustrate what theoretical reason cannot achieve.[1] He proves to his satisfaction that we have an experience of time but that we can offer no adequate philosophical account of time. A comparable conclusion emerges from his consideration of theories of vision and insight in *De Trinitate* 11. The lengthiest demonstration of this type occurs in *Confessions* 10. With the aid of memory, he makes an inventory of the things that he has experienced in the world in an effort to rise above himself. This mental exercise offers no solution to the enigma of memory itself, and he subsequently abandons this hopeless quest in favour of a pragmatic approach through remembering.

As a means of charting the growth of Augustine's interests through reading, chapters 8 and 9 can be viewed as an extension of my discussion of his oral recitation of the Psalms in *Confessions* 9.4; these chapters are also a preface to the extended moral interpretation of Genesis in books 12 and 13, which I do not treat in detail. The treatise on memory thus plays a pivotal role in linking the ethical contributions of the *Confessions*' two major segments. In a comparable way, books 10 and 11 offer a theory of narrative against the background of the autobiographical account of books 1–9.[2] The later books of the *Confessions* and *De Trinitate* are agreed on the human inability to achieve objectivity in thinking about time, memory, or the self;[3] thus it appears appropriate to consider them together in taking up the issues of asceticism and the blessed life.[4]

Possidius, in simplifying the account of Augustine's conversion and retirement,[5] nonetheless notes his evolution toward an outlook in which study, reflection, and recollection of biblical writings played a central role.[6] After Monica's death, he delayed his return to Africa for about a year. The times were unsettled as a result of the revolt of Maximus, who was declared emperor by his troops in Britain in 385 and subsequently allied himself with Gildo, the count of Africa, before being defeated by Theodosius.[7] Augustine retraced his steps from Ostia to Rome, where he devoted his time to a comparative study of the "moral" traditions of Manichaeans and Catholics.[8] He also wrote *De Quantitate Animae*[9] and book 1 of *De Libero Arbitrio,* which was completed in Hippo.[10] He left the city for good around mid-August 388,[11] arriving in Thagaste in September.[12] Between the autumn of 388 and the end of 390, he wrote *De Genesi contra Manichaeos* and *De Vera Religione;* he also redrafted *De Magistro* and finished six of the twelve intended books of *De Musica*.[13] Little of this was known at home, where he was nonetheless remembered for his secular literary talents. Eulogius, a former student who had become a professor of rhetoric, even dreamt that his sometime master had solved difficult problems in Cicero's rhetoric for him as he was preparing a lecture.[14] For his part, Augustine believed that he and Alypius, if they were "not yet clerics," were "already in God's service."[15] Along with Evodius, a convert from the secret police, they were searching for an appropriate place to take up the contemplative life. *Confessions* 10–13 informs us about the individual rather than the institutional side of his reflections as his programme of ascetic reform gradually came into focus.[16] For Augustine the priest and later bishop, the reading of scripture was part of the daily routine of liturgy and pastoral care. Against the background of this activity, the statements about reading in the later books concern not the acquisition but the application of his skills.

Changes in the literary structure of the *Confessions* accompany this transformation. With book 9 concluded, Augustine ceases telling a story based on events that he recalls and begins to question the truth-value of all personalized recollections. Book 10 is a study of the individual's memory of past events, in contrast to the discussion of present memory in *De Trinitate* 12–14 and social memory in *De Ciuitate Dei*. Through the traces left in the memory, each of us is able to recall the images by which the original events were recorded, together with the enjoyable (or unenjoyable) features of the sensations. Such pleasures (or pains) are thereby embedded in habitual patterns of response, which become their narrative frameworks.[17] When we recall images that give us pleasure, we illustrate our dependency upon such mental patterns, and our habits subsequently inhibit our ability to redirect our conduct toward other ends. Personal memory can thus act as an impediment to self-improvement.

As a consequence, having a good memory does not necessarily mean that bad habits will be overcome. The key to self-improvement lies in replacing one type of patterned behaviour with another and, in Augustine's view, in attaching improvement through memory to a nonpersonal framework through the institution of reading. In this endeavour we are aided by another feature of memory, its capacity for storing, along with the sense impressions of many ordinary things, a mental record of the highest sources of pleasure, to which we give the names "God" and "the blessed life."[18] If such notions did not somehow find their way into our memories, we would be unable to recognize the realities that the words designate when their verbal images appear in our conscious thoughts. Augustine argues that such "realities" are found in memory because we have learned about them. If memory is to play a role in self-improvement, other edifying information has to be recorded and made accessible. Since scripture and philosophy are the chief sources of such beneficial knowledge, the reader's role in the process of mental incorporation is highly important, whether one reads for oneself or is the member of an audience. The discussion of memory in book 10 confirms the view implicit in his dialogue with Monica in book 9 that the blessed life is a state to which one can look forward if one is chosen and the right path is wilfully followed; this idea is in his mind when he speaks of a life in which one's thoughts and actions are shaped by an ethically informed, world-denying design. Book 10 initiates a phase of the inquiry that is completed in book 11, where he asks that God reveal to him "the rules for living" in the "law,"[19] thereby making scripture his official guide to correct behaviour. Having described the role of memory, he proceeds to show how the temporal and the eternal, which coexist in the artificial memory of scripture, can live within the human memory of the individual reader.

*Confessions* 1–9 and 10–13 have a similar goal, but they employ different literary strategies. Book 10 turns to the subjects that concerned Augustine at the time of composition, in 397–401. Many reasons have been advanced to account for the change,[20] including the largely unsupported notion that he abandoned autobiography in order to pursue discursive theology.[21] Although the *Confessions* is not a unified literary work by modern standards, the disunity between the two major segments is more apparent than real. As a literary stylist, Augustine is as fond of representing debate in a dramatic fashion as he is expert at relating a series of personal experiences having a deeper, spiritual significance. A mixture of discussion and reminiscence is characteristic of many works written between 386 and 401. We learn more about his everyday life at Cassiciacum from the "philosophical dialogues" than from the brief account of *Confessions* 9.4. The letters and the anti-Manichaean books of this period, while presenting philosophical and theological material, provide precious details of his early years as bishop of Hippo. We read about the results of his exegesis in *Confessions* 12–13, but we follow the evolution of his thinking step by step in the "imperfect" commentary on Genesis (393) and in his three glosses on Paul (394–395). There is no work that refers to the self more intimately than the *Enarrationes in Psalmos*.

There is nonetheless a change that he deliberately introduces into the *Confessions* alone: this concerns the literary notions of "author" and "authority." In books 1–9, he contrasts two types of self-understanding: these are widely understood to be lodged respectively in the Augustine in the story and the Augustine who tells the story. The person who tells the story entertains the idea that he is the author (that is, the cause) of the life that he lives. The other Augustine, who comments on what is taking place, knows that this is not the case. As he sees things, the story of the youthful Augustine contains a meaning that is known to God but not apparent to him. In books 10–13, when the double narrative ends, this type of irony ends too. Augustine the actor and Augustine the narrator become one,[22] and the viewpoint presented to the reader in books 10–13 is that of the bishop, who identifies himself as the inventor of the autobiographical books. Within his Pauline design, he is no longer recounting an "old" life but constructing a "new" one.

The transformation appropriately takes place during a discussion of the achievements and limitations of memory. The value of an account of one's personal past is inseparable from the ability of memory to detach itself from one's participation in events and to provide a means of reflecting on the events themselves. Augustine offers decisive proof that this is impossible. Memory, in his view, is able to reconstruct the past as a series of events recorded in mental images. Yet, when dealing with the self or the soul, the individual's memory is incapable of displaying everything that it contains. In this respect, our narratives concerning ourselves desire completion but remain incomplete. Furthermore, our personal reconstruction creates the illusion of self-authorship. We find the story plausible, despite our awareness that its beginning and end are arbitrarily chosen: we trust in the self's continuity by means of a narrative account, which, as it is not fully knowable, is, in this respect at least, discontinuous.[23] Believing in the existence of our selves over time without the aid of a supplemental authority is an expression of faith. Augustine's narrative theory of the self thereby questions its own theoretical assumptions. Moreover, he believes that stories appeal to us through the sensory and linguistic understanding of things with which we are familiar, and in ethically informed narratives, the surface effect is intended to lead the hearer or reader toward what he or she does not yet know and which, given human limitations, will never be known completely (compare 9.1.14–22). Books 10 and 11 thus take up a question that is approached in another manner in the "philosophical dialogues" and *De Trinitate* 8–15: the degree to which an otherworldly ideal can be experienced in our thoughts while we are in this world.

In addition to changing literary notions of authority, book 10 rethinks authority's relation to human reason. From the moment of first self-consciousness to the mental ascent at Ostia, the Augustine who believes he is the source of his actions attempts to find the solution to his difficulties through rational analysis. For the convert to philosophy, the Manichaean enthusiast, and the professor of rhetoric, there is no higher authority. The beginnings of serious doubts about rationalism coincide with the influence of Ambrose. Each subsequent episode—the debate over neoplatonism, the conversion to the religious life, the dialogues at Cassiciacum, and his baptism—are steps away from the earlier position. After Ostia and in books 10–13, Augustine abandons reason as his principal guide to self-understanding. The bishop knows that he is just an actor in his narrative; he cannot pretend to be outside it, unaffected by its events. If his life has an author and an authority, they must be located beyond the reason's limits, as are the sources of his ethical imperatives. He experiences these forces in a mediated form in which reason offers logistical support for his thinking but provides no solutions in itself. In Book 11, it is through the impermanence of this mediated experience that he encounters the permanence of a meditative presence.

All of this gives rise to a set of potential connections between lives and writings that is unparalleled in the literature of late antiquity. In Augustine's view, reading the self is like reading a body of writing, not because the soul is in any sense a text but because humans understand the ineffable in souls only as expressed in comprehensible images or words. Reason and authority are aspects of the literary understanding of the resulting narratives. The relationship of the life that Augustine has led to the life that he desires to lead is like a gloss on a text that he has previously read (or a text that he has had read to him or has viewed through narrative images): This commentary has no autonomy; it too is a part of the temporal flow of images and words. Its purpose is to permit him to set up a hierarchy of values within his differing narratives about himself.

## Remembering

Augustine's attempt to transcend his "nature" through memory (10.7.3–4; 10.8.1) has to be viewed against the background of the ascents at Cassiciacum and Ostia. The one is an ascetic withdrawal in which he reinterprets classical *otium;* the other is a contemplative transcending of the world.[24]

Book 10 can be divided into three segments in the elaboration of this theme: 10.8–17 describes the contents of memory under the topics of images, methods, and emotional states; 10.18–25 argues that, on the topics of God and the blessed life, memory consists in the recollection of something previously learned and now forgotten; 10.25–43 distinguishes this type of memory, which orients us toward the future, from memory which looks to the past through remembered habits and their sensory associations. These reflections are preceded by an introductory devotion (10.1–7) which analyses the human and divine audiences for confession[25] and complements the prayers that begin books 1 and 5, thereby providing a bridge to books 10–12.

In 10.1, Augustine prays once again to know God as his maker knows him:[26] he asks God to enter his soul and to fit his soul to his design, once it is rid of its flaws (10.1.2–3). The hope that this will come to pass provides the rationale for his speaking "before God" in "the confession" of his "heart" and "before many witnesses" through his "pen."[27] Although nothing is unknown to God, his confession is necessary because he cannot understand his acknowledgement of his shortcomings unless it is made in human words that are potentially speakable, even if they are not spoken audibly.[28] "To you, God, therefore, do I manifest myself, whoever I am," he states, "and the words that I have spoken are the profit that I derive from my confessing." As they reach his maker, the same words are retransformed into "the words of the soul and the clamour of thought, familiar to God's ear" (10.2.6–9). They are "made silently and not silently: there is an absence of noise, but my affection cries out"[29] to be heard. He does not "utter" anything to other men that he has not said to God; and he does not say anything to God that God has not first said to him (10.2.14–17).

He then turns from an audience of one to a potential audience of many, that is, the larger public,[30] of which he speaks at 9.12, when, grieving for his dead mother, he states, "I confess to you, O Lord, now, in what I have written. Let him read it who wishes to do so and interpret what I have said as he wills."[31] His ambivalence about expression in words, a theme introduced in *De Utilitate Credendi,* is reformulated as a mistrust of communication between a confessing author and his public. Should he be concerned if others hear his confession, since none of them can cure his spiritual ills? Are they more eager to pry into another person's life than to examine their own? Why should his readers wish to hear from him what he is, when they will not listen to God telling them what they are? Finally, what criteria may be used for judging the truth or falsehood of confessional discourse? When others hear him speaking of his inner self, how do they

know whether he is telling the truth or not? For "no one knows what is
in man but the spirit of man that is in himself" (1 Cor. 2:11; 10.3.4–7;
compare 10.3.9)?

Just as we assume that the writer communicates with his readers, so, in
conceptualizing our relations with God, we make an assumption of faith
concerning the confessional discourse among those whose "ears" charity
has opened to him (10.3.10–14; compare 10.3.34–35). Words thus create
the possibility of belief *between* men, but this trust rests on a similar basis
for belief *within* each person[32] which is undemonstrable by words alone.
The audience is alleged to support an objective reality, since what is shared
among his hearers or readers is judged to be "true." Moreover, his readers
mirror his intentions in their desires: they do not merely "hear": they also
listen.

One speaks or writes the self, then, because minds are unknowable.
What takes place in the hearer's or the reader's mind is a type of mimesis:
not the imitation of outer action, as in a set speech, a rhetorical debate, or
a dramatic performance, but, as proposed in books 7 and 8, the recreation
of the self from within, by which an already existing narrative, one's past
life, is traced over by the shape of another, a life to come. Both are
representations, one pointing to the past, the other to the future—whence
the centrality of memory in sorting them out. Moreover, the relationships
work within the individual as well as between individuals. To the
hearer/reader, for whom his or her own life is a mental representation built
on experienced events, Augustine's life is a fiction built of unexperienced
ones, since that life, as a text heard or read, is recreated subjectively within
the auditor's imagination. Yet it is through this secondary representation
that the recipient's life is reformed. As individuals contrast what they want
to be with what they were, and with what, from the viewpoint of their
intentions, they no longer are, they are drawn towards the narrative that
they wish to live (10.3.21–23).

But what purpose can *litterae* serve for him? He knows that he is no
longer the person he was, and he has "seen" and "commemorated" the
"fruit of confession" in his own life.[33] Is the text anything more than the
transcript of a lived experience? If that is so, what is the mechanism by
which his readers can hope to gain "fruition," should they wish to read or
hear his story?[34]

His readers cannot know what he is, since their ears are not tuned to
his heart. They can only wish to hear him "confessing" what is within him,
that is, to hear what neither their eyes, ears, nor minds understand (as did
Alypius at his conversion). From his side, reading is a "manifesting," a

making apparent, of his self, just as, from the reader's side, it is a "discovery," an inquiry from outside, into the self. The homology arises from the dispositions of those engaged in discourse rather than from the text itself.[35] And the disclosure is an act of interpretation by both parties. For Augustine, the life to be interpreted is recorded in his personal memory; for his readers, it is a life transcribed in writing, which is a type of artificial memory. His reading is based on the study of the Bible and on events experienced, while theirs applies the consolidated text of his life (that is, the combination of biblical models and lived experience) to their life histories. In each instance, it is the life-informing *process* that is imitated, not the *content* of a narrative. Augustine's audience reads his *Confessions,* but each person rethinks his or her own life; and thus, the creation of a subject for him is viewed as the creation of an object by them, as they engage in the process of constructing narrative selves—new objects, so to speak, out of their own subjects. Giving birth to renewed lives is one purpose of his "daily confession of conscience." That is why, he reiterates, his confessing "takes place before God" through his "writings."[36]

In sum, the charitable trust that exists between author and reader can be described as a community around a text: it is interpretive in formation and behavioural in possibilities. The readers are conceived as an audience that is present before Augustine, expressing emotions of joy or sadness at events (10.4.6–12). His intentionality, which appears in writings, is thus transferred to a community that reads and orally prays (compare 10.4.29). He confesses to God "in secrecy, fear, and joy" and openly to other "believers": to the sons of men, who share in his happiness and in the body's death—those who partake of his story as a "pilgrimage," on whose account he asks to be heard (10.4.3–4, 20–37).

He knows within himself that he loves God. Creation—the heavens, the earth, and all they contain—likewise instructs him to praise his maker (10.6.2–4). Yet, as his consideration of audiences transcends literal speakers and hearers, so his expression of devotion begins with the senses but differs from purely sensory pleasures. He speaks mystically of the light in his soul that touches no place, the voice that sounds but does not fade in time, and the fragrance that endures but is not dispersed in the air (10.6.7–19; compare 1.6.20–40). He is clear on the role of the senses: "I, yes, the interior I, knew all this, I, that is, the soul that is my 'I,' through my body's sense."[37] Yet a new ascent seems appropriate (10.7.1–3): To reach God, he says, I must somehow "transport myself beyond my soul, whose power inheres in my body and vitally fills out my frame."[38]

On that upward journey, he encounters memory,[39] which is a bridge he must cross en route to a deeper understanding of the blessed life; it is the last in a series of such possibilities that appears in the *Confessions,* which include the false starts of philosophy, his student friendships, and the confraternal association held out to him by the Manichaeans. Only when the alternatives are exhausted does he come to place his faith uniquely in scripture.

Just as the mind is inseparable from thinking, so, he argues, memory is inseparable from remembering.[40] Moreover, if we cannot recall everything that is in our memories, there is something that is uncontained by our recollections. How can this be so (10.8.58–63)?

In 10.9–16, he divides the problem into the knowledge of things through sensory images *(imagines),*[41] the knowledge of disciplines through the presence of their methods *(praesentia),* and the knowledge of emotional states through notions or notations, which constitute a mental shorthand (*notiones uel notationes,* 10.17.8).[42] He proves that images are derived from the senses, but not from methods, emotions, or the activities of remembering and forgetting. Some knowledge in the memory must therefore arise from a nonsensory source (10.9–12, 14).

How then is memory a "container"? Augustine agrees with the ancient theory of places in the mind,[43] and he knows that the memory contains the fact that we have memories.[44] However, as his analysis proceeds, the metaphor of static containment is increasingly at variance with his understanding of the dynamics of recollection.[45] What emerges is a working distinction between memory as a place and remembering as a process. His concern thus shifts from locality, as such, to functional localization and, in particular, to what can be known of memory's store through the self-instructive process of recall. For, if our grasp of memory is imperfect, our conscious knowledge of what memory contains must be incomplete. The senses, though essential to recording and to recall, furnish only clues to the operations of memory.

He restates his conclusions from 10.1–7 by proposing that, in acts of remembering, there is always something we cannot recall and do not know. It is possible to conceive a mind capable of grasping everything that is in the human memory, including how we remember, but this would not be a human mind. He asks whether he can understand such a superior being through an instrument that he does not fully understand. He cannot; he realizes that he has ascended beyond his "nature" through memory only to find that memory must be transcended in turn (10.17.14–27). Its record of a better life is not quite an illusion, but it is not a reality either.

The problem arises from the notion of memory as a container. Augustine refers in the discussion to several types of repository,[46] and he employs different metaphors to describe them.[47] But he normally has in mind the manner in which memory acts as a storage place for the impressions of things produced by one of the five senses.[48] Each sense acts as a separate "gateway" to the mind, where the likenesses of things are formed (10.8.4–7, 18–30). Before entering memory's vault, the images are classified in two ways. What the senses perceive is either "enlarged" or "diminished"[49] as required by the mind, and the representations are filed away, individually and generically, within sensory channels.[50]

The implication is that our access to memory arises chiefly from the activities of forgetting and remembering. These furnish occasions when we are aware that images have left our conscious thoughts or return through deliberate acts of recall.[51] Even the operations are partly hidden from our view. What we "know" is sensory (that is, transitory) in nature. We have an awareness that images are in our conscious thoughts when we remember them. They can be summoned at will, even when the original stimuli are no longer present, and the types of recall are remarkably varied: for instance, I can see a colour when it is dark or hear a melody when there is silence.[52] Furthermore, just as the senses provide separate entry-points for images, so, when we recall them, we are able to keep their effects apart: I can momentarily put the image of the colour that I have in mind out of my thoughts while I listen to a melody, and vice versa. Also, I can separate sensory channels through memory alone, distinguishing, for instance, the scents of the lily and of the violet, or expressing a preference for the taste of honey over wine. The diverse operations are carried out "in the great court of memory," where one encounters "the heavens, the earth, the sea, and everything within them knowable by means of the senses" (10.8.31–45).[53]

Such observations considerably weaken the metaphor's force.[54] For, in addition to the images of objects in the external world, memory contains "realities" of a different sort, consisting of methods, principles, and practices, for which there is no external referent for recall (at least none that can be recalled).[55] These are the disciplines of the liberal arts[56] and the principles of number and measure,[57] for which memory is "a remote, interior place, and yet not a place" (10.9.3). The same principle of nonlocalization governs memory's record of emotional experiences—desire, joy, fear, and sadness (10.14.25)—which are preserved chiefly as a capacity for reexperience: this is neither a reality nor an image but a power of the mind, akin to the force of memory itself.[58]

Further thoughts along these lines occur in his consideration of memory as a "meeting-place" with the understanding of the self.[59] "I come upon myself," he remarks, "as I recall what, where, and when anything was done by me, together with my state of mind at the time" (10.8.45–47). Within his memory, he can "locate" everything he has experienced (or what he believes to have been experienced), on the basis of others' accounts. Memory thus emerges as the point of coordination for mental narratives. Weaving together the images of events that have taken place at one time or another, he is able to meditate on them as if they were still present and, as a result, to speculate on their potential influence on himself (10.8.45–52). These already constructed stories act as guides to his thoughts, to his consideration of alternatives, and to his decisions, which, as he sees it, are based on probabilities. Taken together, they comprise an intentional discourse of the self.

He can ask anything that he wishes of his memory (provided, of course, that the information has not been forgotten). Moreover, the internal operations of the memory appear to take place as they will, not as he wills.[60] Some memories appear at once, while others are delayed (stored in a remote part of the brain); the former may appear in sequence, as if memorized lines were being recited. Other recollections "rush forward" into his thoughts, asking, "Is it us you want?" If this happens, he has to will what he does not want out of his conscious thoughts before memory can will what he wants into them.[61] Only after this is done can the facts he desires to know emerge from the hidden wells of memory (10.8.7–17). Images are recalled like temporarily forgotten words. "While I speak," he notes, "the images of the things of which I speak are present, all drawn from the same treasury; and, were they not present in my mind, I would be unable to speak of them" (10.8.55–57). By contrast, in referring to realities such as "a knowledge of letters" or "a skill in argument," he knows what these are and he knows that he knows, without having access to sense impressions (10.9.4–9).

His argument parallels that in *De Magistro,* where, reinterpreting reminiscence, he proposes that we are taught by a type of recall. Having argued that signs imply such a recognition, he now proposes that recognition involves only types of signs. The critical example is in 10.10, where he places himself in the situation of being asked three standard logical questions about a hypothetical object: does it exist, what is it, and what is it like? On hearing what is said, he retains the phonic images; and he knows that the words pass through the air by means of sound, which starts and then stops. Yet what is signified (that is, the meaning of the questions asked) is not arrived at by means of hearing, sight, touch, or the like; it exists in his mind. There is no adequate explanation of how it got there by means of sense-impressions (10.10.1–8), nor did he rely on what anyone else had in mind. The knowledge was already in himself; it was he who confirmed its truth and entrusted it to safe-keeping, so that it could be brought forth whenever he wished. Moreover, its meaning was out of the reach of his faculty of recall. The inquirer's words acted as a reminder, calling to his mind something that he might possibly not have thought about at all (10.10.14–22; compare 10.14.9–14).

The human memory contains many objects in disorder. When we instruct ourselves through recollections, we think about these things as if we were "gathering them together" and "directing our attention" toward them. In this way, things that were "dispersed," "neglected," and "unnoticed" are placed in a position that permits them to be recalled. If I wish to recall them a second time, I have to go through the process of excogitation again, collecting the scattered items of information into one mental location and coordinating my thoughts. Augustine believes that the combined effort of willing, collecting, and thinking provides an etymological link between the verbs *cogo* (I compel), *colligo* (I collect), and *cogito* (I think) 10.11.1–15).[62] He is able to recall the laws of mathematics and of geometrical proportion (10.12.7–13), which he knows are true, along with incorrect opposing views.[63] Memory thereby permits him to distinguish his past thinking about truth and falsehood from that of the present (10.13.1–11).

His mental record of emotions is also nonsensory. His past feelings are contained in his memory as they are recreated (10.14.1–3), not as they were experienced. Their potential exists in his mind before recollection takes place (10.14.24–31). If that were not the case, his memory of his emotional states would depend entirely on the recovery of sense-impressions. Proof arises from the fact that he can experience one emotion while thinking about another: he can recall sadness while happy or recall fear without actually being afraid; he can look back upon a period of physical pain with joy (10.14.3–10). He does not store images of his previous emotions in the way in which a cow temporarily retains undigested food (10.14.19–22).[64] If our past emotions were placed in a mental "belly,"[65] we could experience the same emotions again, just as a cow, on chewing its cud, tastes the food that it has already swallowed. The uniqueness of human emotional recollections consists in our metacognitive awareness that the present reiterates the past without reduplicating it (10.14.31–42).[66]

What is the precise role of images in this process? When one names things that are not present to the senses, the images can nonetheless exist in memory. It is possible to have an image of pain without actually feeling pain; the distinction between pain and pleasure is made through memory (10.15.1–6). Even the central terms of the subject, memory and forgetting, appear to depend on recall.[67] Otherwise one would not understand the respective words. When I remember what memory is, memory itself is presented to my self through itself; but when I remember forgetfulness, both memory and forgetfulness are presented—that is, memory, by which I recall, and forgetfulness, which I recall. But if forgetfulness is remembered as a reality rather than as an image, then its presence, which is the absence of memory, should make it impossible for us to bring it to mind, to recognize the word, and to connect the signifier with the signified. That is clearly not the case. Does this mean that forgetfulness, in order to be remembered, is present as an image, rather than as a reality (10.16.4–16)? That too cannot be.

The problem is complicated[68] by another factor, which brings Augustine back to his point of departure. Knowing what is in his memory is not like measuring the distance between the stars.[69] It is a personal matter. "It is I who remember," he notes: "I, my mind."[70] In other words, the distance in question is mental, it is measured by the subject, and it arises between a past and present experience. In "forgetfulness," therefore, he has an example of a more general paradox of self-knowledge (10.16.25–32). He is unable to comprehend the force of his memory because he is unable to get outside the boundary of his mind; yet he is not able to speak "himself" without it, since the knowledge that he has of himself is contained in his mind.[71] If he finds God outside his memory, he will not be able to claim that he has a memory of God. Yet how is he to find him, if he does not remember him (10.17.25–27)?

## Conduct

Augustine takes up these issues in two subsequent discussions, 10.18–25 and 10.25–43, which complete his analysis of memory in the *Confessions*. But before turning to them, it is necessary to assess the relation between the views expressed in 10.8–17 and other statements on memory in the *Confessions*.

In general, there are two approaches to the problem of memory. These are identical with his divisions of the problem of reading, the analytical and the narrative, since reading, in his view, is always accompanied by some sort of recall. In the analytical approach, statements from within his writings, irrespective of the date at which they were written, can be taken as illustrations on memory's relation to perception, image-formation, remembering, forgetting, and language.[72] In the narrative treatment, the evolution of his ideas can be related to specific purposes and occasions. In *Confessions* 10, both approaches are employed: in 10.8–17, he attacks the issues within an analytic framework; in 10.18–43, however, he refers at length to the memory of his own imperfections. The change in emphasis reflects a historical shift in his interest in memory toward the present, which is completed in his other major exploration of the theme, *De Trinitate* 12–14.

As the previous section of this chapter indicates, the analytical scheme concerns analogies between memory and language.[73] The images in memory arise through perception or imagination; in either case, they have links with the senses. Augustine offers no clear explanation of how such impressions become incorporeal traces in the mind; however, just as we represent objects in the external world through signs, we retrieve the images stored in the memory by attaching the appropriate word to the object recalled. The images in the mind exist in a language of thought, which is translatable into a spoken language through the operation of the will. Memory is the basis both of our understanding of language and of our ability to express ourselves in words: it acts as a "guarantor" of the continuity of what we perceive through our senses,[74] as well as offering us indirect evidence of the immateriality of mind.

The situating of such thinking within a life that furnishes specific occasions for recall is taken up in the second segment of book 10. Proceeding through the topics of images, methods, and emotions, Augustine turns to the problem of "containment" in a fresh perspective. He also introduces the idea that we remember by a type of seeing within the mind. This process is distinguishable from "illumination," that is a knowing within that depends on a force beyond the human mind. Seeing through memory involves the recollection of an image, a method, or an emotion that is fully knowable. Such remembering is a desire for knowledge and the satisfaction of that desire, in which the individual is an audience for himself. In taking up the metaphor of seeing within memory, Augustine complements the discussion of self-expression in 10.1–7; and he looks forward to books 11–13, in which reading and remembering become the preferred means of satisfying his desire to seek and find God in scripture.

## The Inner View

The steps by which Augustine connects memory, inner vision, and the implied role of reading in 10.8–17 are consequently of some importance in linking the two phases of the discussion of memory, the theoretical and the practical. They can be summarized as follows.

1. Outer and inner sight are distinguished. Viewing a scene differs from

one's description based on others' reports. The one image is the result of direct observation, while the other is seen inwardly as it was once presumably seen outwardly.

2. When we see inwardly, therefore, we express a belief in the veracity of what we see on the basis of the evidence of mental images (10.8.64–70). The verbal and iconic signs are the outer representations of interior knowledge. The inner view is part of a narrative, inasmuch as the scenes are displayed in our conscious thoughts in sequence in the way that a story is told to us in a succession of words.

However, the normal manner of representing reality in narrative is reversed. In the case of a story that is told to us, we believe what we hear or read, trusting in what we cannot know; in seeing within, we believe in something that we know with certainty, out of which we create trustworthy sequences of words or images. It is this externalized narrative within our thoughts that explains interior matters: it is like a text that is read to us by someone else, except that in this case the someone is an "other" within us whom we do not empirically know.

3. The inward narrative works in one way with the images of things that we have seen and in another way with methods, principles, or laws, where no sensory exemplars are involved.[75] In the first instance, words are the signs *(signa)* of mental images; in the second, they are examples (as in 10.43.2), illustrating verifiable rules. A consequence of this difference is that a hierarchical relationship exists between the *type* of knowledge that we have in memory and the *status* of our verbal exposition of this knowledge to ourselves. As we move from the sensory to the nonsensory, we place faith increasingly in interior discourse. For, with sensory confirmation denied, only two sources of verification remain: the teaching and learning that take place entirely within us, that is, by and for ourselves (10.10.15–17); and the sensory world that we recreate by putting into words again what we know by interior means.[76]

4. Within the mind, words stand in the same inferior relationship to inner vision as do images. The words are arranged so that they inform Augustine about what he asks to have brought forth from memory, and they coordinate his deliberations with himself about what is received; also, the memories "ask" whether they are "wanted" (10.8.7–12, 48–57; 10.14.10–14). The personified senses likewise speak in the language of verbal signs, as they look in at memory from the perspective of the images that they create (10.10.7–14). When unwanted notions appear, the hand of his "heart" must "wipe clean the face" of his "reflections" (10.8.12–14)— the "face," that is, of his self-expression.

5. Drawing out the realities in memory so that we can express them in words is therefore an interpretive process. The inner world of memory is a place of contemplative silence (10.8.31, 35–36), out of which desired recollections "come into view" before they are expressed in language (10.8.12–14). It is also a place where images are "collected" (10.8.40) and classified by species and genera (10.8.18–19). Remembering imposes a type of coherence (10.11) and contextualizes past events as parts of narratives that have been lived or related (10.8.47–52). Memory images, as the sense-impressions of words, are "written" on the memory (10.16.40–41); to be brought back, they have to be seen within and reexpressed. Augustine would argue that thinking and remembering are virtually inseparable.

In the movement from 10.8–17 to 10.18–25 and 10.26–43, the purpose of this transition is clarified: it is the first stage of a broader reorientation of the issues in book 10 from memory toward acts of remembering. This strategy permits Augustine to bypass the major weakness in human memory—our inability to know all that memory knows—and to focus on the more manageable question of how we recall information that we have actually forgotten. In his view, it is within these boundaries that the issue of locating God within memory can be answered.

## Of Containers and Continence

Augustine's concern is not with the pure theory of memory, any more than it is with the philosophy of signs in *De Magistro*. These are decoys, behind which his practical objectives remain concealed. In *De Magistro*, this strategy leads to the demystification of signs within an acknowledgement of their utility. In the discussion of memory, it brings him to the paradox that God cannot be contained in memory. Yet recourse to memory is necessary if we are to know anything about God. The learner is like a student who has read, memorized, and temporarily forgotten a text. To know what he can know of God, he has to recall what he once knew.[77]

Augustine's priorities are clear from his choice of a biblical example with which to introduce 10.18–25: he reuses the parable of the woman who lost one of her ten silver coins.[78] When she found it, she invited her neighbours to share her joy (Luke 15:8–10);[79] her happiness depended on her recognition of what she had mislaid (10.18).[80] The woman stands for the desire to find anything in memory, as well as the necessity of forgetting;[81] the house is the place where the object is lost and the search is carried out. The "coin" that Augustine is looking for is the memory of the blessed life.[82] As we move forward to books 12–13, the house effectively comes to mean scripture; the woman is the reader's desire to locate meaning in an artificial memory, namely a text.[83]

This shift in thinking brings new questions to mind. Is he to look for happiness among his recollections, as if he has forgotten something but remembers that he has forgotten it? Or is he to seek happiness through a desire to learn about something that he does not know, either because he never knew it or because he has now forgotten that he once knew it?[84] How does he know what he wants; and how does he know that others want, have wanted, and will want the same thing? Does happiness arise from the fact that he knows his memory or from his experience of a memory shared by all (10.20.9–19)?

Augustine's thinking on these issues went through two stages. In *De Beata Vita,* in which the goal of the happy life is first introduced, his immediate objective was "a state of ontological plenitude."[85] The goodwill was identified with a "spiritual habit" within the mind, which was synonymous with stability and virtue.[86] Within two years of his ordination in 391, he had Christianized this classical idea.[87] He likewise distinguished between the satisfaction of desire *(appetitus)* out of habit *(consuetudo)* and the orientation of the will *(uoluntas)* toward the love of God.[88] These ideas were transformed in the *Confessions,* together with the view first expressed in *De Libero Arbitrio,* according to which the morally beneficial operation of free will consists in resisting the sinful habits of the flesh.[89] His assumption is that we cannot attain a truly happy life while on earth; however, inasmuch as we are made in God's image, we can retrieve an image of happiness from our memories. In order to do so, we have to overcome one type of constancy and work towards another. We have to put behind us all that is habitual, corporeal, and geared to satisfying outer needs, and create habits that are spiritual and interior. Memory is the vehicle for achieving this goal, while scripture provides the material on which it works.

It is necessary to be precise about what one remembers of happiness or blessedness. Of the three previously designated ways in which information exists in memory in book 10—through images, methods, and emotions—Augustine rejects two. Happiness is not an image of anything else, like a recollection of the city of Carthage.[90] Nor is happiness retained like a method (such as the rules of rhetoric or mathematics). We do not apply knowledge that we have attained; instead, what we have attained leads us only to desire something that we have not yet enjoyed (10.21.3–6).

The third option presents a different challenge. Our memory of happiness may not be an image or a method, but it is in some sense an emotional state. The memory of happiness and the feeling of happiness are very difficult to separate. But what is the nature of this emotion? How can we know whether what we feel is "good" or "bad"? Augustine realizes that, although we recognize such experiences to belong to our past, we nonetheless pass judgement on them in the present.[91] We temporize (as he does in *Confessions* 1–9). Our judgements about the moral qualities of pleasurable events thus take place through our artificial reconstruction of the modalities of "past" and "present." He was once happy to perform acts that he now finds disagreeable; he did honorable deeds, which he enjoys looking back upon, although they no longer make up a part of his life (10.21.14–28; compare 10.21.34–40).

How, then, are we to distinguish the universal desire for happiness, which all humans share, from the particular circumstances with which individuals associate happiness in their memories? His answer is by orienting our thinking away from the axis that links the past and the present toward that which joins the present to the future. Only through the memory's recognition of happiness can a person know what he or she lacks. In this respect, happiness exists in the past of our experience, whence it is brought to bear on the present. However, if we believe that we proceed from flesh to spirit (compare Gal. 5:7), then bodily habits are the burden of the past on memory, while the desire for spiritual happiness is both a rediscovery of something forgotten before incorporation and of something to come afterwards.

It is clear why individuals are not happy. They are unable to break with the past. They take greater pleasure in things that will not make them permanently happy, since they are easy to recall, than in abstract, spiritual, or conceptual happiness, which, being unconnected to sensory images, is hardly remembered at all (10.23.20–22). Their inability to reconcile the past and the present (that is, to interpret two different narratives concerning their behaviour) leads to a divided self. To privilege the past over the present is to prefer a fiction to reality. Instead of judging the failures of the past by the standards of the present, we reshape the past to offer the most attractive image of ourselves. In Augustine's view, practicing this sort of make-believe is like living a surface narrative that fails to recognize a story's inner design (10.23.29–37).

In expressing such ideas, his thinking about memory comes full circle. He has begun book 10 by praising memory's infinite capacity to contain past experience. He now belittles this faculty, whose reinforcement of bad habits orients the individual toward vice rather than toward virtue. He also reorients classical reminiscence.[92] Only by limiting the discussion to what memory can effectively recall is it possible to transcend memory's limitations.[93] "I discover nothing about you, O God," he observes, "but what I remember of what you have taught me; and I have never forgotten you, since the moment that I learned of you . . . Moreover, from what I have learned of you, I have maintained you in my memory; and I find you there, whenever I reminisce on you and take delight in you" (10.24.1–7).

The metaphor of memory as a container is likewise abandoned, at least as a characterization of how one seeks and finds God within memory.[94] If God endures in memory, and if memory, in some sense, contains the knowledge that God endures, Augustine can ask where within memory he resides. For, despite his changeless nature, God evidently agrees to remain in his changeable mind; otherwise, Augustine could not learn of him from resources within himself. But in what sense is God "there"? Not as an image, a mental state, a metacognitive awareness, or even as mind itself.[95] And if this is the case, then in what sort of a "place" does he dwell, if indeed it is a place at all?[96] "Where would I find you," he asks, "that I might have learned of you? For you were not already in my memory before I learned of you. Where indeed . . . unless it was above and beyond myself, within you? Whether we go backwards or forwards, no such 'location' can be found."[97]

He thus localizes God by delocalizing him.[98] God is not a place in the mind; he exists in the mental activity by which a mind desires to know him (10.26.6–10). In *Contra Academicos* Augustine asks whether happiness consists in finding truth or in searching for it.[99] He now answers that it arises through redirecting the inquiry from a disputation on the outside to one within oneself.[100] In the reading process the intentions of the writer and the reader are supposed to converge. In remembering God, similar relations hold, only they now exist internally between Augustine and God. The text has merely been replaced by memory. Also, as in reading, he looks on this possibility as an ideal. Its presence is a mystical anticipation of things to come. Only in this sense is it a solution to the problem of relating ethics, time, and personal narrative. "When I inhere in you in all my being," he confesses to God, "I shall nowhere exhibit sorrow and travail: my life will be wholly alive, and wholly filled with you" (10.28.1–2). It is then that the "places" of memory will become the "no places" of an eternal present. Yet, as he contemplates this ideal, he is aware that "the sorrows that arise from evil are at war within my soul, and I am not sure where victory lies" (10.28.4–5).

Asceticism

Finding a way out of this dilemma is the programme of the final segment of book 10 (10.27–43). Augustine's answer is a personalized version of the ascetic life,[101] which involves a shift of interests from memory to acts of remembering.[102] There is no standardized "rule": its place is taken by short texts drawn from his reading. The ascetic principles by which he disciplines himself are first read, then codified in the mind, and finally recalled from memory. He memorizes precepts in order to prevent transgression,[103] as well as to stimulate right thinking. In this way they become the primary instruments of reform.[104] As recollections, they are able to participate in two narratives, one arising from his readings in the Bible, the other from the experiences of his life. Memory is the location in which the narratives of his reading are imposed on the narratives of his experience. The operation enables him to direct his thoughts about his future away from habits,[105] which are locked in his personal past and its sensory associations, and to orient them toward moral progress. The possibility of a better life is realized as he becomes his own reader and, through memory, his own audience.[106]

This is an important turning point in the reading programme in the *Confessions*, which brings the discussion of memory to a conclusion and prepares the way for the theological readings of books 12 and 13. Its immediate aim is to make a coherent plan of Augustine's often expressed belief that scripture is a "medicine for the mind," which acts jointly through "coercion" and "instruction."[107] He gives notice of the pragmatic direction of his thinking through a critical reinterpretation of the metaphor of containment in 10.27–29. The notion of memory as a "container" of events yields to the idea of continence as a way of "containing" unruly behaviour (10.29.5–9).[108] Book 10 thus complements the earlier appearance of Continence just before the conversion scene at 8.11. A comparison with the initial discussion of containment in the book is suggested by the nearly identical terms that are used to describe memory and continence as "collectors" and "unifiers" of disordered experience.[109] Through this symmetry, the paradox of memory, which cannot contain itself, is conveniently resolved. For the analysis of memory and the command to remain celibate have this in common: they demonstrate in different spheres that man's inability to contain himself can be overcome only with the help of God.[110] The simplicity of Augustine's solution lends support to the idea that the lengthy praise of memory's capacities in 10.8–17 has a rhetorical purpose, despite its many psychological insights.

The need to discipline the body is a persistent theme in the *Confessions* and other writings.[111] As a young student, Augustine loathed his teachers' beatings but recognized their value (1.9). Later, when he delighted his students without instructing them, God again "broke his bones" with "the rod of discipline."[112] As he moved from Manichaean materialism to neoplatonic intellectualism in his theological views, so he evolved from a corporeal to a cognitive type of ascetic discipline. The culmination of this development is the programme for reform through memory outlined in *Confessions* 10.30–39. It is a largely personal list of his correctable shortcomings under three headings: the pleasures of the senses, the attractions of the mind,[113] and the sins associated with pride. In the first category fall his dreams, as sensory fantasies, as well as the enticements of taste, smell, hearing, and sight (10.30–34); in the second, his curiosity for theologically irrelevant knowledge (10.35); in the third, his oversensitivity to the praise and criticism of others, and his self-love (10.36–39). The remedy for these is obedience to God's commands.

Only at this point in the *Confessions* is the relevance of Augustine's discourse on physical objects and their attractions in book 2 apparent. There, in the context of his adolescent theft of pears, he states that all things in the world have their respective sources of charm, to which each of the senses responds in appropriate ways. Temporal honour and the power to govern each have their "beauty." But neither these nor other socially acceptable modes of conduct can be allowed to deviate from God's commandments (2.5.1–7). Nor should the inferior objects be sought at the expense of the superior ones. The loftiest ideal is God's "truth and law" (2.5.11–14; Ps. 118:42). At the top of the Platonic ladder, therefore, stand the lessons derived from scripture. Their superiority must be kept in mind when considering the wide range of human behavioural responses, whether they consist of pride, fear, and love, or whether they seek fulfilment between curiosity and ignorance, idleness and labour, prodigality and avarice, or anger and regret. The human soul abuses itself whenever it seeks its fulfilment except by returning to God (2.6.18–45).

In the anti-Manichaean treatise *De Continentia,* written two years before the *Confessions,* Augustine recognized the difficulty of satisfactorily describing "the virtue of the soul called continence."[114] His point of departure was Psalm 140:3: "Set a guard over my mouth, O Lord, and a door of continence about my lips." This is not a custodian for the "bodily mouth" *(os corporis)* but "the mouth of the heart, within" *(intus . . . os cordis).* "There are many things that we do not speak with the mouth of the body but cry out from the heart. Yet no word about anything proceeds from the body's mouth when the heart is silent. What does not emanate from within does not sound outside; but what does emanate from there defiles the soul, even though the tongue does not move. The place of continence is where the conscience speaks—even if no outward speech takes place."[115] To verse 3, therefore, the psalmist added "Do not incline my heart to evil words" (Ps. 140:4). This "inclination" of the heart is nothing but "consent."[116] For, if the individual has not spoken within, his heart has not surrendered to evil intentions; and, if he has consented, he has framed the words of his sin within his heart, even though no sounds are heard.[117] This "evil interior word" is "the consent of thought."[118]

In *De Continentia,* Augustine takes up only sexual continence. In *Confessions* 10, he explores the manner in which our behaviour as a whole is patterned by internal representations that work against virtuous self-control. The negative effects are well illustrated by dreams. The images formed from the mental record of habitual activities can influence our actions, but their effectiveness depends on our state of mind. Images frequently "invade" his thoughts when he is awake; but then his rational faculties are alert and temptations are repelled. However, when he is asleep and unable to resist, he succumbs more readily to the enticements of his fantasy life (10.30.5–9). He wonders why these "false visions" that occur in a make-believe world are able to excite him in a way that "true visions" cannot.[119] He concludes that the changes take place within himself rather than through an exterior force. It is as if he ceases to be one person and temporarily becomes another.[120] He asks which of the two is really himself, and in doing so he implies that the self as we know it in everyday life is a little of both.

Food and drink satisfy needs and give pleasure (10.31), and fasting is a method of self-control. Yet, during the passage from hunger to satiety, he again appears to be two people (10.31.14–24). In his response to this problem he effectively summarizes his ascetic programme. Because gluttony originates in the mind rather than the body, it is there that a remedy is to be found. Habitual actions, lodged in memory, must be countered by an alternative food for thought. The relevant texts cannot always be before his eyes; they have to be memorized, in which case they influence his behaviour as he reperforms them. He follows the "voice" of God,[121] imagining that the deity speaks to him each time a verse is recalled. The restating of the words is an ascetic activity, a discipline of mind over body. He can focus his attention on only one thing at a time; and his mental rereading effectively shifts his attention away from the sensory appeal of food, to which, as long as his mind is occupied, it cannot return. Finally, the relevant passages of scripture are not recalled and enunciated in the order in which they appear in the text: an oral debate or dialogue takes place in his mind, resulting in an amalgam of brief quotations interspersed with his own comments. The collected texts may refer to a single theme—food and drink—but they are bound together by his involvement in them, indeed, by his interpretation. Augustine is honest enough to admit that he more than occasionally relapses (10.31.75–79). The directives are written "in God's book," but humans are a weak link in the chain of command.[122]

One of the questions that naturally arises from these discussions is whether he can "know" his own desires. The subject is taken up in 10.32 and 10.33, which deal respectively with attractions of the nose and the ear. When fragrances are not present in the air, he does not miss them (10.32.1–3). But is this a sure sign that he is able to resist? No: his intentions are not fully accounted for in his conscious thoughts. Their force can be demonstrated only subsequently, when he (or someone else) explains them. Moreover, if no one has sure knowledge of the mind's inner world, then life, with its many trials and errors, must be looked upon as a series of temptations whose final outcome is not knowable by man (10.32.3–8). The idea of an inscrutable inner self is reinforced by what he says about the pleasures of the ears.[123] In this case he is unable to resist, even when he consciously wishes to do so. As a result, he is not attracted to music by what he senses alone, but principally by a preexisting affinity for its harmonies, which is in his mind before he hears the notes. If he were not so predisposed, it would be impossible to associate the sensory effects of what he hears with higher religious sentiments, which are obviously not what he listens for (10.33.1–7, 10–13). He is aware that all individuals possess such "affinities," but he cannot say how they arise. They are an aspect of God's predestined knowledge for man.

Only when he takes up the temptations of the eyes does he clarify the distinction between the sensible and intelligible origins of pleasures (10.34–35). He thus returns to the theme of the final segment of De Magistro in a different context. He is aware that sight has a power to tempt that other senses lack. As long as there is daylight, the stimulus for the sense of sight is present; and, because of the mind's tendency to form images in the absence of objects (for example, 10.34.16–34), there is no equivalent of silence, which gives his sense of hearing a rest (10.34.8–10).[124] Among inner visions, temptations that operate within the mind are satisfied intellectually (10.35.1–7), and these represent a type of curiosity. Just as sight is taken to represent other sensory satisfactions,[125] curiosity is a gratification of the mind, often attracting us by beauty as well as by the ugly, the bizarre, or the bogus. The pleasure is entirely mental; it is "a drive to experience and to acquire knowledge,"[126] as in the case of theatricals, magic, and divine interventions when viewed as performances (10.35.21–36). Ocular curiosity thereby distracts him from the path of self-discipline, which is likewise dependent on the eyes, through the reading of scripture.

The final topic in his review is pride (10.36–39).[127] In taking up the cardinal sin, he also returns to his initial concerns: both 10.1–7 and 10.33–39 are concerned with the dual audience of God and other men. In the opening chapters, the subject is the audience's reaction to his confession; in the closing ones, it is his expectations from the words of others. In both, the problem arises from the inability to know thoughts by means of one's words alone. These chapters also deal with variants of a single issue: the compromises involved in allowing our actions to be determined by the desire to be feared or loved by other men (10.36.13–16, 20–22). In such errors, a special place is reserved for the role of false ideas supported only by words (10.38) and one's overreaction to praise or blame without adequate cause (10.39). Lies of any sort are incompatible with divine truth (10.41), as are human mediators between God and man that depend on language. When words are our only evidence of truth, man is unable to distinguish between what is religiously and magically intended (10.42). Self-love, too, is criticized: in this case, the words of an outer audience are merely replaced by one within oneself (10.39). Augustine concludes that the only "true mediator" between God and man is Christ (10.43).

In all these temptations, "the furnace" in which his virtue is daily tested is human language.[128] Accordingly, his decisions are made in a special type of ignorance. When he is confronted with other enticements, he is at least able to question his intentions, even if he cannot fully know them, since they arise within himself; moreover, whether the pleasure he receives is sensory or intellectual, he is able to perceive what he has gained. However, when his satisfaction depends on others' opinion (10.37.7–12), truth pleases him more than praise, but he loves to be praised nonetheless. This vanity is another form of self-deception, since God commands him to observe both continence and justice (that is, to withdraw his love on some occasions and to offer it on others), while the continual reversals of his thinking permit him to disguise his love of praise as love for his neighbour (10.37.24–39). He thus concludes the lengthy dialogue with himself that began in 380–81 with his self-questioning over his "love" and "praise" of Hierius.

In 10.40 he again summarizes the lengthy intellectual journey that he has taken in the earlier books. It is God, he observes, who teaches him what he is to desire and to avoid in the search for truth in life. To the degree that his senses permit, he has taken an inventory of the world and, in particular, of the life of his body conveyed by his senses (10.40.1–4)—an oblique reference, perhaps, to the narrative of books 1–9, which is experienced through his senses, with the exception of earliest infancy and the final seconds of the vision at Ostia. From there, he withdrew into the inner regions of memory and explored its vast riches. He found nothing within memory without the help of God; yet within the contents of memory, God was nowhere to be found. Through this inquiry, he realized that he was not the "discoverer" of what he learned through his senses or his memory, even though he laboured to distinguish them and to assign each its place in a system of values. The ability to inquire was in himself, but its source was in God (10.40.5–16). The highest pleasure in moments of leisure, he notes, is to retreat into this "safe refuge for my soul": to "collect the scattered bits of my self" in one place, and "not to let anything of myself be withdrawn from God."[129] At times he has a mystical intuition of the deity, a "sweetness" which is not something of this life but of the life to come. Such moments do not last; his habits drag him earthwards again (10.40.21–25). He is not happy in either condition: he is able to remain in the one state, but unwilling to do so, and he is willing to proceed to the other, but unable.[130]

## Time

The exemplary use of theory that characterizes Augustine's discussion of memory reappears in a different context in his account of time in book 11. In book 10, ascetic routine is a practical means of disciplining the body through a combination of study and memory. Links are forged between reading, meditation, and ascent. The text is to reading as the content of memory is to recall.

An abstract discussion of the temporal and the eternal in these modes of communication is a next logical step.[131] Reading a text is a way of linking the past and the future of the self by means of an activity in the present. A text is a plan, a guide, and a map; it is also a puzzle, a labyrinth, "an immense wood filled with snares and dangers" (10.35.37). Right reading leads from the historical to the nonhistorical senses; right thinking, from the past to the future as realized in thought and action. This is a "historicizing" of the self and an attempt to remove the individual temporarily from the flow of events.[132] Explaining how this is possible is the task of Augustine's discussion of creation, time, and eternity.[133]

God and Narrative: 11.1–2

The problem involves a restatement of book 10.1–7. Because God is eternal, he must have a complete knowledge of the words that are spoken to him. At what level does this awareness operate? Does he see what takes place in time, as humans do (11.1.1–2)? If not, why does Augustine place so many "narratives" before him (including, presumably, books 1–9)?[134]

If he is eternal, then his Word is changeless. It is inappropriate to refer to his discourse in the way in which we speak of human words that are uttered in a temporal sequence in syllables.[135] Moreover, by the same criteria, our words, thus uttered, can have no affect on God. Their purpose is to stimulate our affections toward him. The *Confessions* is written to express Augustine's praise and love for God (11.1.3–5; compare 1.1.1), not to inform God of what he has done.

Accordingly, when he (as narrator) and his readers (as audience) write and read respectively, they "lay" themselves "open" so that God can "wholly set" them "free." Furthermore, the value of his lengthy narrative (11.1.3–16; compare 10.1–7) differs in relation to its divine and human audiences.[136] With respect to God, it is insufficient: "the tongue of his pen" cannot disclose everything that God has inspired in him—the fears, reassurances, and subsequent inspiration "to preach the word and dispense the sacrament to the people" (11.2.1–4). Yet for his human audience (which includes himself), the "droplets of time"—the words by which, in the course of an ordered narrative discourse, time is measured[137]—reveal what he has learned.

This thinking is consistent with the "innerwordly" plan in 10.27–43; yet it introduces a new theme, which is pursued in the final books of the *Confessions* and in *De Trinitate* 8–15, namely the supersession of reading. Augustine is aware that he cannot understand everything in scripture any more than he can understand all that is in his memory. Far from completing his narrative, his activity as a reader is a witness to his inability to reach a point of closure (11.2.5–10). In the transitions in his thinking he asks God to heed his "prayer," again offering him "the sacrifice of his thought and tongue," even speaking of a "circumcision of his inner and outer lips";[138] at the same time, scripture is to be his "chaste delight."[139] Its abundant obscurities are a divinely inspired "forest" into which inquiring "harts" may "amble about and feed at will," "finding repose and the time to digest" what they have taken in.[140] He thus asks God to enable him "to confess" to him what he finds in his "books."[141]

## Genesis and Creation in Time

The two major segments of book 11 develop out of these topics.[142] In 11.3–8, Augustine analyses what is meant by God's Word in the sequences of words that constitute the narratives in scripture. In 11.9–31, he turns to the related philosophical issue of time and eternity.[143] His arguments concerning time can be compared with those of Aristotle's *Physics* 4.1–14,[144] Plotinus' *Enneads* 3.7 (45),[145] and Stoic views;[146] however, there is no parallel in earlier discussions for his combination of the everyday experience of time with the temporal relations of speaking and reading.[147]

The first phase of his argument involves a recognition of the mediated nature of the statement that "in the beginning" God "made the heavens and the earth" (Gen. 1:1).[148] Moses, who spoke it, is dead; the text is a witness to what he said. Even if he could be questioned, one would depend on his words for establishing the facts (11.3.1–16).[149]

What then is meant by "creation"? The narrative statement and the reality have to differ. Moreover, if God is eternal, we cannot think of his creative activity as a type of craftsmanship,[150] since he is responsible for the matter, the model, and the artisan.[151] When the Bible states that God "spoke" and that "things were made" in his "word" (11.5.21–22), we should reason by analogy with the creation of meaning out of human words. The sound begins and ends, motion takes place through the air, and a measurable period of time elapses; then, if a group of sounds has meaning, a principle *(ratio)* emerges: the meaning is brought *to mind* by the words but is not brought *into being* by them, since this principle existed before they were uttered. In the case of God's words, there is a similar division between what we hear and what is meant: the impermanent element is sound; the permanent organization is his reason and will.[152] Scripture offers a variant of this scheme in writing rather than in speech: God's word is to our words as scripture's meaning is to our thoughts about it.[153]

In principle (that is, *in principio*), the message is in our minds before we hear words or read texts; the signs are reminders. This type of reasoning is a subtle reversal of Augustine's position on reminiscence. In book 10, our inability to understand everything that is in our minds is judged to be an irremediable weakness, just as our desire to recover lost knowledge is the basis of our moral improvement. In book 11, viewing matters in a more positive light, he acknowledges the advantages of human forgetfulness.

When scripture is read aloud, graphic symbols are transformed into sounds, which are heard in order that the words of the text may be believed, sought after, and found inwardly, that is, in eternal truth, where "the one good teacher instructs all his pupils."[154] The unfinished argument of *De Magistro* would appear to be that, in the individual seeking reform, these two interiorities become one.

The simultaneous process of "speaking" and "making," then, is beyond human comprehension (11.9.1–3). Where the intelligence falters, the mind is bound to rely on another sort of enlightenment (11.9.3–15). Questions nonetheless remain in Augustine's mind. What was God doing before the creation?[155] If he is eternal, he is at rest in his desired state. Why does he not remain as he is? If he creates, something is evidently changed; for, in acting, he wills to act, and in the act of will there is mental motion.[156] If there is no change, why are created things not eternal?

## Time and Eternity

Augustine's reply[157] is summed up in the well-known paradox, "What, then, is time? If no one asks me what it is, I know what it is. But, should I wish to explain it to someone asking me what it is, I do not know."[158]

The ambiguity depends on two senses of *scire*, to know. In the second sentence of the statement, *scire* means "to have an awareness" of time; in the third, it refers to one's ability "to explain" or "to account for" the awareness of time. There is a similar parallel between the uses of *quaerere*, "to ask": the question at once concerns knowing and not knowing and not being asked and being asked. The third element in the paradox is *commemorare*, which combines the other two in meaning "to bring something to mind by speaking of it."[159]

We find ourselves before the model of the classical disputation of *De Dialectica* and *De Magistro*. The question "What is time?" is meaningful in the logical situation of someone indicating the sign of a thing by means of words. Augustine asks what time is as if the question were being put to someone else (or as if he were putting it to himself).[160] His initial question is: "What is time? Who can explain what it means, simply and briefly? Even when there is an understanding in thought, who can express it adequately in words? Yet there is no word that we recognize more readily or know better than 'time.' We understand it well enough when we are talking about it ourselves, or when we hear it mentioned by someone else."[161] We have an awareness of time, but we cannot give expression to *what* experience and memory tell us *that* we know.

A response to the paradox is offered at 11.10–11. In the last analysis, humans cannot understand time. In order to accomplish this, they would have to understand what time is not, namely eternity. As matters stand, the sequence of words by which they make their inquiry into time is the mirror image of their mode of existence as creatures living in time. The human awareness of time, in which a mortal's sense of being arises, is, in eternal perspective, a "nonbeing" (11.13.15–27; 11.14).[162]

We "sense" that the past is propelled toward the future and that the future follows hard upon the past.[163] This is what we mean when we speak of a "long" or a "short" period of time (11.15.1–2). If we wish to be precise, we should use the past or the future tense (that is, the model of speech). Each division of time contains within itself a smaller division, and, within each, one part is past and another is to come.[164] Only if an instant is indivisible can it be said to be "present" (11.15.36).[165] Intervals can be compared,[166] but time can be measured only while it passes: once it is past, we cannot measure it, because it no longer exists (11.16.5–10). By this reasoning, the past and the future can be said to exist in the present (11.17; compare 11.19). But that present affords no opportunity for measurement.

We understand the past and the present indirectly, through images and signs. When we give a correct account of something that has taken place in the past, we draw on our recollection of the event; this consists of words and images created when it took place (11.18.7–10).[167] In a comparable manner, the future exists in the present as a set of preconceived words and images. When Augustine reflects on what he is about to do, a "fore-thought" is in his mind although no action has taken place. If it is stated that events are foreseen, it is not the realities that are "seen" but their *causae* or *signa*. The future, therefore, which does not exist in the present, can nonetheless be spoken about in the present (11.18.16–40).

These *signa, imagines,* and *causae* are parts of narratives. In the case of the past, the story is created in words from an already organized set of images in the memory.[168] In the future, past experience provides a model for what is likely to take place, but the narrative components exist in the present, that is, in speech, sense perception, and thought.[169] When we speak of the past or the future in this way, we employ conventions of speech *(consue-tudo)*. The present of past time is what we recall *(memoria);* the present of present time is what we see *(contuitus);*[170] the present of future time is what we think will happen *(expectatio,* 11.20.1–7).[171]

The present is a space of time that has no measurable duration *(nullum spatium,* 11.21.19–20). Consideration of this problem takes Augustine to the most original feature of his understanding of time, the relationship between the "objective" and "subjective" perceptions.[172] He does not "substitute subjective time for the time of history and physics":[173] he is well aware of external regulators of time such as physical laws,[174] historical events,[175] and God's providential will;[176] he also distinguishes between the permanence of mathematical ratios and the impermanent measurement of time's passage.[177] His position is that the human understanding of temporal change is largely if not entirely an internal matter. Consequently, he differs from Plato, Aristotle, and Plotinus[178] in linking the problems of time and memory.[179] We can speak of objective time only as something concerning which we have no personal knowledge (or as something that subjective time is not).[180] And, if our understanding of time is "relational,"[181] so is our understanding of the self or soul.[182]

As a consequence, talk about time cannot help determine what time is.[183] Augustine carries this argument to an extreme, proposing that even the movements of the heavenly bodies are measured by the passage of time.[184] On this view, there are as many indices of measurement as there are bodies in motion and observers to look at them. The lights of heaven may go out, but the potter's wheel continues to turn; and, even without the movements of the heavenly bodies as a guide, we can tell whether its rotations follow a regular rhythm. The words with which I relate the issues likewise punctuate temporal intervals through the length of the syllables I voice: there is no way to separate the measurements from the statements made about them.

The critical role of the observer is proven by our ignorance of initial conditions. The points at which one begins and ends the measurement of an interval of time are arbitrary. Let us say that I hear that there is no body that is moved except in time. I hear the words; but I do not hear the fact that the motion of a body should be measured by time. The latter requires that I observe what is taking place: for, when a body is moved, it is I who measure when it begins to move and when it ceases. Measurement presupposes an observer who visually perceives the start and finish of the motion registered by the lapse of time.[185] While I am observing the motion of a body, I cannot indicate in words how long a time it takes. I can say only that it is either "long" or "short." If I wish to give an accurate account of the length of time, I have to engage in a comparison with other known lengths of time (11.24).[186]

The attempt to understand time provides a practical illustration of another theme of book 10—the mind's inescapable confinement. A clue to Augustine's eventual solution is offered at 11.25. In admitting that he does not understand time, he notes that he has experienced the passage of time as the words of his discourse have flowed by.[187] In what sense does he "know" this, if he is ignorant of time's nature? Is his problem not knowing what time is, or not being able to put what he knows into words (11.25.1–5)? Common sense suggests the latter. He can "measure" the length of time of a passage of quantitative verse by its lines, feet, and syllables (11.26.1–16). His conception is formed while he reads it aloud.[188] Is time then just an awareness of "duration," that is, an extension of thought?[189]

The discussion reaches a turning point at 11.27, where he summarizes his position and solves the problem of time's measurement to his satisfaction. This is accomplished by a closer examination of the reading of a line of verse.[190] The argument consists of two parts, a summary and restatement of his earlier argument and a concluding illustration.

Let us say that the sound of a voice begins, continues for a period of time, then stops. Before it began, it was in the future and could not be measured; afterwards it was past and could not be measured either. The only time when it was measurable was in the present, through its extension (11.27.3–11; compare 11.15). If another voice is heard, Augustine can in theory measure its duration from beginning to end. However, before it ends, it cannot be measured, and after it ends, it will have ceased to be (11.27.11–25; compare 11.24). The paradox of 11.14 is thus reaffirmed.

Yet, if Augustine recites the first line of the hymn *Deus creator omnium*,[191] he discovers that it has eight syllables, of which 1, 3, 5, and 7 are short and 2, 4, 6, and 8 are long; and that the long syllables are twice as long as the short ones.[192] It would appear that this is the evidence of the ears:[193] closer examination reveals that when the long syllable of *de/us*—that is, *us*—is sounding, the short syllable, *de*, is no longer sounding. When he compares the two and arrives at the right answer concerning their quantities, he is evidently not depending on his ears alone. Indeed, when the first and second syllables have begun and ceased to sound, he is able to measure the length of time that each sound was heard (11.27.31–43) through a recollection.[194] Therefore, it is not the sounds that he measures, since they no longer exist, but something "imprinted" on his memory.[195] He concludes that all measurement of time really takes place in the mind[196] (an argument reiterated and expanded from *De Immortalitate Animae*[197] and *De Musica* 6.8).[198]

This is clear from our ability "to measure silence." Let us say that he recites the text of a poem silently to himself. He supposes that the words take as long to pronounce as they did when they were spoken: he lengthens his thoughts to match the length of time that he thinks the sounds would take.[199] Even after the voice and tongue cease, he is able to review the poem in his thoughts, verse by verse, giving the same dimensions of motion and time to the words as when they were spoken.[200] If he is about to utter a lengthy sound and he reflects beforehand how long it should be, he has already expended a period of time in thought. When committed to memory, this mental sound provides the basis for the uttered sound, which begins and ends in time measurable by the senses. He is aware that the sound is passing in and out of existence in thought and in reality (11.27.59–67).

Suppose that the text is a psalm (as at 9.4). Before the recitation begins, Augustine's mind is preoccupied with what is to take place. However, once he has begun, his attention is divided between the past and the future. He focuses on the past, inasmuch as some of the words have been taken from the text and recited, and on the future, inasmuch as others remain to be savoured.[201] Yet, while he is reciting, he is aware that the remembered psalm is the focus of his attention. As he reads, the part of the text that lies in the future becomes smaller. The part that is past grows, until, at the end, everything is just a memory.[202]

The reciting of a psalm involves an awareness of the parts in relation to the whole. This is true of activities that take longer than the reading of a single psalm,[203] for example, the narrative of a person's life, in which the parts are individual actions, or the narrative of a period of history, in which the parts are individual lives.[204] Life is a text, whose living is its reading; for, if the mind is the measure of time, the internalization of scripture can set up a narrative structure by which the self is guided from within. Lacking such guidance, the awareness of time is only an extension of the mind (*distentio . . . animi,* 11.26.20–21).[205] And that is what is wrong with it.[206] It is not a beneficial "extending" or "intending," but rather a "swelling."[207] Book 11 ends with the hope of using present time as a pathway to wisdom (11.29.5–10). Through a simple set of experiments, Augustine alerts us to the fact that our lives unfold in moments. If we are not fully present for those moments, we are unable to realize the potential of our personal narratives.

He thus brings to a close a discussion of ethics and literature that is undertaken in the earlier books and reaches an important turning point at 3.7. There, he notes that he was ignorant in his youth of "true, interior justice, which bases its decisions not on custom, but on the infallible law of the almighty."[208] Echoing Cicero, he proposes that the conventional arrangements for administering justice vary with times, places, and peoples, but that eternal justice is changeless, operating everywhere in the same way.[209] The "times" over which justice presides cannot be alike, because they take place at different "times."[210] Humans, who live brief lives (Wisdom 15:9), lack the capacity to make sense of the causes of events in former times among peoples whom they have not known. His term for this harmonization is *contexere*, (to weave, intertwine, make coherent, or place in a context), a verb that provides a symbolic link to the example of literary composition by which he illustrates his point. For when he composed verse, he was not allowed to put the poetic feet where he wished, but had to obey the rule of metre—an "art" that did not vary (3.7.53–57).[211]

## Books 12 and 13

When Augustine takes up the question of time in the abstract, his thinking concludes with a paradox, whereas when he examines the practical example of reading scripture, he arrives at a working solution.[212] If past usage is a guide, this mental exercise suggests that his discussion of the paradox of time is intended to be a philosophical interlude between two passages of exegesis, one at 11.3, the other in book 12, where he returns to the topic of the creation.[213]

The plan is confirmed by the repetition of the transition from speech to writings. Again he speaks of scripture's "words": his heart "beats" to their reverberations; they open the door to truth as often as he desires to hear them "knocking."[214] Yet his faith resides "in sacred books and their demonstrable mysteries."[215] It is his oral reading of God's words through which he hears "the thundering voice" of his maker addressing him in his "interior ear" (12.11.1–2; compare 12.11.15–16). We are reminded of his excitement on reading the Psalms aloud at Cassiciacum. These same words are now "confessed" to his maker by his "mouth and pen."[216]

Words, he reminds us, are the necessary but imprecise constituents of human thinking (12.5.1–2). They do not relieve our ignorance; they are a kind of "learned ignorance" *(docta ignorantia)*. At best, they tell us what we do not know (12.5.4–6). The only sure thing about human communication is its inherent incompleteness. He addresses his maker through "the humbleness" of his "tongue" (12.2.1–2): God replies through scripture in a language that he can understand. Texts are nonetheless subject to interpretation.[217] Writing and reading act as mediators for thought, but they are not in themselves thoughts about anything: they merely permit the elucidation of the less familiar by analogy with the more familiar. For example, in Genesis 1:2, where God commanded that it be "written" that "darkness was over the abyss," the absence of light can be understood by comparison with silence, which is the absence of sound (12.3.1–9); however, the implied notion of formlessness is more difficult to clarify by a single analogy, since the "matter" in question is both material and immaterial (12.5.1–4). If texts vary, so do readers' minds: the slower their wits, the more straightforward explanations have to be (12.4.1–2). Working with interpretive analogies is basic to human thought; this is the thinking that takes place when a reader is before texts and decides on a preferred sense through an internal dialogue with himself (12.13.1–2; compare 12.16).

In summarizing Augustine's thinking about relations between words, readings, and writings, book 12 draws attention to the interchangeable metaphors with which he speaks of cognitive and spiritual awakening throughout the *Confessions*. This discussion confirms the gradualist trans-formation of the soul in steps of ascent as a supplement to the idea of instantaneous conversion. The human soul normally rises with the aid of biblical texts.[218] Contemplative bliss is achieved through arduous study: the steps of the ladder are the lines of the text.[219] Readers are like infants; they lack the words to express their desires.[220] Beginners can appreciate earthly beauties but not those of the heavens (12.2.7–9). Augustine sees himself passing through just such an evolution, which book 12 recapitulates through the discussion of aesthetics (12.2), Manichaeism (12.6; 12.16), Platonism (12.3–5; 12.7–8; 12.10–14), and views within Catholicism (12.15–32).

In books 1–9, Augustine frequently reminds his readers that there are no impartial observers of events. Objectivity is an illusion, but it is one through which differing subjectivities are clarified. In book 11, this con-viction is framed within a theory of the manner in which we experience time. Book 12, in parallel with *De Doctrina Christiana* 2, offers another variant, the ideas that theological realities are inseparable from the language in which they are expressed (compare 12.6.22–24) and that self-under-standing and the understanding of biblical texts are mutually supporting activities. He returns to this theme at 13.15, where the problem of book-learning is addressed in the context of Genesis 1:7, God's making the firmament. In completing the hermeneutic development of the later books,[221] he reasons that only God could have erected "the solid firmament of authority" over us "in holy scripture."[222] The metaphor is strengthened by two quotations from the Hebrew Bible, Isaiah 34:4 and Psalms 103:2. Taken together, these state that heaven "will fold up like a book," which is "now stretched over us like [a tent] of skins."[223] The survival of the covering bears witness to God's eternity while it recalls the humans to whom he entrusted his word, since Adam and Eve, in becoming mortals, were clad "in skins" (*Fecit . . . tunicas pelliceas,* Gen. 3:21). The symbolism of the skin is also the affirmation of God's enduring will in readership: he extends "the firmament of the book," that is, "brings harmony to his words," which he places in a position of authority over us "through ministry of mortals," that is, through his interpreters and preachers.[224] After the death of those to whom he spoke directly, his words acquire a new life through publication. His prophet's words are likewise "stretched over the heavens like a skin" (13.15.9–14).

A cycle of thought is thus completed:[225] the metaphor of the book and the reader provides Augustine with a way of distinguishing between those who have to read and those who do not.[226] The angels have no need of reading in order to know God's word. They see his face directly (Matt. 18:10), and "there they read, without the syllables that mark time," whatever his will desires. "They read, they choose, they love: they read forever, and what they read never passes away. In reading, they choose, and, in choosing, they love. Their codex is never shut, their book never closed: for God is their text in himself and eternally so."[227] Similarly, preachers pass away, but scripture is "stretched out" eternally over the people (13.15.39–41). In this statement, which employs the triad *legunt, eligunt, diligunt* (13.15.30–31), Augustine brings to the surface a trinitarian interest that grows through the *Confessions'* later books and in *De Doctrina* 1. The topic is directly introduced at 13.11, where, after speaking of the themes of love and happiness announced in scripture, he asks "who can understand the omnipotent trinity?" Who does not "talk about it," to the degree it can be talked about (13.11.1–2)? His wish is that those who do so first think about "the threes" within themselves.[228] The triads in our minds differ greatly from the trinity, and, by thinking systematically about them, his readers can be brought to an understanding of just how wide the gulf is between the human and the divine (a reiteration of the paradoxes of memory and time). The triad that bears examination is "being, knowing, and willing" *(esse, nosse, uelle)*. For, when I think about myself, I am, I know, and I will; knowing and willing, I exist; I know that I exist and that I will; I will to exist and to know. The three are inseparable—one in life, mind, and essence—yet they can be thought about distinctly.[229] What was God's intention in designing us to think in this way? The answer is found in *De Trinitate,* to which I now turn.

# 9

# THE SELF

❧

The later books of the *Confessions* outline Augustine's "psychology of reading": they tell us how the mind analyses, stores, and retrieves what is read, and how these activities influence intentions and behaviour. Books 10 and 11 are the high point of the discussion of these issues, providing an analytical account of the type of recall at work in books 1–9.

Yet throughout Augustine's writings, reading is a means to an end. The reader's objective is a better understanding of the self and its relationship to God through the medium of scripture, in which he or she hopes to gain some insight into the nature of "the blessed life." In the works of his maturity, Augustine has two approaches to this problem, the social and the individual. The social dimension is taken up chiefly in *The City of God,* where he argues that Christian civilization, through the logic of its historical development, is destined to fulfil a divinely inspired plan. His longest account of the part played by individual thinking occurs in *De Trinitate* 8–15. In this chapter, I deal with three topics in this work as they pertain to problems of reading and interpretation: mental representations (books 8–9), the proof of the mind's existence (book 10), and the role of memory in the pursuit of wisdom (books 12–15).

The dates of *De Trinitate* have been the subject of considerable discussion. It is safe to say that it was begun by 399 and very probably completed after 422.[1] The book has long fascinated students of Augustine's theology,[2] but it is not easy to read,[3] as he acknowledged.[4] It is divided into two roughly symmetrical parts: books 1–7 consist of a commentary on biblical texts dealing with the trinity, while books 8–15 explore a number of tripartite relationships in affectivity, perception, and cognition. However, these segments are interdependent: the "trinities" in the Bible and in the mind descend from the same theological source, God's creation of humans in his "image" and "likeness."[5] In Augustine's view, we are informed about the trinity in one way in scripture and in another way through our mental activities.[6]

This dual perspective is attainable in only one sort of person—a reader. It is the reader who is able to recall the trinitarian teachings in sacred texts while reflecting on those arising out of his or her thoughts. The reader thereby engages in an interpretive and a metacognitive activity. In books 1–7, the implied reader is configured as a student who follows his master step by step through an outline of dogmatic theology. In books 8–15, the same person is asked to reflect on the desire to learn, the love of the knowledge acquired, and the understanding of wisdom or blessedness that results. In order to perform these tasks effectively, he or she has to keep in mind the lessons learned in books 1–7, since they provide the background information for the internal inquiries. At the same time, the subject is led through a group of topics in theory and psychology which have instructive value on their own. It is this reorientation that Augustine has in mind when, at the beginning of book 8, he speaks of looking "in a more inward manner" *(modo interiore)* at material in books 1–7.[7] What is envisaged is not an independent group of philosophical statements, but an investigation in which the mind has become the subject, object, and "instrument of research."[8]

In this and other respects, *De Trinitate* invites comparison with the *Confessions*. The prayer of submission at the end of *De Trinitate* stresses man's ignorance and God's omniscience in terms that recall the magnificent devotions which begin the autobiography.[9] *De Trinitate* is informed by the notion of a fictional reader, and it shares some of the "dramatic form" of the *Confessions*.[10] The principle of trust in accounts whose truth cannot be verified is invoked,[11] and in both works there is a reasonably clear division between narrative and analysis. The life related in *Confessions* 1–9 corresponds roughly to the technique of narration of *De Trinitate* 1–7; the psychology of *Confessions* 10–13 takes up themes similar to those found in *De Trinitate* 8–15. The later books of both works deal with the same problem—the limits of human memory. Augustine began *De Trinitate* about a year before finishing his life history, when the narrative segment was complete; then, in parallel with *Confessions* 10–13, he may have engaged in a further exploration of the way in which the soul progresses upwards to an appreciation of divine wisdom through the study of the Bible.[12]

In both works, too, an evolution occurs in the relations between readers and audiences. *Confessions* 1–9 is concerned with the progress of a reader who begins with non-Christian writings and finishes with the Bible. *De*

*Trinitate* reflects the outlook of a thoroughly Christian reader and corresponds to Augustine's state of mind in *Confessions* 10–13. In the autobiography, there are essentially two audiences: God, to whom Augustine's words are directed from within; and the reader, to whom they are addressed through the written text.[13] In *De Trinitate,* God is not Augustine's intended audience except for prayer (for example, 15.28). A dual audience is nonetheless configured in the intended reader (thereby making the reader the equivalent of the dual narrator in the *Confessions*). Augustine refers to us as his readers and, through us, to himself. He sees in his putative younger reader the type of student that he might have been in the spring of 386 when he set off on a theological journey into himself.

In *De Trinitate,* the developmental metaphors that underpin the notion of progress through reading do not reiterate what Augustine says in either the *Confessions* or *De Doctrina Christiana.* In the life history, he asks why his spiritual growth did not keep pace with his physical development. In *De Trinitate,* the comparable evolution is entirely within the reader's mind; the physical component in the autobiography reappears only as the literal sense of the texts that are commented upon.[14] It can be argued that books 1–7 and 8–15 correspond loosely to the division between literal and figurative signs outlined in *De Doctrina Christiana* 2–3. Yet, in *De Trinitate,* Augustine does not discuss how the truths of scripture are communicated by reading and preaching, but how the student of scripture gains some idea of "blessedness" as a postreading experience.[15] The "enjoyment" that is unique to the trinity[16] is concealed within the mind, just as, for the exegete, it is concealed in scripture.[17]

Continuity between the author and the audience is maintained through the activities of writing and reading, about which he speaks directly in the prefaces to books 1–3. He refers to the reader's mind in the familiar metaphor of "a child," which is lured, encouraged, and led upwards by easily recognizable "things" mentioned in scripture.[18] Until the student's mind is cleansed of error, the writer's pen "invigilates" over "the intended reader," lest, valuing reason above faith (1.1.1–4), he misconceive the nature of God, either visualizing him in sensory terms (2.6.66–69) or thinking of him through inappropriate analogies with the incorporeal, the preconceived, or the inauthentic.[19] The commentator's role is to reinforce scripture's "authority" with "rational arguments."[20] The figurative grows out of the literal, and the act of signifying *(actio significatiua)* is "added to what exists" (2.6.59–60).

As the discussion proceeds, the intended reader emerges as a participant[21] in an interpretive process that is organized in part by Augustine's fictional configuration of the manner in which the student rewrites what his master says. He progresses with his teacher when he is certain of the sense; he hesitates and inquires with him when he is not. If he errs, he can return for further guidance. He can point out his mentor's errors,[22] emending the gloss by a combination of faith and his own reasoning.[23] Reading and writing thereby become indeterminate activities, separable from the finite commentary that results: the parts are seen in relation to a whole whose continuity depends on the reader/writer's thinking.[24] Augustine does not want the reader to be enslaved by his habits of thought (3, prologue, 35–36). The difference between his reading of the Bible and the reader's understanding of his commentary permits considerable latitude: it is possible for him to imagine several commentaries on a single subject directed to specific audiences (1.3.11–25). Divided in response, readers are united in assumptions. Reading is an aural and visual confirmation of things that are unheard and unseen (13.2).

Augustine speaks of practicing "a twofold charity of word and pen" toward his brethren. They travel the same road together (3, prologue, 16–19). Their unity is a "pious accord" to which he pledges himself in God's presence "with all who read" what he writes "and in all the texts of those writings" (1.3.5–8; compare 2.1.11–19). His potential readers, who presumably are religious, oblige him to gather the "fruits" of his reading and to write them down. He responds to their inquiries concerning matters unclarified in previous Latin exegesis. A reluctant "authority," he much prefers reading for himself to dictating to his secretaries what others are to read. He would gladly "give his pen a holiday" if he could (3, prologue, 2–16). All the same, he is committed, as he was in the "philosophical dialogues," to preserving a record of his ideas. "Meditating," he notes, if not "day and night, at least when time permits, I pin down my thoughts with my pen, lest, through forgetfulness, they vanish forever."[25] In a remarkable statement, he admits that he learns many things during the creative process of writing.[26]

The prologues to the early books suggest that Augustine began *De Trinitate* with a reasonably clear exegetical programme in mind. During composition over some two decades, new material was added. Repetitions appeared (for example, 13.20.19–21; 15.3.72–74). Yet his long-range objectives are never in doubt, as is demonstrated by a comparison of books 1 and 15, both of which are concerned with the functions of words. In book 1, he cautions his potential readers against a devotion to reason for its own sake (1.1.1–4), reminding them of his published views on error, doubt, and uncertainty. Scripture is the answer to scepticism (1.1.21–41), but only if faith results from the demonstration of an authoritative interpretation, through which "garrulous rationalists" are confounded (1.2.13–14). His advice to the reader is an extension of the programme outlined in *De Doctrina Christiana* 1.1.69–98. Words are the vocal renderings of texts; the rule for understanding scripture *(regula intellegendarum scripturarum)* resolves the problems potentially raised by confusions of the ear (1.11.1–6). From the "many modes of divine speech" in the Bible a unified view of the trinity results (1.12.54–57).

In book 15, the focus is almost entirely on mental words, and, through them, a single, divinely inspired Word.[27] Mental words do not belong to the spoken or written forms of specific languages like Greek or Latin (15.10.64–68). They constitute a language of thought that exists along with images, emotions, and methods.[28] In theological terms, they are the imperfect "likenesses" in man of the original Word in God.[29] As Augustine reviews the evolution of his thinking through the previous fourteen books, his arguments buttress an "essentialist"[30] position in which he speaks of an inward expression of the heart,[31] that is, a "speech" of "truth" (15.10.73).[32] This theme is explored in numerous writings and is succinctly summed up in *Sermon* 119, where he explains the mechanism[33] in the following way: "The word that I myself speak to you, I have in my heart beforehand: it proceeds toward you, yet it does not withdraw from me. Something that was not in you begins to exist in you, and it remains in me while it goes outwards toward you. Just as my word, after being spoken, exists in your senses without leaving my mind, so the Word, when spoken, exists in the sense without leaving its father. My word was with me, yet proceeded into speech. The Word of God was with the father, and proceeded into flesh."[34]

The problem of *De Trinitate* is how to proceed from outer to inner words, from the words that we speak to the word of God. What role can scripture play in enhancing our understanding of relations between them? For it is reading (or hearing texts read) that makes the transition possible, since this is our only access to the mediating elements. The final goal is contemplation, which is announced in book 1 and reemphasized in books 13–15.[35] The intervening books are intended to lead the student of scripture upward in steps.[36] Books 1–4 demonstrate the "unity" and "equality" of the trinity according to "verifiable" statements. Books 5–7 deal with differences in interpretation in biblical and ecumenical passages concerning the language of the trinity in the Bible—for instance, the notions of "substance," "begetting," "wisdom," and "power" (15.3.13–56). Books 8–15 proceed from the text to the mind as one psychological trinity yields to another in the search for a contemplative ideal. Taken together, the two major segments of *De Trinitate* "train the reader" in understanding created things through sacred writings so that he can eventually know their creator (15.1.1–6).

## A Language of Thought

Books 8 and 9 take the initial steps toward a language of thought. They are linked by the now familiar notion of the "love" of God that is created in the reader when texts of scripture are studied and meditated upon.[37] Their relationship to the subsequent books is similar to that of *De Doctrina Christiana* 1 to 2–3, where an inquiry into the nature of human and divine love is completed by a discussion of matters dealing with interpretation.[38] In *De Trinitate* 8–9, the exploration ends with patterns of thinking rather than with patterns in texts. Accordingly, each book expresses its conclusion by means of a trinitarian arrangement; the concept of love acts as the link between the two symmetrical triads. In book 8, the trinity consists of the lover, the object loved, and love itself;[39] in book 9, it is mind, knowledge, and love.[40] Augustine thus begins with a model of how we express our intentions; he then reiterates that model in the context of other mental activities.

This type of thinking can be traced to book 5, where, in opposition to Arianism,[41] he distinguishes between "substance" and "accidents" when referring to God. It is incorrect to speak of anything's taking place in God's substance "through an accident." There are many examples of such terms: quantity and quality, friendship, proximity, services, likenesses, equalities, places, times, actions, feelings, and so forth (5.4.24–32). These are the "names" given to aspects of the divine when the field of reference is temporal rather than eternal. Augustine calls this type of term *appellatio relatiua*.[42] The notion is his point of departure in book 8[43] and underpins his subsequent reflections on the relational nature of self-knowledge.

What does it mean to speak of God "relationally"? It is possible to reason by analogy with signs. As there are three elements in signs—the giver, the receiver, and the sign—so, it becomes apparent, there are three elements in each of the steps by which the mind ascends toward wisdom. However, signs deal with spoken or written words and their analogies (music, dance, gesture, and so on), whereas, in *De Trinitate* 8–15, Augustine is concerned with a broader group of problems involving perception, cognition, and memory. In *De Doctrina*, moreover, the threefold scheme for signs is subordinated to a twofold plan based on the literal and figurative senses of scripture, which effectively places them under the rubric of relations between readers and audiences. In *De Trinitate,* mental ascent from *scientia* to *sapientia* is accomplished through the triads themselves. The logic of the discussion moves away from texts and towards mental activities before returning to biblical texts in the final chapters. In this way, he places his theory of reading in a psychological context.

Evidence of a change in interests arises from his handling of a familiar topic, the contrast between a sudden, fleeting "illumination" and a gradual if less spectacular progress toward higher knowledge. The first alternative is presented at 8.2.28–40, where he asks the reader if he is able "to see" what truth is, even though his soul is burdened with the body and its "earthly thoughts" (8.2.28–29). Can the "light" that is God (John 1:5) be "seen" visually, or is it seen "not as your eyes see it, but in the manner in which the heart sees it, when it hears said, 'He is truth'" (8.2.30–32)?

What is new in this reiteration of a familiar contrast is his image of himself reading the passage aloud and anticipating the audience's response (almost as if he were preaching). In order to understand the type of thinking that is at work, we should not ask what truth is, but instead reflect on what is taking place in *our* minds when *he* quotes the text of John and says the word "truth." As we comprehend, the notion of "truth" fills our thoughts: "the mists of corporeal images" and "the clouds of phantasms" (that is, untruths) evaporate with the first beam of light; yet, as we tremble before truth's incomparable radiance, we are unable to steady our gaze; we fall back on mundane, habitual types of reflection (that is, seeing the ideal through the copies). For Augustine, this is evidence that we are deadened by the weight of accumulated sin.[44]

The statement is comparable to the failed Plotinian elevation of *Confessions* 7.[45] Yet here there is no comparison between neoplatonic and Christian texts, nor does Augustine have in mind a potentially successful ascent of the soul. Instead, he asks what we experience when we form a mental image of the spoken word "truth." In 8.3, his answer leads him to the idea of gradual reform through the careful study of scripture[46] (as a gloss on the expression "seeing again").[47] There is a difference between something unattainable, such as "truth," and something that can be realized in life, such as self-betterment.

The point can be illustrated if we change examples from "truth" to "the good." We cannot understand what "the good" means by comparing the good things that we experience through our senses (any more than we can measure the true nature of time). Take the notion of "a good mind," for instance: we understand what is meant through implicit judgements about "better" and "worse" minds; but unless we impose a standard, the concept has no meaning. Furthermore, the comparisons are internal, since there is no sensory equivalent of qualities of mind.[48] When we ask whether one mind is better than another, we imply that minds have an inherent desire to improve (or the opposite). In asking the question, the mind that seeks an answer is already becoming something that it inherently is not; it is reacting to an image of its own potential betterment anticipated in the reply. From this chain of reasoning, Augustine concludes that self-knowledge begins with the recognition of the mind's alienation from something superior to itself.[49] His term for this desire is *studium,* for the transformation, *conuertere* and, for what is to be done, *assequi*[50]—words that recapitulate, abstractly, the steps taken toward conversion to the religious life in *Confessions 6–9.*

This is nonetheless a new perspective on the soul's elevation. Hearing (*audire,* 8.3.46, 50) leads to seeing (*perspicere,* 8.3.48, 51), proceeding, as in the momentary ecstasy of 8.2, from aural to visual channels. The initial impression of the statement at John 1:5, "God is light," can be interpreted as the final stage in a progressive enlightenment, in which, by means of a vision, the normal steps of upward "participation"[51] (that is, the studies we undertake) are withdrawn. It is by "clinging" to this good, rather than by a momentary flash of inspiration, that one can remain "continuously blessed."[52] The goodness of our inner natures cannot be lost, but the human will can lose whatever it has acquired through its own effort (that is, the image). We see within "what ought to have been or what ought to be" (8.3.66–78). Through our desire, we adhere to the good; in doing so, we enjoy "the presence" of the being from which we derive our existence, in whose "absence" we cannot exist at all. In the *Confessions,* presence and absence are configured in the alternating narratives of speech and silence; the main direction of Augustine's thinking is toward the past. Here, where "we walk by faith, not by sight" (2 Cor. 5:7), he looks to the future. The result is to replace a narrative of despair with one of hope.

He also argues for a different sort of inward knowledge. It is possible to know a thing without loving it, he observes. But is it possible to love something that is completely unknown?[53] It would appear that if one loves God, in some sense one already knows him as a changeless reality (8.4.8–10).[54] Not surprisingly, the means by which we cleanse our vision is itself an ocular activity having an external and an internal perspective on things—namely reading. Combining a quotation from Matthew 5:8 with the second half of Paul's statement at 1 Corinthians 13:12–13 (quoted a few lines before, 8.4.3–5), Augustine speaks of the "clean in heart," who "will see God," and of the need for "faith, hope, and charity," which is reinforced in the mind of the person desiring God through "the stratagems of all the divine books": the purpose is to permit the mind to believe what it does not as yet see, and to love and hope for what it believes. It is through these virtues that God is loved as someone in whom we believe but do not know (8.4.16–20).

In reading scripture, error can arise if the mind trusts an image that reflects something not seen but invented.[55] However, in principle it does not matter whether a mental image faithfully represents an object or not. We do not retain the impression for its own sake; its "use" is to "prepare the way" for something better (as in the comparison of "better" and "worse" minds above). Anyone who reads or hears what Paul wrote (or what has been written about him) is bound to create a mental picture of him among his companions. Because the audience of his writings is very wide (8.4.26–35), many such mental portraits are possible, while none is necessarily correct. Moreover, our confidence in our image of Paul does not depend on such configurations but from our interpretation of his life and deeds, as witnessed by scripture.[56] The same can be said of the many potential likenesses of Christ based on the evidence of his life recorded in the Bible.[57] If this approach is adopted, the potential for error through images is avoided: when the meaning of the story is the issue, we immediately "recognize" what "we see."[58] If we believe that God was made as an *exemplum* of humility in order to demonstrate his love for us, our thoughts are correctly "informed."[59]

A key term here is *notitia* (8.4.48; 8.5.1), which recurs later in *De Trinitate* and refers to the certainty of the mind's ability to recognize internal knowledge. In this sense, *notitia* represents the actual or habitual understanding of the soul by itself[60] and is inseparable from remembering, since "the soul's knowledge of itself is a memory of itself."[61] However, this is not a repetition of the views expressed in *Confessions* 10. Augustine's attention is focused on what memory represents to the thinking mind in the present (8.4.28). His preferred verbs are *cogitare* (to think, 8.4.47) and *cognoscere* (to know, 8.4.49). He speaks of beliefs that are caused by thinking (*cogitatio*, 8.5.1) and retained in the heart (*corde retinere*, 8.5.5), thereby preparing the way for his defence of the *cogito* in book 10, after which he will argue that a link between memory and self-improvement can arise only within the subject's present configuration of the self.

The logic of his discussion in books 8–11 is to drive a wedge between interior and exterior types of evidence for reasoned judgements. The critical phase occurs in the subsequent chapters of book 8, where he argues that beliefs arise from the interpretation of inner narratives.[62] The purpose of the story of Christ's life is to cure us of pride and to acquaint us with the mystery by which sin's chains can be broken. Knowing the meaning of God's omnipotence, we can believe him capable of miracles and of the resurrection; the rest of the story makes sense as facts "collected through experience," obedient to the rules of plausibility with which we normally understand the specific and the general. In this respect, our faith is genuinely "uncontrived" (8.5.9–13).

In the case of Paul, it is necessary to ask if there is any "likeness" or "comparison" with known things that influences our views (8.5.74–76). The aspect of Paul that would normally be accessible to our minds is his "human form"; yet that cannot be the answer, since his body has departed and only his qualities of mind endure (implicitly, through his works, 8.6.1–6). In this sense, Augustine can assert that we "believe that what we love in Paul is what lives even now."[63] This is Paul's "just mind,"[64] which we understand internally as we would any "good mind."[65] His "justice" is not a social virtue but a quality of soul, through which, both Plato and Plotinus argued, responsibility for harmony results from a division of labour within oneself between what rules and what is ruled.[66]

This is to test beliefs through our assumptions about other minds. As no one has seen a mind, there is no "specific" case on which to base "general" knowledge. We know what a mind is only because each of us has one (8.6.9–13). Can I have any internal understanding of what minds are like? How do I know that anyone else's mind is like mine, which knows what it knows through itself?[67] One possible answer lies through inference. I am aware that my mind exists through a principle of life in itself, and I can assume that other souls or minds exist in the same way (8.6.20–22). Yet, in this conclusion, Augustine again trusts in something he cannot empirically know.[68] Moreover, there are clear limits to what we can learn through such intellectual procedures.[69] We can desire justice without being just ourselves; but to love a "just soul," we must already have some experience of justice. We have to have wanted justice, to have willed ourselves to be just, and to have derived the interior knowledge of what constitutes justice (8.6.7–48). In other words, if someone asks me what a just man is and I am able to provide an answer, it is clear that I have searched for the concept of justice in myself and found it (8.6.48–68).

This means that in some sense I am able to visualize justice. I do not see it with my eyes, of course, as I would perceive colours, figures, or physical objects (8.6.48–51). How then does such "sight" come about? To illustrate what he means Augustine provides two counterexamples of seeing from within; these are configured by the cities of Carthage and Alexandria.[70]

1. He has seen Carthage; therefore, when he pronounces the word that names the city, the image *(phantasia)*[71] springs readily to mind. This image originated in his sense of sight and is lodged in his memory, where he can locate the corresponding word whenever he wishes. The word does not consist of the syllables *Car/tha/go* either as sounded out or pronounced silently; it is a word-image that is seen internally when he utters the syllables (or even before he utters them; 8.6.68–77).

2. By contrast, Alexandria is a city that he has not seen; yet an image corresponding to the name exists in his mind which is based on others' firsthand descriptions. No less than "Carthage," the impression is a mental word, which exists before the syllables of Alexandria are pronounced aloud or in silence. If he attempts to describe the city, those who know it can either agree or disagree with what he says. The principle of verification, as in the case of Carthage, is the city's actual appearance. His mental impression may be no less clear than in the case of Carthage, but it may be entirely inaccurate. If he wants to correct it and cannot visit the city personally, he has no choice but to rely on what others tell him (8.6.77–89).[72]

From these examples it may appear that he is contrasting two types of exterior verification for mental images. In reality, he is pronouncing a negative judgement on all images that arise from sense-perception in comparison with those originating in the mind; and, through the latter, he consolidates a critical idea in *De Trinitate* 8–9, the existence of a language of thought. In the cases of Carthage and Alexandria, the means of verification is outside the observer's mind; in the case of justice, the process is reversed. He notes: "I did not seek in this way to find out what a just man was, nor did I find it out in this way. I did not speak of anything that I saw, and nothing that I said was taken as proof. Nor was I able to recognize anything that was said to me, as if justice were something I had seen, learned through my senses, or heard about from others who knew it" (8.6.89–94). Also, in contrast to the case of the absent cities, in which he is aware that he is utilizing his memory, his understanding of justice appears to be in his conscious thoughts in the present. He is able to communicate this knowledge with certainty to others, who, when they recognize it, concur with him, although they too are aware that they are not seeing what is actually "in" themselves (8.6.94–101).

These statements clarify the relationship between the aural and visual metaphors that he uses throughout this discussion (though not necessarily elsewhere). Aural channels are instructive about inner knowledge when communication is envisaged to be taking place between individuals, whereas the visual refers to the knowledge in a single person's mind. The visual is higher on the scale of inwardness than the auditory and is therefore closer to absolute truth. The light of truth penetrates via the eyes before speaking in the heart—an arrangement that replicates the essential functions of reading: the equivalent of the aural is oral reading, which is directed toward a community of listeners; the equivalent of the visual is one's initial contact with the text, which takes place in a flash of word recognition. The marvellous thing about inner knowledge, Augustine notes, is that the mind sees within itself what it has not seen anywhere else as a truth (8.6.105–106). This process differs little from what happens when the truth of a biblical text is discovered through illumination.

Inwardness is explored further in book 9 in comments on 1 Corinthians 8:2–3, "If anyone thinks he knows something, he does not yet know it as he should. Yet, if someone loves God, this is known by him." For Augustine, Paul's meaning is summed up in the grammar of the final clause, *hic cognitus est ab illo*. Paul does not say, "He knew him," as if he had seen God face to face; instead he deliberately employs the passive. With a similar intention, he corrects himself at Galatians 4:9, when he speaks of "knowing God," since he means "to be known by God." An even more significant expression of the idea occurs at Philippians 3:13–15, where, speaking of the mystery of the resurrection, he admits to his brethren: "I do not think that I have personally grasped it—except in one respect: forgetting what is behind, I press forward to what lies before; it is my intention to pursue the goal of God's heavenly calling in Jesus Christ. Let us share this knowledge, as many of us as are perfected" (9.1.15–19).

In his gloss on the last of these quotations, Augustine plays with two of Paul's terms, *extentus* and *intentio,* changing the adjective to a verb and introducing a third term, *tendere* (9.1.23).[73] Paul speaks about perfection "in this life,"[74] while Augustine refers to the "the seeker's intention,"[75] that is, his and his reader's intentions (which are mentioned in the opening lines). The search for the trinity, which he is pursuing "with certitude" (*certe,* 9.1.1), thus becomes "the certain faith" (*certa fides,* 9.1.24), pursued with "a correct intention" (*recta intentio,* 9.1.24). This faith is the beginning of knowledge; but "certain knowledge" is not attainable until the next life, as Paul makes clear.[76] The knowledge that the *perfecti* share, therefore, is a knowledge that is by definition incomplete. It is more important to have the right "inclination" for seeking truth than to seek truth with the "presumption" that it will be found. Accordingly, he asks the reader "to seek" as if he were about "to find, and to find," as if he were "about to seek" (9.1.28–29).

In the phrase *extentus secundum intentionem* (extended, according to intention), his interpretation of Paul also invites comparison with his use of the term *distentio* in the discussion of time at *Confessions* 11.29. In both passages, a philosophical idea associated with Plotinus[77] is placed in a literary context: in the *Confessions,* this takes place through the example of the first line of Ambrose's hymn *Deus creator omnium* and, in *De Trinitate* 9.1, through a return to the principle of faith announced in the prologue to book 8. Let us not express doubt, he tells the reader, concerning what is to be believed, nor hesitate to declare without fear what is to be understood. In the one, authority is to be upheld, in the other, truth is to be sought (9.1.31–34). The terms for "upheld" and "sought," *tenenda* and *exquirenda,* mirror the contrasts of a few lines before (*quaerentis intentio/quo tendimus et quo extendimur,* 9.1.21–22). He seeks an understanding of a trinitarian formula in us (9.1.34–38). This is the context in which he then restates his goal, *Quaeramus hoc . . . intellegere,* "Let us seek to understand the [trinity]," moving from the indicative to the imperative mood: it is a wish to understand and a wish to express what is understood, despite the inevitable imprecision of language (9.1.38–43).

The chapters that follow echo these statements by discussing first the problem of knowledge (9.2–5) and then forms of expression (9.6–12).[78] Augustine's point of departure is the state of mind of the reader/inquirer (*ego qui hoc quaero,* 9.2.1) as he reflects on the three relations involved in love: the lover (*ego, amans*), the object loved (*quod amo*), and love (*amor,* 9.2.1–4). In the subsequent analysis, which is chiefly of logical interest, two solutions are proposed. The three-sided relationship is reduced to two (9.2),[79] and this duality is incorporated into a triad consisting of mind, knowledge, and love (9.5). When the mind loves itself, two things are present, the mind and its love; and when the mind knows itself, two things are likewise present, the mind and its knowledge. Therefore, the mind, its love, and its knowledge are a kind of threesome. They are also one, perfect and coequal (like the trinity); for although we may talk about "love" as if it existed in relation to mind, in reality it is a part of mind's "essence."[80]

As convenient as the three-sided analogy seems, it gives rise to further problems. Augustine turns to these in 9.6–12, moving toward the paradox of self-consciousness taken up in book 10 and away from the recognizable world of the reader. If I think about the inner life of my mind, he proposes, I make my mind known in one way by speaking and I define it in another way through my specific or general knowledge of minds. Although my speech is temporal and subject to change, my formal conception of "mind" is not. The problem is complicated if, instead of thinking about myself, I listen to another person speaking about his mind. If he says that he understands or does not understand something in his mind, I may believe what he says or not: once again, I have to believe what I do not know. Yet, when he talks about the specific and general features of a mind, because I have a mind myself, I recognize what he says as referring to something about which I have direct knowledge; and, if his statement corresponds to what I know, I agree with it (9.6.1–13). Clearly, then, what one sees within oneself one sees individually, and the fact that we understand ourselves relationally does not rule out the possibility of an autonomous self. Another person cannot see what I see; he has to believe what he is told about my mental state. Yet, what one perceives from within as "truth," that is, the essential features of mind, are perceivable by others, since each person, looking within himself, is able to see the same thing, that is, a human mind.[81]

Although we think about minds as individuals, we can conceive their likeness to the model of mind only through relations. In this respect, a knowledge of minds differs from knowledge of places, such as Carthage or Alexandria, in which cases it is nonetheless provable that the rules for judging the correctness of our images are independent of the observer. At the root of this difference is the "ought" of intentions; for the "impressed notion," as Robert Markus noted, "is clearly both a concept and a criterion of judgement."[82] Augustine illustrates this by another type of communication between minds, an affective bond of charity.[83] Let us suppose that what is in the mind of another man is the story of his sufferings, of which I learn. If we later meet, the love aroused in me on hearing his story finds expression, and I trust that my love is reciprocated (9.6.32–44). However, let us now suppose that the person reveals that he has deceived me, whether through his beliefs, desires, or pride. His love is proven "false," and my affection, accordingly, is withdrawn. Yet my love endures in my mind in the "form" in which it existed when I believed him to be what he said he was. He can improve, and I can still offer my love to him—no longer for pleasure but as counsel.[84] This state of affairs can exist because there is an ideal of justice, directed from above, understood by us both. And this "form of truth," being eternal, is responsible for the rightness of my response, rather than my temporary emotional state, which is determined by external events. Something similar takes place when I recall a well-proportioned arch that I once saw in Carthage. A reality, perceived by the eyes, is transferred to my memory, whence I experience an imaginary view of it. Yet while I reflect on the beauty of the image, I am also conscious of a faculty, likewise within my mind, by whose criteria I judge whether the reproduction is adequate or not. This is "the inner eye of the rational mind": it operates similarly on the images of things present, those recalled from memory, and those configured as likenesses of things we know, permitting us, in each case, to distinguish between the images of objects, which are viewed from within sensorially, and their types or forms, which are grasped intellectually (9.6.66–79).[85]

It is important to note Augustine's language for describing these relations. His starting-point is speaking *(loquor)* and knowing *(cognitio,* 9.6.1–5), again recalling *De Magistro.* We are led through a now familiar linguistic cycle, which begins when the subject hears something *(audio,* 9.6.37). An elementary level of meaning is established by showing *(digito ostendatur,* 9.6.38), after which comes an exchange of words *(sermonem confero,* 9.6.40; *inter nostras loquelas,* 9.6.46). Words, in turn, are outer expressions of intentions *(studeo mihi coniungere,* 9.6.39; *possum exprimi . . . atque exprimi uolo,* 9.6.41–42). But they fail to communicate the inner life *(interiora non possum,* 9.6.44). The gap between what we think and what we say is overcome, not by flashes of "illumination," but by a modelling process, in which, in *De Trinitate* 9, the Carthaginian arch provides the theoretical example. The problem is one of minds and worlds: something one saw *(uidi)* is reexperienced as thought *(animo reuoluo).* The components are the thing *(res),* the senses *(per oculos),* memory *(memoria),* and imaginary views *(imaginarius conspectus,* 9.6.66–69). A critical role is played by reason *(regulae, rationabiliter,* 9.6.25–28), directed by the will.

"Speaking" and "thinking," therefore, are signposts of the twins, the one mutable, the other eternal, that coexist in the mind, respectively determining outer expression and inner thought. With a different emphasis from that in *Confessions* 11, Augustine refers in 9.7 to the formal truth by which we see created things "in the mind's eye" as a kind of word: we have it in us, and we "give birth to" it by speaking from within.[86] Yet "in being born" it does not depart: when we speak to others, the voice or some other form of bodily sign enters the service of this inner speech, with the result that in the listener's mind there is a "sensible commemoration" of these permanent words. Indeed, there is nothing concerning the gestures, actions, or words with which we approve or disapprove the moral standards of others that does not arise from "the word" that is within us. As a result, we can say that no one intends anything in the moral sphere that is not already willed in his heart (9.7.1–14). The statement also provides a rationale for linguistic interchange between minds whose individual knowledge is not interchangeable.

What is the nature of this "word," which Augustine deliberately refers to only in the singular? In reality, it is more like a principle than a word: it shares linguistic qualities with the verbal images of "Carthage" and "Alexandria," but it possesses an intentional capability that they lack. For, he notes, we speak of "words" in one sense as the syllables that fill a measurable space of time when they are sounded out or thought about and in another when we refer to a "word imprinted on the mind," as long as what is in the memory can be produced and defined.[87] Not surprisingly,[88] his preferred example of such a verbal concept is love (9.10.1–2). When the mind knows and loves itself, its "word" is united with it in love; and, since it loves what it knows and knows what it loves, the word is in the love and the love in the word, both of them present in "loving" and in "speaking" (9.10.30–33). This type of knowledge can arise from what we know or from what we are aware we do not know (9.11).

As we proceed from outer to inner knowledge, our soul ascends through levels of understanding (compare 8.2.28–40); we move from inferior images, those we know best, to superior ones, whose "changeless illumination" demands greater mental acumen (9.12.12–16), finally reaching a trinitarian plateau consisting of mind, knowledge, and love (9.12.75–78).[89] To be known at all, a thing must be knowable; and each thing that we know gives birth to the knowledge of itself within us at the same time as we know it. Knowledge is generated from both the knower and the known. Self-knowledge, therefore, is paradoxical, inasmuch as it arises from things we know and from things, like ourselves, which we cannot know completely. Once again, relations take the place of absolutes. The mind, in knowing itself, is the "sole parent" of its own knowledge, for it is, with respect to itself, both knower and known. Yet the mind also fulfils the preconditions of knowing anything: it was, even before it knew itself, knowable to itself; however, since it did not yet know itself, its knowledge was not yet within it (9.12.27–34). When the mind loves itself, it gives birth to the love of itself, just as, in knowing itself, it begets its own knowledge, but with an important qualifier, namely that love is a principle proceeding from the mind, not discovered, like knowledge, within it (9.12.43–50).

In this talk about the mind, Augustine appears to have forgotten the reader, with whom he began. At 9.12 he returns to his point of departure in 9.1, the problem of seeking and finding the trinity, God, and truth (9.1.1–6); in doing so, he clarifies the metaphors of "parenthood," in which he has carried on the last phase of the discussion, and offers a parallel within the endeavours of study and learning (9.12.67–70). If love represents the intentionality of mind, then the reader's inquiry is "a desire for finding out," that is, "for the discovery" of knowledge. This "birth" takes place through factual knowledge: what is born is, so to speak, formed by being "represented" in the mind (9.12.53–56). The things that we seek already exist, but, as "offspring" of our minds, they do not exist until we find them. The desire to find proceeds from the mind of the seeker and waits in suspense for union with its desired, the knowledge discovered;[90] it is not the same as the love by which something that is known is loved, since love is an eternal quest, whereas the desire for facts can be satisfied. However, it is the same act of will by which we learn (9.12.64–67).

## The Reader and the *Cogito*

Book 9 introduces the subject that is at the centre of Augustine's interests in the later books of *De Trinitate,* the manner in which the image of God can be discovered in man's mind through inner "trinities" (15.3.71–72). He believes that we understand ourselves to the degree that we are able to do so through such perceptual and conceptual intermediaries, since direct "enlightenment" concerning our inner nature is rare, unpredictable, and fleeting.

Book 10, developing this theme "more thoroughly and with a more precise intention,"[91] replaces the trinity of "mind, knowledge, and love" with that of "memory, understanding, and will."[92] In book 14, elements from each of these triads are combined in a final arrangement consisting of *memoria, intellegentia,* and *amor* (14.8.14–26). Books 11–14 alter the direction of the discussion from triads as such to mental ascent by means of them. At 12.14, major phases of this upward movement are distinguished as *scientia* (knowledge) and *sapientia* (wisdom); in books 13–14, the exploration of wisdom broadens into an inquiry into the nature of the blessed life, in which a key role is played by memory.[93] Book 15 summarizes the material covered in books 8–14 and returns to the theme of books 1–7, the holy trinity in scripture.

Books 8–15 present a wide variety of analytical schemes, in which mental triads are matched with a number of dichotomies (for example, inner/outer, body/soul, sensory/mental, time/eternity).[94] Yet throughout the discussion a single pattern successively asserts the different means by which the spiritual progress of the fictional student in books 1–7 can be brought about. By book 14, this reader is merged with Augustine as he mentally retraces the stages of his youthful reading and examines the role of memory in the reconstitution of his own self.

Augustine has no term for the elusive notion of the self, frequently designating it by pronouns *(se, ipse)* or by *mens, animus, anima,* or *spiritus.* An attempt at definitions, possibly an afterthought, is made in the opening lines of book 15, where, following "not a few Latin authors,"[95] he asserts the commonplace that "man is superior to the other animals in reason, understanding, and whatever pertains to the rational or intellectual soul, normally called *mens* or *animus.*"[96] Elsewhere, his use of terms for talking about the self or the soul is both original and somewhat inconsistent.[97] In book 10, where important shifts in meaning take place, it is difficult to say where the jurisdiction of the mind *(animus)* ends and that of the soul *(anima)* begins.[98] Yet, throughout the later books, there is no doubt that his principal concern is with the self as the intrinsic nature operating in each of us, that is, the source of permanence that we know to exist apart from the transitory constituents of our understanding.[99] If we were unable to separate this enduring substratum from the self's temporal constituents, he argues, we could not distinguish our love of ourselves from the love of God.[100]

In the exploration of this theme, books 12–15 have a special role: they lead the reader back to scripture after the lengthy detour into psychology of books 8–11. Their "structure . . . is governed by the thought that if God's image is to be found in man, it must be in man as capable of sharing in the wisdom which is Christ."[101] Augustine is convinced that we do not really understand ourselves through trinities, nor do we understand the trinity through ourselves. All that we know are trinitarian relations.[102] This conclusion is logically foreshadowed in *De Magistro,* where a discussion of the nature of words demonstrates the limitations of words for conveying the meaning that is lodged in the mind; also, in *Confessions,* where a personal memoir prefaces comparably negative conclusions regarding the dependency of memory on words and images. In *De Trinitate,* the mind is led upwards by trinitarian analogies, but it proves incapable of superseding them (except, in 8.2, through a brief, tantalizing glimpse of the reality that lies behind the word "truth").[103] In book 15, Augustine's restless heart is still searching, as it is in the opening prayer of his life history, for a tranquillity unattainable in this life (15.2.3–6; compare 15.28.15–17).

In Augustine's view, the relationship between the knowledge gained from reading, from writing, or from other types of signs is relational, and the knowledge arising from the evidence of consciousness is not. The issues are addressed chiefly in book 10, where he stresses the irreconcilable difference between the two modes of thought. It is here, rather than in *Confessions* 11–13, that he provides the concluding chapter to his theory of reading. His position is one that allows a certain optimism to colour an essentially pessimistic outlook on human communication. Using the reader as his implicit model, he attempts to balance the demands of empirical information arising in the senses, despite its uncertainties, with those of inward self-knowledge that is certain but unprovably so by empirical criteria. In its paradoxical nature, his argument anticipates the two later thinkers who are most celebrated for their contributions to the issues, Montaigne and Descartes. Like Montaigne, he is convinced that his self-construction is inseparable from his activities of reading and writing. But, like Descartes, he is persuaded that nothing essential to proving the self's existence can arise out of the methods of book-learning. Certainty can come only through a type of rational proof.

In pursuit of this goal, Augustine divides book 10 into two parts. In the first, he offers a demonstration of the way in which the mind knows itself (10.1.1–10.5.19); in the second, he examines the role of memory in maintaining the continuity of that internal knowledge (10.5.19–10.11).[104] Phase one links the problems of reading and self-definition. At 10.1–3, he demonstrates the mind's self-knowledge in a pair of model situations, dealing respectively with written and oral communication. In 10.4–5, on the basis of these examples, he presents a general proof of the mind's knowledge of itself.

It is not just any "mind" that Augustine places under examination, but the mind of a reader of scripture in books 1–7. This becomes clear in 10.1–3, which begins by reminding us of the impossibility of loving something entirely unknown.[105] Instead of reiterating the abstract discussion of the lover, the object loved, and the nature of love in book 9, Augustine proceeds directly to one instance, "the love" demonstrated by "those who study." These are not students, narrowly defined; their numbers include all who wish to master a field of learning, but who have not as yet done so (10.1.2–5). They are "studious" because they desire to learn (in implicit contrast to the merely curious).[106] In acquiring knowledge, they have two means at their disposal, also detailed in book 8: they can compare something they learn about outwardly to a generic type or form already present in their minds, or they can recognize something inwardly "in truth itself." The two ways of knowing Paul come to mind, the picture of a man based on what we know of other men, and the understanding of his good character, which is based on our experience of goodness (10.1.5–13; compare 8.3).

In the opening lines of book 10, as in books 8–9, intentions are thus described in metaphors of desire and love. At the same time, Augustine approaches his theme in a spirit of pragmatism, reiterating and developing his argument about reading communities from *De Utilitate Credendi* 16. A desire to learn is implanted in us through the authority of those who recommend and communicate their teachings.[107] Unless something is known about a subject beforehand, students display little interest in proceeding further. Who would take the trouble to acquire the discipline of rhetoric, if he did not know beforehand that this was "a knowledge of public speaking"?[108] Often we marvel at the results that we see arising from such instruction, both from programmes that we know personally and from those that we have heard about. As a result, we are eager to acquire the faculty ourselves.

In support of this view, he presents two examples:

1. *Literacy and nonliteracy.* If an illiterate person were told that he could transmit words written silently by hand, and that someone far away, to whom they were sent, could make sense out of them by using his eyes rather than his ears, would he not be eager to learn how this is done? Could we not say that he knew about this skill already, at least in the sense that he had heard about it and had the idea in his mind (10.1.21–29)?

Through this example, Augustine offers illustrations of the two sorts of "study" already mentioned: the type that we learn about through applying ourselves to doctrines, and the type that we consider desirable on the basis of what others have told us. The literate and nonliterate persons stand for the alternatives. The link between their interests is provided by two types of memory, one artificial, the other personal. For the literate, writing creates an external memory, which permits signs encoded at one place to be decoded at another. The nonliterate has no access to this type of memory; however, he has a recollection of what he has heard concerning it, and this arouses his desire to acquire the skill of literacy. If he does so, personal memory, based on speech, will be replaced by artificial memory, based on writing.

2. *Temetum.* In a second example, Augustine proposes that a comparable principle operates in the case of verbal communication. To prove his point, he reuses the archaic word *temetum* (wine) from *De Dialectica* 8.[109] In general, he reminds us, if a person hears the verbal expression of an "unknown sign,"[110] that is, the sound of a word whose meaning he does not know, he desires to know the thing that the word has been "instituted" to call to mind. When *temetum* is heard, he must already know that it is not a "meaningless utterance" but "that it signifies something." In one

sense, therefore, the word is already known, since the listener has heard the three syllables that make it up; it has been "imprinted" on his mind through their articulation.[111] Hearing, he knows; and, knowing a little, he desires to know more (10.1.35–41).

These examples are variants of a single type. In both cases, Augustine deals with what he elsewhere calls "signs of words."[112] Here he adds one element to what he proposes concerning such indirect conveyers of meaning in *De Dialectica* and *De Magistro*: in accordance with the guidelines for the internal recognition of external objects laid down in book 8 (for example, 8.5.26–28), he provides general and specific instances of *signa uerborum*. The general case is writing (and reading), in which graphic symbols are substituted for sounds.[113] The specific case is the archaic term *temetum*, the understanding of which, beyond the sound of its syllables, requires a knowledge of its literary context (10.1.101–105). In both, however, the indirectness is a result of the presence of writing. (This is less obvious in the case of *temetum*, until we realize that, in order to find out what the word means, we have to examine the Latin of an earlier period, which is preserved only in a text).

The examples are also a reminder that he has in mind two sorts of readers: the beginner, who has to learn to read and write, and the mature commentator, who searches for the meaning of obscure words as outlined in *De Doctrina Christiana* 2–3. The logic of memory is likewise transformed into a two-stage process in parallel with the sensory and nonsensory components of the reading of scripture. In the first stage, either written characters or sounded syllables can suggest the possibility of meaning; in the second, meaning is firmly established by a previous knowledge of the skill of writing or of the literary background to a word's use.

If the argument had ended with these observations, it could be considered only a set of footnotes to what is outlined elsewhere. However, on the issue of learning and self-knowledge, Augustine strikes out in a new direction, distinguishing between the innate desire to learn and the pragmatic deployment of a means of communication. Whereas in previous writings on language he was concerned chiefly with the signs, he now focuses on mental intentions. If something is known but not known fully, he argues, the mind desires to know more about it: its "knowing" consists both of the knowledge that results from the inquiry and the knowledge constituted by its inherent wish to know. For example, if, on hearing the word *temetum*, we do not know that the sound signifies a thing, our desire to know about it ceases. However, if we know beforehand that *temetum* is not just sound *(uox)* but rather a sign *(signum)*, we normally wish to have a complete understanding of its meaning, which we cannot acquire unless we know the object *(res)* that it represents (10.1.41–47, 51–53). Our desire, therefore, is for the knowledge of the object in its absence.[114] This desire to know what it does not know, Augustine is convinced, is a defining characteristic of the human mind.

True, we recognize the usefulness of the literate skills that have the practical purpose of enabling members of human societies to avoid isolation. Yet another force is at work while we are engaged in the learning process, which distinguishes means from ends—the soul's ability "to see, to know, and to love" learning itself. In Augustine's view, a person who seeks to understand a word that he or she does not know is therefore striving toward self-improvement; within limits (10.1.58–66, 85–87), however, since desiring specific knowledge within a faculty of human understanding differs from seeing "in the light of truth." We "see" that it would be useful to be able to speak all the world's languages (1.10.67–70: we can visualize the beauty of the knowledge in our thought *(cogitatio)*; it is loved as a thing that is known *(res nota)*; it acts as a stimulus to those engaged in study *(studia discentium)*; and they, on acquiring the faculty *(facultas)* of speaking a language, put into practice *(usus)* what they know beforehand in principle *(ratio,* 10.1.70–76). Although we know that such a goal is unattainable, our reflections on the learning process are normally guided by such thoughts (10.1.63–64, anticipating 10.1.87), about which Augustine speaks in Platonic terms as principles that "bring to light the beauty of minds that have been assembled in order to hear and to respond to the sounds of things that are known." This beauty "has the effect of stimulating [minds] to desire what they do not know while they behold what they know" (10.1.87–91).

The link between theory and practice appears in our intentions. Take the example of *temetum.* If someone inquires about its meaning and the opposite party replies, "What does it matter to you?" the first speaker should say, "I may hear it spoken and not understand, or read it and not know what the author meant" (10.1.91–95). The cause of confusion is the indirectness of "signs of words": however, there is also a connection to written language, which is clarified when Augustine so much as asks why we would want to know the word's meaning if our interest were limited to what arises in verbal conversation. The answer lies in the word's written context, that is, in the philological knowledge that relates its past and present linguistic usage. In discussing the meaning of *temetum,* therefore, we engage in a grammatical exercise in which the words between speakers are based on a desire to arrive at a common understanding of a text. This is the situation of *De Dialectica* 8 (10.1.101–105).

Yet a more fundamental question remains unanswered, to which Augustine turns his attention in the second phase of the discussion (10.4–5). What is the nature of the learner's desire? How does it arise? What is its true object? Is the mind merely curious? At the root of the problem is what I mean when I say that I know something. How can I confidently assert "I know" or "I do not know" concerning anything (10.1.124–131)? In resolving the problem, Augustine takes as his point of departure the model situation in which I state that there is something I do not know, but that, in making this statement (as in the case of *temetum*), there is something that I already know. He sees three possible avenues by which this knowledge is gained; these reiterate the cases he has already taken up but then turn to a decisively different solution:

1. Knowledge through a genus, with ignorance of a specific thing that falls under the genus. In this case, I know a genus, which is already a source of my "love"; and I desire to know a particular thing within this genus. I do not as yet know it, but I have heard it praised by others. As an expression of my desire, I represent the particular object in my mind by creating an image of what it looks like. This desire is the form in which I express my "love" (10.2.3–6).

2. Knowledge through an eternal design, with ignorance of how it is to manifest itself. In this case, I see something that falls within the purview of eternal reason, and that is where my love for it arises. When this love is expressed in a likeness of that design existing in time, I believe in it and love it on account of those who, having experienced it, have offered it their praise (10.2.15–19).

3. Knowledge of something via the senses, with ignorance of something not accessible to the senses. In this case, I express my devotion toward something that is known, like the sound of a word, and, on account of it, I seek something that is unknown, which is the word's meaning. This the case of *temetum*, where it is the love of what is known that catches my attention, together with its potential relevance to what I do not know (10.2.19–23).

To these three, Augustine adds a trivial fourth, namely that "everyone loves knowing" (10.2.23–25). But it is possibilities 1, 2, and 3 that he wants to be taken seriously.

The three invite comparison to the pair of examples of inward seeing at 8.6, namely the cities "Carthage" and "Alexandria." However, only 3 works in this way, reasoning via the linguistic sign from the known to the unknown. Alternatives 1 and 2 differ from those of 8.6 in moving beyond the mental representation of actual objects (that is, cities) to the sensory manifestation of what is already generically or essentially known (compare 10.1.1–14). In placing 3 in a subordinate position, Augustine implicitly devalues sensory knowledge in favour of knowledge that arises within: this is his first move toward isolating the problem of inwardness. His argument is introduced as a qualifier to case 1, but, *mutatis mutandis,* it applies equally to 1 or 2. The direction of his thinking contrasts with the examples of Carthage and Alexandria. There, the accuracy of the description depends on the faithfulness of the mental configuration of what the cities actually look like. By contrast, in generic recognition, it is possible that I, as subject, will not love the thing that was praised if I discover that it differs from the configuration in my mind, since it is the mental object that I see most clearly in my thoughts. Internal, not external, considerations come first (10.2.7–15; compare 8.6).

The role of the audience in 1 and 2 is also reversed. In the cases of Carthage and Alexandria, it is others who approve or disapprove of what I present as a faithful description of two cities. In examples 1 and 2, it is the thinking subject who has become the audience. His or her intentions depend on others' reactions: in 1, to the reaction to the particular thing which others have seen; in 2, to the reaction to the eternal quality which others have experienced. In each case, the mind of which Augustine speaks reacts to "praise," that is, the report of others, recalling *Confessions* 4.13–14, where he reflects on his flattery of another unknown, the orator Hierius, to whom he dedicated *De Pulchro et Apto.*[115] There he draws attention to the negative side of audience relations, whereas here, within a discussion of the mutual interpenetration of minds (for example, 10.1.60–61), he focuses on the positive aspects, recognizing, as becomes clear in the next phase of the discussion, that mental configurations play a major part in creating self-understanding and in orienting human behaviour.

These reflections bring him to the problem of self-knowledge, in which he undertakes a critical review of options 1 and 2 respectively at 10.3.8–18 and 10.3.18–34. The basic question comes back to what the mind loves when it ardently seeks to know itself, while remaining unknown to itself. Is there an object of its desire, apart from itself, that is the subject of that desire? If so, how can it know what it is, since it does not yet know itself (10.3.1–5)?

With the paradox of knowing and not knowing thus engaging his thoughts, he reconsiders option 1. He asks whether the mind is acquainted with its own "beauty" by means of a report that has come its way, as we might hear about individuals who are absent. If that is so, does it love itself, or does it love an image that it forms of itself, which may represent something quite different?[116] In other words, how can we overcome the dissimilarity between rival mental configurations of the same desired object (compare 10.2.6–10)?

His reply casts doubt upon the proposed solution 1. One can argue that if the mind forms an image that is similar to itself, and if it attaches itself to this figment of the imagination before it knows the reality that is itself, then perhaps it knows itself in the way in which it knows of the existence of other minds, inferring that the mind exists from the observation of others like it (compare 8.6.1–30). In that case, it already knows itself "in genus" (10.3.8–11).

Augustine has an obvious objection to this view, which is a restatement of an earlier position. If the mind knows other minds, and if its own mind is more present to itself than they are, how can it know them without knowing itself? To reason in this way is tantamount to thinking of the mind as a body: it is as if the mind had eyes, he reminds us, enabling it to see the eyes of others, whereas it is unable to see its own (compare 9.3–4).[117] If that were so, there would be no point in its seeking itself, since it would never find itself. The only way we can see our own eyes is by looking in a mirror, that is, by replicating something in the body. It is not possible that a mind, which is by definition incorporeal, could be physically observed in this way (10.3.13–18).

Having criticized option 1, he turns to 2. He asks whether the mind perceives within "the reason of eternal truth" that the most beautiful thing is knowing itself. Does it express its desire by "studying" how it might become this "reason"? An argument in favour of this view is that the mind, though perhaps not knowing itself, knows that it is good to be known to itself (compare 8.3.26–44); in that respect at least, it has some knowledge of itself.[118] He postpones a further discussion of this possibility and turns instead to an alternative, asking whether the mind perceives some supremely good objective, full "security" for itself or "blessedness," for instance, which its peregrinations have not obliterated from memory. If so, does it believe that it cannot attain this objective unless it knows itself, and thus, while loving the knowledge, is it seeking the distant goal (10.3.27–28)?

However attractive, this option is also unacceptable. How would it be possible for something like the mind's "memory of its blessedness" to be perpetuated over time, while the mind's memory of itself was forgotten (10.3.28–31)? Option 2 would appear to be as unsatisfactory as 1. He then considers a third possibility that has not been previously mentioned. Its introduction appears to be entirely rhetorical; yet it is within his response that he frames his solution to the problem of the mind's self-knowledge.

It is conceivable that when the mind loves to know itself, it does not actually love itself, since it does not yet know itself, but that it loves the notion of "knowing." The mind's frustration may arise from a lack of this sort of self-knowledge,[119] since it recognizes that this knowing within the mind is the basis for all certain knowledge. In this respect, the mind knows what it is to know, and although it loves what it knows, it also desires to know itself (10.3.33–34). The critical question concerning the mind's knowledge of itself is this: "from where does it derive its knowing, if it does not know itself"?[120]

In reply, he presents a detailed version of his *cogito,* his "proof" that the mind knows itself (10.3.39–45):

1. The mind knows that it knows things other than itself. Thus, it knows what it is to know.

2. It follows that the mind, which does not know itself, nonetheless knows itself as a state of "knowing."

3. It is not possible that another mind experiences this "knowing." Therefore, to the degree that the mind knows that it knows, it knows itself.[121]

4. In seeking itself, therefore, the mind already "knows" itself. It knows this without any doubt. Yet it also knows that, in seeking knowledge of itself, something remains that it does not know. If this were not so, there would be no reason for it to seek self-knowledge.

Does this imply, like option 3, that the mind has a partial knowledge of itself, just as the sound of the word *temetum* is a starting-point for understanding what it means? Augustine rejects this possibility as well. If the mind knows itself through the life-principle within itself, this is something that it knows entirely, all at once.[122] Furthermore, it is able to distinguish the fact that it is alive from other facts that it knows.[123]

At 10.5, these considerations lead Augustine to reassess the meaning of the maxim "Know thyself." He is aware that the question is normally asked of the individual. He prefers to ask why the mind or soul *(mens)*[124] should be commanded by the oracle to acquire knowledge of itself.[125] In response to his interpretation of what he thinks the question means, he reinterprets a standard Stoic reply, namely that one should "live according to nature": in his view, this means that the mind should live in accordance with *its* nature. Finally, he glosses this interpretation, stating that it means that the mind has to "be ordered according to its nature," that is, to be ruled by God, who is above it, and to rule over the corporeal, which is below (10.5.2–5). Needless to say, this statement places him in neoplatonism:[126] in confirmation he presents a version of the now familiar narrative of the soul's failed attempt to transcend its limitations.

In the revised story, the soul is said to perform many actions by yielding to perverse desire; in this respect, it has lost touch with its true self. The latter is capable of beholding beautiful things in a nature that excels its own, and as long as these are kept in focus as a source of enjoyment, the soul is said to have a perception of God. However, in acting against its intrinsic nature the soul attributes such objects to itself; it thereby desires to be in itself what it is in God alone. It turns away from God, slips downwards, and becomes something "lesser" than it is. Furthermore, in its need and distress, it becomes too attentive to its own actions and to their unsatisfying pleasures: it has an unhealthy desire to seek knowledge in things outside itself, and as a result it loses its one sure source of security (10.5.51–59).

This is his response to option 2, which was postponed at 10.3.18–28, namely that the mind tries to keep its "gaze" fixed on what is above it, but is unable to do so. The narrative recalls the failed elevation of the soul at 8.2, and both 8.2.28–40 and 10.5.6–19 invite comparison with the experience of neoplatonic ecstasy and its consequences in the *Confessions*.[127] The elevation of the soul at *Confessions* 7.10 and at *De Trinitate* 8.2 both depend on a Plotinian moment of ecstasy, and both end in frustration. The soul is able to attain the glimpse of "being" and of "truth" respectively, but only momentarily. *De Trinitate* 10.5 reincorporates the metaphors of ascent and decline into a slightly different scenario. Its point of departure is the "crooked desire" of the soul, against the background of which its momentary elevation offers an unsustainable, if utopian, image of betterment.

A comparison of 8.2.6–19 and 10.5.28–40 brings to light some differences. The earlier passage makes extensive use of metaphors of seeing and light: attention is focused on words such as *lux* (light), *caligo* (mist), *nubila* (cloud), and *coruscatio* (glittering flash). The later passage uses the metaphor of seeing within (*Videt . . . intrinsecus*, 10.5.6–7), but the metaphysics of light is virtually absent. Although both passages mention *cupiditas* (desire, 8.2.39; 10.5.6), in 10.5 a cause of perverseness is singled out, the will: the narrative turns on a single participle, *uolens* (10.5.8), whose consequences include the sin of pride, the desires of the flesh, and intellectual doubt. The transitions likewise differ. Both passages refer to a slippage from higher things.[128] At 8.2, however, the soul returns to what is "earthly and habit-

ual," while at 10.5 it seeks "outside" what can be found only "inside."[129]
There is a significant contrast in the means of access to higher knowledge.
At 8.2 it arises through a sudden moment of illumination, in which the
soul is overcome and must withdraw; at 10.5 it is the soul itself, being
depraved, which wilfully withdraws from a nature that it knows to be
better than itself. At 8.2, therefore, the soul is largely acted upon from
outside; at 10.5, it is both acted upon and an agent itself.[130] Finally, whereas
8.2 focuses on the theme of transcendence, 10.5 stresses the ethical relationship of means to ends, a notion summed up in Augustine's use of the
verb *frui* (10.5.8). At 8.2 the soul is asked to see and to hear truth inwardly
in the instant that the words *deus, lux,* and *ueritas* are sounded. At 10.5, this
is recognized to be a transient moment: in the more regular procedure the
things of this world are used, so that the realities of the spiritual world can
be enjoyed.

De Trinitate 8.2.28–40 and 10.5.5–19, taken as successive statements
about *cupiditas*,[131] also relate back to the *Confessions* in an interesting way.
The earlier passage is not a reworking of Augustine's inward journey at
*Confessions* 7.10; rather, it implies a criticism of that type of vision, which
is taken over in turn and extended at 10.5.5–19. Thus both 8.2.28–40 and
10.5.5–19 employ elements of the Plotinian ascent of the soul, but they do
so for somewhat different purposes. At 8.2 the emphasis is on the failure
of momentary illumination, in parallel with *Confessions* 7.10 (as well as with
the preface to *De Doctrina Christiana,* where inspired interpretation is
subjected to a critique). *De Trinitate* 8.2.28–40 makes extensive use of
metaphors of sight and light: at 8.2.31, Augustine quotes John 1:5 ("God
is light"), one of the texts that is incorporated into his Christian alternative
to Plotinus at *Confessions* 7.9–10. By contrast, 10.5.5–19, in its verbal echoes
as well as its dramatiziation, more closely resembles *Confessions* 8. There
are a number of echoes: the mind, "weighed down by habit,"[132] discoursing
at length on its failure of will; its sin of believing that it can appropriate
higher truth to itself; and its turning away (*auertere,* 10.5.10)[133] instead of
turning toward (*conuertere*) God. This is the point in *De Trinitate* at which
Augustine begins a rewriting of the itinerary in the *Confessions.* This
journey is completed in *De Trinitate* 12–15.

With these thoughts in mind, he begins the second phase of his argument
at 10.5.20. He points out that it is one thing not to know of oneself (*se
nosse*); it is another not to think of oneself (*se cogitare*).[134] The situation is
like that of knowing two fields of knowledge, say grammar and medicine,
while thinking only of one. If I am curing a patient, I have not forgotten
my grammar, but at the moment of healing I (presumably) have another

discipline in mind. Similarly, in thinking of itself, the mind does not forget what it has learned.[135]

To consider "disciplines" in this way is to analyse thinking as it is directed outwards from the mind to the world. However, we can also ask how it appears on the inside, where a different relationship obtains, namely a nearness to or remoteness from pure being. As God is superior to mind, so the mind, in its self-reflection, is superior to what is learned via the senses. This knowledge is "woven" into the mind by our daily familiarity with sensible things; yet, on entering the mind, it finds itself in the unfamiliar territory of the spirit. The mind responds actively to this challenge by forming images of information conveyed by the senses "in itself and from itself."[136] These incorporate the dual perspective of the mind on itself: by forming them, the mind gives them something of its own substance; at the same time it retains its "rational understanding," through which they can be judged (10.5–34). For, should the mind identify with its own images, it would lose the detachment critical for self-understanding (10.6.1; 10.7.1–4; 10.8.4–11).

The essential question, then, concerns intentionality. How does the mind seek and find itself? Where can it be said to arise, where to go (10.8.1–3)? Augustine's solution to this problem lies in a process of mental replication: the mind simultaneously withdraws from images arising in the senses and attaches itself to images of those images formed and retained in itself. As he puts it, the mind somehow gets outside itself when it directs its affections toward what may be termed the "traces of its many intentions." These are imprinted on the memory, so that, when the impressions vanish, the vestiges remain in the mind actively thinking about them.[137] The mind, therefore, in order to know itself, does not seek itself as if it were absent; instead, it engages in reasoning about its own intentions, which might otherwise remain directionless.[138]

These intentions depend on the mind, in which they arise, and on speech, by which they are conveyed to other minds. When we say, "Know thyself," we do not mean knowing something absent, either genuinely absent like a heavenly power, or merely absent from sight, like our own face, which we cannot see without a mirror; nor do we mean knowing the will of someone else, since we cannot know what is in his or her mind unless intentions are clarified by "corporeal signs" (10.9.5–16); on the contrary, the mind knows itself in the very instant that "thyself" is spoken because the mind is in this sense immediately present for itself (10.9.16–18; compare 10.7.42–44). However, in that instant of self-recognition, the mind does not necessarily understand what is said: therefore, the moment of understanding may differ from the moment of obedience. The mind understands itself through its inherent intentionality, but it fulfils commands through an act of conscious will (10.9.18–21).

Therefore, when the mind hears the words "Know thyself," it knows something with certainty, namely that it is alive and that it understands.[139] It is not a corpse, lacking life, nor a beast, having life but no way of distinguishing between living and understanding. This is Augustine's answer to corporeal or material conceptions of mind (10.10.8–10): he argues that men know that they understand as well as that they exist and are alive; however, they refer understanding to what they understand, and being alive to their selves.[140] Further, they know with certainty that they have wills. Someone who exercises his will knows equally that he exists and is alive, and he refers his act of will to something that the will wills. Similarly, someone who remembers knows that he has existed and has lived and refers memory to something remembered (10.10.15–20). This self-understanding, by which we know we are living, is particular to each of us: it is an *intima scientia* (15.12.18).

There is a difference in these three operations: in memory and understanding are found "many facts and fields of knowledge"; but in the will is located the decisions as to whether they are "to be used or enjoyed" (10.10.20–23). All three have their source in the same principle, namely that what the mind knows concerning itself it knows with certainty (10.10.28–31). It is in this context that the anticipation of the "Cartesian" *cogito* makes its appearance in book 10: one does not doubt that one lives, remembers, wills, thinks, knows, and judges. If one doubts, one is alive; if one doubts, one recalls why one doubts; and, if one doubts, one also understands that one doubts. But also if one doubts, one wishes to be certain, one focuses one's thoughts on doubt, one knows that one does not know, and one does not unknowingly consent to anything.[141]

In Gilson's view, this is "the most elaborated form" of Augustine's several statements of the doctrine of the *cogito*:[142] it is one in which memory, understanding, and will emerge at the end of book 10 as a psychological trinity of interdependent entities (10.11.29–63). In the sphere of education, these are mirrored by invention *(ingenium),* learning *(doctrina),* and use *(usus,* 10.11.16). The better a child remembers, Augustine notes, the better he understands; and the more he exercises his will to study, the more his talent deserves praise (10.11.5–7). When we inquire into an individual's *doctrina,* we ask not about the quality of his memory or mental agility—lessons he vividly records in the *Confessions*—but about what he remembers and understands (10.11.7–10). Moreover, a young mind is admired both for what it knows and for the uses to which its knowledge is put: attention must be paid to the learner's will—not how ferociously he wills, but what he chooses to will and to what degree the will is engaged (10.11.10–14). The Delphic oracle "Know thyself" seems to have led Augustine back once again to the practical problems of education and book-learning.

## The Road toward Wisdom

With these thoughts behind him, Augustine approaches the intellectual challenges of the final books of *De Trinitate*. Two of the themes taken up in books 11–15 provide an appropriate conclusion to this study. These are his abandonment of psychological trinities and his reassessment of the role of memory in the pursuit of wisdom.

The context of his argument is his attitude toward *credibilia*,[143] in which his views are summed up in a much-quoted biblical aphorism which I have noted as a foundation of his theory of narrative: "Unless you believe, you will not understand."[144] If we are trying to make sense of a set of events that we have not witnessed ourselves, we are obliged to rely on the accounts of others.[145] We place our trust in what we do not know,[146] thereby supporting our reasoning with a type of faith. Christ, he reminds us, wrote nothing himself. He asked others to record his deeds; our knowledge of him depends on them.[147]

The awareness that our knowledge of events is often mediated influences Augustine's manner of approaching the classical question of self-understanding.[148] In order to defend the radical opposition between the certainty of self-consciousness and the uncertainties of modes of interpretation, he responds to the Delphic imperative "Know thyself" as a problem both in philosophy and in communication. In this respect, he differs from two other spokesmen for "inwardness" in Western tradition with whom he is often compared, namely Plato and Descartes.[149] The relevant contrast is not between a secular and a religious outlook: Plato and Descartes hold religious beliefs, while Augustine's view of the self depends on his affirmation of the reality of self-consciousness, for which he argues through logic, not through preexisting beliefs.[150] What distinguishes him from purely philosophical thinkers on this issue is the link that he perceives between self-knowledge and an appreciation of God's word, in which the reading of scripture plays a privileged role. Throughout the lengthy period of his intellectual development after 386–87, his main guide was scripture. And it is through his scriptural studies that he discovered problems involving texts, acts of reading, and reflective minds, which, as noted, brought him close to the position of Montaigne.

One purpose of the interlocking triads of De Trinitate 8–15 is to lead us in stages from the senses to the mind. Another is to teach us how far we can ascend through instruments of thinking. We discover that there are no direct links between worldly scientia and otherworldly sapientia, just as, in Confessions 11, there are none between time and eternity. The reflective individual can proceed to the highest realm of understanding only through faith. Can any role be played, therefore, by the images (book 11) and the memories (books 12–14) that are encountered by the seeker after truth?[151] This is one of the key questions that Augustine asks himself as De Trinitate nears its end.

He asks how sensory images instruct us about abstract representations, such as "will," "understanding," and "memory,"[152] and whether it is possible for such images to retain "a trace" of a still loftier concept, the trinity itself (11.1.1–2)? In 11.1–4, he compares "outer" and "inner" vision; then he explains the manner in which memory images coordinate will, reason, and imagination (11.5–11). His discussion of vision, like his analyses of signs and human memory elsewhere, primarily illustrates what information gathered by the senses cannot do.[153] He focuses on parallels (or their lack) between outer and inner sight, in which the "mind's vision" (uisio mentis, 11.1.34–35) involves an object seen (res), an act of seeing (uisio), and an intention (intentio, 11.2.1–8);[154] the intention to see differs from the object, the sense of sight, and the resulting impression in being entirely mental in origin (11.2.32–36);[155] reason distinguishes the thing and the image.[156]

A comparable division of labour is proposed between inner vision, will, and memory, whose collective activity precipitates thought (cogitatio).[157] The will is shaped from within by means of a likeness, just as the visual sense is informed when the object is present (11.2.161–165). The form, created in the sense, is thus taken over by the memory; the sighting, originating outside, is reproduced within as the mind focuses on the content of memory; and the will, which moves the sense to see, now turns the mind's attention to remembering (11.3.8–17). Reason enables the separation of the two components of the mental representation (phantasia) that is, the likeness of the object retained in the memory and the likeness formed during an act of recall (which are not necessarily the same);[158] otherwise, the sense of sight, acting alone, might confuse them (11.2.71–75; 11.3.18–21; 11.4.1–9). As he tentatively proposed in Soliloquia,[159] there is a danger that is not present when the external senses help us to perceive objects. When both images arise from within, the will lacks an external referent (compare 11.4.9–15, 18–20)[160] and has no criterion for judging which (if either) is correct. The ethical and narrative consequence of this view[161] is that the will, operating on memory images—residing above them, so to speak, but adapting itself to what is below—refers the impressions to a superior form of knowledge. The images thereby become the source of "a better and truer life" (11.5.16–22; compare 11.5.66–69).[162]

Let us say that I believe a story told to me by someone who was an eyewitness (11.8.38–40). I conceptualize the events on hearing them narrated;[163] I follow what the narrator says because I have a general recollection of the individual things about which he spoke, not because I have heard his connected statements before.[164] If he had described a mountain that was once forest but is now covered in olive trees, I would have grasped what he said because I had already lodged in my memory the general features of mountains, forests, and olive trees (compare 9.6). I should have failed to understand his words only if I had forgotten what these things were (11.8.54–58). It follows that there is no difference in reconceiving objects or events whether I myself form an image of them directly or whether I hear or read what someone else says about what took place or will take place.[165] Through the will, access to our senses or minds can be cut off, just as, when reading, we can cover a page of scripture or a letter while ignoring the text's import.[166] The reader is like a person on a journey through a familiar landscape who arrives at an unforeseen destination (11.8.72–105).

The nature of the itinerary is the central theme of books 12–15, which effectively reintegrate the theoretical material in books 10–11 with the biblical theology of books 1–7.[167] Augustine thus returns by an indirect route to the problem of narrative and to the problematic status of the reader: he leads us on a last journey through selected texts of scripture and, by means of this, to a rethinking of relations between mediated and lived experience. There is some evidence for considering these reflections as a reversal of the priorities in *Confessions* 1–9, that is, as a type of "unwriting" in which spiritual or psychological education in the pursuit of wisdom is placed before the narration of actual events. This impression is created by the reiteration of details, as well as through a deliberate (if hesitant) attempt to rethink his earlier method for dealing with past experience. Among the details can be placed references to infancy, adolescent learning, acting, praise, and the city of Carthage, as well as the occasionally reutilized metaphor, etymology, or thought-experiment;[168] among the methods are the reintroduction (and revision) of Plotinian ecstasy and the utilization of key texts such as John 1:1–14, the *Hortensius,* and the opening chapters of Genesis.[169]

Whereas the narrative books of the autobiography consist of a search for

intellectual certainty during a lengthy period of sceptical doubt, the final
books of *De Trinitate* view the uncertainties of temporal existence (and
their memories) against the background of the irrefutable knowledge of
the mind's existence. In the autobiography, the introduction of the christological theme at 7.9 is followed by the narrative of the events preceding
the conversion at 8.12, including the reading of Paul. In *De Trinitate,* there
is no single moment of conversion, but instead a gradual process of spiritual
evolution: in this respect, the pattern is similar to that of *Confessions* 9–13.
Accordingly, books 12–15 build on the notion of the thinking subject
established in book 10 and, in particular, on the distinction between the
mind's knowing *(nosse)* and thinking of *(cogitare)* itself (10.5.). Augustine's
final reflections on memory (14.8–19) confirm the merits of the gradualist
scheme of religious enlightenment. What makes the moment of conversion
so remarkable—its brevity and unpredictability—is what renders it unreli-
able as a guide for everyday spiritual progress. As neoplatonic visions are
fleeting, so the goal of pure contemplation remains beyond his grasp.

The internal reader reestablishes his presence in the commentary on the
opening verses of Genesis in book 12. This is another way to return to
beginnings and to rethink matters afresh: the commentary on Genesis plays
a role in *De Trinitate* that is comparable to learning to speak, read, and
write in *Confessions* 1. The material is approached in an intertextual arrangement made up of three layers of interpretation. In the first (12.1–3),
the topics of memory and reason are approached in a largely abstract
manner; these distinctions guide the reader through the second and third,
which consist of a reading of the story of the first couple as it is told in
Genesis (12.3.19–12.6.22) and retold by Paul (12.6.23–12.13). Within this
scenario, a broader transition takes place, which concerns the status of the
self-conscious reader. In *De Trinitate* 1–7, the reader is chiefly a student,
and in books 8–11, he is asked to keep in mind what he has learned as
Augustine explores the inner and outer images of the trinity in man. In
books 12–15, it is the lessons in psychology from books 8–11 on which he
has to focus as his master returns to scripture. The reader thus reaches a
new stage of interpretation *interiore modo* (8.1.29).

As Paul comments on Genesis, Augustine understands Paul to be talking
about an image in man; at the same time, he is talking about an image that
he is reading about in Paul. He reinforces this view by turning the story
of the Fall into a set of illustrations about the activity of the human soul
in which readings underpin principles of psychology.[170] When, through
baptism, one is renewed in God's image, there are no sexes or races.[171] In
Adam and Eve, "a common nature is acknowledged," while "in their

bodies, the division of a single mind is configured" (12.7.107–109). The neoplatonic ascent that is reassessed at 8.2. and 10.5 is thus transformed into a normal method of intellectual progress: "Ascending inwardly, so to speak, by steps of contemplation through the soul's regions, we note the beginnings of an experience . . . through which reason, arising in us, permits us to recognize the inner man."[172]

The distinction between *scientia* and *sapientia* is thus framed by the intellectual activities of reasoning and remembering.[173] The interpretation that results is a compromise between a distant and desirable christological goal and a disappointing realization.[174] Like the several versions of his life history but operating in reverse, the text of Genesis becomes a testing ground for a model of thinking that was once embedded in historical events. Briefly, when the "inner man" paid too much attention to external and temporal affairs, the divisiveness of gender entered Eden.[175] Knowledge was used as an end in itself, not as a means to attain higher things (12.12.17–23). This was science, not wisdom,[176] and related to action rather than to contemplation (12.14.20–21). The drama of Genesis is transformed into an attempt at self-improvement which is enacted in "the marriage of contemplation and action in the mind of each and every person" (12.12.57–59). And, within that interpretation, a primary role is inevitably given to human disciplines.[177] The point is illustrated by a simple thought-experiment that reiterates the essentials of the proof for the experience of time at *Confessions* 11.27. Assume that an artificial melody exists outside time but that its rhythm is understood through temporal intervals. As long as it is within earshot, it can be an object of thought *(cogitari)*. What is caught *(rapere)* by the mind's gaze can be stored in the memory, from which it is able to reemerge as something learned *(doctrina)* in a branch of knowledge *(in disciplinam)*.

These passages domesticate the process of ascent, while they undomesticate their objective. The mind has a memory of itself which is unlike the manner in which we retain or recall such events; and it is within this memory, in which the mind, present to itself (14.11), remembers, understands, and loves God, that it finds its image of him in itself (14.12.1–4). The mind, in recalling God, does not remember its original state of blessedness, but instead the words of God's prophets, which are passed on "through historical tradition."[178] These texts are reminders of the actions they record and of higher principles of conduct, permitting us to see them as "changeless rules" that are "written in the book of light called Truth" (14.15.40–52). In the *Confessions,* the reading of the first line of *Deus creator omnium* is an example of the inseparability of time from the memory of the observer: its reiteration becomes a proof for the establishment of the doctrine of experiential time as relational time. In *De Trinitate,* the example is not the reading of the text but the reader himself, as he attempts to ascend from *scientia* to *sapientia* with scripture as his guide. Time's relationship to eternity is therefore a question of purification in which applications of one's readings of scripture play the principal role in disciplined ascent. The word of God, a changeless truth, is thus incorporated into the changefulness of the time in which we live, taking on our mortality while retaining its immortality. In the vision at Ostia, this otherworld lies beyond reading; in *De Trinitate* 15, it lies beyond the reader.

Even so brief an account of Augustine's intellectual evolution in *De Trinitate* 12–15 indicates that his thinking betrays some of the vicissitudes, misdirections, and unanswered questions of his earlier writings. Yet if we bear in mind his use of scripture to overcome scepticism in the "philosophical dialogues," his approach to *scientia* and *sapientia* some thirty-five years later appears to reaffirm a type of scepticism. He is no more convinced in *De Trinitate* than he was in *De Magistro* that we can learn anything of permanent value about reality from signs. He also restates the strongly anti-utopian view of reading that is implicit in *Confessions* 10–13 and *De Doctrina Christiana.* The use of theory teaches that the problems of reading and interpretation cannot be solved through the imposition of a conceptual scheme; they can be addressed only by means of a system of deferrals in which the authority for the text is ultimately removed from the reader's control. Augustine believes that reading is essential for "spiritual" development in the individual, but he is pessimistic about the degree of "enlightenment" that reading itself confers. As a consequence, his notion of "illumination" is an expression of hope as well as an acknowledgement of the hopelessness of human interpretive efforts. Even if he had made no other contribution to the field, this relational view of reading, writing, and self-expression would assure him a lasting place in the history of human understanding.

ABBREVIATIONS

NOTES

BIBLIOGRAPHY

INDEX

# ABBREVIATIONS

*❧❧❧*

| | |
|---|---|
| *Ad Sim.* | *Ad Simplicianum* |
| *AL* | *Augustinus-Lexikon,* vol. 1, ed. Cornelius Mayer (Basel and Stuttgart, 1986) |
| *AM* | *Augustinus Magister, Congrès international augustinien Paris, 21–24 septembre 1954,* vols. 1 & 2: *Communications;* vol. 3: *Actes* (Paris, 1954–55) |
| *BA* | *Bibliothèque Augustinienne. Oeuvres de saint Augustin* (Paris, 1936–) |
| *C. Acad.* | *Contra Academicos* |
| *CCSL* | *Corpus Christianorum, Series Latina* (Turnhout, 1954–) |
| *CEA, SA* | *Collection des Etudes Augustiniennes, Série Antiquité* (Paris, 1954–) |
| *C. Ep. Fund.* | *Contra Epistulam Manichaei quam Vocant Fundamenti* |
| *C. Faustum* | *Contra Faustum Manicheum* |
| *C. Fel.* | *Contra Felicem Manicheum* |
| *C. Iul.* | *Contra Iulianum* |
| *Conf.* | *Confessiones* |
| *CSEL* | *Corpus Scriptorum Ecclesiasticorum Latinorum* (Vienna, 1866–) |
| *De Ag. Chr.* | *De Agone Christiano* |
| *De Cat. Rud.* | *De Catechizandis Rudibus* |
| *De Ciu. Dei* | *De Ciuitate Dei Contra Paganos* |
| *De Con.* | *De Continentia* |
| *De Cons. Eu.* | *De Consensu Euangelistarum* |
| *De Cura pro Mor. Ger.* | *De Cura pro Mortuis Gerenda ad Paulinum* |
| *De Dial.* | *De Dialectica* |
| *De Diu. Quaes.* | *De Diuersis Quaestionibus Octoginta Tribus* |
| *De Doct. Christ.* | *De Doctrina Christiana* |
| *De Dua. An.* | *De Duabus Animabus contra Manichaeos* |
| *De F. et Sym.* | *De Fide et Symbolo* |
| *De Gen. ad Litt. Imper.* | *De Genesi ad Litteram Liber Imperfectus* |
| *De Gen. ad Litt.* | *De Genesi ad Litteram* |

| | |
|---|---|
| *De Gen. c. Man.* | *De Genesi contra Manichaeos* |
| *De Haer.* | *De Haerisibus ad Quoduultdeum* |
| *De Im. An.* | *De Immortalitate Animae* |
| *De Lib. Arb.* | *De Libero Arbitrio* |
| *De Mag.* | *De Magistro* |
| *De Mor. Eccles. Cath.* | *De Moribus Ecclesiae Catholicae et de Moribus Manichaeorum* |
| *De Mus.* | *De Musica* |
| *De Nat. Boni* | *De Natura Boni* |
| *De Nat. et Or. An.* | *De Natura et Origine Animae* |
| *De Octo Quaes.* | *De Octo Quaestionibus ex Veteri Testamento* |
| *De Op. Mon.* | *De Opere Monachorum* |
| *De Ord.* | *De Ordine* |
| *De Praes. Dei* | *De Praesentia Dei ad Dardanum* (= *Ep.* 187) |
| *De Quant. An.* | *De Quantitate Animae* |
| *De S. Dom. in M.* | *De Sermone Domini in Monte* |
| *De Sp. et Litt.* | *De Spiritu et Littera ad Marcellinum* |
| *De Trin.* | *De Trinitate* |
| *De Util. Cred.* | *De Utilitate Credendi* |
| *De Ver. Rel.* | *De Vera Religione* |
| *De Vid. Deo* | *De Videndo Deo* (= *Ep.* 147) |
| *En. in Ps.* | *Enarrationes in Psalmos* |
| *Enn.* | *Plotini Opera,* ed. Paul Henry and Hans-Rudolf Schwyzer, 3 vols. (Scriptorum Classicorum Bibliotheca Oxoniensis, Oxford, 1964, 1977, and 1982) |
| *Ep.* | *Epistulae* |
| *In Io. Eu. Tract.* | *In Iohannis Euangelium Tractatus CXXIV* |
| *PL* | *Patrologia Cursus Completus, Series Latina,* ed. J.-P. Migne, 221 vols. (Paris 1844–1864) |
| *R Aug* | *Recherches Augustiniennes* (Paris, 1958–) |
| *REA* | *Revue des études augustiniennes* (Paris, 1955–) |
| *Retr.* | *Retractationes* |
| *S. de Dis. Chr.* | *Sermo de Disciplina Christiana* |
| *Sol.* | *Soliloquiorum Libri Duo* |

# NOTES

❧

Augustine's works are spelled out in the Abbreviations. Other sources are cited by author's last name and date. For full documentation, see the Bibliography.

## Introduction

1. Augustine defended the certainty of self-existence through the logical proof of the *cogito* as well as through the theological doctrine of the imprint of God's "image" and "likeness" on human souls. For a summary of his thinking, see *De Ciu. Dei* 11.26, *CCSL* 48.1–17, and, for a discussion of the manner in which he incorporates the reader's viewpoint, see Chapter 9.

2. As does writing, but the problem of the writer differs because of the ancient practice of oral composition through secretaries; on Augustine's practice, see Dekkers (1952), 128–131 and Hagendahl (1971), 34–35; cf. Deferrari (1922) and *Retr.* 1.2, *CCSL* 57.5.16–17.

3. Cf. *Retr.* 1.8.3, *CCSL* 57.22.26–28, commenting on *De Quant. An.* 1.1, *CSEL* 89.131. Augustine's argument can be interpreted as an adaptation of scepticism to reading theory; see *De Util. Cred.* 4.10–5.11, *CSEL* 25.13–16. Good general introductions to his refutation of scepticism on other issues are found in Diggs (1949–1951); Solignac (1958), 126–128; and Andresen (1968), 81–95.

4. An idea beautifully expressed by Plotinus, though not as a reading experience; *Enn.* 6.9.11, vol. 3, 288–290.

5. E.g., *In Io. Eu. Tract.* 22.1.2, *CCSL* 36.223.8–12. For a general introduction to Augustinian contemplation, see Cayré (1954). On the Plotinian background, see the elegant essay of Hadot (1993), 22–34; cf. *Enn.* 3.6.4, vol. 1, 311–313.

6. The classic description remains Leclercq (1961), 19–32, though based mainly on medieval texts; see also Parkes (1993), 18.

7. Cf. Plotinus, *Enn.* 3.8.4 (vol. 1, 365.1–8); cf. 3.8.6 (368.9–14).

8. Cf. *Enn.* 5.3.13, vol. 2, 226.12–14.

9. Cf. Vessey, "Conference" (1993), an excellent marshalling of the evidence from within Augustine's biblical theology.

10. As well as other subjects; cf. Possidius, *Vita* 18, *PL* 32.49. On the place of reading in Augustine's liberal arts education, the standard account remains Marrou, *Saint Augustin* (1958), 3–26, 47–104, 237—275.

11. Cf. Körner (1963), 1–40, 249–257, with a large bibliography, pp. xiii–xxvi; his replacement of a historical with an "existential-phenomenological" viewpoint is strenuously opposed by Mayer (1969), 65–66 n. 66, 186–187 n. 59, 240 n. 61, 347–348 n. 494. For different approaches to the phenomenological element in Augustine, see Schöpf (1965); Maxsein (1966), 1–35; and Zekiyan (1976). A sensitive study of the sermons is Boros (1958); on the much-discussed question of time in *Conf.* 11, see Lampey (1959), 119–148, with a review of the literature, 2–16. The best recent review of the issues is E. A. Schmidt (1985).

12. Cf. Benveniste (1966), 250–266, on the problem of self-presentation through pronouns. For thoughtful reflections on the notion of the subject in the *Conf.* and a review, see Madec (1988), 51–62; less useful is Daraki (1981).

13. For a philological review of antecedents, see Courcelle (1957), 24–33, with an extensive bibliography. On Augustine's place in the history of autobiography, see Misch (1951), vol. 2, 625–667, and the studies cited in Chapter 1. Approaches to ancient biography before Augustine are reviewed by Cox (1983), 45–65.

14. Husserl (1973), 18; on Augustine, see 157. Cf. Zepf (1959), 105–107 and esp. 130; Körner (1959), a major treatment; Körner (1962), 86–91, 101–109; and Berlinger (1962), 12–15.

15. The potential of these themes was realized during the Middle Ages; see Vance (1982) and the outstanding study of Zink (1985), 5–23, 171–264. Religious explorations of the self are ably discussed by Worthen (1992), 1–88.

16. Burnaby (1947), 34 and n. 1.

17. On reading as on other themes; a dated but useful general survey is Portalié, (1923); cf. de Lubac (1959). On later Augustinian traditions, see Schulz (1913) on Alcuin, Longpré (1932) on the Franciscans, Arquillière (1934) on medieval political thought, and Grabmann (1936) on philosophy. Material on the use of *De Doct. Christ.* in subsequent centuries is assembled by Opelt (1974). A brief bibliography on the *Conf.* is Guirau in *Sant'Agostino* (1992), clvii–clxi. A recent study of Augustine's influence on medieval vernacular literature is Gray (1988); cf. Madec, "Malin génie" (1992), 283–288.

18. See Leclercq (1961), 11–43, and, on prayer, Butler (1924), 59–74; a good introduction to the twelfth-century practices (through the eyes of Hugh of St. Victor) is Illich (1993), esp. chaps. 1, 3, and 4. However, Augustine differs from many medieval monastic thinkers in not advocating reading as a substitute for manual labour; see the interpretation of Paul's statements on the subject in *De Op. Mon.* 13.14–18.21, *CSEL* 41.554–567. Reading and work are nonetheless viewed as antidotes to sloth and as an application of theory to practice; ibid., 17.20, p. 565.2–13. On the general approach to work in Augustine, see de Veer, *BA* 3 (1949), n. 40, 467–469; on *lectio divina* in attempts at forming a monastic community, see Lawless (1987), 48; cf. *Ep.* 211 (A.D. 423), *CSEL* 57.356–371.

19. Gilson (1955), 447–471.

20. See Hillgarth (1971), 135–320.

21. On the latter three, see Abercrombie (1938), chaps. 2–4; cf. Kristeller (1956), 361–363 (on Petrarch).

22. Cf. Brunner (1955), 63–64, and, for a wide-ranging review of the issues, Bruns (1992), 139–158.

23. See Béné (1969), 62–66, 78–103, 143–154, 162–194, 210–228, and 381–426.

24. Martz (1962), xiii–xix, and, for a recent review with special reference to John Donne, see Vessey, "John Donne" (1993).

25. See Courcelle (1963), 641–688 and illustrations, 1–54.

26. E.g., Paul Ricoeur and Hans Georg Gadamer; for a reflection on the "Augustinian" element in their ideas, see Herzog (1984), 242–248. Cf. Fish (1972), 21–43, and, for a theological perspective, Mayer (1985), 197–200.

27. In preference to a "synthetic" picture, the disadvantages of which have been frequently noted; e.g., Holte (1962), 64–65; du Roy (1966), 9; TeSelle (1970), 22.

28. The best introduction to this subject remains di Capua (1931). On the unlettered and lettered configured in Augustine's writings, see Finaert (1939), 41–76; on the appropriateness of the style of address, see the enduring contribution of Auerbach (1965), 25–66, and the recent discussion, from a different viewpoint, of Banniard (1992), 65–101.

29. In response to the influential thesis of Wundt (1921), I merely point out that Augustine's reading habits were well established before his break with classical studies occurred; cf. Hagendahl (1967), 714–715, and Pfligersdorffer (1970). For a corroborative view of the importance of Augustine's priesthood and early bishopric, see Madec, "Augustin prêtre" (1992), 186–188, 190–192, 194–199, briefly and cogently summarizing earlier views.

30. One of the advantages of beginning with the narrative segment of the *Conf.* rather than with Augustine's discursive statements about reading is that the bishop's original audience may have proceeded in a comparable manner. Solignac, *Le Confessioni X–XIII* (1987), 11 ff., suggests that Augustine recalls his intention of having bks. 1–9 read orally at *Conf.* 10.3, *CCSL* 27.156.16–18; he adds: "Il est aisé d'imaginer une telle lecture dans l'entourage de l'évêque: les membres de son clergé et des monastères d'Hippone et Thagaste, les amis très chers comme Alypius, Evodius, Possidius. Peut-être même des copies sont-elles parvenues, par des voies indiscrètes, jusqu'aux cercles donatistes de Carthage"; cf. *En. in Ps.* 36, s. 3.19–20, *CCSL* 38.380–382, from the autumn of 401.

31. Madec (1975), 78.

32. Hagendahl (1967), 690, 707–709.

33. O'Donnell (1980), 145–146, with many useful observations on specific readings, 149–172.

34. See the nuanced essays of O'Meara (1963) and Bennett (1988).

35. Hagendahl (1967), 695, 697. For a statement against the editorial practice of artificially signalling quotations in modern editions of Augustine, see Madec (1982).

36. This can be described as the stylistic equivalent of the notion of predestination, in which the biblical text rather than God's will plays a central role.

37. Knauer (1955), which remains the most important study of the use of a single book of the Bible in the *Conf.*

38. Definitively reviewed by Solignac (1958).

39. Courcelle (1950), 11 n. 3. For estimates of Augustine's knowledge of Greek, see Altaner (1967), 129–153, and Courcelle (1968), 149–165; cf. Courcelle (1969), 149–223.

40. Altaner, "Augustins Methode" (1952), 6; cf. Altaner, "Griechische Patristik" (1952), and for specific studies of patristic authors, the fourteen papers reunited in Altaner (1967), 181–331.

41. Madec (1977), 550. On the evolution of classical terms, see Finaert (1939), 19–39.

42. Notably by Marrou, *Saint Augustin* (1958), 3–26; less negatively by Curtius (1953), chaps. 3–5. Cf. di Capua (1931), 607–612; Semple (1950), 138–144; and Oroz Reta (1963), 17–33.

43. On the task and status of the grammarian in antiquity and late antiquity, see Kaster (1988), 15–31, 106–134; within Christianity, ibid., 70–88; on the concept of grammar and its evolution as a tool of literary analysis, see the thorough review of Irvine (1994), chaps. 1–3; on Augustine, ibid., 169–189, 265–271.

44. E.g., *Conf.* 3.6, *CCSL* 27.32.51.

45. E.g., *De Mag.* 1–10, *CCSL* 29.157–194; see Collart (1971), 279–284.

46. *Conf.* 1.13 (*CCSL* 27.11.11), 1.16 (p. 15.35–36).

47. Ibid., 1.18 (p. 15.3–4).

48. *De Util. Cred.* 17, *CSEL* 25.21.25–27.

49. *Conf.* 1.17, *CCSL* 27.15.6–7.

50. Whence, possibly, the emphasis on the mechanism of recomposition as a part of the exercise, which Augustine was so brilliantly to transform; e.g., the anonymous *Epistula Didonis ad Aeneam,* in *Poetae Latini Minores,* ed. A. Baehrens, vol. 3 (Leipzig, 1881), 272.15–17.

51. *Ep.* 118.26, *CSEL* 34/2.690.5; for a useful contrast between the attitudes of Augustine, Jerome, and Basil, see Kaster (1988), 77–88.

52. *De Ord.* 2.17.45, *CCSL* 29.131.9–11. Monica is not one of the "highly talented and studious from youth"; ibid., 2.16.44 (p. 131.25–27). Cf. *De Beata Vita* 2.10, *CCSL* 29.70–71. On the implications of this view of Monica, see Chapter 4.

53. For a corrective to the view that silent reading was virtually unknown in antiquity, see Knox (1968); on the varieties of oral reading, Paoli (1922) and di Capua (1959). Plotinus makes silent reading an example of self-absorption; *Enn.* 1.4.10, vol. 1, 82.24–26; cf. Augustine, *De Trin.* 11.8, *CCSL* 50.352.94–96, quoted in Chapter 9, note 166.

54. Cf. Banniard (1992), 65–104, with many useful distinctions on Augustine's technique of oral preaching.

55. See Raihle (1991) and Parkes (1993), 9–19; also Kenney (1982), 15–16, 23–27, 30–31.

56. Suggesting a relationship between the function of the *grammaticus* as a teacher of reading and levels of literacy; see Kaster (1988), 32–50.

57. I.e., *praelectio;* on which, see Parkes (1993), 11–12; on a means of early Christian instruction, ibid., 14–15.

58. Based on Varro; Marrou, *Saint Augustin* (1958), 20–21; for a recent review of the issues, see I. Hadot (1989) and, on the stages of early education in different accounts, Kaster (1988), 325–336; on Augustine, 333. The essentials are covered in S. Bonner (1977), 212–249.

59. Cf. *In Io. Eu. Tract.* 1.1, *CCSL* 36.1.11–12: "Quare ergo legitur, si silebitur? aut quare auditur, si non exponitur? sed et quid exponitur, si non intellegitur?"

60. Ibid., 20.1 (p. 202.8–11).

61. Di Capua (1931), 622–623, 629–632 (on Augustine).

62. Leclercq (1961), 23–28.

63. Saenger (1990), 55–74. Cf. Saenger (1991), 199–200, 206–211; also Raible (1991).

64. Parkes (1993), 20–29.

65. Cf. Wilmart (1931), 295 and n. 2; cf. Mohrmann (1961) on *praedicare, tractare,* and *sermo;* on *tractare* in Latin rhetoric and *De Doct. Christ.,* see Press (1980), 107–118. Among Augustine's oral genres may be mentioned *Psalmus contra Partem Donati* (393–94), which abandoned classical metre and pioneered rhythmical verse in an attempt to acquaint those lacking a literary education with the tenets of Donatism; *Retr.* 1.20, *CCSL* 57.61.2–5; critical text in Lambot (1935). Useful studies include Ermini (1931), Vroom (1933), and Tréhorel (1939); on hymnody, see Rose (1926–27). Again, in describing a lost work, the *Admonitio Donatistarum de Maximianistiis* (ca. 407), he noted difficulties "in reading" and made his message brief and easy to remember; *Retr.* 2.29 (p. 114.3–7). Cf. *De Ag. Chr.* described in *Retr.* 2.3 (p. 91.2–3).

66. For an analysis, see Chapter 4, "Cassiciacum."

67. Roughly one in fourteen of the originals; Verbraken (1987), 830, who estimates that he preached on some 8,000 occasions. On the oral element, see Deferrari (1915), 45, Pontet (1945), 2. nn. 5–6; cf. Oroz Reta (1963), 160–162. A recent analysis is Banniard (1992), 76–92.

68. On the popular element, see Charles (1947), with useful notes on potential audiences; on the theology of the sermons, see Pontet (1945), 35–110, and Madec, *La patrie* (1989), 155 ff.

69. *Ep.* 73.5, *CSEL* 34/2.269.9–12.

70. *In Io. Eu. Tract.* 69.4, *CCSL* 36.502.7–8: "Cum autem tacuero, quodam-modo ad me redeo."

71. Pontet (1945), 73–79, 388.

72. Normally a person in minor orders; Andrieu (1925), 256–257. On Augustine's instructions, see Banniard (1992), 70–72, 96–97, and 95 for the equat-ing of *dictor* and *lector* in *Sermo* 356.1, *PL* 39.1574; see also Parkes (1993), 35.

73. See Le Landais (1953), 38–48, and Poque (1978), 152. Some brethren, he

noted, could read biblical texts aloud but were incapable of thinking deeply about them; *De Doct. Christ.* 4.29.62, CCSL 32.165.4–5.

74. See the instructive tables in Olivar (1966), 166–167.

75. Berrouard, *BA* 71 (1969), 35; for an analysis, see ibid., 318–335.

76. Deferrari (1922), 110–123, 193–210, arguing persuasively against the view that Augustine wrote and dictated his sermons before they were delivered. On the relation of his modes of delivery to his audiences, see Comeau (1933); on the *notarii,* see Altaner (1967), 41–44. On the library catalogue at Hippo, see Wilmart (1931), 158–160; also Altaner (1948), 75.

77. *In Io. Eu. Tract.* 38.8, CCSL 36.342.17–18: "Legistis quod audistis, et nostis; commemoro tamen."

78. Chartier (1984), 247–248; on earlier printing practices, see Eisenstein (1983), 3–40; and, for a model of oral and silent reading functioning together in early modern society, see McKenzie (1990).

79. Marrou (1949), 221. For a concise review of Augustine's editing principles, see de Ghellinck (1948), 352–361. In a letter to Firmus, ed. Lambot (1939), 112.1–2, Augustine speaks of the care with which he proofread: "Libros De ciuitate Dei quos a me studiossisime flagitasti etiam mihi relectos sicut promiseram misi." On "author and public" earlier, see Kenney (1982), 10–27, and the important summary of evidence in Petitmengin and Flusin (1984), 247–255, on methods of collation by one person or by a team. Dekkers (1990), 236, summarizes Augustine's typical editing practices as follows: first, dictation to a stenographer, who took coded notes on wax tablets or *schedae,* i.e., bits of parchment; next, a literal transcription, after which the text was carefully reread; corrections, additions, and other changes, after which a new copy was made; and a final revision by Augustine, completed by a letter of dedication to a friend whose wealth was sufficient to ensure the production of other copies, some of which were given away while others went to a bookseller. Certain works in one or more volumes (e.g., *De Ciu. Dei*) were bound.

80. On dating the introduction of silent reading in the Middle Ages, see Saenger (1982) and Saenger, *Space between Words* (forthcoming).

81. From the large bibliography on the subject, see the especially valuable reviews of Ong (1982), 6–30, and Goody (1987).

82. For an application of the linguistic approach, see Colish (1983), 37–54; for an integration of "théories de la lecture," see Schobinger (1980).

83. Cf. Lorenz (1955–56), 232–239, who succinctly compared the value of "spoken" and "mental" words in Augustine's theory of knowledge; in *De Trin.,* see Chapter 9.

84. E.g., Cassirer (1953), 117–226.

85. Schobinger (1980), 43–45.

86. Derrida (1967), 15–16; a recent criticism is Schildgen (1994).

87. See, for example, Gadamer (1965), 450, and, for a discussion, Palmer (1969), 3–45; within the history of education, see Marrou (1956), 210–242.

88. In general, see Eno (1981), 134–140; on reason and authority in theology, a balanced view is Lorenz (1955–56), 218–221; also Lorenz (1964), 26–31.

89. E.g., *C. Acad.* 3.19.42, *CCSL* 29.60.10–19; cf. *De Ord.* 2.9.27, *CCSL* 29.122.28–34. On the presentation of Christ as a figure of authority in Augustine's early writings, see the lucid account of Madec, *La patrie* (1989), 52–78.

90. *De Ord.* 2.8.25, *CCSL* 29.121.1–3: "Haec autem disciplina ipsa dei lex est, quae apud eum fixa et inconcussa semper manens in sapientes animas quasi transcribitur."

91. Ibid., 2.9.26 (p. 122.4): "Tempore auctoritas, re autem ratio prior est." For a discussion, see du Roy (1966), 123–130.

92. *De Ord.* 2.11.30 (p. 124.1–2): "Ratio est mentis motio ea, quae discuntur, distinguendi et connectendi potens."

93. Ibid. (p. 122.4–6).

94. Possibly revised in 389; see Bardy, *BA* 12 (1950), n. 12, p. 566.

95. *De Mor. Eccles. Cath.* 1.2.3, *PL* 32.1311.

96. Ibid., 1.7.11 (col. 1315).

97. Cf. ibid., 1.28.56 (col. 1333).

98. See Mazzeo (1962), 190–192.

99. There are other suggestions—although they are only that—concerning silent reading, which include *De Trin.* 11.8.15, *CCSL* 50, 352.94–96: "Nam et legentibus euenit et mihi saepissime ut perlecta pagina uel epistula nesciam quid legerim et repetam." Could the reverie have taken place if the reading was not silent? Also *Ep.* 3.1, *CSEL* 34/1.5.8–10 (to Nebridius): "Legi enim litteras tuas ad lucernam iam cenatus; proxime erat cubitio, sed non ita etiam dormitio; quippe diu mecum in lecto situs cogitaui"; cf. *Ep.* 191.1, *CSEL* 57.163.9–15 (to the future Pope Sixtus III in 418). The relative speeds of reading and writing are compared at *De Mus.* 6.4.6, *PL* 32.1166: "Melior est unius diei lectio, quam plurium scriptio, si eadem res uno diei legatur, quae pluribus scribitur." As both oral reading and oral composition would have implied vocal pronunciation, a more rapid rate of reading would presumably not have been oral. For the parallel of silent chant in prayer, see *Conf.* 10.8.13, *CCSL* 27.162.36: "Et quiescente lingua ac silente gutture canto quantum uolo"; Lawless (1980), 55 n. 66; cf. O'Donnell (1992), vol. 2, 345, for contemporary and later examples. Augustine, of course, recognized that written letters were inherently "tacit"; *De Dial.* 5, ed. J. Pinborg (Dordrecht, 1975), 88.6. He also acknowledged the role of silence in interpreting readings orally, e.g., *De Cat. Rud.* 10.14.3, *CCSL* 46.136.16–24; cf. *Conf.* 11.27, *CCSL* 27.213.56–59. The recollection of a text was likewise silent; on the silence of memory see among other statements, *Conf.* 10.8 (p. 162.31): "Nam et in tenebris atque in silentio dum habito."

100. *De Gen. c. Man.* 1.4.7, *PL* 34.176–177; cf. 1.9.15 (col. 180). Cf. *C. Ep. Fund.* 31 (*CSEL* 25/1.233.12–23) and 32 (p. 234.7–14), where Augustine explores connections between the physical and theological aspects of silence and the absence of light; also *De Cat. Rud.* 17.28, *CCSL* 46.153.48–51: "Fecit autem omnia per

uerbum suum . . . in sancto silentio"; cf. ibid., 25.47, (pp. 170–171.38–44) (on the trinity). For a discussion of related texts, see Madec, *BA* 11.1 (1991), n. 5, p. 255; a striking example is *De Ciu. Dei* 10.13, *CCSL* 47.287.1–5, where Augustine equates God's invisibility with "sonus, quo auditur sententia in silentio intellegentiae constituta."

101. *De Gen. ad Litt.* 10.1, *CSEL* 28.295.4–5: "Tacuit [scriptura] de anima, multo magis nos fecit intentos."

102. *De Lib. Arb.* 2.13.35, *CCSL* 29.261.18–24.

103. *De Gen. ad Litt. Imper.* 5.25, *PL* 34.229: "Sicut in cantando interpositiones silentiorum certis moderatisque interuallis, quamuis uocum priuationes sint, bene tamen ordinantur ab iis qui cantare sciunt, et suauitati uniuersae cantilenae aliquid conferunt. Et umbrae in picturis eminentiora quaeque distinguunt, ac non specie, sed ordine placent." By contrast, if I prefer the sounds, I am like the member of an audience at a recital of poetry, who, struck by a well-turned phrase, asks to have a single syllable pronounced again and again; *De Vera Rel.* 22.43; *CCSL* 32.213.14–214.21.

104. If God had desired utter noiselessness, the gospel's instructive texts would serve no purpose; *In Io. Eu. Tract.* 4.2, *CCSL* 36.31.14–15.

105. On the role of dialogue in achieving this state of mind, a lucid exposition is Lerer (1985), 46–51. An amusing account occurs at *Sol.* 2.7.13–14, *CSEL* 89.61–63, where Reason states that there is no better way to reach a philosophical conclusion than through the Socratic method of questions and answers. In open debate, however, emotions often run high, and the result is a disordered shouting match. Reason therefore prefers a dialogical inquiry within the individual's mind.

106. E.g., *Sermo* 289.3, *PL* 38.1309: "Quae est autem uox quae dicitur uerbum? Ubi intelligitur aliquid, uox significans uerbum est."

107. Cf. Markus (1957), 82–83 (on anticipations of Peirce), and Alici (1976), 117–154 (on Wittgenstein).

108. Often accompanied by enlightenment; e.g., *In Io. Eu. Tract.* 35.9, *CCSL* 36.323.27–31: "Sentio uestros affectus adtolli mecum in superna . . . Depositurus sum et ego codicem istum, discessuri estis et uos quisque ad sua. Bene nobis fuit in luce communi." For a brief account of these relations in Augustine's formative *De Mag.,* see Alici (1976), 15–38.

109. *De Quant. An.* 32.68, *CSEL* 89.215–216; see Gilson (1960), 56–58.

110. See Madec (1963), 285–293.

111. I draw chiefly on *De Doct. Christ.* 1.2 and 2.1–3, *CCSL* 32.7–8.32–34. For an overview of the various terms for designating signs and their frequency, see the table in Mayer, *Die antimanichäische Epoche* (1974), 44; on these distinctions, 97–104.

112. *De Doct. Christ.* 1.2, *CCSL* 32.7.2–5.

113. Ibid. (p. 7.8–10): "Sunt autem alia signa, quorum omnis usus in significando est, sicuti sunt uerba."

114. Ibid. (p. 7.11–12): "Ex quo intelligitur, quid appellem signa, res eas uidelicet, quae ad significandum aliquid adhibentur."

115. *De Quant. An.* 24.45, *CSEL* 89.187.10: "A[ugustinus]. Aliud est ergo sentire, aliud cognoscere?" (where the examples of smoke and fire are utilized).

116. *De Doct. Christ.* 1.3, *CCSL* 32.33.19–20: "Signorum igitur, quibus inter se homines sua sensa communicant." Cf. Markus (1957), 72.

117. *De Doct. Christ.* 2.1.2 (p. 32.12–13).

118. *De Trin.* 9.12.18, *CCSL* 50.309.28–31.

119. *De Doct. Christ.* 2.2.3, *CCSL* 32.33.1–3: "Data uero signa sunt, quae sibi quaeque uiuentia inuicem dant ad demonstrandos, quantum possunt, motus animi sui uel sensa aut intellecta quaelibet."

120. Ibid., 2.10.15 (p. 41.10–12).

121. Ibid., 2.1.2 (p. 33.15): "uolens significare id facit."

122. Augustine does not allow the linguistic consensus that underpins the receiver's understanding to supersede the meaning in the text. Yet in the case of the Bible he argues that widespread readership (even in translation) is evidence of the truth of its teachings; *De Mor. Eccles. Cath.* 1.29.60–61, *PL* 32.1335–36; cf. *De Vera Rel.* 3.5, *CCSL* 32.191.75–76. For the Hebrew precedent, see *De Ciu. Dei* 10.13, *CCSL* 47.287.11–15.

123. A notion introduced by Engels (1962), 371–372.

124. *De Gen. ad Litt.* 7.20, *CSEL* 28.216.18–24. On the possible dependence of the idea on Porphyry's *Aphormai,* see Agaësse and Solignac, *BA* 48 (1972), n. 32.4, pp. 703–704. In the context of reading, *intentio* frequently designates the reader's attention, e.g., *De Gen. ad Litt.* 9.19, *CSEL* 28.294.21: "intentionem legentium."

125. Searle (1983), viii.

126. This means that in principle natural signs are as intentional as given ones, although the context of the intentions differs.

127. E.g., *De F. et Sym.* 3.4, *CSEL* 41.7.10–8.4.

128. Cf. Possidius, *Vita* 15, *PL* 32.45–46, which relates that one day after mass when Augustine was at table with friends, he asked whether they noted that in expounding his sermon's text he had shifted the entire discussion to the Manichaeans. A few days later a merchant called Firmus appeared at the monastery in Hippo and thanked the bishop for winning him away from dualism and back to Catholicism. God's design was revealed to him privately on hearing Augustine's words, while it was made known to the bishop only during the interview. For other examples of literary predestination, see Chapter 3, "Alypius."

129. Not to be confused with the apparitions of dreams or delusions, which only represent or imitate sense impressions; *De Gen. ad Litt.* 8.25, *CSEL* 28.263.1–8. On the notion of *excessus,* see Agaësse and Solignac, *BA* 49 (1972), n. 42.5c, pp. 528–530.

130. Cf. Madec, *BA* 6 (1976), n. 4, p. 539: "[Augustin] n'a pas développé, pour elle-même, une théorie des signes ou du language. Ses remarques à cet égard sont circonstantielles et utilitaires."

131. For an abstract statement, see *De Gen. ad Litt.* 1.21, *CSEL* 28.31.13–24;

for a practical example, the commentary on the phrase "et sint in signa" (Gen. 1:14), ibid., 2.14 (pp. 54–56). Cf. *De Gen. ad Litt. Imper.* 13.38, *PL* 34.236, where, commenting on the same text, he equates *signa* and *tempora* in parallel with the Platonic view of time as a moving image of eternity.

132. For an exploration, see Cambronne, vol. 1 (1982).

133. *Ep.* 102.6, *CSEL* 34/2.573.7–12.

134. E.g., *Ep.* 138.7, *CSEL* 44.131.9–11 (to Marcellinus).

135. For a systematic discussion, see Pontet (1945), 257–383.

136. Couturier (1953), 169; also Féret (1940), 223–234, and Visentin (1957), 405–409. By contrast, Mayer (1969), 284–331 and (1972) takes a more systematic approach, stressing the links between Augustine's teaching on signs and a developing neoplatonic hermeneutics; for a criticism of this view, see Sieben (1975). Another conceptualization, based on Allard (1976), is de Margerie (1983), 62–63, who sees in *De Doct. Christ.* a distinction between the "sens litéral subjectif" and the "sens litéral objectif."

137. E.g., describing the sin of Adam, *De Gen. ad Litt.* 8.16, *CSEL* 28.255.21–256.6. Cf. ibid., 11.32 (p. 366.24–25), on the symbolism of clothing Adam and Eve in fig-leaves.

138. In which he may have been influenced by Ambrose; see Madec (1974), 90–95, 245–246, 339–347, and, on the programme, Madec, *Saint Augustin et la philosophie* (1992), 8–9.

139. E.g., Porphyry, *Vita Plotini* 7–8, in *Enn.* vol. 1, 10–13; cf. Plotinus, *Enn.* 3.7.13 (vol. 1, 359.15–18), describing ancient practice.

140. P. Hadot (1992), 51–68, and *Plotinus* (1993), 9–10; more generally, see P. Hadot, "L'histoire de la pensée," (1987).

141. P. Hadot (1992), 16.

142. E.g., *De Quant. An.* 31.63, *CSEL* 89.210.22–211.4. See Mayer (1985), 200–207.

143. See Kälin (1921), 13–14 and Rohmer (1954); cf. Vanni Rovighi (1962), 24–29. His preferred example is vision; e.g., *De Quant. An.* 23.43, *CSEL* 89.185.4–8. For an excellent bibliography of Stoic influences on Augustine, see Colish (1985), 142–238, 309–328. On the neoplatonic element, a good illustrative text is *De Diu. Quaes.,* q. 9, *CCSL* 44a.16–17; see also the comparative note on Plato and Philo by Beckaert, *BA* 10 (1952), 706.

144. For a summary of Augustine's views on the soul and a full bibliography, see O'Daly (1987), 7–79; useful sketches are found in Kälin (1921), 12–20; Geyser (1935); Armstrong (1940), 109–120 (on Plotinus alone); Holte (1962), 233–250; and Markus (1967), 354–361; earlier accounts are Thimme (1908), 108–152, and Nörregaard (1923), 183–241. The essentials of Augustine's position are outlined in *De Diu. Quaes.* (*CCSL* 44a), q. 1, 7, 20, 23, 46, 54, and 78. On the Plotinian reminiscences in the critical q. 46, see Pépin (1992), 121–127, 133–134.

145. For a full review of this complex subject, see Madec, "Ascensio, ascensus,"

in *AL* 1.3 (1986), 465–475, with an excellent bibliography, pp. 474–475. A fundamental early study is Theiler (1933).

146. *De Quant. An.* 34.77, *CSEL* 89.225–226.

147. Vividly summed up at *In Io. Eu. Tract.* 19.11, *CCSL* 36.194–195.

148. *De Ciu. Dei* 14.6, *CCSL* 48.421.

149. E.g., *De Mor. Eccl. Cath.* 2.6.8, *PL* 32.1348.

150. Ibid.

151. *De Diu. Quaes.*, q. 8, *CCSL* 44a.15.

152. I summarize *De Quant. An.* 32.68, *CSEL* 89.215–216. On the dependence of the neoplatonic ideas in this work on Porphyry, see the convincing exposition of Pépin (1964), 56–92.

153. Ibid., (pp. 215.24–216.2): "Quare si hoc significatione uiuit in ea deminutione temporis, quae diuisio illo sono facta est, cum eadem significatio divisa non sit—non enim ipsa per tempus distendebatur, sed sonus."

154. Ibid. (p. 216.7–10): "Sicut illa significatio non distenta per tempus, omnes tamen nominis litteras suas moras ac tempora possidentes, uelut animauerat atque compleuerat." On the later reuse of the notion of *distentio* at *Conf.* 11.26, *CCSL* 27.211.19–21, see Chapter 8, "Time." For comparable thinking in Plotinus, see *Enn.* 6.4.12, vol. 3, 129–131.

155. *De Quant. An.* 28.55, *CSEL* 89.201.8–14.

156. A view restated by Ricoeur (1981), 131–164, on which see Stock (1990), 101–112.

157. *De Trin.* 15.11.20, *CCSL* 50a.486–489.

158. See Strauss (1959), 44–73, for a full review of the issues.

159. *En. in Ps.* 144.17, *CCSL* 40.2100.6–13.

160. Ibid., 8.7, *CCSL* 38.52.2–8: "Legimus digito Dei scriptam legem, et datam per Moysen . . . Conuenienter intellegimus hoc loco caelos dictos libros utriusque Testamenti." The angels, of course, have no need of reading or books; *De Ciu. Dei* 16.6, *CCSL* 48.507.19–22.

161. *De Ciu. Dei* 18.39 (p. 634.1–12). It is within this context that Augustine's numerous oral metaphors are to be understood; ibid., 9.19 (p. 267.6–7): "Nos autem, sicut scriptura loquitur, secundum quam Christiani sumus."

162. *In Io. Eu. Tract.* 30.1, *CCSL* 36.289.9–10. Cf. *Sermo Denis* 17.1, ed. G. Morin, *Miscellanea Agostiniana*, vol. 1 (1930), 81.26–29.

163. *De Cons. Eu.* 1.1.1, *CSEL* 43.1.9–2.9, where, speaking of the apostles' role in the change from the oral to the written gospels, Augustine effectively summarizes his guidelines for the use of narrative memory in *Conf.* 1–9.

164. *De Trin.* 3.4.10, *CCSL* 50.136.37–40: "Nec linguam quippe eius nec membranas et atramentum nec significantes sonos lingua editos nec signa litterarum conscripta pelliculis corpus Christi et sanguinem dicimus."

165. E.g., Possidius, *Vita* 22, *PL* 32.51–52. Cf. *De Cons. Eu.* 2.28.67, *CSEL* 43.171–172.

166. *Retr.* 1.1, *CCSL* 57.5.2–6. He felt that he had written too much; ibid., (p. 5.20–23), subsequently quoting Matt. 12:36 and James 1:19 and 3:1–2. He would often have preferred to remain silent had he been allowed to do so; ibid. (p. 6.30–34).

167. To which one can add, to the degree that it is understood, the catalogue of his library, which, following the *Indiculum,* was carefully annotated, recalling "the occasion of each work, the date or dates of composition, the object, the recipient," etc.; Wilmart (1931), 158.

168. See de Ghellinck (1948), a thorough review.

169. *Ep.* 224.2, *CSEL* 57.452.18–453.2.

170. *Ep.* 143.2, *CSEL* 44.251.22–252.4.

171. Harnack (1905), 1103.

172. He was perhaps the first to speak of ink and parchment as "media"; *In Io. Eu. Tract.* 23.9, *CCSL* 36.238.6; cf. 23.11 (p. 240.25). Cf. *De Vera Rel.* 31.58, *CCSL* 32.225.40–43.

173. For instance, when Augustine first reads scripture, he notes: "Itaque institui animum intendere in scripturas sanctas et uidere, quales essent"; *Conf.* 3.5, *CCSL* 27.30–31.1–2; cf. ibid; 6.5, (pp. 78–79.34–44), and Bolgiani (1956), 36 n. 72. Another instance is his description of Ambrose reading silently; ibid., 6.3 (p. 75.18–20); cf. ibid. (p. 75.23): "ne auditore suspenso et intento . . ." Similar phrasing occurs during his Manichaean experiments: 5.7.13 (p. 63.22–23), 5.14.25 (p. 71.22–23). A striking example occurs at 6.7.2 (p. 81.27–29), when Alypius' thoughts are reshaped by Augustine's classroom reading of a set text; the scene is analysed in Chapter 3, "Alypius"; cf. ibid., 3.5 (p. 31.6–8). Reading is sometimes described through improvised terms such as *intellector,* meaning "an attentive reader"; Finaert (1939), 28; *De Mor. Eccles. Cath.* 2.3.5, *PL* 32.1347; *In Io. Eu. Tract.* 24.6, *CCSL* 36.246.1–2.

174. *Conf.* 10.4, *CCSL* 27.156.16–18: "Confessiones . . . cum leguntur et audiuntur."

175. *Retr.* 2.6.1, *CCSL* 57.94.5: "Hoc in me egerunt cum scriberentur et agunt cum leguntur."

176. Possidius, *Vita* 31, *PL* 32.63.

177. In addition to Dihle (1982), 123–144, useful discussions of Augustine's doctrine of free will and related questions include de Plinval (1955), Huftier (1966); and Rist, "Augustine on Free Will" (1969); for an overview, see Gilson (1960), 127–164, and on the possible reaction to Manichaeism, see Koenen (1978), 154–161.

178. Cf. *De Im. An.* 3.4, *CSEL* 89.105.17–20. As a consequence of this view, the will is the primary determinant of human emotions; *De Ciu. Dei* 14.6, *CCSL* 48.421.

179. *De Diu. Quaes.,* q. 40, *CCSL* 44a.62.6–7.

180. *Sol.* 1.9.16, *CSEL* 89.24.22–25.1.

181. E.g., Plotinus, *Enn.* 3.1.6 (vol. 1, 242.20–23), where the meaning of the stars is likened to a type of writing that is accessible to those who know how to read it.

182. After 415, Augustine argued against the preservation of faith through miracles; van Bavel (1986), 5–6.

183. For an example of the complexities, see *De Cura pro Mor. Ger.* 17.21, *CSEL* 41.657.6–658.7.

184. Whence the famous prayer "Deus semper idem, noverim me, noverim te"; *Sol.* 2.1.1, *CSEL* 89.45.11.

185. *Retr.* 1.4.4, *CCSL* 57.15.45–50 (referring the reader to *De Trin.* 12.15.24). For a review of the history of the doctrine of reminiscence from Plato to modern thinkers, see Oeing-Hanhoff (1965); on Augustine, 252–255; on Augustine's early views, Gilson (1960), 71–72, is corrected by Teske (1984), 220–226.

186. E.g., *De Cura pro Mor. Ger.* 4.6, *CSEL* 41.630.12–16.

187. E.g., *Ep.* 7.1–2, *CSEL* 34/1.13–14; cf. Markus (1967), 370–371.

188. For the basic texts, see Rossi (1983), 31–36; a lucid commentary is provided by Yates (1966), 17–41; cf. Carruthers (1990), 1–15. Useful introductions are found in Solignac, *BA* 14 (1962), 557–567; Doucet (1987), 50–52; Coleman (1992), 80–116; and O'Donnell (1992), vol. 3, pp. 174–178; cf. Schmidt-Dengler (1968), 81–89. A knowledge of memory treatises is suggested by *Conf.* 10.8.12, *CCSL* 27, 161.1–4, where Augustine makes reference to the standard image of memory as a "treasure-chest": "Transibo . . . ubi sunt thesauri innumerabilium imaginum. . . ." Cf. *Rhetorica ad Herennium* 3.16.28, ed. H. Caplan (Cambridge, Mass., 1989), 204: "Nunc ad thesaurum inuentorum atque ad omnium partium rhetoricae custodem, memoriam, transeamus." However, Augustine introduces the image only to criticize its use; see Chapter 8, "Remembering."

189. On the theory, see Tulving (1984), 223–224, summarizing his and others' previous positions.

190. Bartlett (1932), 197; and on Augustine, see Kaiser (1969), 83–90.

191. *De Cat. Rud.* 2.3, *CCSL* 46.122–123.17–34.

192. Brewer (1986), 26.

193. See Kaiser (1969), 78–83, 91–111; Pelikan (1986), 19–33.

194. *De Lib. Arb.* 2.19.51, *CCSL* 29. 271.30–35.

195. On Plotinus' resistance to "autobiography," see P. Hadot, *Plotinus* (1993), 24–26.

196. Brewer (1986), 30.

197. *De Quant. An.* 33.72, *CSEL* 89.220.1–19.

198. Cf. Burnaby (1947), 45–46, and, on anticipations in the early dialogues, Rief (1961), 303–317.

199. For a magnificent review of the different dimensions of this topic, of which the readerly is only one, see Brown (1988).

200. *De Mor. Eccles. Cath.* 1.30.62, *PL* 32.1336: "Nam Christianis haec [scriptura]

data est forma uiuendi." On the notion of rule in Augustine's thought, see Mayer, *Augustiniana* 24 (1974).

201. He may also have derived the idea in part from his experience as a catechumen, when he learned of the ancient Christian habit of not writing but memorizing the creed. In *Sermo* 214, which was intended to be a model for young priests giving instruction (Verbraken, 1962, 7), he stated that the creed "builds up" what the unbaptized "ought to believe and to confess in order to be saved": it was a set of "truths, entrusted to memory and professed in speech." This type of message was also intended to be drawn from daily sermons; e.g., *Sermo* 214.1, *PL* 38.1066 (= Verbraken, 1962, p. 14.11–15). Cf. *Sermo* 215.1, *PL* 38.1072. The roles of reading, writing, and books are made even more explicit in *De Symbolo ad Catechumenos,* 1.1, *PL* 40.627: "Et cum acceperitis, in corde scribite, et quotidie dicite apud uos . . . Symbolum nemo scribit ut legi possit: sed ad recensendum, ne forte deleat obliuio quod tradidit diligentia, sit uobis codex uestra memoria." In a comparable manner, he explains that memorials or monuments to the dead "admonish" us to call to mind those who have been taken out of our sight, lest, through forgetfulness, they vanish from our hearts; *De Cura pro Mor. Ger.* 4.6, *CSEL* 41.630.8–12.

202. On *lectio diuina* in Palladius, see Meyer (1970); on the discipline of the body, Brown (1988), 213–240.

203. Although it appears not have influenced him; on Stoic views, see Inwood (1985), 105–126, 182–215; P. Hadot (1992), 66; and Erler (1993).

204. On the techniques of meditation and oral reading, see Hadot, *Exercices spirituels,* (1987), 206–211; as a practical "philosophy," pp. 217–227. Cf. Foucault (1984).

205. Gerhardsson (1961), 25, and, among his many publications, Neusner (1986), 1–28. On the Christian handling of Jewish notions of tradition, see Congar (1967), 5–26.

206. Wilder (1964), 21–22. On the use of the metaphor of the book to describe God, fate, or destiny, see Koep (1952), 40–100.

207. Foucault (1988), 27–28, to which add the reserves of Hadot (1989), 261–268. For a summary of the issues, see Brown (1985).

208. Bardy (1949), 99, 107–108; cf. du Roy (1966), 111 n. 4.

209. Van Bavel (1959), 75. African Christians could compare their efforts to those of the Manichaeans; see Stroumsa (1983), 189–197. For the story in Christian sources, see the nuanced views of Folliet (1961), 31–43.

210. Gilson (1960), 127–132; cf. van Bavel, "And honour God" (1987), 195.

211. See Boros (1958), 328–331, 337–339.

212. See Mausbach (1930), 170.

213. E.g., *In Io. Eu. Tract.* 19.14, *CCSL* 36.197–198; cf. *Ep.* 102.1: *De Resurrectione* 2–7, *CSEL* 34/2.545–551.

214. Cf. Marrou (1966), 5–6.

215. E.g., *Ep.* 143.2, *CSEL* 44.251.13–14: "qui proficiendo scribunt et scribendo proficiunt."

216. Poulet (1969–70), 55.

217. Cf. Chastaing (1961), 121–124; (1962), 96–98; G. Matthews (1992), 107–124, with a comparison to Descartes's solution.

218. On the senses, see *De Lib. Arb.* 2.7.15, *CCSL* 29.247.1–11; on the mind, *En. in Ps.* 100.12, *CCSL* 39.1416.28–29. Cf. *In Psalmum* 41.13, *CCSL* 38.470.20–22; cf. *In Io. Eu. Tract.* 18.6 (*CCSL* 36.183.23–27); 19.1 (p. 188.11–12): "Aliquando quippe sermo deficit, ubi etiam intellectus proficit."

219. *In Io. Eu. Tract.* 6.2, *CCSL* 36.53.15–16: "Insinuat enim nobis quia peregrinamur, et docet nos in patriam suspirare."

220. *En. in Ps.* 55.9, *CCSL* 39.684.8–9: "In hac peregrinatione carnalis uitae quisque cor suum portat, et omne cor omni cordi clausum est."

221. *Ep.* 140.36.82, *CSEL* 44.230–231; cf. de Margerie (1983), 121–126, for an interesting contrast with Heidegger. For a historical and phenomenological approach, see Zum Brunn (1984), 77–97.

222. *In Io. Eu. Tract.* 2.2, *CCSL* 36.12.20–25.

223. Ibid., 5.1 (p. 40.10): "et in hac peregrinatione interim consolati." Cf. di Giovanni (1967), 502–508, 511–517, on the "interpersonal" aspects of language and thought.

224. *Ep.* 140.6.15, *CSEL* 44.166.18–23, where, commenting on Ps. 21:2 ("Deus, deus meus, respice me: quare me dereliquisti?"), scripture is effectively dissolved into the life of Christ.

225. *Politicus,* 273d; Augustine is generally thought to have derived the notion from Plotinus, *Enn.* 1.8.13, vol. 1, 122.16–17. On the idea's considerable afterlife, see above all Courcelle (1957), with an important repertoire of texts, 24–33; cf. Dumeige (1956); on Augustine's use of the notion at *Conf.* 7.10, see Chapter 2, "Neoplatonism."

226. See Markus (1966), 433–434, 445–450.

227. E.g., *Sermo* 253.2, *PL* 38.1180.

228. Gilson (1960), 71–75.

229. Reviewed briefly by Halliburton (1962), 329 336, in detail by Lawless (1987), 9–62.

230. *De Diu. Quaes.,* q. 52, *CCSL* 44a.83–84; *De Gen. ad Litt.* 8.17, *CSEL* 28.256.13–28. On Augustine's doctrine of original sin, see Sage (1967), 213–242, and, for a discussion of the latter's developmental scheme, Rigby (1987), 20–28.

231. Madec, *Saint Augustin et la philosophie* (1992), 47, correcting Duchrow (1961). There is an interesting parallel with Plotinus' argument for the beginning of evil in "audacity," through which intellect acquires an independent, self-conscious existence; *Enn.* 5.1.1, vol. 2.185.3–5. In both authors, otherness is linked to fictions about the self, and restoration begins with meditative presence. Plotinus' discussion is nonetheless very abstract; e.g., *Enn.* 5.2.1, vol. 2, 203–204.

232. *De Gen. ad Litt.* 8.18 (*CSEL* 28.258.1–3) and 8.27 (p. 266.16–267.3); cf. 9.2 (pp. 269.2–270.19) and 11.33 (p. 367.3–20), where Augustine distinguishes between God's normal manner of communicating with the first couple before the fall, which was "possibly interior and ineffable," and afterwards, when he appeared as "a voice walking in the garden at dusk"; cf. *De Gen. c. Man.* 2.4.5, *PL* 34.198–199 (and, for a similar expression in describing God's communication with the angels, *De Ciu. Dei* 16.6, *CCSL* 48.507.19–22). Augustine nonetheless saw the first couple's type of speech "talibus uocum signis" (*De Gen. ad Litt.* 8.27, *CSEL* 28.267.3) as an intractable problem; e.g., *De Trin.* 2.10.18, *CCSL* 50.104.61–63. Cf. *De Diu. Quaes.*, q. 47, *CCSL* 44a.74, and the discussion of Duchrow (1965), 149–151. On the anticipation of these views in *De Mag.*, see Madec, *BA* 6, (1976), n. 5, pp. 540–543.

233. *De Vera Rel.* 23.44, *CCSL* 32.214.7–10.

234. Cf. Strauss (1959), 44–73, and, on the historical theory behind the idea, Markus (1970), 22–44, 154–186.

235. On the manuscript evidence for careful reading, see Parkes (1993), 15–16.

236. As noted by Mayer (1969), 43–46.

237. Taylor (1989), 35–36.

238. Cf. Zepf (1926), 1–17.

239. E.g., *Conf.* 8.6.13, *CCSL* 27.121.3: "narrabo et confitebor nomini tuo, domine." See Herzog (1984), 215–231, with interesting literary reflections.

240. *Conf.* 2.3.5, *CCSL* 27.19.9: "Vt uidelicet ego et quisquis haec legit."

241. *In Io. Eu. Tract.* 90.1, *CCSL* 36.551.17–19: "Non igitur in eius facie corporali nobis intimatur cuiusque notitia. Sed tunc nobis ad cognitionem patet, quando eius mores et uita non latet."

242. Except infancy; *Conf.* 1.6.7, *CCSL* 27.4.8–9.

243. Bruner (1991), 129. In historical perspective, see Adam (1954), 9–10, 21–23; on literary issues, Spengemann (1980), 1–32; on the theory of discourse implied, White (1987), 1–6.

244. De Ghellinck (1948), 345–349.

245. *Ep.* 231.6, *CSEL* 57.508.26–509.3.

246. Note, however, that although Augustine has a notion of "representation," he does not use the term *repraesentatio;* Wienbruch (1971), 76–77.

247. *De Lib. Arb.* 2.19.52, *CCSL* 29.272.

248. *S. de Dis. Chr.* 1.1., *CCSL* 46.207.1–6, on Ecclesiasticus 51:31 and 51:36.

249. E.g., *De Diu. Quaes.*, q. 25, *CCSL* 44a.31.1–2; cf. Flores (1975), 6–7.

250. Screech (1991), xvii.

251. E.g., *Conf.* 13.22, *CCSL* 27.260–261, on which see O'Donnell (1992), vol. 3, 394–395. Cf. *Sol.* 1.4, *CSEL* 89.9.1–3: "<Deus>, qui fecisti hominem ad imaginem et similitudinem tuam, quod qui se ipse nouit agnoscit." For discussions of the theme's development, see Kusch (1953), 130–131; Ladner (1959), 185–203; Markus (1964), 130–137; Schindler (1965), 61–74; and Mayer (1969), 271–284; on later tradition, see above all Javelet (1967), vol. 1, 1–66 (on Augustine, pp. 56–63).

Augustine conveniently summarizes his way of distinguishing *imago* and *similitudo* at *De Diu. Quaes.*, q. 74, *CCSL* 44a.213–214.

252. Markus (1967), 361. Augustine's views were also influenced by the theme of self-mastery in Plotinian aesthetics, in which the soul is trained (or, as Augustine would have it, retrained) to envisage a superior way of life and to appreciate its design from within, just as an artist progressively models a statue; *Enn.* 1.6.9, vol. 1, 103.1–22.

253. E.g., *De Vera Rel.* 26.49, *CCSL* 32.218–219; *De Diu. Quaes.*, q. 51, *CCSL* 44.78–82. On Augustine's reinterpretation of Paul, see the enduring study of Ladner (1959), 153–283; for recent literature, see Fredriksen (1986), 3–4 nn. 1–2, and, for a brief review of Augustine's itinerary, Fredriksen (1988), 89–98.

254. See Bochet (1993), 29–50. On the role of Simplicianus in this transformation, see Pincherle, "Intorno alla genesi." (1974); cf. (1976), 122. On Paul in *Conf.* 8, see Fredriksen (1986), 3–6, 20–34, a discerning study; on the notion of person, see Drobner (1986), 103–126.

255. Madec, *Saint Augustin et la philosophie* (1992), 46; cf. Madec, *BA* 6 (1976), 540–542.

256. *De Diu. Quaes.*, q. 44, *CCSL* 44a.65.11–15.

257. Eph. 3:17. For quotations in Augustine, see Manrique (1973).

258. *De Vera Rel.* 40.74, *CCSL* 32.235.2–3: "Interior exteriorem [hominem] respicit et in sua comparatione foedum uidet." Cf. Holl (1965), 94; Ladner (1954). To make this view possible, Paul's complexities had to be rendered as "a seemingly unambiguous text, an intricate synthesis of grace, freewill and predestination"; Brown (1967), 154.

259. In this respect, reading is not an organization of thinking, as it is in standard commentary. Augustine begins, not with the text, but with the knowledge of his own mental restlessness (e.g., *Conf.* 1.1). The incessant stream of thoughts passing through his mind leaves him little opportunity for inner tranquility. Reading, studying, and meditating on passages of scripture begin the process of withdrawal from this sensory world, in which he realizes that he is lost to his true self. Through meditative self-awareness, he temporarily achieves a state of contemplation in which the physical (i.e., phonic or visual) qualities of the biblical text are superseded.

260. On the notion of *peregrinatio animae* as a principle of unity between Bks. 1–9 and 10–13, see Knauer (1957); cf. Crouse (1976), Hanson-Smith (1978). A comparable view, based on the presence of trinitarian thinking in bks. 2–4 and 10–13, is brought forward in an important study by Kusch (1953), 129–150; more briefly, by Valgiglio (1980). One of the chief sources for the admittedly commonplace metaphor of the soul's journey is Plotinus, *Enn.* 1.6.8, vol. 1, 102–103, variants of which are reiterated at *Conf.* 1.18 and 8.8; cf. *De Ciu. Dei* 9.17. And surely Augustine must have had in mind the rare, deeply moving statement that begins *Enn.* 4.8.1 (vol. 2, 165.1–4, 166.17–22), in which Plotinus speaks of exile and return as the awakening to the pleasures of the inner self.

261. *De Vera Rel.* 24.45, *CCSL* 32.215.15–216.

262. Cf. Madec, "Le communisme spirituel" (1987), 227–238.

263. Augustine has well-publicized doubts concerning female intellectual activity; e.g., *De Beata Vita* 2.10, *CCSL* 29.71.101–103; *De Ord.* 1.11.31, *CCSL* 29.105.4–6, where Monica herself remarks, implicitly connecting philosophizing with literate activity: "Quid agitis? inquit; numquidnam in illis quos legitis libris etiam feminas umquam audiui in hoc genus disputationis inductas?" For a discussion, see Lamirande (1989), 9–10. Cf. *De Gen. ad Litt.* 9.5, *CSEL* 28.273.13–14. For a contrasting view, see *De Vera Rel.* 41.78, *CCSL* 32.238–239. Cf. Børresen (1981), 2–49, for the relevant texts and, for a theological approach to Augustine's views on marriage and sexuality, Solignac, *BA* 49 (1972), n. 42, pp. 516–553. On Augustine's lack of a circle of female friends, see E. A. Clark, "'Adam's Only Companion'" (1986), 158; and Bonner (1987), 259–266. For recent discussion of other gender issues in Augustine, see Soennecken (1989), van Bavel (1989), and Zumkeller (1989).

264. Recall, however, that Augustine maintained that "things" are ungendered; *In Io. Eu. Tract.* 38.11, *CCSL* 36.344.16–18: "Consuetudo locutionis ideo per diuersas linguas uariat genera uocabulorum, quia in ipsis rebus non inuenis sexum." Significantly, the *res* in question was *sapientia,* which Monica elsewhere represents.

265. *De Trin.* 14.9.12, *CCSL* 50a.438–440. There again, it is a female configuration, *sapientia,* that is his partner in discussion.

266. See *De Vera Rel.* 34.63, *CCSL* 32.228.10–13.

267. E.g., Montgomery (1914), v. On Augustine's notion of individuality generally, see Weintraub (1978), 45–48.

268. Mommsen (1959), 294–295, 297.

269. Possibly, as well, the cult of Mani's personality among his African followers; there is just a hint of this at *De Util. Cred.* 3.7, *CSEL* 25.10.40–44.

270. Von Harnack (1888) and (1916). For a review of Harnack's position on the *Conf.,* see Blaser (1964); on his view of Augustine as a "reformer of Christian piety," see Geerlings (1978), 12–20.

271. Courcelle (1950), 47 (my translation), restated at 247; cf. J. Matthews (1975), 219–222, who pertinently summarizes the details.

272. For a review of essentials, see Bonner (1963), 42–48, updated by Doignon (1989) (the dialogues) and Madec, "Le néoplatonisme" (1989) (the *Conf.*).

273. For a criticism of Courcelle's approach within a recognition of his major contribution, see, *inter alia,* Mohrmann, "The *Confessions*" (1958), 375–381, who distinguishes between *factum* and *mysterium* in *Conf.* 8.

274. Cf. Löhrer (1957), 393–394.

## 1. Learning to Read

1. The analysis of the problem of reading is not facilitated by referring to the *Confessions* as an autobiography, although avoiding the term does not make a

positive contribution either; on its late appearance, see Voisine (1963), 280–282; cf. Olney (1980), 3–27, 343–352 (for bibliography). For criticism of Romantic views, see Vance, "Augustine's *Confessions.*" (1973), 1–5, and "Le moi comme langage" (1973); cf. Zumthor (1973) and the observations of Fredouille (1993), 167–171. The standard history of autobiography in antiquity remains Misch (1951); for early literature, see Courcelle (1963), 9–11; an intelligent recent review of the issues is Sturrock (1993), 1–19; a dated account of medieval lives, some of which depend on Augustine, is Lehmann (1953).

The theme of reading has been noted by a number of commentators, e.g., Courcelle (1950), 15–20, 24–25; Flores (1975); Consolino (1981), 135–140; Morrison (1992), 20–32; O'Donnell (1992), vol. 2, 341; and Sturrock (1993), 24–36. Note, however, that Possidius does not give reading prominence; on his limitations, see Courcelle (1951–52); Brown (1967), 408–409; and Bastiaensen (1985), 481–482.

In suggesting that the reader provides a principle of unity in the *Conf.,* I differ little from the "plan général" of Cayré (1953), 25–28; I add the instrument of reading to clarify the division between "chercheur" after God (bks. 1–9) and "témoin" (bks. 10–13). Cf. Cayré, "Mystique et sagesse" (1951–52), 443–448, 451–457; Pincherle (1955–57), 189–190; and, based on Augustine's reading of scripture, Kienzler (1989). For a review of other problems connected with the *Confessions'* unity, see Solignac, *BA* 13 (1962), pp. 19–26; Luongo (1976), 286–290, with an extensive bibliography, and Ferrari (1984). Solignac, *Le Confessioni X–XIII* (1987), wisely notes: "Plusieurs commentateurs ont proposé divers schémas pour expliquer la construction; mais la multiplicité même de ces schémas suffit à montrer qu'aucun d'eux ne réussit parfaitement à rendre compte de la succession logique des livres."

2. Throughout Part I, I refer to the *Conf.* by book, chapter, and line numbers of the edition of L. Verheijen (*CCSL* 27.)

3. Verheijen (1949), 21, distinguishes *confiteri* as *uerbum dicendi* and as *recordare, narrare;* for typical passages, see 11–21; Courcelle (1950), 19–20, rightly challenges this schematization, but, in brilliantly assembling the evidence for Augustine's use of *confessio* (ibid., nn. on 14–19), he sees Augustine's need after bk. 10 only "de revenir longuement sur la notion même de confession et de systématiser sa pensée" (p. 17) rather than to move from oral confession to a recorded, literary genre. On the first of Verheijen's distinctions, see Ratzinger (1957), 376–378, who notes classical *fontes* (esp. Cicero). Other useful studies include Böhmer (1915); Wundt (1923); Zepf (1926); Wolf (1928); Williger (1929); Knauer (1955), 78–79; Ratzinger (1957), 385–392; Maxsein (1966), 281–292; and O'Donnell (1992), vol. 2, 3–7. A brief summary is G. Bonner (1963), 48–51. Cf. Mohrmann, *Etudes* 1 (1958), 371–373, sensitive to literary issues; Kahn (1968), 225–230; and Bakhtin (1986), who speaks of "speech genres" but, oddly, does not include the formative influence of the *Conf.* Texts of literary confessions earlier than the *Conf.* are brought together by O'Donnell (1992), vol. 1, li–lvi; they are *De Beata Vita* 1.4, *C. Acad.* 2.2.3–6,

*De Util. Cred.* 1.2 and 8.20, *De Dua. An.* 9.11, and *C. Ep. Fund.* 3.3. Overlooked are the prayer in *Sol.* 1.2–6, *CSEL* 89.4–11, on which see Doignon (1987), and *Ep.* 3.

4. E.g., *Conf.* 5.10.70–72 (reading): "Nunc spiritales tui blande et amanter ridebunt me, si has confessiones meas legerint; sed tamen talis eram"; and 10.1.7–8 (writing): "Volo eam facere in corde meo coram te in confessione, in stilo autem meo coram multis testibus." Cf. 7.20.13–27; 10.3.16–19; 12.24.5–12. On this aspect of Augustine's "confession," see Weintraub (1978), 24, 26–27.

5. On the prayer's other features, see Pincherle (1968); for a line-by-line exposition, see Bouisson, *BA* 13 (1962), n. 1, pp. 647–650, and n. 3, pp. 652–656; cf. O'Donnell (1992), vol. 2, 9–32, with philological observations; also Finaert (1939), 76–79, and Ripanti (1974), 88–89. Early literature is reviewed by Courcelle (1963), 91 n. 2; cf. Solignac, *BA* 13 (1962), n. 2, pp. 650–652.

6. *Conf.* 1.1.1–7; Ps. 47:2, 95:4, 144:3, 146:5 (lines 1–2), and 118:34, 73, 144 (line 7). References throughout are to the Latin Vulgate of Jerome, completed in 384, although Augustine did not adopt it for general use until later; see la Bonnardière, "Augustin" (1986), 304. A reasonably accurate sense of Augustine's interest in *confessio* in the Psalms can be derived from a sermon of 397 in Dolbeau (1991), 244–249, on Ps. 117:1 ("Confitemini Domino . . .").

7. See Herzog (1984), 215–218, and Simon (1982), 132–144.

8. *Conf.* 1.1.6–7: "Tu excitas, ut laudare te delectet, quia fecisti nos ad te et inquietum est cor nostrum, donec requiescat in te." Cf. 13.38.10–11. On interior peace, see Lawless (1980); on the management of the heart, see de la Peza (1961), 344–368, and Maxsein (1966), 13–21; for a commentary on these lines, see Pizzolato in *Le Confessioni I–II* (1984), 12–15, and the excursus by Ceriotti, ibid., 79–88.

9. Cf. Cicero, *Tusc. Disp.* 3.1.2; however, Augustine does not mention "insight" and "perception" arising out of "nature." For an index of Augustine's critical dependence on this text, see Testard (1958), vol. 1, 117–128.

10. The other sense of *infans;* cf. *De Praes. Dei* 7.25 (= *Ep.* 187), *CSEL* 57.102.13–15: "Cum articulatae uocis qualiacumque signa edere coeperint [paruuli] atque ad initium fandi transire ab infantia."

11. Cf. Magass (1984), who succinctly relates the "confessional discourse" of the thirteen books to specific situations in Augustine's life.

12. See Pellegrino, "Aspectos pedagógicos" (1960), 53–59.

13. Of the six (*infantia, pueritia, adulescentia, iuuentus, grauitas,* and *senectus*), Augustine omits old age, although the scheme is fully presented in the six ages of the world in *De Cat. Rud.* 17.28; see Combès and Farges, *BA* 11 (1949), n. 13, pp. 552–554, supplemented by Cranz (1954) and, more briefly, *De Diu. Quaes.,* q. 58.3, *CCSL* 44a, 107–109. On Augustine's reasons for not adhering to the six ages based on *Ad Sim.,* see Pincherle (1976), 122–123, 132–133; the outstanding attempt to integrate them into a theological scheme is Pizzolato (1968). The literature on the "ages of man" is fully reviewed by Mayer (1969), 51–53, with a comparison

to other typologies of time in Augustine's works, 53–60; see also Rousseau (1958), Luongo (1976), 290–292. A typically Augustinian formula is *Ep.* 138.2, *CSEL* 34/3.128.1–5, where it is not only the succession of periods of life that is stressed but God's foreknowledge. One of the most interesting parallels for *Conf.* 1–9 is found in *De Gen. c. Man.* 1.20–25, *PL* 34.187–194, where he first speaks of the seven ages of the world as aspects of the life-cycle (chaps. 20–24), then in terms of education (chap. 25), passing in seven days through the awareness of the light of faith *(lux fidei)*, the foundation of discipline *(firmamentum disciplinae)*, resistance to temptations of the senses *(a tentationibus secernere)*, spiritual understanding *(spirituales intelligentiae)*, withdrawal from the world's turbulence into a fraternal society *(propter utilitatem fraternae societatis)*, the attainment of stability of mind *(stabilitas mentis)* and good thoughts *(bonae cogitationes)*, and, finally, repose *(requies)*. On these relations, see O'Donnell (1992), vol. 2, 52–56, and Burrow (1986), 80–85; on their diffusion in later ancient and medieval art, see Sears (1986), 54–79.

14. *Conf.* 1.6.8–9; 1.7.37–38; *De Gen. c. Man.* 1.23.36, *PL* 34.190; *De Trin.* 14.5, *CCSL* 51a.430.24–25. Cf. Paul on the memory others may have had of his life "a juuentute"; Acts 26:4–5. For accounts of Augustine's infancy, see Miles (1982), 351–352; Cristiani (1984), 405–406. The best commentary on bk. 1 as a whole is Pizzolato in *Le Confessioni I-II* (1984), 9–78.

15. *De Quant. An.* 20.34, *CSEL* 89.173.10–13. Running through *Conf.* 1.6–8, therefore, is an understated argument against classical reminiscence. Augustine's remarks on infancy parallel his cosmological views, which are based on humans' lack of knowledge of initial conditions. Just as our personal narratives begin at an arbitrary moment, the written record of world history in Genesis begins with the birth of time.

16. *Conf.* 1.6.43–44 (on pregnancy); 1.6.9–15, 1.7.7–9 (on breast-feeding); and 1.6.21 (on sleep).

17. Despite this limitation, we are aware that we have passed from infancy to childhood, etc. The growth states are not simultaneously alive in us, but we are easily able to situate them in our life narratives; on the temporal and existential dimensions, see Boros (1954). In bk. 11 Augustine argues that this memory is like the mental record of a spoken word whose meaning remains after we cease to have a recollection of the passage of sound; see Chapter 8, "Time."

18. *Conf.* 1.7; cf. 1.12.12–13: "tantillus puer et tantus peccator." Pelagianism sharpened the issues; see *Sermones* 323 and 324 and the comments of Cayré (1952), 132–139; also Busch (1938), 393–394. Augustine's doctrine is succinctly summarized by Burnaby (1947), 219–220; numerous passages are listed by Pellegrino, *Les Confessions* (1960), 63 n. 15; for thorough reviews, see Sage (1967), 217, 230–232, and Rigby (1987), 38–58. Congar (1967), 53 and 53 n. 4, speaks of infant baptism as "unwritten apostolic tradition."

19. *Ep.* 140.2.3, *CSEL* 44.157.2–4.

20. Infants cannot think *(cogitare)*, but they are not wholly ignorant of themselves *(non ignorare)*; they record sensory impressions. At *De Trin.* 14.5, *CCSL*

50a.429–430.4–15, Augustine explains that the evidence is their attraction to objects outside themselves, as observed in their eye movements. One only needs to perform the following experiment: at night, when the infant is lying down, place a light source nearby in such a way that it can direct its eyes toward it without moving its head. The infant's eyes will invariably follow the light. (He adds that some children thus acquire the habit of squinting.)

21. *Conf.* 1.7.10–11; see also *De Trin.* 14.5, *CCSL* 50a.430.15–23.

22. This becomes a hagiographical topos; e.g., Thomas of Celano, *Vita Prima S. Francisci* 1.1, *Analecta Francescana* 10, *Legendae* 1 (Quaracchi, 1926–1941), 5, 13–15.

23. E.g., *Conf.* 6.4.11–17. The idea appears in a number of variations: 7.18.5–7; 12.27.16–18.

24. *In Io. Eu. Tract.* 15.21, *CCSL* 36.158.9–13.

25. *De Doct. Christ.* 2.12, *CCSL* 32.43.25–27, utilizing 2 Cor. 5:7 and Gal. 3:24. A similar idea was voiced by Quintilian, *Institutio Oratoria* 1.1.21. Cf. *Conf.* 8.5.6 and, on childhood in the same light, *Ep.* 118.2.9, *CSEL* 34.2, 674.4–6, written to Dioscorus in 410 or 411.

26. E.g., *Sermones ad Infantes* 127, 190, 223, 227, 260, 272, 294, etc. For the essentials, see Busch (1938), 396–397; cf. Audet (1954), 151–153; van der Meer (1961), 381.

27. Monachino (1947), 179–181.

28. *Sermo* 228.1, *PL* 38.1101. For a review of images suited to infants, see Charles (1947), 89–90.

29. *Sermo* 228.3, *PL* 38.1102; *Sermo* 227, *PL* 38.1099.

30. For an analysis, see Comeau (1933).

31. Colish (1983), 25, notes that "rightly ordered speech . . . is a consequence of the Incarnation."

32. E.g., *Ep.* 4.2, *CSEL* 34/1.10.13–14: "Pueri enim sumus, sed, ut dici adsolet, forsitan belli; et non male"; *Ep.* 21.1 (p. 50.3–7). Such expressions were reasonably common among Christian correspondents; e.g., *Ep.* 25.4 (pp. 81–82), from Paulinus of Nola and Therasia to Augustine; *Ep.* 32.4, *CSEL* 34/2.11.14–20, from Paulinus to Romanianus, on Augustine's education of the latter's son, Licentius. Cf. *Ep.* 36.26 (ibid., pp. 55–56) (on Mattt. 11:18–19).

33. It is also possible to speak of three states of self-consciousness, although the claim has to be made with caution. In the first phase, there is little or no connection between language and self-awareness (1.6.8–9); in the second, there is a vague sense of time, place, desire (1.6.23–24); in the third, a threshold is crossed when the child speaks and realizes that its period of speechlessness is ending. Self-consciousness is not only an awareness of being located at a stage of development but initially at least a sense of dislocation that is expressed inwardly and subjectively. The appearance of memory marks the end of the infant's sense of timelessness, just as in scripture the writing of the historical record takes the first couple out of paradise and into the world of time.

34. *Conf.* 1.6.18–20; *De Quant. An.* 22.39, CSEL 89.179–180.

35. Although how the infant can be aware of this without any genuine self-awareness is unclear.

36. *Conf.* 1.7.20–22. Acutely observant, Augustine may have concluded that infants recognize different types of facial expression; for the contemporary psychological literature, see Oatley (1992), 94–98.

37. *Conf.* 1.6.27–29. These "signs" mimic his desires, although the similarity that he will subsequently find between reality and language is only apparent.

38. The implicit contrast is with learning Greek, which proceeds by coercion. Quintilian took the opposite view, arguing that Latin speakers would learn their language without instruction; therefore, it was best if children started off with Greek; *Inst. Orat.* 1.1.12–14. The echoes of Quintilian in *Conf.* 1 are not noted in Keseling (1954); a full review would be useful. One clue that Augustine depends on previous accounts of language learning is the omission of any mention of Punic.

39. Banniard (1992), 100. Quintilian places great weight on nurses' diction; *Inst. Orat.* 1.1.4–5.

40. *In Io. Eu. Tract.* 7.23, CSEL 36.80–81.31–35. Augustine may have anticipated a point later established by experiment, namely that infants of two months or more regulate their emotions in relation to their mothers' expression of feeling; see Trevarthen (1984), 142–145.

41. Cf. Quint., *Inst. Orat.* 1.1.22. Emotion plays a large role in this gesturing; he expressed his feelings, but he did not know whether they were effectively transmitted; 1.8.10–14. He also suggests that there is a relationship, if ill-defined, between such linguistic gestures and the acoustic or imagistic patterns that produce meaning in the mind; later, he adds writing to this class of gesture.

42. A view forcefully anticipated in *De Mag.*, though not in a developmental context; see Chapter 6. In general, Augustine's view of the earliest phases of speech acquisition is close to the position of Lev Vygotsky (1978), 107, who remarked that "gesture is the initial visual sign that contains a child's future writing, as an acorn contains the future oak."

43. Bruner (1983), 31–32. Not, in any case, an original idea; cf. Quint., *Inst. Orat.* 1.1.5; 1.1.16 (based on Chrysippus). There is no parallel for Augustine's account of learning to speak by imitating the speech gestures of adults; Quintilian's advice begins with teaching children to recognize letters, (1.1.24–26) and penmanship (1.1.27–29). See also *Inst. Orat.* 1.3.1, where, after memory, the best sign of intelligence is a child's ability to imitate what he is taught (again at 10.2.1); the contrast is with gestures such as walking. On mimesis generally, see Morrison (1982), 59–60.

44. See also *Ep.* 166.17, CSEL 44.570.7–12.

45. Cf. Quint., *Inst. Orat.* 1.1.31, 1.1.36, where it is stressed that memorization is important at an age at which higher reasoning is not possible. In contrast, Plotinus believes that children are often better than adults at remembering because their attention is directed to a few things rather than many—a view that makes

childlike memory a first stage in meditative concentration; *Enn.* 4.6.3, vol. 2, 133.21–24.

46. *Conf.* 1.8.10–14; on the manuscript and syntactical difficulties, see O'Donnell (1992), vol. 2, 57–58. Augustine speaks of relations between words and things, in contrast to Quintilian, who focuses on the memorization of syllables through reading, writing, and oral repetition; only when the vocal and visual recognition of syllables is assured can the child proceed to building words; *Inst. Orat.,* 1.1.30–32.

47. I.e., of their desire "to seek, possess, reject, or flee."

48. *Conf.* 1.8.18–20: "Ita uerba in uariis sententiis locis suis posita et crebro audita quarum rerum signa essent paulatim conligebam measque iam uoluntates edomito in eis signis ore per haec enuntiabam."

49. This includes vocalization, although, like Quintilian, he does not at this point discuss the problems of reading aloud; *Inst. Orat.,* 1.1.32–35. For my suggestion that this occurs in *De Dial.,* see Chapter 6, "Dialectic."

50. In his terms, this is the problem of how it is that we know what we know, even when the source of our knowledge is provably beyond our experience.

51. A point noted by Wittgenstein in a much-quoted statement in which he claims that Augustine "describes the learning of human language as if the child came into a strange country and did not understand the language . . . that is, as if it already had a language, only not this one . . . or, as if the child could already *think,* only not yet speak"; *Philosophical Investigations,* trans. G. E. M. Anscombe (1953), par. 32, pp. 15–16. For a statement in favour of Augustine's view of language learning among children against Wittgenstein, see Fodor (1975), 64. The best of the numerous discussions are Alici (1976), 117–126, and Burnyeat (1987); cf. Hallett (1977), 108–109; G. Matthews (1992), 152–153; and Erneling (1993). For a comparable metaphor in Plotinus (closer in some respects to Wittgenstein than Augustine), see *Enn.* 5.1.1, vol. 2, 185–186.1–15.

52. See Morrison (1988), 72–76.

53. In his belief in the infant's capacity for linguistic competence, Augustine may have anticipated Noam Chomsky; see Fodor (1975), 58–64. Other possible comparisons include de Saussure; see Kelly (1975), who unfortunately does not deal with *Conf.*

54. There is just a suggestion of Piaget's stages of sensorimotor development associated with children under two years of age, although this stretches the evidence. These include (1) reflexes, such as sucking and making sounds (1.6.9–12 and 1.6.21, respectively); (2) focusing on the body and reacting vocally to sounds made by others (1.6.22–23); (3) secondary reactions to external objects or to reiterated movements by others (1.6.23 and, by implication, 1.7.7–19); (4) the coordination of secondary reactions to achieve simple goals (1.6.12–15; 1.7.12–20); (5) an interest in novel objects or events and in the orienting of goals around them (1.8.5–14); and (6) elementary problem-solving by anticipating movement and by an awareness of the independent existence of objects (1.8.14–20). On these dis-

tinctions, see in general Piaget (1952), (1954), and (1962); I draw on the summary in Ingram (1978), 261–262. For an attempt to read Piaget into Augustine, in my view unsuccessfully, see Dombrowski (1980), 128–130.

55. I.e., Vygotsky's distinction between internal and external speech in infants based on social conventions; (1978), 212, 218, 224–225, 243, and 249.

56. *Conf.* 1.6.23–26: "Et ecce paulatim sentiebam, ubi essem, et uoluntates meas uolebam ostendere eis, per quos implerentur, et non poteram, quia illae intus erant, foris autem illi nec ullo suo sensu ualebant introire in animam meam." Cf. 1.6.6–20, 1.7.10–12, 1.8.18–20.

57. E. Clark (1978), 87; see *Conf.* 1.8.13–18, where it would be more appropriate to speak of deictic gestures *(ex motu corporis)* than of deixis in terms of place, individuation, or reference.

58. See Bruner and Scaife (1975); for Augustine, *Conf.* 1.6.31–33 and 1.7.20–22.

59. See Bates et al. (1979); *Conf.* 1.6.29–31.

60. See Trevarthen and Hubley (1978), 183–184, 212–216, and *Conf.* 1.7.5–19, esp. 1.7.12: "Nam extirpamus et eicimus ista crescentes," where *ista* refers to sinless, i.e., thoughtless, play.

61. *Conf.* 1.8.10–14. For a summary of research in the area, see Bretherton and Beeghly (1982), 906–907.

62. A term I borrow from Forguson and Gopnik (1988). Cf. *De Mor. Eccles. Cath.* 2.8.11, *PL* 32.1349–50.

63. See Pramling (1988), 151.

64. On the difference between factual and nonfactual knowledge in children, see Abbeduto and Rosenberg (1985), 621–625, 636–640. Augustine's first use of *nescio* refers to factual situations (e.g., 1.6.5). In 1.6 and 1.7, "to know" means primarily to know a thing or a fact; by contrast, in 1.8 knowledge is also founded on semantic relations.

65. For a discussion, see Wellman (1988) and, for an opposing view, C. Johnson (1988).

66. Perner (1988), 167–168.

67. See Shultz (1980). For the developed version of intentionality, see my discussion of *De Trin.* 10.8, Chapter 9, "The Reader and the *Cogito.*"

68. Rist, "Augustine on Free Will" (1969), 421.

69. *Conf.* 1.9.5–6; for a brief review, see Pincherle (1955–57), 191–193.

70. On the other events of book 2, see "Self-Improvement," later in this chapter.

71. The milieu of Augustine's studies is vividly brought to life by Brown (1967), 19–39; on memorization, see 36–37. Other useful accounts include Bardy (1940), 1–34; Courcelle (1950), 49–52; O'Meara (1954), 20–60; and G. Bonner (1963), 36–41, the last judiciously reviewing the sources. The best documented synthesis remains Alfaric (1918), 1–38; the historical background is described by Marrou, *Saint Augustin* (1958), 3–157.

72. For his general view of the reader's talent, see Chapter 6, "Defining the Reader."

73. *Conf.* 1.9.30–31: "Non enim deerat, domine, memoria uel ingenium."

74. Ibid., 1.12.2–4: "Non amabam litteras . . . . . . nec faciebam ego bene: non enim discerem, nisi cogerer."

75. Ibid., 1.9.6–7, 16–19, 26–27. Cf. Quint. *Inst. Orat.* 1.3.14–18, where corporeal punishment is discouraged; on its widespread practice, see S. Bonner (1977), 143–145; on the social context, see Brown (1992), 51–54. Is Augustine here foreshadowing the severity of his later bishopric?

76. Possidius, *Vita* 1, *PL* 32.35: "et diligentia impensisque, secularibus litteris eruditus apprime."

77. The family property evidently consisted of a vineyard (*Conf.* 2.4.8) and a few fields (*Ep.* 126.7, *CSEL* 44.13.1: "paucis agellulis").

78. *Conf.* 1.9.35–41; 1.10.5–6. Cf. Quint., *Inst. Orat.* 1.3.10–13.

79. *Conf.* 1.10.7–9; cf. 1.19.10–14.

80. Cf. Quintilian, who notes that a clever child, even if ill-behaved, is preferable to one who is dull-witted; *Inst. Orat.* 1.3.2.

81. *Ep.* 93.13.51, *CSEL* 34/2.494.22–495.2, quoting a letter from his friend Vincentius: "'Cum optime,' inquis, 'te nouerim longe adhuc a fide Christiana sepositum et studiis olim deditum litterarum quietis et honestatis fuisse cultorem cumque postea conuersus ad Christianam fidem, ut ex multorum relatione cognoui, disputationibus legalibus operam dare.'"

82. *De Ord.* 2.12, *CCSL* 29, 127.20–22 and 128.38–40. For a reconstruction of Augustine's grammatical knowledge from indirect evidence, see Marrou, *Saint Augustin* (1958), 11–17, 20–26. However, Kaster (1988), 332, notes that "the supposedly normal pattern of schooling deduced from Aug. *Conf.* 1.9.14ff. and 13.20f. is notably at odds with Augustine's own teaching activity at Thagaste."

83. *S. de Dis. Chr.* 11.12, *CCSL* 46.219–220, 287–305; cf. *Sermo* 178.7.8, *PL* 38.964; Courcelle (1950), 84–85.

84. *S. de Dis. Chr.* 1.1, (*CCSL* 46.207.1–6).

85. *Conf.* 1.9.35–38; cf. Quint., *Inst. Orat.* 1.1.20. *Ludus* can mean "play" or "school"; see S. Bonner (1977), 56–57, 125, 136; on sources, Chadwick, *Saint Augustine* (1991), 12 n. 17, to which add Jerome, *Epp.* 81, 82.2–3.

86. There is a parallel in the discussion of Ishmael and Isaac; *In Io. Eu. Tract.* 11.12, *CCSL* 36.117–118; see also Courcelle (1950), 50 and n. 4; Rothfield (1981), 215–221.

87. Cf. Brown (1967), 68.

88. *Conf.* 8.6.26: "supra mensam lusoriam."

89. Ibid., 8.12.22: "in aliquo genere ludendi cantitare tale aliquid." Courcelle (1953), 208–209, sees a version of the "sorts bibliques," in which the *pueri* represent the lowest degree of the clergy. On play in the meaning of a text, see *Ep.* 82, *CSEL* 34/1.351–387, discussed by O'Connell (1978), 357–358; also *De Vera Rel.*

51.100, *CCSL* 32.252.5–6. On the pattern of play, see Morrison (1988), 72–89 and passim.

90. In the background of these ideas is the ancient notion of man or woman as the plaything of the gods; e.g., Plato, *Laws* 4.712B 1–2 and 7.803C–D, as well as Plotinus' sense of philosophical discussion as a kind of interplay, *Enn.* 3.8.1, vol. 1, 362.1–18.

91. The transition effectively implants into his childhood an axiom of Plotinian contemplation, i.e., transcending the senses, while omitting the typically ancient division between students capable of only manual crafts and those capable of seeking higher knowledge; cf. *Enn.* 3.8.4–5, vol. 1, 366.43–47 and 366–367.1–8, respectively.

92. Cf. Quint., *Inst. Orat.* 1.1.17, speaking of children before their seventh year. Augustine reverses the priorities, though referring to himself at a later age.

93. The poverty of Augustine's mathematical and scientific education is perhaps overestimated by Marrou, *Saint Augustin* (1958), 136–141, 143–146, 248–251. His refutation of Manichaeism was based on his growing ability to perceive their cosmological doctrines as pseudo-science; see Chapter 2, "Manichaeism."

94. *Conf.* 1.13.3–6; see Semple (1950), 136–140.

95. *Conf.* 1.13.36–37; cf. Quint., *Inst. Orat.* 1.2.3–4. On the educated literary milieu of Madaura, see Alfaric (1918), 15–23.

96. Cf. *De Ord.* 2.12–13, *CCSL* 29.127–128.

97. *Conf.* 1.13.25–27: "Talis dementia honestiores et uberiores litterae putantur quam illae, quibus legere et scribere didici."

98. Ibid., 1.13.29–31: "Melior est prorsus doctrina illa prior. Nam ecce paratior sum obliuisci errores Aeneae atque omnia eius modi quam scribere et legere." Cf. Quint., *Inst. Orat.* 1.4.3, who links writing to speaking and reading to interpretation: "Nam et scribendi ratio coniuncta cum loquendo est, et enarrationem praecedit emendata lectio." For other references to the value of reading and writing among rhetoricians in late antiquity, see Quacquarelli (1972), 194–197.

99. The preferred poet of Africans; Romanelli (1955), 23–24.

100. *Conf.* 1.13.8–10: "Nam utique meliores, quia certiores, erant primae illae litterae, quibus fiebat in me et factum est et habeo illud, ut et legam, si quid scriptum inuenio, et scribam ipse, si quid uolo."

101. E.g., Quint., *Inst. Orat.* 1.1.19: "initia litterarum sola memoria constant"; 1.3.1: "Ingenii signum in paruis praecipuum memoria est." For a useful summary of Quintilian's views, see Gwynn (1926), 189–200; on memory devices, 190–192; cf. S. Bonner (1977), 165–166, 177, 190–191, 220, 253.

102. *Ep.* 166.17, *CSEL* 44.570.11–17.

103. Although he admired his adolescent friend Simplicius, who was capable, it would appear, of reciting Virgil and Cicero forwards and backwards; *De Nat. et Or. An.* 4.7.9, *CSEL* 60.389.7–16.

104. He did not overcome this attitude until 380–81, according to his reflections

on his unanswered dedication to Hierius. All the same, he claims that it did not matter to him that he excelled in competitive performances; *Conf.* 1.17.11–13; cf. Quint., *Inst. Orat.* 1.2.9.

105. See also Quint., *Inst. Orat.* 2.10.5–6; for a comment, Gwynn (1926), 204–206.

106. Cf. *De Util. Cred.* 1.2, *CSEL* 25/1.4.10–11: "quae mihi puerulo a parentibus insita erat."

107. Cf. Prendiville (1972), 57–61, although his remarks are limited to *Conf.* 8; for current applications, see Connerton (1989), 22–25, 29–31.

108. *Conf.* 1.15.6–10; *Ep.* 21.1–2, *CSEL* 34/1.49–51. The relevance of the point is driven home in *De Trin.* 13.20, *CCSL* 50a.418.33–419.59, where Augustine states that anyone who has merely committed to memory the sounds of the words of his faith (in the way in which a person not knowing Greek might memorize Greek words) does not utilize an inner "trinity" of memory, will, and thought but just a relationship based on the senses (i.e., on signs). However, here he is concerned with the moral vacuum in which much ancient education took place (*Conf.* 1.15.11–12; cf. Quint., *Inst. Orat.* 1. 9–20), despite his insistence as a teacher of rhetoric on traditional memory exercises. These are described at Cassiciacum and in the story of Alpyius, ibid., 6.9.14, where his friend, mistaken for a thief while rehearsing some memorized lines, may symbolize the aimless peregrinations of Augustine's untutored soul; see Chapter 3, "Alypius."

109. Psychological research suggests that this is the primary goal of reading in modern culture; see Nell (1988), 73–195. The ascetic can be absorbed into the aesthetic, as in Ingarden, *Literary Work* (1973), 24–25, and *Cognition* (1973), 187–200; or its autonomy can be insisted upon, as in Burke (1961), 43–171, and Harpham (1987), 3–18, 107–134. Augustine opts for the latter position.

110. For discussions of these texts, see Chapters 6 and 7.

111. *Conf.* 1.13.6–8; Ps. 77:39.

112. Ibid., 1.13.22–23. O'Donnell (1992), vol. 2, 79, notes the "literal citation" from *Aen.* 6.456–457, adding: "He says thereby not merely 'for the dead Dido,' but 'for the dead Dido as incorporated in the text of the *Aeneid*.' It was not just a story or a figure of myth that appealed to him, but a text: the authorized version." On the conflict between literary artistry and theology, see O'Meara (1963), 254–256. Although Augustine cites Virgil, he may also have in mind Horace, *Ars Poetica* 128–135.

113. Thus forcing himself on the woman who is the object of his desire; Terence, *Eunuchus* 583–591; for Augustine's version of the text and its commentaries, see O'Donnell (1992), vol. 2, 88–89; for a sensitive discussion, see Bennett (1988), 57–58. However, in bks. 7–8 Augustine finds his way out of his difficulties, not by appropriating any single classical text, but by applying notions of figuration to the inner and outer enactments of his life within God's design. Against a strong reading of classical influences, the play, the reperformance by the student, and the

commentary are also examples of overlapping "signs of words," whose indirect force is described in *De Dial.* and *De Mag.*

114. In this he hints at something new in ancient criticism, the idea that the outer reading of a text can conflict with the manner in which the reader is predestined to interpret it.

115. *De Util. Cred.* 6.13, *CSEL* 25.18–19. See Fichter (1982), 49, and, for an extensive analysis of Augustine's use of Virgil, Bennett (1988), 47–48, 57–68.

116. He notes that he did not offer his love to God but to a book; *Conf.* 1.13.19.

117. If he learned Homer in the original; Hagendahl (1967), 445, is justifiably sceptical. It is possible, therefore, that the question of translation plays an underground role in this description, just as it surfaces about the same time in *De Doct. Christ.*

118. Which includes laws as well as a range of actions from the trivial level of the teacher's rod to the exemplary sacrifice of a martyr; *Conf.* 1.14.15–19.

119. Ibid., 1.13.40–43: "At si quaeram, quibus litteris scribatur Aeneae nomen, omnes mihi, qui haec didicerunt, uerum respondent secundum id pactum et placitum, quo inter se homines ista signa firmarunt." Cf. Quint., *Inst. Orat.* 1.5.3.

120. For an outline of the notion of *lex aeterna,* see Schubert (1924), 3–20, and Madec, *BA* 6 (1976), n. 10, pp. 551–554.

121. Cf. *Conf.* 1.8.20–24, where he speaks of the "procellosa societas" and, along with it, parental authority.

122. An argument reproduced more extensively in *De Trin.;* see Chapter 9.

123. Hof (1964), 184–189, 191–195, attempts to unite Augustine's use of Rom. 2:14 ff., the notion of *conscientia,* and *lex naturalis.*

124. Cf. *De Octo Quaes.,* ed. de Bruyne, in *Miscellanea Agostiniana* (1931), 333.

125. *Conf.* 1.18.29–30: "Quam tu secretus es, habitans in excelsis in silentio." On silence in this context, cf. *En. in Ps.* 7.1, *CCSL* 38.36.30–31: "silentio . . . id est altissimo secreto."

126. A theme frequently evoked in the later writings; for references, see F. Jansen (1930), 287–292.

127. Rom. 2:15. Cf. *Conf.* 2.4.1–2 (the narrative of the theft of pears): "Furtum certe punit lex tua, domine, et lex scripta in cordibus hominum"; cf. 2.5.7, 13–14. For further parallels, see O'Donnell (1992), vol. 2, 128–129, and, for a discussion, Maxsein (1966), 93–103.

128. On the range of meanings, see Stelzenberger (1959), 47–86; also Fortin (1970), 143–145, and, on relations between *ordo* and *lex* in Augustine's earlier writings, Holte (1962), 221–231. Cf. *Enn.* 5.3.4, vol. 2, 210.1–3, where Plotinus states that we become like kings when we act in accord with intellect through writing inscribed in us like laws.

129. *Conf.* 1.19.17: "Istane est innocentia puerilis?"

130. The alternative view is that Augustine began with the plan of moving chronologically through *infantia, pueritia* (ibid., bk. 1), *adulescentia* (bk. 2), and

*iuuentus* (bks. 6–7), but later abandoned the idea. In a narrative segment so obviously well designed this seems unlikely, as noted by Pincherle (1955–57), 197–198, 202. Augustine still considered himself *iuuenis* when he began *De Trin.;* Pincherle (1976), 132 n. 35, and (1968). One of the assumptions of *Conf.* 1–9 is that the body and the soul both age, but at different rates and according to different principles; this accords with *De Quant. An.* 15.25–26, CSEL 89.161–163. On the link between the soul's growth and the individual's renewal in God's image, see *De Quant. An.* 3.4, CSEL 89.134–136; the chief influence is learning via study; ibid., 19.33 (pp. 172.1–3); cf. 22.40 (p. 180.14–22). Thoughts similar to *Conf.* 3 are admirably summed up in *Ep.* 140.2.3, CSEL 44.157.1–13, esp. 4–6.

131. *De Vera Rel.* 26.49, CCSL 32.218.31–34: "Iste dicitur nouus homo et interior et caelestis habens et ipse proportione non annis, sed prouectibus distinctas quasdam spiritales aetates suas."

132. For a parallel interpretation of bks. 2–4 and 10–13 as a programme of trinitarian thinking, see Kusch (1953), 147–183, which is convincing on individual points but overly schematic; on bks. 2–3 as illustrations of *superbia* and *curiositas,* see ibid., 151–156. A balanced commentary is de Capitani in *Le Confessioni I–II* (1984), 105–121.

133. *Conf.* 2.3.1–6, 11–15. On Patrick's economic circumstances as a *curiale* (Possidius, *Vita* 1.1), see Romanelli (1955), 19–21; G. Bonner (1963), 37–38. The problem of education and power is thoughtfully evoked by Brown (1992), 41–78, 126–146.

134. His morality was questionable; *Conf.* 9.8.5–6; cf. *Sermo* 9.12, CCSL 41.131.444–446.

135. *Conf.* 2.2.42–44; 2.3.60–66. In Milan, Monica wished him to marry, then to be baptized; 6.13.1–5. On Augustine's withdrawal from physical sexuality, see E. A. Clark (1986), 142–143, 152–157.

136. Pincherle (1955–57), 199–202.

137. For a convincing analysis of the pear theft and sexual symbolism, see Buchheit (1968); on the potential symbolism of fall/salvation and pear/fig tree, see Ferrari (1970), 240–241; also de Capitani in *Le Confessioni I–II* (1984), 108–119.

138. Burke (1961), 93–123.

139. *Conf.* 2.4.16–17: "ut essem gratis malus et malitiae meae causa nulla esset nisi malitia."

140. See F. Russell (1990), 698–699, 701–704.

141. As in the conspiracy of Catiline; *Conf.* 2.5.17–33; on its attraction for Augustine, see Hagendahl (1967), 482.

142. Because Augustine had turned his back on him; ibid., 2.3.33–34.

143. Ibid., 2.2.12–16; 2.3.22–29, 42–43, 68–69; cf. 2.3.55–56.

144. Ibid., 10.8.45–47: "Ibi mihi et ipse occurro meque recolo, quid, quando et ubi egerim quoque modo, cum agerem, affectus fuerim."

145. A similar example appears in *De Util. Cred.;* see Chapter 7, "Tradition and Beliefs."

146. Monica acts as a catalyst for this type of literary predestination; *Conf.* 2.3.27–28, 34–36.

147. Ibid., 3.3.16–25. Cf. 5.8.15–20, where Augustine states that he took no part in rowdy student "customs" in Carthage.

148. Cf. Weismann (1972), 134–166, who competently reviews the issues. One can compare the remarks on drama to Augustine's ethical thinking, in which he also moves in a different direction from Aristotle; see Beierwaltes (1981), 16–29, 34–40.

149. There are other examples; cf. on dance and pantomime, *De Doct. Christ.* 2.25, *CCSL* 32.60.7–11; *En. in Ps.* 32, en. 2, serm. 1, *CCSL* 38.247.18–21; on oral poetry, see *De Util. Cred.* 6.13, *CSEL* 25.18.

150. The focus shifts from the ear to the spectacle; *Conf.* 3.2.1; on the visual aspect, see O'Donnell (1992), vol. 2, 152–153. Augustine notes the change, *De Ciu. Dei* 2.4, *CCSL* 47.37.14–23; cf. *De Gen. ad Litt.* 12.22.47, *CSEL* 28/1.413; cf. Courcelle (1950), 52–55.

151. For a vivid evocation of these years and the role of rhetoric, see F. Jansen (1930), 282–287.

152. In this respect, the member of an audience resembles two other model recipients of signs, observers of likenesses and interpreters of gestures; see Chapter 6, "The Teacher."

153. Cf. *De Trin.* 13.3, *CCSL* 50a.387.6–25, where Augustine uses the example of an actor who offers to give a performance in which the thoughts and desires of his audience are revealed. The explanation is in terms of the "great expectation" in their minds; see also Quint., *Inst. Orat.* 6.1.9 ff.

154. *Conf.* 3.2.2–4: "Quid est, quod ibi homo uult dolere cum spectat luctuosa et tragica, quae tamen pati ipse nollet?"

155. *Sol.* 2.10.18, *CSEL* 89.68.2–20; for a discussion, see Chapter 5. This position, however, is abandoned in favour of the sterner moralism of *De Ciu. Dei* 1.32 and 2.8 (*CCSL* 47.32–33 and 40–41), where he distinguishes between comedies and tragedies produced mainly for entertainment and theatrical performances as an integral part of pagan religious ceremonies "commanded" by immoral gods. Cf. ibid., 2.26–27.

156. The literature on this topic is masterfully summarized by Feldmann (1975), vol. 1, 14–43. For subsequent studies, see Madec, *Saint Augustin et la philosophie* (1992), 17–20.

157. See Lapeyre (1931), 92–94.

158. Madec (1988), 46.

159. See Feldmann (1975), vol. 1, 381–393, 530–534.

160. For a philosophical reconstruction of the Ciceronian text, see Feldmann (1975), vol. 1, 77–100.

161. *Conf.* 3.4.1–14. Cf. *De Beata Vita* 1.4 and *De Util. Cred.* 8.20; Courcelle (1943–44), 156–158.

162. It is also a topos by which Augustine charts the passage from immature to mature reflection, as in the case of the youthful Trygetius and Licentius; *C. Acad.*

1.1, *CCSL* 29.5.93–98; 3.4 (p. 39.12–17). Also, could he be unaware that Cicero wrote the book on his retirement from public life following Tullia's death?

163. See O'Connell (1972), 40–42.

164. Nock (1933), 179; see also Brown (1967), 40–45, and, on conversions within Jewish and Christian tradition, Haas (1980), 225–229, with a review of the literature, 225 n. 1.

165. Nock (1939), 177.

166. Nock (1933), 184; but see Préaux (1957), 315–316, who finds an anticipation in Plato's *Phaedo*. The connection between the later ancient dialogue and conversion is explored by Schäublin (1985); on the *Hortensius,* see 123–125.

167. Madec, *Saint Augustin et la philosophie* (1992), 21–26, succinctly traces these developments.

168. Ibid., 17, with an account of the relevant literature, 17–20; cf. Courcelle (1950), 58–60.

169. See Madec, *BA* 6 (1976), n. 11, pp. 554–557: "Souvenirs de l''Hortensius'''; an early study is Ohlmann (1897).

170. *C. Acad.* 1.1.4, *CCSL* 29.5.94–98.

171. See Madec (1969). A favorite maxim is: "Beati omnes esse uolumus"; Testard (1958), vol. 1, 209 n. 1.

172. *Conf.* 3.4.1; compare this to the manner in which he approaches scripture, 3.5.1–5.

173. See also *De Beata Vita* 2.10, *CCSL* 29.71.92–104. On Augustine's employment of *affectus,* see Feldmann (1975), vol. 1, 416–425.

174. See also Nock (1933), 181–183.

175. For this reason, one must be more cautious than Feldmann is in speaking of the *Conf.* as "a Christian protreptic," while nonetheless admitting the relevance of his argumentation, vol. 1, 103–208.

176. For a summary, see Madec, *BA* 6 (1976), n. 2, pp. 554–557, supplemented by Doignon (1981), 810–813. Cf. Testard (1958), vol. 1, 19–39; vol. 2, 1–2, 4–5, 7–8, 10–11, 16.

177. Cf. O'Meara, *The Young Augustine* (1954), 57–60.

178. Gwynn (1926), 118–119.

179. Doignon (1984–85), 117 and n. 14, and, on the classical background, Zepf (1959), 106–110, 114–116, 124–130.

180. *Conf.* 8.7.13–17: "Quoniam multi mei anni mecum effluxerant—forte duodecim anni—ex quo ab undeuicensimo anno aetatis meae lecto Ciceronis Hortensio excitatus eram studio sapientiae et differebam contempta felicitate terrena ad eam inuestigandam uacare."

181. Cf. Hök (1960), 105–108; Holte (1962), 29–44; Doignon (1981), 813–816.

182. E.g., *Conf.* 1.13 (Virgil).

183. Hagendahl (1967), 484, 571.

184. For a comparison, see Testard (1958), vol. 1, 11–48, 131–162, and 174–176, together with the revisions of Hagendahl (1967), 486–497, 578–588. A similar conclusion can be drawn from the analysis of Doignon (1981), 807–810.

185. For a parallel use of Stoic sources, see Chapter 6, "The Teacher."

186. Hagendahl (1967), 489.

187. Courcelle (1950), 60–62; for an outline of Augustine's acquaintance with the Bible from the time of this episode until 391, see Douais (1893), 62–81, and la Bonnardière, "L'initiation" (1986).

188. *Sermo* 51.5, *PL* 38.336: "Loquor uobis, aliquando deceptus, cum primo puer ad diuinas Scripturas ante uellem afferre acumen discutiendi, quam pietatem quaerendi: ego ipse contra me peruersis moribus claudebam ianuam Domini mei: cum pulsare deberem, ut aperiretur, addebam, ut clauderetur. Superbus enim audebam quaerere, quod nisi humilis non potest inuenire."

189. *Conf.* 3.5.5–7; see di Capua (1931), 614–622, and Vogels (1930), 412–413, where related statements are collected and discussed.

190. *Conf.* 3.4.4–5. On the possibility of a mildly disdainful use of *cuius* in quotations of Virgil, see O'Donnell (1992), vol. 2, 77; on this passage, ibid., 164. On *quidam* as a style of citation, see the summary of Hagendahl (1967), 697–698. For other examples of indirection as a form of disrespect, see Courcelle (1950), 41–42 and nn. Augustine's attentive reading of Cicero may have been the exception rather than the rule; yet if he saw the danger of vanity in reading the pagan thinker, he also sensed the possibility of moral benefits, as he suggests between the lines of his dismissive summary in *Ep.* 118.2, *CSEL* 34/2.666.1–3.

191. Cicero, *Brutus* 320: "Summum illud suum studium remisit, quo a puero fuerat incensus."

192. Peters (1986), stresses the theme of curiosity in *Conf.* 3.5–10.

193. See also Laín Entralgo (1970), an enduring review of the issues.

194. *Ep.* 118.2, *CSEL* 34/2.666.1–3: "Ecce enim tot dialogi lecti si ad uidendum finem et capessendum omnium actionum tuarum nihil te adiuuerunt, quid prosunt?"

195. Cf. Peters (1984), who sees the theme reappearing as a response to Manichaean interpretations of Genesis at *Conf.* 11.10 *et seq.*

196. Nock (1933), 182: "It is noteworthy how often philosophers use the metaphor of initiation or of a series of initiations to describe the apprehension of a philosophical truth: its attainment is an *epopteia*, a seeing."

197. Auerbach (1965), 25–81.

198. *Conf.* 1.1.4–5: "quia superbis resistis [1 Peter 5:5]."

199. Ibid., 3.4.18–19: "Sunt qui seducant per philosophiam." Cf. 2 Col. 2:8.

200. *Conf.* 7.9.4–19.

## 2. Intellectual Horizons

1. Attitudes toward Manichaeism since the sixteenth century are reviewed by Ries (1957) and (1959). Earlier studies of the North African movement are superseded by Decret (1970, 1978), with the exception of Alfaric (1918), 73–358, which remains fundamental. Good general introductions are found in A. Jackson (1932), 3–20; Puech (1949) and (1972); Widengren (1965); Ries (1967); also

Schaeder (1927) and Gnoli (1987). Among specialized studies, there are illuminating pages in Frend (1953); Menasce (1956); Brown (1967), 46–60, and (1969); and Courcelle (1968), 60–78; for a comparative perspective, see Asmussen (1965) and the perceptive study of Lieu (1992). A sensitive interpretation of the "antimanichaean" elements in the *Confessions* is Vecchi (1965), 103–115, and Mayer, *Die antimanichäische Epoche* (1974), 62–96, the latter in relation to signs.

2. He may still have been a fellow-traveller during his first sojourn in Rome, in 383–84; Courcelle (1950), 78.

3. Succinctly summarized by Feldmann (1975), vol. 1, 3–5.

4. See Courcelle (1950), 238–245, and Frend (1954), 861–866; also Ries, "La Bible" (1964), 317–320. On Julian's argument against his notions of reproduction, see Clark, "Vitiated Seeds" (1986), 297–319.

5. On the parallel between Hellenistic *sapientia* and Manichaean *sophia,* see Ries in *Le Confessioni III–IV* (1984), 8–9.

6. See Koenen (1978), 165, 168, and 179.

7. In his view, their message was more convincing to those who knew the gospels; *C. Ep. Fund.* 5, CSEL 25/6. 197.19–22.

8. Courcelle (1968), 65–67, and, for a somewhat fuller review, Allgeier (1930), 3–13. Augustine's relationship to Jewish thought and religious practices merits a serious review, which cannot be attempted here.

9. For a review of the issues, see Mandouze (1968), 165–242, and Lawless (1987), 45–58.

10. Douais (1894), 110–135, traced the knowledge of the Bible in Faustus of Mileu that is relevant to monastic discipline.

11. Ries (1961), 231–233.

12. A lesson that was not forgotten; *De Mor. Eccles. Cath.* 1.2.3, PL 32.1311.

13. E.g., ibid., 1.1.1 (cols. 1309–11); cf. *In Io. Eu. Tract.* 1.16, CCSL 36.9.17–18: "Solent enim delirantes dicere, et cum repressi fuerint et resulsi, quasi de scripturis proferunt, dicentes."

14. Both lettered and unlettered are manipulated; *De Gen. c. Man.* 1.1.1, PL 34.173: "Cum uero illi et doctos litteris et indoctos errore suo persequantur, et cum promittunt ueritatem, a ueritate conentur auertere."

15. Cf. *In Io. Eu. Tract.* 29.4, CCSL 36.285–286.

16. *Conf.* 3.6.1–6. Cf. *De Mor. Eccles. Cath.* 1.10.16, PL 32.1317–18.

17. "Loquaces muti"; *Conf.* 1.4.17. On the application to the Manichaeans, see the learned notes of O'Donnell (1992), vol. 2, 26–28 and 177; and vol. 3, 75–76. For the Manichaean source in the *Kephalaia,* see Ries in *Le Confessioni III–IV* (1984), 11. However, Augustine is equally critical of his former loquacity, e.g., *Conf.* 4.2.1–2: "Docebam in illis annis artem rhetoricam et uictoriosam loquacitatem uictus cupiditate uendebam"; cf. 9.2.1–3 and 8.5.5–6 (on Victorinus).

18. Ries, "La Bible" (1964), 321–325, summarizes the biblical themes in recently discovered Manichaean writings; these are explored in detail by Koenen (1978), 161–176.

19. An error that he avoided by adapting the Western Aramaic script which was used for texts in Syriac, Middle Persian, Parthian, Sogdian, and Old Turkish; see Ries (1967), 158. On the formative role of Mani in developing the notion of scripture between the early Judeo-Christian period and Islam, see Smith (1993), 45–59; on the Manichaean distrust of oral tradition, see Tardieu (1987), 128–129.

20. Widengren (1965), 74. A recent review of the discoveries is Gnoli (1987); an excellent overview of texts accessible to North African Manichaeans is contained in Decret (1978), vol. 1, 239–346. A comparative synthesis is presented by Lieu (1992), chaps. 1, 7–9, while the literary asceticism of the *electi* is succinctly outlined by Vööbus (1958), 128–130. On the penetration of Manichaeism into Egypt, see Stroumsa (1983), 187–197.

21. Quispel, "Mani. The Apostle" (1972), 668. Augustine, *De Haer.* 46.16, *CCSL* 46.318.166, notes: "Vnde seipse in suis litteris Iesu Christi apostolum dicit [Mani]." Cf. Koenen (1978), 167–176. Augustine rejected the anti-Hebraism of the Manichaeans; he was nonetheless aware of the Jewish refusal to accept the divinity of Christ; see Blumenkranz (1958), 227–228.

22. See Klimheit (1982) and generally Mair (1988), 50–53.

23. Widengren (1965), 109. Cf. *C. Ep. Fund.* 23, *CSEL* 25/1.220.29–221.8.

24. E.g., *De Natura Boni* 44, *CSEL* 25/2.881–884.

25. These are identified with a commentary by Feldmann (1989).

26. *Cod. Theod.* 16.5.7 (8 May 381) and 16.5.9 (31 March 382).

27. *C. Faustum* 13.6, *CSEL* 25/1.384.12–13. However, is there any evidence to support the view of Decret (1989), 126, who states: "L'auditeur Augustin fut un remarquable fureteur des bibliothèques manichéennes africaines de son temps?"

28. Translated into Greek and Coptic in the fourth century; on its christological emphasis, see Ries, "Jésus-Christ" (1964), 441–452. Decret (1989), 130, notes that the remarkable feature of the ms. of Tebessa is "l'accumulation des [loci] scripturaires"; cf. 130–135 and nn.

29. Decret (1989), 127.

30. *Retr.* 2.8, *CCSL* 57.97.5; *De Mor. Eccles. Cath.* 2.19.71, *PL* 32.1375.

31. *C. Fel.* 2.22, *CSEL* 25/2.852.19–26; cf. Lieu (1988), 154–155.

32. *De Haer.* 46.10, *CCSL* 46.315.89–90.

33. Puech (1949), 66, my trans. Cf. Alfaric (1918), 270.

34. One reason is that the notion of unethical eloquence is a topos, e.g., at *Ep.* 118.26, *CSEL* 34/2.690.4–5, where he speaks of the "big-mouthed" teachers *(litteriones)* who exaggerate the reputation of Anaxagoras because of the "literary antiquity" *(propter litteratam uetustatem)* of his reputation.

35. As in his anti-Donatist and anti-Pelagian writings, Augustine may have adopted a refutation procedure here that was calculated to appeal to less educated readers; cf. A. C. de Veer, *BA* 31.4 (1968), n. 49, p. 835.

36. *De Util. Cred.* 1.2, *CSEL* 25/1.4.14–19.

37. A standard accusation of anti-Christian writers, e.g., the non-Christians Celsus and Porphyry and the heterodox Christian Marcion.

38. See Courcelle (1968), 63–65.

39. *De Util. Cred.* 1.2, *CSEL* 25/1.21–22; cf. *De Dua. An.* 11, *CSEL* 25/1.65.19–66.11.

40. The classic account, despite overstatements, remains Alfaric (1918), 279–320.

41. *Secundini Epistula CSEL* 25/2.894–895.

42. Vööbus (1958), 130–135.

43. Stroumsa (1986), 156, ably discusses the issues. Augustine's views obviously changed over the years. In 386, writing to Hermogenianus, he advocated restricted access; *Ep.* 1, *CSEL* 34/1.1.8–14. Yet in 390, replying to Maximus, a teacher in Madaura, he criticized the secret worship of Bacchus; *Ep.* 17.4, *CSEL* 34/2.43.9–14. He summed up his position in the same year in *De Vera Rel.* 1.1, *CCSL* 32.187.1–17.

44. E.g., *C. Ep. Fund.* 5, *CSEL* 25/1.197.5–10: "Uideamus igitur, quid me doceat Manichaeus, et potissimum illum consideremus librum, quem Fundamenti epistulam dicitis, ubi totum paene, quod creditis, continetur. Ipsa enim nobis illo tempore miseris quando lecta est, inluminati dicebamur a uobis." I assume that *nobis* is dative, indicating that the *Epistula* was read *to* them, whence they were "enlightened" by the others. For a careful reconstruction, see Feldmann (1975), vol. 1, 239–357.

45. E.g., *C. Ep. Fund.* 23, *CSEL* 25/1.5–6.

46. Suggested by ibid., 5 (p. 198.7–10).

47. Ibid., (p. 198.20–24): "Si autem aliquid inde manifestum pro Manichaeo legeris, nec illis nec tibi [credam]: illis [i.e., Catholicis], quia de te mihi mentiti sunt; tibi autem, quia eam scripturam mihi profers, cui per illos credideram, qui mihi mentiti sunt."

48. Ibid., chaps. 9, 11, 12, 13.

49. *C. Fel.* 1.1, *CSEL* 25/2.801.17–20: "'Haec sunt salubria uerba ex perenni ac uiuo fonte: quae qui audierit et iisdem primum crediderit, deinde quae insinuata sunt custodierit.'" Cf. *C. Ep. Fund.* 14, *CSEL* 25/1.211.8–14.

50. *C. Faustum* 33.9, *CSEL* 25/1.796.28–797.1.

51. E.g., *C. Ep. Fund.* 5, *CSEL* 25/1.199.4–6: "Lege mihi iam, si potes, in euangelio, ubi Manichaeus apostolus dictus es, uel in aliquo alio libro."

52. Ibid., 14 (p. 211.25–27): "Offundit nebulas inperitis, primum pollicens rerum certarum cognitionem, postea et incertarum imperans fidem." Cf. *De Haer.* 46.12, *CCSL* 46.316–317.118–138.

53. *Secundini Epistula CSEL* 25/2.899.17: "Illud tamen notum facio tuae sagacissimae bonitati, quia sunt quaedam res, quae exponi sic non possunt, ut intellegantur; excedit enim diuina ratio mortalium pectora." In this respect, Augustine's criticism of the Manichaeans echoes Plotinus' severe rejection of gnosticism; *Enn.*, 2.9, vol. 1, 203–232.

54. *De Ag. Chr.* 28.30, *CSEL* 41.130.16–18. Yet there is no doubt that these existed; for an authoritative summary based mainly on *C. Faustum,* see Tardieu (1987), 128–145.

55. *Secundini Epistula* CSEL 25.899.24–900.4: "Quis autem admittat inter diuina praecidi, scilicet nisi figuram facias interpretantis ad auditorem, quia ab hoc uerba praeciduntur et in illo conponuntur? Et quamuis tractator multa dixerit, quae teneat apud se auditor, tamen a tractatore non recesserunt."

56. Hebblethwaite (1985), 513.

57. *C. Fel.*, CSEL 25/2, referred to in the text by chapter and paragraph; on the dating, see Decret (1970), 78 n. 2.

58. For a discussion, see Decret (1970), 104–115.

59. *De Mor. Eccles. Cath.* 1.1.2, PL 32.1311: "Sed quoniam duae maxime sunt illecebrae Manichaeorum, quibus decipiuntur incauti, ut eos uelint habere doctores; una, cum Scripturas reprehendunt, uel quas male intelligunt uel quas male intelligi uolunt; altera, cum uitae castae et memorabilis continentiae imaginem praeferunt."

60. Menasce (1956), 80–83.

61. See the intensely spiritual rhetoric of *Contra Secundinum* 2, CSEL 25/2.906–908.

62. Eloquently summarized by Brown (1967), 61–64; cf. Brown (1992), 45–47. For an excellent account of the forces directing Augustine toward the monastic life, see Mandouze (1968), 165–242.

63. *C. Acad.* 2.2, CCSL 29.19.9–11.

64. *De Dua. An.* 9.11, CSEL 25/1.65–66.

65. But see the evidence from the ms. of Tebessa assembled by Decret (1989), 143–150.

66. Frend (1954), 865, sees the letter as evidence of Manichaeism's survival, despite Donatism.

67. *Ep.* 236.3, CSEL 57.525.

68. Ibid., 236.2 (pp. 524–525).

69. Anticipating Islam? See Tardieu (1981), 85; cf. Stroumsa (1983).

70. Classical topoi are discussed by Carena (1967).

71. Cf. Nolte (1939), 19–20, 23.

72. For a similar theme, *Ep.* 2 CSEL 34/1.3–4, written to Zenobius in 386.

73. Yet he was unable to draw nourishment from "books and poetry" on his own; *Conf.* 4.7.6–9.

74. His Manichaean friends played a similar role in Milan; ibid., 6.6.46–50.

75. For a summary of these, see Vööbus (1958), 115–130. The implied contrast is with Christian monasticism; see Folliet (1961).

76. On the possible composition of the group and the suggestion that they preceded the community at Cassiciacum, see Mandouze (1968), 125 nn. 5–6, 126 nn. 1–4, 193 n. 1.

77. *De Mor. Eccles. Cath.* 1.31–32, PL 32.1337–39.

78. On the dream's context, see Dulaey (1973), 158–165, and Ferrari (1975), 197–201; on the interpretation of the wooden ruler as *regula fidei,* see Ferrari, "The Dreams of Monica" (1979), 14–15. The range of senses of *regula* in Augustine is fully analysed by Mayer (1991), 131–153; on *regula fidei* as the doctrine of *traditio*

*Christi* among post-apostolic authors, see Congar (1967), 26–30. Poque (1984), 483–485, argues that at the source of Augustine's image is a tool employed by a carpenter, a mason, or a stone-cutter, possibly a *chorobates,* a levelling device measuring about 1.40 m. On the analogous notion of the *regula ueritatis,* see A. C. de Veer, *BA* 31.4 (1968), n. 48, pp. 832–834.

79. The play on teaching and learning recalls *De Mag.;* see Chapter 6, "The Teacher."

80. On the connection between the interpretive possibilities in biblical texts *(exercitatio legentium)* and the rule of faith *(fidei regula),* as the standard against which they are to be measured, see *De Ciu. Dei* 11.32, *CCSL* 48.352.25–31.

81. As Augustine acknowledged, after his bookish conversion, *Conf.* 8.12.52– 54: "Conuertisti enim me ad te, ut nec uxorem quaererem nec aliquam spem saeculi huius stans in ea regula fidei, in qua me ante tot annos ei reuelaueras."

82. On the chronological problems in Augustine's account of astrology in the *Conf.,* see Pellegrino, *Les Confessions* (1960), 118–120 n. 2.

83. *Ep.* 138.3, *CSEL* 44.128–129.

84. For a survey of Augustine's views on astrology, see de Vreese (1933). The statements in Augustine's other writings relevant to the passages examined below are analysed by Hendrikx (1954), 114–129.

85. See *Ep.* 55.4.7, *CSEL* 34/2.176–177.

86. Augustine's disagreement with Manichaean astrology also resulted from a broader acquaintance with mainstream astronomical writings; see Alfaric (1918), 231–238. It is difficult to know how great their influence was on his thinking before 401.

87. On the Jewish and Christian origins, see Dihle (1982), 68–98.

88. *De Ciu. Dei* 5.9–11, *CCSL* 47.136–142; *Ep.* 246, *CSEL* 57.583–585.

89. *CCSL* 44a.67–69; on the episode of the twins, see pp. 68–69.32–44. For a vigorous restatement of his opposition, see *De Gen. ad Litt.* 2.17–18, *CSEL* 28.59–62.

90. Koenen (1978), 167–187, based on the Cologne Mani Codex, replacing earlier views.

91. Grondijs (1954), 395–407, summarizes the chief components. Put briefly, the stage was set through the elemental conflict of God and matter, i.e., light and darkness (*C. Faustum* 11.1, *CSEL* 25/1.313–314; *De Haer.* 46.7, *CCSL* 46.314.39– 54). Astrology entered the picture when God, having permitted the prince of darkness to overcome his son, created primeval man, and through him undertook a rescue (or redemption) of the particles of light entrapped in matter—a process by which the once divine souls of men would be released from their material bodies. This was interpreted as the meaning of Christ's life and death. The principal instruments of the recovery were the sun and moon, to which prayers were addressed, whereas the planets and signs of the zodiac obeyed the laws of the material world. Manichaean astrology simplistically located the twelve signs among some five worlds of darkness in an effort to forecast the disasters of the lower world.

92. See Widengren (1965), 69–72; Lieu (1992), 177–179; and, on the possible popular background, Frend (1953), 17–20. During the period in which he wrote the *Conf.*, Augustine spoke of "astrologers and other kinds of vain and evil diviners" among the charlatans who were to be kept out of church; *De Cat. Rud.* 7.11, *CCSL* 46.132.18–28.

93. *Ep.* 138.1.3, *CSEL* 44.128.11–12. On the traces of his teaching, see Beccaria (1959), 44–56, and, on Augustine's medical knowledge, for which we lack a thorough study, see the note of Agaësse and Solignac, *BA*, 48 (1972), n. 34, p. 710–711.

94. Cf. *C. Acad.* 1.6.17–18, *CCSL* 29.13, where Licentius facetiously suggests that the diviner Albericius can be considered "wise" because he occasionally reveals "a knowledge of divine and human matters."

95. Cf. *De Ciu. Dei* 5.2 and 5.5, *CCSL* 47.129–130 and 131–133, where Augustine discusses the case of two brothers, whose simultaneous illness and recovery led Hippocrates to deduce that they were twins. As they could not have been born at the same moment, he notes, how could they have had the same medical history? Also *De Ciu.* 5.6 (pp. 133–134). The reiteration of the example suggests a common source, which may be Plotinus, *Enn.*, 2.3.14, vol. 1, 159–160.

96. *Conf.* 4.3.35–44. Augustine may not have been fully convinced by Vindicianus; see Chadwick, *Saint Augustine* (1991), 55–56 n. 7; however, he elaborates the distinction about the same time at *De Doct. Christ.* 2.28.44, *CCSL* 32.63.45–48, where he acknowledges that both history and astrology are both related in books, though differently. In historical narratives, the authority relies on the factual content, whereas in progostications it relies on our faith in someone else's audacity to predict the future: "Historia facta narrat fideliter atque utiliter, libri autem haruspicem et quaeque similes litterae facienda uel obseruanda intendunt docere, monitoris audacia, non indicis fide." Needless to say, a variant of arbitrary interpretive procedure turns up in the final conversion scene, *Conf.* 8.12.

97. For a brief review of the documentation on Faustus, see Alfaric (1918), 83–85.

98. *Conf.* 3.4.32–33: "Et hoc solum me in tanta flagrantia refrangebat, quod nomen Christi non erat ibi."

99. Secundinus maintained that Augustine remained more interested in *sermo* than in *scientia*; *Secundini Epistula, CSEL* 25/2.895.13–15.

100. *Conf.* 5.3.15–19, 39–57. Cf. 1.5.7: "curiosa peritia." Peters (1986), 48–53, draws attention to the earlier appearance of the term in *De Mus.*, 6.13.39 and *Conf.* 3.3.2.

101. Ries (1963), 208; Tardieu (1987), esp. pp. 123–127, on Reformation Catholic and Protestant theologians.

102. *Conf.* 5.13.1–6; Courcelle (1950), 79 n. 1. On the "cercle milanais," see the useful note of Solignac, *BA* 14 (1962), n. 1, pp. 529–536.

103. P. Hadot (1971), 203–204.

104. See Holte (1962), 23–44.

105. On this question, Marrou, *Saint Augustin,* (1958), 237–275, remains fundamental; for a summary, see Solignac, *BA* 13 (1962), 88–92.

106. On the probable sources, see Solignac (1958), 126–128.

107. *Conf.* 5.10.24–27. Cf. Solignac, *BA* 13 (1962), 97–98 and 499 n. 2, who argues that Augustine saw in their doctrines only an apparent scepticism, which sheltered the spirituality of neoplatonic doctrines from Stoic and Epicurean "materialism." If this was the case, it may have been a retrospective view.

108. For a comparison of the philosophical formation of Ambrose and Augustine, see above all Madec (1977), 551–559.

109. Courcelle (1950), 106–138, expressing what Madec (1985), 51, calls "an excess of precision." For other illustrations of borrowings by Ambrose from Plotinus, see Courcelle (1956), P. Hadot (1956), and Solignac (1956); cf. Ries, "La Bible" (1964), 312–313; Madec (1974), 66–71, 292–293; and McCool (1959); cf. O'Meara (1954), 118–121. Scholars are now agreed that both thinkers influenced Augustine's ideas.

110. See Ries (1963), 203–207, on the transition and the scholarship related to it.

111. For a cogent summary, see Madec, *Saint Augustin et la philosophie* (1992), 21–26.

112. In bk. 11 he attacks this distinction from another angle in his explanation of our experiential understanding of time; see Chapter 8, "Time."

113. Cf. *Sol.* 2.14.26, *CSEL* 89.80–81.

114. On the problems within Augustine's chronology of these years, see the judicious remarks of Courcelle (1950), 43–45.

115. Ibid., 155 n. 2, where Courcelle notes a distinction in terminology between *libri ecclesiastici* and *codices* (*Conf.* 6.11.11, 15). However, this is not evidence of "lecture à deux" with Plotinus and Ambrose, but, as is more likely, a reference to two different sorts of Christian text, commentary and scripture.

116. The change is mirrored in *Ep.* 5, *CSEL* 34.11.9–11, from Nebridius in 388, and in letters such as *Epp.* 13.1 (p. 30.2–11) and 21.3 (p. 51.7–11); in the last, he writes to Valerius in 391 regretting the lack of free time "for prayer and reading" before his ordination, after which he intends to spend his leisure hours "becoming thoroughly acquainted with sacred scripture."

117. *Conf.* 4.16, *CCSL* 27.54.1–3; cf. *De Util. Cred.* 4.13, *CSEL* 25.17.20–23. Possibly the translation of Marius Victorinus; see Solignac, *BA* 13 (1962), 87 n. 1; sources in O'Donnell (1992), vol. 2, 265.

118. *Conf.* 4.16.6–7: "Legi . . . solus et intellexi."

119. Ibid., 4.16.9–10: "nihil inde aliud mihi dicere potuerunt, quam ego solus apud me ipsum legens cognoueram."

120. Ibid., 4.16.30–32: "Et quid mihi proderat, quod omnes libros artium, quas liberales uocant, tunc nequissimus malarum cupiditatum seruus per ipsum legi et intellexi, quoscumque legere potui?"

121. Ibid., 4.16.36–39: "Quidquid de arte loquendi et disserendi, quidquid de

dimensionibus figurarum et de musicis et de numeris sine magna difficultate nullo hominum tradente intellexi." Compare the intentional naïveté of this view with the irony at *De Util. Cred.* 7.17 (*CSEL* 25.21.24–25), quoted as the epigraph to this study.

122. *Conf.* 4.13.9–13; 4.15.51–52. For a brief summary of the three books and their possible sources, see Alfaric (1918), 221–225, Svoboda (1933), 10–16, and Solignac, *BA* 13 (1962), n. 16, pp. 670–673, notwithstanding the views of Cress (1976); for observations on Svoboda in the light of Plotinus' aesthetics, see O'Connell (1978), 14–20, 28–30. Early literature on the work is well summarized by Mayer (1969), 94–95 n. 6, and by O'Donnell (1992), vol. 2, 249–250. Ciceronian themes are traced by Testard (1958), vol. 1, 49–66; cf. Katô (1966), 233, who draws attention to the rather differently oriented Manichaean preoccupation with beauty; however, the possibility of dualist influence is rightly rejected by Fontanier (1989), 413–414. It is tempting to think of Hierius as a foil for Ambrose, whom Augustine praises for his eloquence, or for Victorinus, the rhetorician who converts; but the comparison is weakened by the fact that Augustine knew Hierius only by report.

123. The notion of friendship would be another potential connection to Cicero, whose influence is rightly stressed by Fontanier (1989), 416–418. A fourth element is the sensory nature of some beauty, on which see Tscholl (1964), 73–74, 76–80.

124. A similarity that remained in Augustine's thoughts; see e.g., *De Trin.* 13.3, *CCSL* 50a.387–389, where audience reactions to acting and praise form part of the same discussion.

125. On the background see Fantham (1978), 2–22; on style, see Auerbach (1953), esp. chaps. 2–4.

126. *De Mus.* 1.3.6, *PL* 32.1086.

127. Ibid., where the contrast is between the singing of a bird and the playing of an instrument; the one is *imitatio,* the other is *ars,* since *ratio* is involved.

128. The illustration is reused in the episodes concerning Alypius; see Chapter 3, "Alypius."

129. At *De Cat. Rud.* 25.49.95–100, *CCSL* 46.172–173, Augustine compares the love of a charioteer, a hunter, or an actor to uniting oneself with those who love God.

130. Here again, the influence is Ciceronian, not Manichaean; see Testard (1958), vol. 1, 49–60; cf. Fontanier (1989), 418–420, for parallels elsewhere in his writings.

131. The theme appears well before *De Diu. Quaes.,* q. 30, discussed thoroughly by Canning (1983); e.g., *De Beata Vita* 4.34, *CCSL* 29.84.265–266: "Hoc est animis deum habere, id est deo perfrui"; reiterated in *De Ord.* 2.7.20, *CCSL* 29.118.14–15; cf. *Sol.* 1.13.22, *CSEL* 89.34.16–17. On the parallels in Cicero, *De Officiis* 1.125, etc., see Testard (1958), vol. 1, 62–64. For an excellent analysis of the context, see Mayer (1969), 95–104; cf. Tscholl (1964), 85–91.

132. An echo of this thinking may be found at *De Vera Rel.* 40.74, *CCSL*

32.235.8–11: "Et per uitalem motum diiudicantur quodam modo, ut ex eis in structuram huius uisibilis *pulchri,* quae *apta* sunt, assumantur, non *apta* uero per congruos meatus eiciantur" (my italics).

133. *Conf.* 4.15.5–10; see Hornstein (1960), 289–290.

134. Courcelle (1950), 86, 88–89.

135. *Conf.* 5.13.10–11: "Ad eum autem ducebar abs te nesciens, ut per eum ad te sciens ducerer."

136. See O'Meara (1954), 117–118, and the skilful recreation of Brown (1967), 81–84.

137. *De Beata Vita* 1.4, *CSEL* 29.67.91–92; cf. *Sol.* 2.14.26, *CSEL* 89.80.15–18; and, for an excellent analysis, Mayer (1969), 115–122.

138. *C. Iul.* 6.21, *PL* 45.1549: "Meus est praeceptor Ambrosius, cuius non solum libros legi, sed uerba etiam loquentis audiui, et per eum lauacrum regenerationis accepi." Cf. Possidius, *Vita* 1, *PL* 32.35.

139. Alfaric (1918), 371–372; Courcelle (1950), 93–94. For a more positive assessment, see Paredi (1964), 285–286, 291; but this is based on Monica's reverence.

140. *Conf.* 6.2; a practice opposed because of drunkenness, a problem that Augustine later faced in Hippo; see *Ep.* 17.4, *CSEL* 34/1.43; *Ep.* 22.2–3 (pp. 55–57); *Sermo* 104, *PL* 38.616–618, now datable to 393 by Halporn (1976), 106–108. Another African custom discussed was fasting on Saturday; see *Ep.* 36.32, *CSEL* 34/1.61–62, written ca. 397.

141. *Conf.* 9.5.4–8. Cf. *Ep.* 31.8, *CSEL* 34/2.8.1–4, where Augustine writes to Paulinus of Nola in 395, regretting he has not been able to read certain of Ambrose's anti-Platonist books, to which may be added *De Util. Cred.* 8.20, *CSEL* 25.25.21–22, where he notes some six years after meeting the bishop: "Opportunissimum ergo me ac ualde docilem tunc inuenire posset, qui posset docere."

142. *Conf.* 5.13.1–6; on the date and circumstances, see Palanque (1933), 130–132, 510; cf. Mommsen (1959), 288–290. The background is discussed briefly by Bloch (1963), 196–199, and in detail by Matthews (1975), 203–215. Barnes (1992) argues that Ambrose and Symmachus may have been cousins, a factor that would have affected their relationship.

143. While combatting Arianism; see Madec (1974), 48–51.

144. *Conf.* 5.10.29–44. Cf. *De Trin.* 13.4, *CCSL* 50a.390.32–33: "cum academicis omnia dubia sint:" not only complaint about scepticism or an echo of Cicero's thoughts on the New Academy as proposed by Testard (1958), vol. 1, 93–97, but also a schoolteacher's disappointment at the absence of discipline and instruction in the liberal arts among Academic philosophers in Rome; this is noted in letter of 386 to Hermogenianus, *Ep.* 1.2, *CSEL* 34/1.2.15–18. Cf. *C. Acad.* 3.37–42, as well as *De Beata Vita* 1.4 and *De Util. Cred.* 8.20, discussed by Courcelle (1943–44), 161–164. On Augustine's knowledge of the New Academy, see Solignac (1958), 126–128; for a review of Augustine's repudiation of scepticism and its literature, see O'Daly (1987), 162–171, together with the qualifications of Mourant (1966), 67–71, 76–80.

145. *Conf.* 6.6.10; for a discussion, see Courcelle (1950), 80–83.

146. Ibid., 5.13.11: "Suscepit me paterne ille homo dei." Simplicianus is described similarly, *Ep.* 37.1, *CSEL* 34/2.63.9; cf. Courcelle (1950), 173 and 173, n. 6.

147. An anticipation of bks. 10–13, where only one Augustine speaks and, by turning to exegesis himself, succeeds his mentor.

148. *Conf.* 5.13.16: "eius facundiam"; 5.13.21: "ad dicendi modum."

149. Ibid., 5.13.15: "non intentione."; 5.13.18: "rerum autem incuriosus et contemptor."

150. E.g., *De Util. Cred.,* discussed in Chapter 6, "Defining the Reader."

151. Cf. Mayer (1969), 117–118, who traces the sources of metaphors of obscurity in other writings.

152. *Conf.* 5.14.4–5: "Veniebant in animum meum simul cum uerbis, quae diligebam, res etiam, quas neglegebam; neque enim ea dirimere poteram."

153. Cf. *De Doct. Christ.* 2.28.43, *CCSL* 32.63.21–39 (despite the error corrected in *Retr.* 2.30.4).

154. If, that is, he heard them, on which there is no solid evidence; for the positive view, see Courcelle (1950), 106–120.

155. McCool (1959), 64–79.

156. See Ripanti (1972), 225.

157. *Conf.* 5.13.15: "audiebam disputantem in populo."

158. Cf. Mayer (1974), 357–367. For a criticism of Verbeke (1945), who sees a Stoic orientation here, see Masai (1961), 15–31. Pontet (1945), 150, notes the predominant influence of Paul.

159. *Conf.* 5.14.22: "Tum uero fortiter intendi animum."

160. See Markus (1966), 435–445, on the Ambrosian element among other influences on Augustine's notion.

161. On the range of *spiritualis,* esp. in Augustine's sermons, see Schumacher (1957), 143–208.

162. Recalling *Conf.* 1.9.13–16 and possibly alluding to Manichaean snares.

163. Or, more accurately, recognized that he had been a catechumen since infancy.

164. *De Mus.* 4.13–15, *PL* 32.1138–43.

165. Cf. *En. in Ps.* 9.8, *CCSL* 38.62.35–37: "Non enim transit ad summam pacem, ubi summum silentium est, nisi qui magno strepitu prius cum suis uitiis belligerauerit." Cf. ibid., 91.2, *CCSL* 39.1280.

166. On this question, see the Introduction, notes 53 and 99.

167. *Conf.* 6.3.15–16: "Sed cum legebat, oculi ducebantur per paginas et cor intellectum rimabatur, uox autem et lingua quiescebant."

168. Ibid., 6.3.18–19: "Sic eum legentem uidimus tacite et aliter numquam sedentesque in diuturno silentio."

169. Ibid., 6.3.13–14: "Aut corpus reficiebat necessariis sustentaculis aut lectione animum."

170. *In Io. Eu. Tract.* 17.11, *CCSL* 36.176.8–10: "Difficile est in turba uidere

Christum; solitudo quaedam necessaria est menti nostrae; quadam solitudine in-
tentionis uidetur Deus."

171. This was true much later as well; see *Ep.* 132, *CSEL* 44.79–80, where he
asks Volusian in 412 to send him his queries on biblical theology in writing, to
which he will reply in writing. Neither of them has time to meet, Augustine
because he finds himself "inundated" by persons who prefer "battles of words" to
"the light of knowledge." Writings and readings have no such unwelcome presence
(p. 80, 10–12): "Quod autem scriptum habetur, semper uacat ad legendum, cum
uacat legenti; nec onerosum fit praesens, quod cum uoles, sumitur, cum uoles,
ponitur." Cf. *Ep.* 137, (pp. 96–97).

172. *Sol.*, 1.15.30, *CSEL* 89.44.3–4: "Et ista mecum adeo tecum, quando in
silentio sumus, diligenter cauteque tractabo."

173. See Chapter 3, "Augustine."

174. *Conf.* 6.3.44: "carnalium cogitationum figmenta."

175. Ibid., 6.3.37–50. On Augustine's debt to Ambrose's teaching on "image"
and "likeness," see Markus (1964), 137–139; and see O'Daly (1983), esp. 188, for
the parallel account in *De Gen. ad Litt.,* begun in 401.

176. For a statistical survey of Augustine's usage, see Mayer (1987), 5–8, and,
on the various contexts, 12–56.

177. On the combination of hermeneutics and realism, see de Margerie (1983),
27–33, 36, 72–87.

178. *Conf.* 6.4.21: "tamquam regulam."

179. The complexities of Augustine's interpretation of 2 Cor. 3:6 cannot be
dealt with here; see O'Donnell (1992), vol. 2, 350–351.

180. For an analysis, see Hök (1960), 104–105, 116–118.

181. Cf. Löwith (1954), 405–410, with criticisms of Augustine's position.

182. Cf. O'Donnell (1992), vol. 2, 353, who sees Augustine's statement concerning the authority of scripture (6.5.16) as envisaging "a profoundly and publicly
textual and historical community."

183. Augustine attests to his reputation in the letter to Dioscorus in 410 or 411;
*Ep.* 118.33, *CSEL* 34/2.697.4–5.

184. On the transformation of the Platonic tradition down to the second
century, see Dillon (1977), 114–340. Augustine's links with Plato's own themes are
surveyed by Hadot (1979) and O'Daly (1987), 190–199, while his differences with
neoplatonic doctrines are succinctly summarized by Booth (1977), 396–400; on
Porphyry, see his comments (1979), 101–106; and, for a full review, see Madec,
"Augustin et Porphyre" (1992), as well as the cautionary note on the notion of
neoplatonism as applied to Augustine in Madec (1981), 231–233; cf. Madec (1988),
47–50, who reminds us that some of Augustine's ideas are as close to Plato as they
are to his successors.

185. A full bibliography on the *libri Platonicorum* cannot be attempted here.
Influential studies include Alfaric (1918), 361–382, 515–127; Theiler (1933); Henry
(1934), 63–145; and Courcelle (1950), 153–174, in part following Alfaric (see

p. 94); other contributions of importance are Grandgeorge (1896), Nörregaard (1923), Svoboda (1933), Dahl (1945), and Courcelle (1954); a useful review of the early literature is Pincherle, *AM,* vol. 3 (1954–55), 71–93 (with discussions, 94–102); also Mayer (1969), 127–132; Madec (1985), 59–63; and, with judicious observations on every phase of the discussion, Madec, *Saint Augustin et la philosophie* (1992), 27–33. On the neglect of Porphyry, the best account remains Theiler (1933); cf. O'Meara (1958), 91–101; Dörrie (1962), 38–46; and Pépin, "Une nouvelle source" (1977). For Courcelle's replies to his critics, see (1954), 225–231, and (1963), 28–31; and, on Porphyry's influence on Victorinus, P. Hadot (1971), 206–210. For further bibliography, see Courcelle (1963), 27–88; du Roy (1966), 61–88; Mandouze (1968), 473–491; and O'Daly (1987), 1–130, all of whom make substantial contributions; for briefer resumes, see Solignac, *BA* 13 (1962), 145–149, 679–693; O'Meara, *The Young Augustine* (1954), 131–155; and P. Hadot (1979), 272–279. The difficulty of sorting out the influences is stressed by de Capitani (1984), 244, after a thorough review. An enduring study in comparative theology is Guitton (1971).

186. Cf. Havelock (1963), 215–233, who, in my view, exaggerates the force of alphabetic literacy, which is not isolated by Augustine or his predecessors in the Platonic tradition.

187. See Jolivet (1936) and Evans (1982); Nédoncelle (1962), 17–21; Bezançon (1965), 133–144; and Russell (1990).

188. See di Giovanni (1974), 285–286. I would argue that these influences are chiefly Platonic and relatively straightforward; significantly, there is little or no echo of Plotinus' geometric metaphor of the circle, the centre, and the radii for describing relations between the immaterial and material world, whose hermeneutic possibilities were less easy to develop; cf. *Enn.* 4.1, vol. 2, 8–9; 5.1.11, vol. 2, 201–202.

189. See Henry (1937), 15; cf. Rist (1967), 130–168, esp. 150; however, Augustine speaks positively of Plotinus' metaphors of alienation and return; *De Ciu. Dei* 9.10 and 9.17, CCSL 47.258–259 and 265–266.

190. E.g., *De Ord.* 2.5.16, CCSL 29.115–116.42–46.

191. E.g., *De Beata Vita* 4.34, CCSL 29.84.255–262.

192. *De Vera Rel.* 1.1–5.8, CCSL 32.187–193; ably summarized by Madec, *Saint Augustin et la philosophie* (1992), 13–14.

193. See Frend (1952), 18–19; G. Bonner (1963), 237–239; Mandouze (1968), 340–341.

194. Perhaps a result of his interest in Porphyry; see Theiler (1933), 11–32; and, also O'Meara, *The Young Augustine* (1954), 136–154; for criticisms, P. Hadot (1968), 24–27; recent literature is summarized by Madec, *Saint Augustin et la philosophie* (1992), 28 nn. 8–13.

195. The view summarized at *De Ciu. Dei* 10.2, CCSL 47.274.

196. Ibid., 10.24 (p. 297.12–22, 30–35).

197. Cf. Madec (1985), 45–49.

198. *Conf.* 7.9.20–23; cf. du Roy (1966), 61, and, for parallels in *De Doct. Christ.,* M. Jordan (1980), 177–178, 182–191.

199. *Conf.* 7.3.1–2; 7.4; 7.6.63–85.

200. Discussed with Simplicianus in 386; Courcelle (1950), 170–174; Hadot (1971), 236–241.

201. Madec, "Notes" (1971), 128 ff., and *Saint Augustin et la philosophie* (1992), 29. On Stoic views reflected in 7.1 and 7.5, see Baguette (1970), 53–77.

202. *Conf.* 7.9.20–49; 7.17; 7.20.13–22. This point has been the subject of a series of outstanding commentaries by Madec, most recently in *La patrie* (1989), 36–50, and, for a review of Augustine's christology, "Christus" (1992). On the notion of a mediator, see *De Ciu. Dei* 9.17, *CCSL* 47.263–264.2–29, where, freely conflating doctrines drawn from *Enn.* 1.6.8 and 2.3, Augustine concludes that man and God can approach each other only through a *mediator* (1 Tim. 2:5). For Augustine's criticism of Porphyry on the subject in contrast to his partial assimilation of Plotinus, see *De Ciu. Dei* 10.24 (ibid., pp. 297–298) and 10.28 (pp. 303–304).

203. On the role of silence in this recreation, see *Conf.* 9.8.8–9; see also the discussion of narrative in Chapter 3, "Reading and Conversion."

204. Courcelle (1950), 99–110; on the source, see Solignac, *BA* 13 (1962), n. 1, p. 589. The debate on evil and free will (7.13 *et seq.*) may be a commentary on Ambrose's sermon for 30 March 386 (Holy Saturday); the reflections on the spiritual nature of the soul (7.1.28 *et seq.*) may reflect the topic for 4 April 386. On the complexity of Ambrose's philosophical outlook in this period, which would appear to work against such rapports, see Pépin (1964), 21–78. Madec, *Saint Augustin et la philosophie* (1992), 27, notes that "les emprunts . . . sont strictement anonymes." How then would Augustine have known that they were drawn from Plotinus?

205. *De Mor. Eccl. Cath.* 1.3 (*PL* 32.1312), 1.10, (cols. 1317–18), 2.1–9 (cols. 1345–53).

206. Briefly recapitulated by Solignac, *BA* 13 (1962), 100–112, 145–149; cf. du Roy (1966), 68–72.

207. Du Roy (1966), 61. For a useful chart of *superbia* in the *Conf.* see Testard (1987), 137.

208. See Dörrie (1962), 28–31, who comments perceptively on *imitatio* among Porphyry's ideals.

209. The most detailed of the various analyses are those of McCool (1959), 63–65, 74–75; du Roy (1966), 72–81; Mandouze (1968), 686–699; and van Fleteren (1974), 33–54. Cf. Verbeke (1954), 279–287. An earlier analysis of value is Henry (1937). Plotinus' only autobiographical passage is *Enn.* 4.8.1 (vol. 2, 165–167); see P. Hadot (1973), 26–27; on possible Plotinian and Porphyrian influences on the notion of self-knowledge as early as *De Ord.*, see Solignac (1957), 455–464. Views similar to those advanced in the text are expressed by Burnaby (1947), 29–30, Mayer (1969), 144–149, and Madec, *La patrie* (1989), 43–46. For a

recent review of tendencies of interpretation with pertinent remarks on "the way this 'reading' is presented," see O'Donnell (1992), vol. 2, 413–418.

210. *Conf.* 7.7.10–11: "Quae illa tormenta parturientis cordis mei, qui gemitus, deus meus! Et ibi erant aures tuae nesciente me."

211. Ibid., 7.7.11–13: "Et cum in silentio fortiter quaererem, magnae uoces erant ad misericordiam tuam, tacitae contritiones animi mei."

212. For an excellent literary analysis, see di Giovanni (1974), 289–297.

213. *Conf.* 7.7.19–20: "Intus enim erat, ego autem foris, nec in loco illud." On the possible source in Porphyry, see Solignac, *BA* 13 (1962), n. 23, pp. 679–681.

214. *Conf.* 7.7.20–21: "At ego intendebam in ea, quae locis continentur, et non ibi inueniebam locum ad requiescendum."

215. Ibid., 7.7.22–35 (Job 15:26 and Ps. 88:11); 7.8.1–2 (Eccles. 18:1 and Ps. 84:6).

216. Ibid., 7.8.2–5: "Et placuit in conspectu tuo reformare deformia mea [Ps. 18:15]. Et stimulis internis agitabas me, ut impatiens essem, donec mihi per interiorem aspectum certus esses."

217. Ibid., 7.9.4–6: "Procurasti mihi per quendam hominem immanissimo typho turgidum quosdam Platonicorum libros ex graeca lingua in latinam uersos." A common metaphor for human pride in Augustine; cf. *De Trin.* 8.5, *CCSL* 50.276.7–8: "quo superbiae nostrae sanaretur tumor"; for a discussion, see O'Donnell (1992), vol. 2, 420–421. Courcelle's suggestion of Mallius Theodorus, (1950), 153–156, has met with a mixed reception. Cf. O'Meara (1954), 125–126; Solignac, *BA* 13 (1962), 102–103; and du Roy (1966), 64. For a sympathetic assessment, see Mandouze (1968), especially 471 n. 3. This and other suggestions are weighed by O'Donnell (1992), vol. 2, 419–420, together with a judicious summary of rival positions, 421–424.

218. *Conf.* 3.4.1–3: "Inter hos ego imbecilla tunc aetate discebam libros eloquentiae, in qua eminere cupiebam fine damnabili et uentoso per gaudia uanitatis humanae." Cf. 3.5.7–8: "Tumor enim meus refugiebat modum eius et acies mea non penetrabat interiora eius." The reference to overweening pride in 7.9.4–6 may therefore be topical. Augustine describes himself in similar terms again at 7.20.11–15. Cf. *De Trin.* 8.5, *CCSL* 50.276.7–8.

219. For a summary of discussions relative to *De Beata Vita* 1.4, *CCSL* 29.67.98–99 ("Lectis autem Plotini paucissimis libris"), see Doignon, *BA* 4.1 (1986), n. 3G, p. 138.

220. See du Roy (1966), 64 n. 1.

221. Lods (1976), 4–12.

222. *Conf.* 7.9.6: "et ibi legi." Cf. 7.9.20, 23, 32, 36, 38, 49, 55–56, 63; 7.19.8, 17, 18; 7.20.1–2, 14–18, 22–27; 7.21.25, 26, 29.

223. For a comparison of "Plotinian" visions, excepting those of the *Conf.* and the steps to wisdom in *De Doct. Christ.* 2.2–9, see Maréchal (1930), 93–102, 192–194.

224. For a brief review of the interpretations of this *locus classicus,* see Doignon,

*BA* 4.1 (1986), nn. 3B–4, pp. 135–140. The most important discussion remains Courcelle (1968), 269–290.

225. *De Beata Vita* 1.4, *CSEL* 29.66.75–79: "Ego ab usque undeuicesimo anno aetatis meae, postquam in schola rhetoris librum illum Ciceronis, qui Hortensius uocatur, accepi, tanto amore philosophiae succensus sum, ut statim ad eam me ferre meditarer." Cf. *C. Acad.* 2.2.5, *CCSL* 29.20.45–57, where the "libri . . . pleni" are those of the neoplatonists; on the interpretation, see Madec, "Pour l'interprétation," (1971), 323–325.

226. We are not told what this superstition was. Alfaric (1918), 70, interprets it as "une sorte de terreur . . . devant la philosophie purement rationelle." Cf. Courcelle (1968), 273. My interpretation is based on *De Util. Cred.* 1.2, *CSEL* 25.4.16–18: "nisi quod nos superstitione terreri et fidem nobis ante rationem imperari dicerent."

227. Not a reference to Manichaean astrology, as Courcelle thought, (1968), 275, but a Ciceronian reminiscence, intermingling astronomical lore with the theme of contemplating the heavens.

228. *De Beata Vita.* 1.4, *CCSL* 29.66.79–67.87: "Sed neque mihi nebulae defuerunt, quibus confunderetur cursus meus, et diu, fateor, quibus in errorem ducerer, 'labentia in Oceanum astra' [Virgil, *Aeneid* 3.515] suspexi . . . Non adsentiebar sed putabam eos magnum aliquid tegere illis inuolucris, quod essent aliquando aperturi." For other interpretations of "labentia . . . astra," see Doignon, *BA* 4.1 (1986), n. 3B, p. 135.

229. *De Beata Vita* 1.4 (p. 67.86–94).

230. Ibid. (p. 67.98–103): "Lectis autem Plotini paucissimis libris . . . conlataque cum eis, quantum potui, etiam illorum auctoritate, qui diuina mysteria tradiderunt, sic exarsi, ut omnes illas uellem ancoras rumpere, nisi me nonullorum hominum existimatio commoueret." On the crux "paucissimis," see Doignon, *BA* 4.1 (1986), n. 3G, p. 138; also O'Meara (1954), 140, and O'Connell (1963), 3–4; on metaphors of rupture and philosophical conversion, see Chapter 3. If the *libri* were scrolls, several "books" might make up the work of a single author. For a discussion of the possibility and its consequences for Augustine's "kinesthetics," see Morrison (1992), 28–32.

231. For a similar connection in the more normal setting of preaching, see *In Io. Eu. Tract.* 23.5, *CCSL* 36.234–235. Augustine, discussing yesterday's reading *(hodierno lectio),* asks his audience to lift up its soul in humility and piety toward God, spilling it out over themselves, where his texts are Ps. 41:4–5 and 24:1. His hearers are to attempt to withdraw their senses from the many in order to focus their attention on the One, i.e., the Word.

232. Courcelle (1950), 157–167; see the judicious evaluation of the notion in Solignac, *BA* 13 (1962), n. 28, pp. 698–703; also O'Donnell (1992), vol. 2, 434–437.

233. Cf. du Roy (1966), 61.

234. E.g., *Conf.* 3.4.33: "Nomen Christi non erat ibi."

235. Du Roy (1966), 61 n. 2. Cf. Madec (1975), 78, and, for a general review, Markus (1967), 333–340.

236. On its source, see Gilson (1946), 43–46; and, on the relationship of pagan knowledge in book 7 to *De Doct. Christ.* 2, see the assessment of previous scholarship in Bochet (1993), 23–29.

237. *Conf.* 7.9.6–8: "Et ibi legi non quidem his uerbis, sed hoc idem omnino multis et multiplicibus suaderi rationibus." See Madec (1981), 233–235.

238. *Conf.* 7.9.20–23; John 1:13–14.

239. *Conf.* 7.9.23–32; Phil. 2:6–11.

240. An idea expressed concisely in *Ep.* 140.6.15, *CSEL* 44.166.18–23 (written to Honoratus in 412).

241. See Brown (1988), 164–167.

242. Cf. Courcelle (1950), 177–178 and 178 n. 1.

243. Du Roy (1966), 64–66 and 64 n. 6, whom I follow here. For general collations of references to Paul and Christ in bks. 7–8, see Lods (1976), 4–15 and 15–34, respectively.

244. In order, these are: (1) John 1:1–10 and 1:11–12; (2) John 1:13 and John 1:14; (3) Phil. 2:6 and 2:7–11; and (4) John 1:16 and Rom. 5:6, 8:32; du Roy (1966), 64–65. Cf. Courcelle (1950), 173 and n. 2, who sees a reference to the teaching of Simplicianus "au cours de leurs entretiens." In this case, Augustine would be reading and recollecting at once. The reconstruction of Lods (1976), 16–17, is somewhat reductive.

245. Du Roy (1966), 65.

246. Kunzelmann, *Miscellanea Agostiniana,* vol. 2 (1931), 437.

247. *De Gen. c. Man.* 2.24.37, *PL* 34.215–216; *De F. et Sym.* 4.5–6, *CSEL* 41.8–11; *Sermo* 292.3, *PL* 38.1321; *En. in Ps.* 130.9.30–51, *CCSL* 40.1905–06. Other texts are listed by du Roy (1966), 65 n. 6.

248. La Bonnardière (1965), 45.

249. See Solignac, *BA* 13 (1962), n. 25, pp. 682–689.

250. Cf. Madec, *BA* 6 (1976), n. 5, pp. 540–543.

251. *Conf.* 7.10.1–2, quoted in the previous paragraph.

252. Du Roy (1966), 72, and, for supporting texts, 72 n. 3, 161–165; van Fleteren (1974), 36–41. Cf. Solignac, *BA* 13 (1962), n. 2, who signals the derivation from Plotinus, *Enn.* 5.1.1 (vol. 2, 206–207). Augustine does not always use the term in a philosophical sense, e.g., *Conf.* 7.20.2; 7.21.10; *Sol.* 1.3, *CSEL* 89.6.2: "quem nemo quaerit, nisi admonitus"; ibid., 1.6 (pp. 10–11). The normal use in *De Trin.* is to be "admonished" through scripture, e.g., 12.1, *CCSL* 50.356.11–12: "Qua in re admonemur ab eo qui nos fecit." Morán, *Augustinus* (1968), 258–259, stresses the closeness to terms such as *monere, indicare, aduertere, insinuare, commonere, commemorare,* and *demonstrare;* cf. Morán, *Augustinianum* (1968), 148. With respect to problems of reading, a perceptive study of the issues down to the *Conf.* is

Schobinger (1977), 70–89. On the relation of *admonitio* to *auctoritas,* see Holte (1962), 318–320. For a recent review of the issues, see Madec, "Admonitio," in *AL* I (1986), 95–99.

253. *De Mag.* 7.20, *CCSL* 29, 178.45–46: "Ex quo admoniti sumus aut signis signa monstrari aut signa alia"; see Morán, *Augustinus* (1968), 263–269; du Roy (1966), 214.

254. *Conf.* 3.4.21–23: "Notantur in eo libro [i.e., in *Hortensio*] et demonstrantur, et manifestatur ibi salutifera illa admonitio spiritus tui per seruum tuum bonum et pium." As in 7.10, a pagan philosopher discredits irrelevant pagan teachings. The statement is followed by an early references to the incarnation, Col. 2:8–9.

255. Ibid., 8.12.26–28: "Audieram enim de Antonio, quod ex euangelica lectione, cui forte superuenerat, admonitus fuerit, tamquam sibi diceretur quod legebatur."

256. See Chapter 3, "Alypius."

257. *Conf.* 8.12.44–45: "Sed tali admonitione firmatus est."

258. Ibid., 7.20.1–2: "Sed tunc lectis Platonicorum illis libris posteaquam inde admonitus."

259. *Enn.* 1.6.9 (vol. 1, 103–104); van Fleteren (1974), 42; cf. du Roy (1966), 77 n. 1.

260. Cf. Thonnard (1962), esp. 132–135.

261. For analyses in neoplatonic terms, see Mandouze (1968), 692 ff., and du Roy (1966), 72.

262. *Enn.* 1.6.7 (vol. 1, 100–120), 6.9.9 (vol. 3, 285–287).

263. *Conf.* 7.10.13: "Tu es deus meus, tibi *suspiro* die ac nocte." Cf. Ps. 1:1–2: "Beatus uir . . . in lege Domini . . . *meditabitur* die ac nocte"; my italics. The subtexts on creation, night, and day, are of course Gen. 1:5 and 1:14. For echoes of similar phrasing, see Job 17:11, Ps. 31:4, 54:11, 77:14, 87:2, 138:11, 12, and Rom. 13:12.

264. Ably reconstructed by Lods (1976), 4–11.

265. The texts are conveniently tabulated by Chadwick, *Saint Augustine* (1991), 123 nn.; see also O'Daly (1985), 530–532.

266. *Conf.* 7.10.13–17: "Et cum te primum cognoui, tu assumpsisti me, ut uiderem esse, quod uiderem, et nondum me esse, qui uiderem. Et . . . contremui amore et horrore: et inueni longe me esse a te in regione dissimilitudinis." The sources are *Enn.* 1.6.7 (vol. 1, 101.12–19) and 1.8.13 (ibid., 122.15 f). (Cf. Plato, *Statesman* 273d). The connection to hermeneutics is recognized by Mayer (1969), 47–50. The large literature on *regio dissimilitudinis* is summarized by Knauer (1955), 15–16, and Solignac, *BA* 13 (1962), n. 26, pp. 689–693; see also TeSelle (1975), 153–154 n. 1, who also traces the early history of the idea. For a more recent analysis of Plotinian themes, see Perler (1980), 243–251. On the connection to reading, compare the phrasing with 9.4.42–43 (after reading Ps. 4 at Cassiciacum): "Inhorrui timendo ibidemque inferui sperando et exultando in tua misericordia, pater."

267. *Pace* Courcelle (1950), who saw this type of reconstruction at work chiefly in the garden scene.

268. *Enn.* 6.9.4, vol. 3, 276–278; cf. *Conf.* 10.40.21–27.

269. Cf. *De Lib. Arb.* 2.3.8.25–2.6.13.51, *CCSL* 29.240–246. See O'Daly (1985), 528–531, and, on the sources, (1987), 102–105.

270. O'Daly (1987), 1.

271. Quispel, "Mani. The Apostle." (1972), 667, and, in relation to Courcelle, 667 n. 4.

272. *Conf.* 7.17.2: "Et non stabam frui deo meo." Cf. 7.18.1–2; 7.20.9.

273. Ibid., 7.17.2; cf. O'Daly (1987), 106–107.

274. *Conf.* 7.17.4–5, 30–32.

275. Another anticipation of the two segments of bk. 10, which deal in turn with memory's ascent and the use of outside sources as aids in recollecting pertinent moral lessons.

276. Suggesting, perhaps, that 7.7 and 7.18 originally formed parts of a commentary on John 1:1–14, into which the neoplatonic material was later introduced. The dates of *In Io. Eu. Tract.* and *En. in Ps.* 130 do not rule out the possibility; see la Bonnardière (1965), 32–33.

277. *Conf.* 7.18.1–8: "Et quaerebam uiam comparandi rorboris, quod esset idoneum ad fruendum te, nec inueniebam . . . hominem Christum Iesum . . . uocantem et dicentem: 'Ego sum uia et ueritas et uita' [John 14:6], et cibum, cui capiendo inualidus eram, miscentem carni, quoniam uerbum caro factum est [John 1:14], ut infantiae nostrae lactesceret sapientia tua, per quam creasti omnia."

278. Incidentally reinterpreting his narrative of his intellectual progress in *De Beata Vita;* 1.2–6, *CCSL* 29.65–68.

279. Cf. *De Ciu. Dei* 10.30–31, *CCSL* 47.307–309.

280. *Conf.* 7.19.3–6. Augustine may have associated these views with Photinus; 7.19.30–33. However, the notion of charismatic teaching was also familiar in Manichaeism, which was still in his thoughts; e.g., 7.21.2–6.

281. Ibid., 7.20.3–4: "quid per tenebras animae meae contemplari non sinerer."

282. Ibid., 7.20.7–9: "Hoc solo firmissimo documento, quia sunt, certus quidem in istis eram, nimis tamen infirmus ad fruendum te."

283. Ibid., 7.20.11–13 and 7.9.4–5. Cf. 1 Cor. 8:1. The parallel is with his discovery of the *Hortensius,* where pride also prevented him from perceiving the alternative message of scripture.

284. This paragraph summarizes 7.20.15–27.

285. *Conf.* 7.20.22–27: "Nam si primo sanctis tuis litteris informatus essem . . . fortasse aut abripuissent me a solidamento pietatis, aut si in affectu, quam salubrem imbiberam, perstitissem, putarem etiam ex illis libris eum posse concipi, si eos solos quisque didicisset." Cf. 8.12.32: "Arripui, aperui et legi" On the background, see Ambrose, *De Fide* 1.1.4, *CSEL* 76.6.27–28.

286. Cf. *C. Acad.* 2.2.5, *CCSL* 29.21.63–67: "Itaque titubans properans haesitans arripio apostolum Paulum . . . Perlegi totum intentissime atque castissime." Mayer

(1969), 149–152, rightly speaks of "die neue Ontologie"; excellent analysis in Dönt (1969), 186–188.

287. *Conf.* 7.21.6: "Et coepi et inueni, quidquid illac uerum legeram."

## 3. Reading and Conversion

1. *Conf.* 4.11.15–16. Yet Augustine realizes that a word, heard by many people, is heard in its entirety by each of them; *De Diu. Quaes.*, q. 42, CCSL 44a.63. Augustine's attitude toward *narratio obliqua* here contrasts sharply with that of his Manichaean adversaries; on their views, see Tardieu (1987), 130–140 and 142.

2. A hermeneutic notion doubtless derived from Plotinus, where it frequently recurs; e.g., *Enn.* 1.6.1 (vol. 1, 93.26–30); 5.3.13 (vol. 2, 226.12–16).

3. This provides another parallel with sound and silence; *Conf.* 4.12.24–30; see also *De Diu. Quaes.*, q. 43, CCSL 54a.64.8–10.

4. *De Gen. ad Litt.* 1.15, CSEL 28.21.7–8; also *Conf.* 12.19.

5. *De Gen. ad Litt.*, ibid. (p. 21.9–12): "Sicut enim uox materia uerborum est, uerba uero formatam uocem indicant, non autem qui loquitur prius emittit informem uocem, quam possit postea conligere atque in uerba formare: ita et deus creator non priore tempore fecit informem materiam et eam postea per ordinem quarumque naturarum quasi secunda consideratione formauit; formatam quippe creauit materiam." Cf. *Conf.* 12.29.27–32 (the similar example of song, stressing that its "being" arises from a relationship of matter and form, parts and whole).

6. *De Gen. ad Litt.* (p. 21.16–17); also *Conf.* 12.29.38–39.

7. *De Gen. ad Litt.* (p. 21.17–19): "Potuit diuidere scriptura loquendi temporibus, quod deus faciendi temporibus non diuisit."

8. Ibid., 6.16 (p. 190.17–20).

9. Ibid., (pp. 190.20–191.4); on secondary causes, not directly dependent on God, see 12.17 (p. 191.12–13). On nature and grace, 9.18 (p. 292.15–19); cf. ibid. (p. 293.1–5).

10. Cf. O'Brien (1978), who sees a deliberate contrast between Catholic and Manichaean views on Genesis.

11. He was living in 428–29; *C. Jul.* 1.42, PL 45.1066. Good narrative accounts of his life are found in Bardy (1940), 36–40, 64–66, 82–88, and Brown (1967), 67–68, 107–109, 124, 144–145, 163–164, 200–202; also McNamara (1964), 74–85, 129–132; on his appearance in Augustine's letters, see Nolte (1939), 24–27. The sources are judiciously weighed by Courcelle (1950), 29–32; for a full review, see E. Feldmann, A. Schindler, and O. Wermelinger, "Alypius," in *AL* 1.1/2 (1986), 245–267.

12. See *Conf.* 6.7.7–8 and 6.10.4–5, from the period of his legal studies; also 6.12.1–2 and 8.12.46: "quibus a me in melius iam olim ualde longeque distabat."

13. Paulinus and Therasia, *Ep.* 24.4, CSEL 34/1.76.2–3.

14. *Ep.* 27.5, *CSEL* 34/1.101.7: "onus ab illo [i.e., Alypio] in umeros meos transtuli."

15. Courcelle (1950), 30–32, summarizes the evidence; also Courcelle (1963), 561–563; both based on Williger (1929). Pincherle (1930), 25, noted the insufficiency of the evidence; cf. Pincherle (1976) and O'Donnell (1992), vol. 2, 360–362.

16. *Ep.* 24.4, *CSEL* 34/1.76.3.

17. Ibid. (p. 76.4–10).

18. Ibid. (p. 76.4); *Aen.* 8.114. On the metaphor of the sea journey and navigation as an expression for the philosophical life, see Doignon, *BA* 4.1 (1986), n. 1, pp. 133–134.

19. O'Meara (1963), 254–255, 257–259; Bennett (1988), 63–66.

20. On the internal dating see *Conf.* 6.7.4–6 and 6.8.1–2.

21. *De Ord.* 2.10, *CCSL* 29.123.23: "ut ego tibi uerborum, tu mihi rerum magister effectus sis."

22. *Conf.* 6.7. In the summaries of 6.8 and 6.9, I have made minor rearrangements of details.

23. Ibid., 6.7.6–8; a detail possibly directed toward Paulinus of Nola; cf. 6.7.49–51.

24. A theme linking the stories, to which Augustine returned; *En. in Ps.* 50.1 (*CCSL* 38.599–600.12–14) and 80.2–3 (*CCSL* 39.1121–22), where he speaks of Christians leaving church services to attend the games; see also 147.7 (*CCSL* 40.2144.9–10) on the equally wasteful selling of villas to finance ritual gift-giving; on the sociological links among these practices, see Veyne (1976), 469–490.

25. No precise reason is given; *Conf.* 6.7.21. Nor we do learn the source of the quarrel with Alypius' father, although 6.8.2 suggests that Augustine discouraged Alypius from the *terrena via*. But this may be a retrospective view; there is nothing in 6.7.13–15 to suggest that the Augustine of 376 had spiritual goals in mind for his pupil. Also, he may have been sensitive to public opinion in his home town, where Alypius' father was an important man; 6.7.3–4.

26. See ibid., 6.8.4–8, and the suggestions later in the story.

27. *Vitae Philosophorum* 4.16, ed. H. S. Long (Oxford, 1964), vol. 1, 173; also Valerius Maximus 6.9, quoted in Courcelle (1950), 59 n. 3. There may be an echo of the original at *Conf.* 6.7.46: "Excussit animum forti temperantia." On Polemon (c. 350–267 B.C.), see Dillon (1977), 39–40.

28. *C. Jul.* 1.4.12 (*PL* 44.647), 1.7.35 (p. 666).

29. *De Helia et Ieiunio* 12.45, *CSEL* 32/2.437.19–438.7. Solignac, *BA* 13 (1962), 543 n. 1, suggests that Augustine's source was the manual of Cornelius Celsus; see also Courcelle (1950), 158 n. 5, and Solignac (1958), 145–148. This may be the case in *Conf.* 6.7–8, but *C. Jul.* 1.4.12 quotes Ambrose. Is the reference to drunkenness in the anecdote partly responsible for Augustine's quoting of Rom. 13:13–14 at *Conf.* 8.12.33–36?

30. Courcelle (1950), 59.

31. The change subtly criticizes the notion of reminiscence, which is formally attacked elsewhere, and reinforces Augustine's view that the study of memory is inseparable from remembering.

32. Diog. Laert., *Vit. Phil.* 4.16: *ton logon;* Ambrose is closer to Augustine in referring to the "auditorium" and the "listener."

33. *Conf.* 6.7.21: "Sed enim de memoria mihi lapsum erat agere cum illo."

34. Ibid., 6.7.33–34: "quod tunc de Alypio . . . non cogitauerim."

35. Ibid., 6.7.27: "Nam quodam die cum sederem loco solito."

36. Ibid., 6.7.29: "lectio in manibus."

37. Ibid., 6.7.31–32: "et iucundius et planius fieret."

38. Ibid., 6.7.10–11: "Ego . . . professus publica schola uterer."

39. Ibid., 3.2.1–2: "Rapiebant me spectacula theatrica plena imaginibus miseriarum mearum et fomitibus ignis mei."

40. Ibid., 6.7.25–26: "ut aperte tibi tribueretur eius correctio, per me quidem illam sed nescientem operatus es."

41. On Augustine's dislike of the games, see *C. Acad.* 1.1.2, *CCSL* 29.4.34–38.

42. *Conf.* 6.7.37–39; Prov. 9:8.

43. *Conf.* 6.7.34–35: "At ille in se rapuit meque illud non nisi propter se dixisse credidit."

44. Ibid., 6.7.29: "forte."

45. Ibid., 6.7.23–24: "Verum autem, domine, tu, qui praesides gubernaculis omnium, quae creasti."

46. Ibid., 6.7.33: "sanando."

47. Ibid., 6.7.21; 6.7.28–29: "In ea quae agebantur intendit animum."

48. The terms in which Augustine describes Alypius' youthful admiration for his teaching suggest a reversal of those by which Augustine describes his initial impression of Ambrose: Cf. ibid., 5.13.12–14: "Et eum *amare* coepi primo quidem non tamquam *doctorem* ueri . . . sed tamquam hominem *benignum* in me" and 6.7.6: "Et *diligebat* multum, quod ei *bonus et doctus* uiderer" (my italics).

49. Ibid., 4.12.4–5; for other early examples of *rapere,* see O'Donnell (1992), vol. 2, 241.

50. Cf. 2 Cor. 12:2–4; for Augustine's comments, see "Augustine," later in this chapter.

51. For examples, see O'Donnell (1992), vol. 2, 475–476; vol. 3, 66.

52. I.e., to his words as a teacher; compare his criticism of Faustus, Chapter 2, "Manichaeism."

53. *Conf.* 6.7.29; cf. 6.7.46 and 6.8.9–10: "et animum et oculos . . . potestis intendere." For other examples, see the Introduction.

54. Cf. ibid., 6.7.34–35: "At ille in se *rapuit* meque illud non nisi propter se dixisse *credidit*." and 6.8.2–3: "Et ibi gladiatorii spectaculi hiatu *incredibili* et *incredibiliter abreptus est*" (my italics).

55. Ibid., 6.8.28: "unus de turba."

56. Ibid., 6.8.5: "forte"; Cf. 6.7.29.

57. Summarizing 6.8.3–20, 25–32.

58. A frequent theme; see du Roy (1966), 469–470, and O'Donnell (1992), vol. 2, 22–23.

59. *Conf.* 6.8.21–22: "qui per eius aures intrauit et reserauit eius lumina."

60. Auerbach (1953), 60.

61. See Chapter 8, "Conduct."

62. Summarizing *Conf.* 6.9.2–44.

63. *Conf.* 6.9.3–4: "Et medio die cogitaret in foro quod recitaturus erat."

64. Ibid., 6.9.4: "sicut exerceri scholastici solent"; also 6.7.27: "solito."

65. Ibid., 6.9.6: "uir tantus futurus"; also 6.9.1; 6.9.42–44.

66. Ibid., 6.9.3; 6.9.19: "stans atque admirans considerabat."

67. Ibid., 6.9.10: "fur uerus." Cf. 6.9.21–22: "tamquam furem manifestum se comprehendisse gloriantur."

68. Ibid., 6.9.27: "cura publicarum fabricarum."

69. Was the student thief the perpetrator of those crimes? Or is Augustine suggesting that the public domain has more than one false self? Cf. the role of the public in Victorinus' conversion, discussed in "Simplicianus," later in this chapter.

70. Cf. *De Sp. et Litt.* 10.17, *CSEL* 60.169.21–26, where Augustine refers metaphorically to the beaters and refiners of silver products, i.e., *exclusores* or *artifices argentarii*, in the contexts of being tested by the Lord's words (Ps. 67:31) and of oracles tested by fire (Ps. 11:7).

71. *Viuere: Conf.* 6.12.3, 7, 25, etc.

72. *Experientia:* ibid., 6.12.5, 30; *expertus:* 6.12.22; *experiendi:* 6.12.30. Cf. 6.9.42–44.

73. Ibid., 8.1.1: "recorder . . . et confitear." Cf. Is. 63:7.

74. Who is invited to express gratitude; *Conf.* 8.1.5: "Et dicunt omnes, qui adorent te, cum audiunt haec."

75. See Schmidt-Dengler (1969), 196–199, an excellent stylistic analysis.

76. Not a foreign idea to Augustine, who traces it to Stoic sources; see Chapter 6, "Dialectic."

77. *Conf.* 8.1.1–6, referring to Ps. 85:13, 34:10, 115:16–17, 71:18, 134:6, and 75:2.

78. Paralleling the triune pattern of the life of Alypius and subtly introducing a trinitarian motif.

79. On the dating, see Courcelle (1950), 181 n. 2.

80. Book 8 proceeds by alternating narrative and nonnarrative segments, as if Augustine were preparing the way for the completion of the narrative segment in bk. 9 and the beginning of the discursive segment in bk. 10.

81. Another pattern first introduced in the stories about Alypius.

82. Just as, having passed through the philosophical and Christian aspects of his lengthy conversion, we now turn to the metaphorical ones; Madec, "La conversion d'Augustin" (1987), 185.

83. Which is divisible into five sections: (1) 8.1.14–22, introduction of Simplicianus; (2) 8.1.23–48, Augustine's state of mind; (3) 8.2.1–72, the conversion of Marius Victorinus; (4) 8.3.1–8.4.27, reflections on the story; and (5) 8.5.1–54,

completion of the story and Augustine's self-analysis. For the historical details of Victorinus' conversion, see the thorough summary by Hadot in the edition of his trinitarian works by Henry and Hadot (1960), 7–18; on the theme of humility, see van Bavel (1986), 11–26.

84. This accentuation is made possible through the repetition of *uiuere, uita,* and *uia;* the point is emphasized by the musical cadences of 8.1.14–22, in which there is a repetition of other words beginning with *u.* The studiousness of Simplicianus was remarked by Ambrose, *Ep.* 65.1, *PL* 16.1275: "Cum fidei et acquirendae cognitionis diuinae gratia totum orbem peragraueris et quotidianae lectioni nocturnis ac diurnis uicibus omne uitae hujus temporis deputaueris."

85. Perhaps anticipating the visit of Ponticianus, whose deliberate lack of historical context is thereby supplied by Augustine's visit to Simplicianus. This would be another example of subtle prefiguration.

86. *Conf.* 8.2.3–9: "Vbi autem commemoraui legisse me quosdam libros Platonicorum, quos Victorinus quondam, rhetor urbis Romae, quem christianum defunctum esse audieram, in latinam linguam transtulisset, gratulatus est mihi, quod non aliorum philosophorum scripta incidissem plena fallaciarum et deceptionum secundum elementa huius mundi [Col. 2:8] in istis autem omnibus modis insinuari deum et eius uerbum." Cf. 7.9.4–6. Augustine does not dwell on the problem of translation, which he discussed about the same time in *De Doct. Christ.*

87. *Conf.* 8.1.36–38 (where "uani homines" are neoplatonists) and 8.1.41–43 (where "aliud genus impiorum" refers to Manichaeans).

88. Ibid., 8.1.24–26; cf. 8.1.7–8.

89. Ibid., 8.1.29–30; 1 Cor. 7:26–38 and 7:7–8. Castration is ruled out; 8.1.34–36.

90. Compare: *Conf.* 5.13.11–14: "Suscepit *me paterne* ille homo dei . . . Et eum *amare coepi* . . . hominem benignum in me" and 8.2.1–2: "ad Simplicianum *patrem* in accipienda gratia tunc episcopi Ambrosii et quem uere ut *patrem diligebat*" (my italics).

91. On the possible development of such views in Ambrose's lost work, *De Sacramento Regenerationis siue de Philosophia,* see Madec (1974), 247–337.

92. O'Donnell (1992), vol. 3, 7–10.

93. *Conf.* 8.2.11: "Victorinum ipsum recordatus est." Cf. Henry and Hadot (1960), 8–10.

94. Ibid., 8.2.3: "Narraui ei circuitus erroris mei."

95. Ibid., 8.2.12–13: "Deque illo mihi narrauit quod non silebo."

96. Presumbably sometime before 362, when he resigned his rhetorship.

97. *Conf.* 3.4.5–6: "Sed liber ille ipsius exhortationem continet ad philosophiam." Cf. 3.4.28–29.

98. Ibid., 8.2.14: "ille . . . senex"; cf. 8.2.24. 8.2.25–26: "Non erubuerit esse puer Christi tui et infans fontis tui." P. Hadot estimates that he was over seventy when he converted; Henry and Hadot (1960), 14.

99. The passages are *Conf.* 8.2.14 (cf. 8.2.15–16); 8.2.26: "ad humilitatis iugum"; and 8.2.28–29 (Ps. 143:5).

100. *Conf.* 1.1.4–5: "quia superbis resistis [1 Peter 5:5]."

101. The two descriptions are *Conf.* 8.2.14–16: "Ille doctissimus senex et omnium liberalium doctrinarum peritissimus quique philosophorum tam multa *legerat et diiudicauerat*" and 8.2.30–31: "*Legebat . . .* sanctam scripturam omnesque christianas litteras *inuestigabat studiossime et perscrutabatur*" (my italics).

102. Summarizing 8.2.32–68. P. Hadot speculates that his reading of Christian texts was sympathetic from the outset; Hadot in Henry and Hadot (1960), 15–16.

103. On the anecdote, see O'Donnell (1992), vol. 3, 21–22.

104. With this may be compared Augustine's reasons for withdrawing quietly from his own chair, *Conf.* 9.2.22–24.

105. Hadot in Henry and Hadot (1960), 17.

106. Was this the type recommended by Augustine? See Chapter 7, "The 'Uninstructed.'"

107. Poque (1985), 140–142, suggests two possibilities for the audience, either the candidates for baptism or, as Augustine indicates, the entire congregation.

108. *Conf.* 8.2.41–42: "Sed posteaquam legendo et inhiando."

109. Which may distantly foreshadow Augustine's approach to the ascent in bk. 10, and anticipates his handling of the story of Anthony in the following two episodes.

110. *Conf.* 8.1.16: "Audieram."

111. Ibid., 8.2.49–50. For a discussion of the role of memory in catechism, see the Introduction and Chapter 7, "The 'Uninstructed.'"

112. Ibid., 8.2.55–57: "Denique ut uentum est ad horam profitendae fidei, quae uerbis certis conceptis retentisque memoriter de loco eminentiore in conspectu populi fidelis Romae reddi solet." Of course, the profession is oral, as is the public's approval.

113. Ibid., 8.2.32: "Dicebat Simpliciano non palam, sed secretius et familiarius"; 8.2.58–59: "Dicebat Victorino . . . ut secretius redderet." In a similar manner Augustine compares Manichaean secrecy to Ambrosian openness.

114. Ibid., 8.2.61–63: "Non enim erat salus, quam docebat, in rhetorica, et tamen eam publice professus erat." Cf. 8.5.7–8, implying a contrast with the leisured reading of Ambrose, 6.11.14–15.

115. This looks back to the contrast between *abscondo* and *reuelo,* and, through the use of oral memory in Simplicianus' account, to the link between oral reminiscence and *rapere* in the *tolle, lege* episode at 8.12.

116. Where phrases are also taken from Ps. 118:176 and 25:8.

117. On the echoes of the story in the *Conf.* see Knauer (1957), whose views are reiterated in O'Donnell (1992), vol. 2, 95–98; on its critical role in bk. 10, see Chapter 8, "Conduct."

118. *Conf.* 8.3.15–16: "Quid ergo agitur in anima, cum amplius delectatur inuentis aut redditis rebus, quas diligit, quam si eas semper habuisset?"

119. See Chapter 1, "Self-Improvement."

120. *Conf.* 8.3.40–41: "Quid est, quod haec rerum pars alternat defectu et profectu, offensionibus et conciliationibus?"

121. Ibid., 8.1.21: "aptus modus."

122. Ibid., 8.3.47–48: "Et nusquam recedis, et uix redimus ad te."

123. Ibid., 8.4.8–9. Cf. *De Util. Cred.,* discussed in Chapter 6, "Defining the Reader."

124. *Conf.* 8.5.1–2: "Sed ubi mihi homo tuus Simplicianus de Victorino ista narrauit, exarsi ad imitandum: ad hoc enim et ille narrauerat." There is no mention of the fact that Victorinus voluntarily resigned his chair in response to the legislation of Julian the Apostate, who banned Christians from teaching literature and rhetoric.

125. Ibid., 8.5.20–22: "Sic intellegebam me ipso experimento id quod legeram, quomodo caro concupisceret aduersus spiritum et spiritus aduersus carnem."

126. Augustine emphasizes the point by returning to the twofold address of bk. 8's opening prayer; ibid., 8.6.3–4: "Narrabo et confitebor nomini tuo, domine, adiutor meus et redemptor meus."

127. He makes this clear only afterwards; ibid., 8.7.34–36.

128. For an extensive review of these relations dating from 413, see *De Vid. Deo (Ep.* 147) 6.18–15.37, *CSEL* 44.289–312.

129. The story divides naturally into three phases: (1) 8.6.1–21, Augustine's introduction; (2) 8.6.22–33, Ponticianus' recognition of Augustine as a Christian; and (3) 8.6.33–86, the stories of Anthony, the Milanese brethren, and the conversion of the *agentes in rebus.*

130. In his case, the deception may have involved a theory of learning as well, since he appears to have been persuaded that eloquence is an inherited talent which is moulded only by a good teacher; *De Mag.* 14.45, *CCSL* 29.202.1–16.

131. See the correspondence from 387 through 389 examined by Gonzague (1954).

132. The little that is known about him is summarized by O'Donnell (1992), vol. 3, 38.

133. Sizoo (1954), 241–254, correctly drew attention to Augustine's adherence to the norms of rhetorical *narratio* in this episode; however, the resulting schema, (254) does not explain its significance in bk. 8.

134. *Conf.* 8.6.22: "Quodam . . . die"; 8.6.25: "Nescio quid a nobis uolebat"; cf. 8.7.36–37. He does not even recall why Nebridius was absent; 8.6.22–23.

135. Ibid., 8.6.24: "Ponticianus quidam, ciuis noster, in quantum Afer."

136. Familiar in his foreignness, he appears to recapitulate the abstract motifs that are brought into play in the previous operations of predestination.

137. *Conf.* 8.6.26–29: "Et forte supra mensam lusoriam, quae ante nos erat, attendit codicem: tulit, aperuit, inuenit apostolum Paulum, inopinate sane; putauerat enim aliquid de libris, quorum professio me conterebat." For a reconstruction of the role of Paul in bks. 7–8, see Lods (1976), 11–15.

138. Note that the trinitarian formula is introduced as a narrative device before it is taken up theologically in bk. 9.

139. The parallels may extend to the gaming table, which anticipates the children's playful *tolle, lege; Conf.* 8.12.22: "in aliquo genere ludendi."

140. Ibid., 8.6.29–31: "Tum uero arridens meque intuens gratulatorie miratus est, quod eas et solas prae oculis meis litteras repente comperisset." The illuminative connection between the eye and the mind, is used again elsewhere; see Chapter 9, "The Reader and the *Cogito.*"

141. Compare the description of the reading of Victorinus at *Conf.* 8.2.30–31, quoted above, note 101.

142. Ibid., 8.6.33: "Cui ego cum indicassem."

143. Ibid., 8.6.35–36: "Nos autem usque in illam horam latebat."

144. *Sermo:* ibid., 8.6.34, 37, 43; 8.7.36.

145. Ibid., 8.6.34–35: "Ortus est sermo ipso narrante de Antonio Aegyptio monacho."

146. Monceaux in *Miscellanea Agostiniana,* 2 (1931), 61–89, provides an authoritative account.

147. *Conf.* 8.6.40–42: "Omnes mirabamur, et nos, quia tam magna erant, et ille, quia inaudita nobis erant."

148. Ibid., 8.6.44–45: "quorum nos nihil sciebamus"; 8.6.46–47: "Et non noueramus."

149. *De Mor. Eccles. Cath.* 1.33.70, *PL* 32.1339: "Vidi ego diuersorium sanctorum Mediolani, non paucorum hominum." On the other communities visited by Augustine in this period, see Monceaux (1931), 66–67.

150. *De Op. Mon.* 28.36, *CSEL* 41.585–586. Cf. *Ep.* 262.5–6, *CSEL* 57.624–626.

151. Compare *Conf.* 8.6.43–44: "Inde sermo eius deuolutus est ad . . . greges . . . et ubera deserta heremi." and Ps. 77:52: "Et abstulit sicut oues populum suum, et perduxit eos tanquam gregem in deserto."

152. *Conf.* 8.6.47: "Pertendebat ille et loquebatur adhuc."

153. Ibid., 8.6.47–48: "Et nos intenti tacebamus."

154. Ibid., 8.6.48: "Vnde incidit, ut diceret nescio quando."

155. This is another example of the audience's taking from a story a meaning not intended by the teller.

156. On the division and its textual problems, see Courcelle (1950), 181 n. 4. Augustine appears to reiterate the type of division that characterizes his reduction of biblical texts from combinations of four quotations to two from bk. 7; see Chapter 2, "Neoplatonism."

157. Or, possibly, had been lived in; the point is unclear, perhaps deliberately so. If the house's history were spelled out, the book would memorialize its inhabitants' lives instead of providing a stimulus to conversion for others.

158. *Conf.* 8.6.53–55: "Sed illos uagabundos inruisse in quandam casam, ubi habitabant quidam serui tui spiritu pauperes, qualium est regnum caelorum [Matt. 5:3]."

159. Ibid., 8.6.55–56: "Et inuenisse ibi codicem, in quo scripta erat uita Antonii."

160. *Vita Antonii (Versio Euagrii)* 2, *Patrologia Graeca* 26.841–842: "Intrauit in ecclesiam, et accidit ut tunc Euangelium legeretur."

161. It can be divided into four sections: two passages in which mental events are recounted (8.6.56–60, 8.6.66–70), and two of direct discourse in which one of the officials addresses the other (8.6.60–66, 8.6.70–72).

162. Ibid., 8.6.59: "Tum subito repletus amore sancto et sobrio pudore iratus."

163. Ibid., 8.6.60: "Sibi coniecit oculos in amicum."

164. See Courcelle (1950), 182, n. 2.

165. *Conf.* 8.6.67–68: "Reddidit oculos paginis: et legebat et mutabatur intus, ubi tu uidebas, et exuebatur mundo mens eius." *Mutare* is used twice at 3.4.7 and recurs at 7.10.19–20.

166. Ibid., 8.6.68–70: "Namque dum legit et uoluit fluctus cordis sui, infremuit aliquando et discreuit decreuitque meliora."

167. Ibid., 8.6.72: "Te si piget imitari, noli aduersari."

168. The watershed in the complex literature of interpretation of *Conf.* 8 is Courcelle (1950), 175–202; replies to critics are found in Courcelle (1963), 17–234. Both volumes contain a full bibliography. For more recent contributions, see Mara in *Le Confessioni VI–IX* (1985), 71–87, and Guiraud in *Sant'Agostino Confessioni* (1992), cli–cliii. Madec, "La conversion d'Augustin" (1987), sums up a number of early interpretive traditions succinctly in suggesting that there are four ways of looking at the conversion, i.e., as an event, an image, a prayer, and a spiritual exercise. Among specific contributions that are not concerned with Courcelle's hypothesis about the *tolle, lege* episode, important reviews include Bolgiani (1956), Lods (1976), Madec, "La conversion d'Augustin" (1987) and "La conversion et les Confessions" (1987); van Bavel (1986); and Fontaine in *Sant'Agostino Confessioni* (1992), ix–cxxxiv.

169. *Conf.* 8.7–12 can be divided into four sections: (1) 8.7, Augustine's reflections on the story of Ponticianus; (2) 8.8.1–11, his statement to Alypius and the change of location to the garden of their house; (3a) 8.8.11–8.10, his internal debate on the mind, the body, and the will, and (3b) 8.11, the allegory of Continence; and (4) 8.12, the double conversion of Augustine and Alypius. Of course, it is possible to look upon (1) as both the conclusion to the episode of Ponticianus and the beginning of the story of his own conversion; see Sizoo (1954), 38.

170. Reminding the reader of bk. 2; cf. Schmidt-Dengler (1969), 205, and, as a stylistic manifestation of Augustine's *sermo humilis,* Auerbach (1953), 43–66, and (1965), 27–66.

171. Cf. Schmidt-Dengler (1969), 196–197, and, in detail, Knauer (1955), 96–132, on the role of quotations, allusions, and parallels with the Psalms, which, to the knowledgeable reader of the Bible, adds another layer of memory. It is also worth noting that Augustine was won over to the study of philosophy at about the time that the civil servants in Trier converted. Ponticianus' words are a reminder that some twelve years have passed during which he has searched for truth in an intellectual manner but failed to be true to himself in the way that he lived.

172. *Conf.* 8.7.34–37: "Ita rodebant intus . . . cum Ponticianus talia loqueretur."

173. Matt 11:12: "A diebus autem Joannis Baptistae usque nunc, regnum

caelorum uim patitur, et uiolenti rapiunt illud." For Matt 5:3, see *Conf.* 8.6.54–55; cf. 8.8.22–23, based on Ps. 34:10.

174. *Arripui: Conf.* 8.12.32; see Courcelle (1950), 168–169, 199–200 n. 1, 308–309, and, for a pertinent comparison of other texts, Courcelle, "Les 'voix'" (1952), 44–45.

175. His state of mind is reflected in bodily signs—through his forehead, cheeks, eyes, colour, and voice; 8.6.7–11. This external agitation becomes a symbol of inner activity.

176. On the repeated mention of *utor/frui,* see Chapter 7, "Christian Doctrine."

177. *Conf.* 8.8.14–15: "qua tu sciebas, ego autem non."

178. The private nature of his struggle is dramatized when it is transferred from an enclosed to an open space. One of the garden's symbolic functions may be to remind the reader that before God all human thoughts are public.

179. Note, however, the change from indirect to direct narrative style. Augustine listened to Ponticianus' words, whereas here the reader follows Alypius as he observes what takes place.

180. *Conf.* 8.8.18–19: "Neque enim secretum meum non erat, ubi ille aderat."

181. An issue that Augustine first raises in *Conf.* 3.1–3, when he is deciding among competing worldy interests.

182. For other texts on the problem of evil in the dialogues and the *Conf.* see Evans (1982), 93–98 and 1–6 respectively.

183. The argument is reproduced philosophically in bk. 11; see Chapter 8, "Time."

184. See O'Donnell (1992), vol. 3, 31.

185. Cf. *Conf.* 8.11.28: *abripere,* and 8.11.29: *excutere.*

186. Ibid., 8.11.7–9: "Dicebam enim apud me intus: 'Ecce modo fiat, modo fiat,' et cum uerbo iam ibam in placitum."

187. Persius, *Satires* 5.66–69. A favorite quotation of Augustine's; see O'Donnell (1992), vol. 3, 59.

188. Thereby maintaining the parallel between two narratives in dialogue, which begins when Ponticianus speaks.

189. *Conf.* 8.11.30, "consuetudo uiolenta," recalling 6.8.6, where he speaks of Alypius, taken off to the games by his friends, as "familiari uiolentia."

190. Including, of course, those of bk. 3; on which, see Shanzer (1992), 43–46. On the more general transformation, see the illuminating pages in Brown (1992), 74–78.

191. On Continence as a female allegorical figure, see Courcelle (1950), 192 n. 2.

192. Which will reappear at *Conf.* 9.10 in Monica's company; see Chapter 4, "Ostia."

193. Compare: Custom, *Conf.* 8.11.30: "'Putasne sine istis poteris?'" and Continence, 8.11.40: "Tu non poteris, quod isti, quod istae?'"

194. Just as, in taking up the internal dialogue, he heard the last words of Ponticianus.

195. It is tempting to see a dim reflection of the timeless youth of Monica's dream (4.11–12). This would be another connection to Manichaeism.

196. *De Nat. Boni* 44, *CSEL* 25.2.881.24–884.2. For an analysis of the sexual implications of the original Manichaean myth, see E. A. Clark (1986), 320–324. Another possibility, noted by Courcelle, "Source" (1952), 174, is *De Sancta Virginitate* 27.27, *CSEL* 41.263.7–264.4, written in 401; here again, the *pueri et puellae* may be "the continent" (Courcelle) or just "boys and girls" (Bolgiani [1956], 38–39 nn. 81–82).

197. *De Nat. Boni* 44, *CSEL* 25/2.882.4–12.

198. *Conf.* 8.12.1–2; cf. Ps. 15:8, 18:15: Acts 2:25.

199. His tears are a way of communicating with himself through emotions, i.e., through nonverbal communication; they cease later, when verbal communication takes over.

200. *Conf.* 8.11.49–50: "At Alypius affixus lateri meo inusitati motus mei exitum tacitus opperiebatur"; cf. 8.12.6.

201. Ibid., 8.12.3–6: "Et ut totum effunderem [= totam miseriam meam, 8.12.2] cum uocibus suis, surrexi ab Alypio—solitudo mihi ad negotium flendi aptior suggerebatur—et secessi remotius, quam ut posset mihi onerosa esse etiam eius praesentia."

202. Not knowing how he got there, ibid., 8.12.9–10. A remarkable feature of the scene is the shift in the literary devices reflecting predestination from the deity to the narrator.

203. On the rhetorical tradition, see, *inter alia,* the classic account of Curtius (1953), 183–202.

204. Cf. John 1:47–48; on the possibly sexual symbolism, see Buchheit (1968). The fullest review of the possible sources is Bolgiani (1956), 104–110, excluding only the Manichaeans, to whom there may be a lingering reference at *Conf.* 3.10.5–6: "Quam tamen ficum si comedisset aliquis sanctus alieno sane."

205. *Conf.* 8.12.12: "non quidem his uerbis."

206. Compare: ibid., 8.12.13–14: "'Usquequo, domine, irasceris in finem" and Ps. 78:5: "Quousque, domine, irasceris perpetuo?" Compare *Conf.* 8.12.4: "totum effunderem" and Ps. 78:3, 6: "Effuderunt . . . Effunde iram." Compare *Conf.* 8.12.14–15: "'Ne memor fueris iniquitatum nostrarum antiquarum'" and Ps. 78:8: "Noli recordari contra nos culpas majorum."

207. *Conf.* 8.12.19–20: "Et ecce audio uocem de uicina domo cum cantu dicentis et crebro repetentis quasi pueri an puellae, nescio: 'Tolle lege, tolle lege.'" Possible antecedents of this literary device are tabulated by Courcelle (1953); cf. Préaux (1955), 558–563 (and, on the opposite topos at *Phaedo* 97b–99d, Socrates' nonconversion in similar circumstances, see Préaux [1957]); a full review of possible sources is found in Bolgiani (1956), 110–117. On the controversial literature that followed Courcelle's interpretation, see Marrou, "La querelle" (1958), 47–48, where Courcelle's numerous contributions are listed. For a criticism of his position (subsequently modified), see Cayré, "La conversion" (1951–52); the detailed dis-

cussion of Bolgiani (1956), and Marrou, "La querelle" (1958), 50–56, as well as Courcelle's reply, (1963), 137–197. Cf. Ferrari (1983) and O'Donnell (1992), vol. 3, 59–61.

208. For a brilliant analysis of the range of "the voices," see Courcelle "Les 'voix'" (1952), 31–37.

209. *Conf.* 8.6.67: "Legebat et mutabatur intus"; cf. 8.11.7–8.

210. I.e., *cogitare;* ibid., 8.12.21.

211. Whence the tendency to favour one or the other among commentators; e.g., Courcelle (1963), 179–198.

212. Giving rise, in its wake, to a large controversy over the meaning of the scene as a whole. It is generally agreed that Courcelle's position was impaired by defending the Sessorianus reading, e.g., (1950), 195–196; (1963), 165–168; (1968), 299–310. For a refutation, see Bolgiani (1956) and Marrou, "La querelle" (1958), 49–50; and, for a brief summary of the extensive debate, see O'Donnell (1992), vol. 3, 62–63. For a recent defense of *diuina* as a symbolic intention, see Chadwick, "History and Symbolism" (1991), 52–55.

213. It is also a statement about misinterpretation, which distantly echoes the discussion of error in *De Util. Cred.;* see Chapter 6, "Defining the Reader."

214. *Conf.* 8.12.23–25: "Repressoque impetu lacrimarum surrexi nihil aliud interpretans diuinitus mihi iuberi, nisi ut aperirem codicem et legerem quod primum caput inuenissem." The command would normally refer to oral reading; Bolgiani (1956), 117–120. The idea is anticipated at 4.3.39–44, where it is voiced by Vindicianus, then attempting not altogether successfully to refute Augustine's belief in astrological prediction: "Si enim de paginis poetae cuiuspiam longe aliud canentis atque intendentis, cum forte quis consulit, mirabiliter consonus negotio saepe uersus exiret, mirandum non esse dicebat, si ex anima humana superiore aliquo instinctu nesciente, quid in se fieret, non arte, sed sorte sonaret aliquid, quod interrogantis rebus factisque concineret."

215. *Conf.* 8.12.20, 25, 26, 31, 32, 36, etc.; cf. Bolgiani (1956), 46.

216. For a brief review of biblical passages containing connections between hearing and conversion, see Tombeur (1965), 159–160.

217. *Conf.* 8.6.27. Ferrari (1980), 11–12, notes the frequency of citation of Romans in earlier writings. The choice of a codex may also be significant; a roll (or scroll) would have made the arbitrary choice of a text cumbersome.

218. Cf. Chadwick, "History and Symbolism" (1991), 48–49, who sees light shed by *De Gen. ad Litt.* 12.22, *CSEL* 28/1.412–414. But there are possible objections: (1) Augustine is not here dealing with prophecy, but predestination; and (2) he is not speaking of images or visions, the topics of *De Gen.* 12, but of external and internal voices.

219. Cf. *De Doct. Christ.,* proem., *CCSL* 32.2.51, where he notes that Anthony was "sine ulla scientia litterarum."

220. Rom. 13:13–14. Could there be an echo of Augustine's rejection of the ceremony of *laetitia,* whose excesses he the Council of Hippo had condemned in

393? In *Ep.* 29.5–11 (*CSEL* 34/1.116–121) he describes how he tackled the problem during a Lenten sermon. There were three stages of reading: first, Exod. 32:6, presumably read by the lector; then, after his disappointment at the audience's response, a "laying aside of the book of Exodus, and . . . as much as time allowed, taking up Paul," in which he himself read 1 Cor. 5:11, 6:9–11, 11:20–22 (as well as Matt. 7:16)—all texts speaking out against "rioting and drunkenness" in a manner similar to Rom. 13:13–14; and finally, "when this was done, and the book returned" to the lector, a calling for prayer, in which, after quoting Ps. 88:31–34, he added the words "in eum [i.e., Christum] me fidere, quod, si haec tanta, quae sibi essent lecta et dicta, contemnerent, uisitaturus esset in uirga et in flagello nec eos permissurus cum hoc mundo damnari" (29.7, p. 118.28–32). When the congregation threatened to relapse on the feast-day, he urged them to become *imitatores* of overseas churches (29.10, p. 120.21); and to break with their disreputable "custom" (ibid., 120.27, 121.11), he asked them "to pass the noon hour in *lectio diuina* and prayer" (ibid., p. 121.12–13). This was continued into the afternoon, when a greater number of people had assembled (29.11, p. 121.19). Support for some contemporary relevance is summarized by O'Donnell (1992), vol. 3, 67, including *Ep.* 22.1.2, to Aurelius, quoting Romans 13:13, as well as the possibility that Augustine's mind was drawn to the verse through Ambrose, *Exameron* 1.10.38 (notwithstanding the difficulty of its dating).

221. *Conf.* 8.12.34–35 (quoting Paul): "sed induite dominum Iesum Christum." Cf. Eph. 4:24 and Gal. 3:27.

222. *Conf.* 8.12.30–32: "Itaque concitus redii in eum locum, ubi sedebat Alypius: ibi enim posueram codicem apostoli, cum inde surrexeram."

223. Ibid., 8.12.32–33: "Arripui, aperui et legi in silentio capitulum, quo primum coniecti sunt oculi mei."

224. Ibid., 8.12.36–38: "Nec ultra uolui legere nec opus erat. Statim quippe cum fine huiusce sententiae quasi luce securitatis infusa cordi meo omnes dubitationis tenebrae diffugerunt."

225. Ibid., 8.12.39–41: "Tum interiecto aut digito aut nescio quo alio signo codicem clausi et tranquillo iam uultu indicaui Alypio. At ille quid in se ageretur—quod ego nesciebam—sic indicauit."

226. Ibid., 8.12.41–42: "Petit uidere quid legissem: ostendi, et attendi etiam ultra quam ego legeram"; another triune arrangement, anticipating the psychological trinities of *De Trin.* 8–15.

227. *Conf.* 8.12.42–43: "Et ignorabam quid sequeretur."

228. Ibid., 8.12.44: "Quod ille ad se rettulit mihique aperuit." On the drama of the silent exchange, see Vecchi (1965), 106–107.

229. Thereby completing the symbolism of enclosure/disclosure that is brought into play when Augustine leaves the house and enters the garden.

230. For a review of the philosophical issues, see Chastaing (1961), 120–124; (1962), 93–97. The fact that we cannot think another person's thoughts is logically related to Augustine's belief in the self's existence through the affirmation of the *cogito*.

231. Cf. *Sol.* 3.8, *CSEL* 89.14.12–19, where Reason, speaking of Alypius, has an exchange with Augustine on this very point.

232. As contrasted with Wittgenstein, who argues that a language game depends on a form of life.

## 4. From Cassiciacum to Ostia

1. His other literary endeavours include his unsuccessful attempt to read Isaiah and the dialogue that became *De Magistro*.

2. In 9.7, the truth of Catholicism is confirmed by the bishop's discovery of the remains of the second-century martyrs Gervasius and Protasius. Dug up and, according to Augustine, miraculously preserved, they countered the influence of the Arian heresy then menacing the Milanese church through Justina, the mother of the boy emperor, Valentinian. The martyrs' graves were so powerful a memorial to the divine that demons allegedly tried to outwit the bishop by making use of them to further their ends; *De Cura pro Mor. Ger.* 12.17.21, *CSEL* 41.655–658. This type of memorial is paralleled at the end of bk. 9 by the monument of Augustine's *Confessions* as a written text. On the connection between baptism and the vision of paradise, another theme of bk. 9, see ibid., 12.15 (p. 646.4–5); for a review of the issues, see the brilliant pages of Courcelle (1950), 141–151.

3. Augustine thus reflects two of the principal ways of describing the earthly paradise in patristic writings, i.e., as a physical location and as a state of mind; see *De Ciu. Dei* 13.21–22, *CCSL* 48.404–405.

4. Cf. *Conf.* 10.9.3, where Augustine reuses and criticizes the topos: "quasi remota interiore loco, non loco." A possible source of the imagery is Lactantius (or pseudo-Lactantius), *Carmen de Aue Phoenice* 1–32 (*CSEL* 27.11); for a discussion of the political symbolism, see Kantorowicz (1957), 388–395. The use of the topos to describe paradise, and thus to ornament the account in Genesis, was popular with Christian Latin poets in the following century; e.g., Avitus, *De Mundi Initio, Monumenta Germanica Historica, Auctores Antiquissimi* 6/2.203.

5. *Conf.* 9.3.13–17: "Gratias tibi, deus noster . . . .: fidelis promissor reddis Verecundo pro rure illo eius Cassiciaco, ubi ab aestu saeculi requieuimus in te, amoenitatem sempiterne uirentis paradisi tui."

6. Ibid., 9.10.7–11: "Conloquebamur ergo soli ualde dulciter et praeterita obliuiscentes in ea quae ante sunt extenti quaerebamus inter nos apud praesentem ueritatem, quod tu es, qualis futura esset uita aeterna sanctorum, quam nec oculus uidit nec auris audiuit nec in cor hominis ascendit."

7. Ibid., 9.2.10–12: "quamquam tu nobis a conualle plorationis ascendentibus [Ps. 119:3–4] et cantantibus canticum graduum dederas sagittas acutas et carbones uastatores [Ps. 119:3–4]." Cf. TeSelle (1970), 37–38. Psalms 119–133 are the *canticum graduum.*

8. To which he may be giving a reluctant, backward glance in the language in which he phrases his compositional activities at Cassiciacum; *Conf.* 9.4.4–5,

quoted in note 9 below. The tone is noted by O'Donnell (1992), vol. 3, 85. On the role of this reading in bk. 10, see Sieben (1977), 489–492.

9. I.e., to the degree we can judge from *Conf.* 9.4.20–25; on soliloquy, cf. 9.4.4–7: "Ibi quid egerim in litteris . . . testantur libri disputati cum praesentibus et cum ipso me solo coram te." I revert to my earlier suggestion that Augustine may be reading into the episode some of his later experience as a preacher.

10. This note is sounded at ibid., 9.1.16–19; cf. 1.18.29–30: "Quam tu secretus es, habitans in excelsis in silentio" 6.3.46–47: "Tu enim, altissime et proxime, secretissime et praesentissime." O'Donnell (1992), vol. 3, 75, sees a parallel between the trio *dulcior, clarior, sublimior* and the undercurrent of oblique references throughout bks. 1–9 to 1 John 2:16: "concupiscentia carnis, concupiscentia oculorum, ambitio saeculi"; for a discussion, see ibid., vol. 1, xxii–xxiii, vol. 2, 65–66. Also Bolgiani (1956), 54–55. By contrast, Alypius, also awaiting baptism (9.4.22–23), adopted reading but resisted composition (9.4.16–17).

11. *Conf.* 9.7.1–3; cf. *De Ord.* 1.7.22 (*CCSL* 29.99.11–13), 1.10.29 (pp. 103–104). Again, in emotional, i.e., wordless, communication with his inner self.

12. Obliquely foreshadowed, perhaps, at *Conf.* 9.2.3, where he refers to his former pupils as "not reflecting on your law" *(pueri meditantes non legem tuam); meditor* more aptly describes his study habits than theirs.

13. O'Donnell (1992), vol. 3, 91, with a useful reconstruction of Augustine's text of Ps. 4 (91–92).

14. This is to elevate the readers' role one step beyond that in bk. 8, where Alypius is present as an interpreter. The readers are singled out again at the end of bk. 9.

15. *Conf.* 9.4.42–44: "Inhorrui timendo ibidemque inferui sperando . . . Et haec omnia exibant per oculos et uocem meam."

16. See Madec (1974), 90–95, 170–175, 207, 254, 325–326.

17. Something of the spirit of this type of reading is captured at *En. in Ps.* 128, s. 19.4, *CCSL* 40.1728.15–25: "'Quia lex,' inquit, 'tua meditatio mea est [Ps. 118:77].' Haec meditatio nisi esset in fide, quae per dilectionem operatur, numquam propter eam posset ad illam uitam quispiam peruenire. Hoc dicendum putaui, ne quisquam, cum totam legem memoriae mandauerit, eamque creberrima recordatione cantauerit, non tacens quod praecipit, nec tamen uiuens ut praecipit, arbitretur se fecisse quod legit . . . Haec meditatio amantis est cogitatio."

18. *Conf.* 10.33.10–13: "Et omnes affectus spiritus nostri pro sui diuersitate habere proprios modos in uoce atque cantu, quorum nescio qua occulta familiaritate excitentur."

19. Ibid., 10.33.13–16; to which compare the temptations of Alypius, discussed in Chapter 3, "Alypius."

20. Ibid., 10.33.25–27: "Verum tamen cum reminiscor lacrimas meas, quas fudi ad cantus ecclesiae in primordiis recuperatae fidei meae, et nunc ipsum cum moueor non cantu, sed rebus quae cantantur." The experience reiterates his initial and subsequent impression of Ambrose's preaching, which was auditory and emotional before becoming intellectual.

21. This is magnificently illustrated in the emotional connections between the sermons of *En. in Ps.,* of which a full study would be useful.

22. *Conf.* 9.4.6, 8: "Testantur libri . . .; testantur epistulae."

23. I.e., the prayer that he wrote on wax tablets in an effort to be cured of a toothache, when he was unable to pray orally; *Conf.* 9.4.104–105: "Et scripsi hoc in cera et dedi, ut eis legeretur."

24. Ibid., 9.4.82–83: "inchoata meditatione renouationis." Former conversations are not excluded; 9.3.28–32; 9.4.10–19, 27–44, 59–64.

25. Ibid., 9.4.20–27; 9.4.65–69, 74–75, 84, 88–91, 94.

26. On this subject, see the exhaustive survey of Knauer (1955), esp. 111–161; and, on *Conf.* 9.4, p. 184.

27. *Conf.* 9.4.99–9.6.27; biblical texts cited in the notes, *CSEL* 27, pp. 138–40, include Ps. 118:103, 105 (9.4.97), Ps. 37:23–24 (9.4.104), Ps. 144:2 (9.4.108).

28. Other quotations refer to God's goodness (1 Peter 2:3 at 9.4.78) and to God's light, illuminating us all (John 1:9 at 9.4.76).

29. A similar sequence of ideas is incorporated into the scheme for freedom after death; *Conf.* 9.4.90–98.

30. Ibid., 9.4.84–85: "Et exclamabam legens haec foris et agnoscens intus."

31. Ferrari (1991).

32. I utilize O'Donnell's reconstruction (1992), vol. 3, 91–92.

33. For a perceptive portrait of Monica, see Brown (1967), 28–31.

34. E.g., *De Beata Vita* 2.10, *CCSL* 29.70–71; *De Ord.* 1.11.31 (ibid., p. 105); emphasized by O'Meara (1954), 33–39.

35. Gwynn (1926), 14–16.

36. *De Ord.* 2.1.4–7, *CCSL* 29.106; cf. 2.17.5–6 (p. 131).

37. Alfaric (1918), 8–10; Henry (1938), 4–7; a succinct but discerning sketch is offered by G. Bonner (1963), 38–41.

38. *De Ord.* 2.17.46, *CCSL* 29.132.24–28.

39. E.g., *De Beata Vita* 2.10, *CCSL* 29.70–71.

40. *Conf.* 9.8.13–14: "Neque enim se ipsa fecerat aut educauerat se ipsam: tu creasti eam."

41. Cf. Quint., *Inst. Orat.* 1.1.6–7, who, by contrast, stresses the value of educated women as beneficent influences on the young.

42. Dyroff (1930), 16–18; O'Donnell (1992), vol. 3, 123.

43. This fact raises the issue of Augustine's views on female spirituality and literacy, which require a fuller exposition than can be attempted here; but see Chapter 5, "The Letters," for the case of Paulina. For the negative side, in addition to the discussion in the Introduction, see *Ep.* 20.3, *CSEL* 34/1.48–49, where he speaks disparagingly of the wife of a certain Antoninus, who should have a "not unreasonable fear of God" instilled in her "through divine reading and serious conversation." Cf. *De Util. Cred.* 6.13, *CSEL* 25.17–18, where he relates an anecdote concerning a Manichaean woman, *religiose simplex* who mistakes the sun's rays for their divine cause. By contrast, one thinks of the brief description of Therasia, the wife of Paulinus of Nola, in *Ep.* 27.2, *CSEL* 34/1.97–98: her

potential "softness" becomes his "strength," as the pair are linked by bonds as "spiritual" as they are "chaste."

44. *De Ord.* 2.17, *CCSL* 29.131–132.23.

45. It is worth drawing attention to an inversion of customary gender relationships. In general, Monica represents a rational, if spontaneous, faith, while Augustine succumbs to temptations of sensuality even as he is reflective.

46. There are many commentaries on this text. Henry (1938), remains the basis for most subsequent judgements; for reviews of different approaches to the allegedly "mystical" elements in the scene, see Morati (1960); Zangara (1979), 64–76; and the lucid pages in Louth (1981), 133–141.

47. *Conf.* 9.10.3–5: "procurante te occultis tuis modis, ut ego et ipsa soli staremus incumbentes ad quandam fenestram, unde hortus intra domum, quae nos habebat, prospectabatur."

48. The occasion is brilliantly recreated by Henry (1938), 1–7; however, the dependence of the scene on Plotinus (chaps. 2–4) remains a hypothesis. On the notion of a sacred landscape that may help to understand the scene, see Cancik (1985–86), 260.

49. *De Ord.* 2.17, *CCSL* 29.131.3–9.

50. *Conf.* 9.10.5–7: "Illic apud Ostia Tibertina, ubi remoti a turbis post longi itineris laborem instaurabamus nos nauigationi." See Capánaga (1966), 359–363.

51. Cf. de Margerie (1983), 146*–157*.

52. See Boyer (1932), 276–278.

53. Significantly, he cannot recall just what was said; *Conf.* 9.10.52.

54. And omitting needless detail, ibid., 9.8.7–8.

55. For the similar perspective in a different context in *De Trin.*, see Chapter 9, "A Language of Thought."

56. *Conf.* 9.10.11–13: "Sed inhiabamus ore cordis in superna fluenta fontis tui, fontis uitae, qui est apud te, ut inde pro captu nostro aspersi quoquo modo rem tantam cogitaremus." The idea is spelled out at *De Gen. ad Litt.* 12.12, *CSEL* 28.396.13–16: "Sed cum spiritalis uisio penitus, nalienato a sensibus corporis animo imaginibus corporalium detinetur siue in somnis siue in extasi . . . ipsius animae sunt imaginationes." Cf. Fontaine (1954), 120–122.

57. *Conf.* 9.10.19–25: "Et adhuc ascendebamus interius cogitando et loquendo et mirando opera tua et uenimus in mentes nostras et transcendimus eas, ut attingeremus regionem ubertatis indeficientis, ubi pascis Israhel in aeternum ueritate pabulo, et ibi uita sapientia est, per quam fiunt omnia ista, et quae fuerunt et quae futura sunt [John 1:3]." The psychological trinity, "thinking, speaking, and marvelling," anticipates *De Trin.* 8–15, where the goal is likewise wisdom.

58. *Conf.* 9.10.25–27: "Quin potius fuisse et futurum esse non est in ea, sed esse solum, quoniam aeterna est."

59. Ibid., 9.10.27–32: "Et dum loquimur et inhiamus illi, attingimus eam modice toto ictu cordis; et suspirauimus et reliquimus ibi religatas 'primitias spiritus' [Rom. 8:23] et remeauimus ad strepitum oris nostri, ubi uerbum et incipitur et

finitur. Et quid simile uerbo tuo, domino nostro, in se permanenti sine uetustate atque innouanti omnia?"

60. See Henry (1934), 63–145, and, more generally, Henry (1938) and Armstrong (1954); also Courcelle (1950), 222–226; Pépin, "'Primitiae spiritus'" (1977), 155–202, and (1964), 262–268; for a word-by-word analysis of the text, see Mandouze (1954). Henry's weaknesses are emphasized by Cavallera (1939), 182–194.

61. *Conf.* 9.10.10–11; 1 Cor. 2:9. On the differences between Plotinian and Augustinian conversion, see the classic account of Guitton (1971), 127–140.

62. See O'Meara (1954), 202–203, and, for a review of opinions, G. Bonner (1963), 98–99. Mandouze (1954) and Capánaga (1966), 369–376, 387–392, argue in favour of mysticism; cf. Louth (1988), 133–141, who ably situates Augustine's experience within Christian mystical tradition.

63. See Pépin, "'Primitiae spiritus'" (1951), and the judicious note of Solignac, *BA* 14 (1962), 552–555.

64. Suggested by the quotation of 1 Cor. 15:51 at 9.10.50–51.

65. Cf. Chadwick, *St. Augustine* (1991), 171 n. 25.

66. For a summary of the relevant texts on this theme beginning with *Sol.* 1.12–13 and 1.23–25, see Cavallera (1939), 186–187 n. 10.

67. Against a philosophical interpretation, Cavallera points out (1939), 183: "Le point de départ en est un texte scriptuaire [1 Cor. 2.9] et c'est la donnée qu'il contient qui va servir de thème à tout le développement."

68. See Chapter 7, "Christian Doctrine."

69. *Commemoratione:* 9.10.16–17; on its role in Augustine's theory of language, see Chapter 6, "The Teacher."

70. E.g., *perduceretur, perambulauimus, ascendebamus, uenimus, transcendimus, attingeremus/attingimus, reliquimus, remeauimus.*

71. On memory, see Chapter 8, "Remembering."

72. *Conf.* 9.11.14–16: "Cumque hanc sententiam uerbis quibus poterat explicasset, conticuit et ingrauescente morbo exercebatur."

73. Ibid., 9.10.33–51. In my paraphrase, I reverse the order of first two clauses. Nowhere else in *Conf.* does Augustine so emphasize the role of silence, 9.10.33–39: "Dicebamus ergo: 'Si cui *sileat* tumultus carnis, *sileant* phantasiae terrae et aquarum et aeris, *sileant* et poli et ipsa sibi anima *sileat* et transeat se non se cogitando, *sileant* somnia et imaginariae reuelationes, omnis lingua et omne signum et quidquid transeundo fit si cui *sileat* omnino . . .'—his dictis si iam *taceant*" (my italics). Note as well the emphasis on "transition."

74. Ibid., 9.10.44–45: "sicut nunc extendimus nos et rapida cogitatione attingimus aeternam sapientiam."

75. Omitting the death of Adeodatus, which does not notably influence the narrative.

76. *Conf.* 9.12.74: "Et nunc, domine, confiteor tibi in litteris."

77. Ibid., 9.13.47–51: "Et inspira, domine meus, deus meus, inspira seruis tuis

... quibus et corde et uoce et litteris seruio, ut quotquot haec legerint, meminerint ad altare tuum Monnicae, famulae tuae, cum Patricio."

## 5. Beginnings

1. Taylor (1989), 4.

2. Cf. *En. in Ps.* 99.10, *CCSL* 39.1399.11–15.

3. On his unusually high social status, see Kaster (1988), 112; on the Milanese friendships continued at Cassiciacum, see Nolte (1939), 27–29, 33–37.

4. *Conf.* 9.2, *CCSL* 27.134.29–32. Cf. *De Beata Vita* 1.4, *CCSL* 29.67.105–106; *C. Acad.* 1.1, ibid., pp. 4–5, 70–71. For a further discussion, see Legewie (1931), 10–13.

5. *C. Acad.* 3.7, *CCSL* 29.43.23–24.

6. *Conf.* 9.1, *CCSL* 27.133.19–21.

7. Ibid., 9.3, pp. 135.5–6 (Verecundus) and 31–34 (Nebridius).

8. But not Nebridius, Verecundus' assistant; cf. Halliburton (1962). Was he kept in Milan for academic reasons? See O'Meara (1954), 192.

9. For a magisterial review, see Mandouze (1968), 165–242.

10. On the notion of *otium* at Cassiciacum, see the texts assembled by Folliet (1961), 36–37; also Voss (1970), 281–283, and J. Matthews (1975), 1–12 (on Symmachus). The period is brilliantly recreated by Brown (1967), 115–127; the theme of meditative withdrawal is discussed by Halliburton (1967), 257–261; an example is *Ep.* 5, *CSEL* 34/1.11.16, where Nebridius echoes Augustine's desires, stating: "Vellem ego te in rus meum uocare ibique adquiescere."

11. *Conf.* 9.4, *CCSL* 27.136.2–3: "Eruisti linguam meam."

12. Possibly also *De Grammatica;* see Law (1984).

13. *Conf.* 9.4, *CCSL* 27.136.4–7: "Ibi quid egerim in litteris iam quidem seruientibus tibi ... testantur libri disputati cum praesentibus et cum ipso me solo coram te."

14. Just as his literary image of friends and friendship was modeled on the *Laelius;* van Bavel, "Influence" (1987), 59–71.

15. Cf. Dönt (1969), 188.

16. For an enduring evocation of these themes in a now abundant literature, a good point of departure remains Alfaric (1918), 414–513.

17. On the topics of the correspondence between the pair, see Folliet (1987), 194–214, who classifies them under three headings (194): the return to oneself; the world, the faculties of the soul, and human understanding; and the trinity and the incarnation.

18. Among the other topics discussed are his opposition to materialism, numerology, and aspects of neoplatonism; *Ep.* 3.2.4, *CSEL* 34/1.6–8.

19. Ibid., 3.1 (p. 5.8–10): "Legi enim litteras tuas ad lucernam iam cenatus; proxime erat cubitio, sed non ita etiam dormitio; quippe diu mecum in lecto situs cogitaui."

20. Ibid., 3.4 (p. 8.24).

21. Ibid., 3.1 (p. 5.10–11).

22. Ibid., 3.1 (p. 5.18–6.2).

23. Compare his mental state to that of the dreamer at *Sol.* 2.6.12, *CSEL* 89.60–61; cf. 2.9.17 (pp. 66–67).

24. *Ep.* 6.1, *CSEL* 34/1.11.21; cf. Seneca, *Epistulae ad Lucilium* 4.40.1. Cf. *Ep.* 27.1–2, *CSEL* 34/1.95–98.

25. This is one of the points of departure for the notion of illumination; e.g., *Sol.* 1.6.12–13, *CSEL* 89.19–22.

26. *Ep.* 10.1, *CSEL* 34/1.23.11–12: "Tu enim potes et apud tuam mentem suauiter habitare." Cf. 11 (ibid., p. 25.23–24), 12 (p. 29.14–15).

27. *Ep.* 4.1 (p. 10.4–8).

28. *Ep.* 12 (p. 29.8–19); cf. 9.5 (p. 22.15–16).

29. *Ep.* 4.1 (pp. 9.21–10.2), 4.2 (p. 11.2–6).

30. *Ep.* 11.1 (p. 25.16–22).

31. *Ep.* 9.5 (p. 22.13–21).

32. *Ep.* 12 (p. 29.1–2); cf. 14.1 (p. 32).

33. *Ep.* 4.2 (p. 11.3–6), 8 (p. 18.21), 13.1 (p. 30.1–2), 14.1 (p. 32).

34. *Ep.* 15 (p. 35.15–20) (to Romanianus).

35. Cf. Augustine's letter to Hermogenianus in 386, *Ep.* 3.3 (pp. 2–3), or to Caelestinus in 390, 18.1 (pp. 44.1–45.6).

36. *Ep.* 9.1 (p. 20.1–2); cf. 1 (pp. 1–3), 10 (pp. 22–25), and, movingly, to Gaius, ca. 390, 19 (p. 46.1–2).

37. *Epp.* 10, 11 (pp. 22–28).

38. *Retr.* 1.1.1, *CCSL* 57.7.2–3.

39. On the gaps in the record, see Courcelle (1951); on the uncertainty of dating, see Fabre (1948), 14–19, and the revisions of Courcelle (1963), 599–607; on the significance, see Nolte (1939), 55–69.

40. Although she scarcely appears to be a separate person in either male's statements to the other.

41. *Ep.* 24.2–3, *CSEL* 34/1.74–75.

42. *Ep.* 25.2 (p. 79.9–12).

43. Brown (1967), 161–162; J. Matthews (1975), 211–215.

44. Marrou, *Saint Augustin* (1958), 99–100.

45. The situation bears some similarity to the personal relating of stories about asceticism by Ponticianus. The literary sequence of events is also paralleled, inasmuch as the oral versions lead to a reading about Paulinus through his letters. Augustine's letter was written in 396, close to the time he embarked on the *Conf.*

46. *Ep.* 31.2, *CSEL* 34/2.2.14–15; cf. 216.3, *CSEL* 57.398.14–21.

47. *Ep.* 27.2, *CSEL* 34/1.97.1–6: "Legi enim litteras tuas fluentes lac et mel . . . Legerunt fratres et gaudent infatigabiliter et ineffabiliter . . . Quotquot eas legerunt, rapiunt, quia rapiuntur, cum legunt." On this use of *rapere,* see Chapter 3, "Augustine."

48. *Ep.* 27.3 (ibid., p. 98.8–9).

49. E.g., *Ep.* 29 (ibid., pp. 114–122). Cf. 121.1, *CSEL* 34/2.723, from 410.

50. *De Diu. Quaes.,* q. 71.6, *CCSL* 44a.205–206. For a positive evaluation, see Nolte (1939), 38–115.

51. *Ep.* 258.1, *CSEL* 57.605.10–11. Cf. Cicero, *Laelius* 20, and, for a discussion, van Bavel, "Influence" (1987).

52. *Sol.* 1.12.20, *CSEL* 89.31.3–6. Cf. *De Mor. Eccles. Cath.* 1.26.48, *PL* 32.1331.

53. *Ep.* 19, *CSEL* 34/1.46.18–21. Cf. Maximus, a grammarian of Madaura, *Ep.* 16 (p. 39.10–13), who argues that his writing *(chartula)* may perish, but a copy *(exemplar)* will remain in the memories of all devotees of paganism.

54. *Ep.* 37.2 (ibid., p. 63.13–20).

55. Cf. Monica's dream, *Conf.* 3.11–12, *CCSL* 27.37–39.

56. *Ep.* 21.3, *CSEL* 34/1.51.4–10. Cf. *Ep.* 21.6 (p. 53.20–24) and the similar demand at *Conf.* 6.11, *CCSL* 27.85–87. For a vivid recollection of the tensions, see *Ep.* 139.3, *CSEL* 44.152–153 (to Marcellinus in 412).

57. Cf. *Ep.* 9.1, *CSEL* 34/1.20.8–13; 13.3–4 (pp. 31–32); 14.2 (p. 32.20–21); 22.1 (p. 54.10–12).

58. *Ep.* 147.1, *CSEL* 44.275.11–15.

59. Ibid., (p. 276.1–6).

60. Ibid., (p. 276.7–11): "Nolo auctoritatem meam sequaris, ut ideo putes tibi aliquid necesse esse credere, quoniam a me dicitur; sed aut scripturis canonicis credas, si quid nondum, quam sit uerum, uides, aut interius demonstranti ueritati, ut hoc plane uideas." For a similar doctrine in the preface to *De Doct. Christ.,* see Chapter 7, "Christian Doctrine," Needless to say, both ideas return to the notion of teaching from within in *De Mag.*

61. *Ep.* 147.3, *CSEL* 44.276.15–16, 147.4 (p. 278.6).

62. *Ep.* 147.3 (p. 276.18–277.6).

63. This is another employment of the proof of the *cogito,* even if some of the argument's stages are assumed.

64. *Ep.* 147.7 (p. 281.9–10): "Creduntur ergo illa, quae absunt a sensibus nostris, si uidetur, idoneum, quod eis testimonium perhibetur."

65. *Ep.* 147.8 (p. 282.2–3): "Dantur signa uel in uocibus uel in litteris uel in quibusque documentis."

66. *Ep.* 147.5 (pp. 278.21–279.1).

67. *Ep.* 147.7, (p. 281.221–224).

68. *Ep.* 147.6 (p. 279.14–18).

69. *Ep.* 147.9 (p. 282.20–21); cf. pp. 282.24–283.1: "Scripturae ad uisa pertinent corporis: oculorum, si eas legit, uel aurium, si audiuit."

70. *Ep.* 147.10 (p. 283.13).

71. Ibid., (p. 283.1–6). Cf. 147.42–43 (pp. 316–318).

72. *Ep.* 147.14 (p. 286.15).

73. *Ep.* 147.17 (p. 289.2–3): "Cum euangelium exponens beatus Ambrosius, Mediolanensis episcopus." The text is Luke 1:11; *Ep.* 147.18–19; cf. Ambrose,

*Expositio Euangelii secundum Lucan* 1.24–27, *CSEL* 32/4.25.15–28.7. The same principles are reaffirmed later, *Ep.* 147.41 (p. 315).

74. For an analysis of the literary qualities of the dialogues, see Voss (1970), 197–225, 233–245; P. Schmidt (1977); and Lerer (1985), 46–56; also Dyroff (1930), 16–20; M. Hoffmann (1966), 135–159; and Gunermann (1973) on *De Ord.*

75. Cf. Possidius, *Vita* 17, *PL* 32.47–48, where the Arian count, Pascentius, refused to have the debate with Augustine recorded. The bishop was required to set down his conclusions in writing and to circulate them as letters. The technique was well advanced by the time of Cicero; see Lerer (1985), 38, in a perceptive account. On the fictional elements in the dialogues which are not incompatible with their historicity, see O'Meara (1950), 23–32, and "The Historicity" (1951), 160–178; also Marrou, *Saint Augustin* (1958), 309 n. 1. On the historical, see above all Madec (1986), a definitive analysis. Cf. Gessel (1966), 93–117, who introduces the idea of a eucharistic "community."

76. *C. Acad.* 2.7, *CSEL* 29.27.40–45; for a detailed portrait of the young "enthusiast," see Bardy, "Un élève" (1954), 61–69. In *Ep.* 33.4, *CSEL* 34/2.20.24–21.12, using similar language, Augustine tells Proculeianus that a written exchange of views between them is preferable to a verbal one, not only because they are apt to forget what they have said, but because of the potentially detrimental effect of a public quarrel on their listening audience.

77. Cf. Starr (1987), 213–215, who outlines the practice among earlier authors.

78. E.g., *C. Acad.* 1.1, *CCSL* 29.5.98–99; 2.9 (p. 30.26–29); *De Beata Vita* 2.15 (ibid., p. 74.228), 2.18 (p. 75.47–48); *De Ord.* 1.2 (ibid., p. 91.41–43). It is difficult to know when Augustine is referring to real stenographers and when the idea is a literary convention, i.e., a way of drawing attention to the historicity of the dialogues. Cf. *Ep.* 44, *CSEL* 34/2.109–121; 66 (ibid., pp. 235–236). Nonetheless, this was Augustine's normal method of composition; for a review of the evidence, see Dekkers (1952), 127–131; also Dekkers (1990), 236.

79. *De Beata Vita* 2.15, *CCSL* 29.74.229–230 (Alypius); *De Ord.* 1.10.30, ibid., p. 104.58–60 (Licentius).

80. *C. Acad.* 1.5 (ibid., p. 12.54–56).

81. *De Ord.* 1.11 (ibid., p. 106.61–62).

82. E.g., ibid., 2.1 (pp. 106.4–107.4–12).

83. *C. Acad.* 2.11 (ibid., p. 31.3–4).

84. *De Vera Rel.* 20.39, *CCSL* 32.211.27–29.

85. *C. Acad.* 2.7, *CCSL* 29.27.40–43.

86. Ibid., 1.1 (p. 5.99); cf. Virgil, *Aen.* 9.312. He also foresaw the dangers of publication; *Ep.* 143.3, *CSEL* 44.252–253.

87. *C. Acad.* 2.9.22, *CCSL* 29.30.26–27: "Sed propter memoriam, quae infida custos est excogitatorum, referri in litteras uolui." Cf. *Sol.* 1.1.1, *CSEL* 89.3.12–14; *De Quant. An.* 18.31 (ibid., pp. 167.23–168.1).

88. This too may be a literary convention; see *C. Acad.* 1.2 (ibid., p. 25.34–35), which does not reiterate anything that Trygetius has previously said.

89. *De Ord.* 1.9 (ibid., p. 102.19–22), speaking of those absent. See also his

dedication to Zenobius, ibid., 2.4 (p. 91.55–60). Was this in his mind when he approved of Paulinus' plan to write a "life of Alypius"? See *Ep.* 27, *CSEL* 34/1.101.3–6.

90. *De Beata Vita* 1.4, *CSEL* 29.67.98–103; *C. Acad.* 2.10 (ibid., p. 31.25–29); cf. 3.14 (p. 53.28–31).

91. *C. Acad.* 2.4 (ibid., p. 23.14–16).

92. See Doignon (1984–85), 118–119.

93. *De Beata Vita* 2.8, *CCSL* 29.69–70.

94. *De Ord.* 1.8.26 (ibid., p. 102.110–116). The only nonreader appears to be Monica, who complains that the discussions give no role to women; ibid., 1.11.31, (p. 105.4–6).

95. Ibid., 1.3.6 (pp. 91.1–92.27); cf. 1.9.29 (pp. 103.15–104.57).

96. Ibid., 2.10.28 (p. 123.23): "ut ego tibi uerborum, tu mihi rerum magister effectus sis."

97. Printed in *Ep.* 26, *CSEL* 34/1.89–95. For a discussion, see Romano (1961), 13–22.

98. Cf. Bardy, "Un élève" (1954), 73–75.

99. *Ep.* 26, *CSEL* 34/1, lines 52–55.

100. Ibid., lines 29, 86, 102; cf. line 75, *docte*.

101. Ibid., lines 1–4. Cf. G. Bonner (1963), 93–94.

102. *Ep.* 26, *CSEL* 34/1, lines 108–109: "Sed labor interiora legens uulgata libellis / atque animis inuenta tuis." Licentius' functions in the dialogues are subtly interpreted by Hübner (1987), 42–48.

103. E.g., *De Beata Vita* 1.4, *CCSL* 29.66.80–81 (cf. *Aen.* 3.515); *C. Acad.* 1.5.14 (ibid., p. 11.25) (cf. *Aen.* 1.401); 2.1.1 (p. 18.16–17) (cf. *Aen.* 8.535); 2.7.18 (p. 28.61) (*Aen.* 11.424); 3.4.9 (p. 39.51) (*Eclogues* 3.104–107); *De Ord.* 1.4 (ibid., p. 94.19) (*Aen.,* 10.875), etc.; for a review of quotations from the *Aeneid,* see Schelkle (1939), 57–175.

104. *C. Acad.* 2.3.7, *CCSL* 29.22.14–15; cf. *De Ord.* 1.8.26 (ibid., p. 102.106–116).

105. E.g., *C. Acad.* 3.4.7 (ibid., pp. 38.1–39.12); *De Ord.* 1.3.8 (pp. 92.43–93.66); *Ep.* 26.1–3, *CSEL* 34/1.83–85. The same complaint is registered by Paulinus of Nola, *Ep.* 32, *CSEL* 34/2.8–18.

106. On the theory that may lie behind the notion, see *Sol.* 2.11.19, *CSEL* 89.70.16–17; on the Ciceronian background, see Comeau (1930), 1–3.

107. *De Ord.* 1.3.6, *CCSL* 29.91.10–11: "ut aliquid et praeter codices secum agerent et apud sese habitare consuefacerent animum." A point overlooked by Hagendahl (1967), 446–447, who contrasts the use of Virgil for embellishment with Augustine's later references to content, 449–450.

108. A frequent occurrence; see Henry (1938), 48–56, and, recently, Lamirande (1989); on *De Beata Vita,* pp. 5–9.

109. *De Beata Vita* 2.8, *CCSL* 29.69.43–46.

110. Cf. I. Hadot (1984), 114–115 (based on *De Ord.* 2).

111. In general, see Gilson (1960), 3–10, 115–126; Lorenz (1964), 34–38; and Madec, *Saint Augustin et la philosophie* (1992), 9–16, 100–103. Augustine would have subscribed to Plotinus' identification of wisdom with the contemplation *(theoria)* of what is in the intellect and with self-activity; *Enn.* 1.2.6, vol. 1, 62.12–15.

112. For a review of his position in the dialogues, see van der Linden (1957), 17–30.

113. On their range and application, see the classic accounts of Cayré: (1943), where some thirty-one definitions are tabulated (434–448) and a synthesis attempted (448–456); also (1951–52) and (1954), 52–103. On the notion *sedes sapientiae,* see la Bonnardière (1972), 119–120.

114. See Diggs (1949–1951), 76–93, drawing attention to the strengths and weaknesses of Augustine's position. On the notion of *scientia,* see Marrou, *Saint Augustin* (1958), 561–564.

115. *C. Acad.* 3.2.5, *CCSL* 29.36.1–5.

116. *De Beata Vita* 1.1, ibid., p. 65.1–6; *C. Acad.* 2.1.1 (p. 18.6–17).

117. *C. Acad.* 2.1.1 (p. 18.20–23).

118. *Ep.* 26.2, *CSEL* 34/1.84.13–17.

119. Cf. Sorabji (1983), 289; admitting, however, Burnyeat's distinction between Augustinian and Cartesian answers to scepticism (1982), 33, which reiterates the position of Gilson, *Etudes* (1930), 191–201; *Discours* (1930), 295–298. Cf. Gilson (1960), 38–43, 54. For an approach through analytic philosophy, see G. Matthews (1992), chaps. 2–3.

120. *Sol.* 2.1.1, *CSEL* 89.46.24–25: "Non igitur uiuere propter ipsum uiuere amas, sed propter scire." For a discussion, see du Roy (1966), 172–196, and, for possible gnostic analogies, see Majercik (1992).

121. *De Im. An.* 1.1, *CSEL* 89.101–102.

122. *De Lib. Arb.* 2.3.27, 29, *CCSL* 29.241.87–91; cf. 2.12.33 (p. 260.6–15).

123. Cf. Rief (1962), 19–40, 305–324, with a full discussion of the background, 40–73; and, more recently, the excellent analysis of I. Hadot (1984), 101–136, with a useful criticism of Dyroff (1930), on 132–135. On the autobiographical element, see Hübner (1987), 23–28.

124. *De Ord.* 2.8.25, *CCSL* 29.121.1–7: "Haec autem disciplina ipsa dei lex est, quae apud eum fixa et inconcussa semper manens in sapientes animas quasi transcribitur . . . Haec igitur disciplina eis, qui illam nosse desiderant, simul geminum ordinem sequi iubet, cuius una pars uitae, altera eruditionis est."

125. Ibid., 2.9.26 (pp. 121.2–122.13). Cf. the lucid account in Löhrer (1954), 61–78, 83–84 (on authority), and 101–106 (on reason); cf. Lütcke (1968), 64–108, 128–146.

126. *De Ord.* 2.11.31 (p. 125.28–30): "Nam rationale esse dixerunt, quod ratione uteretur uel uti posset, rationabile autem, quod ratione factum esset aut dictum."

127. Ibid. (p. 125.30–32).

128. Ibid., 2.12.35 (p. 127.1–5).

129. *De Vera Rel.* 39.72, CCSL 32.235.48–50: "Non enim ratiocinatio talia facit, sed inuenit. Ergo antequam inueniantur, in se manent, et cum inueniuntur, nos innouant."

130. Cf. Arendt (1929), 75–90, on relations with inner charity and love.

131. *De Ord.* 2.12.35, CCSL 29.127.6–15. Cf. *Conf.* 1.6–8, where the same argument is made of infant speech acquisition; discussed in Chapter 1, "Words."

132. *De Ord.* 2.12.35 (p. 127.15–17): "Sed audiri absentium uerba non poterant; ergo illa ratio peperit litteras notatis omnibus oris ac linguae sonis atque discretis."

133. Ibid. (p. 127.18–19).

134. Ibid. (p. 127.20–22); cf. Varro, *De Grammatica,* frag. 92.

135. *De Ord.* 2.11.36 (pp. 127.24–128.37).

136. Ibid., 2.11.37 (p. 128.38–41): "Poterat iam perfecta esse grammatica sed, quia ipso nomine profiteri se litteras clamat—unde etiam Latine litteratura dicitur—factum est, ut, quicquid dignum memoria litteris mandaretur, ad eam necessario pertineret." Cf. Varro, *De Gramm.,* frag. 92.

137. *De Mus.* 1.4.6, PL 32.1086: "Nam uideo tantum ualere in artibus imitationem, ut, ea sublata, omnes pene perimantur. Praebent enim se magistri ad imitandum."

138. *De Ord.* 2.14.39, CCSL 29.129.1–2: "Hinc se illa ratio ad ipsarum diuinarum rerum beatissimam contemplationem rapere uoluit." On *rapere,* see Chapter 3, "Augustine."

139. Their cacophony symbolizes Augustine's often reiterated distrust of purely verbal persuasion.

140. *De Ord.* 2.14.39, CCSL 29.129.4–10.

141. Ibid. (p. 129.10–12): "At ista potentissima secernendi cito uidit, quid inter sonum et id, cuius signum esset, distaret."

142. Ibid., 2.14.40 (p. 129.20–22).

143. Both as a rational system and as a form of mental punctuation (between sound and silence) based on sensory data.

144. Cf. *De Im. An.* 1.1, CSEL 89.101.1–3. Metre may be Augustine's closest analogy to Cartesian rational principles.

145. Including the original "art" of divine creation; see *De Vera Rel.* 22.42, CCSL 32.213.2–9; 30.55 (p. 223.30–31), and, for this principle, 32.57 (p. 224.4–5).

146. *De Ord.* 2.16.44, CCSL 29.131.2–3.

147. Ibid., 2.14.44 (p. 131.1–6). Others may not be able to proceed upwards beyond transitory phenomena; ibid. (p. 131.6–18).

148. Ibid., 2.18.48 (p. 133.21–27): "Hunc igitur ordinem tenens [i.e., ordo studiorum sapientiae, p. 133.16], anima iam philosophiae tradita primo se ipsam inspicit et, cui iam illa eruditio persuasit aut suam aut se ipsam esse rationem . . . ita secum loquetur: 'ego quodam meo motu interiore et occulto ea, quae discenda sunt, possum discernere uel conectere et haec uis mea ratio uocatur.'" Cf. 2.19.50 (p. 134.22–36).

149. Ibid., 2.19.50 (p. 134.36): "anima bene erudita."

150. Ibid., 2.19.51 (p. 135.46–47).

151. Ibid. (p. 135.52): "Cotidiana uerba."

152. Ibid. (p. 135.47–48).

153. Ibid. (p. 135.55–56): "Hanc [pulchritudinem] quisquis uiderit—uidebit autem, qui bene uiuit, bene orat, bene studet."

154. Ibid., 2.20.52 (p. 135.2–3): "Deus enim noster aliter nos exaudire non poterit, bene autem uiuentes facillime exaudiet."

155. Sol. 2.3.3, CSEL 89.50.14–15.

156. Ibid. (pp. 51.20–52.2).

157. The uneducated soul is like a wife who has to put up with five husbands, i.e., the senses, until she ascends from the temporal to the eternal and is wed to wisdom "through doctrine and discipline"; In Io. Eu. Tract. 15.21, CCSL 36.158.2–159.24 Wisdom has conveniently become masculine.

158. Sol. 2.3.3, CSEL 89.49–52; 2.4.5 (pp. 52–53); 2.5.7 (pp. 54–55). The status of the observer is crucial for Augustine's resolution of the problem of time in Conf. 11; see Chapter 8, "Time."

159. Sol. 2.4.6 (p. 54.9–12).

160. Ibid., 2.5.8 (p. 55.18): "A. Verum est quod ista se habet, ut cognitori uidetur."

161. Ibid., 6.9 (p. 56.14–15).

162. De Diu. Quaes., q. 1, CCSL 44a.11.4–7.

163. Sol. 2.6.10, CSEL 89.57.21–22: "R. Nam certe, quod oculi uident, non dicitur falsum, nisi habeat aliquam similitudinem ueri."

164. Ibid. (pp. 57–58).

165. Ibid., 2.6.11 (pp. 58.22–59.1). Inferior likenesses are further divided into those produced by the senses and the mind; ibid. (pp. 59–60).

166. Ibid., 2.9.16 (pp. 65.20–66.2): "Video enim . . . non remansisse quod falsum iure dicatur, nisi quod . . . se fingit esse quod non est."

167. Ibid. (p. 66.9–10): "Omnis fallax adpetit fallere; non autem omnis uult fallere, qui mentitur." Cf. ibid. (p. 66.13–14): "Sed fallax uel fallens is recte dicitur, cuius negotium est, ut quisque fallatur." Deliberate falsification arises in man through reason, in beasts through nature. Non-deliberate falsification occurs through mimes, comedies, poems, or jokes; ibid. (p. 66.10–12); cf. 2.10.18 (p. 68.2–4). A second class of falsifications consists of "things which attempt to exist but do not," such as mirror images, pictures, and hallucinations in dreamers and the mentally ill; 2.9.17 (pp. 66–67). He judges pictorial representations to be inferior to certain writings, possibly because he subscribed to the widespread belief that meaningful images should bear captions; 2.10.18 (p. 68.1–6).

168. Ibid., 2.10.18 (p. 68.16–18).

169. Ibid. (p. 69.8–9): "quia in exemplis istis nihil imitatione dignum uideo."

170. Cf. Lerer (1985), 50–51, on the implicitly literary design.

171. However, in parallel with the example of mathematical regularities in De Ord.

172. *Sol.* 2.11.20, *CSEL* 89.71.8–10.

173. Ibid., 2.11.19 (p. 70.12–13): "An ignoras omnia illa fabulosa et aperte falsa ad grammaticam pertinere?"

174. Ibid. (p. 70.14–16): "Non per grammaticam falsa sunt, sed per eam, qualiacumque sunt, demonstrantur."

175. Ibid. (p. 70.17–22). Cf. ibid., 2.35 (pp. 95.14–96.12) and, for a line-by-line exposition, Doignon (1984–85). The view implicitly contrasts with Plotinus (following Plato), for whom art is depreciated, as it arises later than the soul and can imitate it only "as an image of nature"; *Enn.* 4.3.10, vol. 2, 16–19.

176. *Sol.* 2.11.20 (p. 72.13–15).

177. Ibid. (p. 73.1–5).

178. Ibid. (p. 71.11–14).

179. Ibid. (p. 71.15–16), where Reason asks ironically, using terms that Augustine will employ to describe Christ's teaching in *De Mag.*: "Numquidnam magister noster nolebat nos credere, quae docebat, et nosse?"

180. *Sol.* 2.12.22 (pp. 75–76).

181. Ibid. (p. 75.15–20).

182. Ibid., 2.13.24 (p. 79.2–6): "Et omnis in subiecto est animo disciplina. Necesse est igitur semper animus maneat, si semper manet disciplina. Est autem disciplina ueritas et semper . . . ueritas manet. Semper igitur animus manet."

183. Ibid., 2.18.32 (pp. 90–91).

184. Cf. ibid., 2.10.18, (pp. 67–70).

185. Ibid., 2.12.22 (p. 75.11–14).

186. Ibid., 2.14.26 (p. 80.9–17).

## 6. Speaking and Reading

1. On its authenticity, see Jackson (1975), 1–75, and, for authoritative reviews of the early scholarship, Pinborg (1962) and Pépin, *Saint Augustin* (1976), 21–60. I quote by chapter and, where appropriate, line number from the edition of J. Pinborg in Jackson (1975). I have occasionally repunctuated the text.

2. *De Mag.* 14, *CSEL* 29.202.17–18. I quote from this edition by chapter and line number throughout Chapter 6.

3. *De Dial.* 1.1: "Dialectica est bene disputandi scientia. Disputamus autem utique uerbis." On the possible Stoic origins of the definition, see Barwick (1957), 8, and Jackson (1975), 121–122 n. 2. Antecedents known to him include Cicero, *De Orat.* 2.38.157, and Quint., *Inst. Orat.* 2.15.34. The emphasis on words is Augustine's; cf. Markus (1957), 64–65, on the similar approach of *De Mag.*

4. *De Dial.* 4; cf. Jackson (1975), 122 n. 3: (1) simple words *(De Loquendo)*; (2) compound words (a) which do not make a statement or (b) which make a statement (a) not true or false *(De Eloquendo)* or (b) true or false consisting of simple statements *(De Proloquendo)* or compound statements *(De Proloquiorum Summa)*.

5. The possible sources and analogues are briefly tabulated by Jackson (1975),

122 n. 3; Stoic echoes are noted by Barwick (1957), 8–10; on Varro, see 21–26, and Solignac (1958), 120–126. A useful commentary is Ruef (1981), 44–81, while Nuchelmans (1973), 109–112, provides comparisons with Martianus Capella on the transition of Stoic vocabulary into Latin. Close parallels with Augustine's statements are found in the pseudo-Augustinian *Categoriae Decem* 1, PL 32.1419–21, and in Martianus Capella, *De Nuptiis Philologiae et Mercurii* 388–392, ed. A. Dick (Leipzig, 1969), 184–188.

6. For a review of the relation between logic, rhetoric, and sign theory in Aristotle and the Stoics, see Simone (1969), 90–95; for thoughtful reflections on the contrast between dialectic and rhetoric based on manuscripts of *De Dial.*, see Oroz Reta (1963), 144–152.

7. For the parallel in *De Mag.*, see Baker (1969), 469–471.

8. He may be called a speaker because of the ancient habit of reading aloud.

9. See Oroz Reta (1963), 144–145, who isolates the relevant phrases.

10. See Wienbruch (1971), 76–77, who notes the centrality of the problem of representation.

11. These include the difference between simple words *(simplicia)* such as "man" or "horse" and combinations of words *(coniuncta)* such as "a man walks" (considered to be "compound" because a single statement refers to two things, i.e., "a man" and "walking"; 2.1–3; 3.1–4). Third-person Latin verbs are simple, since no subject is designated (e.g., *ambulat*), while those in the first and second persons are conjoined because specific subjects are speakers (e.g., *ambulo, ambulas,* 1.5–21). Some compound expressions are sentences *(sententiae),* others are not; some sentences affirm truth or falsehood; others are commands, wishes, or curses, etc. (2.9–14). Sentences are simple or compound (e.g., "Every man walks" and "If one is walking, one is in motion"). Important among these examples is *loquor* (1.6–7), which is reused in *De Mag.* 1.71–76, 3.73–83, and 10.38–47.

12. Markus (1957), 60–64, briefly outlines the three major positions on these issues, i.e., the Aristotelian, Epicurean, and Stoic.

13. The topic is introduced in chap. 1, where, in a brief paragraph, *significare* and *significatio* are used seven times; *res* is mentioned in connection with sentence meaning at 1.5–6 and 2.1.

14. A point rightly stressed by Kretzmann (1967), 365–366, but with misreadings; also, briefly, by Kneale and Kneale (1962), 188.

15. A good review of *uerbum* is found in Cataldo (1973); on this definition, see 171 n. 5 *et seq.* On the concept of *uerbum* in other texts, see Schindler (1965), 76–86; on the schema *uox/uerbum,* see Mayer, *Die Zeichen II* (1974), 233–249. D. Johnson (1972), 31–32, does not adequately discuss *De Dial.*

16. Cf. *De Dial.* 6.89–91: "Innumerabilia sunt enim uerba, quorum origo, de qua ratio reddi possit, aut non est, ut ego arbitror, aut latet, ut Stoici contendunt." Concealment here means potentially made evident.

17. Ibid., 5.1–5: "Verbum est uniuscuiusque rei signum, quod ab audiente possit intellegi, a loquente prolatum. Res est quidquid uel sentitur uel intellegitur

uel latet. Signum est quod et se ipsum sensui et praeter se aliquid animo ostendit. Loqui est articulata uoce signum dare. Articulatam autem dico quae comprehendi litteris potest."

18. On the sources, see Barwick (1957), 10–11; Jackson (1975), 125 n. 4, and Ruef (1981), 84–85.

19. Cf. Kretzmann (1967), 366.

20. Whence he speaks of "given signs" in *De Doct. Christ.* 2.2.3, *CCSL* 32.33.

21. We lack the section (to which he refers at 5.5–8) in which word, sign, and thing were defined; 5.27–45 deals with their place in dialectic rather than in grammar and raises the question of understanding through written sounds as a comment on 5.5 *(quae comprehendi litteris potest).*

22. Cf. Diomedes, *Artis Grammaticae* 2: *De uoce,* in *Grammatici Latini,* ed. H. Keil, vol. 1 (1857; reprint, Hildesheim, 1961), 420.11–12, where *articulata uox* (in contrast to *confusa* or *inrationalis*) is defined as "litteralis uel scriptilis . . . quia comprehendi litteris potest," an idea possibly derived from Varro; Jackson (1975), 125 n. 4.

23. Cf. Duchrow (1965), 46–50, where the relevant texts are assembled and discussed but the purely verbal elements are overemphasized; cf. D. Johnson (1972), 25–27.

24. On the transfer of Aristotle's text through the Greek and Latin world and its interpretations, see the careful analysis of Magee (1989), 7–63.

25. Diogenes Laertius, *Vit. Phil.* 7.57, ed. H. S. Long (Oxford, 1954), vol. 2, 321. Plotinus held a comparable view; *Enn.* 6.1.19, vol. 3, 27.26–29.

26. See Jackson (1975), 125 n. 4; Kneale and Kneale (1962), 139; and, for criticism of Barwick's Stoic interpretation, Ruef (1981), 89–93.

27. By a close reading of his text; *De Dial.* 5.8: "Nunc quod instat accipe intentus."

28. Duchrow (1965), 56–62, omits the parallel in an otherwise excellent analysis; see Ruef (1981), 95–97.

29. *De Dial.* 5.8–9: "Omne uerbum sonat." Cf. 5.19–20.

30. Ibid., 5.16: "quamuis omnino tacita sit [littera]"; i.e., when read silently rather than aloud?

31. Ibid., 5.9: "Cum enim est in scripto, non uerbum sed uerbi signum est."

32. Ibid., 5.9–14: "Quippe inspectis a legente litteris occurrit animo, quid uoce prorumpat. Quid enim aliud litterae scriptae quam se ipsas oculis, praeter se uoces animo ostendunt. Et paulo ante diximus [i.e., 5.3–4] signum esse quod se ipsum sensui et praeter se aliquid animo ostendit. Quae legimus igitur non uerba sunt sed signa uerborum." Such thinking was typical of the Alexandrian application of Stoic logic to the analysis of texts; see Baratin (1981), 263–264.

33. An adaptation of the division of Stoic logic into rhetoric and dialectic; see Diog. Laert., *Vit. Phil.,* vol. 2, 315–316. His intention is not evident from 1, although it can be inferred from 2 through the parallel between speaking and reading.

34. *De Dial.* 5.31–33: "Cum ergo uerbum ore procedit, si propter se procedit,

id est, ut de ipso uerbo aliquid quaeratur aut disputetur, res est utique disputationi quaestionique subiecta, sed ipsa res uerbum uocatur."

35. Ibid., 5.33–35: "Quidquid autem ex uerbo non aures sed animus sentit et ipso animo tenetur inclusum, dicibile uocatur." Cf. *De Quant. An.* 32.66, *CSEL* 89.213.20–22: "Cum ergo nomen ipsum sono et significatione constet, sonus autem ad aures, significatio ad mentem pertineat." On the Saussurean connections, see Baratin (1981), 261.

36. *De Dial.* 5.35–36: "Cum uero uerbum procedit non propter se sed propter aliud aliquid significandum, dictio uocatur." A clue to Augustine's usage may arise from his frequent replacement of *orator* with *dictor;* see A. C. de Veer, *BA* 31.4 (1968), n. 6, pp. 748–749.

37. *De Dial.* 5.36–39: "Res autem ipsa, quae iam uerbum non est neque uerbi in mente conceptio, siue habeat uerbum quo significari possit, siue non habeat, nihil aliud quam res uocatur proprio iam nomine."

38. A pillar of Augustine's theory of memory; see Chapter 8, "Remembering."

39. *De Dial.* 5.40–45: "Quod dixi uerbum, et uerbum est et uerbum significat. Quod dixi dicibile, uerbum est, nec tamen uerbum, sed quod in uerbo intellegitur et animo continetur, significat. Quod dixi dictionem, uerbum est, sed quod iam illa duo simul, id est, et ipsum uerbum et quod fit in animo per uerbum significat. Quod dixi rem, uerbum est, quod praeter illa tria quae dicta sunt, quidquid restat significat."

40. On this topic within Stoic influences, see Barwick (1957), 10–14; also Orth (1959); Nuchelmans (1973), 116–117; Jackson (1975), 126 n. 4; and Baratin (1982), 77–79. O'Daly (1987), 141 n. 23, ably summarizes diverse views. On *lekta* in Stoicism itself, see Long (1971), 77–98, 104–106, and Nuchelmans (1973), 45–74. On the moral implications of the theory, important in Augustine's subsequent thought, see Inwood (1985), 43–44, 61–66, 92–99.

41. A favorite quotation; for other examples, see Hagendahl (1967), *testimonia* 813 and p. 424.

42. See Collart (1971) on the "grammatical" dialogue in *De Mag.*

43. *De Dial.* 5.53–61. Cf. 8.47–62 and 10.6–24, where further examples implying reading are adduced.

44. Diog. Laert., *Vit. Phil.* 7.42–43, vol. 2, 315–316.

45. See Bucher (1982), 29–33, who traces the same pattern in *De Doct. Christ.* 2.

46. The explanation deals with language, while the description of reading concerns ethical issues.

47. See D. Johnson (1972), 29–36.

48. *De Dial.* 6.7: "De origine uerbi quaeritur, cum quaeritur unde ita dicatur."

49. The process is likened to interpreting dreams; ibid., 6.13–14: "Huc accedit quod ut somniorum interpretatio ita uerborum origo pro cuiusque ingenio iudicatur."

50. Though how seriously, one is not sure; cf. ibid., 6.33–34: "Stoici autumant, quos Cicero in hac re ut Cicero inridet."

51. Similarities occur through sound, touch, or taste; examples (based on sound) include expressions like "the whinnying of horses," "the bleating of sheep," "the blare of trumpets," "the rattling of chains," etc., where one is able "to perceive" that "the words sound like the things that they signify." Touch can also be a basis for similarity, e.g., smoothness or roughness in the ears (6.37–44). Examples of smoothness include *lene* (smoothly) and *uoluptas* (pleasure); of roughness, *asperitas* (roughness) and *crux* (cross, 6.44–46; cf. 6.52–56). Both sounds and things affect us as their word-names are perceived (6.46–47): honey has a pleasant taste, and its name, *mel,* touches the ears smoothly; *acre* (bitter) is harsh to the taste and to the ears.

52. *De Dial.* 6.38: "ut res cum sono uerbi aliqua similitudine concinat."

53. The word "cross" *(crux)* sounds harsh because of the pain that it produces; the word "legs" *(crura)* is like a cross because of the similarity between legs, which are long and strong, and the wood of the cross. Examples of proximity include the words *paruum* and *minutum,* which signify small, or *piscina,* which derives its name from the fact that baths contain water, the living environment of fish *(pisces,* 6.56–64); an example of contrariety is *bellum* (war) and *bella* (beautiful), where a similarity of spelling is drawn to our attention by the fact that wars are not pretty (6.71). Augustine lists some seven types of proximity, divided roughly into pairs (6.75–85), concluding that the origin of a word cannot be traced beyond similarities in sound (6.117–119, reiterating 6.10–12). Many word origins are not discoverable at all; in other cases, the origins are concealed; 6.89–91. Jackson (1975), 128–129, notes the difficulties in this sentence; I would translate without his added "non," assuming that "quorum origo, de qua ratio reddi possit" is echoed at 6.116, "reddetur ratio," etc.

54. Using examples based on the initial letter *u* (6.100–117), in which only one works, i.e., *uis,* where the powerful sound represents the notion signified (6.115–119, criticized at *De Mag.* 5.47–49).

55. The shift is marked by referring to *uis* in different contexts; in chap. 6, it is the origin in sound of the word's signifying effects; in chap. 7, it is "the power of words" *(uis uerborum,* 7.1–3; cf. 5.1–2). The presentation of Stoic views can be looked upon as an example of a rhetorical, i.e., nonargumentative introduction of philosophical material. A similar strategy is deployed in *De Mag.*

56. *De Dial.* 7.4–6: "Sed cum secundum se mouet, aut ad solum sensum pertinet aut ad artem aut ad utrumque. Sensus aut natura mouetur aut consuetudine."

57. Ibid., 7.12–14: "Nam hic ad soni suauitatem uel insuauitatem nihil interest, sed tantum ualent aurium penetralia, utrum per se transeuntes sonos quasi hospites notos an ignotos recipiant."

58. Ibid., 7.17–18: "At uero ex utroque id est et sensu et arte de uerbo iudicatur, cum id, quod aures metiuntur, ratio notat et nomen ita ponit."

59. An implicit argument from memory, reused at *Conf.* 11.

60. *De Dial.* 7.21–23: "Iam uero non secundum se, sed secundum id quod

significat uerbum mouet, quando per uerbum accepto signo animus nihil aliud quam rem ipsam intuetur, cuius illud signum est quod accepit"; a definition reiterated, with minor variations, in *De Mag.* and *De Doct. Christ.*

61. See Jackson (1975), 129 n. 5; the manuscript tradition may be confused, but the sense of the examples is clear.

62. Sallust, *Catilinae* 14.2, ed. L. D. Reynolds (Oxford, 1991), 13.

63. A somewhat different explanation is given at *De Mag.* 9.34–62. These examples are not as trivial as they would first appear. Augustine effectively introduces a topic of importance in his subsequent theory of reading; this is the role of the reader (or speaker) in supplying the ethical background for any meaning established by a text; see my discussion of *De Util. Cred.* in this chapter.

64. *De Dial.* 7.38–41: "Duplex hinc ex consideratione sensus nascitur: partim propter explicandum ueritatem, partim propter conseruandum decorem; quorum primum ad dialecticum, secundum ad oratorem maxime pertinet."

65. Augustine will reiterate this warning in *De Cat. Rud.* and *De Doct. Christ.*

66. *Pictus, De Dial.* 8.17, 20, 21, 24; *pictura,* 8.19.

67. Ibid., 8.26: "Refer nunc animum ad uerba, quorum sunt istae similitudines."

68. For the reuse of the example, see *De Trin.,* discussed in Chapter 9, "The Reader and the *Cogito.*"

69. The example is reworked by Augustine in a critical discussion of the presence of God, *De Praes. Dei* 6.19 (*Ep.* 187), CSEL 57.97–98. God, Augustine proposes, can be likened to sound, even though sound is a corporeal and transitory thing. For, when there is sound, it is equally present to all who are within its range, despite individual differences in the ability to hear it. Similarly, God is omnipresent for himself, but in a much more complete way, since his nature is incorporeal and everlasting.

70. On the Latin translations of Aristotle's terms, see Jackson (1975), 131–132 n. 7. Univocals are words that fall under one name as well as those that are covered by a single definition of that name, even though distinctions exist among them, for instance, "boy" and "man" (9.61–64). Equivocals are of three kinds, depending on whether they arise from art, use, or both of these (10.3–5). Grammarians can define a word as a name, a poetic foot, or a homonym; for instance, "Tullius" is a man, a dactyl, and the person who suppressed Catiline's conspiracy.

71. *De Dial.* 10.26: "Usum nunc appello illud ipsum propter quod uerba cognoscimus."

72. In the ensuing examples, Augustine reiterates the basic formulas from chaps. 5 and 7, distinguishing in "art" between names like *nomen,* which can be models of themselves and others like *aduerbium,* which cannot; 10.47–60. Ambiguities from "use" are divided into those that arise from the same source (as in transference or declension) or from different sources (e.g., unrelated languages or different parts of speech; 10.67–121). Special types of ambiguity pertain to writings; 10.125–134.

73. Cf. Markus (1957), 60–65, who ably sketches the background; other introductions include Simone (1969), 90–96, and Baratin (1981), 265–266.

74. Cf. Baratin, (1981), 260–265, and (1982), thereby anticipating Saussure's "signifier" and "signified," on which see Simone (1969), 115–116, and the nuanced assessment of Kelly (1975).

75. *De Dial.* 5.42–45, cited above, note 39.

76. See the overview of Quacquarelli (1972), 197–218, and, on Augustine, 213–215; more generally, Colish (1983), 15–29.

77. For parallels between *De Dial.* and *De Mag.,* see Madec, *BA* 6 (1976), n. 1, pp. 533–535. For an excellent introduction to this work within Augustine's intellectual evolution, see Madec, *Saint Augustin et la philosophie* (1992), 41–47, who notes (42) that, while the linguistic issues in chaps. 1–37 have received a great deal of attention, "on ne prêtait attention naguère à la théorie augustinienne de la connaissance thématisée dans la deuxième partie" (i.e., chaps. 38–46). I attempt to reverse this bias.

78. On the historicity of the dialogue, see the succinct summary of Madec, Intro., *BA* 6 (1976), 11–16.

79. *Conf.* 9.6, *CCSL* 27.141.5–11; cf. *De Mag.* 8.1–4.

80. Barwick (1957), an invaluable study; cf. Mayer (1969), 234–241.

81. The issues have been much discussed. For brief reviews based on secondary sources, see Kretzmann (1967), 362–365, and Colish (1985), 181–198; a balanced assessment is Baratin, (1981), 262–266. The neoplatonic element is thoroughly analysed by Mayer (1969), 225–247; for a bibliography on earlier research, see 226–227 n. 23, while the relevant sources are summarized by Madec, *BA* 6 (1976), 21–30. For the parallel transformation of Stoic views on morality in *De Diu. Quaes.,* q. 30, *CCSL* 44a.38–40, see Holte (1962), 201–203. A good analysis of the oral element of the work and its background is found in Duchrow (1965), 62–73, 89–99.

82. *De Dial.* 6.33–35; cf. 6.1–6. The derisive attitude, though not the source, may have been inherited from Plotinus; see *Enn.* 6.1.26, vol. 3, 36.22–27.

83. *De Dial.* 6.50, the pluperfect, "crediderunt," etc.

84. See Barwick (1957), 16–28; cf. Baratin (1982), 84–85, who summarizes the differences between chap. 5 and later chaps. on *uerbum* overlooked by Johnson (1972), 32–33. For a parallel transition at a later date, cf. *De Ciu. Dei* 9.4, *CCSL* 47.251–253.

85. *C. Acad.* 1.2, *CCSL* 29.6.17–18.

86. Ibid. (p. 6.20–21).

87. *De Beata Vita* 2.14, *CCSL* 29.73.183–191.

88. *C. Acad.* 2.5 ibid., p. 24.27–28.

89. Does Augustine's response predate the dialogues? See *C. Acad.* 3.20 (pp. 60.1–61.24).

90. Madec, Intro., *BA* 6 (1976), 33.

91. Specifically, *Meno* 81d–84.

92. For an authoritative commentary, see Huber (1964), 3–11, 41–44, 307–340, 455–487.

93. *Ep.* 7.1.2, *CSEL* 34/1.13–14. Cf. *Sol.* 1.5.11, *CSEL* 89.18–19, for the example of the geometer; on memory, 1.4.9 (pp. 15–18).

94. E.g., *De Trin.* 12.15.24, *CCSL* 50a.378.8–13, where, recalling Plato's solution, he objects that all who reveal a knowledge of geometry cannot have been geometers in a previous life (which is not Plato's position). Earlier objections to the theory of reminiscence include *De Quant. An.* 20.34, *CSEL* 89.173–174; cf. *Retr.* 1.8.2, *CCSL* 57.22.

95. Cicero, *Tusc. Disp.* 1.24.57.

96. For a review of the issues, see O'Daly (1976). Augustine may never have considered the doctrine more seriously than a hypothesis; this is suggested by the syntax of *Ep.* 7.1.2, *CSEL* 34/1.13–14, where the relevant statements are put in the negative for rhetorical emphasis.

97. Vlastos (1965–66), 156–157, 160–161.

98. For an excellent outline, see Madec, "Analyse" (1975), 66–71; on this division, 65. The alternative division of Crosson (1989), 126, does not affect the argument that follows.

99. Note the similarity to Augustine's approach to conversion in *Conf.* 3.5 and 8.12. There, reading, as an activity that uses signs, is necessary to trigger conversion, but is not its causal mechanism.

100. *De Mag.* 1.24–25: "aut ut doceamus aut ut commemoremus uel alios uel nos ipsos."

101. Augustine's comment takes the form of a criticism; *De Mag.* 10.18–48, discussed later in this chapter.

102. On the meaning of *docere* in classical Latin, see Hus (1965); on later usage, see Marrou (1934) and Mandouze (1975), 792–793; on the evolution of the term within *De Mag.*, see Madec, *BA* 6 (1976), n. 2, pp. 535–536.

103. On *commemoratio*, see Madec, *BA* 6 (1976), 536–538. Cf. *Ep.* 7.1.2, *CSEL* 34.14.1–6, where, writing to Nebridius in 389, Augustine fills in a gap in this argument, proposing against the critics of Plato that our memories are of both past and present events. What we learn is not new; it is recalled into memory from what is recorded there *(in memoriam recordatione reuocari)*. These ideas are developed in different directions in *Conf.* and in *De Trin.*

104. Cf. *Conf.* 1.9, *CCSL* 27.8.10–16.

105. *De Mag.* 1.45–48: "Qui enim loquitur, suae uoluntatis signum foras dat per articulatum sonum, deus autem in ipsis rationalis animae secretis, qui homo interior uocatur." Cf. 11.44–51.

106. An allusion to interior dialogue? See Chapter 5, "The Letters."

107. Consideration is limited to words that signify things and excludes words like prepositions or conjunctions which are "names" but which themselves do not

signify; 2.1–72; on the background and contemporary philosophical implications, see Burnyeat (1987), 9–13; for a reconstruction based on the ancient teaching of grammar, see Collart (1971), 284–292.

108. The background is *De Mag.* 4.7–10: "Cum ergo de quibusdam signis quaeritur, possunt signis signa monstrari; cum autem de rebus, quae signa non sunt, aut eas agendo post inquisitionem, si agi possunt, aut signa dando, per quae animaduerti queant." Cf. 7.45–49.

109. For linguistic observations on this discussion, see Simone (1969), 106–109.

110. Cf. *De Dial.* 5.27–45 and 10.50–60.

111. Throughout this section, Augustine plays on two definitions of a noun: it is the first part of speech and a source of knowledge about things. On the grammatical source in Diomedes, see Bellissima (1954), 36–37; for a lucid summary, see Crosson (1989), 122–124.

112. On *uocabulum,* cf. *De Gen. ad Litt. Imper.* 6.26, *PL* 34.230: "Omne quippe uocabulum ad distinctionem ualet. Vnde etiam nomen quod rem notet, appellatum est, quasi notamen. Notet autem, id est distinguat et doctitantur ad discernendum adiuuet."

113. On the derivation of *significabilis* and *audibilis* from Varro, see Finaert (1939), 30.

114. *De Mag.* 8.149–150: "ea scilicet regula, quae naturaliter plurimum ualet, ut auditis signis ad res significatas feratur intentio."

115. See Baratin (1982), 84.

116. *De Mag.* 9.1–2: "Proinde intellegas uolo res, quae significantur, pluris quam signa esse pendendas." Augustine approaches this issue through the contrast between dialectic and rhetoric in *De Dial.* 7.29–37; cf. *Sol.* 1.15.27, *CSEL* 89.40–41, where he argues that "truth" is superior to "being true."

117. *De Mag.* 5.100: "Verba certe sono et litteris constant."

118. Ibid., 1.63–66, alluding to Matt. 6:9–13; cf. Lk. 11:2–5.

119. *De Mag.* 1.42–61, drawing in order on Matt. 6:6, Rom. 7:22, 1 Cor. 3:16, Eph. 3:16–17, and Ps. 4:5–6. Augustine's thinking is effectively summed up at *Conf.* 11.8, *CCSL* 27.199.6–9: "Sic in euangelio per carnem ait, et hoc insonuit foris auribus hominum, ut crederetur et intus quaereretur et inueniretur in aeterna ueritate, ubi omnes discipulos bonus et solus magister docet."

120. Cf. *Conf.* 1.1, and, by extension, *De Ciu. Dei* 10.19, *CCSL* 47.293.4–10, where Augustine proposes that visible sacrifices are the signs of invisible offerings, just as words are the signs of things. In prayers, we address signifying sounds to God, while, in our hearts, we offer him realities.

121. See the discussion in Chapter 1, "Words."

122. *De Mag.* 4.37–39: "Ita fit, ut cum scribitur uerbum, signum fiat oculis, quo illud, quod ad aures pertinet, ueniat in mentem."

123. See Madec, *Saint Augustin et la philosophie* (1992), 42–43, who notes: "il s'agit là d'un paradoxe d'ordre tactique"; cf. Simone (1969), 96.

124. Cf. *Sol.* 2.14.25, *CSEL* 89.79.11–14.

125. Cf. *Conf.* 7.19, *CCSL* 27.108–109.13–16, where Augustine defines gesture along these lines but emphasizes the contrast between gesture and silence rather than between words and sound. A parallel contrast is implied in the observer's role in silent reading at *Conf.* 6.3. In general, the indirect links between gestures and writings strengthen the connections between gesture and language acquisition that are suggested in *Conf.* 1.8, especially in view of Augustine's privileging of scripture.

126. Cf. *De Doct. Christ.* 2.37, *CCSL* 32.70–71, where the example of walking is better explained. His point is that a principle is of little use without a demonstration; also, in such cases, we learn better from demonstrations than from attempting to master rules. For a similar statement applied to eloquence, see 4.3 (p. 118.28–33), where he adds that, while an eloquent person may speak according to the rules of eloquence, he or she is not reflecting on the rules while speaking; cf. *De Dial.* 6.1–4, and, on the division, Quint., *Inst. Orat.* 1.4.2.

127. Cf. Burnyeat (1987), 12–14, with interesting reflections on Augustine and Wittgenstein.

128. *De Mag.* 10.32–33: "Si ergo significamus, ut doceamus, non docemus, ut significemus, aliud est docere aliud significare." I translate *docere* in a manner that suggests the latent intentionality.

129. Perhaps a veiled reference to the verbal entrapments of the Manichaeans; e.g., *De Util. Cred.* 2, *CSEL* 25.5.16–18: "Itaque nobis faciebant [Manichaei], quod insidiosi aucupes solent, qui uiscatos surculos propter aquam defigunt, ut sitientes aues decipiant"; cf. *In Io. Eu. Tract.* 1.14, *CCSL* 36.8.3–5; *Conf.* 3.6 (*CCSL* 27.31.1–4) and 6.6 (p. 79.5–6). It is tempting to see these associations elsewhere; cf. Ferrari (1984), 21–22; however, Augustine is fond of the metaphor itself; see *Ep.* 2, *CSEL* 34/1.4.6–8.

130. For a further development of the notion of the observer, see Chapter 8, "Time."

131. *De Mag.* 10.96–97: "Satis est namque ad rem et de quibusdam rebus tametsi non omnibus et quosdam homines doceri posse sine signo."

132. Ibid., 10.114–117: "Quod si diligentius consideremus, fortasse nihil inuenies, quod per sua signa discatur. Cum enim mihi signum datur, si nescientem me inuenerit, cuius rei signum sit, docere me nihil potest, si uero scientem, quid disco per signum?"

133. Dan. 3:94 (10.119): "Et sarabarae eorum non sunt commutatae." On the spelling (*sarabarae* or *saraballa*), Knauer (1954), 102–106, traces the philological and manuscript evolution.

134. *Conf.* 1.8; see Chapter 1, "Words."

135. *De Mag.* 10.141–144: "In quo tamen signo cum duo sint, sonus et significatio, sonum certe non per signum percipimus, sed eo ipso aure pulsata, significationem autem re, quae significatur, aspecta."

136. Ibid., 10.153–157: "Et id maxime tibi nitor persuadere si potero, per ea signa, quae uerba appellantur, nos nihil discere; potius enim ut dixi uim uerbi, id est significationem, quae latet in sono, re ipsa, quae significatur, cognita discimus,

quam illam tali significatione percipimus." Cf. *De Dial.* 7.21–22: the one stresses cognition, the other, audience relations.

137. *De Mag.* 10.168–71: "Non enim, cum rem ipsam didici, uerbis alienis credidi, sed oculus meis; illis tamen fortasse ut adtenderem credidi, id est ut aspectu quaererem, quid uiderem."

138. Even if one accepts that Augustine is working within "a semantic version of Meno's paradox"; Burnyeat (1987), 16.

139. This may be compared to the "grammatical" interest in the quotations from Terence (4.89) and Persius (9.89).

140. Cf. *De Mag.* 12.43–67, where the limits of questions and answers between interlocutors concerning the parts and the whole of a reality under discussion are pointed out.

141. Ibid., 11.1–3: "Hactenus uerba ualuerunt, quibus ut plurimum tribuam, admonent tantum, ut quaeramus res, non exhibent, ut norimus."

142. This is a subtle shift in the direction of the argument, which takes Augustine away from the issues in *De Dial.* and toward those of *De Cat. Rud.* and *De Doct. Christ.* Although the implications of this position are followed up in *De Doct.* 1, the argument itself is not reiterated.

143. *De Mag.* 9.59–60: "Quanto est igitur melius docere quam loqui, tanto melior quam uerba locutio."

144. Ibid., 11.25–26: "Respondebo cuncta, quae illis uerbis significata sunt in nostra notitia iam fuisse."

145. Ibid., 11.32–34: "Haec autem omnia, quae in illa leguntur historia ita illo tempore facta esse, ut conscripta sunt, credere me potius quam scire confiteor." Cf. Is. 7:9.

146. *De Mag.* 11.37–43, a passage that illustrates the close connections in style and thought between the proof for the *cogito* and the trust in intermediaries for beliefs.

147. For a further discussion of this point, see Chapter 7, "Tradition and Beliefs."

148. As later emphasized; cf. *De Mag.* 12.43–45: "quod ut partibus faciat, admonetur, cum de istis partibus interrogatur, quibus illa summa constat, quam totam cernere non ualebat." See the pertinent remarks of Baker (1969), 471–473.

149. *De Mag.* 12.8–10, quoted in note 152.

150. Ibid., 11.44–46; cf. Jansen (1930), esp. 125–126, where later texts are fully discussed.

151. Cf. *De Ord.* 2.3.10, *CCSL* 29.112–113; *Sol.* 1.6.12, *CSEL* 89.19–21.

152. *De Mag.* 12.7–10: "Namque omnia, quae percipimus, aut sensu corporis aut mente percipimus. Illa sensibilia, haec intellegibilia siue, ut more nostrorum auctorum loquar, illa carnalia, haec spiritalia nominamus." Who "our authors" are remains a mystery.

153. This is one of Augustine's earliest statements of a theoretical basis for thinking of interlocked images as instructive stories, which underpins the application of his ideas about narrative to didactic art.

154. A full account of the controversies over this doctrine cannot be attempted here. For an excellent orientation, see Jolivet (1931) 52–104, 115–153, Gilson (1960), 77–96; Bourke (1978), 16–23, the last with connections to ethical issues. The tendencies of research are summarized by Schützinger (1962) and Madec, *BA* 6 (1976), n. 6, pp. 543–545, with a succinct bibliography, 545; cf. O'Daly (1987), 204 n. 115. On the Plotinian background, see Beierwaltes (1977).

155. Gilson (1960), 77; Kälin (1921), 53–66; and Lorenz (1964), 46–53, who distinguishes the major types of inner knowledge in Augustine's thought. On the Plotinian background, see P. Hadot, *Plotinus* (1993), 35–47. More general treatments include B. Jansen (1930), 111–114, and Miles (1983), the latter on mind/body relations. Madec, *Saint Augustin et la philosophie* (1992), 44–46, cautions against interpreting "illumination" in the fashion of medieval scholastics.

156. E.g., *In Io. Eu. Tract.* 15.19, *CCSL* 36.157.30–33; cf. 47.3 (p. 405.15–17), describing Christ.

157. *C. Acad.* 3.6.13, *CCSL* 29.42.3–4.

158. *De Beata Vita* 4.35, *CSEL* 29.84.268–271; see Alesanco (1968), 19–23.

159. E.g., *Sol.* 1.1.3, *CSEL* 89.5.13–15; cf. 1.13.23 (pp. 35–36). For further references, see Gilson (1960), 77–80 and nn.

160. *De Im. An.* 10.17, *CSEL* 89.119.3–5.

161. *De Mag.* 11.46–49: "Ille autem, qui consulitur, docet, qui in interiore homine habitare dictus est Christus, id est incommutabilis dei uirtus atque sempiterna sapientia." For a summary of similar statements in other writings, see Madec, *BA* 6 (1976), 35–38, and, more generally Thonnard (1962), 126–129, 156–173.

162. *Sol.* 1.13.23, *CSEL* 89.36.13–15: "Nam ordine quodam ad eam peruenire bonae disciplinae officium est, sine ordine autem uix credibilis felicitatis." On the role of the "teacher," see *Sol.* 2.11.20 (p. 71.15–16).

163. *De Trin.* 4.2, *CCSL* 50.163.2–3: "Inluminatio quippe nostra participatio uerbi est." Cf. 14.15, *CCSL* 50a.449–450.17–30.

164. Scripture cannot be the cause of illumination because of the conditions in which it arose; *In Io. Eu. Tract.* 1.6, *CCSL* 36.3.15–20: "Oculos nostros cum leuamus ad scripturas, quia per homines ministratae sunt scripturae, leuamus oculos nostros ad montes, unde auxilium ueniet nobis [Ps. 120:1]; sed tamen quia ipsi homines erant, qui scripserunt scripturas, non de se lucebant; sed ille erat lumen uerum, qui illuminat omnem hominem uenientem in hunc mundum."

165. Ibid., 2.6 (p. 14.4–5).

166. Ibid., 3.5 (p. 22.7): "Lux non est absens, sed uos absentes estis in luce."

167. They are nonetheless aids to seeing within; cf. *De Diu. Quaes.*, q. 46.2, *CCSL* 44a.73.65–71.

168. See Holte (1962), 329–334, who draws attention to the similarity of thinking in *De Ord.* Augustine adds that when words are spoken in this context, the hearer has only three options: not knowing whether what is said is untrue, knowing that it is untrue, or knowing that it is true. As a result, his beliefs depend

on opinion or doubt, on opposition or refutation, and on bearing witness to the truth; *De Mag.* 12.67–72.

169. *In Io. Eu. Tract.* 54.8, CCSL 36.463.16–23. Similar thoughts occur in *De Gen. c. Man.* 2.4.5 (PL 34.198) and 2.5.6 (ibid., 199), which was written in 388 or 389.

170. For illustrations, see the Introduction.

171. *De Mag.* 13.4–5: "Quisquis autem cernere potest, intus est discipulus ueritatis, foris iudex loquentis uel potius ipsius locutionis."

172. Ibid., 14.1–3: "Num hoc magistri profitentur, ut cogitata eorum ac non ipsae disciplinae, quas loquendo se tradere putant, percipiantur atque teneantur?"

173. See Jolivet (1931), 80–82.

174. *De Mag.* 14.18–27; *De Lib. Arb.* 2.14.38, CCSL 29.263.19–53.

175. See Lerer (1985), 55–56.

176. See Rief (1961), 287–303.

177. In Chapters 6 and 7 references to *De Util. Cred.* are taken from the edition of Joseph Zycha, *CSEL* 25 (Vienna, 1925), cited by paragraph numbers and by consecutively renumbered lines within those paragraphs. A good general introduction is Batiffol (1917); recent studies include Consolino (1981), 121–123, and Gigon (1985); problems of reading are noted by Schobinger (1977) and analysed by Schäublin (1989).

178. *De Util. Cred.* 1.13, where Augustine refers to their common search for truth "ab ineunte adulescentia"; cf. 13.5–6: "nobis tunc pueris."

179. The work's autobiographical setting (chap. 20) is often noted. Here, Augustine introduces the theme by recalling that the dualists claimed to tackle scripture with pure and simple reason *(mera et simplex ratio)*, while Catholicism (they maintained) relied on superstition *(superstitio)* and blind obedience to authority *(auctoritas)*. He was proud, needlessly argumentative, and disillusioned with school, whence he was an easy prey. There may be a touch of irony at ibid., 2.16 *(in schola doctorum hominum)*; cf. 10.2–3: "sicut ego possum, non sicut doctissimos uiros posse miratus sum"; and, on the Manichaeans as manipulators of words, another frequently evoked theme, see 2.7–14. The combination of autobiographical reminiscence and anti-Manichaean rhetoric, which appears here for the first time, was polished in the *Conf.*

180. There are many other echoes, e.g., "amore flagrauimus," ibid., 1.14; "progressi atque lapsi." 1.15–16; "recedere a sensibus," 1.19, etc.

181. Ibid., 4.5: "quasi uagientium."

182. Ibid., 4.5–10: "Et quia sunt ibi quaedam, quae suboffendant animos ignaros et neglegentes sui—quae maxima turba est—populariter accusari possunt; defendi autem populariter propter mysteria, quae his continentur, non a multis admodum possunt." Throughout the discussion Augustine argues that the Bible's true doctrines are present and decipherable through skilled analysis, but not always explicit—a view that echoes Origen (e.g., *De Principiis* 1.3) as well as Plotinus, *Enn.* 5.1.8, vol. 2, 197–198 (on Plato).

183. *De Util. Cred.* 4.10–13: "Qui uero pauci hoc facere nouerunt, non amant

propatula et famigerula quaedam in disputatione certamina et ob hoc minime noti sunt, nisi his, qui eos instantissime requirunt."

184. This, I believe, is his sole reference to Manichaeism as a sudden conversion experience rather than a gradual introduction to sectarian beliefs.

185. *De Util. Cred.* 4.15–23. He may be asserting that the spirit of what he says is sincere in view of the tentative nature of his employment of the four senses of scripture; 5.9–10.

186. Ibid., 5.1–4: "Omnis igitur scriptura, quae testamentum uetus uocatur, diligenter eam nosse cupientibus quadrifariam traditur: secundum historiam, secundum aetiologiam, secundum analogiam, secundum allegoriam." Cf. *De Gen. ad Litt. Imper.* 2.5, *PL* 34.222. On the use of the notion of the sign in Augustine's *allegoria,* see Mayer (1969), 341–349; for an argument in favour of the neoplatonic orientation of the fourfold distinction, see Mayer, *Die antimanichäische Epoche* (1974), 334–349.

187. De Lubac (1959), 178. Medieval authors, exploiting Augustine's reticence, lauded him as the originator of the fourfold system of biblical exegesis; their reinterpretations are sympathetically reviewed by de Lubac, 179–187.

188. He is certain that Latin speakers have no equivalent terms; *De Util. Cred.* 5.4–9: "Ne me ineptum putes graecis nominibus utentem. Primum quia sic accepi nec tibi hoc aliter audeo intimare quam accepi. Deinde tu quoque animaduertis non esse harum rerum apud nos usitata nomina: quae si fabricassem interpretando, essem profecto ineptior; si autem circumloquerer, minus essem in disserendo expeditus." He also takes care to define the terms as they are "handed down"; 5.5, 5.6, "accepi"; 5.11, "traditur."

189. Ibid., 5.11–12: "Secundum historiam ergo traditur, cum docetur, quid scriptum aut quid gestum sit; quid non gestum, sed tantummodo scriptum quasi gestum sit."

190. Ibid., 5.13–14: "Secundum aetiologiam, cum ostenditur, quid qua de causa uel factum uel dictum sit."

191. Ibid., 5.14–16: "Secundum analogiam, cum demonstratur non sibi aduersari duo testamenta, uetus et nouum."

192. Ibid., 5.16–18: "Secundum allegoriam, cum docetur non ad litteram esse accipienda quaedam, quae scripta sunt, sed figurate intellegenda." On "intellectus figuratus" in *De Doct. Christ.* and other texts, see Ripanti (1972), 220–224, 226–230.

193. See de Lubac (1959), 178–179. In his application of the fourfold scheme, Augustine only partly answers Manichaean claims. While he responds adequately to their allegation that the Old Testament text is corrupt (8.16–45), on theological issues he selects his illustrative texts from Matthew, Acts, and Paul alone (in order Matt. 12:3, 19:18; Acts 2:2 *et seq.;* Matt. 12:39; 1 Cor. 10:1; Gal. 4:22 *et seq.* and 3:24). The Hebrew Bible is used only for corroboration; cf. Allgeier (1930), 7, on *Conf.* 12–13; and, on *C. Faustum,* Tardieu (1987). The bias of the examples is thereby incorporated into his response.

194. As well, perhaps, as other texts; cf. Lev. 24:5–9; Deut. 23:26.

195. The situations, of course, are not the same. In 1 Sam. 21:4–5, David and his followers eat the loaves reserved for the temple priests (Lev. 24:5–9). The priest makes no effort to prevent them from doing so; however, he asks whether the soldiers are "pure," i.e., whether they have "kept themselves from women" (1 Sam. 21:47). Purity is not an issue in Matthew; rather, it is Christ's claim, as "the son of man," to be "master of the sabbath" (Matt. 12:8).

196. *De Util. Cred.* 6.9: "fornicationis causa," 6.12: "hic enim causa reddita est," both echoing Matt. 19:4, "ex causa."

197. Ibid., 7.12–16; cf. *De Mor. Eccles. Cath.* 1.29.61, *PL* 32.1335; *C. Faustum* 11.2, *CSEL* 25/1.314.11–21; cf. *De Doct. Christ.* 2.11.16, *CCSL* 32.42.

198. *De Util. Cred.* 7.16–19: "Si enim dicerent eas sibi penitus accipiendas non putasse, quod ab his essent conscriptae, quos uerum scripsisse non arbitrarentur, esset utcumque tergiuersatio eorum rectior vel error humanior."

199. Though far from flawless: in the absence of manuscripts "in tam recenti memoria" (ibid., 7.15), his evidence is no stronger than theirs; also, the argument ad hominem (7.29–45) is a non sequitur, even though urged "placidissimo et serenissimo iudicio" (7.30–31).

200. He is aware that he makes their views sound more illogical than they are; 7.40–45.

201. I use the text of 1 Cor. 10:1–10 in Augustine's version of the Latin Bible, *De Util. Cred.* 8.11–28.

202. Interpreted as "fornication" by Paul, 1 Cor. 10:8.

203. Paul makes no reference to the sacrifice that preceded the other activities.

204. The Pauline origins of his usage are clear from *En. in Ps.* 103, s. 1.13, *CCSL* 40.1486.14–16: "'Quae sunt,' inquit, 'in allegoria [Gal. 4:24].' Allegoria dicitur, cum aliquid aliud uidetur sonare in uerbis, et aliud in intellectu significare" [cf. Quint., *Inst. Orat.* 8.6.44; 9.2.92]. Cf. *De Trin.* 15.9.15, *CCSL* 50a.480–482.

205. The phrase *secundum carnem* (*De Util. Cred.* 8.36) is of course Paul's; *per promissionem* (8.37 = Vulgate "per repromissionem") is derived from Gen. 21:1.

206. Augustine does not subsequently emphasize the fact that the notion arises in the context of a response to a Manichaean misinterpretation of dualist notions.

207. Cf. Rom. 3:19–26 and 9:6 and, in view of previous quotations, Matt. 3:9–11.

208. A point taken up in *De Cat. Rud.;* see Chapter 7, "The 'Uninstructed.'"

209. *De Util. Cred.* 10.4–11: "Tria genera sunt erroris, quibus homines errant, cum aliquid legunt. De singulis dicam. Primum genus est, in quo id quod falsum est uerum putatur, cum aliud qui scripsit putauerit. Alterum est, quamuis non tam late patens, non tamen minus noxium, cum id quod falsum est uerum putatur, id tamen putatur, quod etiam ille qui scripsit putauit. Tertium est, cum ex alieno scripto intellegitur aliquid ueri, cum hoc ille qui scripsit non intellexerit."

210. Ibid., 10.11–12: "In quo genere [i.e., tertio], non parum est utilitatis; immo si diligentius consideres, totus legendi fructus est integer."

211. Cf. *De Diu. Quaes.*, q. 30, *CCSL* 44a.38.1–2: "Vt inter honestum et utile

interest, ita et inter fruendum et utendum." On the theological context, see the lucid discussion of di Giovanni (1965), 29–51.

212. A frequently evoked Augustinian theme, appearing as early as *De Pulchro et Apto* in 380–81 (*Conf.* 4.13; cf. *De Mus.* 6.46, *PL* 32.1187) and given as advice in his senior years; e.g., the letter to Dioscorus, in 410 or 411; *Ep.* 118.1–2, *CSEL* 34/2.665.16–23, 666.1–3; for a further discussion, see Chapter 7, "Christian Doctrine." For the context within the tripartite division of philosophy (physics, logic, and ethics), see *De Ciu. Dei* 11.25, *CCSL* 48.344–345, where there may be another link in Augustine's argument, namely his view that, in any artist, one should look at three characteristics, "natura, doctrina, usus" (p. 344.22), the first and third reiterated and transformed from *De Dial.* 10, ed. Jackson (1975), 114.38–44.

213. *De Dial.* 8 (ibid., p. 104.15–25). Cf. *C. Acad.* 3.15, *CCSL* 29.54.22–23: "Non solum enim puto eum errare, qui falsam uiam sequitur, sed etiam eum, qui ueram non sequitur."

214. *De Util. Cred.* 10.13–17: "Primi generis exemplum est, ut si quisquam uerbi gratia dicat et credat Rhadamanthum apud inferos audire ac diiudicare causas mortuorum, eo quod Maronis in carmine id legerit. Hic enim errat duobus modis: quod et rem non credendam credit neque id putandus est credidisse ille quem legit." No reason is given as to why Virgil would not have believed what he said.

215. Ibid., 10.18–19: "Si quis, quia Lucretius animam ex atomis esse scribit." Cf. Lucretius, *De Rerum Natura* 1.1021–51; 2.1058–63; 5.419–431.

216. On the relevance of continence as an example, see Chapter 8, "Conduct."

217. While it is open to the same objection, i.e., one set of prior beliefs can be substituted for another without harming its internal logic.

218. The opposite of the situation in *Conf.* 1–6.

219. It is assumed that the death occurs before he can question him on his motivations.

220. *De Util. Cred.* 10.34: "nuntiaretur"; 10.45: "nuntiatum est."

221. Ibid., 10.46–47: "quisquam . . . qui mihi suscenseret."

222. Ibid., 11.1; Augustine deliberately plays on *scripturae,* which refers to "writings" and to "scriptures."

223. Ibid., 11.3–5: "Aut enim utiliter scripsit quispiam et non utiliter ab aliquo intellegitur, aut utrumque inutiliter fit, aut utiliter intellegit lector, cum ille contra, qui legitur, scripserit."

224. Ibid., 11.5–6: "Horum trium primum non inprobo, ultimum non curo." Yet the third possibility is not so very different from the third type of error in reading, in which, he notes, utility chiefly arises. Cf. 10.9–11: "Tertium est, cum ex alieno scripto intellegitur aliquid ueri . . . In quo genere non parum est utilitatis"; and 11.4–5: "aut utiliter intellegit lector."

225. I.e., not "aut utrumque inutiliter fit" (ibid., 11.4), but understood as "utiliter fit." It is possible that Augustine is referring to a fourth type, i.e., something beyond 11.3–5. But if that were the case, why introduce the division at all; and why refer to *primum* and *ultimum,* leaving only one choice?

226. Ibid., 11.9–11: "Unum igitur genus est probatissimum et quasi purgatissimum, cum et bona scripta sunt et in bonam partem accipiuntur a legentibus." The focus on intentions reflects the good arising out of reading errors as well as the metaphysical position outlined in *De Mag.*

227. Ibid., 11.13–15: "Nam euenit plerumque, ut cum bene senserit scriptor, bene etiam lector sentiat, sed aliud quam ille et saepe melius, saepe inferius, utiliter tamen."

228. Augustine is not entirely clear here. The statement "tamen adhuc in duo diuiditur" (ibid., 11.12) is not followed by two logically distinctive types at 11.12–15 and 11.15–27; however, when he discusses the second alternative, two different possibilities are raised, i.e., obscurity in the text and the unknowability of the author's intentions.

229. Ibid., 11.18–20: "Quod genus cum de rebus obscurissimis lectio est, rarissimum omnino est neque id mea sententia liquido sciri, sed tantummodo credi potest."

230. Ibid., 11.24–25: "Illud autem nihil ad rem cognoscendam ualere arbitror, qualis fuerit ille, qui scripsit."

231. Ibid., 5.10–13. This is what Augustine did when he read Sallust's *Catilinae* as a student; he refused to take notes, to proceed slowly through the text, or to listen to received opinions; *Conf.* 4.16, *CCSL* 27.54.1–10.

232. Cf. *De Util. Cred.* 13.35–53, where the example of Virgil is discussed at length.

233. Ibid., 13.16–17: "An istae scripturae legis planissimae sunt, in quas isti quasi uulgo expositas inpetum faciunt frustra et inaniter?" Cf. 13.27–28: "quia eis inperiti plaudunt."

## 7. *Toward Theory*

1. The argument develops in stages: chap. 8 recapitulates his change from Manichaeism to Catholicism; he then touches on the problems of authority (introduced in chaps. 14–19 and developed in chaps. 33–34), faith, reason, and related issues (chaps. 21–22 and 25), belief and credulity (chap. 23–24), understanding, beliefs, and opinions (chaps. 25–29), and the functions of signs in religious reading and writing (chaps. 30–32 and passim).

2. *De Util. Cred.* 14.5–7. The argument roughly parallels the distinction in *De Mag.* 3.53–83 and 10.1–17 between speaking and showing.

3. *De Util. Cred.* 10.4–5: "Tria genera sunt erroris, quibus homines errant, cum aliquid legunt." This is the first of several trinitarian formulas.

4. I.e., an Augustine who, as an unsympathetic reader, was unable to appreciate the message of scripture; *Conf.* 3.5, *CCSL* 27.30–31.

5. The problem is envisaged from the outset as one of dissemination, not as a search for absolute truth as in *De Doct. Christ.*

6. *De Util. Cred.* 16.1–2: "At enim apud paucos quosdam est ueritas. Scis ergo iam quae sit, si scis, apud quos sit."

7. The introduction of the observer anticipates Augustine's interpretation of his experience with St. Ambrose; *Conf.* 6.3.

8. *De Util. Cred.* 16.3–4: "Sed si ex ipsa ui ueritatis paucos eam tenere coniectas, qui uero sint, nescis, quid?"

9. Ibid., 21.9–10: "ut aliquam concilient multitudinem nomine rationis."

10. The model is Cicero, whose preeminence is confirmed by "ancestral authority"; ibid., 16.12–13.

11. Ibid., 16.13–14: "Eadem inperitorum turbae discere moliuntur, quae a paucis doctis discenda recepta sunt."

12. I.e., the proof of Catholicism's truth arises from the number of adherents; ibid., 19.8–10.

13. Ibid., 17.3–4, quoted in the epigraph to this volume.

14. Ibid., 17.10: "sine duce"; 17.11: "sine praeceptore." Cf. 17.15–17.

15. A rare reference to scrolls, ibid., 13.56–57: "non euolutis . . . illis litteris." Augustine is presumably referring to pagan (or perhaps to Manichaean) texts, since the books of the Bible were by this time regularly copied by Christians into codices.

16. A point emphasized in a different context in *De Doct. Christ.*, proem. 3–4, *CCSL* 32.2–3.

17. *De Util. Cred.* 17.27–31. The problem of esotericism is thus shifted from individuals (e.g., Faustus) to biblical texts.

18. Cf. Batiffol (1917), 3–5.

19. Which culminates at *De Util. Cred.* 20.33–35; see Courcelle (1950), 275–281.

20. *De Util. Cred.* 20.11–15: "Rationem ipse mecum habui magnamque deliberationem iam in Italia constitutus, non utrum manerem in illa secta, in quam me incidisse paenitebat, sed quonam modo uerum inueniendum esset, in cuius amorem suspiria mea nulli melius quam tibi nota sunt."

21. Ibid., 20.15–17: "Saepe mihi uidebatur non posse inueniri magnique fluctus cogitationum mearum in academicorum suffragium ferebantur."

22. This is a restatement and a subtle inversion of his former position with respect to the Academics.

23. *De Util. Cred.* 20.17–21: "Saepe rursus intuens, quantum poteram, mentem humanam tam uiuacem, tam sagacem, tam perspicacem, non putabam latere ueritatem, nisi quod in ea quaerendi modus lateret, eundemque ipsum modum ab aliqua diuina auctoritate esse sumendum."

24. Ibid., 20.21–22.

25. Ibid., 20.33–37.

26. Ibid., 21.13–16: "Nam uera religio, nisi credantur ea, quae quisque postea, si se bene gesserit dignusque fuerit, adsequatur atque percipiat, et omnino sine quodam graui auctoritatis imperio inire recte nullo pacto potest." The theme of authority is well documented by Batiffol (1917), 9–18.

27. On the method of construction, see the suggestions in Chapter 5, "The Letters."

28. Augustine frequently contrasts "curiosity" and "study." For a review of the early literature on curiosity, see Mayer (1969), 88–89 n. 157, and, on the use of *curiositas* in classical authors, Labhardt (1960), 206–216; also Joly (1961), 33–38. The rare use of the term in Christian authors before Augustine is noted by Labhardt, 216–220. On the use of the notion in *Conf.*, see O'Donnell (1992), vol. 2, 150–151, 158, 209–210; vol. 3, 223–224. Augustine's influence is examined by Blumenberg (1961), Newhauser (1982), and in a wide-ranging essay by Peters (1985).

29. The term *studiosus* (22.13) suggests the reader of scripture; see the discussion of *De Doct. Christ.* in this chapter.

30. *De Util. Cred.* 22.16–18: "Curiosus tamen ea requirit, quae nihil ad se adtinent, studiosus autem contra quae ad sese adtinent requirit."

31. Cf. Plotinus, *Enn.* 4.3.32, vol. 2, 52.1–2. If this is the illustration's source, it would provide a link between the incidental discussion of memory in *De Util. Cred.* and the more extensive account in *Conf.* 10, where Augustine's debt is clearer.

32. On the necessity of reiteration and its relation to memory in Augustine's programme of reform, see Chapter 8, "Conduct."

33. *De Util. Cred.* 22.46–49. On the sense of *cura* and its relationship to *curiositas*, see *Ep.* 118.1 (datable to 410 or 411), *CSEL* 34/2.665.11–15.

34. In my view, there is an unacknowledged link in the argument between Augustine's initial premise concerning the seeker after truth and his admittedly limited definition of studiousness as reiterated knowledge. The missing element concerns the nature of this knowledge, which must presumably deal with the individual's salvation and thus devolve from some aspect of the soul's immortality, mentioned at the outset. An example of this sort of knowledge would be prayer.

35. *De Util Cred.* 22.7: "uitium"; 23.13: "culpa."

36. Ibid., 23.13–15: "Quid existimes in grauiore culpa esse, religionem tradere indigno, ad id quod ab eis, qui illam tradunt, dicitur credere."

37. Ibid., 23.15–16. This notion follows from the fact that the argument deals with potential believers.

38. Ibid., 23.23–25. The situation is analogous to that of Epicurus in *De Util. Cred.* 10.

39. Ibid., 23.25–26: "Non enim animi tui latebras, ita ut intime sciaris, homo homini aperire possis."

40. Ibid., 23.26–29: "At ille si dixerit: ecce credo tibi; sed nonne est aequius, ut etiam tu credas mihi, cum tu beneficium, si aliquid ueri teneo, sis accepturus, daturus ego? Quid respondebimus nisi esse credendum?"

41. Ibid., 24.1–2: "Sed, inquis, nonne erat melius, rationem mihi redderes, ut ea quocumque me duceret, sine ulla sequerer temeritate?"

42. Ibid., 24.13–17. Cf. *De Mor. Eccles Cath.* 1.7.11, *PL* 32.1315.

43. *De Util. Cred.* 24.29–30: "Vix enim est, qui de se tantum sentiat, quantum potest."

44. Cf. Gigon (1985), 154–156.

45. *De Util. Cred.* 25.6–9: "Duae sunt enim personae in religione laudabiles: una eorum, qui iam inuenerunt, quos etiam beatissimos iudicare necesse est; alia eorum, qui studiosissime et rectissime inquirunt."

46. Ibid., 25.10–15: "Tria sunt alia hominum genera, profecto inprobanda ac detestanda. Vnum est opinantium, id est eorum, qui se arbitrantur scire quod nesciunt; alterum eorum, qui sentiunt quidem se nescire, sed non ita quaerunt, ut inuenire possunt; tertium eorum qui neque se scire existimant nec quaerere uolunt."

47. Ibid., 25.18, 19; cf. 27.15, with *peccatum* related to "right reason."

48. Ibid., 25.17–19: "Quae si per se ipsa considerentur, primum semper sine uitio est, secundum aliquando cum uitio, tertium numquam sine uitio."

49. Ibid., 25.27–29, reiterating what he maintains elsewhere on belief and trust. I may believe that conspirators against Rome were executed as a result of the courageous intervention of Cicero on behalf of the republic. But if I say that I know this, I express an opinion, not a fact; and this opinion indicates my trust that these events took place as they are related. Moreover, this reasoning is a demonstration of my ability to convince myself (25.29–38). Augustine generalizes his position on past knowledge, which prepares the way for his argument about scripture at 25.38–41.

50. Ibid., 25.41–42: "Quod intellegimus igitur, debemus rationi, quod credimus, auctoritati, quod opinamur, errori." For an excellent résumé of this theme, see Camelot (1958). In a gloss on these statements in *Retr.*, Augustine argues that when we say that we believe something on the authority of witnesses, we mean that we grasp the point by means of reason; however, in the case of scripture, reason cedes to genuine authority; *Retr.*, 1.14, CCSL 57.43.54–62

51. *De Util. Cred.* 25.57–59: "Quamquam in illis etiam qui se in agendo probabilia sequi dicunt, scire potius nihil posse quam nihil credere uolunt uideri."

52. These appear elsewhere in Augustine's writings. In the first occurrence, chap. 26, he asks why children display obedience and affection toward their parents, since a child knows who its father is only on the mother's authority. Admitting this type of credulity as a general principle of human beliefs (26.15–17), he introduces a second example from chap. 7, namely the fool's inability to select a wise person among those who claim to be wise (chaps. 27–28). The question of audience relations is thereby reintroduced in a manner that brings together the notions of signs and illumination in defence of his position on authority and belief (28.8–17), putting the argument of *De Mag.* in a slightly different context. Finally, on the biblical narrative concerning Christ, he argues that believers are obliged to trust the "report" of those who actually saw him (chap. 31). Such beliefs are supported by fame, consensus, and the strength of antiquity (31.30–31), as well as by authenticated miracles; he adds that the type of miracle best suited to persuading the masses operates through the senses (34.30–34).

53. Datable to 399 or possibly 400; see Madec, *BA* 11.1 (1991), n. 1, pp. 233–237.

54. On earlier hypotheses concerning the relationship between *Conf.* 11–13

and *De Cat. Rud.* (e.g., Wundt [1923] and Williger [1929]), see Pincherle (1955–57), 203–205.

55. For an argument that *De Doct. Christ.* anticipates Augustine's views in *De Ag. Chr.*, written in 396 or 397, see Kleinberg (1987), 16–29. A useful note on Augustine's employment of *sermo humilis* with rural, unlettered audiences is MacMullen (1966).

56. See Folliet (1962).

57. Although its institutional form remains a topic of discussion; for a review, see Lawless (1987), 47–62.

58. On this aspect of Augustine's career, good introductions are found in Monachino (1947), 164–183, and van der Meer (1961), 347–387, 453–467; cf. Eggersdorfer (1907), 153–200, which has not been superseded.

59. For early bibliography, see Negri (1961), 7–9, and his discussion, 11–17; Cranz (1954), 308–311, is unfortunately omitted. The most important philological commentary is Christopher (1926), 122–238. Recent studies are noted by J.-B. Allard (1976), 11–15, and Madec, *BA* 11.1 (1991), 38–41, the latter providing an excellent introduction, 9–38. Little attention has been paid to the potential debt to Ambrose, although Augustine was his catechumen; but see Hellemo (1989), 253–258.

60. Cf. Madec, *BA* 11.1 (1991), 15–17, who compares the technique of reading advocated in the treatise to Augustine's own experience at *Conf.* 3.5, *CCSL* 27.30–31 (the *Hortensius*) and 5.13.14–24, 70–71 (hearing Ambrose preach).

61. On the identity, see J.-B. Allard (1976), 37–40. Madec, *BA* 11.1 (1991), 9–10, is favorably disposed to identify him with the recipient of *Ep.* 102. See the comments of Goldbacher in his edition, *CSEL* 58.31.

62. The treatises are also comparable in being divided into segments devoted to theory and practice: in *De Mag.*, these are respectively chaps. 1–10 and 11–14, in *De Cat. Rud.*, chaps. 1–14 and 15–27. In *De Mag.* the introductory section is an actual dialogue; in *De Cat. Rud.* it is a theoretical discussion of dialogic communication between the catechist and the catechumen.

63. *De Mag.* 10.30, *CCSL* 29.188–189; 11.36 (p. 194.1–8).

64. *De Cat. Rud.* 5.11–12; 8.12–16; 25.1–6; cited in this section from *CCSL* 46, by chapter and line.

65. Hebrews 6:4, 10:32. On the rites at Hippo, as discussed in Augustine's baptismal sermons, see Audet (1954); cf. van der Meer (1961), 353–382. On similar vocabulary in Cyril regarding Jerusalem and Ambrose, see Hellemo (1989), 188–196, 259–262.

66. *De Mag.* 12.40, *CCSL* 29.197–199.

67. *De Cat. Rud.* 2.50–61; 9.16–21; 25.10–12.

68. Marrou (1966), 5.

69. Cf. Quint., *Inst. Orat.* 1.4.2. On the rhetorical figures in the work, see Cordovani (1968), 289–300, and, on *narratio*, 297–299. On the relation of this instruction to Augustine's later critique of the teaching of history in his time, see Green (1944), 317–327.

70. This outline deals mainly with points in my discussion; for a general guide, see Madec, *BA* 11.1 (1991), 20–21.

71. The sermons are included in the treatise but presumably were not delivered; for a discussion, see Negri (1961), 23.

72. Schematically represented by Banniard (1992), 76–77.

73. Chap. 2 is omitted from discussion in van der Meer (1961) and Negri (1961); but see Reil (1989), 8–12, and Madec, *BA* 11.1 (1991), n. 3, pp. 241–244, noting (242–243): "On se trouve . . . au croisement de l'axe vertical de la contemplation et de l'axe horizontal de la communication," in which *De Cat. Rud.* "marquerait . . . une évolution par rapport au *De magistro.*"

74. Cf. *In Io. Eu. Tract.* 1.1, *CCSL* 36.1.19–25.

75. *De Cat. Rud.* 2.6–10: "Nam et mihi prope semper sermo meus displicet. Melioris enim auidus sum, quo saepe fruor interius, antequam eum explicare uerbis sonantibus coepero: quod ubi minus quam mihi motus est eualuero, contristor linguam meam cordi meo non potuisse sufficere"; also 10.54–60, where the failure to express oneself in words is preeminent among the sources of "tedium" for speakers; discussed by Banniard (1992), 68–69.

76. *De Cat. Rud.* 2.10–18: "Totum enim quod intelligo, uolo ut qui me audit intelligat; et sentio me non ita loqui, ut hoc efficiam; maxime quia ille intellectus quasi rapida coruscatione perfundit animum, illa autem locutio tarda et longa est, longeque dissimilis, et dum ista uoluitur, iam se ille in secreta sua condidit; tamen, quia uestigia quaedam miro modo impressit memoriae, perdurant illa cum syllabarum morulis; atque ex eisdem uestigiis sonantia signa peragimus"; on *coruscatio,* see Chapter 9, "The Reader and the *Cogito.*"

77. I.e., through a type of gesturing in relation to acoustical patterns.

78. Augustine maintains that facial expressions of emotion are universal, since they transcend the limitations of particular languages. If this is the case, his view anticipates conclusions of contemporary research; see Ekman (1993), 384–385.

79. This view differs in emphasis from that of *Conf.* 10, discussed in Chapter 8, "Remembering."

80. *De Cat. Rud.* 2.66–69, 10.4–5; J. B. Allard (1976), 67–70.

81. A point developed during this period in *De Trin.* 8–9; see Chapter 9, "A Language of Thought."

82. One point remains unclear: is the speaker's understanding, as his thoughts become words, the same as the hearer's, as a message is received and decoded?

83. Cordovani (1968), 297–299. Augustine's source may have been Quintilian; on his usage, see Gwynn (1926), 200–202; Oroz Reta (1963), 83–86; cf. S. F. Bonner (1977), 253, who notes the importance of memory. On the background, see Combès and Farges, *BA* 11 (1949), n. 3, pp. 547–548; and, on Augustine's development out of classical rhetoric, Siniscalco (1974), 614–622.

84. See Reil (1989), 12–16, 22–24, and 103–148, who outlines the features of Augustine's implicit "narrativity."

85. Green (1944), 315–327; Markus (1970), 5–7, 32–33.

86. For a brief review of the idea in Augustine's thought, see Combès and Farges, *BA* 11 (1949), n. 13, pp. 552–554.

87. Cf. *Ep.* 102, *CSEL* 34/2.544.

88. *De Cat Rud.* 3.6–8: "uel, si ad uerbum edidicimus, memoriter reddere, uel nostris uerbis omnia quae his uoluminibus continentur narrando euoluere et explicare."

89. Ibid., 3.14–19; cf. 6.14–19, 9.11–16. Although too much weight must not be placed on a single statement, the metaphors utilized in 3.5.3–15 (i.e., the contrast between *euoluere* and *in inuolucris ostendere*) suggest that the codex is better suited to interpretive discussion than the roll.

90. This is also the theme of the first specimen sermon, chaps. 16–22.

91. 1 Cor. 10:11; *De Cat. Rud.* 3.58–62: "Quapropter omnia quae ante scripta sunt, ut nos doceremur scripta sunt, et figurae nostrae fuerunt; et in figura contingebant in eis: scripta sunt autem propter nos, in quos finis saeculorum obuenit."

92. *De Cat. Rud.* 4.56–59: "Omnisque scriptura diuina quae ante scripta est, ad praenuntiandum aduentum domini scripta est, et quidquid postea mandatum est litteris et diuina auctoritate firmatum, Christum narrat et dilectionem monet."

93. This is a twofold statement about readership, not about "society"; cf. Cranz (1954), 308–309; for an extensive analysis, see Cordovani (1967); cf. G. H. Allard (1966), 331–339. The point has implications for the understanding of Augustine's political theology which cannot be treated here; on this topic, see Markus (1967), 406–419 and (1970). For a recent review of the issues but not of the secondary literature, see van Oort (1991), 176–198. Texts on the two cities in Augustine's sermons are found in Lauras and Rondet (1953).

94. Cf. *C. Faustum* 13.13, *CSEL* 25.392–393.

95. See *De Doct. Christ.* 1 and *De Trin.* 8–9, discussed in Chapters 7 and 9 respectively.

96. E.g., *De Cat. Rud.* 5.32–33: "Faciamus eum delectari esse se talem, qualem uideri cupit."

97. Ibid., 5.16–17: "Et occultum est quidem nobis est, quando ueniat animo quem iam corpore presentem uidemus." A commentary on his own conversion?

98. Di Capua (1931), 673.

99. A good example is Honoratus in *De Util. Cred.,* although Augustine takes a different view of his reeducation.

100. E.g., *De Cura pro Mor. Ger.* 12.15, *CSEL* 41.644–647; however, this was a priest, Curma.

101. Cf. *Conf.* 4.3.5, *CCSL* 27.42.19–36; *De Gen. ad Litt.* 12.24–25, *CSEL* 28.416–418.

102. *De Cat. Rud.* 6.20–25, discussing *fictas poetarum fabulae* taught by *grammatici* as in *Conf.* 1.

103. Cf. ibid., 19.9–12: "Duae itaque ciuitates, una iniquorum, altera sanctorum, ab initio generis humani usque in finem saeculi perducuntur, nunc permixtae

corporibus, sed uoluntatibus separatae." Cranz (1954), 308–311, takes the statement somewhat out of context; Augustine is discussing the meaning of the resurrection in a sermon for *accedentes,* those preparing for the twin baptismal ceremonies of *traditio* and *redditio symboli;* cf. Marrou (1966), 5–6, and, for other examples, Audet (1954), 152 n. 6. A possible background text is Plotinus, *Enn.* 4.4.17, vol. 2, 72.35–37.

104. Banniard (1992), 73–74, who sees in *indoctus* and *imperitus* "désignations précises d'une culture écrite très pauvre," in which "le sens religieux du mot cède ici à la place au sens linguistique." I do not envisage Augustine aiming at quite such a sweeping designation.

105. In general, *rudes* means "those uninstructed in religion," e.g., *De Cat. Rud.* 1.2, 11.9; on one occasion, "the unconverted," 23.62–63. In the phrase *tamquam rudem et ignarum* (5.35–36), an implicit link is made between lack of information and lack of skills to understand it, a notion also suggested by the verbs *imbuo, insinuo,* and *instruo,* e.g., 2.57–58, 10.24, and 26.24–25. References to *rudis* are listed in J.-B. Allard (1976), 46–49; also Cordovani (1966), 491–504; and Combès and Farges, *BA* 11 (1949), 545–546.

106. *De Cat. Rud.* 27.3–4, uniting the notions of reading and seeing.

107. Ibid., 8.4–6, an idea echoed in *De Doct. Christ.* 1–2.

108. Ibid., 8.26–28: "Sane etiam exprimendum de illo est, ut indicet quem maxime legerit, et quibus libris familiarius inhaeserit, unde illi persuasum est, ut sociari uellet ecclesiae." Cf. 11.1–2, 54–57.

109. See *Ep.* 102, *CSEL* 34/2.544–578, where, writing possibly to the same Deogratias between 406 and 412, Augustine outlines how the questions of a *paganus eruditus* are to be answered.

110. Di Capua (1931), 673.

111. *De Cat. Rud.* 9.11–16. Augustine suggests that "quidam de scholis usitatissimis grammaticorum oratorumque uenientes" (9.1–2), like himself, though not being among the truly learned, are well prepared to proceed from a grammatical to a deeper interpretive understanding of biblical texts; which is to recapitulate the message of *Conf.* 1.1, *CCSL* 27.1.4–5; 3.5 (pp. 30–31).

112. An allusion to the difficulty of visual reading without oral clues; see the Introduction.

113. *De Cat. Rud.* 11.16–18: "Plerumque autem nos ipsi recolentes quae diximus, reprehendimus aliquid, et ignoramus quomodo cum diceretur acceptum sit."

114. Ibid., 12.4–6. This is an answer, through emotional rather than cognitive union, to the isoluble problem of communication through signs in *De Mag.*

115. *De Util. Cred.* 4.10, *CSEL* 25.14.21–15.19.

116. For a detailed analysis see Negri (1961), 26–86.

117. *De Cat. Rud.* 15.4–7: "Quod priusquam faciam, uolo cogites aliam esse intentionem dictantis, cum lector futurus cogitatur; et aliam loquentis, cum praesens auditor adtenditur."

118. Oroz Reta (1963), 171, and, for an excellent analysis of the "psychological qualities" in Augustine's sermons, 171–190. The topic of audiences is taken up by Banniard (1992), 76–85.

119. Cf. M. D. Jordan (1980), 177–179, 182–191. For an outline of the work's argument, see Combès and Farges, *BA* 11 (1949), 151–167; on the possible stages of composition, see Pincherle, "Sulla composizione" (1974). In the following section of this chapter I refer to *De Doctrina Christiana* in the edition of J. Martin, *CCSL* 32, quoting by book, chapter, and line.

120. Eggersdorfer (1907), 97–200.

121. See Marrou, *Saint Augustin* (1958), 387–413; on the divergences between Eggersdorfer and Marrou, see Kevane (1966).

122. Verheijen (1974), 11; my translation.

123. The numerous studies of this theme are summarized by Press (1980), 99–100 nn. 2–3 and 100 nn. 6–7. Marrou, *Saint Augustin* (1958), 329–545, provides background; a useful supplement is Oroz Reta (1963), 18–141. Briefer overviews include F. Jansen (1930); Mohrmann, "Eloquentia" (1958); and Fortin (1974).

124. On Augustine's possible reasons for interrupting the treatise, see Hill (1962). In the early draft, written in 396, Aurelius may have discouraged Augustine from borrowing heavily from the interpretative principles of the Donatist Tyconius; *Ep.* 41.2, *CSEL* 34/2.83, 16–18. However, by 426–27, when the revision took place, the Donatist controversy was behind him. A thorough comparison of Augustine and Tyconius on interpretation is beyond the scope of this study. For a brief introduction, see Chadwick (1989); scholarship is reviewed by Bright (1988), 28–31, including the important contributions of Hahn (1900), Pincherle (1925), and Ratzinger (1956). The following discussion concerns the place ˙of *De Doct. Christ.* in Augustine's overall intellectual evolution rather than the work's possible stages of composition.

125. On the notions of *doctrina* and *disciplina,* a useful general review is Marrou (1934); cf. Kevane (1966) and the response of Verheijen (1974); also Prete (1970); Geerlings (1978), 87–91; and Press (1984), 113–115, who is good on *doctrina*'s complexity, 100 ff. In *De Doct. Christ.,* Augustine prefers substantives to verbs for both ideas. On *disciplina,* his thinking is summarized in *S. de Dis. Chr.* 1.1, *CCSL* 46.207.2–7: "'Accipite disciplinam in domo disciplinae [Ecclis. 51:31; cf. 51:36].' Disciplina, a discendo dicta est: disciplinae domus, est ecclesia Christi. Quid ergo hic discitur, uel quare discitur? Qui discunt? a quo discunt? Discitur bene uiuere. Propter hoc discitur bene uiuere, ut perueniatur ad semper uiuere. Discunt christiani, docet Christus." The role of the teaching of letters is made clear in 11.12 (pp. 219–220, 290–305), where he orients the potential reader away from the secular use of literature and toward the religious; *De Trin.* 14.1.1, *CCSL* 50a.421.16–17. On the notion's biblical background see Dürig (1952), 245–254, and de Lubac (1959), vol. 1, 43–56; on the incarnation as *disciplina uiuendi,* see Geerlings (1978), 85–87.

126. Cf. Kaster (1988), 84–88. It is possible that *De Cat. Rud.* furnished him

with a transitional model, i.e., a "dialogue" between catechumen and catechist, whose aim was doctrinal instruction.

127. *De Doct. Christ.*, 1.1. In Augustine, the term normally refers to the written version of oral discourse concerning the Bible; e.g., 4.18.53–57. The passage is misquoted by Bardy (1946), 228, who provides other illustrations, pp. 227–230; cf. Mayer, "'Res per signa'" (1974), 105–106; and the lengthier treatment by Press (1980), 107–113.

128. E.g., *De Doct. Christ.* 2.32.1–3, where *discere* and *docere* concern inferences about a biblical text.

129. On the debate over its dating, relevant scholarship is summarized by M. D. Jordan (1980), 180 n. 9, and Seeliger (1980), 148 n. 1. For an authoritative statement, see Mayer, "'Res per signa'" (1974), 107–112, who supports the view, followed here, that the ideas advanced in the prologue and in bk. 2 are reasonably consistent.

130. *De Doct. Christ.*, prooem. 1.1–4: "Sunt praecepta quaedam tractandarum scripturarum, quae studiosis earum uideo non incommode posse tradi, ut non solum legendo alios, qui diuinarum litterarum operta aperuerunt, sed etiam ipsi aperiendo proficiant."

131. Ibid., prooem., 9.132–134: "Qui legit audientibus litteras, utique quas agnoscit enuntiat; qui autem ipsas litteras tradit, hoc agit, ut alii quoque legere nouerint, uterque tamen id insinuat, quod accepit."

132. I.e., an "office of reading"; cf. Oroz Reta (1963), 87–94.

133. *De Doct. Christ.*, prooem. 9.134–138: "Sic etiam qui ea, quae in scripturis intellegit, exponit audientibus tamquam litteras, quas agnoscit, pronuntiat lectoris officio; qui autem praecipit, quomodo intellegendum sit, similis est tradenti litteras, hoc est praecipienti, quomodo legendum sit." Cf. *De Mor. Eccles. Cath.* 1.1.1, *PL* 32.1311, where as early as 388–390 he argued that the Bible is best taught by professional teachers *(doctores)*.

134. *De Doct. Christ.*, prooem. 9.139–146: "Vt quomodo ille, qui legere nouit, alio lectore non indiget, cum codicem inuenerit, a quo audiat, quid ibi scriptum sit, sic iste, qui praecepta, quae conamur tradere, acceperit, cum in libris aliquid obscuritatis inuenerit, quasdam regulas uelut litteras tenens intellectorem alium non requirat, per quem sibi, quod opertum est, retegatur, sed quibusdam uestigiis indagatis ad occultum sensum sine ullo errore ipse perueniat aut certe in absurditatem prauae sententiae non incidat." Cf. Brunner (1955), 59–61, 65–67.

135. "Tradere": ibid. prooem. 1.2, 1.4, 9.133.

136. Accordingly, *littera* refers both to the written transcription of a minimal unit of sound and to the understanding of a text that is retransmitted vocally; ibid., prooem. 9.122, 138.

137. A rethinking of the triune divisions of reader's and writer's errors in *De Util. Cred.?*

138. See Brunner (1955), 85–103, an excellent discussion. The situation is comparable to that of individuals who are able to gaze directly on reason or truth;

*Sol.* 1.6.13, CSEL 89, pp. 21–22; 1.13.23 (pp. 35–36). The parallel in secular letters is Albericius, who, with scarcely any knowledge of grammar, is able to recite a verse of Virgil that is in the mind of one of Augustine's pupils, Flaccianus; *C. Acad.* 1.6.18, CCSL 29.13.34–55. However, it is important to distinguish feats of memory from inward instruction by Christ; e.g., *De Vera Rel.* 17.33, CCSL 32.207.1–5.

139. *De Doct. Christ.,* prooem. 4.51–58. Cf. *Conf.* 8.12, CCSL 27.131.26–28.

140. Just as he does not deny the possibility of miracles in his own time; *Retr.* 1.13.7, CCSL 57.39. However, inasmuch as inspired interpretation yields to rules, so the age in which his distant predecessors made use of "visible miracles" has been superseded by that of "the Catholic church"; *De Vera Rel.* 25.47, CCSL 32.216–217.24–34.

141. They include first and second languages, among the latter, Greek and Hebrew; 5.60–66; cf. *Conf.* 1.13, CCSL 27.11.

142. Although man does not have to read to be "purified," he cannot achieve purification on his own either; *De Trin.* 4.15, CCSL 50.187.

143. *De Doct. Christ.,* prooem. 6.98–101. Cf. *De Trin.* 10.5, CCSL 50.320–321.

144. Prete (1970), 67; cf. Mayer, *Die antimanichäische Epoche* (1974), 294–298.

145. Mayer, *Die antimanichäische Epoche* (1974), 286–293, a masterful introduction; also M. D. Jordan (1980), 177–178, 182–191.

146. *De Doct. Christ.* I.I. Istace (1956), 291, divides the discussion into three parts: an ethico-dogmatic exposition of three types of object (chaps. 3–21), a reduction of directives to the double precept of charity (22–38), and an accompaniment by hope and faith (39–40). For a response to Mayer's emphasis on Platonic influences in bk. 1, see Sieben (1975), 72–80.

147. Reiterating that the one is the means, the other the goal, in the search for the blessed life (1.3.1–6). To enjoy *(frui)* is "to be closely united with something for its own sake" (1.4.1–2). Of course, only one thing is completely enjoyable, namely the triune God (1.5.1–3). Cf. *De Diu. Quaes.,* q. 30, CCSL 44a.38.9–12.

148. See Istace (1956), 292–294, who notes scriptural *fontes* and possible Plotinian parallels.

149. The idea is reiterated in a number of contexts, among which a little-noted example is *Ep.* 138.5, CSEL 44.129.17–130.1 (to Marcellinus).

150. See Chapter 6, "Defining the Reader."

151. *De Diu. Quaes.,* q. 30 and 35, CCSL 44a.38–40 and 50–53, where the context of the reader is absent. Discussions of *utor* or *frui* normally begin here; e.g., di Giovanni (1965), 21–88. The finest overall review remains Holte (1962), 251–281, whose ideas are in harmony with those of Lorenz (1950–51) and (1952–53); more recent surveys include Canning, "The Augustinian Distinction" (1983), 195–231, and O'Donovan (1982); cf. Pfligersdorffer (1971); a brief outline is Cayré, *BA* 11 (1949), n. 18, pp. 558–561.

152. *De Diu. Quaes.,* q. 35, CCSL 44a.51–52.20–41. For a discussion of differing interpretations with an excellent synthesis, see O'Donovan (1980), 10–36, 137–152. Cf. Canning, "Love of Neighbor" (1983) and (1984).

153. Di Giovanni (1965), 137–199, omits the sign theory and the application to reading, thereby weakening an otherwise outstanding exposition.

154. Markus (1966), 434.

155. Another theme mentioned elsewhere is the lack of an adequate name or noun for the object of our love, namely the trinity (1.5.3–7); on which see Istace (1956), 295–296. *De Trin.* 7.1.2, *CCSL* 50.245–246.57–74. In our attempts to express what is indescribable, we merely bear witness to the limitations of human language (1.6.2–3). It follows that to know God the mind has to be purified. This can take place through a momentary vision of truth, as at Ostia, or through a lengthier voyage of self-discovery, which does not require that we move anywhere except in our thoughts (1.10.3–8).

156. A point of structural importance in *De Trin.*, discussed in Chapter 9, "The Self."

157. *De Doct. Christ.* 1.13.1–8: "Quomodo uenit, nisi quod 'Verbum caro factum est et habitauit in nobis [John 1:14]'? Sicuti cum loquimur, ut id, quod animo gerimus, in audientis animum per aures carneas inlabatur, 'fit sonus' uerbum quod corde gestamus, et locutio uocatur, nec tamen in eundem sonum cogitatio nostra conuertitur, sed apud se manens integra, formam uocis qua se insinuet auribus, sine aliqua labe suae mutationis adsumit: ita uerbum dei non commutatum caro tamen factum est, ut habitaret in nobis." This optimistic scenario in communication, the opposite of what is argued in *De Mag.*, depends on shifting the weight of meaning from words to thoughts. Augustine's affirmation of thought's permanence also depends on the assumption of the *cogito*.

158. See Istace (1956), 305–315, and, from a literary persective, Consolino (1981), 119–123, 128–130.

159. *De Doct. Christ.* 1.17.1–2; also 3.11–23, where the emotions play a part in the interpretation of ambiguous signs.

160. Ibid., 1.36.1–4: "Quisquis igitur scripturas diuinas uel quamlibet earum partem intellexisse sibi uidetur, ita ut eo intellectu non aedificet istam geminam caritatem dei et proximi, nondum intellexit."

161. He reminds us that some do not need sacred books, except to instruct others; ibid., 1 39.1–4.

162. Mayer, *Die antimanichäische Epoche* (1974), 302–321, provides an authoritative commentary on the hermeneutical principles of bk. 2.

163. See Vogels (1930), 414–416, 419, and, on Augustine's increasing attention to precise quotation between the two versions of *De Doct.*, de Bruyne (1912), 301–312.

164. Cf. *De S. Dom. in M.* 1.1.1, *CCSL* 35.1.1–10.

165. For a summary of *De Doct. Christ.* 2.1–3, see the Introduction.

166. Ibid., 2.2.7–9: "quia et signa diuinitus data, quae scripturis sanctis continentur, per homines nobis indicata sunt, qui ea conscripserunt." As noted in the Introduction, only given signs operating among humans are relevant (2.2.9–18). In principle, these can convey information through any of the senses; however,

the vast majority are words, whereas signals given by others means (e.g., nods, theatrics, or banners) are considered to be visible words. It is through words that humans convey their inner states to each other (2.3.1–21).

167. Ibid., 2.4.1–4: "Sed quia uerberato aere statim transeunt nec diutius manent quam sonant, instituta sunt per litteras signa uerborum. Ita uoces oculis ostenduntur non per se ipsas, sed per signa sonantia."

168. Cf. *De Trin.* 4.20.29, CCSL 50.201.140–148, where Augustine cites Ps. 18:4–5 in favour of the thesis that, when God first spoke to man, the holy spirit transcended the differences among human spoken languages; see the Introduction.

169. Cf. *De Trin.* 12–15, discussed in Chapter 9, "The Road toward Wisdom."

170. See Maréchal (1930), 96–102, 192–194, who draws attention to a Plotinian component in successive visions of ascent.

171. Cf. *De S. Dom. in M.* 1.4.11, CCSL 35.9–11, proceeding through *timor, pietas, scientia, fortitudo, consilium, intellectus,* and *sapientia.*

172. For a full analysis with sources, see du Roy (1966), 256–260.

173. See the Introduction and Chapter 8, "Remembering."

174. *De Vera Rel.* 20.38, CCSL 32.210.

175. Ibid., 24.45 (p. 215.1).

176. Ibid., 26.48 (p. 217.1–2).

177. Ibid., 20.38 (p. 210.11–13).

178. Ibid., 24.45 (p. 215.3–6).

179. Ibid., 26.48 (p. 217.3–6): "Primo unius hominis cuiuslibet nascentis natura et eruditio cogitatur. Prima huius infantia in nutrimentis corporalibus agitur penitus obliuiscenda crescenti. Eam pueritia sequitur, unde incipimus aliquid meminisse." Cf. *Conf.* 1.6–8, CCSL 27.4.

180. *De Vera Rel.* 26.48 (p. 217.7–9).

181. Ibid. (p. 217.14).

182. Ibid. (p. 217.15–16).

183. Ibid. (p. 218.17–18); cf. 26.49 (p. 218.24–27).

184. Ibid. (p. 218.18–23).

185. Ibid. (p. 218.26–31).

186. Ibid. (p. 218.31–34): "Iste dicitur nouus homo et interior et caelestis habens et ipse proportione non annis, sed prouectibus distinctas quasdam spiritales aetates suas."

187. Ibid. (p. 218.34–35): "Primam in uberibus utilis historiae, quae nutrit exemplis." This would also correspond to catechism.

188. Ibid. (p. 218.35–38).

189. Ibid. (p. 21.38–42). Cf. The allegory of Continence in *Conf.* 8 and the discussion in Chapter 8, "Conduct."

190. Ibid. (pp. 218–219.48).

191. Ibid. (p. 219.48–51): "Sextam omnimodae mutationis in aeternam uitam et usque ad totam obliuionem uitae temporalis transeuntem perfecta forma, quae facta est ad imaginem et similitudinem dei."

192. Ibid. (p. 219.51–53).

193. Burnaby (1947), 52; *De Quant. An.* 33.76, CSEL 89.223.17–19.

194. *De Doct. Christ.* 2.7.10–12. Augustine elaborates the formal programme in *Conf.* 10.25–43, CCSL 27.174–193.

195. *De Doct. Christ.* 2.8.3–6. The rest of 2.8 presents Augustine's views on the then unfixed canon of the books of the Bible.

196. Ibid., 2.7.13–35. Cf. *De S. Dom. in M.* 1.3.10, CCSL 35.8.152–159.

197. Cf. *De Trin.* 1.8.17, CCSL 50.50.80–81; cf. 1.8.17 (pp. 51.115–52.127). For a theological synthesis, see Cayré (1931), 4–7, 21–51.

198. *De Doct. Christ.* 2.9.2–5. Cf. 2.39.1–5, on young students' avoiding non-Christian writings.

199. These concern faith, morals for life, hope, and charity—matters, Augustine notes, touched upon in bk. 1. Proceeding in this manner, groups of readers can replace uncertainty with certainty (2.9.8–16).

200. The notion of a sign operating in a literary field thus takes priority over that of a sign in the world and is subsequently imposed on it.

201. On this question, see the masterly analysis of Bucher (1982).

202. E.g., *De Doct. Christ.* 2.12.2–4. On the use of this technique in the *Conf.*, see Chapter 2, "Neoplatonism."

203. The solution is a knowledge of languages, especially Hebrew and Greek (*De Doct. Christ.* 2.11.1–2; 2.13.1–4; 2.15). The student of the Bible is advised to consult native speakers as well as translations (2.11.6–21; 2.16.7–11). A diversity of versions nonetheless has its advantages, among them comparison (2.12.1–4; cf. 2.12.22–23). The reader will at least overcome solecism and barbarism (2.13.16–26). Augustine prefers a mythological to philological account of the origins of translations (2.15.7–11); see Sirridge (1975), 107–108, who notes his awareness of differences between speakers, writers, and authors. On the debate with Jerome over the canon of the Old Testament, see Hennings (1994). Augustine argues that one can translate words *(uerba)* or expressions *(locutiones)*; a harmony is desirable but seldom attained. In any case, the object is realities (2.13.10 13, 29–31).

204. *De Doct. Christ.* 2.16.1–3. When the connections arise from spoken Hebrew (within Judaeo-Christian tradition), his solutions parallel those devised for unknown literal signs: examples include the figurative use of names, animals, numbers, and musical instruments (2.16); however, when they arise from pagan antiquity, the spoken languages in question, Greek and Latin, are those of the Bible's translation, not of its origin. As a consequence, he is obliged to evaluate a wide variety of non-Christian facts and methods under the heading of unknown figurative signs.

205. For a more extensive treatment of Augustine's notion of a religious cult than can be attempted here, see Kobusch (1983), 101–120.

206. *De Doct. Christ.* 2.20.1–5; cf. 3.7. Cf. *Sermo* 141.3, PL 38.777; *De Diu. Quaes.*, q. 78, CCSL 44a.223–224.

207. E.g., enchantments, the fabrication of secret characters, the wearing of

magical objects, such as earrings or ostrich bones, popularly called physics; *De Doct. Christ.*, 2.20.4–9; cf. 2.29.5–21.

208. Ibid., 2.20.3–4, where magic is called "consultationes et pacta . . . significationum." Cf. 2.20.14; 2.29.13; *De Trin.* 4.12.15, *CCSL* 50.180.1–4. Is this an anticipation of contemporary linguistic anthropology? Even if it is not, Augustine's view contrasts sharply with that of Plotinus, who sees magic operating through "sympathy"; *Enn.* 4.4.40, vol. 2, 106–108.

209. The latter are divisible into those amenable to the senses (*De Doct. Christ.* 2.27–30) and those amenable to reason (2.31–39).

210. In earlier times, audiences recognized the story on which such dance was based; in his time, they had to be reminded by means of a narrator. His point is that such a mimetic art cannot communicate its meaning without audience participation; ibid., 2.25.7–19. Cf. Plotinus, *Enn.* 4.4.33, vol. 2, 96–96, for a vivid description.

211. Cf. *De Trin.* 3.10, *CCSL* 50.147.25–29, on the permanence of writings (*litterae*).

212. *De Doct. Christ.* 2.28.1–2; cf. 2.28.40–41. For an analysis, see Seeliger (1980), 151–155.

213. The easiest way to understand the scheme is to work backwards from the fourth class. Augustine argues that it is helpful to know practical skills (e.g., making a dish, a bench, or a house), since a craftman's future course of action is guided by what he has done in the past (2.30.8–10). In dancing, running, and wrestling, the effects are produced by actions (2.30.5–7), whereas arts such as medicine, agriculture, and navigation enable their practitioners to be "God's helpers," i.e., they fulfil a design that they have not made. But this sort of knowledge is of limited use in understanding scripture; an example is astrology, which is useful for ascertaining feast-days but restricted to external causalities (2.29.22–36, 40–45). As a consequence, useful knowledge is found in the first and second options, which relieve ignorance through facts about the past or present; the first comprise places, animals, trees, plants, stones, etc., whose names are found in the Bible (2.29.1–5); included are remedies, which are not magical or superstitious (2.29.13) but consist of notations about medicines that can help the reader solve "enigmas" (2.29.5–8). However, these fail to account for the behaviour of biblical figures found in option two.

214. Ibid., 2.29.19–21. This explanation has to be distinguished from Augustine's position, derived from Paul, that, in creation, man works from the outside, while God works from within; *De Trin.* 3.8.13, *CCSL* 50.141.72–74. It is only demons or men under their influence who reverse this relationship; ibid., (pp. 141.75–142.88); 3.9.10 (pp. 146.11–147.32).

215. I omit his discussion of factual information acquired outside church (*De Doct. Christ.* 2.8.3–4), as well as his well-known view that pagan philosophical sources can fill in the chronological gaps in the gospel; 2.28.4–20 and 2.28.27–32; cf. 2.40.

216. The distinction parallels that between natural and given signs.

217. Augustine argues that what has passed cannot become present, but belongs to the "order of time" created and administered by God, who is outside time; this view is vigorously defended in *Conf.* 11.

218. Cf. *De Trin.* 4.16.21–4.18.24, *CCSL* 50.188–193.

219. They are relevant because they are communicated to others; *De Doct. Christ.* 2.32.1–3; 2.35.1–4; cf. *De Trin.* 4.4.7–4.6.10, *CCSL* 50.169–175. Number is discussed only briefly; *De Doct. Christ.* 2.38.1–13; cf. 2.39.36–38.

220. *De Doct. Christ.* 2.32.24–26: "Et haec regula [i.e., if the consequent is false, the antecedent must be false] pertinet ad ueritatem conexionum, non ad ueritatem sententiarum." Cf. 2.34.1–2.

221. For example, if a pious reader argues that Christ did not rise from the dead, he employs a valid premise but reaches a false conclusion—false, that is, in relation to the literal statements in the Bible. Augustine lists several types of operation of this kind: valid consequences can arise from false antecedents, and vice versa (ibid., 2.33.14–16); definition, division, and partition can likewise lead to error (2.35.1–2); persuasive techniques can be misused (2.36).

222. In support of this argument, Augustine makes the unsual remark (in this context) that experience is a better teacher than precepts. We often master principles in order to explain to ourselves what we already know; his example, reworked from *De Mag.* 3, is trying to learn to walk from instructions rather than from experience. In a comparable manner, an intelligent person recognizes that false conclusions, while an unintelligent one, even with instruction in logic, may fail to do so (2.37.9–26; cf. 2.38.14–24).

223. 1 Cor. 8:1; *De Doct. Christ.* 2.41.3–4; cf. 2.42.12–18.

224. On the theme of pagan knowledge in *De Doct. Christ.* and *Conf.*, see Bochet (1993), 23–29. For an authoritative commentary on bk. 3, see Mayer, *Die antimanichäische Epoche* (1974), 321–334.

225. When the context is no help, the only recourse is faith or arbitrary interpretation (*De Doct. Christ.* 3.3.3–7; cf. 3.2.3–5). Augustine adds that such problems are rare, and can normally be resolved through an understanding of the author's intention or a comparison of translations (3.4.17–22). Elsewhere he underlines the human language of scripture; *De Trin.* 1.12.23, *CCSL* 50.62.24–26.

226. See Ripanti (1972), 220–225.

227. This solution can be understood as a more sophisticated version of the errors of reading and writing in *De Util. Cred.*

228. *De Doct. Christ.* 3.5.5–7: "'Littera occidit, spiritus autem uiuificat [2 Cor. 3:6].' Cum enim figurate dictum sic accipitur, tamquam proprie dictum sit, carnaliter sapitur."

229. Ibid., 3.5.9–12: "Qui enim sequitur litteram, translata uerba sicut propria tenet neque illud, quod proprio uerbo significatur, refert ad aliam significationem."

230. Ibid., 3.5.7–8, 16–17; cf. *De Trin.* 1.11.22, *CCSL* 50.60.1–6; 2.1.2 (p. 81.8–12).

231. On these themes, see the wide-ranging review of issues in Kobusch (1983), and, on the Jews, 104–107. In Augustine's view, the process is historical as well as

psychological and begins with the Jewish adoption of monotheism. The Jews are envisaged as children with their tutor, mistaking signs for things. Some convert; others remain in bondage (*De Doct. Christ.* 3.6.4–8, 19–30; 3.7.20; cf. 3.8). They are like worshippers of statues (3.7.20–23; cf. 3.9.25–27). Yet they left a legacy of laws and precepts. On these issues, see the brief remarks of Blumenkranz (1958), 229–230; also Blumenkranz (1946), 131–133 and nn. A more comprehensive review of Augustine's relationship to Jewish thought would be useful.

232. *De Doct. Christ.* 3.9.6: "homo spiritalis et liber." A notion possibly derived from Tyconius, who uses it in the context of prophecy; see Bright (1988), 9–10.

233. *De Doct. Christ.* 3.15.3–5. In 3.11–29, Augustine provides examples of the "rule" by which literal expressions are to be taken figuratively in accordance with the doctrine of charity, turning to statements of bitterness and anger (3.11), apparent shamefulness (3.12–14), and a variety of precepts condemning vice and crime (3.16–23). He then reiterates key points about ambiguity and obscurity (3.24–28), adding a note on tropes (3.29). Finally he takes up the seven rules of Tyconius, which he finds useful but vague (3.30–37); on which see Hahn (1900), 6–7 and 29–56; other scholarship is summarized by Ratzinger (1956), 173–174. On their role in the composition of *De Doct. Christ.* see Pincherle, "Sulla composizione" (1974), 546–553, and Bright (1988), 55–56, 120–121, 124; cf. 152–154.

234. For an overview, see Kunzelmann (1930), 158–161; for a brief comparison with *De Cat. Rud.,* see Jubany (1942), 11–14; on Augustine's position as a Christian "orator" in contrast to Cicero, see Comeau (1930), 11–18, 23–39, 46–58, 71–84; cf. Fortin (1974). On the ethics of words and its background, see di Giovanni (1968), 23–32.

235. *De Doct. Christ.* 4.3.3–16.

236. *De Doct. Christ.* 4.4.18–25. Among the writings "over and above the canon," does Augustine have his own in mind?

237. Cf. *De Oratore* 3.52–143.

238. Augustine also anticipates his response to the Donatist grammarian Cresconius, who misquoted Prov. 10:19 ("Ex multa eloquentia non effugies peccatum," *Contra Cresconium* 1.2, *CSEL* 52.326.4–5), against his view, evidently adapted from Cicero, that eloquence, if properly used, perfects knowledge, just as adequate knowledge complements one's oratorical skill. Augustine may not have known that Cicero's Crassus based his theory on the New Academy, whose teachings he rejected; see Gwynn (1926), 112–115.

239. *De Doct. Christ.* 4.5.29–33; however, it is unethical to memorize the wise sayings of others and to offer them to the audience as one's own; 4.29.5–8.

## 8. Memory, Self-Reform, and Time

1. The model is announced in *De Dial.* and *De Mag.;* see Chapter 6.

2. For a major exploration of this theme and its philosophical implications, see Ricoeur (1983).

3. He is well aware of this when bk. 10 begins. His shift from theoretical to

practical concerns is a trick of "reminiscence," i.e., a recognition of something that he knew but had not spelled out for himself.

4. On the link with his statements on the monastic life, see Verheijen (1976), 1–4.

5. Courcelle (1963), 609–621; Bastiaensen (1985), 481–482.

6. Possidius, *Vita* 1–2, PL 32.34–36.

7. On the circumstances, see G. Bonner (1963), 104–105.

8. *Retr.* 1.7.1, CCSL 57.18.3–8.

9. Ibid., 1.8.1 (pp. 21.1–22.5).

10. Ibid., 1.9.1 (p. 23.6–11). For a résumé of scholarship on this work and pertinent reflections on the subsequent period, see Madec, *Saint Augustin et la philosophie* (1992), 48–59.

11. Perler and Maier (1969), 147.

12. Ibid., 149.

13. *Retr.* 1.10.1, CCSL 57.29.1–2; 1.11.1 (p. 33.1–2); 1.12.1 (p. 36.1).

14. *De Cura pro Mor. Ger.* 11.13, CSEL 41.641–643 (from 421).

15. *De Ciu. Dei* 22.8, CCSL 48.816.49.

16. On Augustine's institutional interests in this period, see Monceaux (1931), 68–72, supplemented by Lawless (1987).

17. Bezançon (1965), 155–158, with connections to the notion of free will.

18. Augustine's attitude toward memory and self-improvement differs profoundly from that of Plotinus, whom he implicitly criticizes; cf. *Enn.* 1.5.1–2 and 1.5.8–9, vol. 1, 87 and 90. Augustine's ideas sometimes echo those of Plotinus, e.g., on the aesthetics of reminiscence, *Enn.* 1.6.2, vol. 1, 94.7–11.

19. *Conf.* 11.2.6; Ps. 1:2. In this chapter, I again quote the *Conf.* by book, chapter, and line of CCSL 27.

20. These are reviewed by Luongo (1976), 286–294, 296–299.

21. Nor is there a need for the thesis that bk. 10 was written and added to the *Conf.* after the other books were completed; see Courcelle (1950), 25–26 and 25 n. 2, following Williger (1929), 103–106. The fact that bk. 10 may have been circulated separately and that it possesses an autonomous logic is not convincing proof that it does not play an important role, together with *Conf.* 9 and 11, in bridging the narrative and nonnarrative segments. On Williger's thesis, see Pincherle (1955–57), 196–197; cf. Knauer (1955), 154–155, and, for a summary of the controversy, O'Donnell (1992), vol. 3, 153, who notes that "the main difficulty" with the "notion" of separate composition is "the absolute lack of attestation or parallel."

22. This technique has given rise to puzzlement; yet Augustine's aims are reasonably clear. The early and late pictures of himself do not refer respectively to a fiction within the narrative and to a reality outside it. By the manner in which the events are arranged, he makes it appear that as a young man he was living a fiction when he should have known better, whereas in maturity, the reality and its mental representation have come closer together. Within the *Conf.,* both versions of himself have to be recognized as literary configurations. While we are

reading about the spiritual development of an actual person—Augustine of Hippo—the "actuality" is not discoverable from any single characterization of himself in the work.

23. I.e., its continuity inevitably depends upon subjective considerations, and these are separable from the account itself. And, whereas the account may be continuous, this subjectivity makes it impossible for us to prove that it is.

24. See O'Donnell (1992), vol. 3, 151–152, with interesting parallels between the ascents of bks. 9 and 10; cf. Mayer, "Signifikationshermeneutik" (1974), 24–26, 45–51.

25. Cf. Cayré (1931), 19–21; cf. Courcelle (1950), 17, and Oroz Reta (1985) for relations to Augustine's other prayers; a brilliant analysis is Magass (1984), 35–40, 43–45. For an emended text, see O'Donnell (1979), 282–287, and, for commentary, Brabant (1969), 258–277 (based on a comparison with *En. in Ps.* 55), and Mayer, "Signifikationshermeneutik" (1974), 27–30.

26. *Conf.* 10.1.1–2: "Cognoscam te, cognitor meus, cognoscam, sicut et cognitus sum."

27. Ibid., 10.1.7–8: "Volo eam facere in corde meo coram te in confessione, in stilo autem meo coram multis testibus."

28. I.e., described in *De Dial.* 5 as *dicibile* and *dictio*.

29. *Conf.* 10.2.13–14: "Confessio itaque mea, deus meus, in conspectu tuo tibi tacite fit et non tacite. Tacet enim strepitu, clamat affectu."

30. Ibid., 10.3.16–18: "confessiones . . . cum leguntur et audiuntur."

31. Ibid., 9.12.74–75: "Et nunc, domine, confiteor tibi in litteris. Legat qui uolet et interpretetur, ut volet."

32. See Chastaing (1962), 98: "Tes confessions . . . présupposent ma confiance."

33. *Conf.* 10.24–28, see the excellent discussion in Bochet (1993), 30–33.

34. *Conf.* 10.4.1: "Sed quo fructu id uolunt?"

35. Ibid., 10.4.3–4. Cf. 10.4.12; 10.4.34–35; all referring back to 10.3.15–19, where the larger audience is defined.

36. Ibid., 10.3.24–28, quoted above, note 33.

37. Ibid., 10.6.40–42. Is 10.6.20–42 intended as a parallel to the temptations of the senses and the allegory of Continence at 8.11? Augustine will turn to the second theme shortly.

38. Ibid., 10.7.3–4: "Transibo uim meam, qua haereo corpori et uitaliter compagem eius repleo." Cf. 10.7.11.

39. Augustine's account of memory has been the subject of numerous studies. For overviews with useful bibliographies, see Solignac, *BA* 14 (1962), 557–567, which is more accurate than O'Donnell (1992), vol. 3, 174–178; a useful supplement is Solignac, *Le Confessioni X–XIII* (1987), 9–34, and, for bibliography, 10–11 n. 1. Important among early studies are Kälin (1921), 23–33, and Söhngen (1930), the latter using Heinrich Wölfflin's notions to contrast Augustine with Aristotle, Plato, and Aquinas. On the place of memory in the hermeneutic plan of the early dialogues and bks. 11–13, see especially Mayer, "Signifikationshermeneutik"

(1974), 31–42; cf. Teske (1984), 224–229, linking *Ep.* 7 with *De Trin.* 12 and 14. An excellent analysis of the empirical aspects of memory is O'Daly (1987), 131–151; cf. Coleman (1992), 90–100, within a review of ancient conceptions.

40. The critique of memory, rather than Augustine's *cogito,* first examines the limits of self-knowledge in detail. In this respect, both the first phase of the discussion of memory and *De Trin.* 10.3 (*CCSL* 50a.295–296) explore the problem of self-knowledge that is illustrated, *inter alia,* in Plotinus, *Enn.* 5.3.1, vol. 2, 206–207.

41. Not replicated here is the logic by which Augustine earlier distinguishes between types of mental images in memory. At *De Mus.* 6.11.32, *PL* 32.1180–81, he draws a boundary between *phantasia* and *phantasma.* Acknowledging the difficulty of tracing the origin of such images, he nonetheless separates *imagines,* which are *phantasiae,* from *imagines imaginum,* which are *phantasmata.* Another type of distinction is made in *Ep.* 7, where, rejecting the doctrine of reminiscence, he notes the importance of the passage of time in distinguishing successive sets of images in the memory. He subsequently divides *phantasiae* into three classes; ibid., 7.4, *CSEL* 34/1.15.6–9. In the first class are simple memory-images, such as "the mental image of a face or of Carthage," and in the last are mental records "of numbers and dimensions" which occur in nature, in mathematics, geometry, and music. In the second are literary images occurring when we read, compose, or concoct a story, whether it is based on truth or on fiction; ibid. (p. 15.13–17). However, *Conf.* 10–11 concludes this youthful discussion by proposing a way in which images in the memory, while recognized to be mental creations, can nonetheless aid one's self-image in the real world—possibly a reaction to the different view of Plotinus on memory images, e.g., *Enn.* 3.6.15, vol. 1, 329–331.

42. Cf. *Conf.* 10.8.18–42; the material is schematized by Söhngen (1930), 383–388. Augustine, of course, rejects his initial view.

43. On the origin of the notion in Plotinus and Porphyry, see Pépin (1964), 58–62; on the rhetorical background, Doucet (1987), 50–55, with an interesting theory of bk. 10's role in the *Confessions'* circuits of memory.

44. *De Lib. Arb.* 2.19.51, *CCSL* 29.271.30–35.

45. Possibly echoing Plotinus' rejection of a place for the soul, e.g., *Enn.* 4.2.1, vol. 2, 3.15–17 (bearing in mind the latter's view that the soul is indivisible in the intelligible world but divisible in the body; *Enn.* 4.1, p. 8.8–13). Cf. *Enn.* 4.6.1, vol. 2, 130.1–5 (rejecting Aristotle, *De Memoria et Reminiscentia* 1.450a.30–32); 5.5.8 (p. 249.16–24).

46. *Conf.* 10.8.9–10. Cf. 10.8.34–35, where colours and sounds are recalled simultaneously, but presumably from different places in the mind.

47. These include, to ibid., 10.18, *thesaurus* (10.8.3, 38, 56); *receptaculum* (10.8.10); *abditum* (10.8.14); *recessus* (10.8.25); *secretum* (10.8.26); *sinus* (10.8.26, 52); *aula* (10.8.43); *copia* (10.8.48); *penetrale* (10.8.59; 10.11.11); *fundum* (10.8.59); *spatium* (10.8.70); *cella* (10.9.15); *cauum* (10.10.21); *uenter* (10.14.20, 21, 31); *antrum* (10.17.5); *cauerna* (10.17.5). On *praetoria memoriae,* see Hübner (1981), 247–255.

48. Ibid., 10.8.3–4: "ubi sunt thesauri innumerabilium imaginum de cuiuscemodi rebus sensis inuectarum."

49. Ibid., 10.8.4–6. Memory thereby acquires an interpretive function—an idea that has many contemporary parallels.

50. He elsewhere adds that memory, in dealing with these images in an incorporeal form, provides evidence for the incorporeal power of the soul; *C. Ep. Fund.* 17, *CSEL* 25/1.214.16–25 (from 396).

51. *Conf.* 10.8.27–29: "Nec ipsa tamen intrant, sed rerum imagines illic praesto sunt cogitationi reminiscenti eas."

52. These are presumably colours and melodies with which we are already familiar, since, in Augustine's view, we remember only what we know.

53. Does it follow that *Conf.* 10.6.6–40 is a mental image of God's creation rather than the reality? If memory is the source of information, that would appear to be the case.

54. As he suggests at ibid., 10.9.14–16.

55. I add the caveat because Augustine states that although we cannot recall such methods, it is clear that we once learned them; ibid., 10.10.15–17.

56. Ibid., 10.9.2–4: "Hic sunt et illa omnia, quae de doctrinis liberalibus percepta nondum exciderunt . . . nec eorum imagines, sed res ipsas gero."

57. Ibid., 10.12.1–3: "Item continet memoria numerorum dimensionumque rationes et leges innumerabiles, quarum nullam corporis sensus impressit."

58. Ibid., 10.14.1–3. On the implications of this theme, see Maxsein (1966), 177–215.

59. An idea subtly anticipated by Plotinus in his philosophical interpretation of *Odyssey* 11.601 ff.; *Enn.* 4.3.27, vol. 2, 48.13–14.

60. Cf. Plotinus, *Enn.* 4.4.17, vol. 2, 71.11–17.

61. As he did in *Conf.* 8.11, just before conversion.

62. Augustine argues that *cogo* (I compel) and *cogito* (I think) have the same relation to each other as *ago* (I put into motion) and *agito* (I impel), and *facio* (I do) and *factito* (I practice); ibid., 10.11.14–15.

63. Thereby returning to the initial paradox and suggesting that the discussion is an intellectual exercise.

64. Despite his criticism of digestive metaphors for depicting memory, Augustine is fond of employing the biblical language of "rumination" (e.g., Lev. 11:3, Deut. 14:6); e.g., *En. in Ps.* 46.1, *CCSL* 38.529; *De Trin.* 11.7, *CCSL* 50.348.40–42.

65. Yet again, he clings to the metaphor; *De Trin.* 12.14, *CCSL* 50.377.76: "quasi glutiens in ventre."

66. An idea foreshadowed in Plotinus, though in the context of his defence of the idea that neither God nor the soul has humanly definable memories; *Enn.* 4.3.26, vol. 2, 46.29–47.54.

67. *Conf.* 10.15.16–18. On forgetting, see 10.16.1–4; cf. 10.19.

68. Though not insolubly so; it is another example of verbal sophistry designed

to preface a nonlogical approach to faith. Augustine has already distinguished between two types of reality, that of the world and that of memory, in pointing out that he is able to recall false arguments as well as the fact that they are false (10.13.2–4). An application of this distinction would simplify the problem of remembering memory and forgetfulness.

69. On the measurement of time as a development of this argument, see this chapter, "Time."

70. *Conf.* 10.16.21: "Ego sum, qui memini, ego animus."

71. Ibid., 10.16.23–24: "Et ecce memoriae meae uis non comprehenditur a me, cum ipsum me non dicam praeter illam."

72. Good examples of analytic schemes include Gilson (1960), 11–111, and G. Matthews (1972); the finest study is O'Daly (1987), 87–88, 131–151; on the presentness of memory in the *Conf.,* see Fredouille (1993), 171–175.

73. For diagrammatic representations of these relations, see O'Daly (1987), 144.

74. Ibid., 87.

75. *Conf.* 10.9.4–14; 10.10.4–16. He omits seeing from the first list—an oversight.

76. The divergence between the two is greatest in the case of God, in relation to whom the knowledge within is of the highest certainty, but we are entirely dependent for what we know on an external discourse, i.e., scripture.

77. See Prime (1942), 52–53, with a useful note on the relationship between remembering and illumination as "intellectual apprehension."

78. Cf. *Conf.* 2.10.8; 3.4.10; 4.16.44; and, most relevantly, during the conversion of Victorinus, 8.3.10.

79. On the related theme of the prodigal son (Luke 15:11–18), see Knauer (1957); Ferrari, "Prodigal Son" (1979); and O'Donnell (1992), vol. 2, 95–98.

80. Is Augustine also echoing Plotinus, *Enn.* 3.6.2, vol. 1, 309.42–44, where memory is described as the soul's recognition of what it does not have? Cf. *Enn.* 4.3.25, vol. 2, 43–45.

81. The second message becomes more apparent in the course of bk. 10. In his meditative exploration of biblical writings, Augustine is as concerned with forgetting the desires of the senses as he is with recalling the desires of the spirit.

82. Cf. *Sermo* 331.1.1, *PL* 38.1459: "Quod tenes, perit a te; si perdis, inuenis in te."

83. A point underlined by the grammarian Diomedes, *Artis Grammaticae* 1, ed. H. Keil, *Gramm. Lat.* (1857; reprint, Hildesheim, 1961), 419.23–25: "Memoria est uelox animi et firma perceptio, cuius facultatem fouet exercitatio lectionis enarrationisque intentio, stili cura, redditio sollicita et diligens et iteratio atque repetitio frequens."

84. *Conf.* 10.20.5–9; an alternative means of arriving at this solution appears in *De Trin.* 12–14.

85. Holte (1962), 218, with a useful review of previous scholarly approaches to the issues, 207–214. Cf. *De Beata Vita* 4.31, *CCSL* 29.82.195–198.

86. Holte (1962), 294.

87. E.g., *De Gen. ad Litt. Imper.* 16.59, *PL* 34.242–243.

88. *De Diu. Quaes.*, q. 40, *CCSL* 44a.62.3–6.

89. *De Lib. Arb.* 3.18.52, *CCSL* 29.305.41–45.

90. Cf. *De Trin.* 8.6, *CCSL* 50.281.68–77.

91. Augustine recognizes the authenticity of his emotions, while granting the possible inauthenticity of their source; cf. *Conf.* 3.2.

92. A point made more clearly at *De Trin.* 12.15.24, *CCSL* 50.377.1–378.17.

93. Cf. *De Gen. ad Litt.* 7.22.33, *CSEL* 28.367, where, in parallel with this view, Augustine rejects the container hypothesis to explain the origin of the soul at Gen. 1:26.

94. Söhngen's characterization of Augustine's concept of memory as "open," (1930), 367–369, is therefore inadequate.

95. *Conf.* 10.25.1–15; cf. *De Diu. Quaes.*, q. 20, *CCSL* 44a.25.1–3: "Deus non alicubi est. Quod enim alicubi est continetur loco; quod continetur loco corpus est; deus autem non est corpus. Non igitur alicubi est."

96. *Conf.* 10.25.15–16: "Et quid quaero, quo loco eius habites, quasi uero loca ibi sint?"

97. Ibid., 10.26.1–4: "Vbi ergo te inueni, ut discerem te? Neque enim iam eras in memoria mea, priusquam te discerem. Vbi ergo te inueni, ut discerem te, nisi in te supra me? Et nusquam locus, et recedimus et accedimus, et nusquam locus." Cf. *De Praes. Dei* (*Ep.* 187) 6.18, *CSEL* 57.96.5–8, where, discussing the phrase *in se ipso* as it pertains to God, Augustine summarizes his views on the deity's "uncontainedness" as they appear in *Conf.* 10–11.

98. See du Roy (1966), 469–470.

99. *C. Acad.* 1.2.5, *CCSL* 29.5–6.

100. Cf. Schöpf (1967), 86–87, 91, and, on the force of *quaerere* in bk. 11, see this chapter, "Time."

101. Augustine notes that the hermit's life tempted him, but that God forbade him to take it up (10.43.28–31). Yet he found his desert solitude—in the Bible.

102. See Gilson (1960), 99–104, extending the issues to metaphysics.

103. *De Gen. ad Litt.* 11.30, *CSEL* 28.363.4–5, on the sin of Eve.

104. Cf. *Sermo* 5.1, *CCSL* 41.50.17–21, written sometime between 410 and 419, where Augustine sums up his thoughts concerning reading, repetition from memory, and the purgations of sins: "Istae lectiones quae uobis leguntur, numquid modo primum uobis leguntur, et non eadem cotidie repetuntur? Sicut autem lectiones dei cotidie opus est ut repetantur, ne saeculi mala et spinae nascantur in cordibus uestris et offocent semen quod ibi seminatum est [cf. Matt. 13:7; Luke 8:14]." Cf. *De Ciu. Dei* 10.6, *CCSL* 47.278.11–15.

105. Cf. *De Diu. Quaes.*, q. 73.1, *CCSL* 44a.3–6, where the distinction between habits of mind and body is clarified; on the relation of habit to the incarnation, 73.2 (p. 212).

106. The relationships were neatly summed up in a sermon delivered in 410 on

Gal. 6.1:10. Having read the text aloud to his audience, Augustine then commented as follows; *Miscellanea agostiniana,* vol. 1 (1930), *Sermo* 5.2, p. 213.8–12 (*PL* 46.984): "Huc usque recitatum est de epistola apostoli: huc usque uobis tanquam lector fui. Sed, fratres mei, si intellectus est lector, cui rei necessarius est disputator? Ecce audiuimus, intelleximus: faciamus, et uiuamus. Et quid opus est uestram onerare memoriam? tenete ista, et inde cogitate." Memorization, of course, is also advocated for basic dogma, e.g., *De F. et Sym.* 1.1.1, *CSEL* 41.3.13–15; *De Fide et Operibus* 11.17, *CSEL* 41.54.25–55.1.

107. E.g., *De Mor. Eccles. Cath.* 1.28.56, *PL* 32.1333.

108. Reason thus governs emotion (a Hellenistic commonplace); but he adds the Weberian twist of making this a practically oriented, instrumental rationality.

109. *Conf.* 10.11.3–5 and 10.29.5–6. There may also be an oblique reference to alleged Manichaean claims of continence; *De Mor. Eccles. Cath.* 1.2, *PL* 32.1311.

110. *Conf.* 10.29.3–5; Wisdom 8:21. Cf. *Conf.* 6.11.54–56.

111. E.g., *De Mor. Eccles. Cath.* 1.5.8, *PL* 32.1314, where the importance of discipline in the soul is stressed. The idea was not original with Augustine; Plotinus, his chief source on purification, describes the link between self-control and the pursuit of wisdom as "old thinking" by the time he wrote; *Enn.* 1.6.6, vol. 1, 99.1–3.

112. *Conf.* 6.6.30–34, quoting Ps. 22:4 and 41:11. Cf. 3.11.10–12, where Monica's dream foretells just such a disciplinary rule.

113. "Concupiscentia oculorum," 10.30.2.

114. *De Con.* 1.1, *CSEL* 41.141.3–4.

115. Ibid., 1.2 (p. 142.13–18): "Multa enim corporis ore non dicimus et corde clamamus; nullum autem procedit rei alicuius ex ore corporis uerbum, cuius est in corde silentium. Inde igitur quod non emanat, foris non sonat; quod uero emanat inde, si malum est, etsi non moueat linguam, inquinat animam. Ibi ergo ponenda est continentia, ubi et tacentium loquitur conscientia." Silence thereby acquires a moral dimension.

116. Ibid., 2.3 (p. 142.25): "Declinatio cordis quid est, nisi consensio?" This becomes a cornerstone of Peter Abelard's ethics, which is a bridge between Augustine and modern ethical intentionality.

117. Ibid. (pp. 142.27–143.8): "Si autem consensit, iam corde dixit, etiamsi ore non sonuit . . . Neque enim mendaciter scriptum est: initium omnis operis uerbum."

118. Ibid., 2.4 (p. 145.14–15): "solus inquinat in cogitatione consensus, id est, interioris uerbum malignum."

119. *Conf.* 10.30.9–11. On the linguistic explanation of such images, see *De Gen. ad Litt.* 12.8, *PL* 34.460–461.

120. *Conf.* 10.30.12–14: "Et tamen tantum interest inter me ipsum et me ipsum intra momentum, quo hinc ad soporem transeo uel huc inde retranseo." Augustine's reasoning here is similar to that of Alypius and himself in 6.7–9.

121. Ibid., 10.31.30; 10.31.40; 10.31.53–54.

122. Ibid., 10.31.83–85: "[Deus] . . . numerans me inter infirma membra corporis sui, quia et 'imperfectum eius uiderunt oculi tui, et in libro tuo omnes scribentur [Ps. 138:16].'"

123. On ibid., 10.33, see Chapter 4, "From Cassiciacum to Ostia."

124. He also distinguishes between secular and religious visual temptations; *Conf.* 10.34.35–41.

125. Ibid., 10.35.7–20; 1 John 2:16; Cf. Peters (1986).

126. *Conf.* 10.35.24–25: "experiendi noscendique libidine."

127. On the implications for Augustine as bishop, see the thoughtful remarks of O'Donnell (1992), vol. 3, 229–231.

128. *Conf.* 10.37.2–3: "Cotidiana fornax nostra est humana lingua."

129. Ibid., 10.40.18–21: "Neque in his omnibus, quae percurro consulens te, inuenio tutum locum animae meae nisi in te, quo conligantur sparsa mea nec a te quidquam recedat ex me."

130. Ibid., 10.40.26–27: "Hic esse ualeo nec uolo, illic uolo nec ualeo, miser utrubique."

131. See Chaix-Ruy (1956), 21–23, 27–34; Kaiser (1969), 13–48. The logic is implicit in the difference between the self in the autobiography, which is a being in time, and the self known to God, which is not.

132. For a speculative diagram on how this comes about, see Herzog (1984), 240.

133. The topic of creation is subsequently treated philosophically (*Conf.* 12) and theologically (bk. 13). Cf. Solignac, *BA* 14 (1962), 572–591; Mayer, *Die anti-manichäische Epoche* (1974), 156–171; Meijering (1979), a detailed examination; and Flasch (1980), 263–286.

134. *Conf.* 11.1.2–3: "Cur ergo tibi tot rerum narrationes digero?" This human story is in implicit contrast to the abstract narrative of Plotinus, e.g., *Enn.,* 3.7.11, vol. 1., 354–356, which is nonetheless paralleled in the story of the birth of the arts in the "philosophical dialogues."

135. Cf. *In Io. Eu. Tract.* 29.4, CCSL 36.285.1–3: "Verbum ergo et Deus est, et doctrinae stabilis Verbum est, non sonabilis per syllabas et uolatilis, sed manentis cum Patre."

136. Cf. Gilson (1962), 205–212, on the notion of "being" implied in the language with which God is described in the Bible (e.g., Exod. 3:14: "Qui sum," "Qui est").

137. *Conf.* 11.2.4–5. The metaphor is probably taken from the action of the water-clock; Chadwick, *Saint Augustine* (1991), 221 n. 3.

138. *Conf.* 11.2.12, 15, 17–18; cf. 11.2.20–25. A taunt of Manichaeism in its Hebraic associations?

139. Ibid., 11.2.19: "Sint castae deliciae meae scripturae tuae."

140. Ibid., 11.2.25–29. Cf. Ps. 28:9 and the restatement at 11.2.26, 46–47.

141. *Conf.* 11.2.33–34: "Confitear tibi quidquid inuenero in libris tuis."

142. This section of *Conf.* is much commented upon; in the following discussion I omit superfluous examples and emphasize relations of reading.

143. See Gilson (1947), 25–31.

144. For a comparison of Aristotle's and Augustine's views, see Callahan (1968), 38–87, 149–187; and Sorabji (1983), 17–32, but cf. 253–267. An outstanding review of the issues is found in Weis (1984), 109–147. Heidegger (1982), 232–274, criticizes Aristotle from a viewpoint acceptable to Augustine, if the literary phenomenology of bk. 11 is taken into account; the definition of *Dasein* as "temporality . . . stretched out within itself" (270) is a rough translation of Augustine's *distentio* (*Conf.* 11.26.19–21); cf. Weis (1984), 69, on the same debt in *Sein und Zeit* (1927); neither was acknowledged. For a further discussion of phenomenological issues, see Lampey (1959), 2–7, 119–131, 190–203, and the concise discussion of E. Schmidt (1985), 11–17, 41–63.

145. See Guitton (1971) 45–65, 174–329; more briefly, Solignac, *BA* 14 (1962), 581–584. On Plotinus' views, synthetic statements are found in Callahan (1968), 88–148, and Beierwaltes (1981); on infinity in Plotinus and Augustine, see Armstrong (1954–55) and, on Augustine's use of specific ideas, the valuable notes in Chadwick, *Saint Augustine* (1991), 221–245.

146. On the Stoic sources, see O'Daly (1987), 152–161 (superseding 1981), with bibliography, 153 n. 8. A brief overview is Verbeke (1958). On the Stoic view of time, see Rist, *Stoic Philosophy* (1969), 273–288; Goldschmidt (1977), 30–73; and Sorabji (1983), 21–27, 309–311.

147. A failure to appreciate the combination of literary and philosophical elements in Augustine's account of time may be responsible for the dissatisfaction expressed by some contemporary philosophers, e.g., Heidegger (1982), 231–232, and Wittgenstein (1953), 42. On Wittgenstein's views, see Suter (1962); Mundle (1966); Flasch (1980), 284–286; and McEvoy (1984).

148. On the anti-Manichaean elements in Augustine's exegesis, see Mayer, *Die antimanichäische Epoche* (1974), 157–159; on the development of ideas, see Gilson (1960), 189–190.

149. The Bible refers to God as "speaking the truth" (e.g., John 14:6); nonetheless, Moses' voice is not "truth." On Moses and the implied reader, see the suggestive remarks of de Margerie (1983), 61–87.

150. *De Gen ad Litt.* 6.12, CSEL 28.185.11–14. Augustine nonetheless retained the artisan metaphor to describe the manner in which the world's design, contained in God's wisdom, is fulfilled in space and time; e.g., *In Io. Evang., Tract.*, 1.17, CCSL 36.10.1–13. He may have in mind Plotinus' criticism of artisan analogies; *Enn.* 4.3.23, vol. 2, 40–42, although he does not echo the latter's cognitive explanation; see *Enn.* 5.5.9, vol. 2, 249.1–4, and the continuing discussion, 5.8.1 (pp. 268–269).

151. *Conf.* 11.5.8–13. Cf. *De Octo Quaes.* 2, *Miscellanea Agostiniana*, vol. 2 (1931), 333; cf. *De Lib. Arb.* 2.16.42, CCSL 29.265–266.

152. *Conf.* 11.8.5–6. Augustine expressed a similar idea on many occasions; of particular interest is *De F. et Sym.* 3.4, *CSEL* 41.7.10–16, which not only distinguishes between God's word and our words but also separates the "mental" and "bodily" aspects of our speech, the one producing inner, the other outer narrative.

153. *De Trin.* 15.11.20–21, *CCSL* 50a.487–490.

154. *Conf.* 11.8.6–9, summarizing *De Mag.*, but in a more readerly context. Cf. Matt. 3:17, discussed at 11.6.1–6, where Augustine speaks of Matthew's inner ear, already tuned to God's word when he hears the verbal statement "This is my beloved."

155. *Conf.* 11.10.1–2; cf. 11.12.1–2; 11.13.1–5. For discussion, including the background in Greek and patristic thought, see Peters (1984).

156. True, God's will is part of his "essence" or "substance," but if something takes place in that enduring entity, we cannot say that it is changeless.

157. For a commentary, see Weis (1984), 17–147; a recent alternative is Meijering (1979). Important articles include Christian (1953), R. Jordan (1954–55/1972), Quinn (1969), Boros (1958), Gilson (1962), Casares (1966), and Duchrow (1966); for further bibliography, see Solignac, *BA* 13 (1962), 260–261, and, for a commentary, 14 (1962), n. 18, pp. 581–591.

158. *Conf.* 11.14.8–9: "Quid est ergo tempus? Si nemo ex me quaerat, scio; si quaerenti explicare uelim, nescio." Gilson (1947), 30–32, notes the parallel with Augustine's notions of being and God, with many reflections of perennial value.

159. Cf. *De Mag.* 1.20–21, *CCSL* 29.57.

160. On the soliloquy technique, see Chapter 5, "The Letters."

161. *Conf.* 11.14.4–7: "Quid est enim tempus? Quis hoc facile breuiterque explicauerit? Quis hoc ad uerbum de illo proferendum uel cogitatione comprehenderit? Quid autem familiarius et notius in loquendo commemoramus quam tempus? Et intellegimus utique, cum id loquimur, intellegimus etiam, cum alio loquente id audimus."

162. Heidegger's "ontological priority of the *Dasein*" (1982), 223, may be a secular restatement of this idea, in which the being that Augustine associates with God is imported to the mind.

163. *Conf.* 11.11.1–16. Anticipating Bergson? See Moschetti (1956) and Chaix-Ruy (1930), 81–83, 92–93. For a parallel, see *En. in Psalmus* 2.6, *CCSL* 38.5.4–7; *Psalmus* 101, s. 2.10–11, *CCSL* 40.1444–46.

164. *Conf.* 11.15.3–48; on the Stoic roots of the notion, see O'Daly (1987), 154–155.

165. *Conf.* 11.15.48–52. This infinite regression of intervals of time measured in the present bears some resemblance to fractal geometry.

166. Ibid., 11.16.1–5; cf. *En. in Ps.* 38.7, *CCSL* 38.408–409.

167. See R. Jordan (1954–55/1972), 259.

168. *Narrare: Conf.* 11.17.9; 11.18.7.

169. Ibid., 1.18.13–15, 24–28; cf. Augustine's subtle use of *praedicere,* 11.18.15,

22; *praesentire;* 11.18.16, 18, 19; and *praemeditari,* 11.18.16, 17; also 11.18.12, where he deliberately combines *recolo et narro.*

170. On this term, see O'Donnell (1992), vol. 3, 284–285.

171. This view does not deny the existence of the past and the future; *Conf.* 11.21.1; 11.16.5–6; 11.21.5.

172. See Weis (1984), 11–13, who makes the distinction from a phenomenological standpoint; also Lampey (1959), 119–148, 190–203. For a comparison of Plotinus and Augustine, see Sorabji (1983), 29–32, 157–173.

173. Russell (1951), 228. This is not to argue that Augustine's understanding of time is beyond criticism; see Suter (1962) and Mundle (1966), both based on Wittgenstein.

174. E.g., *De Gen. ad Litt.* 2.14, *CSEL* 28.55.2–22; on the notion of natural law, ibid., 9.17 (p. 291.9–10). By contrast, on the personal experience of time, see *Ep.* 14.2, *CSEL* 34/1.33.3–4; *Ep.* 138.2, *CSEL* 44.127–128.

175. Cf. Duchrow (1966); and the discussion of his views in E. Schmidt (1985), 15–32; Madec, *Saint Augustin et la philosophie* (1992), 77.

176. Although he rejects as naive determinism astrology (*Conf.* 7.6.1–7) and "those whom the Greeks call *physici*" concerning the elements, the heavenly bodies, and natural philosophy; *Enchiridion de Fide et Spe et Caritate* 3.9, *CCSL* 46.52–53.1–10. He likewise distinguishes between practical observations of the heavens, useful for agriculture or navigation, and attempts to predict the future; *Ep.* 55.9.16, *CSEL* 34/1.186–187. However, this type of codified knowledge does not have the instructive power of history; *De Doct. Christ.* 28.44, *CCSL* 32.63.

177. *De Ord.* 2.29.50, *CCSL* 29.134.24–31.

178. Against this view, see O'Daly (1981), 171–175; however, the argument in favour of Augustine's knowledge of Aristotle's *De Memoria et Reminiscentia* is weak. For Plotinus' criticism of the notion of time as movement, the direct source of Augustine's thinking, see *Enn.* 3.7.8–12, vol. 1, 347–359; both Plotinus and Augustine emphasize the definition of eternity and its links with presentness, not time alone. On Augustine's possible debt to Cicero here, see Winkler (1954), 517–519.

179. A modern way of stating the issues would be through the limitations of algorithms and Gödel's theorem; see Penrose (1990), 40–92, 138–141.

180. Cf. R. Jordan (1954–55/1972), 262.

181. O'Daly (1987), 159, notes that "we have no specific Stoic text to compare with these views." It is tempting to link the notion to the special and general theories of relativity, but these are about "objective" time in Galilean and Newtonian mechanics; see, *inter alia,* Einstein (1961); on astronomy, the case that Augustine rejects, 49–50. Augustine's views more closely resemble the mathematics of deterministic chaos, inasmuch as his system is predestined but unpredictable as a result of the subject's ignorance of initial conditions. This is also the case in infancy; *Conf.* 1.6.

182. In order to understand time, he pictures his self as something timeless—as an eternal witness to temporal events; but he knows that our self-understanding is "relational."

183. See Lacey (1972), 280–281, whose argument is weakened by undervaluation of the linguistic dimension. For criticism of Augustine's views, see O'Daly (1987), 155–156.

184. See Plotinus, *Enn.* 3.7.8, vol. 1, 347.8–348.8. Chadwick, *Saint Augustine* (1991), 237 n. 25, notes similar views in Basil and the Latin translation of Plato's *Timaeus;* cf. *Ep.* 102.4 (23), *CSEL* 34/2.564.8–12.

185. See Plotinus, *Enn.* 3.7.9, vol. 1, 351.25, asking "what" the measurer will be.

186. The "relational" aspects of the problem of measurement are better explained in Plotinus than in Augustine; see *Enn.* 6.1.7, vol. 3, 10–11. However, they were clearly understood by Augustine, who uses them as his point of departure for the discussion of self-understanding through mental images in *De Trin.* 8–9, *CCSL* 50.

187. For the analogy of speech *(logos)* and time *(chronos),* see Plotinus, *Enn.* 6.1.5, vol. 3, 7–8.

188. His subsequent experiment recognizes that a short line that is recited slowly can take more time than a long line recited in a hurry.

189. *Conf.* 11.26.16–21; cf. R. Jordan (1954–55/1972), 260; Chadwick, *Saint Augustine* (1991), 240 n. 27.

190. The precedent is *De Ord.* 2.12, discussed in the Introduction.

191. Ambrose, *Hymni* 1.2.1–8; on its occurrence in Augustine's writings, see O'Donnell (1992), vol. 3, 142–143. The obvious precedent is the mourning period after Monica's death; *Conf.* 9.12.59 ff. The idea of abstracting principles concerning time from classical metre may have occurred to Augustine because the understanding of quantity was on the wane; it was therefore necessary for readers of poetry to think about quantity independently of the effect that the sounds made on the ear. Yet no one but Augustine appears to have made the connection with the theory of time; see in general di Capua (1931), 607–612, and, for a succinct review of language and time with a bibliography, Alici (1981).

192. See *De Ord.* 2.12, *CCSL* 29.127.24–31; and *De Mag.* 6, *CCSL* 29.175–177.1–52; cf. Quint. *Inst. Orat.* 1.4.6.

193. *Conf.* 11.27.29–31: "Hae singulae ad illas singulas duplum habent temporis; pronuntio et renuntio, et ita est, quantum sentitur sensu manifesto." On the role of sensation in the example, see Gilson (1960), 64–65.

194. As well as through the will, which is not specifically mentioned. For Augustine is not only hearing; he is also listening, in which case his view is that intentions are involved.

195. *Conf.* 11.27.43–45: "Non ergo ipsas, quae iam non sunt, sed aliquid in memoria mea metior, quod infixum manet."

196. Ibid., 11.27.46: "In te, anime meus, tempora metior." Cf. 11.27.2–3, 48–52;

cf. R. Jordan (1954–55/1972), 261; on the background, see Moreau (1955). For a similarly mentalist view, see *De Gen. ad Litt.* 8.20, *CSEL* 28/1.258–259.

197. *De Im. An.* 3.3–4, *CSEL* 89.103.13–105.22, brilliantly summarized by Madec, "Le spiritualisme augustinien" (1987), 187–188; cf. Pépin (1964), 89–90, and, for other relevant literature, Madec, "Le spiritualisme," 188 n. 28. It is this argument, rather than that of *De Mus.* alone, that is assumed in *Conf.* 11. Augustine defines *uirtus* as the ability to perform an action *(potest aliquid agere)* and *actio* as being moved or bringing about movement *(mouetur aut mouet)*. The *constantiae uirtus* is its ability to resist change *(inmutabilis)*. It follows that not everything that brings about movement is itself subject to change, i.e., to mortality—a point that is illustrated by the difference between body and soul. The body can be moved only in time, and it is moved in parts, just as time flows in intervals. Definitions of future and past follow and, in 3.4, the link with mind.

198. *De Mus.* 6.8.21, *PL* 32.1174–75; on the musical principles involved, see Perl (1954). Other analyses include O'Connell (1978), 65–90, stressing Plotinian influences, Forman (1988), 22–23, and, on the problem of sensation, the commentary of Pizzani and Milanese on *De Musica* (1990), 63–86.

199. *Conf.* 11.27.52–55: "Quid cum metimur silentia et dicimus illud silentium tantum tenuisse temporis, quantum illa uox tenuit, nonne cogitationem tendimus ad mensuram uocis, quasi sonaret, ut aliquid de interuallis silentiorum in spatio temporis renuntiare possimus?" Augustine's use of *tendere* is an expansion of its sense at *De Ord.* 2.11.34–12.37, *CCSL* 29.126–127.

200. *Conf.* 11.27.56–59: "Nam et uoce atque ore cessante peragimus cogitando carmina et uersus et quemque sermonem motionumque dimensiones quaslibet et de spatiis temporum, quantum illud ad illud sit, renuntiamus non aliter, ac si ea sonando diceremus."

201. The pleasure of the text occurs in both time modes.

202. *Conf.* 11.28.14–22; cf. *In Io. Eu. Tract.* 124.5, *CCSL* 36.686.111–113, where the same thinking appears in a theological context; cf. *De Trin.* 15.7.13, *CCSL* 50a.478.98–107.

203. In a footnote to this theory written in 388, Augustine distinguishes between the senses of smell and touch and those of hearing and sight. Only the latter have the potential to create the impression of the parts and the whole at once; *De Lib. Arb.* 2.14.38, *CCSL* 29.263.19–24. Yet hearing and sight likewise differ; ibid. (p. 263.24–28).

204. *Conf.* 11.28.23–27: "Et quod in toto cantico, hoc in singulis particulis eius fit atque in singulis syllabis eius, hoc in actione longiore, cuius forte particula est illud canticum, hoc in tota uita hominis, cuius partes sunt omnes actiones hominis, hoc in toto saeculo filiorum hominum, cuius partes sunt omnes uitae hominum."

205. There appears to be agreement among scholars that Augustine's term is not drawn from Plotinus, *Enn.* 3.7.11, vol. 1, 354–356, although other aspects of his discussion are clearly influenced by the latter's analysis of eternity and time; for a

discussion, see Solignac, *BA* 14 (1962), 588–590, Gilson (1960), 194; Teske (1983), 84–86; O'Daly (1987), 153–154 and 154 n. 11; Chadwick *Saint Augustine* (1991), 240 n. 27; and Madec, *Saint Augustin et la philosophie* (1992), 76–77. Within a full discussion of the term's philological background, O'Daly (1977) makes a case for Augustine's drawing on Philippians 3:12–14; however, see the evidence of Madec, ibid., 76, for dependence on Porphyry on the basis of *De Im. An.* 3.3, *CSEL* 89.103–106. A lucid analysis is provided by Weis (1984), 61–85, with diagrams, 70–71, 84. Cf. Liuzzi (1984), 42–51, and, for a recent review of issues, O'Donnell (1992), vol. 3, 289–290. A neglected Plotinian text relevant to the theme is *Enn.* 5.1.6, vol. 2, 193.8–11, where he speaks of invoking God, not in words, but by "stretching out our souls in prayer toward him alone," a notion that is expressed again in Augustine's metaphor of scripture as a "tent" in *Conf.* 13.15.

206. Augustine seems to imply here the same criticism of *distentio* that he offered for measurements of time, though in a fashion that can be turned against his own argument. For, the moment the mind experiences such a protraction of thought, it implicitly engages in a measurement of the duration of its own experience. Both the beginning and end of this measurement are arbitrary.

207. Cf. *Conf.* 11.29.2: "Distentio est uita mea," etc. The sentiment is well summed up at *De Vera Rel.* 35.65, *CCSL* 32.229.5–230.7; cf. *De Praes. Dei* (*Ep.* 187) 6.19, *CSEL* 57.98.6–10.

208. *Conf.* 3.7.17–18. For a discussion of the idea based mainly on *De Lib. Arb.,* see Fortin (1978), 187–191.

209. Cf. Cicero, *De Republica* 3.11.18–19; 22.33.

210. *Conf.* 3.7.41–42; cf. Virgil, *Aen.* 4.569.

211. *Conf.* 3.7.48–53; cf. *De Vera Rel.* 22.42, *CCSL* 32.213.7–9.

212. A number of structural schemes are clarified in bks. 11–13 which fall outside the scope of this study; on bk. 13, see Cayré (1956), and, on methods and themes, A. Holl (1963), 14–45 and 46–105 respectively.

213. Cf. Grotz (1970), 118–149, for an argument in favour of the *Confessions'* unity based on approaches to Genesis in bks. 12–13, and the brilliant review of the issues in Bochet (1973), 29–50.

214. *Conf.* 12.1.1–3: "Multa satagit cor meum, domine, in hac inopia uitae meae pulsatum uerbis sanctae scripturae tuae, et ideo plerumque in sermone copiosa est egestas humanae intellegentiae"; 12.12.2: "quantum me ad pulsandum excitas quantumque pulsanti aperis [Matt. 7:7–8; Luke. 11:9–10]." The same quotations open and close the *Conf.,* i.e., 1.1.13–14 and 13.38.13–14.

215. Ibid., 12.10.7–8: "Tu me alloquere, tu mihi sermocinare. Credidi libris tuis, et uerba eorum arcana ualde."

216. Ibid., 12.6.1–2: "Ego uero, domine, si totum confitear tibi ore meo et calamo meo." Cf. 10.4.20–24 and 12.3.9–10.

217. Cf. ibid., 12.6.15–32, and, for a discussion, de Margerie (1983), 64–72.

218. On his anticipations of this idea at *Conf.* 3.5. and 6.5, see Shanzer (1992), 46–50; the idea is confirmed in *De Doct Christ.* 2.7–9, *CCSL* 32.36–46.

219. A relationship that is spelled out in detail in *En. in Ps.;* for a study of this aspect of time, see Fontaine (1984), 373–378.

220. *Conf.* 12.12.16–18; cf. 1.6–8.

221. On which see Mayer, "Signifikationshermeneutik" 24 (1974), 56–73, and, for a brief résumé, Magass (1980). For a historical review of Augustine's commentaries on the opening verses of Genesis, see Solignac (1973); on problems of nature and grace, TeSelle (1968), 115–123. On the pastoral reasons for Augustine's shift to exegesis at the outset of his bishopric (e.g., *Conf.* 10.43.28–30), see Cayré (1956), 156–161.

222. *Conf.* 13.15.1–2. For fascinating reflections on the notions of "being" and "narrative" in bk. 13, see di Giovanni (1974), 295–310.

223. *Conf.* 13.15.2–3: "Caelum enim plicabitur ut liber [cf. Is. 34:2] et nunc sicut pellis extenditur super nos [cf. Ps. 103:2]." Cf. *En. in Ps.* 93.6, *CCSL* 39.1305.2–1306.37, for a fuller exposition; and *De Gen. ad Litt.* 2.9.22, *CSEL* 28/1.47.11.

224. *Conf.* 13.15.7–9: "Vnde sicut pellem extendisti firmamentum libri tui, concordes utique sermones tuos, quos per mortalium ministerium superposuisti nobis." This is the completion of the metaphor of distension/extension introduced in bk. 11.

225. In this interpretation, bk. 11 deals with God, i.e., eternity, as contrasted with the human understanding of time; bk. 12 deals with the trinity's second person, contrasting the word of God with human language; and bk. 13 represents the union with God by means of the holy spirit. For a reconstruction of Augustine's version of Gen. 1:1–2:2, see O'Donnell (1992), vol, 3, 344–345.

226. For a remarkable example of reading technique, see *Conf.* 13.19.1–22.

227. Ibid., 13.15.26–34; cf. Is. 34:4; Luke 4:20. Cf. *En. in Ps.* 8.7, *CCSL* 38.52.7–8; 93.6, *CCSL* 39.1305–07.

228. *Conf.* 13.11.4–5. For a discussion of this statement and its relation to later trinitarian writings, see Schindler (1965), 34–41.

229. *Conf.* 13.11.5–11; cf. Kusch (1953), 131–132, who traces the triad in earlier writings.

## 9. The Self

1. La Bonnardière (1965), 166, proposes "between 420 and 426" for the editing of bk. 15; cf. Schindler (1965), 7–10, and, for dates of various groups of books, 10. Cf. Zarb (1934), 48–49. Augustine's terse summing-up is found in Prologue 4–5. On the circumstances of prepublication without permission when he was midway through bk. 12, see ibid., 10–15 (= *Ep.* 174, *CSEL* 44.650); for a discussion, see Dekkers (1990), 237–238. Good introductions to the historical issues are found in Schmaus (1927), 1–76, and Schindler (1965), 1–11. Throughout this chapter, *De Trin.* is cited by book, chapter, and line from the edition of W. J. Mountain and Fr. Glorie, *CCSL* 50–50a.

2. A list of studies up to 1978 is found in *CCSL* 50.lxxxiii–xcvi; cf. *BA* 15 (1955), 77–83; 16 (1955), 663–666. On theological issues, an especially useful set of notes is provided by Agaësse and Moingt, *BA* 16 (1955), 571–661. On Augustine's rapports with Marius Victorinus, see P. Hadot (1962), 424–442.

3. See Marrou, *Saint Augustin* (1958), 315–327, for an explanation of the digressions as examples of *exercitatio animi*.

4. *Ep.* 169.1, *CSEL* 44.612.8–9.

5. Gen. 1:26–27; *De Trin.* 1.7.43, and the extensive discussion in 15.7–16. The history of the "image" and "likeness" problem is thoroughly treated by Ladner (1959), 185–203; cf. Kusch (1953), 137–139. The relevant Augustinian texts are listed by Schindler (1965), 61–62 n. 1.

6. On the sources of Augustine's "analogies," see Schindler (1965), 43–60.

7. *De Trin.* 8, prol. 28–30. The procedure in the later books is inward and upward; cf. 10.1.1–2.

8. Agaësse and Moingt, *BA* 16 (1955), 8–9. Cf. Crouse (1985).

9. *De Trin.* 15.28.12–23, 30–35; cf. *Conf.* 1.2, *CCSL* 27.1.4–16, 2.1–12; and, on this theme generally, the fundamental article of Duchrow, "Der Aufbau" (1965).

10. See Hill (1973), 277 and 281–282, for reflections on this theme.

11. *De Trin.* 8.4.26–31; see Camelot (1958).

12. Cf. O'Connell (1972), 47–48.

13. *Conf.* 2.3, *CCSL* 27.19–20.9–10.

14. In this respect, the later books of *De Trin.* complete the "metaphysics of speech" introduced in the dialogues; see Beierwaltes (1971), 181–192.

15. Chiefly in *De Trin.* 13.4–9; for an excellent synthetic treatment, see Cayré (1931).

16. *De Doct. Christ.* 1.5.5, *CCSL* 32.9.

17. E.g., *De Trin.* 15.1.1–2; 15.4; see Bochet (1993), 34–35.

18. *De Trin.* 1.1.37–41, 51–54; also 1.12.24–26 and 3.9.78–87, where the context is "understanding" what is on the altar during mass.

19. Ibid., 1.1.4–28; cf. 2, prooem. 9–11, where Augustine distinguishes two types of error: believing in falsehoods beforehand, and defending those presumed to be true.

20. Ibid., 1.2.1–18; 3.10.188–200. Cf. *Retr.* 1.1, *CCSL* 57.5.6: "uelut censorio stilo denotem." For a commentary, see de Ghellinck (1948), 360–361.

21. E.g., *De Trin.* 8.3.46–52; also bks. 12–15, discussed later in the chapter.

22. Ibid., 1.3.1–4: "Proinde quisquis haec legit ubi pariter certus est, pergat mecum; ubi pariter haesitat, quaerat mecum; ubi errorem suum cognoscit, redeat ad me; ubi meum, reuocet me."

23. Ibid., 3, prol. 42–43: "Noli meas litteras ex tua opinione uel contentione sed ex diuina lectione uel inconcussa ratione corrigere." Cf. 1.8.51–53; 3.1.25–26.

24. Ibid., 1.7.8–10: "Errauerunt homines minus diligenter scrutantes uel in-

tuentes uniuersam seriem scripturarum." This includes taking account of variant readings in manuscripts; 1.6.107–131.

25. Ibid., 1.3.38–41: "Ego tamen 'in lege domini meditabor,' si non 'die ac nocte' [Ps. 1:2], saltem quibus temporum particulis possum, et meditationes meas ne obliuione fugiant stilo alligo."

26. Ibid., 3, prol. 19–20: "Egoque ipse multa quae nesciebam scribendo me didicisse confitear"; cf. 1.5.36–38.

27. For an outline, see Schindler (1965), 86–104, and, for references in Augustine's writings, 250–251; also *De Doct. Christ.*, 2.5, *CCSL* 32.35. On the oral element in the inner word, see Duchrow (1965), 137–148, although this account is overly concerned with the metaphysics of light. For a general review of interpretations of Augustine's notions of *uerbum* between 386 and 397, see D. Johnson (1972), 25–33.

28. *De Trin.* 15.15.60–78. Cf. G. Matthews (1967), who is correct in essentials but limits himself to bk. 15.

29. Ibid., 15.14.32–39; cf. *In Io. Eu. Tract.* 1.8, *CCSL* 36.5.12–15, where Augustine explains that, just as my words remain within my mind when they are spoken, so God's Word remains eternally with him while it is sounded out. Cf. 14.7 (p. 145.22–24); 20.10 (p. 208.16–18); 20.4 (pp. 285–286). A similar idea is found in Plotinus, *Enn.* 1.2.4, vol. 1, 59.27–30, where the spoken word is described as an imitation of the word in the soul, and the word in the soul as an imitation of a word elsewhere. The spoken word appears to be divided when compared to the word in the soul, which it interprets, etc. For a more detailed exposition see *Enn.* 5.1.3, vol. 2, 189–190; cf. 5.3.10 (p. 221.28–40).

30. E.g., *De Trin.* 15.5.44–75; 15.6.1–12; 15.7.1–22; cf. 15.13.1–20.

31. Ibid., 15.10.36: "Quaedam . . . cogitationes locutiones sunt cordis."

32. In contrast to earlier patristic thinking; see Bavaud (1963), 95–97.

33. *Sermo* 119.7, *PL* 38.675: "Vestem dicas carnem Christi, uehiculum dicas." Cf. *Sermo* 288.4, *PL* 38.1306: "Verbum manens uoces misit, et post multas praemissas uoces, unum ipsum Verbum uenit tanquam in uehiculo suo, in uoce sua, in carne sua."

34. *Sermo* 119.7, *PL* 38.675. Augustine is not referring here, as in *De Mag.*, to the manner in which words, created in one mind, come to exist in another through the medium of signs. His point is that the spoken word exists in our "sense," i.e., it marks the physical passage of time, just as Christ marks the passage of an epoch of history.

35. *De Trin.* 1.8.60–1.10; 15.25; see Cayré (1931), 12–15.

36. *De Trin.* 13.20.27: "Placuit quippe uelut gradatim ascendentibus."

37. Cf. Zepf (1959), 109–116. The anticipations of Augustine's ideas in *De Mor. Eccles. Cath.* are summarized by Burnaby (1947), 85–110.

38. The theory of signs is Augustine's way of telling us that truth is neither in us nor outside us—it exists in both places at once. In other words, truth, as we

perceive it, exists in relations, just as meaning arises between the speaker and the hearer of words. In proceeding from *De Doct. Christ.* to *De Trin.*, we learn that Augustine is concerned not with semantic relations as such nor with cognitive ones, but with relationships themselves, in which he perceives a key to our understanding of reality.

39. *De Trin.* 8.10.3–4. Cf. 9.2.3–4.

40. Ibid., 9.4.3. On Augustine's possible source in Porphyry, see Pépin (1964), 92–107, with a full discussion.

41. See Schmaus (1927), 110–127; Chevalier, *S. Augustin* (1940), 68. Schindler (1965), 3–6, provides a concise survey of Augustine's anti-Arian writings.

42. *De Trin.* 5.16.5–7: "Etiam ista appellatio relatiua ex tempore est deo; non enim sempiterna creatura est." See Chevalier, *S. Augustin* (1940), 10–27.

43. Ibid., 8, prol. 1–3: "Diximus alibi ea dici proprie in illa trinitate distincte ad singulas personas pertinentia quae relatiue dicuntur ad inuicem." For a lucid analysis of texts relevant to trinitarian relations in bks. 1–7, see Chevalier, "La théorie" (1940), 322–364.

44. *De Trin.* 8.2.35–40: "Ecce in ipso primo ictu qua uelut coruscatione perstingeris cum dicitur ueritas mane si potes; sed non potes. Relaberis in ista solita atque terrena. Quo tandem pondere, quaeso, relaberis nisi sordium contractarum cupiditatis uisco et peregrinationis erroribus?" Cf. Plotinus, *Enn.* 1.6.1 and 8, vol. 1, 92–94 and 102–103.

45. See Schindler (1965), 170–172, with a list of sources for typical expressions (*ictus, coruscatio, ecstasis,* and other forms of inwardness), 171 n. 18.

46. For a theological analysis, see the excellent note of Agaësse, *BA* 16 (1955), 576–578.

47. *De Trin.* 8.2.28 and 8.3.1.

48. Ibid., 8.3.26–29. This strategy introduces two established tenets of Augustine's thinking into the discussion. As in *De Mag.,* he takes up the problem of outer, spoken words and inner understanding. He also makes implicit use of the distinction between natural and given signs in *De Doct. Christ.* 2.1–2, since the noun "mind" is the equivalent of a natural sign, the adjective "good," of a given sign.

49. Markus (1966) ably sketches the background.

50. *De Trin.* 8.3.38–40: "Cum uero agit hoc studio et fit bonus animus, nisi se ad aliquid conuertat quod ipse non est non potest hoc assequi."

51. Ibid., 8.3.49: "participatione."

52. Ibid., 8.3.52: "Et si amore inhaeseris, continuo beatificaberis," reading *continuo* in contrast to *statim* and *sed non potes* (8.2.33, 37).

53. Ibid., 8.4.6–7: Cf. *Sol.* 1.2.7, *CSEL* 89.12.9–11.

54. On the implied role of memory here, see Plotinus, *Enn.* 1.6.4, vol. 1, 96–97.

55. *De Trin.* 8.4.21–23; see Löhrer (1957), 393–394, on *De Trin.* 8.4 and 13.1.

56. *De Trin.* 8.4.38–40, with the notion that the lives and deeds of biblical figures are narrative texts before they are witnessed by scripture.

57. E.g., John, the subject of a similar argument in *De Trin.* 13.1.46–62.

58. Ibid., 8.4.47–50, where *notitia* bridges *aspicere* and *cognoscere*.

59. Ibid., 8.5.1–3, where *notitia* leads to *humilitatis exemplum.* On the multiple uses of *exemplum,* see Geerlings (1978), 146–228.

60. Schmaus (1927), 250 ff., on the basis of the evidence of bk. 10; a view that is acceptable if the definition is taken as an aspect of Augustine's "inquiry in progress, and not as the definitive expression of a completed theory"; Agaësse and Moingt, *BA* 16 (1955), n. 17, p. 592 (my trans.). For an excellent discussion, see ibid., nn. 17–19, pp. 591–600.

61. Coleman (1992), 107, with a discussion of the implications for narrative.

62. For an outline of these relations, see Bailleux (1966).

63. On the concept of "life" and its relation to the "subject" and "object" of thought, see Schmaus (1927), 225–229.

64. *De Trin.* 8.6.6–7: "Sed id quod in illo amamus etiam nunc uiuere credimus; amamus enim animum iustum."

65. The argument of 8.2.26–40 is reiterated at 8.5.31–52.

66. Plato, *Republic* 4.427e–434d, quoted in Plotinus, *Enn.* 1.2.1, vol. 1, 55–56. On the eternal quality of justice, see *De Trin.* 14.9.7–8; and, for a succinct summary of Augustine's position, see *De Ciu. Dei* 11.28, *CCSL* 48.347–349.

67. *De Trin.* 8.6.13–15: "Quid enim tam intime scitur seque ipsum esse sentit quam id quo etiam cetera sentiuntur, id est ipse animus?"

68. Ibid., 8.6.27–29: "Animum igitur cuiuslibet ex nostro nouimus, et ex nostro credimus quem non nouimus."

69. Cf. *De Doct. Christ.* 2.31–35, *CCSL* 32.67–69, on "inference." Reworking his argument about subjectivity in *Conf.* 11, he notes that we observe movements that indicate the presence of mind but are unable to see the thinking that brings them about; *De Trin.* 8.6.15–20.

70. On the unresolved issues in Augustine's account of images in these examples, see the perceptive comments of O'Daly (1987), 92–102, 113–114.

71. On the distinction between *phantasia,* the image in memory of an object actually seen, and *phantasma,* the image, created in the imagination and lodged in the memory, of an object not actually seen, see *De Mus.* 6.11.32, *PL* 32.1180–81. In the example of Alexandria, Augustine would appear to introduce a third possibility, namely the image of an object not actually seen but described by others. This type of imagination would make his visual distinctions subordinate to a literary presentation of them.

72. Augustine nonetheless believes that such images are acquired by comparable means; *De Trin.* 9.6.19–31.

73. See Agaësse and Moingt, *BA* 16 (1955), n. 15, pp. 589–590, pointing out the psychological aspect of *intentio.*

74. *De Trin.* 9.1.19–20: "Perfectionem in hac uita dicit."

75. Ibid., 9.1.22: "quaerentis intentio."

76. Ibid., 9.1.24–26, quoting 1 Cor. 13:12.

77. On the text quoted here, see Plotinus, *Enn.* 3.7.11, vol. 1, 354–356; for *distentio,* see Chapter 8, "Time."

78. The enduring discussion of bk. 9 remains Schmaus (1927), 235–264; other good commentaries include Sciacca (1956), echoing Schmaus; and Racette (1956), with useful schematic divisions; also du Roy (1966), 437–450. Possible Aristotelian background is discussed by Booth (1979), 106–111.

79. Again paralleling *De Doct. Christ.* 2, where the triad of sender, receiver, and sign (2.1–3) yields to Augustine's concern with the literal and figurative senses of the biblical text. The example of love also recalls *De Mag.,* where speech is the only self-sufficient sign.

80. *De Trin.* 9.2.32–33: "Mens uero et spiritus non relatiue dicuntur sed essentiam demonstrant."

81. Ibid., 9.6.9–11: "Vnde manifestum est aliud unumquemque uidere in se quod sibi alius dicenti credat, non tamen uideat; aliud autem in ipsa ueritate quod alius quoque possit intueri."

82. Markus (1967), 367.

83. Cf. *De Trin.* 8.4.16–20, quoting the trinity *fides, spes, caritas* from 1 Cor. 13:13.

84. Similar to the example of Epicurus, *De Util. Cred.* 4 (discussed in Chapter 6, "Defining the Reader") except in the inclusion of the abstract notion of truth.

85. On judgement and illumination in Augustine more generally, see the judicious summary of Bourke (1978), 20–23.

86. For a review of Augustine's usage, see Schindler (1965), 97–118.

87. *De Trin.* 9.10.6–9: "Aliter enim dicuntur uerba quae spatia temporum syllabis tenent siue pronuntientur siue cogitentur; aliter omne quod notum est uerbum dicitur animo impressum quamdiu de memoria proferri et definiri potest."

88. Given the paradoxical nature of the example. The knowing and not knowing of the subsequent proof for the *cogito* parallels the discussion of time and eternity in *Conf.* 11, as well as *De Doct. Christ.,* which places loving (bk. 1) above signs (bks. 2–3).

89. On its background, see Pépin (1964), 94–100.

90. Cf. Plotinus, *Enn.* 6.1.7, vol. 3, 10–11.

91. Cf. *De Trin.* 10.1.1–2: "Nunc ad ea ipsa consequenter enodatius explicanda limatior accedat intentio."

92. See Schmaus (1927), 264–281, a full discussion; also Kusch (1953), 136–137.

93. On *memoria* in *Conf.* 10, *De Mus.* 6, and *De Trin.,* a fundamental synthesis is Schmaus (1927), 313–331.

94. For the source of these relations, see the discussion of numerical symbolism in the Bible at *De Trin.* 4.4.

95. Ibid., 15.1.6–7, where possible *fontes* are given in the notes.

96. Ibid., 15.1.2–6. For a brief review of positions on relations between *ratio* and *intellectus,* see van der Linden (1957), 7–11, with a good exposition of Augustine's usage in earlier writings, 11–30.

97. For a brief but exhaustive survey of terms, see O'Daly (1987), 7–8; cf. Beckaert, *BA* 10 (1952), 705–706; Agaësse and Moingt, *BA* 16 (1955), 581–583; Gilson (1960), 56 n. 1; Pépin, "Une nouvelle source" (1977), 235 n. 1. On *mens,* see Schmaus (1927), 310–313; Schindler (1965), 180–181; and the excellent discussion of Biolo (1969), 80–107; on *spiritus,* Verbeke (1945), 489–508, who concludes that Augustine's notion brings together Stoic, neoplatonic, and scriptural elements. On the term *persona* as a combination of "the philosophical and psychological concepts of person and personality," see above all Henry (1960), from which I quote (p. 1); also Schmaus (1927), 107–108; Boigelot (1930), 6–16; Lloyd (1972); and Drobner (1986), where a distinction is made between the use of the term in grammatical and rhetorical interpretation (27–81, 82–102). O'Donnell (1992), vol. 2, 258–259, sees a glimmer of Augustine's trinitarian interests in the discussion of *rationalis mens* at *Conf.* 4.15.12–13. On the related problem of memory and "identity," see O'Daly (1987), 148–151; for a phenomenological approach, not pursued in the following discussion of the text, see Körner (1956), (1959), and (1963); also Maxsein (1966), 37–45. Of course, Augustine has a notion of the "self," but not a modern one; see Outler (1955), 352–353, and, as a corrective to a negative approach, Chastaing (1956), 346–347.

98. Cf. Plotinus, *Enn.* 4.7.1, vol. 2, 138.24–25, for whom "the soul is the self."

99. Cf. ibid., 5.6.1, vol. 2, 257.1–3, which neatly conceptualizes this issue.

100. Burnaby (1947), 116–120. Augustine argues that triads exist in each of us individually, whereas the divine trinity is shared by all through God's "image" and "likeness." The trinity thereby becomes his way of countering a notion of truth which, if relational, might easily deteriorate into subjectivism.

101. Ibid., 61–62.

102. Cf. Chevalier, *S. Augustin* (1940), where the relevant texts from bks. 1–7 are assembled with analogues, 37–65, and critically discussed, 67–86; also Chevalier, "La théorie" (1940), 322–364, a lucid exposition; and Schobinger (1966), 183–192, for philosophical reflections. On the origins in Plotinus and his sources, see P. Hadot, "Etre, vie, pensée" (1960), esp. 124–125 on Augustine. Augustine's interest in the quality of relationships in *De Trin.* may be a consequence of his belief in the personal nature of truth as revealed in the incarnation.

103. However, this example is problematic in subsequent discussions of inner seeing; e.g., *De Trin.* 10.5.6–19 and bk. 11.

104. The topic is treated at length at ibid., 14.6–16. On Augustine's intentions here, see 14.4.36–41; 14.5.29–31; and the reiteration at 15.3.75–84. On Cicero, *Tusc. Disp.* 1, as a source, see Schindler (1965), 246–249.

105. *De Trin.* 10.1.2–3, 29–30; cf. 8.4.6–7; 9.3.1–2; 13.4.9–11; 13.5.31–32; and 13.20.59–60.

106. See the discussion of *De Util. Cred.* in Chapter 7, "Tradition and Beliefs."

107. *De Trin.* 10.1.15–16: "Ad doctrinas autem cognoscendas plerumque nos laudantium atque praedicantium accendit auctoritas." A veiled reference to Ambrose?

108. Ibid., 10.1.18–20. Cf. *De Util. Cred.* 16, *CSEL* 25.20–21.

109. *De Dial.* 8, ed. Jackson (1975), 104, where it provides an illustration of types of obscurity.

110. Cf. *De Doct. Christ.* 2, *CCSL* 32.

111. *De Trin.* 10.1.36–38: "Alioquin iam notum est hoc trisyllabum, et articulatam speciem suam impressit animo per sensum aurium."

112. *De Dial.* 5, ed. Jackson (1975), 88.14: "signa uerborum."

113. See *De Doct. Christ.* 2.4.5, *CCSL* 32.34.3–8.

114. There is a rough similarity between this desire to know and Augustine's theory of narrative, since, minimally, a "narrative" is a string of syllables spoken one after another whose logic and meaning we understand through a comparable orientation of our intentions.

115. On the incorporation of the idea, see *De Trin.* 9.2.22–23.

116. Ibid., 10.3.5–8. Cf. *De Util. Cred.* 23, *CSEL* 25.28–29.

117. The metaphor of "seeing" in these examples is derived from Plotinus, chiefly *Enn.* 5.3.5, vol. 2, 211–213; however, the contextualization in the problem of learning is Augustine's alone.

118. *De Trin.* 10.3.18–21: "An in ratione ueritatis aeternae uidet quam speciosum sit nosse semetipsam, et hoc amat quod uidet studetque in se fieri quia, quamuis sibi nota non sit, notum ei tamen est quam bonum sit ut sibi nota sit?"

119. Ibid., 10.3.31–33. The distinction between the legitimate desire for *scientia* and some illegitimate types of curiosity brings Augustine perilously close to hair-splitting, as he acknowledges, *De Util. Cred.* 22, *CSEL* 25.26–28.

120. *De Trin.* 10.3.35. For an interesting discussion of this notion in Augustine and Descartes, see Chastaing (1956), 350–358; Lloyd (1964), 189–191, does not take account of the intricacies of Augustine's language.

121. *De Trin.* 10.3.35–39: "Nam nouit quod alia nouerit, se autem non nouerit; hinc enim nouit et quid sit nosse. Quo pacto igitur se aliquid scientem scit quae se ipsam nescit? Neque enim alteram mentem scientem scit sed se ipsam. Scit igitur se ipsam." On the connections between this argument and Augustine's refutation of scepticism, see O'Daly (1987), 169–171; G. Matthews (1972), 152–160, likewise discussing scepticism, omits the passage, preferring 15.21.12; cf. Jolivet (1931), 65–66. On the important role of this formulation of the *cogito* in anticipation of Descartes, see Blanchet (1920), 33–47. The relevant antecedent in Plotinus is *Enn.* 5.3.6, vol. 2, 213.1–2 (along with 5.3.5, pp. 211–213); cf. 5.3.7 (pp. 215.18–216.34). A full discussion of Augustine's similarities to and differences from the Plotinian position on the intellect would be useful but cannot be attempted here.

122. *De Trin.* 10.4.1: "Deinde quid eius ei tam notum est quam se uiuere?" Cf. Plotinus, *Enn.* 5.3.6, vol. 2, 214.22–28, for the examples of sight and speech.

123. *De Trin.* 10.4.2–3: "Non potest autem et mens esse et non uiuere quando habet etiam amplius ut intellegat." He also considers the cases in which the mind

seeks itself and knows it is a mind (10.4.5–12) and in which it seeks itself but does not know that what it is seeking is a mind (10.4.13–25).

124. Augustine replaces *animus* with *mens* at 10.3.1; however, the change may not be significant, as his use of *anima, animus,* and *mens* varies considerably; see Gilson (1960), 269–270, n. 1.

125. *De Trin.* 10.5.1: "Vtquid ergo ei [= mente, 10.4.36] praeceptum est ut se ipsa cognoscat?"

126. I.e., Plotinus, *Enn.* 5.3.7, vol. 2, 214–215.1–3.

127. See also his use of hermeneutics to answer doubt at *De Mag.* 10; Baker (1969), 472–473.

128. Compare *De Trin.* 8.2.37–38: "Relaberis in ista solita atque terrena"; and 10.5.10–11; "et labitur in minus et minus."

129. Ibid., 10.5.7: "intrinsecus"; 10.5.15: "ex his quae foris sunt."

130. Ibid., 10.5.13–14: "Ideoque . . . fit nimis intenta in actiones suas."

131. Ibid., 8.2.39; 10.5.6, 15.

132. *Conf.* 8.9.21, *CCSL* 27.127.18: "[animus] consuetudine praegrauatus."

133. Cf. ibid., 8.7.16 (p. 123.6).

134. *De Trin.* 10.5.23: "cum ergo aliud sit non se nosse, aliud non se cogitare"; cf. 10.5.20.

135. The distinction may be an application of Augustine's argument concerning the identity and mutability of the soul, *De Im. An.* 5–7; see O'Daly (1987), 36–37, and, on the use of Aristotle, *Categoriae,* du Roy (1966), 177 ff. The same distinction is made between the independence of disciplines and the relative value of literary knowledge in Augustine's several discussions of grammar.

136. *De Trin.* 10.5.26–31: "Et quia illa corpora sunt quae foris per sensus carnis adamauit eorumque diuturna quadam familiaritate implicata est, nec secum potest introrsus tamquam in regionem incorporeae naturae ipsa corpora inferre, imagines eorum conuoluit et rapit factas in semetipsa de semetipsa." Note the use of *rapere;* on *regio dissimilitudinis,* see Chapter 3, "Neoplatonism."

137. Ibid., 10.8.17–22: "Cum ergo sit mens interior, quodam modo exit a semetipsa cum in haec quasi uestigia multarum intentionum exerit amoris affectum. Quae uestigia tamquam imprimuntur memoriae quando haec quae foris sunt corporalia sentiuntur ut etiam cum absunt ista, praesto sint tamen imagines eorum cogitantibus."

138. Ibid., 10.8.22–24: "Cognoscat ergo semetipsam, nec quasi absentem se quaerat, sed intentionem uoluntatis qua per alia uagabatur statuat in se ipsa et se cogitet." Cf. 10.9.1–2.

139. Ibid., 10.9.22–23: "Certe enim nouit sibi dici, sibi scilicet quae est et uiuit et intellegit."

140. Ibid., 10.10.8–10: "Omnes tamen se intellegere nouerunt et esse et uiuere, sed intellegere ad quod intellegunt referunt, esse autem et uiuere ad se ipsas."

141. Ibid., 10.10.38–43. On the fate of the triad *esse, uiuere, intellegere* down to the twelfth century, see Bell (1985).

142. Gilson (1930), 260–261; cf. Blanchet (1920), 33–47.

143. For a brief review of the issues, see Markus (1967), 350–353; a thorough inquiry is Schöpf (1965), 51–59, 61–73, esp 75–87, 89–91, on the inner criteria for knowing. On the classification of *credibilia* in *De Diu. Quaes.*, q? 48, (*CCSL* 44a.75) and *Ep.* 147.6–8 (*CSEL* 57.85–88), see Coleman (1992), 86–88.

144. Is. 7:9 (in the Septuagint). E.g., *De Mag.* 11.37, *CCSL* 29.194–195; *De Lib. Arb.* 1.2.4 (ibid., p. 213); *De Trin.* 7.6 (p. 267.178–179). For a word-by-word exposition of the text, see *Sermo* 43, *PL* 38.254–258 (with a summary at 43.3, col. 255). On the transition in Augustine's early thinking, see Madec, *BA* 6 (1976), n. 9, pp. 549–551 (bibliography, p. 551); also Ladner (1959), 196, n. 33.

145. Cf. *De Ciu. Dei* 11.3, *CCSL* 48.322–323, where the idea is the philosophical justification for Augustine's notion of biblical authority; on which see Löhrer (1954), 23–65, 106–110 (down to Cassiciacum), and, on terms for belief, 117–132. Cf. Lütcke (1968), 39–45, on Ciceronian sources; on Plotinus as an influence, see O'Meara, "St. Augustine's View of Authority" (1951), 344.

146. E.g., *In Io. Eu. Tract.* 36.7, *CCSL* 36.328.16–17; cf. *De Trin.* 8.4.7 (p. 275.26–31). The principle is valid even in the case of authors whose intentions are not in doubt; *Sol.*, 1.4.9, *CSEL* 89.15.1–10.

147. *De Cons. Eu.* 1.7.12, *CSEL* 43.13.3–6.

148. Cf. K. Holl (1965), 61–63; Bourke (1958); Andresen (1973).

149. For an outstanding review, see Taylor (1989), 3–207; on the classical background, see Zepf (1959) and Booth (1977). On the history of the maxim, a magisterial synthesis is Courcelle (1974–75); on Augustine's sources, see (1974), 125–164.

150. Anticipating Descartes; see Blanchet (1920), 27–47 (relevant texts) and 47–55 (the Augustinian *cogito* in Descartes); also Gilson, *Etudes* (1930), 259–264; Chastaing (1956), 347–352; Gouhier (1962), 34–40; du Roy (1966), 173–177, 242–244; Alesanco (1968), 9–19; and, within analytic philosophy, G. Matthews (1992), 11–38. For a dissenting view, see Abercrombie (1938), 57–66.

151. See Cilleruelo (1966).

152. The topics with which bk. 10 concludes; a "new departure" is necessitated by its length; 10.12.23–24.

153. The penultimate empirical hurdle in *De Trin.*; see Kälin (1921), 8–12, and, on the metaphysics of light, Thonnard (1962). Note that triadic relations appear in early discussions of visions, e.g., *Sol.* 1.6.12, *CSEL* 89.19–20.

154. Or alternately the *corpus uisibile, sensus oculorum,* and *uisio; De Trin.* 11.2.10–13; cf. *De Quant. An.* 23.43, *CSEL* 89.184–185.

155. The point is illustrated by the blind, who have the *uidendi appetitus; De Trin.* 11.2.37–47.

156. The point is illustrated by three thought-experiments: (1) A sealing ring, placed alternately on wax and on water, produces in turn a lasting and an ephemeral image; we recognize that the image-producing process in each case is the same, not through what we see but through our reasoning (ibid., 11.2.76–91). (2) We can look at coloured lights, then close our eyes; the impressions remain until the source vanishes, offering another rational proof of a sense within (11.2.92–

99; cf. 11.2.100–102, where window lattices perform a comparable role). (3) The double image that we see when staring at a candle indicates that separate impressions, one from each eye, are created in the sense of sight. If one eye is closed, only one image appears (11.2.105–116).

157. Ibid., 11.3.1–3. Cf. *Conf.* 11.3, *CCSL* 27.196.1–3.

158. Another role for reason is to distinguish between the total content of memory, which is not all conscious (cf. 11.3.32–41), and specific memory searches (11.3.21–28), which are entirely so.

159. See Chapter 5, "The Dialogues."

160. A theme of bk. 8. As a person decides what sort of clothes he or she will wear, so the will governs the presentation of the body to itself; *De Trin.* 11.4.15–18. The mind focuses on images alone when the will is unable to perform its normal functions, i.e., when the senses are numbed by sleep or bemused by prophets or diviners. This enfeeblement can also occur when one is awake: an imaginary menace is feared as much as a real one; 11.4.19–38.

161. Ibid., 11.1.1–24; 11.5.12–26; see Schmaus (1927), 217–220.

162. Cf. Plotinus, *Enn.* 5.8.11, vol. 2, 284–285, for a beautiful, alternative rendering of this idea.

163. *De Trin.* 11.8.45–46: "cogito cum aliquid mihi narratur." Cf. 11.8.39–42 and *De Util. Cred.* 10.24, *CSEL* 25/1.29–31.

164. *De Trin.* 11.8.51–54: "Neque enim uel intellegere possem narrantem si ea quae dicit et si contexta tunc primum audirem, non tamen generaliter singula meminissem."

165. Ibid., 11.8.58–62: "Ita fit ut omnis qui corporalia cogitat, siue ipse aliquid confingat, siue audiat aut legat uel praeterita narrantem uel futura praenuntiantem, ad memoriam suam recurrat et ibi reperiat modum atque mensuram omnium formarum quas cogitans intuetur."

166. Ibid., 11.8.94–96: "Nam et legentibus euenit et mihi saepissime ut perlecta pagina uel epistula nesciam quid legerim et repetam." The parallel is presumably created by the words spoken and the words read aloud; for a possible analogue in Plotinus, see the Introduction, note 53.

167. In *De Trin.* 12, the significant text is the opening chapters of Gen. (12.4–12); in bk. 13, it is the prologue to John (13.1–2, 9, 14). The alternation of philosophical issues and biblical theology is continued in bks. 14–15: in 14, the dominant themes are wisdom, the blessed life, and memory; in 15, the inadequacy of the human mind and its triadic thinking for coping with divine knowledge.

168. On infancy, see ibid., 14.5 (= *Conf.* 1.6–8); on adolescent learning, 10.11.6–19 (= *Conf.* 1.12–14); on acting, 13.3.1–43 (= *Conf.* 3.2); on praise, 13.3.44–56 (= *Conf.* 4.2, 13–14); on Carthage, 8.6.68–77 (= *Conf.* 10.16.33; 10.21.1–2; cf. 2.3, 3.1, 4.7, 5.8); on the metaphor of memory as a belly, 12.14.75–77 (= *Conf.* 10.14.19–20); on the etymology of *cogo*, 11.3.1–3 (= *Conf.* 10.11.14–15); on thought-experiments, 11.7 (recalling what I ate yesterday) and 11.8 (recalling the appearance of the sun) (= *Conf.* 10.31 and 11.18, 23).

169. Of major themes in earlier reading, only the Manichaeans are absent; this omission is surely deliberate.

170. On parallels between *De Trin.* 12.10–11, *De Ciu. Dei* 11.26, and the *Conf.,* see Kusch (1953), 134–135.

171. *De Trin.* 12.7.88–101; Gal. 3:26–28.

172. Ibid., 12.8.1–4: "Ascendentibus itaque introrsus quibusdam gradibus considerationis per animae partes unde incipit aliquid occurrere quod non sit nobis commune cum bestiis, inde incipit ratio ubi iam homo interior possit agnosci."

173. See Antonelli (1954), 990–1002, with interesting reflections on this inwardness.

174. For a good schematic representation of the goal, see Madec (1975), 81; on the anticipation, see Camelot (1956).

175. *De Trin.* 12.8; cf. 12.11.28–29: "scientia, id est cognitio rerum temporalium atque mutabilium." Cf. 12.12.12–14; 12.15.41–52.

176. Ibid., 12.14.7–9: "Distat tamen ab aeternorum contemplatione actio qua bene utimur temporalibus rebus, et illa sapientiae, haec scientiae deputatur." Cf. Plotinus, *Enn.* 5.8.5, vol. 2, 275–276.14–25.

177. Were it not to find what it originally put there, the mind would have to be reeducated, that is, to rediscover incorporeal truth and to fix it in memory like writing; *De Trin.* 12.14.62–68.

178. Ibid., 14.15.17–26: "Quando autem bene recordatur domini sui spiritu eius accepto, sentit omnino quia hoc discit intimo magisterio . . . Non sane reminiscitur beatitudinis suae . . . Credit autem de illa fide dignis litteris dei sui per eius prophetas conscriptis narrantibus de felicitate paradisi atque illud primum et bonum hominis et malum historica traditione indicantibus."

# BIBLIOGRAPHY

Abbeduto, Leonard, and Sheldon Rosenberg, "Children's Knowledge of the Presuppositions of *know* and Other Cognitive Verbs," *Journal of Child Language* 12 (1985), 621–640.

Abercrombie, Nigel, *Saint Augustine and French Classical Thought* (Oxford, 1938).

Adam, Karl, *Die geistige Entwicklung des Heiligen Augustinus*, 2nd ed. (Libelli 14, Darmstadt, 1954).

Alesanco, Tirso, "Metafísica y gnoseología del mundo inteligible, según S. Agustín. En torno a la teoría agustiniana de la iluminación," *Augustinus* 13 (1968), 9–36.

Alfaric, Prosper, *L'évolution intellectuelle de saint Augustin*, vol. 1: *Du manichéisme au néoplatonisme* (Paris, 1918).

Alici, Luigi, *Il linguaggio come segno e come testimonianza. Una rilettura di Agostino* (Collezione La Cultura 10, Rome, 1976).

———"Linguaggio e tempo in S. Agostino," in *Sprache und Erkenntnis im Mittelalter* (Akten des VI. Internationalen Kongresses für mittelalterlichen Philosophie, 29. August–3. September 1977 in Bonn, Berlin, 1981), vol. 2, 1037–45.

Allard, Guy H., "L'articulation du sens et du signe dans le *De doctrina christiana* de S. Augustin," *Studia Patristica* 14.3 (Berlin, 1976), 377–388.

———"Arts libéraux et langage chez saint Augustin," in *Arts libéraux et philosophie au moyen âge* (Actes du quatrième Congrès international de philosophie médiévale, 27 août–2 septembre 1967, Montreal and Paris, 1969), 481–492.

———"Pour une nouvelle interprétation de la *Civitas Dei*," *Studia Patristica* 9.3 (Berlin, 1966), 329–339.

Allard, Jean-Bernard, *La nature du "De catechizandis rudibus" de saint Augustin* (Pontificia Universitas Lateranensis Facultas Theologiae, Rome, 1976).

Allberry, C. R. C., "Manichaean Studies," *Journal of Theological Studies* 39 (1938), 337–349.

Allgeier, Arthur, "Der Einfluss des Manichäismus auf die exegetische Fragestellung bei Augustin. Ein Beitrag zur Geschichte von Augustins theologischer Entwicklung," in *Aurelius Augustinus* (1930), 1–13.

Altaner, Berthold, "Augustins Methode der Quellenbenützung. Sein Studium der Väterliteratur," *Sacris Erudiri* 4 (1952), 5–17.

———"Augustinus und die griechische Patristik. Eine Einführung und Nachlass zu den quellenkritischen Untersuchungen," *Revue bénédictine* 62 (1952), 201–215.

———"Die Bibliothek des hl. Augustinus (Possidius, Vita s. Augustini c. 31,7)," *Theologische Revue* 2 (1948), 73–78.

————*Kleine patristische Schriften,* ed. G. Glockmann (Texte und Untersuchungen 83, Berlin, 1967).

Andresen, Carl, "Gedanken zum philosophischen Bildungshorizont Augustins vor und in Cassiciacum. Contra academ. II, 6,14 f; III 17–19, 37–42," *Augustinus* 13 (1968), 77–98.

————"Die geoffenbarte Wahrheit und die sich offenbarende Wahrheit oder das Verhältnis von Wahrheit und Autorität bei Augustin," in *Sichtbare Kirche. Für Heinrich Lang zu seinem 80. Geburtstag,* ed. U. Fabricius and R. Volp (Schriftenreihe des Instituts für Kirchenbau und kirchliche Kunst der Gegenwart 3, Gütersloh, 1973), 22–38.

Andrieu, Michel, "Les ordres mineurs dans l'ancien rit romain," *Revue des sciences religieuses* 5 (1925), 232–274.

Antonelli, Maria Teresa, "La dialettica dell'uomo interiore in Agostino," *Humanitas* 9 (1954), 990–1012.

Arendt, Hannah, *Der Liebesbegriff bei Augustinus. Versuch einer philosophischen Interpretation* (Philosophische Forschungen 9, Berlin, 1929).

Armstrong, Hilary, *The Architecture of the Intelligible Universe in the Philosophy of Plotinus. An Analytical and Historical Study* (Cambridge, 1940).

————"Plotinus's Doctrine of the Infinite and Its Significance for Christian Thought," *Downside Review* 73 (1954–55), 47–58.

————"Spiritual or Intelligible Matter in Plotinus and St. Augustine," in *AM* (1954), vol. 1, 277–283.

Arquillière, H. X., *L'Augustinisme politique. Essai sur la formation des théories politiques du moyen-âge* (L'Eglise et l'Etat au Moyen Age 2, Paris, 1934).

Asmussen, Jes P., *XUASTVĀNIFT. Studies in Manichaeism* (Acta Theologica Danica 7, Copenhagen, 1965).

Audet, Th.-André, "Note sur les catéchèses baptismales de Saint Augustin," in *AM* (1954), vol. 1, 151–160.

Auerbach, Erich, *Literary Language and Its Public in Late Latin Antiquity and in the Middle Ages,* trans. R. Manheim (London, 1965).

————*Mimesis: The Representation of Reality in Western Literature,* (1946), trans. W. Trask (Princeton, 1953).

*Augustiniana. Sexto decimo exacto saeculo a die natali s. Aurelii Augustini 354–1954 (Augustiniana* 4.3–4, Louvain, 1954).

*Augustiniana Traiectina. Communications présentées au Colloque International d'Utrecht 13–14 novembre 1986,* ed. J. den Boeft and J. van Oort (Etudes Augustiniennes 119, Paris, 1987).

*Aurelius Augustinus. Die Festschrift der Görres-Gesellschaft zum 1500. Todestage des heiligen Augustinus,* ed. M. Grabmann and J. Mausbach (Cologne, 1930).

Baguette, Ch., "Une période stoïcienne dans l'évolution de la pensée de saint Augustin," *REA* 16 (1970), 47–77.

Bailleux, E., "La sotériologie de saint Augustin dans le 'De Trinitate,'" *Mélanges de science religieuse* 23 (1966), 149–173.

Baker, Peter Harte, "Liberal Arts as Philosophical Liberation: St. Augustine's *De Magistro,*" in *Arts libéraux et philosophie au moyen âge* (Actes du quatrième Congrès international de philosophie médiévale, 27 août–2 septembre 1967, Montreal and Paris, 1969), 469–479.

Bakhtin, M. M., "The Problem of Speech Genres," in *Speech Genres and Other Late Essays,* trans. V. W. McGee, ed. C. Emerson and M. Holquist (Austin, 1986), 60–102.

Balogh, Joseph, "*Voces paginarum*. Beiträge zur Geschichte des lauten Lesens und Schreibens," *Philologus* 82 (1927), 84–109, 202–240.

Banniard, Michel, *Viva voce. Communication écrite et communication orale du IVe au IXe siècle en Occident Latin* (Collection des Etudes Augustiniennes, Série Moyen-Age et Temps Modernes 25, Paris, 1992).

Baratin, Marc, "Les origines stoïciennes de la théorie augustinienne du signe," *Revue des études latines* 59 (1981), 260–268.

———"Sémiologie et métalinguistique chez saint Augustin," in *Signification et référence dans l'antiquité et au moyen âge,* ed. M. Baratin and F. Desbordes (*Langages* 65, Paris, 1982), 85–89.

Bardy, Gustave, "Un élève de Saint Augustin: Licentius," *L'année théologique augustinienne* 14 (1954), 55–79.

———"Les méthodes de travail de saint Augustin," in *AM* (1954), vol. 1, pp. 19–29.

———"'Philosophie' et 'philosophe' dans le vocabulaire chrétien des premiers siècles," *Revue d'ascétique et de mystique* 25 (1949), 97–108.

———*Saint Augustin. L'homme et l'oeuvre* (Bibliothèque Augustinienne, Paris, 1940).

———"Tractare, Tractatus," *Recherches de science religieuse* 33 (1946), 211–235.

Barnes, T. D., "Augustine, Symmachus, and Ambrose," in *Augustine: From Rhetor to Theologian,* ed. Joanne McWilliam et al. (Waterloo, Ont., 1992), 7–13.

Bartlett, Frederic C., *Remembering. A Study in Experimental and Social Psychology* (Cambridge Psychological Library, Cambridge, 1932).

Barwick, Karl, *Probleme der stoischen Sprachlehre und Rhetorik* (Abhandlungen der Sächsischen Akademie der Wissenschaften zu Leipzig, Philologisch-historische Klasse 49, 3, Berlin, 1957).

Bastiaensen, Antoon A. R., "The Inaccuracies in the Vita Augustini of Possidius," *Studia Patristica* 16.2 (Berlin, 1985), 480–486.

Bates, Elisabeth, L. Benigni, I. Bretherton, L. Camaioni, and V. Volterra, "Cognition and Communication from Nine to Thirteen Months," in *The Emergence of Symbols: Cognition and Communication in Infancy,* ed. E. Bates et al., (New York, 1979), 69–140.

Batiffol, P., "Autour du *De utilitate credendi* de saint Augustin," *Revue biblique* 14 (1917), 1–45.

Bavard, Georges, "Un thème augustinien: Le mystère de l'Incarnation, à la lumière de la distinction entre le verbe intérieur et le verbe proféré," *REA* 9 (1963), 95–101.

Beccaria, Augusto, "Sulle tracce di un antico canone latino di Ippocrate e di Galeno. I," *Italia medioevale e umanistica* 2 (1959), 1–56.

Beierwaltes, Werner, "Plotins Metaphysik des Lichtes," in *Die Philosophie des Neuplatonismus,* ed. C. Zintzen (Wege der Forschung 436, Darmstadt, 1977), 75–117.

———"Zu Augustins Metaphysik der Sprache," *Augustinian Studies* 2 (1971), 179–195.

——— ed., *Plotin über Ewigkeit und Zeit* (Enneade III 7), 3rd ed. (Frankfurt, 1981).

Bell, David N., "Esse, Vivere, Intelligere: The Noetic Triad and the Image of God," *Recherches de théologie ancienne et médiévale* 52 (1985), 5–43.

Bellissima, Giuseppina, "Sant'Agostino grammatico," in *AM* (1954), vol. 1, 35–42.

Béné, Charles, *Erasme et saint Augustin ou influence de saint Augustin sur l'humanisme d'Erasme* (Travaux d'Humanisme et Renaissance 103, Geneva, 1969).

Bennett, Camille, "The Conversion of Vergil: The *Aeneid* in Augustine's Confessions," *REA* 34 (1988), 47–69.

Benveniste, Emile, *Problèmes de linguistique générale,* vol. 1 (Paris, 1966).

Berlinger, Rudolph, *Augustins dialogische Metaphysik* (Frankfurt, 1962).

Berrouard, Marie-François, "L'exégèse de saint Augustin prédicateur du quatrième Evangile. Le sens de l'unité des Ecritures," *Freiburger Zeitschrift für Philosophie und Theologie* 34 (1987), 311–338.

Bezançon, J. N., "Le mal et l'existence temporelle chez Plotin et saint Augustin," *R Aug* 3 (1965), 133–160.

Biolo, Salvino, *La coscienza nel "De Trinitate" di S. Agostino* (Analecta Gregoriana 172, Rome, 1969).

Blanchet, Léon, *Les antécédents historiques du "Je pense, donc je suis"* (Paris, 1920).

Blaser, Klauspeter, "Harnacks Augustinbild in der Entwicklung der seitherigen Forschung," *Schweizerische Theologische Umschau* 34 (1964), 117–128.

Bloch, Herbert, "The Pagan Revival in the West at the End of the Fourth Century," in *The Conflict between Paganism and Christianity in the Fourth Century,* ed. A. Momigliano (Oxford, 1963), 193–218.

Blumenberg, Hans, "Augustins Anteil an der Geschichte des Begriffs der theoretischen Neugierde," *REA* 7 (1961), 35–70.

Blumenkranz, Bernhard, "Augustin et les juifs. Augustin et le judaisme," *R Aug* 1 (1958), 226–241.

———*Die Judenpredigt Augustins. Ein Beitrag zur Geschichte der jüdisch-christlichen Beziehungen in den ersten Jahrhunderten* (Basler Beiträge zur Geschichtswissenschaft 25, Basel, 1946).

Bochet, Isabelle, "Interprétation scripuaire et compréhension de soi. Du *De doctrina christiana* aux *Confessions* de Saint Augustin," in *Comprendre et interpréter. Le paradigme herméneutique de la raison* (Philosophie 15, Paris, 1993), 22–50.

Böhmer, H., "Die Lobpreisungen des heiligen Augustinus," *Neue kirchliche Zeitschrift* 26 (1915), 419–438, 487–512.

Børresen, Kari Elisabeth, *Subordination and Equivalence: The Nature and Role of Woman in Augustine and Thomas Aquinas,* texts trans. by C. Talbot (Washington, D.C., 1981).

Boigelot, R., "Le mot 'personne' dans les écrits trinitaires de saint Augustin," *Nouvelle revue théologique* 57 (1930), 5–16.

Bolgiani, Franco, *La conversione di S. Agostino e l'VIII libro delle "Confessioni"* (Pubblicazioni della Facoltà di Lettere e Filosofia 8.4, Turin, 1956).

Bonner, Gerald, "Augustine's Attitude to Women and 'Amicitia,'" in *Homo Spiritalis* (1987), 259–275.

———*St. Augustine of Hippo: Life and Controversies* (The Library of History and Doctrine, Philadelphia, 1963).

Bonner, Stanley F., *Education in Ancient Rome. From the Elder Cato to the Younger Pliny* (London, 1977).

Booth, E., "St. Augustine's 'notitia sui' Related to Aristotle and the Early Neo-Platonists," *Augustiniana* 27 (1977), 70–132, 364–401; 29 (1979), 97–124.

Boros, Ladislas, "Les catégories de la temporalité chez saint Augustin," *Archives de philosophie* 21 (1958), 323–385.

Bourke, Vernon J., "Light of Love: Augustine on Moral Illumination," *Mediaevalia* 4 (1978), 13–31.

———"Wisdom in the Gnoseology of Saint Augustine," *Augustinus* 3 (1958), 331–336.

Boyer, Charles, "La contemplation d'Ostie," in *Essais sur la doctrine de saint Augustin* (Bibliothèque des archives de philosophie, Paris, 1932), 272–296.

Brabant, Oliva, "Confiteri-Enuntiare Vitam Suam chez Saint Augustin d'après l'*Enarratio* LV et le livre X des *Confessions*," *Science et esprit* 21 (1969), 253–279.

Bretherton, Inge, and Marjorie Beeghly, "Talking about Internal States: The Acquisition of an Explicit Theory of Mind," *Developmental Psychology* 18 (1982), 906–921.

Brewer, William F., "What is Autobiographical Memory?" in *Autobiographical Memory,* ed. D. C. Rubin (Cambridge, 1986), 25–49.

Bright, Pamela, *The Book of Rules of Tyconius: Its Purpose and Inner Logic* (Christianity and Judaism in Antiquity 2, Notre Dame, Ind., 1988).

Brown, Peter, "Late Antiquity," in *A History of Private Life,* ed. P. Ariès and G. Duby, vol. 1: *From Pagan Rome to Byzantium* ed. P. Veyne, trans. A. Goldhammer (Cambridge, Mass.: The Belknap Press of Harvard University Press, 1987), 235–311.

————*Augustine of Hippo. A Biography* (London, 1967).

————*The Body and Society: Men, Women, and Sexual Renunciation in Early Christianity* (Lectures on the History of Religions Sponsored by the American Council of Learned Societies, n.s., 13, New York, 1988).

————"The Diffusion of Manichaeism in the Roman Empire," *Journal of Roman Studies* 59 (1969), 92–103.

————*Power and Persuasion in Late Antiquity: Toward a Christian Empire* (Curti Lectures 1988, Madison, 1992).

Bruner, Jerome, *Child's Talk: Learning to Use Language* (New York, 1983).

Bruner, Jerome, and M. Scaife, "The Capacity for Joint Visual Attention in the Infant," *Nature* 253 (1975), 265–266.

Bruner, Jerome, and Susan Weisser, "The Invention of Self: Autobiography and Its Forms," in *Literacy and Orality,* ed. D. R. Olson and N. Torrance (Cambridge, 1991), 129–148.

Brunner, Peter, "Charismatische und methodische Schriftauslegung nach Augustins Prolog zu De doctrina christiana," *Kerygma und Dogma* 1 (1955), 59–68, 85–103.

Bruns, Gerald, *Hermeneutics Ancient and Modern* (New Haven, 1992).

Bucher, Theodor G., "Zur formalen Logik bei Augustin," *Freiburger Zeitschrift für Philosophie und Theologie* 29 (1982), 3–45.

Buchheit, Vincenz, "Augustinus unter dem Feigenbaum (zu Conf. VIII)," *Vigiliae Christianae* 22 (1968), 257–271.

Burke, Kenneth, *The Rhetoric of Religion: Studies in Logology* (Boston, 1961).

Burnaby, John, *Amor Dei. A Study of the Religion of St. Augustine* (The Hulsean Lectures for 1938, London, 1947).

Burnyeat, M. F., "Idealism and Greek Philosophy: What Descartes Saw and Berkeley Missed," *Philosophical Review* 91 (1982), 3–40.

————"Wittgenstein and Augustine De Magistro," *Proceedings of the Aristotelian Society, Suppl.,* vol. 61 (1987), 1–24.

Burrow, J. A., *The Ages of Man. A Study in Medieval Writing and Thought* (Oxford, 1986).

Busch, Benedictus, "De modo quo s. Augustinus descripserit initiationem christianum," *Ephemerides Liturgicae Analecta historico-ascetica Commentarium* 52 (1938), 385–483.

Butler, Cuthbert, *Benedictine Monachism. Studies in Benedictine Life and Rule,* 2nd ed. (London, 1924).

Callahan, John F., "Basil of Caesarea: A New Source for St. Augustine's Theory of Time," *Harvard Studies in Classical Philology* 63 (1958), 437–454.

————*Four Views of Time in Ancient Philosophy,* rev. ed. (Westport, Conn., 1968).

Cambronne, Patrice, *Recherches sur la structure de l'imaginaire dans les Confessions de saint Augustin;* vol. 1: *Texte;* vol. 2: *Notes;* vol. 3: *Annexes* (CEA, SA 92–94, microfiche, Paris, 1982).

Camelot, Pierre-Thomas, "A l'éternel par le temporel (*De Trinitate,* IV, xviii, 24)," *REA* 2 (1956), 163–172.

———"'Quod intelligimus, debemus rationi.' Note sur la méthode théologique de saint Augustin," in *Festschrift für B. Altaner* (Sonderausgabe des Historischen Jahrbuches 77, 1958), 397–402.

Cancik, Hubert, "Rome as a Sacred Landscape," *Visible Religion* 4–5 (1985–86), 250–265.

Canning, Raymond, "The Augustinian *uti/frui* Distinction in the Relation between Love for Neighbour and Love for God," *Augustiniana* 33 (1983), 165–231.

———"Love of Neighbour in St. Augustine. A Preparation for or the Essential Moment of Love for God?" *Augustiniana* 33 (1983), 5–57.

———"'Love your Neighbour as Yourself' (Matt. 22, 39). Saint Augustine on the Lineaments of the Self to Be Loved," *Augustiniana* 34 (1984), 145–197.

Capánaga, Victorino, "El silencio interior en la visió agustiniana de Ostia," *Studia Patristica* 9 (Berlin, 1966), 359–392.

Carena, Carlo, "Fonti classiche di un passo delle *Confessioni* agostiniane," *Rivista di storia e letteratura religiosa* 3 (1967), 65–70.

Carruthers, Mary J., *The Book of Memory. A Study of Memory in Medieval Culture* (Cambridge, 1990).

Casares, Tomás D., "La concepción del tiempo en el libro XI de las Confesiones de san Augustín," *Sapientia* 21 (1966), 169–200.

Cassirer, Ernst, *The Philosophy of Symbolic Forms,* trans. R. Manheim, introduction by C. W. Hendel, vol. 1 (New Haven, 1953).

Cataldo, Giacinto B., "Semantica e intersoggettività della parola in S. Agostino," *Sapienza* 26 (1973), 170–184.

Cavallera, F., "La contemplation d'Ostie," *Revue d'ascétique et de mystique* 20 (1939), 181–196.

Cayré, Fulbert, *La contemplation augustinienne. Principes de spiritualité et de théologie,* 2nd ed. (BA, Etudes, Paris, 1954).

———"Contemplation et raison d'après saint Augustin," in *Mélanges augustiniens publiés à l'occasion du XVe centenaire de saint Augustin* (Paris, 1931), 1–51.

———"La conversion de saint Augustin. Le 'Tolle, lege' des *Confessions,*" *L'année théologique* 12 (1951–52), 144–151, 244–252.

———"Le livre XIII des *Confessions* de S. Augustin," *REA* 2 (1956), 143–161.

———"Mystique et sagesse dans les Confessions de saint Augustin," in *Mélanges Jules Lebreton,* vol. 1 (*Recherches de science religieuse* 39, 1951–52), 443–460.

———"La notion de Sagesse chez Saint Augustin," *L'année théologique* 4 (1943), 443–456.

———"Une rétractation de saint Augustin. Les enfants morts sans baptême," *L'année théologique* 12 (1952), 131–143.

———"Le sens et l'unité des Confessions de saint Augustin," *L'année théologique* 13 (1953), 13–32.

Chadwick, Henry, "History and Symbolism in the Garden at Milan," in *From Augustine to Eriugena: Essays on Neoplatonism and Christianity in Honor of John O'Meara,* ed. F. X. Martin and J. A. Richmond (Washington, D.C., 1991), 42–55.

———"The Influence of Augustine on Ethics," in *Saint Augustine and His Influence in the*

*Middle Ages,* ed. E. B. King and J. T. Schaefer (Sewanee Medieval Studies 3, Sewanee, Tenn., 1988), 10–18.

———"Tyconius and Augustine," in *A Conflict of Christian Hermeneutics in Roman Africa: Tyconius and Augustine* (Center for Hermeneutical Studies in Hellenistic and Modern Culture, Colloquy 58, Berkeley, 1989), 49–55.

———trans. and ed., *Saint Augustine. Confessions* (Oxford, 1991).

Chaix-Ruy, Jules, "Existence et temporalité selon saint Augustin," *Augustinus* 3 (1958), 337–349.

———"La perception du temps chez saint Augustin," in *Saint Augustin* (Cahiers de la Nouvelle Journée 17, Paris, 1930), 71–93.

———*Saint Augustin. Temps et histoire* (*CEA, SA* 4, Paris, 1956).

Charles, Pierre, "L'élément populaire dans les sermons de Saint Augustin," in *Prédication et prédicateurs* (Cahiers de la Nouvelle Revue Théologique 3, Paris, 1947), 63–94.

Chartier, Roger, *Lectures et lecteurs dans la France d'Ancien Régime* (Paris, 1987).

Chastaing, Maxime, "Consciousness and Evidence," *Mind,* n.s., 65 (1956), 346–358.

———"Saint Augustin et le problème de la connaissance d'autrui," *Revue philosophique de la France et de l'étranger* 151 (1961), 109–124; 152 (1962), 90–102; 153 (1963), 223–238.

Chevalier, Irénée, *S. Augustin et la pensée grecque. Les relations trinitaires* (Iubilaria Friburgensia 1889–1939. Travaux publiés à l'occasion du cinquantenaire de l'Université de Fribourg. Collectanea Friburgensia 33, n.s., 24, Fribourg, 1940).

———"La théorie augustinienne des relations trinitaires," *Divus Thomas. Jahrbuch für Philosophie und spekulative Theologie,* 3rd ser., 18 (1940), 317–384.

Christian, William A., "Augustine on the Creation of the World," *Harvard Theological Review* 46 (1953), 1–25.

Christopher, Joseph P., trans. and ed., *S. Aureli Augustini Hipponensis episcopi De catechizandis rudibus liber unus* (Patristic Studies 8, Washington, D.C., 1926).

Cilleruelo, P. Lope, "Pro memoria Dei," *REA* 12 (1966), 65–84.

Clark, Elizabeth A., "'Adam's Only Companion': Augustine and the Early Christian Debate on Marriage," *Recherches augustiniennes* 21 (1986), 139–162.

———"Vitiated Seeds and Holy Vessels: Augustine's Manichean Past," in *Ascetic Piety and Women's Faith: Essays on Late Ancient Christianity* (Studies in Women and Religion 20, Lewiston, N.Y., 1986), 291–349.

Clark, Eve, "From Gesture to Word: On the Natural History of Deixis in Language Acquisition," in *Human Growth and Development. Wolfson College Lectures 1976,* ed. J. Bruner and A. Garton (Oxford, 1978), 85–120.

Coleman, Janet, *Ancient and Medieval Memories. Studies in the Reconstruction of the Past* (Cambridge, 1992).

Colish, Marcia, L., *The Mirror of Language: A Study in the Medieval Theory of Knowledge,* rev. ed. (Lincoln Neb., 1983).

———*The Stoic Tradition from Antiquity to the Early Middle Ages,* vol. 2: *Stoicism in Christian Latin Thought through the Sixth Century* (Leiden, 1985).

Collart, Jean, "Saint Augustin grammarien dans le 'De Magistro,'" *REA* 17 (1971), 279–292.

*Collectanea Augustiniana. Mélanges T. J. van Bavel,* ed. B. Bruning, M. Lamberigts, and J. van Houten, 2 vols. (Leuven, 1990–1991).

Comeau, Marie, "Les prédications pascales de S. Augustin," *Recherches de sciences religieuses* 23 (1933), 257–282.

———*La rhétorique de saint Augustin d'après les Tractatus in Ioannem* (Paris, 1930).

*"Le Confessioni" di Agostino d'Hippona: Libri I–II,* commentary by L. F. Pizzolato, G. Geriotti, and F. de Capitani (Lectio Augustini. Settimana Agostiniana Pavese, ed. L. F. Pizzolato and G. Scanavino, Palermo, 1984); *Libri III–V,* commentary by J. Ries, A. Rigobello, and A. Mandouze (Palermo, 1984); *Libri VI–IX,* commentary by J. M. Rodriguez, G. Madec, M. G. Mara, and P. Siniscalco (Palermo, 1985); *Libri X–XIII,* commentary by A. Solignac, E. Corsini, J. Pépin, and A. di Giovanni (Palermo, 1987).

Congar, Yves M.-J., *Tradition and Traditions: An Historical and a Theological Essay,* (1960), trans. M. Naseby and T. Rainborough (New York 1967).

Connerton, Paul, *How Societies Remember* (Cambridge, 1989).

Consolino, Franca Ela, "Interlocutore divino e lettore terreni: La funzione-destinatorio nelle Confessioni di Agostino," *Materiali e discussioni per l'analisi dei testi classici* 6 (1981), 119–146.

Cordovani, Rinaldo, "Il 'De Catechizandis rudibus' di S. Agostino. Questioni di contenuto e di stile," *Augustinianum* 6 (1966), 489–527.

———"Le due città nel 'De catechizandis rudibus' di S. Agostino," *Augustinianum* 7 (1967), 419–447.

———"Lo stile nel 'De catechizandis rudibus' di S. Agostino," *Augustinianum* 8 (1968), 280–311.

Courcelle, Pierre, "Antécédents autobiographiques des *Confessions* de Saint Augustin," *Revue de philologie de littérature et d'histoire ancienne* 31 (1957), 23–51.

———*Les Confessions de saint Augustin dans la tradition littéraire. Antécédents et posterité* (Paris, 1963).

———*Connais-tu toi-même de Socrate à saint Bernard,* 3 vols. (Paris, 1974–75).

———"L'enfant et les 'sorts bibliques,'" *Vigiliae Christianae* 7 (1953), 194–220.

———"Les lacunes de la correspondence entre saint Augustin et Paulin de Nole," *Revue des études anciennes* 53 (1951), 253–300.

———*Late Latin Writers and Their Greek Sources* (1948), trans. H. E. Wedeck (Cambridge, Mass., 1969).

———"Litiges sur la lecture des 'Libri Platonicorum' par saint Augustin," *Augustiniana* 4 (1954), 225–239.

———"Nouveaux aspects du platonisme chez saint Ambroise," *Revue des études latines* 34 (1956), 220–239.

———"Possidius et les *Confessions* de saint Augustin. Emprunts et compléments," in *Mélanges Jules Lebreton,* vol. 1 *(Recherches de science religieuse* 29, 1951–52), 428–442.

———"Les premières *Confessions* de saint Augustin," *Revue des études latines* 21–22 (1943–44), 155–174.

———*Recherches sur les Confessions de saint Augustin,* (Paris, 1950; 2nd ed., Paris, 1968).

———"Source chrétienne et allusions païennes de l'épisode de 'Tolle-lege,'" *Revue d'histoire et de philosophie religieuses* 32 (1952), 171–200.

———"Tradition néo-platonicienne et traditions chrétiennes de la 'région de dissemblance' (Platon, *Politique* 273 d)," *Archives d'histoire doctrinale et littéraire du moyen âge,* Année 1957 (1958), 5–33.

———"Les 'voix' dans les Confessions de saint Augustin," *Hermes* 80 (1952), 31–46.

Couturier, C., "'Sacramentum' et 'mysterium' dans l'oeuvre de saint Augustin," in *Etudes augustiniennes* (1953), 161–332.

Cox, P., *Biography in Late Antiquity: A Quest for the Holy Man* (Berkeley, 1983).

Cranz, F. Edward, "The Development of Augustine's Ideas on Society before the Donatist Controversy," *Harvard Theological Review* 47 (1954), 255–316.

Cress, Donald A., "Hierius and St. Augustine's Account of the Lost 'De Pulchro et Apto': Confessions IV.13–15," *Augustinian Studies* 7 (1976), 153–163.

Cristiani, M., "L'évocation de l'enfance dans le 1er livre des 'Confessions.' Problèmes culturels et anthropologiques," *Le temps chrétien de la fin de l'antiquité au moyen âge—IIIe–XIIIe siècles* (Colloques Internationaux du Centre National de la Recherche Scientifique 604, Paris, 1984), 399–418.

Crosson, Frederick J., "The Structure of the *De magistro*," *REA* 35 (1989), 120–127.

Crouse, Robert, "*Recurrens in te unum*: The Pattern of St. Augustine's *Confessions*," *Studia Patristica* 14.3 (Berlin, 1976), 389–392.

———"St. Augustine's *De Trinitate*: Philosophical Method," *Studia Patristica* 16.2 (Berlin, 1985), 501–510.

Curtius, Ernst Robert, *European Literature and the Latin Middle Ages,* trans. W. R. Trask (Bollingen Foundation Series 36, Princeton, 1953).

Dahl, Axel, *Augustin und Plotin. Philosophische Untersuchungen zum Trinitätsproblem und zur Nuslehre* (Lund, 1945).

Daraki, Maria, "L'émergence du sujet singulier dans les Confessions d'Augustin," *Esprit* 5 (Feb. 1981), 95–115.

de Bruyne, Donatien, "L'Itala de Saint Augustin," *Revue bénédictine* 30 (1913), 294–314.

de Capitani, Franco, "Platone, Plotino, Porfirio e sant'Agostino sull'immortalità dell'anima intesa come vita," *Rivista di filosofia neo-scolastica* 37 (1984), 230–244.

Decret, François, *L'Afrique manichéenne (IVe–Ve siècles). Etude historique et doctrinale,* 2 vols. (*CEA, SA* 74–75, Paris, 1978).

———"Aspects de l'Eglise Manichéenne. Remarques sur le manuscrit de Tébessa," in *Signum Pietatis* (1989), 123–151.

———*Aspects du manichéisme dans l'Afrique romaine. Les controverses de Fortunatus, Faustus et Felix avec saint Augustin,* (*CEA, SA* 41, Paris, 1970).

Deferrari, Roy J., "St. Augustine's Method of Composing and Delivering Sermons," *American Journal of Philology* 43 (1922), 97–123, 193–219.

———"Verbatim Reports of Augustine's Unwritten Sermons," *Transactions and Proceedings of the American Philological Association* 46 (1915), 35–45.

de Ghellinck, J., *Patristique et moyen âge. Etudes d'histoire littéraire et doctrinale,* vol. 3: *Compléments à l'étude de la patristique* (Gembloux, 1948).

de Margerie, Bertrand, *Introduction à l'histoire de l'exégèse, vol. 3: Saint Augustin,* préface by A.-M. la Bonnardière (Collection "Initiations," Paris, 1983).

Dekkers, Eligius, "Les autographes des Pères latins," in *Colligere Fragmenta. Festschrift Alban Dold zum 70. Geburtstag am 7.7.1952,* ed. B. Fischer and V. Fiala (Texte und Arbeiten Herausgegeben durch die Erzabtei Beuron, 1.2, Beuron in Hohenzollern, 1952), 127–139.

———"Saint Augustin éditeur," in *Troisième centenaire de l'édition mauriste de saint Augustin. Communications présentées au colloque des 19 et 20 avril 1990* (*CEA, SA* 127, Paris, 1990), 235–244.

de Lubac, Henri, *Exégèse médiévale. Les quatre sens de l'écriture. Première partie,* vol. 1 (Théologie 41, Paris, 1959).

de la Peza, Edgardo, "El significado de 'cor' en san Agustín," *REA* 7 (1961), 339–368.

*"De Musica" di Agostino d'Ippona,* commentary by U. Pizzani and G. Milanese (Lectio Augustini. Settimana Agostiniana Pavese 5, ed. L. F. Pizzolato and G. Scanavino, Palermo, 1990).

de Plinval, Georges, "Aspects du déterminisme et de la liberté dans la doctrine de saint Augustin," *REA* 1 (1955), 345–378.

Derrida, Jacques, *De la grammatologie* (Paris, 1967).

Descartes, René, *Discours de la méthode. Texte et commentaire,* ed. E. Gilson (Paris, 1930).

di Capua, Francesco, "Osservazioni sulla lettera et sulla preghiera ad alta voce presso gli antichi," in *Scritti minori,* vol. 1 (Rome, 1959), 1–40.

————"Il ritmo prosaico in S. Agostino," in *Miscellanea Agostiniana,* vol. 2 (1931), 607–764.

di Giovanni, Alberto, "Creazione ed essere nelle 'Confessioni' di sant'Agostino," *REA* 20 (1974), 285–312.

————*La dialettica dell'amore. 'Uti-frui' nelle preconfessioni di Sant'Agostino* (Itinerari Critici 5, Rome, 1965).

————"Parola e fede nel dialogo interpersonale," *Rivista de filosofia neo-scolastica* 59 (1967), 498–520.

————"Per un'etica della parola," *Filosofia e vita* 9 (1968), 23–46.

de Vreese, L. C. P. J., *Augustinus en de Astrologie* (Diss., Maastricht, 1933).

Diggs, Bernard J., "St. Augustine against the Academicians," *Traditio* 7 (1949–1951), 73–93.

Dihle, A., *The Theory of the Will in Classical Antiquity* (Sather Classical Lectures 48, Berkeley, 1982).

Dillon, J., *The Middle Platonists* (Classical Life and Letters, London, 1977).

Dönt, Eugen, "Aufbau und Glaubwürdigkeit der Konfessionen und die Cassiciacumgespräche des Augustinus," *Wiener Studien,* n.s., 3 (1969), 181–197.

Dörrie, Heinrich, "Porphyrios als Mittler zwischen Plotin und Augustin," in *Antike und Orient im Mittelalter. Vorträge der Kölner Mediaevistentagungen 1956–1959,* ed. P. Wilpert (Miscellanea Mediaevalia 1, Berlin, 1962), 26–47.

Doignon, Jean, "Etat de questions relatives aux premiers Dialogues de Saint Augustin," in *Internationales Symposion* (1989), 47–86.

————"Les 'nobles disciplines' et le 'visage de la vérité' dans les premiers dialogues d'Augustin. Un commentaire de *Soliloques* 2,20,35," *Jahrbuch für Antike und Christentum* 27–28 (1984–85), 116–123.

————"La prière liminaire des *Soliloquia* dans la ligne philosophique des Dialogues de Cassiciacum," in *Augustiniana Traiectina* (1987), 85–105.

————"La problématique cicéronienne du protreptique du *De Libero Arbitrio* II, 35 de saint Augustin," *Latomus* 40 (1981), 807–817.

Dolbeau, F., "Sermons inédits de saint Augustin prêchés en 397," *Revue bénédictine* 101 (1991), 240–256.

Dombrowski, Daniel A., "Starnes on Augustine's Theory of Infancy: A Piagetian Critique," *Augustinian Studies* 11 (1980), 125–133.

Douais, C., "S. Augustin et la Bible," *Revue biblique* 2 (1893), 62–81, 351–377; 3 (1894), 110–135, 410–432.

Doucet, Dominique, "L'*Ars Memoriae* dans les *Confessions,*" *REA* 33 (1987), 49–69.

Drobner, Hubertus R., *Person-Exegese und Christologie bei Augustinus. Zur Herkunft der Formel "una Persona"* (Philosophia Patrum, Interpretations of Patristic Texts, 8, Leiden, 1986).

Duchrow, Ulrich, "Der Aufbau von Augustins Schriften *Confessiones* und *De trinitate*," *Zeitschrift für Theologie und Kirche* 62 (1965), 338–367.

———"*Signum* und *Superbia* beim jungen Augustin (386–390)," *REA* 7 (1961), 369–372.

———"Der Sogenannte psychologische Zeitbegriff Augustins im Verhältnis zur physikalischen und geschichtlichen Zeit," *Zeitschrift für Theologie und Kirche* 63 (1966), 267–288.

———*Sprachverständnis und biblischen Hören bei Augustin* (Hermeneutische Untersuchungen zur Theologie 5, Tübingen, 1965).

Dürig, Walter, "Disciplina. Eine Studie zum Bedeutungsumfang des Wortes in der Sprache der Liturgie und der Väter," *Sacris Erudiri* 4 (1952), 245–279.

Dulaey, Martine, *Le rêve dans la vie et la pensée de saint Augustin* (CEA, SA 50, Paris, 1973).

Dumeige, Gervais, "Dissemblance (Regio dissimilitudinis)," in *Dictionnaire de spiritualité, ascétique et mystique,* vol. 3 (Paris, 1956), 1330–46.

du Roy, Olivier, *L'intelligence de la foi en la Trinité selon saint Augustin. Genèse de sa théologie trinitaire jusqu'en 391* (CEA, SA 27, Paris, 1966).

Dyroff, Adolf, "Über Form und Begriffsgehalt der augustinischen Schrift De ordine," in *Aurelius Augustinus* (1930), 15–62.

Eggersdorfer, Franz X., *Der heilige Augustinus als Pädagoge und seine Bedeutung für die Geschichte der Bildung* (Strassburger Theologische Studien 8.3–4, Freiburg im Breisgau, 1907).

Einstein, Albert, *Relativity: The Special and General Theory: A Popular Exposition,* trans. R. W. Lawson (New York, 1961).

Eisenstein, Elizabeth L., *The Printing Revolution in Early Modern Europe* (Cambridge, 1983).

Ekman, Paul, "Facial Expression and Emotion," *American Psychologist* 48 (1993), 384–392.

Engels, J., "La doctrine du signe chez saint Augustin," *Studia Patristica* 6.4 (1962), 366–373.

Eno, Robert B., "Doctrinal Authority in Saint Augustine," *Augustinian Studies* 12 (1981), 133–172.

Erler, Michael, "*Philologia Medicans.* Wie die Epikureer die Texte ihres Meisters lasen," in *Vermittlung und Tradierung von Wissen in der griechischen Kultur,* ed. W. Kullmann and J. Althoff (Tübingen, 1993), 281–303.

Ermini, F., "Il 'psalmus contra partem Donati,'" in *Miscellanea Agostiniana,* vol. 2 (1931), 341–352.

Erneling, Christina, "Why First Language Learning Is Not Second Language Learning—Wittgenstein's Rejection of St. Augustine's Conception of Learning," *Interchange* 24 (1993), 341–351.

*Etudes augustiniennes,* ed. H. Rondet, M. Le Landais, A. Lauras, and C. Couturier (Theologie 28, Paris, 1953).

Evans, G. R., *Augustine on Evil* (Cambridge, 1982).

Fabre, P., *Essai sur la chronologie de l'oeuvre de saint Paulin de Nole* (Publications de la Faculté des lettres de l'université de Strasbourg 109, Paris, 1948).

———*Saint Paulin de Nole et l'amitié chrétienne* (Bibliothèque des Ecoles françaises d'Athènes et de Rome 167, Paris, 1949).

Fantham, Elaine, "Imitation and Evolution: The Discussion of Rhetorical Imitation in Cicero De Oratore 2.87–97 and Some Related Problems of Ciceronian Theory," *Classical Philology* 73 (1978), 1–16.

Feldmann, Erich, *Der Einfluss des Hortensius und des Manichäismus auf das Denken des jungen Augustinus von 373,* 2 vols. (Diss. Münster i. W., 1975).

————"Literarische und theologische Probleme der *Confessiones*," in *Internationales Symposion* (1989), 27–45.

Féret, H.-M., "Sacramentum-Res dans la langue théologique de S. Augustin," *Revue des sciences philosophiques et théologiques* 29 (1940), 218–243.

Ferrari, Leo C., *The Conversions of Saint Augustine* (Saint Augustine Lecture 1982, Villanova, 1984).

————"The Dreams of Monica in Augustine's 'Confessions,'" *Augustinian Studies* 10 (1979), 3–17.

————"'*Ecce audio vocem de vicina domo*' (*Conf.* 8, 12, 29)," *Augustiniana* 22 (1983), 232–245.

————"Isaiah and the Early Augustine," in *Collectanea Augustiniana*, vol. 2 (1991), 739–756.

————"Monica on the Wooden Ruler (*Conf.*, 3, 11, 19)," *Augustinian Studies* 6 (1975), 193–205.

————"Paul at the Conversion of Augustine (*Conf.* VIII, 12.29–30)," *Augustinian Studies* 11 (1980), 5–20.

————"The Pear-Theft in Augustine's 'Confessions,'" *REA* 16 (1970), 233–242.

————"The Theme of the Prodigal Son in Augustine's *Confessions*," *Recherches augustiniennes* 12 (1979), 105–118.

Fichter, Andrew, *Poets Historical: Dynastic Epic in the Renaissance* (New Haven, 1982).

Finaert, Joseph, *L'évolution littéraire de saint Augustin* (Collection d'Etudes Latines, Série Scientifique 17, Paris, 1939).

Fish, Stanley, *Self-Consuming Artifacts: The Experience of Seventeenth-Century Literature* (Berkeley, 1972).

Flasch, Kurt, *Augustin. Einführung in sein Denken* (Stuttgart, 1980).

Flores, Ralph, "Reading and Speech in St. Augustine's Confessions," *Augustinian Studies* 6 (1975), 1–13.

Fodor, Jerry, *The Language of Thought* (Cambridge, Mass., 1975).

Folliet, Georges, "Aux origines de l'ascétisme et du cénobitisme africain," in *Saint Martin et son temps. Mémorial du XVIe centenaire des débuts du monachisme en Gaule, 361–1961* (Studia Anselmiana 46, Rome, 1961), 25–44.

————"La correspondance entre Augustin et Nébridius," in *L'opera letteraria di Agostino tra Cassiciacum e Milano. Agostino nelle terre di Ambrogio (1–4 ottobre 1986)* (Augustiniana, Testi e Studi 2, Palermo, 1987), 191–215.

————"'Deificari in otio.' Augustin, Epistula 10,2," *R Aug* 2 (1962), 225–236.

Fontaine, Jacques, "La pédagogie augustinienne des rhythmes du temps dans les *Enarrationes in Psalmos*," in *Le temps chrétien de la fin de l'antiquité au moyen âge—IIIe–XIIIe siècles* (Colloques Internationaux du Centre National de la Recherche Scientifique 604, Paris, 1984), 369–382.

————"Sens et valeur des images dans les '*Confessions*,'" in *AM* (1954), vol. 1, 117–126.

Fontanier, J.-M., "Sur le traité *De pulchro et apto*: Convenance, beauté et adaptation," *Revue des sciences philosophiques et théologiques* 73 (1989), 413–421.

Forguson, Lynd, and Alison Gopnik, "The Ontogeny of Common Sense," in *Developing Theories of Mind*, ed. J. W. Astington, P. L. Harris, and D. R. Olsen (Cambridge, 1988), 226–243.

Forman, Robert J., "Augustine's Music: 'Keys' to the *Logos*," in *Augustine on Music: An Interdisciplinary Collection of Essays*, ed. Richard C. LaCroix (Studies in the History and Interpretation of Music 6, Lewiston, N.Y., 1988), 17–27.

Fortin, Ernest L., "Augustine and the Problem of Christian Rhetoric," *Augustinian Studies* 5 (1974), 85–100.

———"Augustine, Thomas Aquinas and the Problem of Natural Law," *Mediaevalia* 4 (1978), 179–208.

———"The Political Implications of St. Augustine's Theory of Conscience," *Augustinian Studies* 1 (1970), 133–152.

Foucault, Michel, *Histoire de la sexualité,* vol. 3: *Le souci de soi* (Paris, 1984).

———"Technologies of the Self," in *Technologies of the Self: A Seminar with Michel Foucault,* ed. L. H. Martin, H. Gutman, and P. H. Hutton (Amherst, Mass., 1988), 16–49.

Fredouille, Jean-Claude, "Les *Confessions* d'Augustin, autobiographie au présent," in *L'invention de l'autobiographie d'Hésiode à saint Augustin,* ed. M.-F. Baslez, P. Hoffmann, and L. Pernot (Actes du deuxième colloque de l'Equipe de recherche sur l'hellénisme post-classique, Paris, Ecole Normale Supérieure, 14–16 juin 1990, Paris, 1993), 167–178.

Fredriksen, Paula, "Beyond the Body/Soul Dichotomy. Augustine on Paul against the Manicheans and the Pelagians," *R Aug* 23 (1988), 87–114.

———"Paul and Augustine: Conversion Narratives, Orthodox Traditions, and the Retrospective Self," *Journal of Theological Studies,* n.s., 37 (1986), 3–34.

Frend, W. H. C., *The Donatist Church. A Movement of Protest in Roman North Africa* (Oxford, 1952).

———"The Gnostic-Manichaean Tradition in Roman North Africa," *Journal of Ecclesiastical History* 4 (1953), 13–26.

———"Manichaeism in the Struggle between Saint Augustine and Petilian of Constantine," in *AM* (1954), vol. 2, 859–866.

Gadamer, Hans-Georg, *Wahrheit und Methode,* 2nd ed. (Tübingen, 1965).

Geerlings, Wilhelm, *Christus Exemplum. Studien zur Christologie und Christusverkündigung Augustins* (Tübinger theologische Studien 13, Mainz, 1978).

Gerhardsson, Bitger, *Memory and Manuscript. Oral Tradition and Written Transmission in Rabbinic Judaism and Early Christianity* (Acta Seminarii Neotestamentici Upsaliensis 22, Uppsala, 1961).

Gessel, Wilhelm, *Eucharistische Gemeinschaft bei Augustinus* (Cassiciacum 21, Würzburg, 1966).

Geyser, Joseph, "Die Theorie Augustins von der Selbsterkenntnis der menschlichen Seele," in *Aus der Geisteswelt des Mittelalters. Studien und Texte Martin Grabmann zur Vollendung des 60. Lebensjahres von Freunden und Schülern Gewidmet,* ed. A. Lang, J. Lechner, and M. Schmaus (Beiträge zur Geschichte der Philosophie und Theologie des Mittelalters. Texte und Untersuchungen, Supplementband 3.1, Münster, 1935), 170–187.

Gigon, Olof, "Augustins De utilitate credendi," in *Catalepton. Festschrift für Bernhard Wyss zum 80. Geburtstag,* ed. C. Schäublin (Basel, 1985), 138–157.

Gilson, Etienne, *The Christian Philosophy of Saint Augustine,* trans. L. E. M. Lynch (New York, 1960).

———"Egypte ou Grèce," *Mediaeval Studies* 8 (1946), 43–52.

———*Etudes sur le rôle de la pensée médiévale dans la formation du système cartésien* (Etudes de philosophie médiévale 13, Paris, 1930).

———*History of Christian Philosophy in the Middle Ages* (London, 1955).

———"Notes sur l'être et le temps chez saint Augustin," *Recherches augustiniennes* 2 (1962), 205–223.

————*Philosophie et incarnation selon saint Augustin* (Conférence Albert le Grand 1947, Montreal, 1947).

————*Discours . . .* (1930): see Descartes.

Gnoli, Gherardo, "Manichaeism: An Overview," in *The Encyclopedia of Religion,* ed. M. Eliade, vol. 9 (New York, 1987), 161–170.

Goldschmidt, V., *Le système stoïcien et l'idée de temps,* 3rd ed. (Paris, 1977).

Gonzague, Marie de, "Un correspondant de Saint Augustin: Nebridius," in *AM* (1954), vol. 1, 93–99.

Goody, Jack, *The Interface between the Written and the Oral* (Studies in Literacy, Family, Culture and the State, Cambridge, 1987).

Gouhier, Henri, *La pensée métaphysique de Descartes* (Bibliothèque d'Histoire de la Philosophie, Paris, 1962).

Grabmann, Martin, "Der Einfluss des heiligen Augustinus auf die Verwertung und Bewertung der Antike im Mittelalter," in *Mittalterliches Geistesleben,* vol. 2 (Munich, 1936), 1–36.

Grandgeorge, L., *Saint Augustin et le Néo-platonisme* (Bibliothèque de l'Ecole des Hautes Etudes, Sciences Religieuses 8, Paris, 1896).

Gray, Douglas, "Saint Augustine and Medieval Literature I–II," in *Saint Augustine and His Influence in the Middle Ages,* ed. E. B. King and J. T. Schaefer (Sewanee Medieval Studies 3, Sewanee, Tenn., 1988), 19–58.

Green, William M., "Augustine on the Teaching of History," *University of California Publications in Classical Philology* 12 (1944), 315–332.

Grondijs, L. H., "Analyse du manichéisme numidien au IVe siècle," in *AM* (1955), vol. 3, 391–410.

Grotz, Klaus, *Die Einheit der "Confessiones." Warum bringt Augustin in den letzten Büchern seiner "Confessiones" eine Auslegung der Genesis?* (Diss. Tübingen, 1970).

Guitton, Jean, *Le temps et l'éternité chez Plotin et Saint Augustin,* 4th ed. (Bibliothèque de l'Histoire de la Philosophie, Paris, 1971).

Gunermann, Hans Heinrich, "Literarische und philosophische Tradition im ersten Tagesgespräch von Augustinus' *De ordine,*" *R Aug* 9 (1973), 183–226.

Gusdorf, Georges, "Conditions and Limits of Autobiography," in Olney (1980), 28–48.

Gwynn, Aubrey, *Roman Education from Cicero to Quintilian* (Oxford, 1926).

Haas, Alois, "Streiflichter auf die Struktur der Bekehrung im Geiste Augustins," in *Unterwegs zur Einheit. Festschrift für Heinrich Stirnimann,* ed. J. Brantschen and P. Selvatico (Fribourg, 1980), 225–240.

Hadot, Ilsetraut, *Arts libéraux et philosophie dans la pensée antique* (*CEA, SA* 107, Paris, 1984).

————"Erziehung und Bildung bei Augustin," in *Internationales Symposion* (1989), 99–130.

Hadot, Pierre, *La citadelle intérieure. Introduction aux "Pensées" de Marc Aurèle* (Paris, 1992).

————"L'image de la Trinité dans l'âme chez Victorinus et chez saint Augustin," *Studia Patristica* 6 (Berlin, 1962), 409–442.

————"Etre, vie, pensée chez Plotin et avant Plotin," in *Les sources de Plotin* (Entretiens sur l'Antiquité classique 5, Vandoeuvres-Geneva, 1960), 107–141.

————*Exercices spirituels et philosophie antique,* 2nd ed. (*CEA, SA* 118, Paris, 1987).

————"Introduction," in Marius Victorinus, *Traités théologiques sur la trinité* ed., Paul Henry and Pierre Hadot (Sources Chrétiennes 68–69, Paris, 1960).

————*Marius Victorinus. Recherches sur sa vie et ses oeuvres* (Paris, 1971).

————"La philosophie antique. Une éthique ou une pratique?" in *Problèmes de morale antique. Sept études,* ed. P. Demont (Université d'Amiens, Faculté des Lettres, Centre de Recherches sur l'Antiquité grecque et latine, 1993), 7–37.

——"Platon et Plotin dans trois sermons de saint Ambroise," *Revue des études latines* 34 (1956), 202–220.

——*Plotinus or The Simplicity of Vision,* trans. M. Chase, intro. A. I. Davidson (Chicago, 1993).

——*Porphyre et Victorinus,* 2 vols (*CEA, SA* 32–33, Paris, 1968).

——"La présentation du Platonisme par Augustin," in *Kerygma und Logos. Beiträge zu den geistesgeschichtlichen Beziehungen zwischen Antike und Christentum. Festschrift für Carl Andresen zum 70. Geburtstag* (Göttingen, 1979), 272–279.

——"Réflexions sur la notion de 'culture de soi,'" in *Michel Foucault philosophe. Rencontre internationale, Paris, 9, 10, 11 janvier 1988* (Paris, 1989), 261–268.

Hagendahl, Harald, *Augustine and the Latin Classics:* vol. 1: *Testimonia, with a Contribution on Varro by Burkhart Cardauns;* vol 2: *Augustine's Attitude* (Studia Graeca et Latina Gothoburgensia 20.1–2, Stockholm, 1967).

——"Die Bedeutung der Stenographie für die spätlateinische christliche Literatur," *Jahrbuch für Antike und Christentum* 14 (1971), 24–38.

Hahn, Traugott, *Tyconius-Studien. Ein Beitrag zur Kirchen- und Dogmengeschichte des 4. Jahrhunderts* (Studien zur Geschichte der Theologie und der Kirche 6.2, Leipzig, 1900).

Hallett, Garth, *A Companion to Wittgenstein's "Philosophical Investigations"* (Ithaca, 1977).

Halliburton, R. J., "The Concept of the 'Fuga saeculi' in St. Augustine," *Downside Review* 85 (1967), 249–261.

——"The Inclination to Retirement. The Retreat of Cassiciacum and the 'Monastery' of Tagaste," *Studia Patristica* 5.3 (Berlin, 1962), 329–340.

Halporn, James W., "Saint Augustine Sermon 104 and the *Epulae Venerales,*" *Jahrbuch für Antike und Christentum* 19 (1976), 82–108.

Hanson-Smith, Elizabeth, "Augustine's *Confessions:* The Concrete Referent," *Philosophy and Literature* 2 (1978), 176–189.

Harpham, Geoffrey Galt, *The Ascetic Imperative in Culture and Criticism* (Chicago, 1987).

Havelock, Eric A., *Preface to Plato* (Cambridge, Mass., 1963).

Hebblethwaite, P., "St. Augustine's Interpretation of Matthew 5, 17," *Studia Patristica* 16.2 (Berlin, 1985), 511–516.

Heidegger, Martin, *The Basic Problems of Phenomenology,* trans. and ed. Alfred Hofstadter (Bloomington, 1982).

Hellemo, Geir, *Adventus Domini. Eschatological Thought in 4th-Century Apses and Catecheses* (Supplements to Vigiliae Christianae, vol. 5, Leiden, 1989).

Hendrikx, E., "Astrologie, Waarzeggerij en Parapsychologie bij Augustinus," in *Augustiniana . . . 354–1954,* (1954), 109–136.

Hennings, Ralph, *Der Briefwechsel zwischen Augustinus und Hieronymus und ihr Streit um den Kanon des Alten Testaments und die Auslegung von Gal. 2, 11–14* (Supplements to Vigiliae Christianae vol. 21, Leiden, 1994).

Henry, Paul, "Augustine and Plotinus," *Journal of Theological Studies* 38 (1937), 1–23.

——*Plotin et l'Occident. Firmicus Maternus, Marius Victorinus, Saint Augustin, et Macrobe* (Spicilegium Sacrum Lovaniense. Etudes et Documents 15, Louvain, 1934).

——*Saint Augustine on Personality: The Saint Augustine Lecture 1959* (New York, 1960).

——*La vision d'Ostie. Sa place dans la vie et l'oeuvre de saint Augustin* (Essais d'art et de philosophie, Paris, 1938).

Henry, Paul, and Pierre Hadot *Marii Victorini Opera I: Opera Theologica* (*CSEL* 83.1 1971).

Herzog, Reinhart, "*Non in sua uoce.* Augustins Gespräch mit Gott in den *Confessiones*—Voraussetzungen und Folgen," in *Das Gespräch,* ed. K. Stierle and R. Warning (Poetik und Hermeneutik 11, Munich, 1984), 213–250.

Hessen, Johannes, *Augustins Metaphysik der Erkenntnis,* 2nd ed. (Leiden, 1960).

Hill, Edmund, "De doctrina christiana. A Suggestion," *Studia Patristica* 6 (Berlin, 1962), 443–446.

————"St. Augustine's *De Trinitate.* The Doctrinal Significance of Its Structure," *REA* 17 (1973), 277–286.

Hillgarth, J. N., *Ramon Lull and Lullism in Fourteenth-Century France* (Oxford-Warburg Studies, Oxford, 1971).

Hök, Gösta, "Augustin und die antike Tugendlehre," *Kerygma und Dogma* 6 (1960), 104–130.

Hof, Hans, "Conscientia och lex in corde scripta enligt Augustinus," *Svensk Theologisk Kvartalskrift* 40 (1964), 183–195.

Hoffmann, Manfred, *Der Dialog bei den christlichen Schriftstellern der ersten vier Jahrhunderte* (Texte und Untersuchungen 96, Berlin, 1966).

Hoffmann, Wilhelm, *Augustinus. Das Problem seiner Daseinsauslegung* (Aevum Christianum 6, Münster, 1963).

Holl, Adolf, *Die Welt der Zeichen bei Augustin. Religionsphänomenologische Analyse des 13. Buches der Confessiones* (Wiener Beiträge zur Theologie 2, Vienna, 1963).

Holl, Karl, "Augustins innere Entwicklung," in *Gesammelte Aufsätze zur Kirchengeschichte,* vol. 3 (1922; reprint, Darmstadt, 1965), 54–116.

Holte, Ragnar, *Béatitude et Sagesse. Saint Augustin et le problème de la fin de l'homme dans la philosophie ancienne* (*CEA, SA* 14, 1962).

*Homo Spiritalis. Festgabe für Luc Verheijen OSA zu seinem 70. Geburtstag,* ed. C. Mayer with K. H. Chelius (Cassiciacum 38, Würzburg, 1987).

Hornstein, Herbert, "Immaterialität und Reflexion. Eine Studie zur Geistphilosophie des hl. Augustinus," in *Erkenntnis und Verantwortung. Festschrift für Theodor Litt,* ed. H. Derbolav and F. Nicolin (Düsseldorf, 1960), 285–300.

Huber, Carlo E., *Anamnesis bei Plato* (Pullacher philosophische Forschungen 6, Munich, 1964).

Hübner, Wolfgang, "Der *ordo* der Realien in Augustinus Frühdialog *De ordine,*" *REA* 33 (1987), 23–48.

————"Die *praetoria memoriae* im zehnten Buch der *Confessiones.* Vergilisches bei Augustin," *REA* 27 (1981), 245–263.

Huftier, Maurice, "Libre arbitre, liberté et peché chez saint Augustin," *Recherches de théologie ancienne et médiévale* 33 (1966), 176–281.

Hus, Alain, *Docere et les verbes de la famille de docere* (Publications de la Faculté des Lettres et Sciences Humaines de Rennes, Paris, 1965).

Husserl, Edmund, *Cartesian Meditations. An Introduction to Phenomenology,* (1929), trans. D. Cairns, 5th ed. (The Hague, 1973).

Illich, Ivan, *In the Vineyard of the Text: A Commentary to Hugh's "Didascalicon"* (Chicago, 1993).

Ingarden, Roman, *The Cognition of the Literary Work of Art,* (1968), trans. R. A. Crowley and K. R. Olson (Northwestern University Studies in Phenomenology and Existential Philosophy, Evanston, 1973).

————*The Literary Work of Art: An Investigation on the Borderlines of Ontology, Logic, and Theory of Literature, with an Appendix on the Functions of Language in the Theater* (1965), trans. with an introduction by George G. Graborwicz (Northwestern University Studies in Phenomenology and Existential Philosophy, Evanston, Ill., 1973).

Ingram, David, "Sensori-Motor Intelligence in Language," in *Action, Gesture and Symbol. The Emergence of Language,* ed. A. Lock (London, 1978), 261–290.

*Internationales Symposion über den Stand der Augustinus-Forschung vom 12. bis 16 April 1987 im Schloss Ravischholzhausen der Justus-Liebig Üniversität Giessen,* ed. C. Mayer and K. H. Chelius (Cassiciacum 39.1, "Res et Signa," Giessener Augustinus Studien 1, Würzburg, 1989).

Inwood, Brad, *Ethics and Human Action in Early Stoicism* (Oxford, 1985).

Irvine, Martin, *The Making of Textual Culture. 'Grammatica' and Literary Theory, 350–1100* (Cambridge Studies in Medieval Literature 19, Cambridge, 1994).

Istace, Gérard, "Le livre Ier du 'De doctrina christiana' de saint Augustin. Organisation synthéthique et méthode mise en oeuvre," *Ephemerides Theologicae Lovanienses* 32 (1956), 289–330.

Jackson, A. V. Williams, *Researches in Manichaeism with Special Reference to the Turfan Fragments* (New York, 1932).

Jackson, B. Darrell, trans. and ed., *Augustine. "De Dialectica"* (Synthese Historical Library 16, Dordrecht, 1975).

————"The Theory of Signs in St. Augustine's *De doctrina christiana,*" *REA* 15 (1969), 9–49.

Jansen, Bernhard, "Zur Lehre des hl. Augustinus von dem Erkennen der Rationes aeternae," in *Aurelius Augustinus* (1930), 111–136.

Jansen, François, "Saint Augustin et la rhétorique," *Nouvelle revue théologique* 57 (1930), 282–297.

Javelet, Robert, *Image et ressemblance au douzième siècle de saint Anselme à Alain de Lille,* 2 vols. (Paris, 1967).

Johnson, Carla Nils, "Theory of Mind and Structure of Conscious Experience," in *Developing Theories of Mind,* ed. J. W. Astington, P. L. Harris, and D. R. Olsen (Cambridge, 1988), 47–63.

Johnson, Douglas, "*Verbum* in the Early Augustine," *R Aug* 8 (1972), 25–53.

Jolivet, Régis, "La doctrine augustinienne de l'illumination," in *Mélanges augustiniens publiés à l'occasion du XVe centenaire de saint Augustin* (Paris, 1931), 52–172.

————*Le problème du mal d'après saint Augustin* (Paris, 1936).

Joly, Robert, "Curiositas," *L'antiquité classique* 30 (1961), 33–44.

Jordan, Mark D., "Words and Word: Incarnation and Signification in Augustine's *De Doctrina Christiana,*" *Augustinian Studies* 11 (1980), 177–196.

Jordan, Robert, "Time and Contingency in St. Augustine," *The Review of Metaphysics* 8 (1954–55), 394–417; reprinted in Markus (1972), 255–279.

Jubany, Narciso, "San Agustín y la formación oratoria cristiana," *Analecta Sacra Tarraconensia* 15 (1942), 9–14.

Kälin, Bernhard, *Die Erkenntnislehre des hl. Augustinus* (Beilage zum Jahresbericht der kantonalen Lehranstalt Sarnen 1920–21, Sarnen, 1921).

Kahn, Helmut, "Die Bekenntnisse des heiligen Augustin als literarische Werk," *Stimmen der Zeit* 4 (1968), 223–238.

Kaiser, Hermann-Josef, *Augustinus. Zeit und "Memoria"* (Abhandlungen zur Philosophie, Psychologie und Pädagogik 67, Bonn, 1969).

Kantorowicz, Ernst H., *The King's Two Bodies: A Study in Mediaeval Political Theology* (Princeton, 1957).

Kaster, Robert A., *Guardians of Language: The Grammarian and Society in Late Antiquity* (The Transformation of the Classical Heritage 11, Berkeley, 1988).

Katô, Takeshi, "Melodia interior. Sur le traité *De pulchro et apto*," *REA* 12 (1966), 229–240.

Kelly, Louis G., "Saint Augustine and Saussurean Linguistics," *Augustinian Studies* 6 (1975), 45–64.

Kenney, E. J., "Books and Readers in the Roman World," in *The Cambridge History of Classical Literature,* vol. 2: *Latin Literature,* ed. E. J. Kenney and W. V. Clausen (Cambridge, 1982), 3–32.

Kermode, Frank, *The Genesis of Secrecy: On the Interpretation of Narrative* (Cambridge, Mass., 1979).

Keseling, Paul, "Augustin und Quintilian," in *AM* (1954), vol. 1, 201–204.

Kevane, E., "Augustine's *De doctrina christiana:* A Treatise on Christian Education," *R Aug* 4 (1966), 97–133.

Kienzler, Klaus, "Der Aufbau der 'Confessiones' des Augustinus im Spiegel der Bibelzitate," *R Aug* 24 (1989), 123–164.

Kleinberg, Aviad M., "*De Agone Christiano:* The Preacher and His Audience," *Journal of Theological Studies,* n.s., 38 (1987), 16–33.

Klimheit, Hans-Joachim, *Manichaean Art and Calligraphy* (Iconography of Religions 20, Leiden, 1982).

Knauer, Georg Nicolaus, "Peregrinatio Animae (Zur Frage der Einheit der augustinischen Konfessionen)," *Hermes* 85 (1957), 216–248.

———*Psalmenzitate in Augustins Konfessionen* (Göttingen, 1955).

———"*Sarabara* (Dan. 3,94(27) bei Aug. mag. 10,33–11,27," *Glotta* 33 (1954), 100–118.

Kneale, William, and Martha Kneale, *The Development of Logic* (Oxford, 1962).

Knox, Bernard M. W., "Silent Reading in Antiquity," *Greek, Roman and Byzantine Studies* 9 (1968), 421–435.

Kobusch, Theo, "Das Christentum als die Religion der Wahrheit. Überlegungen zu Augustins Begriff des Kultus," *REA* 29 (1983), 97–128.

Koenen, Ludwig, "Augustine and Manichaeism in Light of the Cologne Mani Codex," *Illinois Classical Studies* 3 (1978), 154–195.

Koep, Leo, *Das himmlische Buch in Antike und Christentum. Eine religiongeschichtliche Untersuchung zur altchristlichen Bildersprache* (Theophaneia. Beiträge zur Religions- und Kirchengeschichte des Altertums 8, Bonn, 1952).

Körner, Franz, "Abstraktion oder Illumination? Das ontologische Problem des augustinischen Sinneserkenntnis," *R Aug* 2 (1962), 81–109.

———*Das Sein und der Mensch. Die existenzielle Seinsentdeckung des jungen Augustin* (Symposion, philosophische Schriftenreihe, Freiburg, 1959).

———"Deus in homine videt. Das Subjekt des menschlichen Erkennens nach der Lehre Augustins," *Philosophisches Jahrbuch des Görres-Gesellschaft* 64 (1956), 166–217.

———*Vom Sein und Sollen des Menschen. Die existentialontologischen Grundlagen der Ethik in augustinischen Sicht* (CEA, SA 16, Paris, 1963).

Kretzmann, Norman, "Semantics, History of," in *Encyclopedia of Philosophy* (New York, 1967), vol. 7, 358–406.

Kristeller, Paul Oskar, "Augustine and the Early Renaissance," in *Studies in Renaissance*

*Thought and Letters* (Storia e Letteratura, Raccolta di Studi e Testi 54, Rome, 1956), 355–372.

Kunzelmann, A., "Augustins Predigttägigkeit," in *Aurelius Augustinus* (1930), 155–168.

——"Die Chronologie der Sermones des hl. Augustinus," in *Miscellanea Agostiniana,* vol. 2 (1931), 417–520.

Kusch, Horst, "Studien über Augustinus, I. Trinitarisches in den Büchern 2–4 und 10–13 der Confessiones," in *Festschrift Franz Dornseiff zum 65. Geburtstag,* ed. H. Kusch (Leipzig, 1953), 124–183.

Labhardt, André, "Curiositas. Notes sur l'histoire d'un mot et d'une notion," *Museum Helveticum* 17 (1960), 206–224.

La Bonnardière, Anne-Marie, "Anima iusti sedes Sapientiae dans l'oeuvre de saint Augustin," in *Epektasis. Mélanges patristiques offerts au Cardinal Jean Daniélou,* ed. J. Fontaine and C. Kannengiesser (Paris, 1972), 111–120.

——"Augustin a-t-il utilisé la 'Vulgate' de Jérôme," in *Saint Augustin et la Bible,* (Bible de Tous les Temps 3, Paris, 1986), 303–312.

——*Biblia Augustiniana A. T.: Le livre de la Sagesse* (CEA, SA 42, Paris, 1970).

——"L'initiation biblique d'Augustin," in *Saint Augustin et la Bible* (Bible de Tous les Temps 3, Paris, 1986), 27–47.

——*Recherches de chronologie augustinienne* (CEA, SA 23 Paris, 1965).

Lacey, Hugh M., "Empiricism and Augustine's Problems about Time," *Review of Metaphysics* 22 (1968), 219–245; reprinted in Markus (1972), 280–308.

Ladner, Gerhart B., *The Idea of Reform: Its Impact on Christian Thought and Action in the Age of the Fathers* (Cambridge, Mass., 1959).

——"St. Augustine's Conception of the Reformation of Man to the Image of God," in *AM* (1954), vol. 2, 867–878.

Laín, Entralgo Pedro, *The Therapy of the Word in Classical Antiquity,* trans. and ed. L. J. Rather and J. Sharp (New Haven, 1970).

Lambot, C., "Lettre inédite de S. Augustin relative au 'De Civitate Dei,'" *Revue bénédictine* 51 (1939), 109–121.

——"Texte complété et amendé du 'Psalmus contra partem Donati' de saint Augustin," *Revue bénédictine* 47 (1935), 312–330.

Lamirande, Emilien, "Quand Monique, la mère d'Augustin, prend la parole," in *Signum Pietatis* (1989), 3–19.

Lampey, Erich, "Das Zeitproblem nach den Bekenntnissen Augustins," *Wissenschaft und Weisheit* 22 (1959), 1–16, 119–148, 190–203.

Lapeyre, G. G., "Saint Augustin et Carthage," in *Miscellanea Agostiniana,* vol. 2 (1931), 92–148.

Lauras, A., and H. Rondet, "Le thème des deux cités dans l'oeuvre de saint Augustin," in *Etudes augustiniennes* (1953), 99–160.

Law, Vivien A., "St. Augustine's *De Grammatica*: Lost or Found?" *R Aug* 19 (1984), 155–183.

Lawless, George P., *Augustine of Hippo and His Monastic Rule* (Oxford, 1987).

——"Interior Peace in the *Confessions* of St. Augustine," *REA* 26 (1980), 45–61.

Leclercq, Jean, *The Love of Learning and the Desire for God: A Study of Monastic Culture,* trans. C. Misrahi (New York, 1961).

Legewie, "Die körperliche Konstitution und die Krankheiten Augustins," in *Miscellanea Agostiniana,* vol. 2 (1931), 5–21.

Lehmann, Paul, "Autobiographies of the Middle Ages," *Transactions of the Royal Historical Society*, 5th ser., 3 (1953), 41–52.

Le Landais, Maurice, "Deux années de prédication de saint Augustin. Introduction à la lecture de l'*In Joannem*," in *Etudes augustiniennes* (1953), 8–95.

Lerer, Seth, *Boethius and Dialogue: Literary Method in "The Consolation of Philosophy"* (Princeton, 1985).

Lieu, Samuel N. C., "An Early Byzantine Formula for the Renunciation of Manichaeism. The *Capita VII Contra Manichaeos* of 'Zacharias of Mitylene.' Introduction, Text, Translation, and Commentary," *Jahrbuch für Antike und Christentum* 26 (1988), 152–218.

————*Manichaeism in the Later Roman Empire and Medieval China*, 2nd ed. (Wissenschaftliche Untersuchungen zum Neuen Testament 3, Tübingen, 1992).

Liuzzi, Tiziana, "Tempo e memoria in Agostino. Dalle 'Confessioni' al 'De Trinitate,'" *Rivista di storia della filosofia* 39 (1984), 35–60.

Lloyd, A. C., "Nosce Teipsum and Conscientia," *Archiv für Geschichte der Philosophie* 46 (1964), 188–200.

————"On Augustine's Concept of a Person," in Markus (1972), 191–205.

Lods, Marc, "La personne du Christ dans la 'conversion' de saint Augustin," *R Aug* 11 (1976), 3–34.

Löhrer, Magnus, *Der Glaubensbegriff des hl. Augustinus in seinen ersten Schriften bis zu den Confessiones* (Einsiedeln, 1954).

————"Glaube und Heilsgeschichte in De Trinitate Augustins," *Freiburger Zeitschrift für Philosophie und Theologie* 4 (1957), 385–419.

Löwith, Karl. "Wissen und Glauben," in *AM* (1954), vol. 1, 403–410.

Long, A. A., *Problems in Stoicism* (London, 1971).

Longpré, Ephrem, "S. Augustin et la pensée franciscaine," *La France franciscaine* 15 (1932), 1–76.

Lorenz, Rudolf, "Fruitio dei bei Augustin," *Zeitschrift für Kirchengeschichte* 63 (1950–51), 75–132.

————"Gnade und Erkenntnis bei Augustinus," *Zeitschrift für Kirchengeschichte* 75 (1964), 21–78.

————"Die Herkunft des augustinischen *frui deo*," *Zeitschrift für Kirchengeschichte* 64 (1952–53), 34–60.

————"Die wissenschaftslehre Augustins," *Zeitschrift für Kirchengeschichte* 67 (1955–56), 29–60, 213–251.

Louth, Andrew, *The Origins of the Christian Mystical Tradition from Plato to Denys* (Oxford, 1981).

Lütcke, Karl-Heinrich, *"Auctoritas" bei Augustin. Mit einer Einleitung zur römischen Vorgeschichte des Begriffs* (Tübinger Beiträge zur Altertumswissenschaft 44, Stuttgart, 1968).

Luongo, Gennaro, "Autobiografia ed esegesi biblica nelle *Confessioni* di Agostino," *La parola del passato* 167 (1976), 286–306.

MacMullen, Ramsay, "A Note on *Sermo Humilis*," *Journal of Theological Studies* 17 (1966), 108–112.

Madec, Goulven, "Analyse de *De magistro*," *REA* 21 (1975), 63–71.

————"Augustin et Porphyre. Ebauche d'un bilan des recherches et des conjectures," in ΣΟΦΙΗΣ *"Chercheurs de sagesse." Hommage à Jean Pépin (CEA, SA* 131, Paris, 1992), 367–382.

————"Augustin prêtre. Quelques notes pour la célébration d'un 16e centenaire 391–1991," in *De Tertullien aux Mozarabes. Mélanges offerts à Jacques Fontaine (CEA, SA* 132, Paris, 1992), vol. 1, 185–199.

————"Christus," in *AL* 1.5/6 (1992), 845–908.

————"Christus, scientia et sapientia nostra. Le principe de cohérence de la doctrine augustinienne," *R Aug* 10 (1975), 77–85.

————"Connaissance de Dieu et action de grâces. Essai sur les citations de l'Ep. aux Romains I,18–25 dans l'oeuvre de saint Augustin," *R Aug* 2 (1963), 273–309.

————"Le communisme spirituel," in *Homo Spiritalis* (1987), 225–239.

————"La conversion d'Augustin. Intériorité et communauté," *Lumen Vitae* 42 (1987), 184–194.

————"La conversion et les Confessions," in *Augustin. Le message de la foi,* ed. G. Madec (Paris, 1987), 17–31.

————"La délivrance de l'esprit (Confessions VII)," in *"Le Confessioni," Libri VI–IX,* (1985), 45–69.

————"Les embarras de la citation," *Freiburger Zeitschrift für Philosophie und Theologie* 29 (1982), 361–372.

————"L'historicité des *Dialogues* de Cassiciacum, 386–1986," *REA* 32 (1986), 207–231.

————"L'*Hortensius* de Cicéron dans les livres XIII–XIV du *De Trinitate*," *REA* 15 (1969), 167–173.

————"'In te supra me.' Le sujet dans les *Confessions* de saint Augustin," *Revue de l'Institut Catholique de Paris* 28 (1988), 45–63.

————"Le néoplatonisme dans la conversion d'Augustin. Etat d'une question centenaire (depuis Harnack et Boissier, 1888)," in *Internationales Symposion* (1989), 9–25.

————"Notes sur l'intelligence augustinienne de la foi," *REA* 17 (1971), 119–142.

————*La patrie et la voie. Le Christ dans la vie et la pensée de saint Augustin* (Jésus et Jésus Christ 36, Paris, 1989).

————"Pour l'interprétation de *Contra Academicos* II, II, 5," *REA* 17 (1971), 322–328.

————*Saint Ambroise et la philosophie (CEA, SA* 61, Paris, 1974).

————"Saint Augustin est-il le malin génie de l'Europe," in *Imaginer l'Europe,* ed. P. Koslowski (Passages, Paris, 1992), 279–290.

————*Saint Augustin et la philosophie. Notes critiques* (Association André Robert, Institut Catholique, Paris, 1992).

————"Si Plato uiueret . . . (Augustin, *De uera religione* 3.3)," in *Néoplatonisme. Mélanges offerts à Jean Trouillard* (Les Cahiers de Fontenay 19–22, 1981), 231–247.

————"Le spiritualisme augustinien à la lumière du *De immortalitate animae*," in *L'opera letteraria di Agostino tra Cassiciacum e Milano. Agostino nelle terre di Ambrogio (1–4 ottobre 1986)* (Augustiniana, Testi e Studi 2, Palermo, 1987), 179–190.

————"'Verus philosophus est amator Dei.' S. Ambroise, S. Augustin et la philosophie," *Revue des sciences philosophiques et théologiques* 61 (1977), 549–566.

Magass, Walter, "Claritas versus Obscuritas. Semiotische Bermerkungen zum Wechsel der Zeicheninventare in den Confessiones des Augustin (*Conf.* XIII, XV, 18)," *Linguistica Biblica* 48 (1980), 7–18.

————"Die konfessorische Rede in den *Confessiones* Augustins," *Linguistica Biblica* 55 (1984), 35–45.

Magee, John, *Boethius on Signification and Mind* (Philosophia Antiqua 52, Leiden, 1989).

Mair, Victor H., *Painting and Performance: Chinese Picture Recitation and Its Indian Genesis* (Honolulu, 1988).

Majercik, Ruth, "The Existence-Life-Intellect Triad in Gnosticism and Neoplatonism," *Classical Quarterly* 42 (1992), 475–488.

Mandouze, André, "L'extase d'Ostie," in *AM* (1954), vol. 1, 67–84.

——"Quelques principes de 'linguistique augustinienne' dans le 'De magistro,'" in *Forma futuri. Studi in onore del cardinale Michele Pellegrino* (Turin, 1975), 789–795.

——*Saint Augustin. L'aventure de la raison et de la grâce* (*CEA, SA* 31, Paris, 1968).

Mannucci, U., "La conversione di s. Agostino e la critica recente," in *Miscellanea Agostiniana,* vol. 2 (1931), 23–47.

Manrique, Andrés, "Presencia de Cristo en los corazones por la fe (Ef. 3,17) según san Agustín," *Revista agustiniana de espiritualidad* 14 (1973), 41–61.

Maréchal, J., "La vision de Dieu au sommet de la contemplation d'après saint Augustin," *Nouvelle revue théologique* 57 (1930), 89–109, 191–214.

Markus, R. A., "'Alienatio.' Philosophy and Eschatology in the Development of an Augustinian Idea," *Studia Patristica* 9.3 (Berlin, 1966), 431–450.

——*Augustine: A Collection of Essays* (Modern Studies in Philosophy, New York, 1972).

——"Augustine on Signs," *Phronesis* 2 (1957), 60–83.

——"'Imago' and 'similitudo' in Augustine," *REA* 10 (1964), 125–143.

——"Marius Victorinus and Augustine," in *The Cambridge History of Later Greek and Early Medieval Philosophy,* ed. A. H. Armstrong (Cambridge, 1967), 327–419.

——*Saeculum. History and Society in the Theology of St. Augustine* (Cambridge, 1970).

Marrou, Henri-Irénée, "'Doctrina' et 'disciplina' dans la langue des Pères de l'église," *Bulletin du Cange* 9 (1934), 3–23.

——*A History of Education in Antiquity,* trans. G. Lamb (New York, 1956).

——"La querelle autour du 'Tolle, lege,'" *Revue d'histoire ecclésiastique* 53 (1958), 47–57.

——*The Resurrection and Saint Augustine's Theology of Human Values* (Saint Augustine Lecture 1965, Villanova, 1966).

——*Saint Augustin et la fin de la culture antique,* 4th ed. (Paris, 1958).

——"La technique de l'édition à l'époque patristique," *Vigiliae Christianae* 3 (1949), 208–224.

Martz, Louis L., *The Poetry of Meditation: A Study in English Religious Literature of the Seventeenth Century,* 2nd ed. (New Haven, 1962).

Masai, François, "Les conversions de saint Augustin et les débuts du spiritualisme en Occident," *Le moyen âge* 67 (1961), 1–40.

Matthews, Gareth, "The Inner Man," *American Philosophical Quarterly* 4 (1967), 166–172.

——"*Si Fallor, Sum,*" in Markus (1972), 151–167.

——*Thought's Ego in Augustine and Descartes* (Ithaca, 1992).

Matthews, John, *Western Aristocracies and Imperial Court, A.D. 364–425* (Oxford, 1975).

Mausbach, Joseph, "Wesen und Stufung des Lebens nach dem hl. Augustinus," in *Aurelius Augustinus* (1930), 169–196.

Maxsein, Anton, *Philosophia Cordis. Das Wesen der Personalität Augustinus* (Salzburg, 1966).

Mayer, Cornelius Petrus, "Augustins Lehre vom 'homo spiritalis,'" in *Homo Spiritalis* (1987), 3–60.

——"Herkunft und Normativität des Terminus *Regula* bei Augustin," in *Collectanea Augustiniana* (1991), vol. 1, 127–154.

————"Philosophische Voraussetzungen und Implikationen in Augustins Lehre von den Sacramenta," *Augustiniana* 22 (1972), 53–79.

————"Prinzipien der Hermeneutik Augustins und daraus sich ergebende Probleme," *Forum Katholische Theologie* 1 (1985), 197–211.

————"'Res per signa.' Der Grundgedanke des Prologs in Augustins Schrift *De doctrina christiana* und das Problem seiner Datierung," *REA* 20 (1974), 100–112.

————"Signifikationshermeneutik im Dienste der Daseinsauslegung. Die Funktion der Verweisungen in den *Confessiones* X–XIII," *Augustiniana* 24 (1974), 21–74.

————*Die Zeichen in der geistigen Entwicklung und in der Theologie des jungen Augustinus* (Cassiciacum 24.1, Würzburg, 1969); vol. 2: *Die antimanichäische Epoche* (Cassiciacum 24.2, Würzburg, 1974).

Mazzeo, Joseph A., "St. Augustine's Rhetoric of Silence," *Journal of the History of Ideas* 23 (1962), 175–196.

McCool, Gerald A., "The Ambrosian Origin of St. Augustine's Theology of the Image of Man," *Theological Studies* 20 (1959), 62–81.

McEvoy, J., "St. Augustine's Account of Time and Wittgenstein's Criticisms," *Review of Metaphysics* 38 (1984), 547–577.

McKenzie, D. F., "Speech-Manuscript-Print," in *New Directions in Textual Studies,* ed. D. Oliphant and R. Bradford (Harry Ransom Humanities Research Center, Austin, 1990), 87–109.

McNamara, Marie Aquinas, *Friends and Friendship for Saint Augustine* (New York, 1964).

Meijering, E. P., *Augustin über Schöpfung, Ewigkeit und Zeit. Das Elfte Buch der Bekenntnisse* (Philosophia Patrum 4, Leiden, 1979).

Menasce, Pierre Jean de, "Augustin manichéen," in *Freundesgabe für Ernst Robert Curtius zum 14. April 1956* (Bern, 1956), 79–93.

Meyer, Robert T., "Lectio Divina in Palladius," in *Kyriakon. Festschrift Johannes Quasten,* ed. P. Granfield and J. A. Jungmann, vol. 2 (Münster, 1970), 580–584.

Miles, Margaret, "Infancy, Parenting, and Nourishment in Augustine's 'Confessions,'" *Journal of the American Academy of Religion* 50 (1982), 349–364.

————"Vision: The Eye of the Body and the Eye of the Mind in Saint Augustine's *De trinitate* and *Confessions,*" *Journal of Religion* 63 (1983), 125–142.

*Miscellanea Agostiniana. Testi e studi pubblicati a cura dell'Ordine eremitano di s. Agostino nel xv centenario dalla morte del santo dottore:* vol. 1: *Sancti Augustini Sermones post Maurinos reperti . . .,* ed. G. Morin (Rome, 1930); vol. 2: *Studi Agostiniani . . .* (Rome, 1931).

Misch, Georg, *A History of Autobiography in Antiquity,* trans. in collaboration with the author by E. W. Dickes, 2 vols. (Cambridge, Mass., 1951).

Mohrmann, Christine, "The *Confessions* as a Literary Work of Art," in *Etudes sur le latin des chrétiens,* vol. 1 (Rome, 1958), 371–381.

————"Praedicare—Tractare—Sermo. Essai sur la terminologie de la prédication paléochrétienne," in *Etudes . . .,* vol. 2 (Rome, 1961), 63–72.

————"Saint Augustine and the 'Eloquentia,'" *Etudes . . .,* vol. 1, 351–370.

Mommsen, Theodor, "St. Augustine and the Christian Idea of Progress: The Background of *The City of God,*" in *Medieval and Renaissance Studies,* ed. E. F. Rice, Jr. (Ithaca, 1959), 265–298.

Monachino, Vincenzo, *La cura pastorale a Milano, Cartagine e Roma nel sec. IV* (Analecta Gregoriana 41, Rome, 1947).

Monceaux, Paul, "Saint Augustin et Saint Antoine. Contribution à l'histoire du monachisme," in *Miscellanea Agostiniana,* vol. 2 (1931), 61–89.

Montgomery, William, *St. Augustine. Aspects of His Life and Thought* (London, 1914).

Morán, José, "La teoría de la 'admonición' en las 'Confesiones' de S. Agustín," *Augustinianum* 8 (1968), 147–154.

————"La teoría de la 'admonición' en los Diálogos de san Agustín," *Augustinus* 13 (1968),
257–272.

Morati, Luciano, "Note sulla struttura della 'Visione di Ostia,'" in *Miscellanea Adriano
Gazzana,* vol. 2 (Archivum philosophicum Aloisianum, 2nd ser., 10, Milan, 1960),
23–49.

Moreau, M., "Mémoire et durée," *REA* 1 (1955), 239–250.

Morrison, Karl F., *Conversion and Text: The Cases of Augustine of Hippo, Herman-Judah, and
Constantine Tsatsos* (Charlottesville, 1992).

————"I Am You": The Hermeneutics of Empathy in Western Literature, Theology, and Art*
(Princeton, 1988).

————*The Mimetic Tradition of Reform in the West* (Princeton, 1982).

Moschetti, A. M., "S. Agostino e il bergsonismo," in *S. Agostino e le grandi correnti della
filosofia contemporanea* (Rome, 1956), 271–277.

Mourant, John A., "Augustine and the Academics," *R Aug* 4 (1966), 67–96.

Mundle, C. W. K., "Augustine's Pervasive Error concerning Time," *Philosophy* 41 (1966),
165–168.

Nédoncelle, Maurice, "L'abandon de Mani par Augustin ou la logique de l'optimisme,"
*Recherches augustiniennes* 2 (1962), 17–32.

Negri, Coian Carlo, *La disposizione del contenuto dottrinale nel "De catechizandis rudibus" di s.
Agostino* (Pontificum Athenaeum Salesianum, Facultas Theologica 57, Rome, 1961).

Nell, Victor, *Lost in a Book: The Psychology of Reading for Pleasure* (New Haven, 1988).

Neusner, Jacob, *The Oral Torah: The Sacred Books of Judaism: An Introduction* (San Francisco,
1986).

Newhauser, Richard, "Towards a History of Human Curiosity: A Prolegomenon to Its
Medieval Phase," *Deutsche Vierteljahrsschrift* 56 (1982), 559–575.

Nock, Arthur Darby, *Conversion. The Old and the New in Religion from Alexander the Great
to Augustine of Hippo* (Oxford, 1933).

————"Conversion and Adolescence," in *Pisciculi. Studien zur Religion und Kultur des
Altertums. Franz Joseph Dölger zum sechzigsten Geburtstage* (Antike und Christentum,
Ergänzungsband 1, Münster, 1939), 165–177.

Nörregaard, Jens, *Augustins Bekehrung,* trans. A. Spelmener (Tübingen, 1923).

Nolte, Venantius, *Augustins Freundschaftsideal in seinen Briefen. Unter Hereinbeziehung seiner
Jugendfreundschaften gemäss den Philosophischen Schriften und den Confessionen* (Cassiciacum
6, Würzburg, 1939).

Nuchelmans, G., *Theories of the Proposition. Ancient and Medieval Concepts of the Bearers of
Truth and Falsity* (North-Holland Linguistic Series 8, Amsterdam, 1973).

Oatley, Keith, *Best Laid Schemes. The Psychology of Emotions* (Studies in Emotion and Social
Interaction, Cambridge, 1992).

O'Brien, William J., "The Liturgical Form of Augustine's Conversion Narrative and Its
Theological Significance," *Augustinian Studies* 9 (1978), 45–58.

O'Connell, Robert J., "Action and Contemplation," in Markus (1972), 38–58.

————*Art and the Christian Intelligence in St. Augustine* (Cambridge, Mass., 1978).

————"*Ennead* VI, 4 and 5 in the Works of Saint Augustine," *REA* 9 (1963), 1–39.

————*St. Augustine's Early Theory of Man, A.D. 386–391* (Cambridge, Mass., 1968).

O'Daly, G. J. P., "Augustine on the Measurement of Time: Some Comparisons with Aristotelian and Stoic Texts," in *Neoplatonism and Early Christian Thought. Essays in Honour of A. H. Armstrong,* ed. H. J. Blumenthal and R. A. Markus (London, 1981), 171–179.

————"Augustine on the Origin of Souls," *Jahrbuch für Antike und Christentum* 10 (1983), 184–191.

————*Augustine's Philosophy of Mind* (London, 1987).

————"Memory in Plotinus and Two Early Texts of St. Augustine," *Studia Patristica* 14 (Berlin, 1976), 461–469.

————"*Sensus interior* in St. Augustine, *De libero arbitrio* 2.3.25–6.51," *Studia Patristica* 16.2 (Berlin, 1985), 528–532.

————"Time as *Distentio* and St. Augustine's Exegesis of *Philippians* 3,12–14," *REA* 23 (1977), 265–271.

O'Donnell, James J., "Augustine Confessions 10.1.1–10.4.6," *Augustiniana* 29 (1979), 280–303.

————"Augustine's Classical Readings," *R Aug* 15 (1980), 144–175.

————ed., *Augustine. Confessions:* vol. 1: *Introduction and Text;* vol. 2: *Commentary on Books 1–7;* vol. 3: *Commentary on Books 8–13, Indexes* (Oxford, 1992).

O'Donovan, Oliver, *The Problem of Self-Love in St. Augustine* (New Haven, 1980).

————"'Usus' and 'Fruitio' in Augustine, 'De doctrina christiana,'" *Journal of Theological Studies* 33 (1982), 361–397.

Oeing-Hanhoff, Ludger, "Zur Wirkungsgeschichte der platonischen Anamnesislehre," in *Collegium Philosophicum. Studien Joachim Ritter zum 60. Geburstag* (Basel, 1965), 240–271.

Ohlmann, D., *De S. Augustini dialogis in Cassiciaco scriptis* (Strasbourg, 1897).

Olivar, Alejandro, "La duración de la predicación antigua," *Liturgica* 3 (1966), 143–184.

Olney, James, ed., *Autobiography: Essays Theoretical and Critical* (Princeton, 1980).

O'Meara, John J., "'Arripui, aperui, et legi,'" in *AM* (1954), vol. 1, 59–65.

————"Augustine and Neo-platonism," *R Aug* 1 (1958), 91–111.

————"Augustine the Artist and the *Aeneid*," in *Mélanges offerts à Mademoiselle Christine Mohrmann* (Utrecht, 1963), 252–261.

————"The Historicity of the Early Dialogues of Saint Augustine," *Vigiliae Christianae* 5 (1951), 150–178.

————"St. Augustine's View of Authority and Reason in A.D. 386," *The Irish Theological Quarterly* 18 (1951), 338–346.

————*Porphyry's Philosophy from Oracles in Augustine (CEA, SA* 9, Paris, 1959).

————*The Young Augustine. The Growth of St. Augustine's Mind up to His Conversion* (London, 1954).

————trans. and ed., *St. Augustine: Against the Academics* (Ancient Christian Writers 12, Westminster, Md., 1950).

Ong, Walter J., *Orality and Literacy. The Technologizing of the Word* (London, 1982).

Opelt, Ilona, "Materialien zur Nachwirkung von Augustins Schrift De doctrina christiana," *Jahrbuch für Antike und Christentum* 17 (1974), 64–73.

Oroz Reta, José, "Prière et recherche de Dieu dans les *Confessions* de Saint Augustin," *Studia Patristica* 16.2 (Berlin, 1985), 533–550.

————*La retórica en los sermones de san Agustín,* introduction by A. Tovar (Colección Augustinus 7, Madrid, 1963).

Orth, Emil, "Lekton = dicibile," *Helmantica* 10 (1959), 221–226.

Outler, Albert C., "The Person and Work of Christ," in *A Companion to the Study of St. Augustine*, ed. R. W. Battenhouse (Oxford, 1955), 343–370.

Palanque, Jean-Rémy, *Saint Ambroise et l'empire romain. Contribution à l'histoire des rapports de l'église et de l'état à la fin du quatrième siècle* (Paris, 1933).

Palmer, Richard E., *Hermeneutics: Interpretation Theory in Schleiermacher, Dilthey, Heidegger, and Gadamer* (Northwestern University Studies in Phenomenology and Existential Philosophy, Evanston, 1969).

Paoli, Ugo Enrico, "'Legere' e 'recitare,'" *Atene e Roma*, n.s., 3 (1922), 205–207.

Paredi, Angelo, *Saint Ambrose: His Life and Times*, trans. M. J. Costelloe (Notre Dame, Ind., 1964).

Parkes, M. B., "The Contribution of Insular Scribes of the Seventh and Eighth Centuries to the 'Grammar of Legibility,'" in *Grafia e interpunzione del latino nel medioevo. Seminario Internazionale, Roma, 27–29 settembre 1984*, ed. A. Maieru (Rome, 1987), 15–30.

———*Pause and Effect: An Introduction to the History of Punctuation in the West* (Berkeley, 1993).

Pelikan, Jaroslav, *The Mystery of Continuity: Time and History, Memory and Eternity in the Thought of Saint Augustine* (Richard Lectures 1984–85, Charlottesville, 1986).

Pellegrino, Michele, "Aspectos pedagógicos de las 'Confessiones' de San Agustín," *Augustinus* 5 (1960), 53–63.

———*Les Confessions de saint Augustin. Guide de lecture*, ann. H. Chirat (Paris, 1960).

Penrose, Roger, *The Emperor's New Mind: Concerning Computers, Minds, and the Laws of Physics* (New York, 1990).

Pépin, Jean, "Augustin, *Quaestio 'De Ideis.'* Les affinités plotiniennes," in *From Athens to Chartres. Neoplatonism and Medieval Thought. Studies in Honour of Edouard Jeauneau*, ed. H. J. Westra (Studien und Texte zur Geistesgeschichte des Mittelalters 35, Leiden, 1992), 117–134.

———"La connaissance d'autrui chez Plotin et chez saint Augustin," *Augustinus* 3 (1958), 227–245.

———*"Ex Platonicorum Persona." Etudes sur les lectures philosophiques de saint Augustin* (Amsterdam, 1977).

———*Mythe et allégorie. Les origines grecques et les contestations judéo-chrétienne*, 2nd ed. (*CEA, SA* 19, Paris, 1976).

———"Une nouvelle source de saint Augustin: le Ζητήματα de Porphyre 'Sur l'union de l'âme et du corps,'" (1964), reprinted in *"Ex Platonicorum Persona"* (1977), 213–267.

———"'Primitiae spiritus.' Remarques sur une citation paulinienne des 'Confessions' de saint Augustin" (1951), reprinted in *"Ex Platonicorum Persona"* (1977), 133–180.

———*Saint Augustin et la dialectique* (Saint Augustine Lecture, 1972, Villanova, 1976).

———*Théologie cosmique et théologie chrétienne (Ambroise, Exam. I,1,1–4)* (Bibliothèque de Philosophie Contemporaine, Paris, 1964).

Perl, C. J., "Augustinus und die Musik," in *AM* (1954), vol. 3, 439–452.

Perler, Othmar, "Contremui amore et horrore. Augustinus, *Confessiones* VII 10,16," in *Unterwegs zur Einheit. Festschrift für Heinrich Stirnimann*, ed. J. Brantschen and P. Selvatico (Fribourg, 1980), 241–252.

Perler, Othmar, with J.-L. Maier, *Les voyages de saint Augustin* (*CEA, SA* 36, Paris, 1969).

Perner, Josef, "Developing Semantics for Theories of Mind: From Propositional Attitudes to Mental Representations," in *Developing Theories of Mind*, ed. J. W. Astington, P. L. Harris, and D. R. Olson (Cambridge, 1988), 141–172.

Peters, Edward, "Aenigma Salomonis: Manichaean Anti-Genesis Polemic and the Vitium curiositatis in *Confessions* III.6," *Augustiniana* 36 (1986), 48–64.

——"*Libertas Inquirendi* and the *Vitium Curiositatis* in Medieval Thought," in *La notion de liberté au moyen-âge*, ed. G. Mahdisi et al. (Paris, 1985), 89–98.

——"What Was God Doing before He Created the Heavens and Earth?" *Augustiniana* 34 (1984), 53–74.

Petitmengin, Pierre, and Bernard Flusin, "Le livre antique et la dictée. Nouvelles recherches," in *Mémorial André-Jean Festugière. Antiquité païenne et chrétienne*, ed. E. Lucchesi and H. D. Saffrey (Cahiers d'Orientalisme 30, Geneva, 1984), 247–262.

Pfligersdorffer, Georg, "Augustins 'Confessiones' und die Arten der Confessio," *Salzburger Jahrbuch für Philosophie* 14 (1970), 15–28.

——"Zu den Grundlagen des augustinischen Begriffspaares uti-frui," *Wiener Studien*, n.s., 5 (1971), 195–224.

Piaget, Jean, *The Construction of Reality in the Child* (New York, 1954).

——*The Origins of Intelligence in Children*, trans. M. Cook (New York, 1952).

——*Play, Dreams, and Imitation in Childhood* (London, 1962).

Pinborg, Jan, "Das Sprachdenken der Stoa und Augustins Dialektik," *Classica et Mediaevalia* 23 (1962), 148–177.

Pincherle, Alberto, "The Confessions of St. Augustine: A Reappraisal," *Augustinian Studies* 7 (1976), 119–133.

——"Da Ticinio a Sant'Agostino," *Ricerche religiose* 1 (1925), 443–466.

——"Il 'decennio di preparazione' di sant'Agostino (386–396)," *Ricerche religiose* 6 (1930), 15–38; 7 (1931), 30–52; 8 (1932), 118–143; 9 (1933), 339–423; 10 (1934), 215–249.

——"Et inquietum est cor nostrum. Appunti per una lezione agostiniana," *Augustinus* 13 (1968), 353–368.

——"Intorno alla genesi della 'Confessioni' di S. Agostino," *Augustinian Studies* 5 (1974), 167–176.

——"Quelques remarques sur les *Confessions* de saint Augustin," *La nouvelle Clio* 7–9 (1955–57), 189–206.

——"Studi agostiniani," *Rassegna di filosofia* 2 (1953), 14–50.

——"Sulla composizione del *De Doctrina Christiana* di S. Agostino," in *Storiografia e storia. Studi in onore di Eugenio Duprè Theseider* (Rome, 1974), 541–559.

Pizzolato, Luigi F., *Le "Confessioni" di Sant'Agostino. Da biografia a "confessio"* (Pubblicazioni dell'Università Cattolica del S. Cuore, Saggi e Richerche, serie III, Scienze Filologiche e Letteratura 7, Milan, 1968).

Pontet, Maurice, *L'exégèse de s. Augustin prédicateur* (Théologie 7, Paris, 1945).

Poque, Suzanne, "L'alternative 'dictées ou prêchées' pour les 'Enarrationes in Psalmos' de saint Augustin," *Revue bénédictine* 88 (1978), 147–152.

——"Au sujet d'une singularité romaine de la 'Redditio Symboli,'" *Miscellanea . . . Agostino Trapè (Augustinianum* 25.1–2, 1985), 133–143.

——"'In quadam regula lignea' ('Conf.' III, 11,19). Essai d'élucidation d'une vision onirique," *Rivista di storia e letteratura religiosa* 20 (1984), 480–488.

Portalié, E., "Augustinisme (Développement historique de l')," in *Dictionnaire de théologie catholique*, vol. 1 (Paris, 1923), 2501–61.

Poulet, Georges, "Phenomenology of Reading," *New Literary History* 1 (1969–70), 53–68.

Pramling, Ingrid, "Entrance into the 'World of Knowledge': Pre-school Children's Conceptions of Learning," in *The Written Word. Studies in Literate Thought and Action*, ed. R. Säljo (Berlin, 1988), 151–160.

Préaux, J.-G., "Du *Phédon* aux *Confessions* de saint Augustin," *Latomus* 16 (1957), 314–325.

———"Nouvelles approximations sur l'épisode augustinien du 'Tolle, lege,'" *Revue belge de philologie et d'histoire* 33 (1955), 555–576.

Prendiville, John G., "The Development of the Idea of Habit in the Thought of St. Augustine," *Traditio* 28 (1972), 29–99.

Press, Gerald A., "*Doctrina* in Augustine's *De doctrina christiana*," *Philosophy and Rhetoric* 17 (1984), 98–120.

———"The Subject and Structure of Augustine's De Doctrina Christiana," *Augustinian Studies* 11 (1980), 99–124.

Prete, Serafino, "'Ars rhetorica' e cultura cristiana nel *De doctrina* di Agostino," *Divus Thomas. Commentarium de Philosophia et Theologia*, 3rd ser., 43 (1970), 59–68.

Prime, P., "*Tenuissima Forma Cognitionis:* Predication in St. Augustine's Theory of Knowledge," *Journal of Theological Studies* 43 (1942), 45–59.

Puech, Henri-Charles, "Le manichéisme," in *Encyclopédie de la Pléiade. Histoire des religions,* vol. 2, ed. H.-C. Puech (Paris, 1972), 523–645.

———*Le manichéisme. Son fondateur, sa doctrine* (Musée Guimet. Bibliothèque de Diffusion 53, Paris, 1949).

Quacquarelli, Antonio, "*Inventio* ed *elocutio* nella retorica cristiana antica," *Vetera Christianorum* 9 (1972), 191–218.

Quinn, John M., "The Concept of Time in St. Augustine," *Studies in Philosophy and the History of Philosophy* 4 (1969), 75–127.

Quispel, Gilles, "Mani et la tradition évangélique des judéo-chrétiens," in *Judéo-christianisme. Recherches historiques et théologiques offertes en hommage au cardinal Jean Daniélou* (*Recherches de science religieuse* 60, 1972), 143–150.

———"Mani. The Apostle of Jesus Christ," in *Epektasis. Mélanges patristiques offerts au cardinal Jean Daniélou,* ed. J. Fontaine and C. Kannengiesser (Paris, 1972), 667–672.

Raby, F. J. E., *A History of Christian-Latin Poetry from the Beginnings to the Close of the Middle Ages* (Oxford, 1953).

Racette, Jean, "Le livre neuvième du 'De Trinitate' de saint Augustin," *Sciences ecclésiastiques* 8 (1956), 39–57.

Raible, Wolfgang, "Zur Entwicklung von Alphabetschrift-Systemen. *Is fecit cui prodest,*" *Sitzungsberichte der Heidelberger Akademie der Wissenschaften, Philosophisch-historische Kl.,* 1991, 1 (Heidelberg, 1991).

Ratzinger, Joseph, "Beobachtungen zum Kirchenbegriff des Tyconius im 'Liber regularum,'" *REA* 2 (1956), 173–185.

———"Originalität und Überlieferung in Augustins Begriff der 'confessio,'" *REA* 3 (1957), 375–392.

Reil, Elisabeth, *Aurelius Augustinus De catechizandis rudibus* (Studien zur Prakischen Theologie 33, St. Ottilien, 1989).

Ricoeur, Paul, *Hermeneutics and the Human Sciences. Essays on Language, Action and Interpretation,* trans. and ed. J. B. Thompson (Cambridge, 1981).

———*Temps et récit,* vol. 1 (Ordre Philosophique, Paris, 1983).

Rief, Josef, "Liebe zur Wahrheit. Untersuchungen zur Ethik des jungen Augustinus," *Theologische Quartalschrift* 141 (1961), 281–318.

———*Der Ordobegriff des jungen Augustinus* (Abhandlungen zur Moraltheolgie, Paderborn, 1962).

Ries, Julien, "La Bible chez saint Augustin et chez les manichéens," *REA* 7 (1961), 231–243; 9 (1963), 201–215; 10 (1964), 309–329.

————"Introduction aux études manichéennes. Quatre siècles de recherches," *Ephemerides Theologicae Lovanienses* 33 (1957), 453–482; 35 (1959), 362–409.

————"Jésus-Christ dans la religion de Mani. Quelques éléments d'une confrontation de saint Augustin avec un hymnaire christologique manichéen copte," *Augustiniana* 14 (1964), 437–454.

————"Manichaeism," in *The New Catholic Encyclopedia,* vol. 9 (New York, 1967), 153–160.

Rigby, Paul, *Original Sin in Augustine's "Confessions"* (Ottawa, 1987).

Ripanti, Graziano, "L'allegoria o l'intellectus figuratus' nel *De doctrina christiana* di Agostino," *REA* 18 (1972), 219–232.

————"Il problema della comprensione nell'ermeneutica agostiniana," *REA* 20 (1974), 88–99.

Rist, John, "Augustine on Free Will and Predestination," *Journal of Theological Studies,* n.s., 20 (1969), 420–447.

————*Plotinus. The Road to Reality* (Cambridge, 1967).

————*Stoic Philosophy* (Cambridge, 1969).

Rohmer, Jean, "L'intentionalité des sensations chez Saint Augustin," in *AM* (1954), vol. 1, 491–498.

Romanelli, Pietro, "S. Agostino nell'Africa del suo tempo," in *Augustiniana. Napoli a S. Agostino nel XVI centenario della nascità* (Naples, 1955), 17–35.

Romano, Domenico, "Licenzio poeta. Sulla posizione di Agostino verso la poesia," *Nuovo Didaskaleion* 11 (1961), 1–22.

Rose, H. J., "St. Augustine as a Forerunner of Mediaeval Hynmology," *Journal of Theological Studies* 28 (1926–27), 383–392.

Rossi, Paolo, *Clavis Universalis. Arti della memoria e logica combinatoria da Lullo a Leibniz,* 2nd ed. (Bologna, 1983).

Rothfield, Lawrence, "Autobiography and Perspective in *The Confessions* of St. Augustine," *Comparative Literature* 33 (1981), 209–223.

Rousseau, Olivier, "La typologie augustinienne de l'Hexaeméron et la théologie du temps," in *Glaube und Geschichte. Festgabe für J. Lortz,* vol. 2 (Baden-Baden, 1958), 47–58.

Ruef, H., *Augustin über Semiotik und Sprache. Sprachtheoretische Analysen zu Augustins Schrift 'De Dialectica' mit einer deutschen Übersetzung* (Bern, 1981).

Russell, Bertrand, *Human Knowledge. Its Scope and Limits.* 2nd ed. (London, 1951).

Russell, Frederick P., "'Only Something Good Can Be Evil': The Genesis of Augustine's Secular Ambivalence," *Theological Studies* 51 (1990), 698–716.

Saenger, Paul, "The Separation of Words and the Order of Words: The Genesis of Medieval Reading," *Scrittura e civiltà* 14 (1990), 49–74.

————"The Separation of Words and the Physiology of Reading," in *Literacy and Orality,* ed. D. R. Olson and N. Torrance (Cambridge, 1991), 198–214.

————"Silent Reading: Its Impact on Late Medieval Script and Society," *Viator* 13 (1982), 367–414.

————*Space between Words: The Origins of Silent Reading* (Figurae, Reading Medieval Culture, Stanford, forthcoming).

Sage, A., "Péché original. Naissance d'un dogme," *REA* 13 (1967), 211–248.

*Sant'Agostino Confessioni,* vol. 1 (Books 1–3), ed. J. Fontaine, M. Cristiani, J. Guirau, L. F. Pizzolato, M. Simonetti, and P. Siniscalco; trans. G. Chiarini (Scrittore Greci e Latini, Fondazione Lorenzo Valla, Vicenza, 1992).

Schaeder, Hans Heinrich, "Urform und Fortbildung des manichäischen Systems," in *Vorträge der Bibliothek Warburg*, vol. 4, 1924–25 (Leipzig, 1927), 65–157.

Schäublin, Christoph, "Augustin. De utilitate credendi, über das Verhältnis des Interpreten zum Text," *Vigiliae Christianae* 43 (1989), 53–68.

————"Konversionen in antiken Dialogen?" in *Catalepton. Festschrift für Bernhard Wyss zum 80. Geburtstag,* ed. C. Schäublin (Basel, 1985), 117–131.

Schelkle, Karl Hermann, *Virgil in der Deutung Augustins* (Tübinger Beiträge zur Altertumswissenschaft 32, Stuttgart, 1939).

Schildgen, Brenda Deen, "Augustine's Answer to Jacques Derrida in the *De Doctrina Christiana,*" *New Literary History* 25 (1994), 383–397.

Schindler, Alfred, *Wort und Analogie in Augustins Trinitätslehre* (Hermeneutische Untersuchungen zur Theologie 4, Tübingen, 1965).

Schmaus, Michael, *Die psychologische Trinitätslehre des hl. Augustinus* (Münsterische Beiträge zur Theologie 11, Münster, 1927).

Schmidt, Ernst A., *Zeit und Geschichte bei Augustin* (Sitzungsberichte der Heidelberger Akademie der Wissenschaften, Philosophisch-historische Kl., 1985, 3, Heidelberg, 1985).

Schmidt, Peter L., "Zur Typologie und Literarisierung des frühchristlichen lateinischen Dialogs," in *Christianisme et formes littéraires de l'antiquité tardive en Occident* (Entretiens sur l'Antiquité Classique 23, Vandoeuvres-Geneva, 1977), 101–190.

Schmidt-Dengler, Wendelin, "Die *'aula memoriae'* in den *Konfessionen* des heiligen Augustin," *REA* 14 (1968), 69–89.

————"Der rhetorische Aufbau des achten Buches der *Konfessionen* des heiligen Augustin," *REA* 15 (1969), 195–208.

Schobinger, Jean-Pierre, "Augustins Begründung der 'inneren Zeit,'" *Schweizer Monatshefte* 46 (1966), 179–192.

————"Augustins Einkehr als Wirkung seiner Lektüre. Die admonitio verborum," in *Esoterik und Exoterik der Philosophie. Beiträge zu Geschichte und Sinn philosophischer Selbstbestimmung,* ed. H. Holzhey and W. C. Zimmerli (Basel, 1977), 70–100.

————"La portée historique des théories de la lecture (Réflexions à la lumière du *De doctrina christiana* de saint Augustin)," *Revue de théologie et de philosophie* 112 (1980), 43–56.

Schöpf, Alfred, "Die Verinnerlichung des Wahrheitsproblems bei Augustin," *REA* 13 (1967) 85–96.

————*Wahrheit und Wissen. Die Begründung der Erkenntnis bei Augustin* (Epimeleia, Beiträge zur Philosophie 2, Munich, 1965).

Schubert, P. Alois, *Augustins Lex-aeterna-Lehre nach Inhalt und Quellen* (Beiträge zur Geschichte der Philosophie des Mittelalters 24.2, Münster, 1924).

Schützinger, C., "Die augustinische Erkenntnislehre in Lichte neurer Forschung," *R Aug* 2 (1962), 177–203.

Schulz, W., *Der Einfluss Augustins in der Theologie und Christologie des VIII. und IX. Jahrhunderts* (Halle, 1913).

Schumacher, William A., *"Spiritus" and "Spiritualis": A Study in the Sermons of Saint Augustine* (Pontificia Facultas Theologica Seminarii Sanctae Mariae ad Lacum, Dissertationes ad Lauream 28, Mundelein, Ill., 1957).

Sciacca, Michele F., "Il principio della metafisica di S. Agostino e tentativi metafisici del pensiero moderno," in *S. Agostino e le grandi correnti della filosofia contemporanea. Atti del Congresso italiano di filosofia agostiniana Roma 20–23 ottobre 1954* (Rome, 1956), 9–24.

————"Trinité at unité de l'esprit," in *AM* (1954), vol. 1 521–533.

Screech, M. A., "Introduction," in M. A. Screech, trans., *The Essays of Michel de Montaigne* (London, 1991), xiii–xlviii.

Searle, John R., *Intentionality. An Essay in the Philosophy of Mind* (Cambridge, 1983).

Sears, Elizabeth, *The Ages of Man: Medieval Interpretations of the Life Cycle* (Princeton, 1986).

Seeliger, Hans Reinhard, "Aberglaube, Wissenschaft und die Rolle der historica narratio in Augustins Doctrina christiana," *Wissenschaft und Weisheit* 43 (1980), 148–155.

Semple, W. H., "Augustinus Rhetor. A Study, from the *Confessions*, of St. Augustine's Secular Career in Education," *Journal of Ecclesiastical History* 1 (1950), 135–150.

Shanzer, Danuta, "Latent Narrative Patterns, Allegorical Choices, and Literary Unity in Augustine's Confessions," *Vigiliae Christianae* 46 (1992), 40–56.

Shultz, Thomas R., "Development of the Concept of Intention," in *Development of Cognition, Affect, and Social Relations*, ed. W. A. Collins (Minnesota Symposia on Child Psychology 13, Hillsdale, N.J., 1980), 131–164.

Sieben, Hermann-Josef, "Der Psalter und die Bekehrung der *uoces* und *affectus*. Zu Augustinus *Conf.* IX,4.6 und X,33," *Theologie und Philosophie* 52 (1977), 481–497.

————"Die 'res' der Bibel. Eine Analyse von Augustinus, De doct. christ. I–III," *REA* 21 (1975), 72–90.

*Signum Pietatis. Festgabe für Cornelius Petrus Mayer OSA zum 60. Geburstag*, ed. A. Zumkeller (Cassiciacum 40, Würzburg, 1989).

Simon, Werner, "Von Gott Reden. Beobachtungen und Bermerkungen zu Augustins Confessiones I,4," *Wissenschaft und Weisheit* 45 (1982), 130–157.

Simone, Raffaele, "Semiologia agostiniana," *La cultura* 7 (1969), 88–117.

Siniscalco, P., "Christum narrare et dilectionem monere. Osservazioni sulla *narratio* del 'De catechizandis rudibus' di S. Agostino," *Augustinianum* 14 (1974), 605–623.

Sirridge, Mary J., "St. Augustine and 'the Deputy Theory,'" *Augustinian Studies* 6 (1975), 107–116.

Sizoo, A., "Augustinus' bekeringsverhaal als narratio," *Augustiniana* 4 (1954), 240–257.

Smith, Wilfred Cantwell, *What Is Scripture? A Comparative Approach* (Minneapolis, 1993).

Söhngen, Gottlieb, "Der Aufbau der augustinischen Gedächtnislehre. X,c.6–27.," in *Aurelius Augustinus* (1930), 367–394.

Soennecken, Silvia, "Die Rolle der Frau in Augustins 'De Genesi ad Litteram,'" in *Signum Pietatis* (1989), 289–300.

Solignac, Aimé, "Doxographies et manuels dans la formation philosophique de saint Augustin," *R Aug* 1 (1958), 113–148.

————"Exégèse et métaphysique. Genèse 1,1–3 chez saint Augustin," in *In Principio. Interprétations des premiers versets de la Genèse* (Centre d'Etudes des Religions du Livre 152, Paris, 1973), 153–171.

————"Nouveaux parallèles entre saint Ambroise et Plotin," *Archives de philosophie* 19 (1956), 148–156.

————"Réminiscences plotiniennes et porphyriennes dans le début du *De Ordine* de saint Augustin," *Archives de philosophie*, n.s., 20 (1957), 446–465.

Sorabji, R., *Time, Creation, and the Continuum: Theories in Antiquity and the Early Middle Ages* (Ithaca, 1983).

Spengemann, William C., *The Forms of Autobiography: Episodes in the History of a Literary Genre* (New Haven, 1980).

Starobinski, Jean, "The Style of Autobiography," in Olney (1980), 73–83.

Starr, Raymond J., "The Circulation of Literary Texts in the Roman World," *Classical Quarterly* 37 (1987), 213–223.

Stelzenberger, Johannes, *Conscientia bei Augustinus. Studien zur Geschichte der Moraltheologie* (Paderborn, 1959).

Stock, Brian, *Listening for the Text: On the Uses of the Past* (Baltimore, 1990).

Strauss, Gerhard, *Schriftgebrauch, Schriftauslegung und Schriftbeweis bei Augustin* (Beiträge zur Geschichte der biblischen Hermeneutik 1, Tübingen, 1959).

Stroumsa, Gedaliahu G., "Esotericism in Mani's Thought and Background," in *Codex Manichaicus Coloniensis. Atti del simposio internazionale, Rende-Amantea, 3–7 settembre 1984,* ed. L. Cirillo and A. Roselli (Cozenza, 1986), 153–168.

———"Monachisme et Marranisme chez les Manichéens d'Egypte," *Numen* 29 (1983), 184–201.

Sturrock, John, *The Language of Autobiography. Studies in the First Person Singular* (Cambridge, 1993).

Suter, R., "Augustine on Time with Some Criticisms from Wittgenstein," *Revue internationale de philosophie* 16 (1962), 378–394.

Svoboda, K., *L'esthétique de saint Augustin et ses sources* (Opera Facultatis Philosophicae Universitatis Masarykianae Brunensis 35, Brno, 1933).

Tardieu, Michel, *Le manichéisme* (Paris, 1981).

———"Principes de l'exégèse manichéenne du Nouveau Testament," in *Les règles de l'interprétation,* ed. M. Tardieu (Centre d'Etudes des Religions du Livre, Paris, 1987), 123–146.

Taylor, Charles, *Sources of the Self: The Making of the Modern Identity* (Cambridge, Mass., 1989).

TeSelle, Eugene, *Augustine the Theologian* (New York, 1970).

———"Nature and Grace in Augustine's Expositions of Genesis I,1–5," *R Aug* 5 (1968), 95–137.

———"'Regio Dissimilitudinis' in the Christian Tradition and Its Context in Late Greek Philosophy," *Augustinian Studies* 6 (1975), 153–179.

Teske, Roland J., "Platonic Reminiscence and Memory of the Present in St. Augustine," *New Scholasticism* 58 (1984), 220–235.

———"The World-Soul and Time in St. Augustine," *Augustinian Studies* 14 (1983), 75–92.

Testard, Maurice, *Saint Augustin et Cicéron,* vol. 1: *Cicéron dans la formation et dans l'oeuvre de saint Augustin;* vol. 2: *Répertoire des textes* (CEA, SA 5–6, Paris, 1958).

———"La 'superbia' dans les *Confessions* de saint Augustin," in *Homo Spiritalis* (1987), 136–170.

Theiler, Willy, *Porphyrios und Augustin* (Schriften der Königsberger gelehrten Gesellschaft, Geisteswissenschaftliche Klasse 10.1, Halle, 1933).

Thimme, Wilhelm, *Augustins geistige Entwicklung in den ersten Jahren nach seiner "Bekehrung," 386–391* (Neue Studien zur Geschichte der Theologie und der Kirche 3, Berlin, 1908).

Thonnard, François-Joseph, "La notion de lumière en philosophie augustinienne," *R Aug* 2 (1962), 125–175.

Tombeur, F., "'Audire' dans le thème hagiographique de la conversion," *Latomus* 24 (1965), 159–165.

Tréhorel, E., "Le psaume abécédaire de saint Augustin," *Revue des études latines* 17 (1939), 309–329.

Trevarthen, Colwyn, "Emotions in Infancy: Regulators of Contact and Relationships with

Persons," in *Approaches to Emotion,* ed. K. R. Scherer and P. Ekman, (Hillsdale, N.J., 1984), 129–157.

Trevarthen, Colwyn, and Penelope Hubley, "Secondary Intersubjectivity: Confidence, Confiding, and Acts of Meaning in the First Year," in *Action, Gesture and Symbol. The Emergence of Language,* ed. A. Lock (London, 1978), 183–229.

Tscholl, Josef, "Augustins Interesse für die körperliche Schöne," *Augustiniana* 14 (1964), 73–104.

Tulving, Endel, "Précis of Elements of Episodic Memory," *Behavioral and Brain Sciences* 7 (1984), 223–238.

Valgiglio, E., *Confessio nella Bibbia e nella letteratura cristiana antica* (Turin, 1980).

van Bavel, Tarsicius J., "'And honour God in one another' (*Rule* of Augustine 1, 8)," in *Homo Spiritalis* (1987), 195–206.

———"De la Raison à la Foi. La conversion d'Augustin," *Augustinianum* 36 (1986), 5–27.

———"The Influence of Cicero's Ideal of Friendship on Augustine," in *Augustiniana Traiectina* (1987), 59–72.

———"Parallèles, vocabulaire et citations bibliques de la 'Regula S. Augustini.' Contribution au problème de son authenticité," *Augustiniana* 9 (1959), 12–77.

———"Woman as the Image of God in 'De Trinitate XII,'" in *Signum Pietatis* (1989), 267–288.

Vance, Eugene, "Augustine's *Confessions* and the Grammar of Selfhood," *Genre* 6 (1973), 1–28.

———"Le moi comme langage: Saint Augustin et l'autobiographie," *Poétique* 14 (1973), 163–177.

———"St. Augustine: Language as Temporality," in *Mimesis: From Mirror to Method, Augustine to Descartes,* ed. J. D. Lyons and S. G. Nichols, Jr. (Hanover, N.H., 1982), 20–35.

van der Linden, L. J., "Ratio et intellectus dans les premiers écrits de saint Augustin," *Augustiniana* 7 (1957), 6–32.

van der Lof, L. J., "The Date of the *De Catechizandis Rudibus,*" *Vigiliae Christianae* 16 (1962), 198–204.

van Fleteren, F. E., "Augustine's Ascent of the Soul in Book VII of the Confessions: A Reconsideration," *Augustinian Studies* 5 (1974), 29–72.

van der Meer, F., *Augustine the Bishop: The Life and Work of a Father of the Church,* trans. B. Battershaw and G. R. Lamb (New York, 1961).

Vanni Rovighi, Sophia, "La fenomenologia della sensazione in Sant'Agostino," *Rivista di filosofia neo-scolastica* 54 (1962), 18–32.

van Oort, Johannes, *Jerusalem and Babylon. A Study into Augustine's 'City of God' and the Sources of His Doctrine of the Two Cities* (Supplements to Vigiliae Christianae 14, Leiden, 1991).

Vecchi, Alberto, "L'antimanicheismo nelle 'Confessioni' de Sant'Agostino," *Giornale di metafisica* 20 (1965), 91–121.

Verbeke, Gérard, "Augustin et le stoïcisme," *R Aug* 1 (1958), 67–89.

———"Connaissance de soi et connaissance de Dieu chez saint Augustin," in *Augustiniana . . . 354–1954* (1954), 279–299.

———*L'évolution de la doctrine du pneuma du Stoicisme à S. Augustin* (Paris, 1945).

Verbraken, Pierre-Patrick, *Études critiques sur les sermons authentiques de saint Augustin* (Instrumenta Patristica 12, The Hague, 1976).

——"Lire aujourd'hui les sermons de saint Augustin. A l'occasion du XVIe centenaire de sa conversion," *Nouvelle revue théologique* 109 (1987), 829–839.

——"Le sermon CCXIV de saint Augustin pour la tradition du symbole," *Revue bénédictine* 72 (1962), 7–21.

Verheijen, L. M. J., "Le *De Doctrina Christiana* de saint Augustin. Un manuel d'herméneutique et d'expression chrétienne avec, en 11, 19 (29)–42 (63), une 'charte fondamentale pour une culture chrétienne,'" *Augustiniana* 24 (1974), 10–20.

——*Eloquentia Pedisequa. Observations sur le style des Confessions de saint Augustin* (Latinitas Christianorum Primaeva 10, Nijmegen, 1949).

——*Saint Augustine's Monasticism in the Light of Acts 4:32–35* (Saint Augustine Lecture 1975, Villanova, 1979).

Vessey, Mark, "Conference and Confession: Literary Pragmatics in Augustine's *Apologia contra Hieronymum*," *Journal of Early Christian Studies* 1 (1993), 175–213.

——"John Donne (1572–1631) in the Company of Augustine: Patristic Culture and Literary Profession in the English Renaissance," *REA* 39 (1993), 173–201.

Veyne, Paul, *Le pain et le cirque. Sociologie historique d'un pluralisme politique* (Univers Historique, Paris, 1976).

Visentin, Pelagio, "'Mysterion-Sacramentum' dai Padri alla Scolastica," *Studia Patavina* 3 (1957), 394–414.

Vlastos, Gregory, "*Anamnesis* in the *Meno*," *Dialogue* 4 (1965–66), 143–167.

Vööbus, Arthur, *History of Asceticism in the Syrian Orient. A Contribution to the History of Culture in the Near East,* vol. 1: *The Origin of Asceticism. Early Monasticism in Persia* (Corpus Scriptorum Christianorum Orientalium 184, Subsidia 14, Louvain, 1958).

Vogels, Heinrich J., "Die Heilige Schrift bei Augustinus," in *Aurelius Augustinus* (1930), 411–421.

Voisine, Jacques, "Naissance et évolution du term littéraire 'autobiographie,'" in *La littérature comparée en Europe orientale. Conférence de Budapest 26–29 octobre 1962,* ed. I. Sötér et al. (Budapest, 1963), 278–286.

von Harnack, Adolf, *Augustins Konfessionen. Ein Vortrag* (Giessen, 1888).

——"Die Höhepunkte in Augustins Konfessionen," in *Aus der Friedens- und Kriegsarbeit. Reden und Aufsätze,* n.s., vol. 3 (Giessen, 1916), 67–99.

——"Die Retractationen Augustins," *Sitzungsberichte der Königlich Preussischen Akademie der Wissenschaften, phil.-hist. Klasse* 2 (1905), 1096–1131.

Voss, Bernd Reiner, *Der Dialog in der frühchristlichen Literatur* (Studia et Testimonia Antiqua 9, Munich, 1970).

Vroom, H., *Le psaume abécédaire de saint Augustin et la poésie latine rhythmique* (Latinitas Christianorum Primaeva 4, Nijmegen, 1933).

Vygotsky, Lev S., *Mind in Society: The Development of Higher Psychological Processes,* ed. M. Cole, V. John-Steiner, S. Scribner, and E. Souberman (Cambridge, Mass., 1978).

Weintraub, Karl Joachim, *The Value of the Individual: Self and Circumstance in Autobiography* (Chicago, 1978).

Weis, Josef, *Die Zeitontologie des Kirchenlehrers Augustinus nach seinen Bekenntnissen* (Europäische Hochschulschriften 20, Philosophie 135, Frankfurt, 1984.

Weismann, Werner, *Kirche und Schauspiele. Die Schauspiele im Urteil der lateinischen Kirchenväter under besonderer Berücksichtigung von Augustin* (Cassiciacum 27, Würzburg, 1972).

Wellman, Henry R., "First Steps in the Child's Theorizing about the Mind," in *Developing Theories of Mind,* ed. J. W. Astington, P. L. Harris, and D. R. Olson (Cambridge, 1988), 64–92.

White, Hayden, *The Content of the Form: Narrative Discourse and Historical Representation* (Baltimore, 1987).

Widengren, Geo, *Mani and Manichaeism,* trans. C. Kessler (New York, 1965).

Wienbruch, Ulrich, "'Signum,' 'Significatio' und 'Illuminatio' bei Augustin," in *Der Begriff der Repraesentatio im Mittelalter. Stellvertretung, Symbol, Zeichen, Bild,* ed. A. Zimmermann (Miscellanea Mediaevalia, Veröffentlichungen des Thomas-Instituts der Universität zu Köln 8, Berlin, 1971), 76–93.

Wilder, Amos N., "Eschatology and the Speech-Modes of the Gospel," in *Zeit und Geschichte. Dankesgabe an Rudolf Bultmann zum 80. Geburstag,* ed. E. Dinkler (Tübingen, 1964), 19–30.

Williger, E., "Der Aufbau der Konfessionen Augustins," *Zeitschrift für die neutestamentliche Wissenschaft* 28 (1929), 81–106.

Wilmart, A., "Operum S. Augustini Elenchus a Possidio eiusdem discipulo Calamensi episcopo digestus, post Maurinorum labores nouis curis editus critico apparatu numeris tabellis instructus," in *Miscellanea Agostiniana,* vol. 2 (1931), 149–233.

Winkler, Klaus, "La théorie augustinienne de la mémoire à son point de départ," in *AM* (1954), vol. 1, 511–519.

Wittgenstein, Ludwig, *Philosophische Untersuchungen (Philosophical Investigations),* trans. G. E. M. Anscombe (Oxford, 1953).

Wolf, Ernst, "Zur Frage nach der Eigenart von Augustins Confessiones," *Christentum und Wissenschaft* 4 (1928), 97–120, 158–165.

Worthen, Jeremy, "The Self in the Text: Guigo I the Carthusian, William of St. Thierry and Hugh of St. Victor" (Diss. Toronto, 1992).

Wundt, Max, "Augustins Konfessionen," *Zeitschrift für die neutestamentliche Wissenschaft und die Kunde der älteren Kirche* 22 (1923), 161–206.

———"Ein Wendepunkt in Augustins Entwicklung," *Zeitschrift für die neutestamentliche Wissenschaft und die Kunde der älteren Kirche* 21 (1921), 53–64.

Yates, Frances A., *The Art of Memory* (London, 1966).

Zangara, V., "La visione di Ostia. Storia dell'indagine e della controversia," *Rivista di storia e letteratura religiosa* 15 (1979), 63–82.

Zarb, S., *Chronologia operum sancti Augustini secundum ordinem Retractionum digesta . . .* (Rome, 1934).

Zekiyan, Boghos L., "L'interiorismo agostiniano e l'autocoscienza del soggetto," *Augustinianum* 16 (1976), 399–410.

Zepf, Max, *Augustins Confessiones* (Heidelberger Abhandlungen zur Philosophie und ihrer Geschichte 9, Tübingen, 1926).

———"Augustinus und das philosophische Selbstbewusstsein der Antike," *Zeitschrift für Religions- und Geistesgeschichte* 11 (1959), 106–132.

Zink, Michel, *La subjectivité littéraire. Autour du siècle de saint Louis* (Collection Ecriture, Paris, 1985).

Zum Brunn, Emilie, *Le dilemme de l'être et du néant chez saint Augustin. Des premiers dialogues aux "Confessions"* (Bochumer Studien zur Philosophie 4, Amsterdam, 1984).

Zumkeller, Adolar, "Die geplante Eheschliessung Augustins und die Entlassung seiner Konkubine. Kulturgeschichtlicher und rechtlicher Hintergrund von *conf.* 6,23 und 25," in *Signum Pietatis* (1989), 37–51.

Zumthor, Paul, "Autobiography in the Middle Ages?" *Genre* 6 (1973), 29–48.

# INDEX